Readings in Canadian History
Post-Confederation

Second Edition

Readings in Canadian History

Post-Confederation

Second Edition

R. Douglas Francis
Donald B. Smith

Holt, Rinehart and Winston of Canada, Limited

Canadian Cataloguing in Publication Data

Main entry under title:
Readings in Canadian history

Contents: [v.1.] Pre-Confederation — [v.2] Post-Confederation
ISBN 0-03-921876-7 ([v.1] — ISBN 0-03-921877-5 ([v.2])

1. Canada-History-Addresses, essays, lectures.
I. Francis, R.D. (R. Douglas), 1944–
II. Smith, Donald B., 1946–

FC164.R42 1986   971   C85-098585-4
F1026.R42 1986

Cover: *North Shore, Baffin Island* by Lawren Harris. Reprinted by permission of
the National Gallery of Canada, Ottawa, Lawren P. Harris and Mrs. James H. Knox.
Publisher: Anthony Luengo
Developmental Editor: Tessa McWatt
Managing Editor: Mary Lynn Mulroney
Copy Editor: Warren Laws
Typesetting and Assembly: Compeer Typographic Services Limited

Printed in Canada
 2 3 4 5 90 89 88 87

Contents

Preface

In this edition of our two volumes *Readings in Canadian History*, as in the first edition, our concern is to provide a collection of articles suitable for introductory Canadian history tutorials. This has meant selecting topics related to the major issues dealt with in such history courses, and providing useful readings of a general nature. We have once again included material that deals with the various regions of the country, and selected, whenever possible, readings that reflect new research interests among Canadian historians. Consequently, we have changed some of the topics, and many of the readings. Unfortunately, these new additions have necessitated the elimination of worthwhile readings in the first edition due to a limitation of space. Still, we hope that this edition will continue to meet the needs of introductory students in Canadian history.

This volume includes two or three selections on each of fifteen topics, thus providing instructors flexibility in choosing readings. Short introductions to each topic set the readings in an historical context and offer suggestions for further readings. It is our hope that this reader will contribute to increased discussion in tutorials, as well as complement course lectures and, where applicable, textbooks.

In preparing the reader, we and the publisher have both sought advice from a number of Canadian historians. Their comments have been generously given and have greatly improved the original outline. We would like once again to thank Douglas Baldwin of the University of Prince Edward Island and Neil Semple of the United Church Archives, Toronto, who helped us with selections for the first edition. In addition, we would like to thank, for the first volume, Olive Dickason of the University of Alberta, Douglas Leighton of Huron College, University of Western Ontario, Richard Reid of the University of Guelph, Hugh Tuck of Memorial University, St. John's Newfoundland, and Christon Archer of the University of Calgary; for the second volume, David Mills of the University of Alberta, and Thomas P. Socknat of Queen's University. All made constructive suggestions for improvement in this second edition. As well, appreciation is extended to the tutorial assistants and students at the University of Calgary, from 1982 to 1984, who offered valuable comments, based on their use of the first edition. Heartfelt thanks also go to Tony Luengo, Brian Henderson and Tessa McWatt of Holt, Rinehart and Winston for their constant encouragement towards the completion of this second edition. Finally we wish to thank those Canadian historians who consented to let their writings be included in this reader. Their ideas and viewpoints will greatly enrich the study and appreciation of Canadian history among first- and second-year university students.

Douglas Francis
Donald Smith
Department of History
University of Calgary

Topic One
Consolidation of Confederation

Canada had just come into existence when it faced some critical challenges:
the only British colony on the Pacific Coast debated whether it wanted to
join Confederation; the tiniest British colony on the Atlantic held out for
"better terms"; and one of the four original partners wanted to leave.

Nova Scotians had consistently opposed Confederation. They had been
brought into the union largely through the efforts of the premier, Charles
Tupper, who had refused to submit the question to a vote in the Legislature. In the federal and provincial elections of September 1867, Nova Scotians recorded their disapproval — eighteen of the nineteen seats for the
federal Parliament went to the separatists (with only Tupper retaining his
seat for the pro-Confederationists) and provincially the electors almost eliminated Tupper's Conservative Party, which retained only two of the thirty-
eight seats. Part of this political protest consisted of an annexation movement ready to join the United States as an alternative to Confederation.
Donald Warner in "The Post-Confederation Annexation Movement in Nova
Scotia" explains the reasons behind this dissatisfaction, and shows the continuity between the pre- and post-Confederation protest movements. He
reveals the deep divisions within the annexation movement, both in personalities and principles, and analyses the movement along geographical and
class lines.

The fulfillment of the motto of the new nation, "from sea to sea," required the entry of British Columbia into Confederation. There was no assurance that British Columbia, a colony on the Pacific Ocean separated
Canada by the vast unsettled territory of the North-West, would join. Yet,
despite considerable opposition, British Columbia did enter Confederation
on 20 July 1871. Walter Sage explains the pro-Confederates' success in "British Columbia becomes Canadian (1871–1901)."

In the early 1870s a series of crises forced Prince Edward Island to re-
consider its opposition to Confederation. Economic and financial collapse
(chiefly as a result of an over-ambitious railway building scheme) forced the

island to re-open negotiations with Canada. Francis Bolger explains the circumstances which led to P.E.I.'s entry in "Long Courted, Won at Last."

The question of Nova Scotian protest at Confederation is examined in the context of later provincial protest movements in Colin D. Howell's "Nova Scotia's Protest Tradition and the Search for a Meaningful Federalism" in *Canada and the Burden of Unity*, edited by D. Bercuson (Toronto: Macmillan, 1977), pp. 169–191. R.H. Campbell's "The Repeal Agitation in Nova Scotia, 1867–1869," Nova Scotia Historical Society, *Collections*, 25 (1942), pp. 95–130 is also useful. George Rawlyk's *The Atlantic Provinces and the Problems of Confederation* (St. John's: Breakwater Press: 1979) provides a good overview of development in Atlantic Canada at the time of Confederation. K.G. Pryke discusses Nova Scotia's relations with the federal government in "The Making of a Province: Nova Scotia and Confederation," Canadian Historical Association *Papers*, 1968, pp. 35–48. The views of Joseph Howe, the leading opponent of Confederation in Nova Scotia are presented in J. Murray Beck's *Joseph Howe*, Vol. II: *The Briton Becomes Canadian, 1848–1873* (Montreal: McGill-Queen's University Press, 1983), and his *Joseph Howe: Anti-Confederate* (Ottawa: Canadian Historical Association, Booklet No. 17, 1965).

A useful contrast to Sage's interpretation of the British Columbia question is Margaret Ormsby's "Canada and the New British Columbia," Canadian Historical Association *Report*, 1948: 74–85. See also her book, *British Columbia: A History* (Toronto: Macmillan, 1958). The views of British officials in the colony of British Columbia are presented in M. Ormsby's "Frederick Seymour: The Forgotten Governor" and Robert Smith, "The Hankin Appointment"; both are in *BC Studies 22* (Summer 1974): 3–25 and 26–39 respectively. *British Columbia and Confederation* edited by W. George Shelton (Victoria: University of Victoria Press, 1967) is a valuable collection of essays.

Francis Bolger presents a comprehensive treatment of Prince Edward Island's decision to join Canada in *Prince Edward Island and Confederation* (Charlottetown: St. Dunstan University Press, 1964) and in the chapters leading up to Confederation in *Canada's Smallest Province: A History of P.E.I.* (Charlottetown: P.E.I. Heritage Foundation, 1973) from which the following excerpt is taken. Ronald Tallman's, "Annexation in the Maritimes? The Butler Mission to Charlottetown," *Dalhousie Review*, 53 (Spring 1973): 97–112, shows the American influence which almost prevented P.E.I. from entering Confederation.

James Hillier reviews Newfoundland's rejection of Confederation in "Confederation Defeated: The Newfoundland Election of 1869," in *Newfoundland in the Nineteenth and Twentieth Centuries: Essays in Interpretation* (Toronto: University of Toronto Press, 1980), pp. 67–94.

The Post-Confederation Annexation Movement in Nova Scotia*

DONALD F. WARNER

The story of the anti-Confederation movement in Nova Scotia and of Joseph Howe's part in it is an oft-told tale. Historians and biographers have related how this agitation was launched and how it rode out gales of denunciation only to founder on the rocks of adamant imperial opposition after the desertion of its captain, Howe. Thus the major outline of this story is well known. One aspect, however, has received too little attention — the lively annexation movement which grew out of the agitation against Confederation. Some writers gingerly skirt this bog of treason barely acknowledging its existence. A few discuss it but seem by brevity, to dismiss it as unimportant; they leave the impression that it was nothing more than an attempt on the part of a few desperate Nova Scotians to frighten the imperial government into permitting their province to secede from the Canadian Dominion as the price for keeping it in the British Empire. It is the purpose of this article to remedy the neglect by analysing this annexation movement, showing its causes and course, and demonstrating that, for a time, it did achieve some strength. To prove the sincerity of the annexationists is, of course, very difficult, involving as it does the nearly impossible problem of the exact analysis of human motives. It is probably true that most of the annexationists were "running a bluff." Yet contemporary evidence indicates that many of them, with their loyalty to the British Empire temporarily gone, viewed the question of joining the United States as a business proposition and were honestly convinced that they would gain materially from such a move. Certainly the alarm which this movement caused to the loyal elements in the province could not have been produced by an agitation which was entirely insincere.

Since the annexation movement had its origin in the agitation against Confederation, it is necessary, first, to glance at the latter. By 1864-5, the plan to unite British North America in a federation had aroused the opposition of the people of the Maritime colonies for several reasons. They realized that they would be a minority in the proposed union and that their interests might be subverted by the majority in Ontario and Quebec. Economically, the colonies by the sea also stood to lose by Confederation. They were, of necessity, wedded to free trade for they depended upon lumbering, mining, ship-building, and fishing for a livelihood, exporting their produce and importing much of what they consumed. Canada, on the other hand, was protectionist, and it seemed likely that its tariff wall

3

* From *Canadian Historical Review*, XXVIII (1947): 156–165. Reprinted by permission of University of Toronto Press.

would be stretched around the new Confederation.[1] Nova Scotia particularly disliked the financial terms of the union, fearing that its government would lose half of its income and would lack money to support such essential functions as education and public works.[2] For these and other reasons, most Nova Scotians preferred to remain as they were, a separate colony, rather than to join in the proposed union. A number of these "antis," as the opponents of federation were popularly called, formed the League of the Maritime Provinces to carry on the fight against Confederation. Joseph Howe, one of the greatest figures in the history of British North America, led this organization, partly, according to tradition, from personal motives. Nearly twenty years before, he had won the fight for responsible government in his province, and his victory had established him as the leader of Nova Scotia. Since then, however, he had accomplished little and his arch-enemy, Dr. Charles Tupper, had risen to dominate the province and to be the leader of its government. Howe, like most Nova Scotians, sincerely opposed Confederation; but he also astutely recognized in the "anti" movement an opportunity to regain his former prestige and to pay off old scores against Tupper, who favoured Confederation.

The first action of the "antis" was an attempt to prevent the passage of the British North America Act by the imperial Parliament, or at least to amend the Act so that it would not include Nova Scotia. For this purpose, the League sent Howe and other delegates to London. There the first mention of annexation occurred; for Howe was to hint to the Colonial Office that Confederation might cause "changes which none of us desire . . . and all of us deplore."[3] As instructed, Howe made the most of this weapon in his correspondence with Lord Carnarvon, the secretary of state for the colonies, by pointing out the "range of temptation" which political union with the United States offered to the Maritimes: they would have free trade with a market of 34 million people, access to American capital, and the benefit of American fishing bounties.[4] These broad hints did not impress the imperial government, which pushed the British North America Act through Parliament with little opposition. Thus Nova Scotia became part of the Dominion of Canada, for Tupper had pledged his province to enter Confederation without consulting the voters.

If Tupper expected the "antis" to accept this *fait accompli* without further ado, he was soon wiser. The "antis" turned from the attempt to prevent the formation of the Dominion to an attempt to withdraw Nova Scotia from it. The secession movement, already strong, was steadily gaining new adherents, largely because the formation of the Dominion coincided closely with the beginning of a severe depression. The termination, in 1866, of the Reciprocity Treaty of 1854 had had the immediate effect of halving the trade with the United States and bringing distress to the merchants, commercial cities, and producers of Canada. This depression was most severe in the Maritime Provinces whose staple exports of fish, coal, and lumber were subject to prohibitive duties after the end of the Treaty. To increase the discontent in these provinces, the fisheries of

1866 and 1867 proved to be complete failures, leaving thousands of families to struggle against hunger and privation.[5] At a time when income was declining, the federal government, as expected, extended the higher tariff of the old colony of Canada to the entire Dominion and considerably increased the price of necessities in the hard-hit Maritime Provinces. This readjustment of the tariff was said to have cost the inhabitants of these provinces $356 000 a year;[6] even the lieutenant-governor and the confederationists in Nova Scotia felt compelled to condemn the tariff because of the hardship that it worked there.[7] A final affliction to the depression-ridden Canadians was the spectacle of the United States which was, at this time, entering a frenzied post-war boom. The contrast was both vivid and suggestive.

It is not strange that the "antis" took advantage of these circumstances to argue that there was a direct connection between the formation of the Dominion and the coming of the depression. Nor is it strange that some Canadians envied the seeming prosperity of the United States and longed to share in it. The result of these factors was a double trend in the "anti" movement. As stated above, it grew steadily; and, secondly, some of its followers began to consider secession not as an end in itself but as a step toward annexation.

For a time, however, most of the "antis" regarded political union with the United States as a last resort and hoped to relieve their distress by other means. There was some foundation for this expectation. The first election in Nova Scotia under the new Dominion had resulted in an overwhelming victory for the opponents of Confederation. This made them confident that the British government would accede to their desire for secession from Canada and that a return to the status of a separate, self-governing colony would solve their economic and political problems. Nova Scotia could restore its revenue tariff, the income of its government would increase, and other provinces could not undermine its interests. More important, Nova Scotians were certain that the United States would be willing to negotiate a reciprocity treaty with their province if it were not part of the Dominion. This belief was based on the notion that the United States and Nova Scotia were complementary in production while the United States and Canada were competitive.

Thus secession was still the key to prosperity and the "antis" again set out to get it. The provincial assembly passed a series of resolutions urging the British government to release Nova Scotia from the Confederation. Howe embarked for London bearing this appeal, and the "antis" waited confidently for news that the British government had granted it. Talk of annexation almost disappeared.

Howe did not share the confidence of his followers that his mission would succeed. He knew from his previous experience in Great Britain that the home government was determined to have Confederation and would oppose the withdrawal of Nova Scotia, which might wreck the new union. This official British attitude was well expressed by Lord Monck,

5

the governor-general of the Dominion, who pressed the colonial secretary to refuse Howe's request graciously but firmly. If the union broke up, wrote Monck, "I have no hesitation in expressing my opinion that . . . the maintenance of British power or the existence of British institutions in America will soon become impossible."[8] This advice from the man on the spot fortified the determination of the imperial government to deny the repeal of Confederation. Obviously, Howe had good reasons for admitting privately before he sailed that he expected his mission to fail,[9] and he was not mistaken. The colonial secretary, the Duke of Buckingham, proved to be courteous and willing to listen to the complaints of Nova Scotia but unmovable in his refusal to dissolve the Confederation or to permit the secession of any of the provinces. Early in June, he informed Monck that the imperial government "could not consider" this, or any other, request for repeal.[10]

The publication of this dispatch, bringing the frustration of their highest hopes, was a terrible blow to most of the "antis." A storm of protest arose in Nova Scotia, and bitter denunciations rained down upon the Canadian and British governments. One newspaper, typical of the organs that favoured repeal of Confederation, vented its wrath and sorrow in the following terms: "Nova Scotians have been proud of their connection with England. What have they to be proud of now? We feel assured that the people of Nova Scotia will never be loyal to the Dominion of Canada. They never have consented, never will consent to such an alliance. The Union, whilst it lasts, can only be one of force, so far as Nova Scotia is concerned."[11]

Many soon went beyond philippics and vowed that their loyalty to Great Britain was now gone. Prominent men and newspapers in the province came out openly for annexation.[12] These advocates of political union frankly stated that, with their hope of secession now blasted, their only remaining chance of rescue from the undesired federation was to join the United States.

This outburst of disloyalty frightened Howe, who realized how much he had helped to blow up this tempest. Even before leaving on his second mission to London, he had been uneasy over the extreme doctrines held by some of his followers; on his return to Halifax he became alarmed at the treasonable talk in the province. At once, he determined to check it. Calling a convention of the "anti" leaders, he lectured them sternly for their sedition. He pointed out that any attempt by Nova Scotia to secure annexation would be forcibly resisted with the whole power of the British Empire and would end in disaster.[13] This plain speaking seemed to have its effect; the convention resolved that the "antis" must continue to attempt to secure secession by "lawful and constitutional means."[14]

The conversion of some of the repealers to "lawful and constitutional means" proved to be very temporary. Soon they were again using violent language, advocating seditious action, casting strong hints that American aid would be forthcoming, and that annexation would result. Members of the provincial government and prominent newspapers led the way towards the edge of treason.[15] Howe soon realized that his efforts to secure secession and to quiet the extremists in his group had failed and that it would be a waste of time to repeat them. The repeal movement was in a *cul-de-sac*, and he faced the necessity of choosing between two lines of retreat: to abandon opposition to Confederation, or to attempt to bring Nova Scotia into the American union. To Howe, the former was distasteful and the latter abhorrent. Choosing the lesser of the two evils, he reluctantly decided to accept Confederation, the pain of transition being assuaged by the willingness of Macdonald to make concessions that would partially redress the grievances of Nova Scotia.[16] In November, 1868, Howe suddenly announced that he could no longer remain in the "anti" movement, which was becoming merely a cloak for annexationism.

Howe had apparently hoped and planned that his action would be imitated by many, if not most, of the advocates of the repeal of Confederation, and that the extremists would be driven to cover. His expectation was disappointed. The "antis" were stunned by this spectacular and unexpected about-face on the part of their leader. Some of the moderates followed him, but many others refused to do so, irked because he had not consulted or forewarned them. Even the confederationists in the province condemned Howe on the ground that his action would have been effective only if he had notified his moderate associates of his intentions, so that they might have been prepared to withdraw gradually from the secession movement and become confederationists with some show of consistency.[17] Contemporary observers, friendly to Howe, estimated that his action had important effects in only two counties — Queens and Lunenburg — where about half of the "antis" followed him out of the movement.[18] The rest, if anything, became more determined in opposition, and the tendency towards political union seemed to increase. Moreover, the tone of the annexationists was changing. In the beginning, they had been inspired by anger and had been hopeful of alarming the British government by the intemperance of their sentiments. But by this time, their wrath had cooled and so had their loyalty to the British Empire. With the hope of repeal gone and economic distress still prevalent, Nova Scotians began to view their future without sentiment and some of them concluded that annexation was the only cure for the depression from which they were suffering. It became the expression of cold self-interest, not of hot wrath.[19]

It is impossible to determine the extent of this movement with exactness. Contemporary evidence indicates, however, that it had considerable strength in some areas. Howe, who knew the political situation in Nova Scotia better than any other man, informed Macdonald that "a clear unfettered vote of the people might take it [Nova Scotia] into the American Union."[20] Three by-elections to the Dominion Parliament in 1869, in each of which annexation was a major issue, seemed to bear out this statement. Having accepted a post in the Dominion Cabinet, Howe was forced to stand for re-election, which he did in the constituency of Hants. Thereupon, both the annexationists and the confederationists determined to make this electoral contest a test of strength, and both strained every resource to win. The victory went to Howe because his personal prestige was highest in this, his home district, and because the Dominion government supported him with all of its resources in his "Holy War."[21] Even so, the margin of victory was not great.

The excitement in Hants partly obscured significant developments in the two other ridings where by-elections were being held. In Richmond a candidate, reputedly an annexationist, was returned after a canvass which seems to have excited almost no outside interest. The campaign in Yarmouth was more closely watched and contested. The confederationists were most anxious to carry this constituency which was known to contain many annexationists; and there, as in Hants, they raised a large campaign fund and secured aid from the Dominion government.[22] The annexationists nominated Frank Killam, a young merchant, and one of the wealthiest men in the province. Both the banks and every man of means in Yarmouth supported him.[23] The confederationists soon lost hope of defeating him at the polls and planned instead to "work on him" after his election.[24] The results of the polling proved the wisdom of this decision.[25]

Their success in two of the three by-elections greatly encouraged the advocates of political union. They were, by this time, numerous enough to control the League of the Maritime Provinces, which had been founded to fight Confederation, and in June, 1869, formally changed it to the Annexation League. This action was accompanied by the issuing of a manifesto which made the motivation of the annexationists clear: "Our only hope of commercial prosperity, material development, and permanent peace lies in closer relations with the United States. Therefore be it resolved that every legitimate means should be used by members of this convention to sever our connections with Canada and to bring about a union on fair and equitable terms with the American Republic."[26]

While these political unionists were fairly numerous, their strength, geographically and socially, was not uniformly distributed throughout the province. The movement apparently was strongest in the southern part of Nova Scotia, particularly about Yarmouth. This area was a centre for the fishing industry which wanted free access to American markets and hoped to attract capital from the United States.[27] The north-eastern portion of the province, including the adjacent counties of Cape Breton Island, also had numerous advocates of annexation. The coal industry of this area wanted duty-free entry into the United States; such a privilege, mine operators estimated, would increase their annual sales in that market from 200 000 to 11 million tons a year.[28] This industry had prospered during the years of the Reciprocity Treaty of 1854; now it was in the depths of depression, with thousands out of work.[29] Reopening of the American market, preferably on a permanent basis, seemed to be the only hope for restoring and maintaining prosperity. Finally, the commercial cities of the province, especially Halifax, contained many advocates of annexation.

They were supplied mostly by the trading and shipping industries, which were then in a serious decline and were particularly anxious to qualify for participation in the lucrative American coasting trade, open only to citizens of the United States.[30]

It is also important to note that the movement in all centres was strongest among the more important economic classes in the province: merchants, ship captains, seamen, commission men, coal operators, and miners.[31] The moneyed interests of Nova Scotia, who had invested capital in the enterprises which would benefit from annexation, financed the movement.[32]

This agitation, however, began to decline as early as 1869 and was a thing of the past by 1872. The first defections took place in the coal region where the annexationist tide began to ebb in December, 1869, and soon disappeared.[33] The agitation was more persistent in southern Nova Scotia but there, also, its strength steadily waned. The *Yarmouth Herald*, most intransigent of the annexationist papers, sounded the death knell in December, 1870, when it declared that the time was not ripe for political union with the United States.[34]

The causes for this decline are not far to seek. As distress and depression had built up the annexation movement, so returning prosperity tore out its foundations. Exports from Canada to the United States, which had reached their nadir in 1867, were strongly reviving. The fisheries, after the complete failures of 1866 and 1867, yielded abnormal catches from 1869 to 1873, and the Treaty of Washington brought a new day of prosperity for the Maritime Provinces by admitting Canadian fish duty-free into the United States. At the same time, exports of coal from Nova Scotia increased greatly. The mine operators reaped heavy profits and were able to employ more men.[35] Finally, the annexationists of Nova Scotia realized that the British government would not stand idly by and see that province secede from the Dominion and join the United States. It seemed that an appeal to force would be necessary, and that it would be bound to fail unless the United States strongly assisted it. When it became apparent that there was no hope of such help, the political union agitation received its *coup de grâce*.[36]

Thus disappeared one of the strongest and most interesting of the Canadian annexation movements. Like most of them, it was born of discontent and it died when the conditions which produced that discontent had disappeared. Unlike most of the others, however, it had considerable and outspoken support and some financial backing. Indeed, for a time, it caused genuine alarm to the loyal majority in the province.

Notes

1. Public Archives of Canada, Howe Papers, vol. 26, pt. 1, Miscellaneous Papers on Confederation, 152-4.
2. The normal annual income of the province, $1 500 000, would be reduced to $750 000 according to the *Yarmouth* (Nova Scotia) *Tribune*, June 27, 1866.

3. Howe Papers, vol. 4, Letters to Howe, 1864–1873, Instructions to Howe from the League of the Maritime Provinces, July 5, 1866.

4. British Parliament, *Accounts and Papers, 1867*, n. XLVIII, 14–15, Howe to Lord Carnarvon, London, Jan. 19, 1867.

5. *Yarmouth Tribune*, May 22 and Dec. 11, 1867 and Jan. 5, 1869.

6. *Saint John* (New Brunswick) *Morning Freeman*, Sept. 7, 1868.

7. P.A.C., Macdonald Papers, Nova Scotia Affairs, vol. I, Lieutenant-Governor Hastings-Doyle to Sir John A. Macdonald, Halifax, Dec. 31, 1867, and P.S. Hamilton to Macdonald, Halifax, Feb. 24, 1868.

8. P.A.C., Series G 573 A, Secret and Confidential Despatches, 1867–1869, Lord Monck to the Duke of Buckingham, Feb. 13, 1867.

9. Howe Papers, vol. 37, Howe Letter Book, Howe to A. Musgrove, Halifax, Jan. 17, 1868.

10. Macdonald Papers, Nova Scotia Affairs, vol. III, Buckingham to Monck, London, June 4, 1868.

11. *Yarmouth Herald*, June 18, 1868.

12. Among the papers outspokenly advocating annexation, the most persistent were the *Yarmouth Herald* and the *New Glasgow Eastern Chronicle*. Others, including the *Halifax Morning Chronicle*, were more reserved but discussed annexation favourably. Among the annexationists of whom I have found mention were Marshall, the former chief justice of the province, and Underwood, a member of the Dominion Parliament. Most of the members of the provincial government frequently spoke favourably of annexation, especially Martin Wilkins, the attorney-general and real leader of the Cabinet. His sincerity, however, seems open to some question, for he likewise protested his loyalty to the Empire when questioned by Hastings-Doyle.

13. Howe Papers, vol. 38, Howe Letter Book, Howe to Livingston, Halifax, Aug. 12, 1868.

14. *Saint John Morning Freeman*, Aug. 11, 1868.

15. Macdonald Papers, Nova Scotia Affairs, vol. I, Hastings-Doyle to Macdonald, Halifax, Sept. 4 and 5, 1868.

16. Macdonald addressed a repeal convention in Halifax in August, 1868, and promised that Nova Scotia would have better terms of union. *Ibid.*, vol. III, Macdonald to Lord Monck, Sept. 4, 1868.

17. *Ibid.*, Hastings-Doyle to Macdonald, Halifax, Feb. 25, 1869.

18. Howe Papers, vol. 4, Letters to Howe, 1861–1873, R. Huntington to Howe, Yarmouth, Dec. 24, 1868.

19. For typical expressions of this view, see M. N. Jackson to F. Seward, Halifax, Aug. 29, 1868. National Archives of the United States, Consular Despatches to the Department of State, Halifax, vol. IX. See also *Halifax Morning Chronicle*, Sept. 16, 1868, and *New Glasgow Eastern Chronicle*, Jan. 9, 1869.

20. Macdonald Papers, Nova Scotia Affairs, vol. II, Howe to Macdonald, Halifax, Oct. 29, 1868 and Nov. 16, 1868.

21. The expression, "Holy War" is Macdonald's. The federal government made 400 appointments to aid Howe in this campaign. See Howe Papers, vol. 4, Letters to Howe, 1864–1873, Macdonald to Howe, Ottawa, Jan. 12, Mar. 8, and Mar. 16, 1869. Also Macdonald Papers, Nova Scotia Affairs, vol. I, Hastings-Doyle to Macdonald, Halifax, Mar. 5 and 30, 1869.

22. Macdonald Papers, Nova Scotia Affairs, vol. III, A. W. Savary to Macdonald, Halifax, Dec. 3, 1868. P.A.C., Macdonald Letter Books, XII, Macdonald to Savary, Ottawa, December 14, 1868.

23. Macdonald Papers, Nova Scotia Affairs, vol. III, J. A. McClellan to Macdonald, Halifax, Feb. 23, 1869.

24. Howe Papers, vol. 38, Howe Letter Book, Howe to Macdonald, Halifax, Mar. 30, 1869. Series G 573 A, Secret and Confidential Despatches, 1867–1869, Young to Granville, Apr. 8, 1869.

25. Killam had a majority in every district in the riding and, in Yarmouth County, polled 1220 votes to 598 for his opponent. *Saint John Morning Freeman*, Apr. 22, 1869.

26. *Ibid.*, June 24, 1869.

27. *Yarmouth Herald*, Apr. 15, 1869 and Apr. 14, 21, 26, and 30, 1870.

28. *New Glasgow Eastern Chronicle*, Nov. 25, 1869.

29. *Boston Daily Advertiser*, Oct. 17, 1868.

30. Series G 573 A, Secret and Confidential Despatches 1867–1869, Young to Granville, Apr. 8, 1869.

31. *Ibid.*

32. Macdonald Papers, Nova Scotia Affairs, vol. III, J. McClellan to Macdonald, Halifax, Feb. 23, 1869.

33. The last annexation meeting in the region seems to have taken place in Feb., 1870. *Yarmouth Tribune*, Feb. 9, 1870.

34. *Yarmouth Herald*, Dec. 5, 1870.

35. *Saint John Morning Freeman*, Nov. 13, 1869.

36. There were annexationists in the United States, but they were in the minority and very few of them were willing to fight Great Britain in order to obtain Canada or any part of it. See L. B. Shippee, *Canadian-American Relations 1849–1874* (New Haven, Toronto, and London, 1939).

British Columbia Becomes Canadian (1871-1901)*

WALTER N. SAGE

In an impassioned speech against federation delivered in the Legislative Council of British Columbia in March, 1870, Dr. John Sebastian Helmcken uttered these prophetic words:

No union between this Colony and Canada can permanently exist, unless it be to the mutual and pecuniary advantage of this Colony to remain in the union. The sum of the interests of the inhabitants is the interest of the Colony. The people of this Colony have, generally speaking, no love for Canada; they care, as a rule, little or nothing about the creation of another Empire, Kingdom, or Republic; they have but little sentimentality and care little about the distinctions between the forms of Government of Canada and the United States.

Therefore no union on account of love need be looked for. The only bond of union outside of force — and force the Dominion has not — will be the material advantage of the country and the pecuniary benefit of the inhabitants. Love for Canada has to be acquired by the prosperity of the country, and from our children.[1]

The last four words are more than prophetic. They are a stroke of genius! Probably in his old age the good doctor was fated to hear the school-children of British Columbia singing:

Our fair Dominion now extends
From Cape Race to Nootka Sound.

The children and children's children were in the process of becoming Canadians. It was not a speedy evolution. At Confederation British Columbians were *not* Canadians. By 1901 Canadianism had spread and penetrated the province. But there were still many in the older age group-ings who remembered the colonial period and were still definitely British Columbians. The youngsters were Canadians, but Canadians with a dif-ference. The barrier of the Rocky Mountains had conditioned them. Their outlook was towards the Pacific and not towards the Atlantic nor even towards Hudson Bay. They were not well acquainted with Ontario and knew little of the prairies or the Maritimes, and probably still less about Quebec. None the less they were becoming increasingly conscious that they were a part of Canada.

Dr. Helmcken was right. Love for Canada was at first not a spontaneous or a natural growth in British Columbia. It did not spring from the native soil of the province as did love for British Columbia. In the colonial days and even for a time after Confederation 'Canadians' were unpopular. They were known as 'North American Chinamen' — a tribute to their thrift.

*From *Queen's Quarterly*, LII (1945): 168–183. Reprinted by permission of the editors.

11

They sent their money home and did not spend it so freely as did the open-handed Americans. But British Columbia could not thrive without the aid of the rest of Canada. She was cut off from American markets by the tariff laws of the United States. Until the completion of the Canadian Pacific Railway in 1885 there was no direct link through Canadian territory between the Coast and Eastern Canada. It is true that during the critical years from 1866 to 1871 British Columbia might have followed 'Manifest Destiny' and as the Territory of Columbia have become a weaker edition of Washington Territory — weaker because, in spite of her huge expanse, she had a smaller and more widespread population. But British Columbia had made her decision. She would remain British even though it entailed paying the high price of becoming Canadian. The only other course open to her was to remain a bankrupt British colony on the edge of nowhere!

A glance at the early history of the British colonies on the Northwest Coast and especially at the so-called critical period between 1866 and 1871 will show that British Columbia was much more British and American in outlook than it was Canadian. In fur-trading days before 1849 there was relatively little Canadian influence. There had been some when the North West Company was operating west of the Rockies, but the union of 1821 left the Hudson's Bay Company in complete control. Very few of the company's officers were from Canada, although there were many French-Canadians among the *voyageurs*. The Colony of Vancouver Island was a British, not a Canadian, venture. The gold-seekers of 1858 were from California. A few of them were Canadians who had been attracted to the placer mines of the Golden State and were now following the paystreak north. The miners' meetings stemmed from California and even 'Ned McGowan's War' had its roots in the troubles between the Vigilantes and the Law and Order Group, rival California organizations, members of which had come north to Fraser River.[2] The United States was omnipresent. The British Isles were half the world away, and Canada, although geographically nearer than Great Britain, was even farther away in spirit. There was a sentimental tie with the Mother Country but as yet practically none with Canada. Joseph Despard Pemberton, former Colonial Surveyor, in a letter to the Victoria *British Colonist* early in 1870, summed up the situation neatly in verse:

True Loyalty's to Motherland
And not to Canada,
The love we bear is second-hand
To any step-mama.

At first sight it would seem that American influences preponderated in British Columbia. The economic tie was with California, and this tie remained until the completion of the Canadian Pacific Railway. As the late Marcus Lee Hansen has penetratingly observed:

The new province of British Columbia, although firmly attached to the empire by political, naval and military bonds, was in commerce and population a part of the Pacific region which had its center at San Francisco.[3]

Hansen also states that

Fully three-fourths of the fifteen thousand miners who in 1864 made up the principal
element in the population were Americans, and half of the business houses were branches
of American establishments.[4]

The only regular steamship communication which British Columbia possessed with the outside world was by American vessels.[5] The express
companies were of American origin, although local express was carried by
British Columbian companies which maintained American connections.
Postal service was through San Francisco. It was necessary for letters
posted in British Columbia, destined for Great Britain, Canada, the United
States, or elsewhere, to bear United States stamps in addition to their local
postage. Governor Musgrave protested against this practice, but it was
found impossible to change it.[6] Telegraph service with San Francisco, by
way of Portland, Oregon, was established in 1865. The completion of the
Union Pacific Railroad in 1869 provided British Columbia, through San
Francisco, with railway connections with the Atlantic seaboard, and put
an end to travel by the tedious, and often dangerous, Panama route.

From California the mining frontier spread eastward and northward to
Nevada, Utah, Colorado, Wyoming, Montana, Idaho and British Columbia. The gold rushes of 1858 to Fraser River and of 1862 to Cariboo
stemmed from San Francisco. Later rushes to Omineca, the Stikine,
Cassiar, and finally to Atlin and the Klondike were closely connected with
California. Mining methods in British Columbia were similar to those in
vogue in California, and the miners who came north were accustomed to
'frontier justice'. In British Columbia, however, they found Judge Begbie,
but not 'Judge Lynch'.

American influences were economic, and, to a less degree, social and
cultural. British influences were political and institutional and also social
and religious. The political and legal structure of British Columbia was
entirely British. The colonial governors were all of British origin. Most of
the government officials had been born in the British Isles. In the Legislative Council of British Columbia, which in 1870 discussed terms of union
with Canada, the majority had come from the Motherland. The Royal
Navy was another link with 'Home'. The part played by the Special
Detachment of the Royal Engineers in the early development of the Crown
Colony of British Columbia is too well known to demand more than a
passing reference. The Church of England was also a link with the Mother
Country. Bishop Hills, the first Bishop of Columbia, was consecrated in
Westminster Abbey and set apart for his work in the far-off colony. In
1860 he arrived in Victoria, where he diligently upheld the traditions and
dignity of his Church, but was unable to secure its establishment as the
State Church of the colony. The first Presbyterian ministers came from
Ireland, but the 'Scottish Kirk' flourished under their ministrations, and
for many years retained a close connection with the Established Church of
Scotland. The Roman Catholics and the Methodists, on the other hand,
had Canadian connections. The first Roman Catholic priests came from

Canada to the Columbia in the 1830's, and later in the 1840's came north to Fort Victoria and the Fraser River. The Methodists were sent from Canada, in the late 1850's, to establish a mission in British Columbia.

Canadian influences were at first relatively weak, but they strengthened as the battle for Confederation was fought. The leading Confederationists were chiefly British North Americans: *e.g.*, Amor De Cosmos, John Robson, Dr. R. W. W. Carrall, Francis J. Barnard, and J. Spencer Thompson. Some Englishmen — *e.g.*, Robert Beaven and Alfred Waddington — also joined the cause of federation. George A. Walkem was Irish by birth but Canadian by adoption. Many of the Confederationist leaders had come to British Columbia by way of California. Their sojourn in the United States had, apparently, not dulled their affection for British institutions, but had strengthened rather than weakened their determination that British Columbia should join Canada.

A mining population is notoriously unstable. It is a case of 'Here to-day and gone to-morrow'. As a rule the American gold-seekers returned to the United States when they had 'made their pile' or had become disgusted with the 'Fraser River humbug'. It was the British and the Canadians who remained and settled down in Cariboo, along the lower Fraser River, or on Vancouver Island. Unfortunately it is not possible to make an accurate check of the birthplace of British Columbians before 1871.[7] Some idea of the national origins of British Columbians at that date may, however, be obtained from a study of J. B. Kerr's *Biographical Dictionary of Well-Known British Columbians*, published in Vancouver in 1890. Of the 242 names listed in this publication, 178 were resident in British Columbia in 1871. An analysis of their birthplaces is rather enlightening: *British Isles*, 94, divided as follows: England, 57; Scotland, 21; Ireland, 16. *Dominion of Canada*: 45, — Nova Scotia, 7; New Brunswick, 3; Prince Edward Island, 1; Quebec, 5; Ontario, 29.[8] *British Columbia*, 7; *Other British possessions*, 5; United States, 12; Other Foreign Countries, 14; no birthplace, 1.

These figures clearly show that British Columbia was *British* in the broadest sense of the term. The Americans had come and gone. The British, including the Canadians, remained.

In the Canadianization of British Columbia from 1871 to 1901 three phenomena are clearly observable: political development, the building of the Canadian Pacific Railway, and the arrival as settlers of large numbers of Eastern Canadians. It must not be thought that British and American influences did not continue to be strong. What happened was that Canadian influence strengthened, especially after the completion of the Canadian Pacific Railway. The period divides naturally at 1886. The first regular transcontinental passenger train from Montreal arrived at Port Moody on July 4th of that year. Vancouver came into existence in April, and was burnt to ashes in June. But nothing could daunt the future Canadian metropolis of the West Coast. It arose triumphantly from its ashes and five years later had a population of 13 709 as compared with Victoria's 16 841. The census of 1901 showed that Vancouver had already surpassed Victoria in population — 29 432 as against 20 919.[9] Since Victoria was the centre of the British-born (natives of the British Isles) Vancouver's rapid advance was a sign of Canadianization. The roots of its people strike deep into Eastern Canada.

The political phase of Canadianization is concerned chiefly with the establishment of the provincial government and with the relations existing between the Lieutenant-Governor of British Columbia and the Government of Canada. Before federation British Columbia had possessed representative but not responsible government. Her political education was, therefore, not so far advanced as that of the eastern provinces. On the other hand, British Columbia had been the only Crown Colony west of the Great Lakes, and was rather more experienced than Manitoba in the art of self-government. Yet British Columbians in 1871 were still politically immature.

The Terms of Union with Canada provided for "the introduction of Responsible Government when desired by the Inhabitants of British Columbia".[10]

15

It was not, however, until after the first provincial elections had been held in October, 1871, that Lieutenant-Governor Joseph William Trutch could claim to have "established a Responsible Cabinet".[11] Actually, it may be doubted whether responsible government was fully established during the régime of John Foster McCreight, the first Premier of British Columbia. McCreight was a distinguished lawyer, Irish by birth, who had no previous political experience. Probably Trutch selected him because he was "a 'safe' man, one whom the Lieutenant-Governor could direct and guide".[12] Trutch virtually ruled British Columbia during the McCreight régime, 1871–1872. When Amor de Cosmos became premier in December, 1872, Trutch found his power challenged. De Cosmos, with his Nova Scotian tradition and his long political experience in British Columbia, was not prepared to yield the reins of power to any Lieutenant Governor, even though he had once held office in colonial days as Chief Commissioner of Lands and Works.

Trutch was in a unique position as regards Ottawa. He considered himself the accredited representative of the federal government in British Columbia. His letters to Sir John A. Macdonald and Macdonald's replies clearly indicate that he was definitely the *liaison* officer between Ottawa and Victoria during the period from July 20th to November 14th, 1871, that is, until the McCreight ministry was formally constituted. The real difficulty was that Trutch did not hand over full authority to McCreight. In his analysis of the situation R. E. Gosnell saw very clearly:

During the transition from Crown Colony government to Provincial autonomy there was a brief interregnum in which it was necessary for him [Trutch] to administer affairs on his own initiative, but he continued this rule much longer than was necessary, or than was constitutionally defensible.[13]

Part of Trutch's difficulties arose from his selection of McCreight as premier. Neither he nor McCreight had any real acquaintance with responsible government. The leading opponents of Trutch and McCreight — Amor De Cosmos and John Robson — possessed this experience. Either of them could, in all probability, have headed a real responsible ministry. In a rather pathetic passage in a letter to Sir John A. Macdonald Trutch unburdened himself as follows:

> I am so inexperienced and indeed we all are in this Province in the practice of Responsible Govt. that we are initiating that I step as carefully and guardedly as I can — and whilst teaching others I feel constantly my own extreme need of instruction on this subject — which must account to you — if you please — for the trouble which I have put you to — and which I know I ought not to have imposed on you.[14]

De Cosmos, for his part, roundly denounced the Trutch-McCreight combination in an appeal addressed to "the Liberals of the Province":

> To rally round their old leaders — the men who have year after year fought their battles and have in no instance deserted the popular cause. To take any other course is to convict themselves of Treason to manhood, Treason to the Liberal party, that year by year for fourteen years have urged Responsible Government, Union of the Provinces, and Confederation with the Dominion. It is no Treason, no public wrong to ignore the nominees of Governor Trutch.[15]

The reference to the "Liberal party" is extremely interesting. Actually there were no political parties, in the federal sense of the term, in British Columbian provincial politics until 1903, when Richard McBride announced the formation of a Conservative ministry. De Cosmos, in his federal career, supported Macdonald and Mackenzie in turn. It is noteworthy, however, that as early as 1871 he could make his appeal to the 'Liberals'.

By the Terms of Union British Columbia was entitled to three senators and six members of the House of Commons. The senators were Dr. R. W. W. Carrall, Clement F. Cornwall and W. J. Macdonald. Carrall was from Ontario, but the other two senators were born in the British Isles. The six Members of Parliament were J. Spencer Thompson, Hugh·Nelson, Robert Wallace, Henry Nathan, Amor De Cosmos, and Charles F. Houghton. Two of them, Thompson and De Cosmos, both Canadians, had been prominent Confederationists. In Ottawa all six were classed as supporters of the Macdonald administration.

In the federal elections of 1872 Sir Francis Hincks was elected by acclamation for Vancouver Island. Six years later, in the well-known National Policy election, Sir John A. Macdonald, defeated in Kingston, Ontario, was elected for Victoria City. His colleague was Amor De Cosmos.

During the Macdonald régime from 1878 to 1891 the British Columbian Members of Parliament were Conservatives. They gave their political allegiance to the party which had promised to build the transcontinental railway. It must be confessed that, with the exception of Amor De Cosmos, the British Columbians do not seem to have played any large part at Ottawa. But their presence there showed that the Pacific province was part of the Canadian federation.

16

As has been noted, federal parties as such took no part in provincial politics until 1903. Political divisions in the provincial area were local rather than national. Until the population of the Mainland had surpassed that of Vancouver Island the division was Mainland vs. Island. But local issues in the 1870's and early 1880's were closely intertwined with the all-important railway question.

The greatest single Canadianizing force in British Columbia during the period 1871 to 1901 was the Canadian Pacific Railway. Its construction had been promised in the Terms of Union. Delay in carrying out those terms almost led to the secession of British Columbia from the Canadian federation in 1878. The change of government in 1873 and the attitude of the Mackenzie administration were largely responsible for this delay, but there is no denying that George A. Walkem in British Columbia made political capital out of the difficult situation. The return of Sir John A. Macdonald and the Conservatives to power in 1878 put an end to the secession movement and led to the chartering of the new company which built the railway. Over that railway from 1886 to 1901 came thousands of eastern Canadians who were to become the cement binding British Columbia more closely to the rest of the Dominion. _17_

The well-known story of the building of the Canadian Pacific Railway need not here be retold. Its terminus was fixed at Port Moody, not Esquimalt. The so-called "Island section of the main line" became the Esquimalt and Nanaimo Railway, constructed not by the Canadian Pacific Railway Company, but by Robert Dunsmuir, the 'coal king' of Vancouver Island, and the 'Big Four' of the Southern Pacific Railway — Collis P. Huntingdon, Mark Hopkins, Leland Stanford, and Charles Crocker. The Yellowhead Pass route through the Rocky Mountains was abandoned in favour of the Kicking Horse. In 1887 the 'branch' line from Port Moody to Vancouver was built.

From the vantage-point of nearly three-quarters of a century after the event the real wonder is that the railway was ever built at all. The total population of the Dominion, including Prince Edward Island, in 1871 was 3 689 257. Of this total 25 228 are listed for Manitoba, 36 247 for British Columbia, and 48 000 for the Northwest Territories.[16] The white population of Western Canada was probably short of 25 000. The four 'original provinces' of Eastern Canada had a population of 3 225 761. It was a tremendous undertaking for Canada to build a transcontinental railway, and it is not surprising that others than Edward Blake had misgivings. But Sandford Fleming blazed the trails before the Canadian Pacific Railway Company was formed and that great group of railway builders who made up the new company built the road. James J. Hill withdrew from the directorate in 1883 when it became evident that the company was determined to build the Lake Superior section. Hill then began to plan the Great Northern Railway, which would invade the prairies and southern British Columbia.

The completion of the main line in 1886 did not, however, end the activities of the Canadian Pacific Railway in British Columbia. There was American competition to be faced, especially in the Kootenays and the Boundary country. In the 1880's and early 1890's the chief American competition was the Northern Pacific Railway, but in the late 1890's the Great Northern had seriously invaded the field. The Canadian Pacific Railway began to buy up, or lease, local lines in the Kootenays, especially the Columbia and Kootenay, the Columbia and Western and the British Columbia Southern. Eventually the south line of the Canadian Pacific from Lethbridge, Alberta, through Crowsnest Pass and through the Kootenays and Boundary country was completed in 1916 by the construction of the Kettle Valley Railway. By that time the Great Northern had been worsted. The Trail smelter, which originally had been an American venture, was in the hands of the Consolidated Mining and Smelting Company of Canada, a subsidiary of the Canadian Pacific Railway. Thus did Canadian interests triumph over American in the Kootenays.

18   For many years there was a story current in British Columbia that an old-timer in Victoria addressed a newcomer from Eastern Canada as follows: "Before you Canadians came, you know, we never had to take the shutters down till ten o'clock." Whether apocryphal or not, the tale illustrates the clash between the early settlers, who usually had come from the British Isles, and the rather more hustling and energetic 'Canadians'. On the whole, this clash was more in evidence on Vancouver Island than on the Mainland. Cariboo had never been so 'English' as Victoria and the lower Fraser Valley after 1886 rapidly absorbed the newcomers from 'the East'. Vancouver was, *par excellence*, the Mecca of the men and women from Ontario and the Maritimes.

In a study of this sort there is no accurate yardstick by which the growth of Canadianism can be measured. Still, it is possible to detect certain tendencies. In 1871 Canadians in British Columbia had made their presence felt. Many of them had come from California during the early gold rushes. Others had come direct to British Columbia by way of Panama and San Francisco. One devoted band — 'The Argonauts of 1862' — had come 'the plains across' through British Territory from Fort Garry. But it was not until after the completion of the Canadian Pacific Railway that eastern Canadians came in large numbers to 'the West beyond the West'.

During the decade from 1871 to 1881 the population of British Columbia increased from 36 247 to 49 459. Manitoba's went up from 25 228 to 62 260. The next decade, 1881 to 1891, witnessed an increase in British Columbia from 49 459 to 98 173, but Manitoba shot up from 62 260 to 152 506. British Columbia from 1891 to 1901 increased from 98 173 to 178 657 and Manitoba from 152 506 to 255 211.[17] But even as late as 1901 British Columbia possessed only 3.33 per cent. of Canada's total population. In 1901 only 12.02 per cent. of Canadians lived west of the Ontario-Manitoba border. The proportion in 1941 was 28.30 per cent., roughly 3 250 000 out of 11 500 000.

The first Census of Canada contained figures dealing only with the four 'original provinces'. It was not until the 1880–1881 Census that information was published regarding Manitoba, British Columbia and Prince Edward Island. The population of British Columbia is given as 49 459. According to birthplace this number was made up as follows:[18]

Born in British Columbia		32 175
Born in the British Isles		5 783
English	3 294	
Irish	1 285	
Scottish	1 204	
Born in other parts of Canada		2 768
Prince Edward Island	23	
Nova Scotia	379	
New Brunswick	374	
Quebec	396	
Ontario	1 572	
Manitoba	24	
Born in The Territories		14
Born in other British Possessions		211
Born in the United States		2 295
Born in other countries and at sea		5 462
Birthplace not given		751
Total		49 459

The Third Census of Canada, 1890–91, gave the population of British Columbia as 98 173, but apparently gave no statistics as regards the birthplaces of the people. It did, however, provide information regarding the numbers born in Canada and in foreign countries. In British Columbia 37 583 are classed as native, born of a native father; 19 268 as native, born of a foreign father; and 41 322 as foreign-born.[19] In this census, as in the previous one, the native Indians of British Columbia are included in the native-born totals. No attempt has been made to separate white men and Indians.

It is from the Fourth Census of Canada, 1900–1901, that most information is obtained regarding racial origins, nationalities and the birthplaces of the people. The population of British Columbia was now 178 657. According to racial origins 106 403 were of British birth (English, 52 863; Irish, 20 658; Scottish, 31 068), 25 488 were Indians, 532 Negroes, 19 482 Chinese and Japanese and the remainder of continental European origins or "unspecified". On the basis of nationality, 144 989 are classed as Canadian, 10 088 as American, 14 201 as Chinese, 3516 as Japanese and the remainder from the continent of Europe. But it is Table XIII — "Birthplaces of the People" — which best tells the story. Of the 99 612 listed as born in Canada 59 589 were born in British Columbia; 2203 in Manitoba; 2839 in New Brunswick; 4603 in Nova Scotia; 23 642 in Ontario; 1180 in Prince Edward Island; 4329 in Quebec; 991 in the North West Territories and 236 in "Canada not given". The total of those born in the British Isles was 30 630 distributed as follows: English, 19 385; Irish, 3957; Scottish, 6457; Welsh, 710; Lesser Isles, 121. From

19

the other British Possessions had come 1843. The foreign-born totalled 46 110, of whom 17 164 were from the United States.

From the statistics given above it is obvious that by 1901 the Canadianization of British Columbia was fairly well complete. A new generation had grown up west of the Rockies since 1871. No matter where their parents came from these young people were Canadians. To be sure, they were British Columbian Canadians, not quite the same as Canadians from the other provinces, nevertheless Canadians. Many of them were destined to prove their loyalty to Canada and to the British Empire in 1914. By 1901 east and west in Canada were really joined and 'the West beyond the West' had become Canadian.

Notes

1. *Debate on the Subject of Confederation with Canada*, Victoria, 1878, p. 13.
2. On this subject see F. W. Howay, *The Early History of the Fraser River Mines*, Victoria, 1926, pp. viii–xvii.
3. Marcus Lee Hansen and J. Bartlet Brebner, *The Mingling of the Canadian and American Peoples*, New Haven, 1940, p. 155.
4. *Ibid*.
5. For a discussion of this topic *cf.* F. W. Howay, W. N. Sage and H. F. Angus, *British Columbia and the United States*. Toronto: Ryerson, 1942, pp. 184–186.
6. *Cf.* A. S. Deaville, *The Colonial Postage Systems and Postage Stamps of Vancouver Island and British Columbia, 1849–1871*. Archives Memoir No. VIII, Victoria, B.C., King's Printer, 1928, pp. 137–143.
7. *The Census of Canada, 1870–1871*, Volume I, does not give figures for British Columbia. In *The Census of Canada, 1880–1881*, the total population of British Columbia, in 1871, whites, Indians, Chinese and coloured is given, however, as 36 247. Of this number 25 661 were Indians. *Cf.* L. T. Marshall, *Vital Statistics of British Columbia*, Victoria, B.C.; Provincial Board of Health u.d. (1932), p. 192.
8. Technically, of course, Prince Edward Island was not part of Canada till 1873, but this seems a hair-splitting distinction.
9. *Canada Year Book 1943–1944* Ottawa: King's Printer, 1944, p. 125.
10. *Journals of the Legislative Council of British Columbia, Session 1871*, Victoria, B.C., 1871, p. 6.
11. J. W. Trutch to Sir John A. Macdonald, Nov. 21, 1871, *Macdonald Papers*, Trutch Correspondence, 1871–1873, p. 98. (Public Archives of Canada.)
12. W. N. Sage, "John Foster McCreight, the first Premier of British Columbia", in the *Transactions of the Royal Society of Canada*, Third Series, Section II, Vol. XXXIV, 1940, p. 177.
13. E. O. S. Scholefield and R. E. Gosnell, *British Columbia, Sixty Years of Progress*, Vancouver and Victoria, 1913, Part II, p. 15, n.1.
14. *Macdonald Papers*, Trutch Correspondence, 1871–73, pp. 101–102.
15. Victoria *Daily Standard*, November 21, 1871.
16. *Canada Year Book, 1943–44*, p. 79.
17. *Canada Year Book, 1943–44*, pp. 79, 80.
18. *Census of Canada, 1880–1881*, Ottawa: McLean, Roger & Co., 1882, Vol. I, pp. 396–7, Table IV.
19. *Census of Canada, 1890–1891*. Ottawa: King's Printer, 1893, Vol. II, p. 228.

Long Courted, Won at Last*
F.W.P. BOLGER

I Mission to Canossa

Lieutenant Governor Robinson, the ever-active crusader in the cause of Confederation, wrote to Lord Kimberley in December, 1872, that he fully expected "unless some hitch occurs, which I do not foresee, to hand the Island over to the Dominion within six or eight months at the latest."[1] In the latter weeks of 1872, a series of events led almost inexorably to the fulfilment of Robinson's prognosis. In the autumn of 1872, unfavorable trade conditions caused serious financial difficulties. The harvest was late and markets were unfavorable. The result was that the farmers, unable to sell their limited agricultural produce at remunerative prices, were deprived of purchasing power. This recession in the agricultural industry seriously affected the whole economy. The government found it increasingly difficult to obtain the exchange needed to meet interest payments. Moreover, this recession almost immediately had serious repercussions on the market for the government's railway securities. The government had an agreement with the railway contractors whereby they were paid in debentures redeemable at par. The contractors, in turn, sold these at the Island banks. When the economy of the Island showed serious signs of strain, these debentures could not be sold except at a discount. Moreover, the Island banks refused to purchase any more of the government debentures. The result was that the contractors refused to continue with the construction of the railway.

21

The banks on Prince Edward Island, large holders of the railway debentures, feared a financial crisis. Charles Palmer, the President of the Union Bank, and a brother of Edward Palmer, went to London to attempt to sell some of these debentures. His mission was an unqualified failure. He was informed that if the Island would join Canada the bonds could be sold at a good rate. It was obvious that London was putting on the pressure. "No one can shut his eyes to the fact," J.C. Pope emphasized, "that influences have been brought to bear on our paper. Baring Brothers will not take one of our bonds."[2] On his return to the Island, Charles Palmer had a number of interviews with the members of the Executive Council with a view to persuading them that Confederation was the only solution to the Island's financial crisis. He later informed Sir John Rose, Canada's unofficial agent in London, "that he was quite certain that the way is open for our joining the Dominion on fair terms, and that, as soon as the matter can be brought about without prominent advances on our part."[3] There cannot be the slight-

*From *Canada's Smallest Province: A History of P.E.I.*, ed. by Francis W.P. Bolger. Copyright 1973 by the Prince Edward Island Museum and Heritage Foundation. Reprinted by permission.

est doubt that the pressure by Palmer and the other Island bankers was of considerable influence in convincing the Haythorne administration that it should reopen negotiations with Canada. While it is incontestable that these negotiations would have been initiated eventually, the pressure of the financial leaders undoubtedly hastened their beginnings.

The Island government spent a number of weeks in a fruitless attempt to save face. Prince Edward Island did not wish to make an open admission that Confederation was a necessity. Such an acknowledgement, the government correctly reasoned, would reduce its bargaining strength with the Dominion authorities. But the government's efforts to present a bold front were undermined from the very outset. Lieutenant Governor Robinson, Governor General Dufferin and Sir John Rose engaged in a triangular correspondence which eventually came across John A. Macdonald's desk. Robinson assumed the initiative with a revealing letter to Lord Dufferin:

22 Looking at the question fairly in the face, my Ministers see that there are only two courses open to them: either they must impose heavy additions to taxes on the people [and this, while it would be exceedingly unpopular would not get over the difficulty of exchange], or seek admission into the Union, provided that Canada would thereupon make our Railway debt her own. One or the other course will have to be adopted at the next session of the Local Parliament. Under these circumstances I shall feel greatly obliged if your Excellency will ascertain for me whether Canada will be prepared to adhere to the offer which she made to us in 1869 [commonly known as the "better terms"], and assume our Railway liabilities in addition, in the event of Prince Edward Island desiring admission into the Union.[4]

Robinson had already shown the Island's hand. The Canadian reply was cautious. Dufferin replied that "while my Ministers would not be prepared themselves to re-initiate any fresh proposals, I am authorized to assure you should your Government be disposed to make any overtures, there is no intention on the part of the Dominion Government to recede from the offer made in 1869, popularly known as "the better terms."[5] Pressed further by Robinson as to whether the Island's railway debt would be regarded as a Dominion or local debt, Dufferin replied evasively that the "railway debt was a subject for consideration and would be considered fairly."[6]

The replies of the Dominion authorities indicated that they intended to exercise extreme caution in their negotiations with the Islanders. Ever since 1864 the Canadians had taken the initiative in offering terms of union. The Islanders had invariably been unreceptive; and now that the "tight little Island" was in financial difficulties, Sir John A. Macdonald and his colleagues resolved that the overtures should come from the Islanders themselves. Sir John Rose told Macdonald of his correspondence with Charles Palmer and advised that "the present condition of things was a favorable opportunity for you to strike."[7] But Macdonald was wary and would not commit the Dominion Government. He indicated his stance in his reply to Rose in London:

Governor Robinson of P. E. Island has written privately and as if off his own bat, to Lord Dufferin, saying that he thought he could bring round his Government to consider the subject of union if Canada were still inclined in that direction. He wrote beyond a doubt, at the instigation of his Council, and, as we know from experience the style of the men, we answered guardedly. . . . You may remember how shamefully old Palmer behaved in '65. Haythorne behaved just as badly to us on the "better terms" matter in '69. He, then, under pretence of union, humbugged Tilley and our government into making an offer. He proved afterwards, that he never had any intention of supporting union, and that his object was by getting a better offer than the terms of the Quebec Conference, to kill our friends Haviland, Col. Gray, W. H. Pope, and others who had agreed to the original arrangement. This treacherous policy was successful, and our friends were for the time being politically snuffed out. Now Haythorne and Palmer are the ruling spirits of the present government, hence our caution. I have little doubt that our policy will be successful and that we will get a proposition before Parliament meets.[8]

The careful policy adopted by Macdonald made it necessary for the Islanders to swallow their pride and make the formal overture.

Robert Haythorne, pressured by Charles Palmer and Lieutenant Governor Robinson, and by now personally convinced that there was really no viable alternative, decided to ask his Executive Council to draft a series of proposals. The task which confronted Premier Haythorne was not an easy one. Robinson described the anti-Confederate complexion of his government:

23

My present Government, as your Lordship is aware, is an anti-Confederate one. Mr. Palmer, the Attorney General, is the same gentleman, who, as a delegate to Canada in 1864, spoke warmly in favor of Confederation and opposed it with equal warmth on his return to the Island. Mr. Haythorne, the Leader of the Government, is not personally opposed to it, but he represents an anti-Confederate constituency, is naturally of a timid disposition, and would not be a likely person to initiate successfully any important movement in opposition to the wishes of his constituents. The remaining members of the Government are personally, and as representatives, strongly anti-Confederate, and would like to remain out of the union as long as possible.[9]

The addition of David Laird to the Executive Council, in mid-December, made Haythorne's assignment even more delicate. As a result, the formal Minute, adopted by the Executive Council, on January 2, 1873, still reflected the spirit of independence which for so many years had characterized the Island's attitude to Confederation.

The Minute opened bravely with the claim that the members of the Executive Council were broaching the discussions on Confederation, because the Lieutenant Governor had initiated a correspondence on the subject with Lord Dufferin. They did acknowledge, however, that they had decided to pursue the subject because of the large railway liabilities. They admitted, moreover, that although the Islanders could undoubtedly sustain the taxation necessary to meet these liabilities, yet the economy would be adversely affected. They, therefore, felt the people of the Island should have the opportunity of choosing between increased taxation and Confederation. In order that the people might have the choice of deciding definitively between these two options at a general election, they asked the Dominion Government for a statement of the commitments it was prepared to make to the Island.[10] Specifically, the Minute requested the Dominion to concede, in addition to the proposals made by the "better terms" offer of 1869, the following terms: an additional annual allowance of $5,000 to bring the subsidy for the expenses of the local Legislature up to $30,000; that the Dominion Government take over the Prince Edward Island Railway and assume its debts, not exceeding $3,250,000; that the Dominion accept the new Law Courts Building and the Post Office, at a cost of $69,000, and the new Steam Dredge under contract, at a cost of $22,000; and that the Island be allowed to retain any sum, which might be awarded under the Washington Treaty, as an equivalent for surrendering the fisheries of the Island.[11] The Islanders managed to present a bold front despite their precarious economic situation.

Meanwhile, before the arrival of the Minute of Council in Ottawa, John A. Macdonald decided that any negotiations between the Island and Dominion Governments should be conducted by a delegation rather than by correspondence. He asked Lord Dufferin to write to Lieutenant Governor Robinson expressing these sentiments. After Robinson informed Haythorne of Macdonald's views, Haythorne replied that "he considered it unnecessary, at the present time, to send authorized agents to Ottawa, but if, hereafter, any circumstances should occur, which would render *viva voce* explanations necessary or desirable, we will not hesitate to adopt Lord Dufferin's suggestion."[12] Robert Haythorne did not have long to wait, however, before packing his luggage for Ottawa. When the Island Minute of Council arrived, it was immediately referred to Leonard Tilley, the Minister of Finance, who was placed in charge of negotiations. He informed the Privy Council "that some of the conditions are inadmissable, while others seemed reasonable, but that, in his opinion, it would be impossible to discuss fully or to settle these terms by correspondence."[13] He, therefore, suggested that the government of Prince Edward Island should send a delegation to Ottawa, and that a Committee of the Privy Council should receive it at once in conference. The Privy Council concurred, and on January 31, 1873, Lord Dufferin sent to the Island government a formal Minute incorporating these recommendations.

The Haythorne administration was disturbed by the request that a delegation should be appointed and sent to Ottawa. The authorization of such a body obviously meant that the negotiations with Canada, heretofore private, would have to be made public. The members of the Executive Council had hoped to avoid any publicity until they were in a position to announce the terms that Canada would concede. But their plan was to no avail. Robert Haythorne, when taunted in the Legislature about his mission to Ottawa, explained:

When the answer to our Minute of Council was received, it became a question whether we would accept the invitation, and send a delegation to Canada, or let the subject drop. However, the Government came to the conclusion that, having put our hand to the plough we should go forward, so that when Parliament would meet, we would be able to state what terms Canada was prepared to offer, and then the representatives of the people would be able to choose between Confederation and a large amount of increased taxation. That was the object of the Government in the first instance, and when it was shown that our object could not be attained without sending a delegation, we determined to put the matter through efficiently.[14]

Thus, since the Island administration had no other choice, Haythorne and Laird "stole away in the night by the ice-boat route to the mainland," George

Howlan sarcastically noted, "and reached Ottawa on February 24, 1873."[15]

Several conferences were held between Haythorne and Laird and a sub-committee of the Canadian Privy Council, consisting of John A. Macdonald, Leonard Tilley, Hector Langevin, Joseph Howe and Charles Tupper. Although the Canadians fully realized that Prince Edward Island's financial crisis had prompted the negotiations, they did not manifest any disposition to take unfair advantage of the situation. After lengthy discussions lasting ten days, generous terms of union were mutually agreed upon. These terms, with minor modifications, became the basis of the political union between Prince Edward Island and the Dominion of Canada.

The Island's debts and liabilities were to be assumed by the Dominion. The debt allowance, which in the other provinces had been set at approximately $25 per capita upon the population of 1861, was fixed for the Island at $45 per head on the basis of the 1871 census.[16] This clause meant that the Island, with a population of 94,021, was entitled to incur a debt of $4,230.95.[17] If the Island, at the time of its entrance into union, had not incurred debts equal to this sum, it was entitled to receive interest at the rate of 5 per cent per annum on the difference between the actual amount of its indebtedness and the amount authorized.[18] Since the debt of the Island amounted to $3,785,576, the net effect of this clause was to concede $22,218.42 annually to the Island.[19] This concession was granted in view of the limited benefits which the Island would receive from Dominion public works, the possibility of a new financial adjustment between Canada and its existing provinces, as well as the Island's "isolation during six months of the year."[20] In return for the transfer to the Dominion of the power of taxation the Island received for the support of its government and legislature an annual grant of $30,000 and a subsidy of 80 cents per capita upon the population of 1871, which was to be augmented in proportion to the increase of population until it reached 400,000.[21]

The terms contained many provisions designed to settle the Island's particular problems. All the railways under contract and in course of construction became the property of the Dominion; and the new Law Courts Building and new Steam Dredge were also transferred to the federal government.[22] "Efficient Steam Service for the conveyance of Mails and Passengers," and "continuous communication" with the mainland was also guaranteed.[23] The allotment of six members in the House of Commons, now warranted by the Island's population, met the Island's principal constitutional objections to Confederation.[24] Finally, to enable the Island to settle its contentious land tenure question, a special provision was mutually agreed upon by the Island and Federal negotiators:

The Island Government holding no lands from the Crown, and consequently enjoying no revenue from that source for the construction and maintenance of Local Works, it is agreed that the Dominion Government pay, in half-yearly instalments, and in advance, to the Government of Prince Edward Island, $45,000 per annum, less five per cent upon any sum not exceeding $800,000, that the Dominion Government may advance to the Island Government for the purchase of Lands, now held by large proprietors.[25]

Prince Edward Island certainly received generous treatment from the Canadian Government. The Dominion took over the railway that had seriously threatened the financial collapse of the Island. While its cost, naturally enough, was charged against the Island as a local debt, yet the Dominion increased the debt allowance by $20 per capita to permit the Island to derive some revenue from the debt allowance clause. The annual grant for the support of the local government and legislature was increased by some $5,000 over the amount promised in 1869. The land settlement was also liberal. The annual subsidy of $45,000 per year in consideration of the absence of Crown Lands on the Island helped to alleviate the loss the Island had suffered in this category since 1767; and, moreover, the provision of $800,000, would enable the government to purchase the proprietary estates. Since the interest on the $800,000 would amount to only $40,000, the net effect of this clause was to add $5,000 if the Island borrowed the whole amount; and if the government elected to repay the principal, it would receive the $45,000 subsidy *in toto*.

Haythorne and Laird, completely satisfied with the negotiations, telegraphed a synopsis of the terms to their colleagues on March 3, 1873, and advised a dissolution.[26] Three days later they received word that their colleagues agreed to the terms and concurred in advising an immediate appeal to the electors.[27] On the next day, March 7, the Island delegates and the sub-committee of the Privy Council formally attached their signatures to the terms; and in Charlottetown, Lieutenant Governor Robinson dissolved the Legislature. Haythorne and Laird returned immediately to defend the new terms before the perplexed and astonished electors of Prince Edward Island.

II Confederation — Yes: Increased Taxation — No

Haythorne and his colleagues fully realized the formidable challenge they faced in attempting to persuade the people of Prince Edward Island to vote for Confederation. Lieutenant Governor Robinson, who now saw his objective nearing realization, lent considerable assistance to his government. "What is now to be feared," he wrote Lord Kimberley, "is intrigue, and the raising of side issues, on the part of the Confederates, who are exceedingly jealous of an anti-Confederate Government having taken up the question, and will do everything to overthrow the present Government and get into office themselves."[28] With characteristic partisanship he enlisted support for the Liberals. He informed Lord Dufferin, that "the standard taken by the Opposition is that the terms are not good enough, and that if in power they could procure better."[29] In order to undermine this campaign strategy, he asked Lord Dufferin to state that "the delegates had procured terms as good as they could expect or are ever likely to receive."[30] Lord Dufferin replied by telegraph, that his "Ministers are of opinion — an opinion in which I fully coincide—that no additional concessions would have any chance of being adopted by the Parliament of Canada."[31] Robinson also cabled Lord

26

Kimberley at the Colonial Office, and asked him to express the pleasure of the British Government that Prince Edward Island was considering Confederation.[32] Lord Kimberley replied on the same day, that "Her Majesty's Government learns with much satisfaction that terms are agreed upon for the admission of Prince Edward Island into the Dominion, and trust that Prince Edward Island will not lose this opportunity of union with her sister colonies."[33] Robinson immediately published these messages in all the Island newspapers with the hope that they would influence the electorate to return the Haythorne administration to power.

The political platform upon which the Haythorne Government based its appeal was outlined by David Laird at a large political rally in Charlottetown. He marshalled two principal arguments, the first of which was, that Confederation was now a financial necessity. "I care not what political party comes into power," he argued, "as sure as the sun rises in the heaven, so surely will this Island enter Confederation, whatever better political "shibboleth" pronounced at the coming election. I will tell you why I know this. It is because our debt is so great that we cannot meet the interest upon it."[34] Secondly, he maintained that the terms were generous and no additional concessions could or should be expected. "Viewing the situation from a financial standpoint," he asserted, "I conclude that the offer of the Dominion Government is very liberal, and that it should be accepted without hesitation on our part."[35] "To attempt to maintain our independence any longer," he insisted," "encumbered as we are, with a debt, so disproportionate to our resources, would be sheer folly. We would be literally dragging out a sickly and miserable existence, quarelling among ourselves and getting more hopelessly and irretrievably involved, and in the end would have to accept the inevitable with loss of prestige and self-respect."[36] Confident that such arguments were irrefutable, the Liberals, under the leadership of Haythorne and Laird, hoped to receive a mandate for Confederation on the proposed terms.

The Conservatives, under the leadership of James C. Pope, were placed in an embarrassing position in this campaign. They realized that Confederation was the only answer to the Island's financial difficulties, and for this reason, they wanted the constituencies to declare in favor of it. "Union with Canada," said J. C. Pope, "will place our securities on a par with those of the Dominion, and our public position will be much better."[37] But the Conservatives also wanted to win the election. Their problem was to defeat a government committed to Confederation without endangering the principle of Confederation itself. Pope, their strong Confederate leader, eventually adopted a two-fold strategy. In the first place, he maintained that the people were being asked by the Haythorne administration to make an irrevocable decision without sufficient knowledge and time. "Parliament should have met," he contended, "and the terms agreed upon by our Government, should have been submitted to the Representatives of the people, as well as the financial state of the Colony. All matters, relating to the state of the Colony, should have been discussed, and then the question of Confederation

27

could properly have been submitted to you at the polls."[38] In the second place, Pope claimed that the terms obtained by Haythorne and Laird were inadequate. He stated that if the Conservatives were elected he would immediately renew negotiations with the Dominion Government in order to obtain "proper terms." He insisted that he, as a Conservative and a close personal friend of Sir John A. Macdonald, could make a much better bargain with the Dominion.[39] Pope and the Conservatives hoped the alluring appeal of "still better terms" would be favorably received by the electorate and that they would gain power without endangering the principle of Confederation.

Although the 1873 campaign was ostensibly contested on the question of Confederation, another controversy intervened that served to cloud, to some degree, the main issue. The second problem was the school question which had been for years a prolific source of bitterness in Prince Edward Island. It seemed to be endowed with a magic charm. No matter what other problems might be raised, it was always a force to be reckoned with at every fresh appeal to the electorate. The 1873 campaign was no exception, and the education question came to the forefront. James C. Pope, in the thick of a desperate fight for office, decided to attempt to turn the school question to his advantage. He realized that he could be assured of his party's victory if he could obtain the support of the Catholic electorate. What better ploy than to promise the Catholics governmental support for their separate schools? He, therefore, took counsel with his supporters, and the Conservative caucus promised that "the Opposition, as a party, was prepared to go for such a modification of the School Law, as will entitle any school, open to Government inspection, to its equitable proportion of the school-tax . . . provided a sufficient number of supporters of the present Government, being dissatisfied with the present policy of the Government, are prepared to join us in carrying such a measure."[40] W. H. Pope even went so far as to draw up a Draft Bill embodying the principles contained in the caucus resolution.

The Draft Bill soon became public and the Conservative proposals were widely circulated in the press. The Protestant clergy, naturally enough, united against the proposals of the Draft Bill. Shortly afterwards, they published a letter in all the newspapers of the Island, in which they recommended that the "unsectarian system of education should be maintained, and that our Protestant brethren and our fellow-colonists, in general, in order to preserve in its integrity the present system, should give their support to those only who, in seeking their suffrages, shall satisfy them that such system will not be interfered with."[41] This letter proved quite effective. The Protestant electors exacted pledges from all Protestant candidates that they would not alter the existing educational system. Every Protestant candidate, even J. C. Pope, agreed to this pledge. Feelings were so embittered at this time that even the least perspicacious could realize that to refuse to do so was to court political disaster. Once again religion and politics were mixed in hopeless confusion and bitterness.

The people of Prince Edward Island, confronted with the confusing is-

28

sues of "just terms" versus "proper terms," "grants" versus "no grants," went to the polls on April 2, 1873. They approved the principle of Confederation but gave a majority to J. C. Pope. L. H. Davies, commenting on the election, remarked that Confederation "was discussed in every hamlet and school house in the country, and there was hardly a man who did not understand it, in all its bearings. The result of that election, was that there is today, in this House, only one man, who opposed a Union with Canada, and he is not to the fore, while the question is being discussed."[42] Although Haythorne had lost the election, he was pleased that Confederation had been approved. He attributed the favorable response of the public opinion to Confederation "not merely to the financial position of the Colony, and the heavy pecuniary obligations she has assumed, but to the fact that for the first time in the history of the question, it can be fairly argued, that the terms of Union, offered for our acceptance, by Canada, are advantageous and just."[43] James Rowe's explanation for the change of viewpoint was less altruistic: "After the terms came down," he told the Assembly, "I went among the people and laid them before them, telling them, they would have to choose these, or increased taxation. I did not try to persuade them, as to what they should do, but placed Confederation or increased taxation before them, asking them to say, which they would choose. They chose the former."[44] Considering the Islanders' previous rejections of terms not dissimilar, it seems safe to assume that their aversion to increased taxation was the impelling motive that led them to declare so unanimously in favor of Confederation.

29

The decision at the polls also indicated that the Islanders wished to place the direction of their public affairs in the hands of the Conservatives. This party, under J. C. Pope's leadership, won a decisive victory. It was placed in command of eighteen of the thirty seats in the Assembly. Since two of the elected Liberals, Cornelius Howatt and A. E. C. Holland, declared themselves independents, Haythorne's supporters numbered only ten. The magnitude of the Conservative victory can be attributed to two principal factors. Firstly, Pope's promise to secure "still better terms" won many votes for the Conservatives. This alluring appeal was not lost on the Islanders, who had demonstrated since 1864 that they were determined to drive a shrewd economic bargain before they would consent to union with Canada. Secondly, the Catholic electors voted almost unanimously for the Conservative party. The Draft Bill, published early in the campaign, pledging aid to Catholic schools brought the Catholics into alliance with the Conservatives; and the situation did not change appreciably when the Conservative Protestant candidates had to pledge they would not alter the school law. The Catholic electors considered that the Protestant candidates were literally forced to make this pledge so they placed their confidence in J. C. Pope's candidates. Thus, the promise of the Conservatives to redress the Catholic grievance gained Pope and five other Conservative Protestant candidates Catholic support. In addition, the twelve Catholic candidates elected were all supporters of J. C. Pope. The *Herald* remarked that "Mr. Pope came into power with a triumphant majority, and the very pith of that majority was Catholic representatives."[45] J. C. Pope had his substantial majority, but his attempts to mollify his Catholic supporters caused him many anxious moments in the next few months.

III J. C. Pope and Proper Terms

On April 15, 1873, Robert Haythorne tendered his resignation to Lieutenant Governor Robinson, and expressed his appreciation "for the frankness and courtesy,"[46] he had displayed during his term of office. In choosing Haythorne's successor, Robinson displayed considerably more frankness than courtesy. He was disappointed that Haythorne had been defeated, and extremely displeased that J. C. Pope had engaged in a criticism of the terms obtained by Haythorne and Laird. He did not like J. C. Pope personally, and would have preferred to have offered the office of Premier to T. H. Haviland.[47] But since Robinson really had no alternative but to accept Pope, he attempted to place conditions on his acceptance so as to ensure the passage of Confederation. Robinson's attempts to impose these conditions introduced an interesting constitutional conflict, in which Pope diplomatically, but firmly, reminded Robinson of the position of the Crown under responsible government.

After accepting Haythorne's resignation, Robinson informed J. C. Pope that he intended to entrust the formation of the new government to him if he promised to do his best "to carry Confederation during the coming session, on the terms which have recently been submitted to the people, if none better can be procured from the Dominion authorities."[48] Although Pope declared that he would do all in his power "to ensure the speedy admission of the Island into the Union on terms just and equitable," he refused to accept "the honor of attempting to form a Government pledged to your Honor to pursue any definite policy. . . ."[49] "I trust that I may be pardoned," he wrote, "if I remind your Honor that the people of this Island have the right to self-government, and that as one of their representatives, I can never undertake, at the instance of the representative of the Crown, to do any act calculated to abridge this right."[50] Robinson was highly incensed by Pope's reply and said he needed such a pledge in view of his assertion during the campaign, that the delegation to Ottawa was "a conspiracy to deprive the people of self-government, *et hoc genus omne.*"[51] He reminded Pope that he was perfectly aware of his constitutional position, but "it was absolutely necessary to the harmonious working of the Constitutuion, that the Crown shall be aware of, and have full reliance on, the personal views of the Minister, in whom it proposes to place its chief confidence."[52] Pope remained unimpressed and simply replied that he "still could not recognize the propriety of your requiring from me any pledge."[53]

J. C. Pope's second refusal convinced Robinson that he should adopt a more threatening approach. He said that some of Pope's election statements required him to make sure that his views, and those of the Assembly, on union, would not "be so wide apart as to be practically irreconcilable."[54] Without such assurance he would "have no alternative but to entrust the formation of the new Administration to some member of your party whose estimate of the relative position of the Crown and its chief adviser shall better accord with my own."[55] Such a threat to a man who had just received an overwhelming mandate, as leader of a party, was remarkably naive. Pope refused to budge. He informed Robinson that he still could not see any propriety in a pledge even if his views and those of the Legislature did not agree.[56] "As a matter of course," Pope wrote, "if I were to fail to acquiesce in the decision of the Legislature upon this or any other question, I would at once cease to be one of your Honor's constitutional advisers."[57] Robinson seemed to be completely disarmed by Pope's astute reply. He removed the condition, retreated gracefully and informed Pope he would be delighted if he would "proceeed to form a Government and submit the names of your proposed colleagues with as little delay as possible."[58] The whole episode reveals not only the strange impression Robinson entertained of his function as head of the government, but also his partisanship and the extent to which he was prepared to interfere in order to bring the Island into Confederation.

J. C. Pope formed an administration at once, and the Legislature was convened on April 22, 1873. The new Conservative government was as determined as its predecessor to unite Prince Edward Island with the Dominion. "Feeling as we do," said J. C. Pope, "that all side issues should give way in order that the public credit may be maintained, and if Confederation will do this, I believe in view of all the difficulties entailed upon the country, this side of the House feels constrained to overcome their scruples against Confederation."[59] But the Conservatives insisted that they intended to seek better terms from Ottawa, and this for two principal reasons. In the first place, they maintained that the present terms were inadequate. Pope insisted that "they did not secure to this Colony a sum sufficient to defray the ordinary and indispensable requirements of its local government, and are by no means an equivalent for the Revenue, present and prospective, which it would be called upon to surrender to the Dominion."[60] "Better terms than those offered," he challenged the Assembly, "we have a right to look for. Better, I feel persuaded, we are entitled to, and if sought for, I am confident better we shall obtain."[61] In the second place, the Conservatives insisted that their mandate from the electorate required them to seek "better terms." "The late Government went to the country with these terms," A. J. Macdonald said, "and I contend that the people voted against them. But while doing do, they also voted in favor of the principle of Confederation, a majority declaring that we were justly entitled to better terms still. Such being the case, I contend that it is the duty of this side of the House to see what better terms can yet be obtained."[62] J. C. Pope then asked the Assembly to endorse a resolution authorizing the appointment of a delegation to proceed at once to Ottawa to confer with the Government of the Dominion of Canada on the securing of "just and reasonable terms."[63]

David Laird, the leader of the Liberals in the Lower House, and his colleagues vigorously maintained that the Conservatives had no justification for resuming further negotiations with the Dominion. They insisted that the terms received were just and liberal and that no additional concessions could or need be obtained. Laird contended that "by accepting the terms now offered, the Island would be placed in a superior position to any of the other Colonies that have entered the Confederacy."[64] "We have some honor and dignity to maintain in this matter," he said, "and have no right to send off a begging delegation to Canada for new Terms. The Colony has already obtained terms which the Governor General has declared cannot be increased, and I, for one, cannot stultify myself in supporting the resolution in favor of another delegation."[65] The Liberals also argued that Confederation should not be delayed in view of the financial and commercial difficulties of the Island. "The business of the country," Arthur Stewart asserted, "is now embarrassed. Trade is encumbered with many difficulties. All this would be relieved, if Confederation was effected. That is why, I am so anxious that no unnecessary delay should take place."[66] For these reasons, David Laird countered J. C. Pope's resolution with an amendment that the Assembly should prepare an Address to the Queen asking her to unite "Prince Edward Island with the Dominion of Canada on terms and conditions approved of in the Minute of the Privy Council, of the 10th March, 1873."[67]

After a spirited debate, Laird's amendment was rejected by the Assembly by a vote of fifteen to ten.[68] Cornelius Howatt and A. E. C. Holland, and two die-hard anti-Confederates, sponsored a resolution "that the best interests and future prosperity of Prince Edward Island would be secured by refusing Terms of admission into union with the Dominion of Canada."[69] This resolution was defeated by a majority of twenty-four to two, an almost complete contrast to the votes registered on similar anti-Confederate resolutions in the past.[70] Pope's original resolution was then adopted on a division of sixteen to ten.[71] In accordance with this resolution, Lieutenant Governor Robinson was requested to appoint a delegation to renew Confederation negotiations with the Dominion of Canada. The Assembly was then adjourned for ten days to await the results of the second mission to Ottawa.

When John A. Macdonald heard the results of the election on Prince Edward Island, he was highly pleased. He wrote to Lord Dufferin:

Pope's party which has triumphed was always in close alliance with us of the Dominion on the subject of Confederation. It was defeated by Mr. Haythorne and his friends who are anti-Confederates. At the last moment Mr. Haythorne took up Confederation as "une planche de salut" fearing defeat in their general policy at the approaching meeting of the Legislature. They had met the just reward of their tortuous policy. The original friends of Confederation have succeeded and will have the credit of carrying the measure.[72]

Apparently Macdonald also heard the rumor, falsely circulated in some quarters, that David Laird intended to join in a coalition with J. C. Pope, for he said in the same letter: "I understand that Laird who was here with Haythorne will join Pope's administration. I hope this is so for the sake of the cause, although it does not raise Mr. Laird in my estimation. His presence there will shield us from attempts at *still better* terms."[73] Laird, of course, did not become a member of Pope's administration, and Macdonald and his colleagues were not shielded from another delegation. On May 3, 1873, Macdonald's friend, J. C. Pope, accompanied by George Howlan and T. H. Haviland, left for Ottawa to seek additional concessions. Prince Edward Island's financial crisis certainly did not prevent the Islanders from doing all in their power to make a shrewd bargain with the Dominion of Canada.

On May 6, the Island delegates arrived in Ottawa to initiate further negotiations with the Dominion government. For the next nine days they held several conferences with a sub-committee of the Privy Council, consisting of John A. Macdonald, Leonard Tilley, Charles Tupper and Hector Langevin. The first proposals of the Islanders were categorically denied, and they were placed in an embarrassing position. They concluded, however, that it would be more humiliating to return home without any concessions than to make further approaches. Accordingly, they submitted two additional memoranda comprising modified demands. The sub-committee relented and granted a few concessions. An agreement was formally reached on May 15, which enabled the Island delegates to return home loudly proclaiming that their mission was highly successful.

The additional concessions agreed upon by the delegations were that Prince Edward Island's debt allowance was to be raised from $45 per capita ($4,230,945) to $50 per capita ($4,701,050) and that telegraphic communications would be maintained by the Dominion Government between the Island and the mainland.[74] The $23,500 realized annually from the increased debt allowance, and the $2,000 for the telegraphic communications represented an annual increase of $25,000 to the original terms conceded to Haythorne and Laird. The additional terms were not impressive. David Laird claimed that the delegates had operated "on the principle that it was better to take half a loaf than to starve."[75] But to the Island delegates, who came so close to registering a zero in Ottawa, the new terms represented a substantial victory. They were now ready to defend their mission in the Island Legislature.

33

IV Confederation Debates

On May 22, 1873, J. C. Pope presented the terms of the union to the members of the House of Assembly. Their approval was a foregone conclusion. The debates revealed that the members almost unanimously considered that Confederation was a necessity. "It has now become a self-evident proposition," said T. H. Haviland, "that we cannot any longer remain out of Confederation. Unless we accept the Terms now before us and go into Confederation, it will be utterly impossible, with the large debt now upon us, to float our debentures, and establish our public credit."[76] "I have held anti-Confederation views," admitted George W. Howlan, "but I find no other course is now open to us as a Colony, but to accept the best terms we can procure, and enter the Dominion."[77] But it was James Rowe, who, perhaps, best expressed the sentiments of most Islanders:

He believed that his constituents would not have gone in favor of the measure [Confederation] were it not for circumstances over which they had no control. Indeed he had reason to believe that his constituents regretted the circumstances which had placed them in their present position, and necessitated their acceptance of the Terms of Confederation now offered to the Colony. Had it not been for the introduction of the Railway Bill, his constituency, and he believed other constituencies also, would still have rejected any offer Canada might make to this Colony to induce us to unite with her, as the people would have preferred to manage their own affairs as in times past. But there is, under our present circumstances, a necessity for our accepting Terms of Confederation, in order to escape financial embarrassment . . . and he would most heartily support the resolution before the committee, in the interest of his constituents, and of the people of the whole Island.[78]

The argument that Prince Edward Island must enter Confederation, *ex necessitate*, was advanced by nearly all the members.

These final Confederation debates also indicated that the large majority of the members of the Assembly considered that they had acted very sagaciously in delaying the Island's entry into the union with Canada. David Laird proudly referred to the merits of the delay and the part he had played in effecting it. "If it had not been for my opposition to Confederation in years gone by," he asserted, "we would, today have the old spavined horse which the Hon. Col. Secretary [T. H. Haviland] was willing to accept, and with that old horse we would now be limping and hobbling along."[79] "The eighty cents per head," he continued, "and the debt equivalent, were all that they were granted under the Quebec Scheme, and I am today proud that I opposed the scheme. The Better Terms of 1869, I also opposed, and I am glad I did so, as the Terms secured by the former delegation were $14,000 better than they were."[80] "Perhaps it is as well," admitted Frederick Brecken, "that we have been allowed our own way and time of joining with Canada. We have not married in haste. No doubt, the hon. member, the Leader of the Opposition [Laird] has rendered good service in opposing the measure so long, and, perhaps, his position and the influence he brought to bear has, more than anything else, contributed to the result now achieved."[81] W. W. Sullivan also maintained that "a great deal had been gained by resisting Confederation as long as we did, but as we now had fair and reasonable terms, we should be satisfied to accept them with good grace."[82]

The members of the Assembly did accept the terms with good grace. They expressed satisfaction with the generous treatment accorded by the Dominion. Henry Beer said "all the members should be satisfied with the handsome sum that had been secured."[83] "It was not probable," he added, "that any additional concession would be made to this Colony for a long time to come, as we had been liberally dealt with by the Government of the Dominion."[84] "I am only too happy," Arthur Stewart informed the Assembly, "to know that Confederation is so nearly consummated on fair and reasonable terms, that our Island is to be freed from its tremendous debt, and that we shall be a free, independent, and well-governed people, retaining all our present rights and privileges."[85] Nearly all the members expressed similar sentiments in different ways.

34

The representatives predicted that Prince Edward Island would enjoy a prosperous future as a province of the Dominion. Peter Sinclair stated that the Island "would improve its agricultural, commercial and fishing operations, at a more rapid rate than it had ever done, and that general prosperity would be the result. The Colony would occupy a better financial position than ever before as it would be entirely free from debt, and would receive a sufficient revenue to meet its requirements for many years to come."[86] The members even asserted that the old bugbear of taxation, that had been so effectively used by anti-Confederates in the past, would not mar the brilliant future. David Laird, the inveterate anti-Confederate of former days, said with confidence: "I am free now to admit that I do not fear any bad results from Confederation. The people of the other Provinces are as afraid of taxation as we are. No increase of taxation can be levied upon us, but what must be imposed upon them, therefore, in that respect we have nothing to fear."[87] The members were so optimistic of the Island's future that it could be said John Lefurgy expressed the sentiments of all when he concluded the debate with the claim that the Assembly had "this night acted wisely for the interests of this Colony."[88]

35

On May 26, 1873, in the early hours of the morning, Premier J. C. Pope moved that the Address to the Queen, embodying the terms of union between Prince Edward Island and the Dominion of Canada, be accepted by the Assembly.[89] David Laird, the leader of the Opposition, magnanimously seconded Pope's motion, maintaining that "as a party we were defeated, but nevertheless the question had been sustained."[90] Only two members, A. E. C. Holland and Cornelius Howatt opposed the motion. Holland maintained that "no reason had been produced, save the glory argument, to show why we should support Confederation."[91] "We have sold our noble little ship," he continued, "and she now stands stripped of all the glory with which for one hundred years, she was adorned."[92] Howatt said facetiously: "I know, Mr. Speaker, that in this House, I occupy about the same position that our representatives will in the Dominion Parliament. They will be left out, and have their views treated in the same way as mine are here."[93] The two anti-Confederates were indeed an insignificant minority. The resolutions in favor of Confederation were carried by a majority of twenty-seven to two.[94] Thus by an almost unanimous majority, a complete contrast to the vote on the Quebec Resolutions, the Assembly decided that Prince Edward Island should become a province of the Dominion of Canada.

The debate on Confederation followed a similar pattern in the Legislative Council. The Councillors unanimously declared themselves favorable to the new terms, but it was evident that necessity prompted their decision. The speeches of the two confirmed anti-Confederates, A. A. MacDonald and Edward Palmer illustrate this emphasis on necessity. "The only thing that induces me to come to the determination that Confederation is our destiny, if not an absolute necessity," said A. A. MacDonald, "is that our other securities, treasury warrants, etc. may become depreciated. . . . I have, therefore, reluctantly come to the conclusion that Confederation is a necessity."[95] "I have always been one of the strongest opponents of the union of this Island with Canada," Edward Palmer declared truthfully, "but I saw that the country was brought into such a state by the great railway debt that Confederation was the only expedient we could resort to so as to maintain the credit of the Colony, and carry on the Government."[96] Every member of the Council expressed similar views.

All the Councillors signified satisfaction with the generous terms conceded to them by Canada. "When Canada engaged to take $3,250,000 of railway debt off our shoulders," said Palmer, "I thought we had reason to congratulate ourselves. I cannot, therefore, have the slightest hesitation in accepting the present proposals."[97] "I was perfectly satisifed when we got $45 per head," Thomas Dodd remarked, "because it was very much more than we had been previously offered, but when the late Delegates got $5 additional, I am better satisfied still."[98] Patrick Walker, with typical Island logic, commented: "All I have to say is that the first Delegation did well, but the second did better."[99]

36   The members of the Council did not display the same optimism as their counterparts in the Assembly with respect to the Island's future in the Dominion. Edward Palmer was the only member who referred to the subject, and his remarks did not manifest much enthusiasm. He said:

> I have been agreeably surprised at the advancement and prosperity in Canada since Confederation was first established. Her manufactures have vastly increased, and her prospects are good. She has maintained her public credit with great ease; and I am of the opinion that upon our going into the union now we will not have the disadvantages we would have had six or seven years ago.[100]

The silence of the rest of the Councillors would seem to imply that they regarded the future with mixed feelings. But they did not hesitate to accept the terms of Confederation for better or worse. On May 27, 1873, the resolutions recommending union with Canada were presented to the Council by A. A. MacDonald and carried unanimously without a division.[101] As in the Assembly, this vote was a perfect contrast to the 1865 vote on the Quebec Resolutions. The Legislative Council on Prince Edward Island had never believed in half-measures.

In Ottawa, the preparations for the entry of Prince Edward Island into Confederation went smoothly. On May 16, 1873, Leonard Tilley, on behalf of the Canadian Privy Council, submitted the terms of union for the admission of Prince Edward Island into Confederation to the Canadian House of Commons for ratification. He informed the House that the terms conceded to the Island differed from those granted to the other provinces in only two particulars. The differences were, he pointed out, a special grant of $800,000 for the settlement of the land tenure question, and a more generous debt allowance arrangement. He elaborated upon the $800,000 provision:

> The Province was in a different position to that of any other Province in the Dominion. What passed to the other Provinces as Crown lands had, in the case of Prince Edward Island, been sold to parties in England by the Imperial Government, so that they had no Crown Lands, and derived no revenue from such a source for local purposes as every other Province did.

These lands being held by absentee proprietors, the only persons living on them were tenants; this was a very unsatisfactory state of things, and had prevented the Island from taking the position it would otherwise have taken. It was in consequence of this that the Legislature, in 1869, authorized the Government to make arrangements for the admission of the Island, including the purchase of the Crown Lands.[102]

Tilley went on to explain the reasons for the special debt allowance settlement:

From the fact that the Dominion Government and Parliament had undertaken the construction of the Intercolonial Railway at a cost of $20,000,000, that the Pacific Railway was to be built with a contribution on the part of the Dominion of $30,000,000, that $20,000,000, or $25,000,000, was to be expended on canals, that is was contemplated to readjust the debts of the Dominion by assuming the surplus of Ontario and Quebec, and giving sums in proportion to the other Provinces, and that the Island would not have public works after it came into the Dominion at all in proportion to the other Provinces, it was agreed to extend the Island debt to be assumed to $50 a head. At the negotiations in January last the sum was fixed at $45 a head. That had been submitted to the people of the Island and the result was that the newly elected Legislature had rejected the terms and authorized another deputation to come to Ottawa with power to enter into negotiations with the Government for the extension of the amount to $50.[103]

37

After making these explanations, Tilley asked the House of Commons to authorize the Canadian Government to admit "this beautiful and fertile Island into the Union."[104] He admitted that the terms were quite generous, but maintained that the Dominion would not need to spend much money on the Island after Confederation. "The great local works there having now been completed," contended Tilley, "there could never be any large local expenditure in the future, and it was in consideration of this fact that the Dominion had granted such liberal terms."[105] Alexander Mackenzie, the leader of the Liberals, graciously stated that "they were all very happy at the prospect of the Island joining the Confederation, and no member of the House, especially amongst those who were the originators of the Confederation project, would be disposed to treat the matter otherwise than in an amicable way."[106] All the members who spoke expressed the same views. On May 17, 1873, the Confederation resolutions were adopted without a division; and John A. Macdonald, Leonard Tilley, Hector Langevin and Charles Tupper were appointed to prepare an Address to the Queen requesting her to unite Prince Edward Island with the Dominion of Canada.

The debate in the Canadian Senate was very brief. On May 21, Senator Campbell moved that the Senate accept the Confederation resolutions in order to effect "the completion of the Union, which we have been endeavouring to bring about ever since 1861, and which remains simply to be completed by the admission of Prince Edward Island."[107] Senator Ferrier referred, with some satisfaction, to the motivation that had prompted the Island's entry into the union: "I am glad that Prince Edward Island has decided upon coming into Confederation. I have said that prosperity is not always an advantage, and, I think, if the seal fishing had been less successful for the last few years, we should have seen Newfoundland wishing to become part of the Confederation, like Prince Edward Island. It got into difficulties a short time ago, and was glad to take hold of the stronger power."[108] Senator Holmes concluded the debate stating that "he felt very glad that the

Island had at least consented to enter the Union. This was the garden of the Lower Provinces, possessing a favorable climate and productive soil . . . and would be a benefit and not a burden to us, as we all knew that union was strength.''[109] The Confederation resolutions were than adopted by the Upper House without a division. With the Senate's ratification of the terms, the Legislature of Canada authorized the entrance of another province into the Dominion of Canada.

While the legislative debates reveal that both Prince Edward Island and the Dominion of Canada were well pleased with the results of the Confederation negotiations, their Governors and the Imperial Government were even more delighted. Lord Dufferin, in a congratulatory letter to Lieutenant Governor Robinson, expressed his enthusiasm. "The union of Prince Edward Island with the Dominion of Canada," he wrote, "is a most fortunate circumstance from whatever point it may be regarded, whether affecting Local, Imperial, or Canadian interests."[110] "I am well aware," he continued, "that it has been in a great measure owing to your wise and administrative counsels, that so happy a consummation has been reached, and in forwarding the duplicate copy of the enclosed Minute to Lord Kimberley, it has been an additional pleasure to me to state how highly conducive your efforts have been to the satisfactory results which have been obtained."[111] Lord Dufferin remarked facetiously to John A. Macdonald, when inviting him to the christening of the newest addition to the Dufferin family, that "this birth with Prince Edward Island's entry into Confederation makes twins."

Lord Dufferin did not need to remind the Colonial Office of Robinson's important role in the Confederation negotiations. Robinson had such a broad concept of humility that he had no hesitation in personally emphasizing the large part he had played in inducing Prince Edward Island to enter the union. "To me it is a matter of no little gratification," Robinson wrote to Kimberley, "that the Union of the Island with Canada has been accomplished during my Administration, and I shall always look back with pride to the share which it has been my good fortune to take in bringing about this beneficial and long wished for result."[112] In another letter he detailed the beneficial results of his influence:

Under these circumstances I may be pardoned, if I refer with a feeling of satisfaction to the large majority by which a question has now been carried, which, when I came here two years and a half ago there would not have been found 1,000 people out of a population of nearly 100,000 to support. The first great point gained was inducing the adoption of a Confederate policy by the then anti-Confederate party, and tho' the scheming of the avowed Confederates at one moment threatened to throw everything back for a time, I never felt any real anxiety as to the result since the day Mr. Haythorne and his Colleagues consented to send delegates to Ottawa.[113]

Lieutenant Governor Robinson was such an ardent promotor of Confederation that it was quite natural that he should derive immense satisfaction from the Island's decision to unite with Canada. He had, moreover, played such a crucial role in influencing the Haythorne government to decide in favor of Confederation, that he could, with perfect justification, feel a real sense of accomplishment. However, in all his Confederation endeavors he was simply being a devoted and faithful public official of the Imperial Government. Since the year 1865 the British authorities had exerted unrelenting pressure to secure the adherence of Prince Edward Island to Confederation, and, therefore, when the Island decided to unite with Canada they were highly gratified. Kimberley expressed their sentiments in a letter to Robinson: "I take this opportunity of congratulating you on the successful result of the negotiations for union which have been carried on between the two Governments, and I have to desire you to make it publicly known that the accomplishment of this further important step towards the complete consolidation of Her Majesty's Possessions in British North America has offered Her Majesty's Government much gratification."[114] The Imperial Government, moreover, did not fail to acknowledge Robinson's faithful instrumentality. On June 30, 1873, Kimberley conveyed to him "the entire approval of Her Majesty's Government, for the ability and judgment you have displayed in this matter;"[115] and as a tangible expression of its approval the Imperial Government appointed him a "Companion of the most Distinguished Order of St. Michael and St. George."[116]

V July 1, 1873

On June 26, 1873, an Imperial Order-in-Council authorized that Prince Edward Island's union with Canada would become effective "from and after the first of July, 1873."[117] The union was proclaimed in due form on that day. The *Patriot* gave a vivid description of the proclamation ceremonies:

On Tuesday, July 1st, whether for weal or woe, Prince Edward Island became a province of the Dominion of Canada. At 12 o'clock noon, the Dominion Flag was run up on the flag staffs at Government House and the Colonial Building, and a salute of 21 guns was fired from St. George's battery and from H. M. S. *Spartan* now in port. The Church and city bells rang out a lively peel, and the Volunteers under review at the city park fired a *feu de joie*. So far as powder and metal could do it, there was for a short time a terrible din. But among the people who thronged the streets there was no enthusiasm. A few moments before 12, Mr. Sheriff Watson stepped forward on the balcony of the Colonial Building and read the Union Proclamation. He was accompanied by two ladies and about half a dozen gentlemen. The audience within hearing consisted of three persons, and even they did not appear to be very attentive. After the reading of the Proclamation was concluded, the gentlemen on the balcony gave a cheer, but the three persons below — who, like the Tooley street tailors who claimed to be "the people of England" — at that moment represented the people of Prince Edward Island responded never a word.[118]

The *Island Argus* also made some revealing comments on the Island's first Dominion Day celebrations:

Confederation has been consummated at last. For the first time the Dominion flag waved from the Colonial Building, on Tuesday last, when the inauguration drama was enacted. The roar of cannon, the sharp rattle of musketry, the reading of the proclamation, the administering of the gubernatorial oath and — presto, the thing is done. . . . There were no unseemly or extravagant demonstrations of joy. The people here are too self-possessed for that. Though they are impressed with the advantages resulting from Union and the financial

39

relief it brings them, they are fully aware of the value of the acquisition to Canada of their fertile and prosperous Island. There was no waste of lung power, therefore, when it was announced to the People of Charlottetown by the High Sheriff of Queen's County that they were Canadians. As the proclamation was being read with due care, interrupted here and there by the reports of the guns on board H. M. S. *Spartan*, furnishing as it were, the note of admiration to the document, the people in the adjoining market place, bought and sold, apparently unmoved. . . . In the evening there was a display of fireworks from H. M. S. *Spartan*, and from the Colonial Building, which were brilliantly illuminated. Altogether the day passed quietly without any particularly noteworthy demonstrations.[119]

Thus with these low-key celebrations, Prince Edward Island became the seventh province of the Dominion.

On July 1, 1873, the people of Prince Edward Island accepted their destiny with mixed feelings of disappointment and satisfaction. They expressed disappointment because economic necessity alone had induced them to declare in favor of Confederation. The *Patriot* accurately commented that "the great majority of the people have accepted Confederation as a necessity. They did not take up the question *cum amore*, and when the day arrived that the union was a *fait accompli*, they did not have a cheer to give."[120] Yet they also displayed satisfaction because the Dominion Government, by its generous terms of admission, had removed their principal economic and political objections to Confederation. The special annual subsidy of $45,000 granted in lieu of the absence of Crown Lands, together with the guarantee of an $800,000 loan, placed the Island in a position to settle the contentious land question that had plagued it since 1767. In 1875, the Island Legislature passed a compulsory Land Purchase Act whereby the system of proprietorship was ultimately extinguished. A Commission was established to evaluate the holdings of the proprietors and to determine the price at which they would be required to sell. In September, 1875, the government purchased 187,699 of the 381,720 acres still held by the proprietors at a cost of $1.63 per acre. The last legal obstacle was cleared away and the last estate purchased by the government in 1895. The Prince Edward Island government borrowed a total of $782,402.33 from the Dominion. It never repaid this loan, even though it received over $600,000 from the sale of the lands to the tenants. The $45,000 subsidy was, therefore, reduced by some $39,000.[121] The settlement of the century-old land question was the greatest blessing that the Island received from the terms granted by the Dominion.

The guarantee of efficient steam service with the mainland, assured the Island that the economic weaknesses caused by isolation would be obviated. The Dominion Government's assumption of the ownership, maintenance and operation of a 200-mile railway system, provided the Island with a much-desired and very adequate means of internal communication. When this railway was finally completed, with its additional branches, more than four-fifths of the province was less than five miles from the line and less than eight miles by road from a station.[122] The Dominion provided the Island with a friendly, leisurely, community railway which each Islander could with reason feel was his very own. The *Island Argus* remarked with wry satisfaction: "That heavy cloud bearing railway indebtedness and a thou-

40

sand other ills on its bosom, which lately loomed up so ominously has dispersed. The burden that threatened to break the back of the little Island has been put on the stout shoulders of vigorous young Canada, who marches off without wavering under the additional load and smiling triumphantly that he has won the *coy little maiden* at last."[123] Since the terms of the Quebec Conference guaranteed neither the settlement of the land question nor efficient communications with the mainland, and since the 1869 offer made no provision for a railway system, it is easy to appreciate the satisfaction with which the Islanders viewed the 1873 terms of union.

When Lord Dufferin visited Prince Edward Island in July, 1873, he was greeted on the Queen's wharf by an arch of welcome adorned with the words, "Courted long, but won at last."[124] These words were an appropriate admission from the newest province of the Dominion. Prince Edward Island had always viewed union with Canada in the light of the settlement that would accompany the marriage. For ten years, in spite of protestations from her mother, Great Britain, the Island had categorically rejected all proposals because she did not consider the terms of union sufficiently attractive to compensate her for her highly prized independence. And it was only when economic forces threatened to undermine her financial security that she consented to unite with Canada. During his visit, Lord Dufferin wrote to Sir John A. Macdonald, that he "found the Island in a high state of jubilation, and quite under the impression that it is the Dominion that has been annexed to Prince Edward Island, and in alluding to the subject, I have adopted the same tone."[125] His attitude must have been consoling indeed to the people of Prince Edward Island, who had so reluctantly relinquished their independent status.

41

Notes

1. Robinson to Kimberley, Secret, December 23, 1872, C. O. 226, vol. 110, p. 78.
2. *Debates and Proceedings of the House of Assembly of Prince Edward Island for the year, 1873*, p. 62.
3. Palmer to Rose, November 16, 1872, *Macdonald Papers*, vol. 119, p. 133.
4. Robinson to Dufferin, Private and Confidential, November 16, 1872, C. O. 226, vol. 110, pp. 69-70.
5. Dufferin to Robinson, Private and Confidential, November 27, 1872, *ibid.*, p. 79.
6. Dufferin to Robinson, Telegraph, December 7, 1872, *ibid.*, p. 80.
7. Rose to Macdonald, November 26, 1872, *Macdonald Papers*, vol. 119, p. 134.
8. Macdonald to Rose, December 13, 1872, *Macdonald Papers*, vol. 522, p. 321.
9. Robinson to Kimberley, Confidential, September 28, 1872, C. O. 226, vol. 110, pp. 37-38.
10. *Executive Council Minute*, January 2, 1873, *Journal of the House of Assembly, P.E.I.*, 1873, Appendix A.
11. *Ibid.*
12. Haythorne to Robinson, January 6, 1873, C. O. 226, vol. 111, p. 25.
13. "Copy of a Report of the Privy Council, January 27, 1873," *Assembly Journal*, 1873, Appendix A.
14. *Legislative Council Debates*, 1873, p. 31.
15. *Assembly Debates*, 1873, p. 25.
16. "Copy of a Report of a Committee of the Honorable the Privy Council approved by his Excellency the Governor General in Council on March 10, 1873," *Assembly Journal*, 1873, Appendix A.
17. *Ibid.*
18. *Ibid.*
19. *Assembly Debates*, 1873, p. 73.
20. *Ibid.*, p. 121.

21. Privy Council Report, March 10, 1873, *Assembly Journal*, 1873, Appendix A.
22. *Ibid.*
23. *Ibid.*
24. *Ibid.* It should be noted that the Island population, having increased by some 15,000 since 1864, was actually entitled to 6 representatives in the House of Commons.
25. *Ibid.*
26. Haythorne and Laird to Edward Palmer, Telegraph, March 3, 1873, *Assembly Journal*, 1873, Appendix A.
27. Robinson to Haythorne, March 6, 1873, *ibid.*
28. Robinson to Kimberley, February 19, 1873, C. O. 537, vol. 104, pp. 12–13.
29. Robinson to Dufferin, March 10, 1873, Telegraph, *Macdonald Papers*, vol. 78, p. 240.
30. *Ibid.*
31. Dufferin to Robinson, Telegraph, March 11, 1873, G. 13, vol. 2, P.A.C.
32. Robinson to Kimberley, Cablegram, March 20, 1873, C. O. 537, vol. 104, p. 103.
33. Kimberley to Robinson, Cablegram, March 20, 1873, *ibid.*, p. 34.
34. *Patriot*, March 20, 1873.
35. *Patriot*, March 8, 1873.
36. *Ibid.*
37. *Assembly Debates*, 1873, p. 62.
38. Letter of James C. Pope to the Electors of Prince Edward Island, March 8, 1873, Published in the *Island Argus*, March 11, 1873.
39. Nomination Day Speech of J. C. Pope, *Island Argus*, April 1, 1873.
40. J. C. MacMillan, *The History of the Catholic Church in Prince Edward Island from 1835 to 1891* (Quebec, 1905), p. 349.
41. *Patriot*, March 15, 1873.
42. *Assembly Debates*, 1873, p. 97.
43. Haythorne to Robinson, April 9, 1873, C. O. 226, vol. 111, p. 86.
44. *Assembly Debates*, 1873, p. 107.
45. Quoted MacMillan, *op cit.*, p. 358.
46. Haythorne to Robinson, April 15, 1873, C. O. 226, vol. 111, p. 108.
47. Robinson to Kimberley, April 9, 1873, *ibid.*, pp. 80–81.
48. Robinson to J. C. Pope, April 15, 1873, *J. C. Pope Papers*. This correspondence is in the possession of H. R. Stewart, Ottawa.
49. J. C. Pope to Robinson, April 15, *ibid.*
50. *Ibid.*
51. Robinson to J. C. Pope, April 15, *ibid.*
52. *Ibid.*
53. J. C. Pope to Robinson, April 15, *ibid.*
54. Robinson to Pope, April 15, *ibid.*
55. *Ibid.*
56. Pope to Robinson, April 16, *ibid.*
57. *Ibid.*
58. Robinson to Pope, April 16, *ibid.*
59. *Assembly Debates*, 1873, p. 62.
60. *Ibid.*, p. 66.
61. *Ibid.*
62. *Ibid.*
63. *Ibid.*, p. 120.
64. *Ibid.*, p. 69.
65. *Ibid.*, p. 123.
66. *Ibid.*, pp. 119–120.
67. *Ibid.*, p. 126.
68. *Ibid.*, p. 149.
69. *Ibid.*
70. *Ibid.*, p. 152.
71. *Ibid.*
72. John A. Macdonald to Dufferin, April 4, 1873, *Macdonald Papers*, vol. 523, pp. 82–83.
73. *Ibid.*
74. "Minutes of Conference between the Committee of the Privy Council of Canada and the undersigned delegates from the Province of Prince Edward Island," May 15, 1873, *Assembly Journal*, 1873, Appendix O.
75. *Assembly Debates*, 1873, p. 176.
76. *Ibid.*, pp. 173–174.
77. *Ibid.*, p. 185.

78. *Ibid.*, pp. 202–203.
79. *Ibid.*, p. 182.
80. *Ibid.*
81. *Ibid.*, p. 228.
82. *Ibid.*, p. 200.
83. *Ibid.*
84. *Ibid.*
85. *Ibid.*, p. 187–188.
86. *Ibid.*, p. 200.
87. *Ibid.*, p. 225.
88. *Ibid.*, p. 232.
89. *Ibid.*, p. 224.
90. *Ibid.*, p. 225.
91. *Ibid.*, p. 231.
92. *Ibid.*, p. 232.
93. *Ibid.*, p. 230.
94. *Ibid.*, p. 232. The Speaker, S. F. Perry, who was in favour of Confederation, was, of course, not allowed to vote.
95. *Debates and Proceedings of the Legislative Council of Prince Edward Island for the Session of 1873*, p. 35.
96. *Ibid.*, p. 88.
97. *Ibid.*
98. *Ibid.*, p. 75.
99. *Ibid.*, p. 79.
100. *Ibid.*, p. 60.
101. *Ibid.*, p. 78.
102. *House of Commons Debates*, May 17, 1873, p. 190, *Canada, Parliament, House of Commons Debates,* March 5, 1873–May 25, 1874, P. A. C.
103. *Ibid.*, pp. 189–190.
104. *Ibid.*, p. 200.
105. *Ibid.*
106. *Ibid.*, p. 190.
107. *Debates of the Senate, Canada, Parliament*, May 21, 1873, p. 202. Campbell admitted that Newfoundland still remained apart, but did not think it was "of so much importance," *ibid.*, p. 202.
108. *Ibid.*
109. *Ibid.*, p. 203.
110. Dufferin to Robinson, May 17, 1873, C. O. 226, vol. 111, p. 226.
111. *Ibid.*
112. Robinson to Kimberley, May 29, 1873, G. 8, D, vol. 55, p. 29.
113. Robinson to Kimberley, Confidential, May 29, 1873, C. O. 226, vol.111, pp. 232 233.
114. Kimberley to Robinson, June 30, 1873, G. 8, D, vol. 42, p. 249.
115. Kimberley to Robinson, June 30, 1873, *ibid.*, p. 261.
116. Kimberley to Robinson, June 30, 1873, *ibid.*, p. 364.
117. Kimberley to Robinson, Telegraph, June 27, 1873, G. 13, vol. 7, P. A. C.
118. *Patriot*, July 3, 1873.
119. *Island Argus*, July 15, 1873.
120. *Patriot*, July 3, 1873.
121. "Precis of Correspondence relating to land tenure in Prince Edward Island," R. G. 7, G. 21, No. 63. P. A. C.
122. A. H. Clark, *op. cit.*, p. 141.
123. *Island Argus*, July 15, 1873. "Italics Mine."
124. *Patriot*, July 19, 1873.
125. Dufferin to Macdonald, July 21, 1873, *Macdonald Papers*, vol. 79, pp. 412–413.

Topic Two
The National Policy

44   The National Policy has been the subject of considerable debate since its inception. Why was it implemented? Was it designed to benefit certain classes or regions at the expense of others? To what extent was the policy truly "national"? Has Canada survived because of, or in spite of, the National Policy? These and other questions have received considerable attention.

John A. Macdonald's Conservative government implemented the National Policy, a policy of tariff protection, in 1879. It imposed a tariff of more than 17½% on many manufactured goods coming into the country from the United States. The policy, aimed at stimulating the growth of Canadian industries, appeared to Conservative politicians to be a logical solution to the problem of the depressed Canadian economy in the mid-1870s. Britain had abandoned the mercantile system of trade with her colonies in the late 1840s in favour of free trade, while the United States had adopted its own highly protectionist policy toward Canada after the abrogation of the Reciprocity Treaty in 1866. Certain Canadian leaders, forced to look within for a solution to their problems, believed that a policy of high protection would foster Canadian industrial growth.

The "National Policy" was part of a broader "national policy," one that included the building of a transcontinental railway, and large-scale immigration to the West. The logic went as follows: the railway would enable east-west trade, while the growing population of the West would provide the necessary markets for Canadian manufactured goods and a ready source of raw materials for the growing industries of Central Canada. The high tariff would force Canadians to buy Canadian products, thus encouraging industrial growth within the nation.

Craig Brown in "The Nationalism of the National Policy" explained its popularity at the time by showing it in a larger historical and international context. In "Canada's National Policies," John Dales questions the logic of the National Policy in terms of its long-range benefits for Canadians.

Craig Brown presents his argument in greater detail in *Canada's National Policy, 1883–1900: A Study in Canadian-American Relations* (Princeton:

Princeton University Press, 1964). John Dales elaborates on his position in his *The Protective Tariff in Canada's Development* (Toronto: University of Toronto Press, 1966). Donald Creighton's works contain the traditional defence of the National Policy: see, for example, *Canada's First Century* (Toronto: Macmillan, 1970). The negative impact of the National Policy on developments in the hinterlands of the Maritimes and the West can be found in *Canada and the Burden of Unity*, edited by D. Bercuson (Toronto: Macmillan, 1977), and in an article by T.W. Acheson, "The National Policy and the Industrialization of the Maritimes, 1880-1910," *Acadiensis*, I (1972):3-28. Kenneth Norrie's "The National Policy and Prairie Economic Discrimination, 1870-1930," in Donald Akenson, ed., *Canadian Papers in Rural History* (Gananoque: Langdale Press, 1978), pp. 13-33, questions whether western farmers had legitimate grievances against the National Policy. An issue of the *Journal of Canadian Studies*, 14 (Fall 1979) is devoted to "The National Policy, 1879-1979."

45

The Nationalism of the National Policy*
CRAIG BROWN

Debating nationalism is the great Canadian national pastime. Since Confederation it has been the pre-eminent preoccupation of politicians, journalists, scholars and plain ordinary citizens. All have wrestled diligently with the problem that Canadian nationalism — if such there be — does not fit any of the classic definitions of nationalism. Common language, religion, and ethnic origin must obviously be rejected. Except for the disciples of Harold Adams Innis, geography provided few satisfactory clues to the Canadian identity. And a common historical tradition, in the words of Mill, "the possession of a national history and consequent community of recollections, collective pride and humiliation, pleasure and regret, connected with the same incidents in the past," raises more questions about a Canadian "nationality" than it answers. There is no great national hero who cut down a maple tree, threw a silver dollar across the St. Lawrence and then proceeded to lead a revolution and govern the victorious nation wisely and judiciously. There are no great Canadian charters of freedom or independence expressing the collective will of the people. But the search goes on. Historians and retired Governors General laboriously attempt to define "the Canadian identity" or "being Canadian." Many nations have manifested their nationalism through great public acts; Canada has asserted its nationalism by looking for it.

Yet there is abundant evidence that Canadians have both thought and

* From *Nationalism in Canada*, edited by the University League for Social Reform. Copyright 1966 by McGraw-Hill Limited. Reprinted by permission of McGraw-Hill Ryerson Limited.

acted like contemporary nationalists in other countries. Much, though by no means all, of the evidence is provided by the politicians.[1] The evidence is mundane, for seldom have Canadian politicians been political theorists or philosophers. Rather, their concerns have been with everyday problems of government. But within this framework their thoughts and acts have been decidedly nationalist in character. A brief look at the men who implemented and carried out the National Policy may serve to illustrate the point.

Writing to a Conservative editor in 1872, Sir John A. Macdonald noted in a postscript that "the paper must go in for a National policy in Tariff matters, and while avoiding the word 'protection' must advocate a readjustment of the tariff in such a manner as incidentally to aid our manufacturing and industrial interest."[2] In this obvious afterthought at the conclusion of a letter devoted to the necessity for finding an appropriate label for Macdonald's party, is the origin of the National Policy. The context is significant. Macdonald was looking for a policy that would attract, at one and the same time, voters and dollars to his party, and the National Policy would do both. The manufacturers would contribute to the party war-chest and the simplicity of the title and concept of the National Policy would appeal to an electorate looking to fulfill the promise of Confederation. Moreover, as a transcontinental railway, immigration and opening of the Northwest were added to the tariff as items in the National Policy, it took on a strikingly familiar complexion that added to its political attractiveness. It was in most respects a duplication of a similar "national policy" designed for continental expansion in the United States. It was "a materialistic policy of Bigness"[3] in an age when expansionism appealed to nationalist sentiment. Canadians could take pride in their ability to compete with their neighbours in the conquest of the continent.

The National Policy was equally attractive because a policy of tariff protection meant another step in the long path from colony to nation within the Empire. As early as 1859, Galt argued for protection less on its economic merits than on the grounds that tariff autonomy was implicit in responsible government. Referring to Imperial objections to the Cayley-Galt tariff of that year, the crux of Galt's argument was that "self-government would be utterly annihilated if the views of the Imperial Government were to be preferred to those of the people of Canada."[4] With tariff autonomy not only achieved but emphasized by protection, in 1911 the ardent nationalist John S. Ewart proudly summed up the elements of "Canadian Independence" by pointing first to the fact that "we are fiscally independent". "By that I mean that we make our own tariffs; that we frame them as we wish; that we tax British, and other goods as we please; and that neither the Colonial Office nor the British Parliament has any right whatever to interfere."[5]

That the National Policy was politically attractive, is, then, evident. By 1886 the Liberal party had been driven so far into a "me too" position that Blake in essence declared his party's policy to be, to borrow a phrase, the

National Policy if necessary, but not necessarily the National Policy. It is true that in 1891, with a new leader and the new policy of Unrestricted Reciprocity with the United States, the Liberals came closer to victory than they had at any time since 1874. But within two years the Liberals had again revised their policy to "freer trade" and in 1897 the Liberal Government admitted the futility of attempting to destroy Macdonald's brainchild. "I not only would not retire from the Government because they refused to eliminate the principle of protection from the tariff, but I would not remain in the Government if they did eliminate the principle of protection entirely from the tariff", wrote Clifford Sifton. He added that "the introduction of a tariff from which the principle of protection would be entirely eliminated would be fraught with results that would be most disastrous to the whole Canadian people."[6] In 1911, Sifton and 17 other "revolting" Liberals issued their manifesto against reciprocity "believing as we do that Canadian nationality is now threatened with a more serious blow than any it has heretofore met with."[7] Robert Borden simply added that "we must decide whether the spirit of Canadianism or of Continentalism shall prevail on the northern half of this continent."[8]

47

In short, the idea of protection embodied in the tariff became equated with the Canadian nation itself. The National Policy, by stressing that Canadians should no longer be "hewers of wood and drawers of water" for the United States, as Tilley put it, recalled and reinforced that basic impulse of survival as a separate entity on this continent that had been born of the American Revolution, made explicit in Confederation, and remained the primary objective of Canadian nationalists. Protection and the National Policy, then, took on a much larger meaning than mere tinkering with customs schedules.

The same idea was evident in the building of the Canadian Pacific Railway and the opening of the Northwest. The Northwest was the key to the future of both the National Policy and the nation, and an expensive and partially unproductive railway through Canadian territory was the price Canada had to pay to "protect" it from American penetration and absorption. It was to be the great market for Canadian industry and the foundation of a "Canadian economy". Emphasizing that building the railway was "a great national question", Sir Charles Tupper remarked that "under the National Policy that Canada has adopted we must look forward not only to building up thriving centres of industry and enterprises all over this portion of the country, but to obtaining a market for these industries after they have been established; and I say where is there a greater market than that magnificent granary of the North-west?"[9] He added that upon the success of the venture "the rapid progress and prosperity of our common country depends".

The United States played an interesting role in the National Policy that emphasized its nationalistic assumptions. Fundamental to the thinking of the framers of the policy was the idea that the United States was much less a friendly neighbour than an aggressive competitor power waiting for a suitable opportunity to fulfill its destiny of the complete conquest of North America. The National Policy was intended to be the first line of defence against American ambitions. And this, I think, is the reason any Canadian alternative to it was unsuccessful. It was the "national" implications of the National Policy that hindered the Liberals in their attempt to formulate an opposition policy before 1896. They could not accept Commercial Union because it meant the total surrender of tariff autonomy. Unrestricted Reciprocity was adopted as a compromise that retained autonomy. But its distinction from Commercial Union was too subtle for much of the electorate to grasp and left the party open to skillful exploitation by Macdonald's "loyalty" cry. More important, the very indefiniteness of what the Liberals meant by Unrestricted Reciprocity caused confusion and disruption in party ranks and eventually led to the revelation that Unrestricted Reciprocity did not mean the complete free interchange of all Canadian and American products after all. Rather, most Liberals simply wanted a more extensive reciprocity agreement with the United States than the Conservatives. Or, to put it another way, the Liberals were only interested in somewhat less protection from American competition than their opponents. W. S. Fielding's budget speech in 1897 had a very familiar ring to Canadian ears: "If our American friends wish to make a treaty with us, we are willing to meet them and treat on fair and equitable terms. If it shall not please them to do that, we shall in one way regret the fact but shall nevertheless go on our way rejoicing, and find other markets to build up the prosperity of Canada independent of the American people."[10]

Other problems in Canadian-American relations in the latter part of the nineteenth century were related to the nationalism of the National Policy. With the abrogation of the fishery articles of the Treaty of Washington by the United States, Canada was forced to adopt what can properly be called a "protectionist" policy for her inshore fisheries. The fisheries and the commercial privileges extended to Americans by the treaty were considered a national asset by Canadians. The object of their Government was to use that asset for the benefit of the whole of Canada, not simply the Maritime Provinces. It was for this reason that from 1871 on the fishery question was always related to reciprocity. On each occasion when Canada participated in negotiations the policy was always the same: Canada's exclusive and undoubted rights in the inshore fisheries would be bargained for the free exchange of natural products.

A different and more complex problem was presented by the Behring Sea dispute arising out of the seizure of Canadian pelagic sealers by United States revenue cruisers. The central problem was one of international law involving the doctrines of freedom of the seas and *mare clausum*. And because the Canadian vessels were of British registry, the British Government assumed a much more active negotiating role than was the case in some other disputes. But Canadian participation was far from negligible, and Sir Charles Hibbert Tupper and Sir Louis Davies made a point of protecting Canadian interests. Significantly, they argued that despite the legal technicalities, it was a Canadian industry that was threatened with destruction by the illegal acts of the United States Government and that the Mother Country had a clear duty to protect that industry.

The Alaska Boundary question also illustrated the relationship between the National Policy and Canada's relations with the United States. All of the evidence available suggests that the Canadian case was hopelessly weak and members of the Canadian Government (Laurier and Sifton) as much as admitted it both privately and in public. Why, then, was the case pressed with such vigour? Part of the answer, it seems to me, is that when the Alaska Boundary question became important for Canadians after the Yukon gold rush began, those responsible for Canadian policy, led by Clifford Sifton, regarded the question less as one of boundary definition than of commercial competition with the United States. Definition of the boundary was important because it was related to control of the growing Yukon trade. The intricate legal details of the boundary dispute were generally ignored by the Canadian Government. Writing during the meetings of the Joint High Commission in 1898, Lord Herschell complained to Lord Salisbury that "I found that the question had not been thoroughly studied or thought out by any Canadian official."[11] The urgent and ill-considered introduction of the Yukon Railway Bill of 1898 providing for a "Canadian" route to the Yukon — a route which was dependent upon trans-shipment privileges at the American customs port at Fort Wrangel and on navigation rights on the American portion of the Stikine River — illustrates the same point. The "imperative reason for immediate action" was that the Yukon trade was at stake, as the Minister of Railways and Canals explained to the House of Commons: "The importance of securing that trade and preserving it to Canada becomes a national question of the greatest interest . . . . It is ours, it is within our own borders and of right belongs to us, if, by any legitimate or proper means we can secure it for the people of our own country."[12]

49

Again, in the negotiations at the Joint High Commission of 1898–99 the Canadians insisted that if the boundary question went to arbitration, Pyramid Harbour should be reserved for Canada to match American insistence that Dyea and Skagway be reserved for the United States. While both sides thus rejected an unqualified and impartial arbitration, it must be admitted that Dyea and Skagway were established and settled communities under American control; Canada could make no such claim regarding Pyramid Harbour. Pyramid Harbour, as a Canadian outlet to the sea with a corresponding Canadian land corridor to the interior, had not arisen in negotiations until the meetings of the Joint High Commission and, as before, the Canadian claim was based primarily on the desire to secure control of the Yukon trade.

Ultimately, of course, Canadian indignation knew no bounds when Lord Alverstone reportedly suddenly changed his mind and awarded Pearse and Wales Islands to the United States in 1903. The settlement of 1903 was unquestionably diplomatic rather than "judicial". Theodore Roosevelt's pressure tactics before and during the meeting of the so-called "judicial tribunal" were certainly deplorable and these factors, combined with the apparent sacrifice of Canadian interests by Great Britain, have supplied grist for the mills of Canadian nationalists ever since. But too often the emphasis in Canadian historiography on this point has been misplaced by concentrating solely on the alleged British sellout. The more interesting point in all the clamour surrounding the Alaska Boundary decision is that, once again, National Policy interests were considered to be threatened by the decision. Alverstone's agreement with Lodge and Root, that Pearse and Wales Islands belonged to the United States, threatened the Laurier Government's first venture in transcontinental railway building. The projected terminus of the Grand Trunk Pacific, chartered just a few short months before, was Port Simpson on Observatory Inlet; Pearse and Wales Islands, which the Canadians believed could be armed by the United States, commanded the shipping lanes into Port Simpson. Thus, though the Yukon trade had drastically declined in value by 1903, from first serious consideration of the problem to final settlement the National Policy — an "all Canadian" trade route to the Yukon or a secure terminus for a new Pacific railway — dominated Canadian consideration of the Alaska Boundary dispute.

50

I have tried to suggest that the National Policy was a manifestation of Canadian national sentiment. Its basic assumptions, protection against the United States, the need for a "Canadian economy" with a strong industrial base and secure markets, and the implicit assumption of achieving greater autonomy within the Empire all crystallized that ill-defined, but deeply felt, sense of difference that set Canadians apart from both their neighbours to the south and the mother country. But why did this desire to proclaim a national identity take its form in economic terms?

Perhaps a part of the answer rests in the dilemma posed at the beginning of this paper. Appeals to a common language, a common cultural tradition or a common religion were simply impossible for Canadians and when they were attempted they were rightly regarded by French Canadians as a violation of their understanding of Confederation. Most Canadians, especially those who built or paid for the building of the transcontinental railways, argued that the Canadian nation would have to be built in spite of its geography and regarded their efforts as "the price of being Canadian". Appeals to national history could also be a divisive rather than a unifying factor for, as often as not, the two ethnic groups disagreed as to what, in their historical tradition, was a matter of pride or of humiliation. What was necessary, then, as Cartier put it in the Confederation debates, was to "form a political nationality". And it is not at all surprising that the political nationalism of the early decades of Confederation was expressed in terms of railways and tariffs.

It is a commonplace to equate the politics of North America in the latter part of the nineteenth century with self-seeking capitalism. But we might remind ourselves that the age of Darwinism and of industrialism was also a great age of nationalism. The nationalism of the large assertive states of the age, the United States, Germany and Great Britain, was assuredly economic in its emphasis. In the United States, in particular, nationalism was equated with the problems of industrialism and industrial expansion. In keeping with Darwinian assumptions, bigness was a virtue for a nation state, and industrialism was the key to bigness. At the very time their own nation was being born, Canadians reasoned that industrialism was the determining factor in the victory of the North in the Civil War and in the apparent reunification of the United States. Industrialism meant power; power to withstand the pressures from the south and power to expand and consolidate the Canadian nation. And a political programme that emphasized expansion and industrialism had the added advantage of ignoring the potentially divisive issues that would disrupt a "political nationality".

In sum, then, the National Policy, a policy for a "Canadian economy" and a "Big Canada", a materialistic policy for a materialistic age, was the obvious policy to give expression to Canadian national sentiment. That policy was adopted in 1878 and accepted by the Liberal party in 1896. Three years later J. I. Tarte urged Laurier to do more than simply accept the National Policy, to expand upon it with more railways, canals and harbour improvements (and presumably with higher tariffs). "Voilà", he observed, "le programme le plus national et le plus populaire que nous puissons offrir au pays".[13]

51

Notes

1. Carl Berger, "The True North Strong and Free", in *Nationalism in Canada*, Toronto, 1966, p. 3ff.
2. *Macdonald Papers*, (P.A.C.) Macdonald to T. C. Patterson, February 27, 1872.
3. John Dales, "Protection, Immigration and Canadian Nationalism", in *Nationalism in Canada*, op. cit. pp. 167–170.
4. A. B. Keith, *Selected Speeches and Documents on British Colonial Policy, 1763–1917*, London, 1953, p. 60.
5. J. S. Ewart, *The Kingdom Papers*, Vol. 1, Ottawa, 1912, p. 3.
6. *Sifton Papers*, (P.A.C.) Sifton to James Fleming, March 13, 1897.
7. *Manifesto of Eighteen Toronto Liberals on Reciprocity*, February 20, 1911; cited, *Canadian Annual Review*, Toronto, 1911, p. 49.
8. Henry Borden (ed.) *Robert Laird Borden: His Memoirs*, Vol. 1, Toronto, 1938, p. 327.
9. *House of Commons Debates*, April 15, 1880, pp. 1424–5.
10. *House of Commons Debates*, April 22, 1897.
11. Cited in R. C. Brown, *Canada's National Policy, 1883–1900*, Princeton, 1964, p. 379.
12. *House of Commons Debates*, February 8, 1898, pp. 191–2.
13. *Laurier Papers* (P.A.C.), Tarte to Laurier, April 3, 1899.

Canada's National Policies*
JOHN DALES

To the infant industry argument for protectionism Canadians have added an infant nation argument. Among Canadian academic historians, journalists, and citizens at large there seems to be a dangerous unanimity of opinion that Canada is a transparently artificial entity whose very existence has always depended on something called a national policy. Canada, in this view, is a denial of geography and a travesty of economics that stands as living proof of the primacy of politics in the affairs of men. Critical comment to the effect that most Canadian manufacturers still depend on protective tariffs is very apt to be greeted first by astonishment that anyone would think the comment worth making, and then by patient explanation that of course many parts of the Canadian economy—not only manufacturing—have *always* depended on government bounty in one form or another, and that Canada simply would not exist as a nation if public support were not continuously made available to key sectors of the economy. Such a policy is necessary, the explanation continues, both in order to overcome the outrageous geography of the country and in order to defend the nation's economy against the formidable efficiency, and thus the natural expansionism, of the American economy. In Canada infant industries are not *expected* to grow up.

I reject this view of Canada. It seems to me to be subversive not only of the nation's wealth but also of the nation's pride. National pride and economic performance I believe to be positively, not negatively, correlated; both efficiency and honour, as the parable of the talents teaches, come from making the most of what one has, not from having the most. And yet Canadian economic policy—and, what is more important, the economic policy of so many developing nations today—aims consistently at maximizing the purse, gross national product, rather than the performance, gross national product per citizen.

Sir John A. Macdonald gave us our first national policy, and our first lessons in the irrelevance of economics. Western lands, he argued, must be controlled by the Dominion because provincial land policies "might be obstructive to immigration," i.e., provinces might actually try to sell land rather than give it away. Canadian railways, in Macdonald's view, were not to be thought of primarily as business enterprises; they were instruments of national development and served this end by providing both attractive objects of government expenditure and reliable sources of party support. As for the tariff, Macdonald rang all the changes on the protectionist fallacies and promised that *his* tariff would benefit everyone, the teachings of the

*From *The Protective Tariff in Canada's Development* by John Dales. Copyright 1966 by University of Toronto Press. Reprinted by permission.

dismal science notwithstanding. Macdonald was the first great Canadian non-economist.

It is hard to believe, though, that Macdonald deserves the whole credit for the low esteem in which economics and economists are held in Canada today. Macdonald has in any event had powerful support from Canadian historians, of both the political and economic persuasions, who have rationalized his national policy and have encouraged Canadians to believe that by disregarding economics they could build a nation that would represent a victory over mere materialism. The national policy originally consisted of government support for three main ventures: railway building, Western settlement, and manufacturing development. (We adopt the original convention of using "national policy" for the famous trinity of Canadian nation-building policies, and of reserving "National Policy" for the protective tariff policy.) The mutual consistency of Western settlement and railway building was perhaps fairly obvious; land grants helped to finance railways, and railway companies encouraged settlement. From an economist's point of view, however, the rationalization has been carried a little far. The government has been praised for using valuable lands as a loss-leader, while the C.P.R. has been praised for selling land to immigrants at prices considerably below those charged by other land owners, and for showing great initiative in developing uneconomic irrigation projects.

What was at first difficult for historians to discover was the consistency between Macdonald's tariff policy and the other two prongs of his national policy. The late Professor H. A. Innis seems to have provided the connecting argument. The role of the tariff in the Canadian economy, he taught, was to inhibit Canadian-American trade, to promote east-west trade in Canada, and in this way to provide revenue for Canadian transcontinental railways. Though I cannot resist a long footnote on the subject, I do not want to make a full textual analysis of Innis' writings in order to try to find out whether he believed that his tariff-railway link was (*a*) the *ex post* result of the two policies — the way things worked out — or (*b*) the *ex-ante* design — the way things were intended to work out — or (*c*) either or both of these combined with the opinion that the link was felicitous.[1] I wish only to suggest that once the Innis link was forged the way was wide open for a full-scale rationalization of the national policy. Thus D.G. Creighton:

[The tariff] was intimately and vitally related to the other national policies. By means of the tariff, the settlement of the west would provide a national market; and this national market would supply east-west traffic for Canadian transcontinental railways and areas of exploitation for eastern Canadian industry.[2]

And J. B. Brebner:

Looking backward from the present, it is easy to see that the very existence of both the Province and the later Dominion of Canada as entities separate from the United States has depended on such expensive transportation services that a large proportion of their cost has had to be met from the public purse. . . . it was [in the exuberant 1850s] that Canadians . . . began systematically to adopt the *only* procedure by which they could surmount this handicap, that is, the imposition of quite high tariffs on manufactured goods.[3]

53

W. T. Easterbrook and H. G. Aitken:

[The detailed program of Canadian nation building] appeared slowly and in piecemeal fashion but by 1879 . . . the parts of the comprehensive and more or less complete pattern had fallen into place: a transcontinental railway, protective tariffs, land settlement policy, the promotion of immigration.[4]

And the present author, who providentially has written very little on the subject:

The Dominion immediately proceeded to fulfil its purposes. A transcontinental railway system was constructed, an energetic settlement policy was adapted to the needs of the West, and the tariff was designed to develop Canadian industry and stimulate Canadian trade. These policies proved effective in the period of prosperity which began towards the end of the nineteenth century.[5]

54

Two features of the historians' stereotype of the national policy should be noted. First, much emphasis is placed on the consistency of the three pillars of the program, while inconsistencies are either ignored or glossed over. Among the authors I have consulted, several mention the regional inconsistency inherent in the policy. V. C. Fowke, in particular, interpreted the national policy as a program designed by and for central Canadians. The national policy is therefore seen not as national at all but rather as a policy of central Canadian imperialism. Fowke comes dangerously close to shattering the whole myth of the national policy, yet in the end he refuses to be an iconoclast. Thus his glosses that the national policy was "prerequisite to western development" and that "the groundwork [for western development] . . . was laid . . . by the institution of the 'National Policy' or tariff protection . . ."[8] seem wildly inconsistent with his main position, particularly in view of his insistence that Macdonald's railway policy was *not* prerequisite to western development: "As far as the western provinces are concerned . . . Canadian railways are expensive alternatives to American railways rather than to no railways at all."[7] Brebner and Careless both hint at the logical inconsistency inherent in protectionism, namely, the attempt to build a wealthy nation by lowering the standard of living of its population. Thus Careless notes that "A protective tariff plainly meant that goods would cost more to buy in Canada," yet after a token flirtation with this line of reasoning he surrenders to the stereotype on the following page and concludes that "as far as Canada is concerned the protective tariff system that was adopted under Macdonald . . . did much in the long run to develop the wealth and encourage the industry of the Dominion."[8] He then goes on to paint the usual picture of the wonderful consistency among Canada's railway, settlement, and tariff policies.

None of the authors I have examined has flatly challenged the national stereotype of the beneficence of the national policy. W. A. Mackintosh, however, writes very cautiously about this subject. He outlines the "Basic National Decisions" and their interrelations in chapter II of his *The Economic Background of Dominion-Provincial Relations*,[9] but adds at the end of the chapter (p.21): "It is not suggested that these national decisions were taken by governments, or still less by electorates, in full consciousness of their implications, nor that the inter-relations among them were fully appreciated. They were in large measure the outcome of conflicts of interest and, to some extent, of political expediency." Later (p. 37) he notes the regional conflicts occasioned by the national policies, and the tendency of these policies to rigidify the economy by creating "vested interests, regional and sectional, which would resist readjustment." Also two other authors, both political historians, have distinguished themselves by refusing to have anything to do with the standard patter. Chester Martin disdains even to mention the tariff in his *Foundations of Canadian Nationhood*[10]; A. R. M. Lower bluntly refers to the National Policy as being a "frank creation of vested manufacturing interests living on the bounty of government," and in exasperation writes that "Macdonald's way of imposing the new tariff was simple: he just invited anyone who wanted a duty to come to Ottawa and ask for it."[11]

55

The stereotype of the national policy is powerful enough not only to bridge logical inconsistencies but also to abridge time. To its defenders the national policy was both a well-designed and a powerful engine of nation-building. Yet it refused to function for some twenty or thirty years. Many authors simply ignore this awkward gap in timing, as I did myself in the quotation above. Others mention it and then ignore it, as for example Easterbrook and Aitken: "The three decades following Confederation. . . seemed to many a prolonged period of marking time . . . Not until the turn of the century did the program of nation-building begin to pay off . . ." (p. 381). After a long account of the Time of Troubles in both its economic and political aspects, Careless finds himself concluding that "conservative nationalism was played out," and thus in imminent danger of rending the stereotype beyond repair. But he draws back at the very brink of the abyss, and proclaims in strident tones that "Macdonald nationalism had not failed. It was the age that had failed . . ." (p. 295).

Why can we not bring ourselves to say quite simply that the national policy was a dismal failure? Everyone admits, for example, that the land settlement policy was a failure before 1900. After 1900 the demand for western land was so brisk, and the C.P.R. and various land companies so zealous in attracting settlers to the region, that it is hard to believe that the homestead policy was in any sense necessary as a means of settling the West. It was, indeed, probably undesirable. After writing of the efficiency and enterprise of the private land companies, Martin notes that "The general opening of 'Dominion lands,' even- and odd-numbered sections alike, to homestead entry after 1908 brought a deluge of less selective migration to Western Canada. In vain the government had sought to reserve vast areas with marginal rainfall in 'Palliser's triangle' for grazing and other purposes. In the queues which formed up at the land offices prospective settlers, as one observer records, 'held their place in the line day and night for two or three weeks to enable them to file on certain lands,' and places in the queue were frequently bought and sold for 'substantial sums of money,' '' Uneconomically low prices inevitably produce queues. No one, I suggest, really believes that without the homestead policy in particular, and the settlement policy in general, the West would not have been settled. These policies were powerless to promote settlement before 1900; after 1900 their chief effect was to promote not settlement but *rapid* settlement, and there is much evidence to suggest that the rapidity of settlement did much short-term and long-term harm in Western Canada. Martin's trenchant criticism of the homestead system certainly permits one to believe that Canada would have been better off without this member of the national policy trilogy.

As with land settlement policy so with tariff policy; the burden of the argument suggests that we would have been much better off still if we had never tangled with the National Policy. Historically, it need only be noted that manufacturing was developing in Canada well before the tariff of 1879; Mackintosh notes that the "Census of 1871 reveals that Canada had made some progress along the path of industrialization," and that "The new protectionist policy intensified, broadly speaking, industrial trends already visible."[12] Moreover, Canadian manufacturing grew less rapidly than American manufacturing both before and after the tariff and net emigration from Canada was a feature of the decades both before and after 1879. To the extent that the National Policy was intended to reverse, or even to reduce, the disparity in Canadian and American growth rates it was clearly a failure. After 1900 the Canadian economy, including Canadian manufacturing, grew more rapidly than the American economy for a dozen years, and Canadian historians have not hesitated to attribute this surge to the beneficial, if somewhat delayed, effects of the National Policy. As Careless wrote,[13] it was the "age that had failed" before 1900 and the rise of a prosperous age after 1900 that "spelt success at long last for the National Policy. . . ." In Canadian history it is heads the National Policy wins, and tails the age loses.

There remains the curious case of the C.P.R. While a Canadian transcontinental railway, as Fowke argues, was not prerequisite to western development, economists and political scientists can agree that as a matter of political economy such a railway was an essential adjunct of nationhood for the new Dominion. The railway had to be built for political reasons, whatever the subsidy involved; sensible economic policy required only that the subsidy be kept as low as possible. The C.P.R. was in fact heavily subsidized. Still, given the lack-lustre performance of Canadian settlement and tariff policies before the middle 1890s one might have expected, on the basis of the national policy stereotype in general and the Innis link in particular, that the C.P.R. would have been unable to survive its first bleak decade. Surely no one would wish to argue that the population of Western Canada in 1895 (perhaps a third of a million people, an increase of something over 100,000 since the completion of the C.P.R.) was able to supply either enough wheat or a large enough market for manufactured goods to make a paying proposition out of even so heavily subsidized a transcontinental railway as the C.P.R.

Yet the C.P.R. was profitable from the minute it was completed and began to pay dividends on its common stock in 1889. The Wheat Boom that began in the closing years of the century was only the frosting on the cake that allowed the Company to raise dividends from 4% in 1897 to 10% in 1911, despite large decreases in railway rates around the turn of the century. The chronology of C.P.R. earnings thus raises a nagging doubt about whether the C.P.R. ever *needed* to be subsidized indirectly by the tariff as well as directly by grants of money and a kingdom in land. Professor Fogel's conclusion that the Union Pacific Railway would have been profitable *without* subsidies, despite unanimous opinion, before the fact, that it would not be,[14] suggests a need for testing the hypothesis that the C.P.R. would have been profitable with direct subsidies alone, or even, subversive thought, without *any* subsidy! Careful analysis of this matter seems to be an urgent necessity. The core of the national policy has always been the protective tariff, and although today the tariff is more and more often brazenly defended simply on the grounds that we must protect the vested interests we have built up, the argument of last resort is still that the tariff is the defender of the railways, and thus of the east-west economy. The defence retains its appeal since the railways still carry a great deal of freight, if not many passengers, and the Innis link remains persuasive. If it were possible to deny the validity of the Innis argument that without the tariff there would be no C.P.R., it would be much more difficult for present-day nationalists to argue that if there were no tariff there would be no Canada.

There are, therefore, reasonable grounds for questioning the validity of the historians' stereotype of the national policy. To stress the consistency of the national policy as an interrelated whole is to ignore all too cavalierly its inconsistencies. And to write as if the wisdom and power of a nation-building program that is ineffective for two or three decades is somehow "proved" or "demonstrated" by a subsequent period of great prosperity is to mislead the public with a monstrous example of the *post hoc ergo propter hoc* fallacy. Moreover, the whole tortuous exercise is so unnecessary, for a much more reasonable, and very much simpler, explanation of the Great Canadian Boom is also standard fare in our textbooks. This explanation runs in terms of a number of world events and developments in the last decade of the nineteenth century, all of which reacted favourably on the Canadian economy — the "closing" of the American frontier, rising world prices, falling shipping rates, the development of the gradual reduction process for milling wheat, and the development of the technique of making paper from wood pulp are perhaps the principal items in the list. None of these factors owed anything to the national policy.

Why, then, do historians insist on overdetermining their explanation of the Great Boom by trying to fit a perfectly straightforward argument into the national policy stereotype, as Fowke, for example, does when he writes that "This conjuncture of world circumstances created the opportunity for Canadian expansion, but a half-century of foundation work along the lines of the national policy had prepared Canada for the opportunity."[15] Economic man does not need to be prepared by government policy before he reacts to opportunities for making profits. Is it crude hero worship, or an unconscious human predisposition to human explanations of history that leads Canadians to believe that what success they have enjoyed "must" reflect Macdonald's wise nation-building policies? Or are we all of us merely prisoners of our own history — as it has been written? It is very odd that, enjoying one of the highest standards of living in the world, Canadians in all walks of life should nevertheless believe that their economy is a frail, hot-house creation, whose very survival depends on the constant vigilance of a government gardener well provided with props and plant food. Who but historians could have created this chasm between reality and belief? It is high time that someone should write the history of Canada since Confederation as a triumph of the forces of economic and political development over the national policies of Macdonald and his successors.

58

II

Our national policies were laid down when Canada was young, both politically and economically. The country looked forward to a long period of what I shall call *extensive* economic growth—a combination of geographical expansion, immigration, the exploitation of new resources, railway building, and the extension of manufacturing and service industries to keep pace with the growth of the national economy. The national policies were adopted to facilitate this "natural" growth process; they were designed to increase natural resources through political expansion, human resources through immigration, social capital by railway building, and private capital by means of the tariff. This "vision" of growth was surely not unreasonable in 1870, even though, as things turned out, it failed to materialize during the next generation. In retrospect it is easy enough to see why the expectation was premature: world demand for wheat had not yet grown to the point where, even with rail transportation, wheat could be profitably exported from the Canadian prairies; technology had not yet released the wealth of the Canadian shield in terms of base metals, pulpwood, and waterpower; and the absence of cheap coal and iron ore hampered manufacturing development. It was only with the "conjuncture" around 1900 that natural economic expansion gave the national policies something to facilitate. For a generation thereafter, extensive growth was the stuff of Canadian economic development.

Extensive growth, which is essentially a process of increasing the quantity of resources, provides the sort of massive economic development that fascinates economic historians. Yet from an economic point of view it is such a simple type of growth that it holds almost no interest for economic theorists, who concern themselves primarily with the efficient use of *a given quantity* of resources, and who therefore tend to think of economic progress not in terms of amassing resources but in terms of making better use of existing resources. Fortunately, however, economic historians and economic theorists *do* have a common interest in an improvement of resource *quality* as a third path to the wealth of nations. Historians have long manifested an interest in technological change, which may be considered as a means of improving the quality of capital resources, and in such things as health, diet, training, and a wide range of institutional factors that affect the quality of human resources. Only recently have economic theorists invaded in force the fields of technology, health, education, recreation, and governmental activities, but already the power of economic analysis is beginning to make itself felt in public policies relating to these matters.

Both better resource allocation and resource improvement, but especially the latter, result in what I shall call *intensive* economic growth, a type of growth that has little to do with the mere multiplying of resources that is the basic characteristic of extensive economic growth. Intensive growth, as against extensive growth, involves better job opportunities rather than more job opportunities, more highly trained people rather than more people, better use of capital and land rather than more capital and land — in brief, a better performance rather than a larger one. Extensive growth implies primary concern with the GNP growth rate; intensive growth implies primary concern with the GNP per capita growth rate. What must now be asked is whether the roughhewn concepts of extensive and intensive growth have any operational significance, and if so whether national policies designed for extensive growth have any place in an age of intensive growth.

It is, of course, true that it would be hard to find historical examples of either pure intensive or pure extensive growth. The important question is whether it is legitimate to characterize certain periods as periods of *predominantly* intensive or extensive growth. Both traditional history and Professor Gallman's quantitative work suggest that for the United States it is meaningful to distinguish between the extensive growth of the last half of the nineteenth century and the intensive growth of the first half of the twentieth. Thus Gallman found that "the rate of increase of commodity output over the first fifty years of the twentieth century was very far below the rate for the last sixty years of the nineteenth," but "the average rate of change of commodity output per capita was about the same in the twentieth as in the nineteenth century."[16] That twentieth-century economic growth in the United States has been mainly of the *intensive* variety is made clear by Gallman's findings that "the twentieth century average decade rate of increase of gainful workers in commodity production was only . . . slightly more than one-fifth as large as that of the nineteenth. The twentieth century increases in commodity output were largely productivity increases. . . . Productivity advance in commodity production was sufficiently high to maintain a high rate of growth of commodity output per member of the population, despite the fact that a sharply declining share of the population was engaged in commodity production."[17]

In Canada we have only the beginnings of a statistical history of our economic growth before 1926 and we cannot with confidence argue from the statistical record. Neverthless the Canadian GNP data, based on Firestone's figures for the pre-1926 period, fail to show any evidence of re-

59

tardation in the growth of GNP since 1900, or even since 1880, and clearly suggest some modest acceleration of GNP growth in the period since the Second World War. Taken at face value — and I find it hard to believe that the general trends of the data are misleading — the suggestion is that Canada has remained in a period of extensive economic growth for the past sixty or seventy years. Qualitative evidence, however, is clearly at odds with this hypothesis. Most economic historians would agree with Fowke's suggestion that 1930 marked "the end of the establishment phase of the wheat economy and the completion of the first national policy"[18] and would even go farther by using 1930 to mark the end of the period of extensive growth that started in Canada in the mid-1890s. By this time the West had been settled, the railways built, and the pulp and paper, hydroelectric, and mining industries established.[19] It is true that since the Second World War there have been some dramatic new mining developments in Canada — petroleum, iron ore, uranium, and potash — but the industries built on these new resources have been neither land-intensive nor labour-intensive and they have had a much smaller impact on the postwar economy than the earlier "staple industries" had on the pre-1930 economy. In retrospect, there seems as much reason to have expected some retardation in the growth of GNP in Canada after 1930 as there was to expect a slowing down of the GNP growth rate in the United States after 1900, that is to say, for a replacement of predominantly extensive growth by predominantly intensive growth.

Yet our growth statistics are still those of a period of extensive growth. In part, the statistics reflect the postwar resource discoveries, mentioned above, and in part, I think, the likelihood that the expansion in manufacturing in Canada after 1940 was unusually large not only because of the war but also because normal growth had been suspended in the 1930s. In a sense, those technological trends that were differentially favourable to Canadian manufacturing had just begun to take hold in the 1920s, were submerged by the depression of the 1930s, and only became fully apparent in the 1940s and 1950s. But when this has been said, there still remains a strong suspicion that Canadian *policy* has had much to do with the perpetuation of very high GNP growth rates characteristic of a period of extensive growth long after our period of extensive growth apparently came to an end.

The change in "national policies" after 1930 was not, perhaps, as sharp as Fowke suggested.[20] Indeed two out of three of the main pillars of the old national policy — tariff protection and the promotion of immigration — are as much a feature of present-day Canadian policy as they were of Canadian policy sixty years ago. As has been argued throughout (the Canadian tariff and Canadian immigration policy operate jointly to "force the pace" of manufacturing growth) and, more generally, of growth in population and GNP. The danger is that in a period of intensive growth, when the growth in natural resources is slower than the growth in population, part of the growth in GNP will be at the expense of growth in GNP per person. American adjustments to the "closing" of their "frontier" included, one might suggest, a rapid extension of birth control practices, severe limitations on immigration, land conservation policies, and, more recently, growing concern for the wise use of air and water. Some of these adjustments have also been in evidence in Canada. But our *national* economic policies today are substantially those of 1900 — more factories, more people, more cities, more GNP. Is it not time to consider whether these are appropriate policies for a country whose "frontier" was "closed" a generation ago?

Notes

1. The Innis link was derived from Galt's argument, made in reply to protests from British manufacturers against his raising of the Canadian tariff in the late 1850s, that increased tariff revenue was necessary to help pay for Canadian canals and railways that could not be profitably built by private concerns, and that British manufacturers ought to be pleased with the arrangement because the cheaper cost of transportation would lower the price of British manufactured goods in Canada and thus increase the market for them. (Innis accepted as profound this economic doubletalk of a suave politician, though with a certain amount of incredulity about its source: ". . . whether or not [Galt's] explanation was one of rationalization after the fact, or of original theoretical analysis, reliance on the customs was undoubtedly the only solution.) Surely it was not the only solution; if the canals had been paid for by domestic taxation, or by import duties that were no heavier than domestic excise duties, the British manufacturers would have been at least as well off, and Canadians would have been better off. A subsidy is always to be preferred to a tariff on both economic grounds and political grounds; on economic grounds because direct payments distort resource allocation less than indirect payments, and on political grounds because direct payments involve less deception than indirect payments.

Galt was talking *mainly* of revenue tariffs. Innis extended the Galt argument to tariffs that were mainly protective, and thereby compounded Galt's error. "The National Policy was designed not only to increase revenue from customs [as in Galt's argument] but also to increase revenue from traffic from the standpoint of the railways. The increasing importance of railways has tended to emphasize the position of protection rather than revenue." As economic theory this is absurd, not only because the railways, like the canals, could have been financed more efficiently by subsidy than by tariff, but also because a tariff cannot at the same time maximize both protection and revenue; the greater the protective effect of a tariff the less the revenue will provide. The charitable interpretation of this passage is that Innis was indulging in "rationalization after the fact." In the article in which these passages occurred, Innis at any rate doubted the *future* application of his argument. "Dependence on the application of mature technique, especially in transport, to virgin natural resources must steadily recede in importance as a basis for the tariff. It will become increasingly difficult to wield the tariff as the crude but effective weapon by which we have been able to obtain a share of our natural resources."

All of the above quotations are taken from an article by Innis published in 1931, and reprinted in H. A. Innis, *Essays in Canadian Economic History* (Toronto, 1956), pp. 76–7. Two years later Innis was in a deep quandary about the effect of the Canadian tariff. "Inflexibility of the tariff downward contributed to the difficulties during the period of prosperity which began . . . in 1896 . . ." (*ibid.*, p. 91). On the following page he wrote that "During a period of prosperity the tariff should be raised to act as a brake. . . . If railroad rates are lowered at the beginning of a period of prosperity tariff rates should be raised accordingly. . . . Lowering the tariff during the period of a depression and raising the tariff during a period of prosperity might do much to alleviate the problem of a staple-producing area" (p. 92–3). The only way I can see of resolving the contradiction between these two quotations is to suppose that in the first Innis was thinking of the combined effect on C.P.R. revenues of the wheat boom and the continued support of the tariff, and the consequent effect of swollen railway revenues in promoting a new, and uneconomically large, railway building program in Canada: had the tariff been lowered, and the C.P.R.'s profits thereby dampened, the incentive to build *two* new transcontinental railways in Canada would have been reduced; and that in the second he was thinking of the Western farmer: the wheat boom might have been dampened by raising farm cost by means of *increased* tariff rates in order to offset the advantages that farmers gained by lowered railway rates. Since the final part of the second quotation recommends a counter-cyclical tariff policy (Innis must have know how politically impracticable *this* was!), with no qualification about how railway rates should be changed, one can only make sense out of this passage by supposing that by 1933 Innis was willing to sacrifice the railways to the farmers during depression and the farmers to the railways during prosperity; his recommended policy would be counter-cyclical for farmers and pro-cyclical for railways! Perhaps the subtlety, or the confusion, was covering a retreat. Realizing that a high tariff may

61

"become inadequate" during depressions (p. 91), and suggesting that the period of resource expansion in Canada had ended, Innis in fact repudiated his linking of the National Policy and railways by reverting to the lesser economic confusions of Galt's position: "Assuming relative stability in the production of raw materials as a result of exhaustion of natural resources the tariff must assume to an increasing extent the position of a toll, as Galt originally planned, and should approximate the deficit on transportation finance" (p. 93). Unfortunately the damage had been done, for textbook writers cannot spare the time to assess qualifications to, or second thoughts on, powerful generalizations.

2. *Dominion of the North* (Toronto, 1944), p. 346.
3. *North Atlantic Triangle* (New Haven and Toronto, 1945), p. 158. My italics.
4. *Canadian Economic History* (Toronto, 1956), p. 383.
5. *Engineering and Society*, Part II (Toronto, 1946), p. 246.
6. *Canadian Agricultural Policy* (Toronto, 1946), p. 8. Fowke may mean that the national policy was a prerequisite from central Canadians' point of view, i.e., that central Canada would not have "invested" in the West without it. At the same time he would not argue that eastern investment was a *sine qua non* of western development; see note 7.
7. V. C. Fowke, *The National Policy and the Wheat Economy* (Toronto, 1957), p. 69.
8. J. M. S. Careless, *Canada* (Toronto, 1953), pp. 277-8.
9. Ottawa, 1939.
10. Toronto, 1956.
11. *Colony to Nation* (Toronto, 1946), pp. 373-4.
12. *The Economic Background of Dominion-Provincial Relations*, pp. 17 and 20.
13. *Canada*, pp. 295 and 312.
14. R. W. Fogel, *The Union Pacific Railroad* (Baltimore, 1960), *passim*.
15. *The National Policy and the Wheat Economy*, p. 70.
16. R. E. Gallman "Commodity Output, 1839-1899" in *Trends in the American Economy in the Nineteenth Century* (Princeton, 1960), pp. 18 and 20.
17. *Ibid.*, p. 20.
18. "The National Policy — Old and New" in the *Canadian Journal of Economics and Political Science*, August, 1952, pp. 277-8.
19. See J. H. Dales, *Hydroelectricity and Industrial Development* (Cambridge, Mass., 1957), chap. 8, esp. p. 166.
20. "The National Policy — Old and New."

Topic Three
The Rise of Western Alienation

Roughly 25,000 Indians and 10,000 mixed-bloods, of Métis, lived in the Prairie West in 1867. The Métis had developed their own sense of nationality and had established their own way of life based on agriculture and the buffalo hunt. The majority of the Métis lived in the Red River colony at the junction of the Red and Assiniboine rivers (present day Winnipeg), the only major permanent settlement in the entire region.

The newly formed Canadian government purchased Rupert's Land (which incorporated all of the present-day prairies) from the Hudson's Bay Company in 1869, for a cash payment of £300,000 plus one-twentieth of the fertile area of the Prairies. This new colony would be administered by a federally appointed lieutenant governor and council, until the granting of provincial status. Without consulting the local western population, the Canadian government arranged for the new lieutenant governor and a group of surveyors to go west to prepare the way for settlement and the building of a transcontinental railway. Donald Swainson in "Canada Annexes the West: Colonial Status Confirmed," provides an overview of the history of the Canadian West in the nineteenth century from the perspective of western alienation.

The Métis resisted the Canadian takeover under the leadership of Louis Riel, a Red River Métis who had been educated in Quebec. They formed their own provisional government to defend their interests and to present their views. Armed conflict arose between the settlers who had recently arrived in the Red River colony from Ontario (and whose interests initially paralleled those of the federal government) and the Métis. Out of the Riel uprising of 1869 emerged the terms for the incorporation of Manitoba as a province the following year. In "Louis Riel: Patriot or Rebel?," George Stanley presents a biographical sketch of the Métis' leader.

The Canadians' takeover of their homeland adversely affected other groups. The Indians, the original inhabitants, also had to adjust to the new conditions. Traditionally historians have favourably regarded the Canadian government's policy of negotiating treaties with the Indians and settling them on reserves, but historian John Tobias offers an alternative viewpoint in "Canada's Subjugation of the Plains Cree, 1879–1885." Looking at this critical period in western Canadian Indian history from the Indians' vantage point, he argues that their subjugation came only after much resistance, and as a result of policies both unjust and dishonourable.

For a short overview of the Métis see D.B. Sealey and A.S. Lussier's, *The Metis: Canada's Forgotten People* (Winnipeg: Metis Federation Press, 1975). A growing literature exists on Louis Riel and the Métis in 1869/70 and 1885. The five-volume, *The Collected Writings of Louis Riel/Les Ecrits complets de Louis Riel*, (Edmonton: University of Alberta Press, 1985), under the general editorship of George F.G. Stanley, is currently available. Secondary studies include: G.F.G. Stanley's *The Birth of Western Canada: A History of the Riel Rebellion* (Toronto: University of Toronto Press, 1961, first published 1936); Thomas Flanagan's *Louis 'David' Riel: 'Prophet of the New World'* (Toronto: University of Toronto Press, 1979); H. Bowsfield's *Louis Riel: The Rebel and the Hero* (Toronto: Oxford University Press, 1971); Joseph Kinsey Howard's *Strange Empire* (New York: William Morrow, 1952); and, for the uprising of 1885, B. Beal and R. Macleod, *Prairie Fire: A History of the 1885 Rebellion* (Edmonton: Hurtig, 1984). An earlier study of 1885 is Desmond Morton's *The Last War Drum* (Toronto: Hakkert, 1972). Hugh Dempsey presents one Indian leader's response in his *Big Bear* (Vancouver: Douglas and McIntyre, 1984). For a critical view of the Métis position see: T. Flanagan, *Riel and the Rebellion: 1885 Reconsidered* (Saskatoon: Western Producer Books, 1983). Douglas Owram presents the central Canadian view of the West in *The Promise of Eden: The Canadian Expansionist Movement and the Idea of the West, 1856–1900* (Toronto: University of Toronto Press, 1980). George Melnyk's *Radical Regionalism* (Edmonton: NeWest Press, 1981) examines the roots of western protest, and its association with a regional identity.

64

Canada Annexes the West:
Colonial Status Confirmed *

DONALD SWAINSON

The early history of the Canadian West[1] is characterized by dependence and exploitation. The area and its resources were controlled from outside, for the benefit of several distant centres, whose relative importance changed from time to time. London, Montreal and Toronto, the major and competing metropolises, were flanked by such lesser competitors as Minneapolis-

* From *Federalism in Canada and Australia: The Early Years*, edited by Bruce W. Hodgins et al. Copyright 1978 by Wilfrid Laurier University Press, Waterloo, Ontario. Reprinted by permission.

St. Paul, Benton and Vancouver. A prime result of this pattern of development has been a continuing resistance to outside controls. At the same time, the character of western people and institutions has been heavily influenced by forces outside western control. Even indigenous peoples were largely defined by the forces that controlled the region. The interplay of these factors has played a large part in moulding the character of the West and in determining fundamentally its role in Canadian federalism.

I

The pattern of dependence preceded federal union and for the West is the context within which federalism must be viewed. It began in the seventeenth century when English traders established themselves in posts around Hudson Bay. Chartered in 1670 as the Hudson's Bay Company, this "Company of Adventurers of England tradeing [sic] into Hudson Bay"[2] tapped an enormously profitable trade in furs. To this prestigious and powerful firm the Crown delegated vast responsibilities and valuable privileges:

[T]he Company was granted the "sole Trade and Commerce of all those Seas Streightes Bayes Rivers Lakes Creekes and Soundes in whatsoever Latitude they shall bee that lye within the entrance of the Streightes commonly called Hudsons Streightes together with all the Landes and Territoryes upon the Countryes Coastes and confynes of the Seas Bayes Lakes Rivers Creekes and Soundes aforesaid that are not actually possessed by or granted to any of our Subjects or possessed by the Subjects of any other Christian Prince or State". They were to be the "true and absolute Lordes and Proprietors" of this vast territory, and they were to hold it, as had been envisaged in the grant of October 1669, in free and common socage. . . . These lands were to be reckoned as a plantation or colony, and were to be known as Rupert's Land; and the Company was to own the mineral and fishing rights there as well as the exclusive trade and the land itself.[3]

For two hundred years, the Hudson's Bay Company was the (more or less) effective government of Rupert's Land, an enormous territory stretching from Labrador through the shield and the prairies and into the Arctic tundra in the West. It included most of what are now the provinces of Manitoba, Saskatchewan and Alberta. Control over the West was thus vested in a firm centred in London and exercised in the interests of commerce.

Montreal businessmen (whether French before the Conquest, or British after) refused to recognize the HBC's trade monopoly, and wanted to share in the profits. In spite of enormous overhead costs French traders penetrated the West in the middle of the eighteenth century, and entered into competition for the favour of the Indian fur gatherers. After the Conquest Montreal's challenge to the Hudson's Bay Company's monopoly was even more serious. Numerous Montreal-based traders entered the field, but the most famous and effective were organized late in the eighteenth century as the North-West Company. This marvel of capitalist organization exploited the wealth of the shield and the prairies. It opened the rich Athabasca country and its agents penetrated north to the Arctic and west to the

Pacific. The Nor'Westers introduced the influence of Montreal into the mainstream of western life. The vicious competition between Montreal and London for the control of the western trade, however, proved too costly; in 1821 the Hudson's Bay Company and the North-West Company amalgamated. But both Montreal and London continued to exercise great influence in the West. And, of course, the officers and men of the re-organized Hudson's Bay Company remained a powerful force in the West until Canada annexed the area in 1870.

Children of mixed white and Indian blood were an inevitable result of the presence of fur traders in the West. By the late eighteenth century these people were a numerous group on the prairies. They can be very roughly divided into two sub-groups: English-speaking half-breeds and French-speaking Métis. The former tended to be relatively settled and to have close ties with the white communities in the Red River Valley. The Métis were more autonomous and distinctive. During this period, they developed into a powerful force.

66

As a people, the Métis were very much a product of the fur trade. Like many other unsophisticated and indigenous peoples, they were manipulated by the great business firms that exploited the natural resources of their area. The North-West Company employed them first as labourers and hunters. The trade war between the fur trading giants increased their utility, especially after Lord Selkirk established his famous settlement in the Red River Valley in 1811–12. Selkirk's colony and the HBC functioned as interdependent units, and challenged the viability of the NWC operations west of the Red River. The NWC could not declare war on one without fighting the other. Consequently it declared war on both, and the Métis became its prime weapon. The leaders of the NWC encouraged the growth of a primitive nationalism; the Métis were encouraged to believe that the Red River settlers threatened their claim to western lands, a claim inherited from their Cree and Saulteaux mothers. Cuthbert Grant, a Scottish-educated half-breed, was appointed Captain of the Métis by the North-West Company, and his followers became a small private army. They harassed the Selkirk settlers, a process that culminated in 1816 in the battle of Seven Oaks where Grant's men massacred Governor Robert Semple and twenty of his settlers. But in spite of its superior military strength, the NWC, primarily for geographical reasons, could not sustain a protracted campaign against the Red River colonists and the HBC. Consequently, the firms united in 1821; the West was pacified.

The four-year struggle (1812–1816) against the Selkirk settlers was a decisive event in western history. It marked the beginning of the Métis as an organized and self-conscious group. After 1821, they continued to accept Grant's leadership. They founded Grantown on the Assiniboine River west of the restored Selkirk settlement and made that village their capital; for the next seventy years they were at the centre of prairie history.

After the union of the firms, Cuthbert Grant and his people were coopted by the controlling interests. The Métis defended the growing and prosperous community of Selkirk settlers, their former enemies, from the

Sioux. In 1828, Grant was made Warden of the Plains of Red River, with responsibility for enforcing the Hudson's Bay Company trade monopoly. During these quiet years of the 1820s and 1830s the Métis of Grantown organized and refined their most important institution, the famous buffalo hunt, which provided important food reserves for settlers and traders alike, and an economic base for the Métis.[4] The implications of the hunt were endless. It was organized along military lines and was easily adaptable to military and political purposes. The Métis, self-confident about their identity and proud of their place in western society, referred to themselves as the "New Nation" but nonetheless they remained dependent on buffalo and fur traders.

The Métis were created as a people only after the arrival of white traders in the West; the Indians had peopled the prairies for several millennia. It might be argued, however, that European influences recreated Indian society; these forces certainly revolutionized Indian history. When white men first came to North America the Indians who inhabited the western plains lacked horses and guns. The acquisition of these items, combined with trade, radically altered Indian society. In some instances, and for a brief period, the result was startling. A recent historian of Alberta illustrates:

67

> For a few vivid decades Blackfoot culture, based upon horses, guns and unlimited buffalo, rose rapidly into the zenith of the rich, colourful and glamorous life which many regard as the apogee of plains culture. Prior to 1730, during the long era which the Blackfoot called the dog-days they travelled on foot and used dogs for transport. About that year, the acquisition of horses and guns swept them rapidly onward and upward until slightly over a century later they were at the peak of their spectacular horse-based culture. . . . Though horses and guns had made the Blackfoot aggressive, they also provided the leisure which led to the flowering of their social life.[5]

Revolutionized Indian societies were highly vulnerable to external forces. They could not manufacture either guns or ammunition; traders could (and did) cause social calamities through the introduction of liquor and a variety of diseases; trading patterns could not be controlled by Indians. More important, the buffalo could be liquidated and settlement could destroy the basis of Indian independence. In the mid-nineteenth century these successful western Indian societies were in a delicately balanced position. European contacts had changed the very character of their society; at the same time they were dependent upon and vulnerable to white society. Further white encroachment in the West could destroy them. That encroachment of course quickly occurred, and in the 1870s the western Indians were swamped. A recent student of Canadian Indians comments: "For the sake of convenience, and recognizing the arbitrariness of the choice, we may use the date 1876, that of the first Indian Act, as the beginning of what we call the "colonial" period. From the point of view of the European, the Indian had become irrelevant."[6]

The full complexity of mid-nineteenth-century prairie society cannot be revealed in a few paragraphs. The main characteristics, however, can be delineated. The West was inhabited by French-speaking Métis, English-speaking half-breeds, officers and men of the Hudson's Bay Company,

Selkirk settlers and a handful of missionaries, retired soldiers and free-traders. Except for the Indians, these groups were all centred around the forks of the Red and Assiniboine Rivers, where a pluralistic society emerged. Reasonable amity usually prevailed, although the Métis could not be controlled against their will by the aging and increasingly ineffective HBC regime. This was a civilized society, with its own churches, schools and law courts. Its various components produced their own indigenous middle-classes, leaders, institutions and traditions. Several religions were sustained within the settlement and promoted amongst the Indians.

At the same time these diverse western societies were fragile and derivative. W. L. Morton describes the Selkirk settlers as "Scottish crofters on the banks of the Red."[7] Indian society had been recreated through European contact and persons of mixed blood were a product of liaisons between fur traders and Saulteaux and Cree women. Employees of the HBC were often of British birth. None of these groups had sufficient cultural integrity or autonomy to retain their distinctiveness and independence without a considerable degree of isolation from the larger North American society. As Bishop Taché observed about immigration into the West: "[T]he movement [of immigration] is an actual fact, and we must cease to be what we have hitherto been, an exceptional people."[8]

They were dependent on more than isolation. Economically they needed the fur trade and the buffalo hunt. Buffalo products were sold to traders, settlers and Americans at Minneapolis-St. Paul. The fur trade supplied cash, employment and markets. Agriculture, "subsistent, riparian, and restricted,"[9] was nonetheless an important enterprise. Markets were obviously extremely limited. The large-scale export of commodities was hardly reasonable and, even within the West, Red River Valley farmers had no monopoly on food production as long as the buffalo survived. The agricultural sector of the western economy thus remained modest.[10]

Within the West some of these groups, particularly HBC officials, Indians and Métis, could exert tremendous authority; their futures, however, were in the hands of forces that could not be contained. They had sufficient group-consciousness to defend collective interests, and to varying degrees they were all willing to resist encroachments from the outside. The Métis revolted against the locally enforced trade monopoly; HBC officials became dissatisfied with the treatment meted out to them by their London superiors. The Scots settlers resented the suggestion that the area could be disposed of without prior consultation. A willingness to resist in spite of dependence and relative weakness was a striking western characteristic long before the West was annexed by Canada. It is an important component of the western context of federalism.[11]

II

The Central Canadian context is equally important. French-Canadian explorers penetrated the West in the eighteenth century, and thereafter the

West was always a concern of at least some Central Canadians. The connection became somewhat tenuous after the union of the fur companies in 1821, but it was never lost; there was always full cognizance of the fact that Rupert's Land was British territory.

A more pointed interest became evident in the late 1840s, and the nature of that interest illuminates Central Canadian attitudes about what the West was, what it should become and how it should relate to what was then the Province of Canada. This interest, while by no means partisan in nature, centred in the Upper Canadian Reformers. It can be illustrated by an examination of two of its representative manifestations: the campaign of the Toronto *Globe* to annex the West and the organization of the North-West Transportation Company.[12]

The *Globe* was the organ of George Brown, who emerged in the 1850s as the Upper Canadian Reform leader. It was a Toronto newspaper that spoke to the farmers of what became western Ontario, but at the same time represented many of the metropolitan interests of Toronto's business elite. Its interest in the North-West tended to be economic and exploitative. Underlying this early tentative interest in the West was the assumption that the West would become an economic and social adjunct of Upper Canada. On 24 March 1847, for example, Brown reprinted Robert Baldwin Sullivan's lecture, "Emigration and Colonization." While primarily concerned with Upper Canada, Sullivan also discussed settlement possibilities in the North-West. He viewed the West as a potential settlement area for Upper Canadians. In 1848 the *Globe* claimed the West for Canada, and dismissed the rights of the Hudson's Bay Company. The West, it argued, was "capable of supporting a numerous population. This wide region nominally belongs to the Hudson's Bay Company, but in point of fact it does not seem to be theirs."[13] The *Globe's* interest petered out in 1850, but revived after a few years. In 1856 it published a series of revealing articles by an anonymous correspondent, "Huron": "I desire to see Canada for the Canadians and not exclusively for a selfish community of traders, utter strangers to our country; whose only anxiety is to draw all the wealth they can from it, without contributing to its advantages even one farthing."[14] He pronounced the charter of the Hudson's Bay Company "null and void" and declared that "[t]he interest of Canada require that this giant monopoly be swept out of existence. . . ." "Huron" was emphatic on this point:

69

The formation of a Company in opposition to the Hudson's Bay Company would advance the interests of Canada; it would consolidate and strengthen the British power on the continent. . . . In the organization of [opposition to the HBC], every patriot, every true Canadian, beholds results the most important to his country.

According to the *Globe*, westward expansion was an urgent need because of a shortage of settlement land "south of Lake Huron." "[Canada] is fully entitled to possess whatever parts of the Great British American territory she can safely occupy. . . ."[15]

Interest in westward expansion was by no means confined to the *Globe*.

In 1856 the Toronto Board of Trade indicated interest in western trade.[16] Various politicians took up the cause and the matter was aired in both houses of parliament.[17]

In 1858 a Toronto-based group made a "quixotic" and "abortive"[18] attempt to penetrate the West through the incorporation of the North-West Transportation, Navigation and Railway Company (known as the North-West Transit Co.).[19] The project, designed to link Central Canada and the Red River Valley by a combination of rail and water transport, was premature and unsuccessful, but its promoters' attitudes towards the West were both representative and persistent.[20] The objects were the exploitation of such likely and unlikely western possibilities as buffalo hides, furs, tallow, fish, salt, sarsaparilla and cranberries, "the opening [of] a direct communication between Lake Superior and the Pacific . . ." and the opening of trade with the Orient. "[W]e place before us a mart of 600 000 000 of people [in China] and [our project will] enable us geographically to command them; opening the route, and leaving it to the guidance of commercial interests, Canada will, sooner or later, become the great tollgate for the commerce of the world." By "Canada," of course, was meant Toronto, and these promoters dreamed of controlling a great empire: "Like the Genii in the fable [the East Indian trade] still offers the sceptre to those who, unintimidated by the terms that surround it, are bold enough to adventure to its embrace. In turn Phoenicia, Carthage, Greece, Rome, Venice, Pisa, Genoa, Portugal, Holland and lastly England, has won and worn this ocean diadem; Destiny now offers [the East Indian trade] to us."

During the 1850s a dynamic and expansive Upper Canada saw the North-West as its proper hinterland. It was regarded as a huge extractive resource, designed to provide profit for the businessman, land for the farmer and power for Toronto.

While cultural attitudes are sometimes difficult to identify, it was probably assumed that the North-West would be culturally as well as economically dependent on the St. Lawrence Valley. J. M. S. Careless, for example, suggests that "Brown used the North-West agitation to complete the reunification of Upper Canada's liberal party, merging Toronto urban and business leadership with Clear Grit agrarian strength in a dynamic party front."[21] Brown's "party front," which wanted "French Canadianism entirely extinguished,"[22] was dedicated to majoritarianism and the sectional interests of Upper Canada. While the nature of Reform attitudes towards French Canada is debatable, it is hardly likely that the same men who strove to terminate duality in Central Canada sought to extend it to the North-West. Some Lower Canadian leaders (both French- and English-speaking), especially those identified with Montreal business, were interested in westward expansion for economic reasons. There was, however, little French-Canadian enthusiasm for expansion westward.[23] French-Canadian attitudes emanated from the nature of Lower Canadian society, which was profoundly conservative and lacked the buoyant and dynamic qualities of Upper Canada: "Not movement but stasis, enforced by the very nature of the task of 'survival', was the keynote of French-Canadian society."[24] French Canadians lacked confidence in the economic viability of the North-West, in major part because of pre-Confederation missionary propaganda that emphasized difficulties related to the West. It was generally assumed that "western settlement was the sole concern of Ontario"[25] and that large-scale French Canadian emigration would threaten French Canada's ability to survive. Thus there existed no Lower Canadian force to counterbalance Upper Canada's drive westward or Upper Canadian assumptions about how the West should be used. The only additional British North American region that could have possessed western ambitions consisted of the Atlantic colonies: New Brunswick, Nova Scotia, Prince Edward Island and Newfoundland. Their traditional orientation was towards the Atlantic, not the interior. The Atlantic colonies were not about to launch an imperialistic venture in the 1860s.

Apart from Montreal business ambitions the field was clear for Upper Canada, but little could be done until a new political order was established in Central Canada. The constitutional settlement embodied in the Act of Union of 1840 broke down during the 1850s. The complexities of Central Canadian politics during the 1850s are not germane to this discussion, although it should be noted that a prime reason for the breakdown of Canadian government was the incompatability between the uncontrollable dynamism and expansionism of Upper Canadian society on the one hand, and the conservative and inward-looking society of Lower Canada on the other. 71

The new order was worked out by the Great Coalition of 1864 that was committed to the introduction of "the federal principle into Canada, coupled with such provision as will permit the Maritime Provinces and the North-West Territory to be incorporated into the same system of government."[26] The solution was Confederation, which was established by the British North America Act of 1867. It created a highly centralized federation that included the Province of Canada (divided into Ontario and Quebec), Nova Scotia and New Brunswick, and that made explicit provision for the inclusion of the remaining British North American territories:

It should be lawful for the Queen, by and with the Advice of Her Majesty's Most Honourable Privy Council, on Addresses from the Houses of the Parliament of Canada, and from the Houses of the respective Legislatures of the Colonies or Provinces of Newfoundland, Prince Edward Island, and British Columbia, to admit those Colonies or Provinces, or any of them, into the Union, and on Address from the Houses of the Parliament of Canada to admit Rupert's Land and the North-western Territory, or either of them, into the Union. . . .[27]

Confederation was thus the constitutional framework within which the West was destined to relate to Central Canada.

The nature of the new confederation had profound implications for the West. The system was highly centralized, so much so that in conception it hardly qualified as a federation in the classic sense. The Fathers of

Confederation wanted a strong state that could withstand American pressure. Heavily influenced by trade considerations, they saw federation in mercantilistic terms. As children of the empire as it existed prior to the repeal of the corn laws, it is not surprising that their federal model was the old colonial system, modified to involve "the citizens of the provinces . . . in the government of the whole entity":[28]

> The purpose of the Fathers of Confederation — to found a united and integrated transcontinental Dominion — was comparable with that of the mercantilists: and in both designs there was the same need that the interests of the parts should be made subordinate to the interest of the whole. The Dominion was the heir in direct succession of the old colonial system. It was put in possession of both the economics and political controls of the old regime. On the one hand, it was given the power to regulate trade and commerce, which had been the chief economic prerogative of Great Britain; on the other hand, it was granted the right to nominate provincial governors, to review provincial legislation and to disallow provincial acts, the three powers which had been the chief attributes of Great Britain's political supremacy.[29]

72   In his more optimistic moments, John A. Macdonald went so far as to predict the demise of the provinces: "If the Confederation goes on, you, if spared the ordinary age of man, will see both local parliaments and governments absorbed in the general power. This is as plain to me as if I saw it accomplished."[30]

It is true that Lower Canada and the Atlantic colonies were part of the new dominion, but the effective pressure for the new settlement came from Upper Canada. French Canada realized the inevitability of change, but generated little enthusiasm for Confederation. She could offer no better alternative and hence acquiesced (not without considerable protest) in the new arrangement.[31] The creative role was played by Upper Canada, and for that section Confederation was a great triumph. The new system was posited on the abandonment of dualism and, through representation by population in the House of Commons, the acceptance of majoritarianism, albeit with limited guarantees for French Canadian culture within the Province of Quebec. Majoritarianism was very much to the advantage of Ontario, which, according to the 1871 census, had 1 600 000 persons — or 46 per cent of Canada's 3 500 000 people. This translated into 82 of 181 seats in the House of Commons. The first prime minister was an Ontarian, as were the leading lights of the opposition — George Brown, Edward Blake and Alexander Mackenzie. In the first cabinet Ontario, the wealthiest province, had 5 of 13 places. Even the capital was an Ontario city.

The Ontario Liberals became the leaders of the nineteenth-century provincial rights agitation and Ontario emerged as the bastion of provincial rights sentiment, but while the federal scheme was being defined most of Ontario's leaders, regardless of party, concurred on the utility of this "quasi federal" scheme.[32] This is hardly surprising. The Reformers or Liberals were the larger of the two Ontario parties, and doubtless looked forward to a great future as the rulers of *both* Ontario and the dominion. Although they realized this aim by 1873 and ruled simultaneously in Toronto and Ottawa for five years, they suffered humiliating defeats in

1867 at both levels. The deep autonomist drives within Ontario society quickly reasserted themselves and Ontario's Liberals began their protracted assault on Macdonald's constitutional edifice. This should not obscure the fact that quasi-federalism met with little Ontario opposition during the mid-1860s.

The acquisition of the North-West would take place within the context of Canadian federalism. The Fathers of Confederation tended to assume that the "'colonial' relationship with the provinces was a natural one. . . . It therefore seems more appropriate to think of the dominion-provincial relationship at that time as similar to the relationship of the imperial government with a colony enjoying limited self-government."[33] Ontario Liberals quickly adopted a different approach to federalism; federal Conservatives did not. The West was to be "annexed as a subordinated territory."[34] Ontario's leaders were anxious that expansion take place quickly, and assumed that Ontarians would benefit through the creation of a miniature Ontario in the West. At the same time the settled portion of the West, shaken by the breakdown of its isolation and possessing a tradition of resistance to outside control, was accustomed to colonial status, exploitation and dependency.

III

Canada's first Confederation government was anxious to honour its commitment to annex the West. William McDougall and George Cartier went to London in 1868 to negotiate the transfer to Canada of Rupert's Land and the North-West Territory. Their mission was successful. The Hudson's Bay Company agreed to transfer its territory to Canada; the dominion agreed to compensate the company with one-twentieth of the fertile area in the West, land surrounding HBC posts and a cash payment of £300 000. The initial transfer was to be to the Crown, which would immediately retransfer the area to Canada.

In preparation for the reception of this great domain, Canada passed "An Act for the temporary Government of Rupert's Land and the North-Western Territory when united with Canada."[35] This short act provided that the West, styled "The North-West Territories," would be governed by federal appointees — a lieutenant governor assisted by a council. It also continued existing laws in force and public servants in office until changes were made by either the federal government or the lieutenant governor. The act was to "continue in force until the end of the next Session of Parliament."

It has been suggested that this statute does not reveal much about the intent of the federal authorities because it was preceded by such phrases as: "to make some temporary provision" and "until more permanent arrangements can be made."[36] At the same time P. B. Waite notes that it was not a temporary provision at all. After the creation of Manitoba, "the

73

rest of the vast Northwest Territories remained under the Act of 1869, that 'temporary' arrangement. It was re-enacted in 1871 as permanent without any alteration whatever."[37] There is no reason to assume that in 1869 Macdonald and his colleagues intended any very radical future alteration in the statute, which, with the appointments made thereunder, revealed much about Ottawa's attitude toward the West. The area, not a crown colony in 1869, was to join Confederation as a federally controlled territory — not as a province. It was not assumed that the West was joining a federation; rather, Canada was acquiring a subservient territory. Local leaders were neither consulted nor considered. These assumptions emerge even more clearly when the initial appointments under the act are studied. Ontario's ambitions to control the West were symbolized by the appointment of William McDougall as Lieutenant Governor. He was a former Clear Grit who represented Ontario Reformers in the first Confederation government. An imperious and sanctimonious expansionist, he had neither the ability nor the desire to take local leaders, especially those who were not white, into his confidence. Certainly the federal government's request that he search out westerners for his council[38] would hardly inspire local confidence. McDougall was regarded as anything but impartial.[39] Initial executive appointments were not likely, with the possible exception of J. A. N. Provencher,[40] to inspire local confidence in a regime that was organized in Central Canada. Two appointments were flagrantly political. A. N. Richards was the brother of a minister in Sandfield Macdonald's Ontario government and Captain D. R. Cameron was Charles Tupper's son-in-law. Even if one accepts the argument that the "temporary" act was indeed temporary, it is difficult to argue that Lieutenant Governor McDougall, Attorney General Richards or Chief of Police Cameron were temporary.

These various decisions made in distant capitals caused an upheaval in the Red River settlement, the only really settled part of Rupert's Land. Red River was, in fact, on the verge of explosion — a point forcibly made to federal and imperial authorities by Anglican Bishop Machray, HBC Governor of Assiniboia Mactavish, and Roman Catholic Bishop Taché.[41] The unsettled state of Red River was a product of many factors. By the end of the 1840s the commercial authority of the HBC had been irretrievably eroded. During the 1850s the isolation of the area was just as irretrievably lost. American traders pushed up from St. Paul and by the late 1850s a Canadian party, allied with the anti-HBC agitation in Canada, had emerged in the settlement. These Canadians, whose attitudes had been previewed in the 1840s by Recorder Adam Thom and were later to merge with those of Canada First, were arrogant, threatening and racist. They led a concerted assault on the authority of the company, and were instrumental in producing political chaos at Red River during the 1850s. To the Métis especially they represented a threat to their rights and way of life. These justified fears[42] were confirmed by Canadian government officials who entered the area prior to the transfer and offended local sensibilities. Instability was abetted by a "breakdown of the traditional economy of the

Settlement" during the late 1860s. In 1868 Red River "was threatened by famine."[43]

The people of Red River could assess Canadian intentions only on the basis of Canadian activities, appointments, and laws. The response was resistance, spearheaded by the Métis but reluctantly supported to varying degrees (or at least tolerated) by most people at Red River, except the members of the Canadian party: "Riel's authority, although it originated in armed force, came within a few months to be based on the majority will of the community."[44]

The details of the resistance of 1869–1870 are well known and are not germane to this paper. What is important is that Louis Riel's provisional government was in such a strong strategic position that it was able to force the federal authorities to negotiate on terms of entry. The results were embodied in the Manitoba Act that created the Province of Manitoba.

Provincehood was a victory (more, it might be noted, for the Métis than for the other sections of the Red River community), but Manitoba nonetheless entered Confederation as a dependency, not as a full partner with a federal system. Two broad circumstances explain the continuation of "subordinate"[45] status. First, Manitoba was not constitutionally equal to the other provinces. The Métis leaders and their clerical advisors placed great emphasis on cultural problems. Anticipating an influx of Ontarians, they demanded and obtained educational and linguistic guarantees. The federal authorities were concerned primarily with such larger issues as the settlement of the West and the construction of a transcontinental railroad. To facilitate these policies, in the formulation of which Manitoba had no say, Ottawa retained control of Manitoba's public lands and natural resources "for the purposes of the Dominion."[46] Professor Eric Kierans comments:

75

The ownership of the land and resources belong [sic] to the people collectively as the sign of their independence and the guarantee of their responsibility. By British law and tradition, the ownership and control of the public domain was always handed over to the political authority designated by a community when the citizens assumed responsibility for the government of their own affairs. . . . During the . . . hearings [related to the *Report of the Royal Commission on the Transfer of the Natural Resources of Manitoba* (Ottawa, 1929)] Professor Chester Martin . . . testified: "The truth is that for 35 years, (i.e., until the creation of the Provinces of Saskatchewan and Alberta), I believe that it will be correct to say, Manitoba was the solitary exception within the British Empire to accepted British practice with regard to control of the crown lands and it still remains in respect of public lands, literally not a province but a colony of the Dominion." . . . In substance, any attempt to grant responsible government to a province or state, while retaining for the Imperial or Federal authority the control of crown lands and revenues, was held to be a "contradiction in terms and impossible."[47]

Just as serious as Manitoba's inferior constitutional position, was her effective status. She was in no way equipped to function as a province with the full paraphernalia of responsible government. She was ridiculously small, limited in 1870 to some 12 000 persons and 13 500 square miles. The province had an extremely limited tradition of representative government and, to complicate matters further, several of her key leaders were fugitives from justice because of their roles in the resistance. As Lieutenant Governor A. G. Archibald explained in 1872: "You can hardly hope to carry on responsible Government by inflicting death penalties on the leaders of a majority of the electors."[48] Perhaps even more important, provincial finances were hopelessly inadequate; the federal government granted "provincial status to an area which was essentially primitive; and it gave financial terms modelled improperly upon those given to the older provinces."[49] Under the Manitoba Act the province received $67 104 per annum in grants. Her own revenue came to only about $10 000. Even by 1875, 88 per cent of provincial revenues were federal subsidies. "During the whole period from 1870 to 1885 Manitoba was little more than a financial ward of the federal government. . . ."[50] The province could not even afford public buildings to house the lieutenant governor and assembly until Ottawa advanced the necessary funds. In 1871 about one-third of provincial expenditures were used to cover legislative expenses.

76   Thus provincehood was granted prematurely to a jurisdiction that could sustain neither its responsibilities nor the kind of status it ought to have occupied with a federal state. The primary fault lay with the federal leaders: "[T]he Manitoba Act bears on its face evidence both of the inexperience of the delegates from the Red River settlement and of the lack of mature consideration given to the measure by the federal government. The former circumstance was unavoidable; the latter can hardly be condoned."[51] During the early years of Manitoba's history even the outward trappings of real provincehood were absent. For several years the province's immaturity prevented the development of responsible government and the first two lieutenant governors, A. G. Archibald and Alexander Morris, functioned as effective governors rather than as constitutional monarchs. Until 1876 the lieutenant governors even attended cabinet meetings.

Early Manitoba was a colony of Central Canada because of constitutional discrimination and because she had neither the maturity nor resources to support provincehood. But that was not all. With the advent of formal provincial status came an influx of settlers from Ontario, a process that started with the arrival of the Anglo-Saxon Ontarian hordes that dominated Colonel Garnett Wolseley's expeditionary force of 1870. That small army had no real military function. It was sent west in 1870 to appease Ontario — to serve as symbolic compensation for the inclusion in the Manitoba Act of cultural guarantees for the Métis. In extreme form, the expeditionary force was a model of what the later Central Canadian influx was to mean. Local traditions were shunted aside as agriculture was commercialized and society revolutionized. The Indians were unable to assimilate themselves; many Métis sold the land they had been granted to unscrupulous speculators and moved into the North-West Territories. In a symbolic action a group of Ontarians who arrived in 1871 seized some Métis land on the Rivière aux Ilets de Bois. In spite of Métis protests they kept the land and sharpened the insult by renaming the river "the Boyne"!

Some Scots settlers sympathized with the Canadians, but like the HBC traders they had to watch the old society die. Within a few years Manitoba was a colony of Ontario demographically as well as constitutionally, politically and economically.

The Province of Manitoba was only a miniscule portion of the territory annexed by Canada. The remaining enormous area was organized as the North-West Territories. With virtually no permanent white settlement, it received even shorter shrift than Manitoba. Its initial government was provided under the "temporary Government" act. That statute was "reenacted, extended and continued in force until . . . 1871" by the Manitoba Act.[52] Prior to its second automatic expiry in 1871 it was again reenacted without major change, this time with no expiry date. Until 1875, therefore, government for the North-West Territories was provided under the initial legislation of 1869. During these six years the administration of the territories was somewhat casual. There was no resident governor — that responsibility was simply added to the duties of the Lieutenant Governor of Manitoba. Most of the members of the council were Manitobans who did not live in the territories. The Indians, the largest group of inhabitants, were managed not consulted.

The Mackenzie government overhauled the administration of the North-West in 1875 by securing the passage of "The North-West Territories Act." Although not "fully thought out"[53] it did provide a fairly simple system of government consisting of a separate governor and a council that was initially appointed but that would become elective as a non-Indian population grew. The capital was established at Battleford until 1882 when it was moved to Regina. Mackenzie appointed David Laird, a federal cabinet minister from Prince Edward Island, as the first full-time Lieutenant Governor of the North-West Territories. His first council included neither an Indian nor a Métis who resided in the NWT. There was no elected councillor until 1881.

Prior to 1869 the West was a dependent area, ruled (if at all) in a casual, chaotic but paternalistic manner for the benefit of a huge commercial firm centred in London. Westerners feared that the transfer involved simply a change of masters, not a change of status. The Métis feared that in the process they would lose their life style and culture through an inundation of Ontario settlers. The result was a movement of resistance led by the Métis, but with broad support within the Red River settlement. For the bulk of the West the resistance resulted in no change whatsoever. For a small district on the Red River the result was a tiny, anemic province incapable of functioning as a viable partner within a federal system.

IV

After 1867 Macdonald and his colleagues were not able to maintain "quasi-federalism" over the original components of Confederation, but for the West annexation to Canada involved the confirmation of colonial status. The fifteen years after the transfer was the launching period for the West in Confederation. During those years federal sway on the prairies was virtually unchallengeable.

Ottawa's most powerful instrument was federal possession of the West's public lands "for the purposes of the Dominion." This enabled Ottawa to implement two policies that were crucial to the Canadianization of the West: rapid settlement and the construction of a transcontinental railroad. Extreme difficulties did not prevent the execution of these policies. Public lands were made available to settlers in a variety of ways. Although settlement did not proceed as quickly as the federal authorities desired, Manitoba experienced rapid growth during the 1870s and 1880s. Within a generation of the transfer the territories west of Manitoba had been populated by Ontarians, Americans and Europeans. Consequently the provinces of Saskatchewan and Alberta were established in 1905. The federal authorities had recognized from the outset that a transcontinental railroad was required if the West was to be properly Canadianized. After several false starts, the Canadian Pacific Railway was chartered in 1880. The CPR was heavily subsidized, receiving from the federal government some $38 000 000 worth of track constructed at public expense, $25 000 000 in cash, a railroad monopoly in western Canada for twenty years and 25 000 000 acres of prairie land. The land grant was considered indispensible to the line's success and the success of the railroad was one of the fundamental "purposes of the Dominion." The federal government designed its transportation policies to suit the needs of Central Canadian business, and was not particularly tender towards western interests. As Charles Tupper, Minister of Railroads, put it in 1883: "The interests of this country demand that the Canadian Pacific Railway should be made a success. . . . Are the interests of Manitoba and the North-West to be sacrificed to the interests of Canada? I say, if it is necessary, yes."[54]

Federal Conservative strategists, who were in power during 1867–73 and 1878–96, tied tariff policy to settlement and transportation. They saw the West as Central Canada's economic hinterland. The area was to be settled quickly and become an exporter of agricultural products and an importer of manufactured goods. Central Canada was to be the manufacturing centre. The CPR was to haul eastern manufactured goods into the West and western agricultural produce to market. High tariffs were designed to protect the manufacturing industries from foreign competition and at the same time guarantee freight traffic to the CPR by forcing trade patterns to flow along east-west, not north-south, lines. These basic decisions determined the nature of post-1870 western development. They were made by federal leaders to serve Central Canadian interests and they perpetuated the status of the West as a colonial region.

Federal management of the West during these years should be looked at in micro as well as macro terms, although it is clear that federal authorities had little interest in day-to-day western conditions. If settlement was to proceed in orderly and rapid fashion the Indian "problem" had to be solved. That task involved extinguishing Indian rights to the land and rendering the tribes harmless by herding them onto reserves. The instrument used for these purposes was the Indian "treaty." During the 1870s a series of agreements was negotiated between the crown and the prairie tribes. Through these treaties the Indians gave up their rights to their traditional lands in return for reserves and nominal concessions, payments and guarantees. However, they tended to resist being forced onto reserves as long as the buffalo, their traditional source of food, remained plentiful. By 1885 the buffalo were on the verge of extermination and most Indians had been coerced to settle on reservations.

In 1873 Canada founded the North-West Mounted Police, another instrument of federal control.[55] The mounties constituted an effective federal presence on the prairies, chased American traders out of southern Alberta, policed the Indians and Métis, and symbolized the stability and order desired by white settlers. In bringing effective federal rule to southern Alberta they abetted the termination of the international aspect of Blackfoot life. This breakdown of regional international societies was part of the process of Canadianization.

The federal political structure also functioned as a control instrument. Until 1887 Manitoba's handful of MPs constituted the West's entire representation in the House of Commons. These members tended to support the government of the day because of its immense patronage and fiscal authority.

Dependent upon federal largesse yet suspicious of eastern dictation, the western attitude towards national politics was often a curious mixture of ministerialism and defiance. Some papers seemed to believe that the electorate should always give a general support to the government, for such support would ensure a continuous supply of federal monies for western projects. At the same time these papers admitted the need to champion regional interests.[56]

During the 1870s and 1880s the West was Canadianized. By the end of the century massive immigration (which incidentally produced a distinctive population mix that helped differentiate the region from Central Canada) combined with basic federal policies had produced a new West, but its status had changed little. The process generated resistance. The government of Manitoba challenged the CPR's monopoly and sought to obtain better financial terms. Farmers in Manitoba and along the Saskatchewan River organized unions and began their long struggle for a host of reforms including lower tariffs and a transportation system sensitive to their needs. Under Louis Riel's leadership a minority of Indians and Métis rose in 1885 in a pathetic and ill-led rebellion. Territorial politicians crusaded for representation in parliament and responsible government for the North-West Territories.

By the end of the century western resistance to federal control and leadership was a well-established tradition. The West, however, was not strong enough to challenge Canada's great national policies successfully. Consequently the West has remained a subordinate region; the Canadian federation retains its imperialistic characteristics. As W. L. Morton suggested: "For Confederation was brought about to increase the wealth of Central Canada, and until that original purpose is altered, and the concentration of wealth and population by national policy in Central Canada ceases, Confederation must remain an instrument of injustice."[57]

Notes

1. In this essay the "West" refers to the territories that became the provinces of Manitoba, Saskatchewan and Alberta. Rupert's Land consisted of the Hudson's Bay Company territories. The North-West Territory included the other British lands in the northwest. British Columbia was separate and is not considered in this essay.

2. E. E. Rich, *Hudson's Bay Company, 1670–1870*, 3 vols. (Toronto, 1960): 1:53.

3. Cited in ibid., 1:53–54.

4. For a superb account of the buffalo hunt, see Alexander Ross, *The Red River Settlement* (London, 1856), Chap. XVIII.

5. James G. MacGregor, *A History of Alberta* (Edmonton, 1972), pp. 17, 24. For further illustrations see Stanley Norman Murray, *The Valley Comes of Age: A History of Agriculture in the Valley of the Red River of the North, 1812–1920* (Fargo, 1967), p. 13: "By 1800 the Sioux and Chippewa tribes also had acquired horses. Because these animals made it possible for the Indians to hunt the buffalo over great distances, these people soon spent most of the summer and fall roaming the vast prairie west of the Red River. As they became more nomadic, the Indians placed less emphasis upon agriculture, pottery making, weaving, and the idea of a fixed dwelling place. In years when the buffalo were numerous, they could live from the hunt alone. Such was the case between 1800 and 1840 when the Sioux and Chippewa experienced degrees of luxury and leisure they had never known."

6. E. Palmer Patterson, *The Canadian Indian: A History Since 1500* (Don Mills, 1972) pp. 39–40. Different dates apply in different areas: "Thus, by 1865 the plight of the Indians in the Red River Valley was a pathetic one, and for the most part their culture no longer had any effect upon this area" (Murray, *Valley Comes of Age,* p. 15).

7. W. L. Morton, "Introduction to the New Edition" of Alexander Ross. *The Red River Settlement* (Edmonton, 1972), p. xx.

8. Cited in A. I. Silver, "French Canada and the Prairie Frontier, 1870–1890." *CHR* 50 (March 1969): 13.

9. W. L. Morton, "Agriculture in the Red River Colony," *CHR 30* (December 1949): 321.

10. Murray, *Valley Comes of Age,* pp. 44 and 48: "[T]here can be little question that the economy of the Selkirk colonies stagnated soon after they were able to produce a surplus. The major reason for stagnation in Red River agriculture was the limited market for farm produce, and this situation developed primarily out of the economic prerogatives of the Hudson's Bay Company. . . . [I]t continued to rely upon supplies brought from England and pemmican furnished by the métis hunters." In short, "agriculture did not become really commercial under the fur company regime. . . ." Morton points out that Red River agriculture lacked both "an export staple and transportation" ("Agriculture in the Red River Colony," p. 316).

11. There has recently been considerable discussion of western "identity." Debate on this question will doubtless continue. It can be argued that this persistent willingness to resist is one of the most distinctive western characteristics and is certainly a part of any western "identity," and that it long antedates Confederation. P. F. W. Rutherford, however, dismisses Métis influence: "Unlike other regions in the dominion, the western community was essentially a product of events set in motion by Confederation" ("The Western Press and Regionalism, 1870–96," *CHR* 52 [September 1971]: 287). Morton, however, comments: "Louis Riel was a more conventional politician than William Aberhart . . ." and "[t]his was the beginning of the bias of prairie politics. The fears of the Métis had led them to demand equality for the people of the Northwest in Confederation" ("The Bias of Prairie Politics" in *Historical Essays on the Prairie Provinces,* ed., Donald Swainson [Toronto, 1970], pp. 289 and 293). What is more "western" than this recurring "demand" for "equality"?

12. For a more detailed discussion by the present author see *Ontario and Confederation.* Centennial Historical Booklet No. 5 (Ottawa, 1967) and "The North-West Transportation Company: Personnel and Attitudes," Historical and Scientific Society of Manitoba *Transactions,* Series III, No. 26. 1969–70.

13. *Globe* (Toronto), 14 June 1848.

14. Quotations from articles by "Huron" are from *Globe,* 18 and 31 October 1856.

15. Ibid., 10 December 1856.

16. Ibid., 4 December 1856.
17. Province of Canada, *Journals of the Legislative Council of the Province of Canada*. Being the Third Session of the 5th Provincial Parliament, 1857, vol. XV, pp. 60, 80, 184, 195; Province of Canada, *Appendix to the Fifteenth Volume of the Journals of the Legislative Assembly of the Province of Canada*. Being the 3rd Session of the 5th Provincial Parliament, 1857, vol. XV, Appendix 17.
18. Joseph James Hargrave, *Red River* (Montreal, 1871), p. 143.
19. Province of Canada, *Statutes*, 1858, pp. 635ff.
20. Material that follows is from *Memoranda and Prospectus of the North-West Transportation and Land Company* (Toronto, 1858): Allan Macdonnell, *The North-West Transportation, Navigation and Railway Company: Its Objectives* (Toronto, 1858) and *Prospectus of the North-West Transportation, Navigation and Railway Company* (Toronto, 1858).
21. J. M. S. Careless, *The Union of the Canadas: The Growth of Canadian Institutions, 1841-57* (Toronto, 1967), p. 206.
22. PAC, George Brown Papers, George Brown to Anne Brown, 27 October 1864, cited in Donald Creighton, *The Road to Confederation* (Toronto, 1964), p. 182.
23. For an analysis of French-Canadian attitudes see Silver, "French Canada and the Prairie Frontier."
24. Ibid., p. 29.
25. Ibid., p. 15.
26. Cited in Chester Martin, *Foundations of Canadian Nationhood* (Toronto, 1955), p. 314.
27. British North America Act, Section 146.
28. Bruce W. Hodgins, "Disagreement at the Commencement: Divergent Ontarian Views of Federalism, 1867-1871," in *Oliver Mowat's Ontario*, ed., Donald Swainson, Toronto, 1972), p. 55.
29. Donald Creighton, *British North America at Confederation* (Ottawa, 1939), Appendix II, *The Royal Commission on Dominion-Provincial Relations* (Ottawa, 1940), p. 83.
30. PAC, John A. Macdonald Papers, 510. Macdonald to M. C. Cameron, 19 December 1864, cited in Creighton, *The Road to Confederation*, p. 165.
31. See Jean Charles Bonenfant, *The French Canadians and the Birth of Confederation*, Canadian Historical Association booklet No. 10 (Ottawa, 1967).
32. See Hodgins, "Disagreement at the Commencement."
33. J. R. Mallory, "The Five Faces of Federalism," in *The Future of Canadian Federalism*, eds., P.-A. Crepeau and C. B. Macpherson (Toronto, 1965), p. 4.
34. W. L. Morton, "Clio in Canada: The Interpretation of Canadian History," in *Approaches to Canadian History*, ed. Carl Berger, Canadian Historical Readings I (Toronto, 1967), p. 44.
35. This act is reprinted in W. L. Morton, ed., *Manitoba: The Birth of a Province* (Altona, 1965), pp. 1-3.
36. See Ralph Heintzman, "The Spirit of Confederation: Professor Creighton, Biculturalism, and the Use of History," *CHR* 52 (September 1971): 256-58. Heintzman comments: "Now even a cursory examination of the text of this Act of 1869 would cast serious doubt upon the worth of this argument" (p. 256) — i.e., that the act revealed the "real intentions of the federal government" (p. 247). "The purely temporary character of the Act is made clear in the preamble. . . . But all of this informed speculation is quite unnecessary. We have an explicit statement of the intentions of the government from the mouth of John A. Macdonald himself. Macdonald told the House of Commons flatly that the 1869 Act was 'provisional' and 'intended to last only a few months' . . ." (p. 257). Heintzman's chief concerns are educational and linguistic rights.
37. P. B. Waite, *Canada 1874-1896: Arduous Destiny* (Toronto, 1971), p. 65. See also Lewis Herbert Thomas, *The Struggle for Responsible Government in the North-West Territories 1870-97* (Toronto, 1956), p. 48. It is clearly possible to debate the implications of the act, but a document that Macdonald's government made the permanent constitution for the North-West Territories cannot simply be dismissed as meaningless. It is interesting to note that when the statute was made permanent in 1871, with only insignificant modifications, and, of course, the exclusion from its provisions of the new Province of Manitoba, it was justified in its preamble as follows: "whereas, it is expedient to make provision for the government, after the expiration of the Act first above mentioned [i.e., An Act for the temporary government of Rupert's Land], of the North-West Territories, that being the name given . . . to such portion of Rupert's Land the North Western Territory as is not included in . . . Manitoba . . ." (*An Act to make further provision for the government of the North-West Territories*, 34 Vict. Cap. XVI).
38. "Instructions issued to Hon. Wm. McDougall as Lieutenant Governor of the North West Territories, Sept. 28, 1869," in *The Canadian North-West: Its Early Development and Legislative Records*, ed., E. H. Oliver (Ottawa, 1914-15), II: 878-79.
39. For his earlier hopeless insensitivity concerning Red River see W. L. Morton, "Introduction" to *Alexander Begg's Red River Journal* (Toronto, 1956), p. 23.
40. Provencher, a nephew of Bishop J. N. Provencher of St. Boniface (1847-53), was a Central Canadian newspaperman. He had only a minimal contact with the West and was described by Alexander Begg, an intelligent and representative citizen of Red River, as "a pleasant sort of a man who had come up

altogether wrongly informed regarding this country . . ." (*Alexander Begg's Red River Journal*, p. 176). Provencher's relationship with the Bishop was his only tie with the West, unless it is assumed that the Métis were French Canadians and therefore identified closely with other French Canadians. The Métis, of course, assumed no such thing, regarding themselves as a New Nation. To assume that the Métis were French Canadian is to commit a sort of historiographical genocide. Heintzman, "Spirit of Confederation," p. 253, for example, comments: "This awareness of the 'canadien' community at Red River was one reason to rejoice in the annexation of the North-West: it meant that the French of the west would be welcomed back into the fold and raised the possibility that colonists from Lower Canada would find themselves 'at home' on the prairies." Presumably, for Heintzman, these 'canadiens' included the Métis. Alexander Begg held the members of McDougall's party in very low esteem. McDougall was characterized as "overbearing," "distant," "unpleasant" and "vindictive." Richards "does not appear to be extraordinarily [*sic*] clever on Law Subjects although appointed Attorney General." Cameron was "a natural ass" and Dr. Jacques "an unmannerly young fellow" (W. L. Morton, "Introduction," *Alexander Begg's Red River Journal*, p. 176). Is it any wonder that Canada's initial attitude toward the North-West was looked at through a jaundiced eye?

41. George F. G. Stanley, *The Birth of Western Canada: A History of the Riel Rebellions* (Toronto, 1936), pp. 63-64.
42. Morton, "Introduction," *Alexander Begg's Red River Journal*, pp. 29, 40-42, 45.
43. Ibid., p. 17.
44. M. S. Donnelly, *The Government of Manitoba* (Toronto, 1963), p. 10.
45. Morton, "Clio in Canada." p. 44.
46. Manitoba Act, Section 30.
47. Eric Kierans, *Report on Natural Resources Policy in Manitoba* (Winnipeg, 1973), p. 1. The severity of this kind of analysis has been questioned. See, for example, J. A. Maxwell, *Federal Subsidies to the Provincial Governments in Canada* (Cambridge, Mass.: 1937).
48. Cited in Donnelly, *Government of Manitoba*, p. 16.
49. Maxwell, *Federal Subsidies to the Provincial Governments*, p. 37.
50. Donnelly, *Government of Manitoba*, p. 161.
51. Maxwell, *Federal Subsidies to the Provincial Governments*, pp. 37-38.
52. Section 36.
53. R. G. Robertson, "The Evolution of Territorial Government in Canada," in *The Political Process in Canada* (Toronto, 1963), p. 139 note.
54. Cited in Chester Martin, "*Dominion Lands*" *Policy* (Toronto, 1938), p. 470.
55. See S. W. Horrall, "Sir John A. Macdonald and the Mounted Police Force for the Northwest Territories," *CHR* 53 (June 1972). Horrall notes, pp. 182-83: "To Macdonald the problem of policing the Northwest resembled that faced by the British in India."
56. Rutherford. "Western Press and Regionalism," p. 301.
57. Morton, "Clio in Canada," p. 47.

Louis Riel: Patriot or Rebel?*

GEORGE STANLEY

The Essence of the Riel Question

Few characters in Canadian history have aroused such depth and bitterness of feeling as that of the métis chieftain, Louis "David" Riel. The mere mention of his name bares those latent religious and racial animosities which seem to lie so close to the surface of Canadian politics. Despite the fact that he identified himself, not with the French Canadians of Quebec, but with the mixed-blood population of the western plains, Louis Riel became, for a few years, the symbol of the national aspirations of French

Canadian Historical Association Booklet No. 2. Copyright 1964 by Canadian Historical Association. Reprinted by permission.

Canada and the storm-centre of political Orangeism. French-speaking Canadians elevated him to the pedestal of martyrdom; English-speaking Canadians damned him as a rebel. In Riel the people of Quebec professed to see another Papineau, a heroic patriot defending on the far away prairies the cause of Canadians living in the valley of the St. Lawrence; the people of Ontario saw in him only the dastard murderer of an Ontario Protestant. Even today the racial controversies which emerged from Riel's actions in Manitoba in 1869–70, and the political turmoils stirred up by his trial and execution in Saskatchewan fifteen years later, make it difficult to assess fairly the contribution of this strange and rather pathetic creature, whose remains now lie but a few steps from those of his grandparents, in the peaceful cathedral yard of St. Boniface.

In essence the troubles associated with the name of Louis Riel were the manifestation, not of the traditional rivalries of French Catholic Quebec and English Protestant Ontario, but of the traditional problems of cultural conflict, of the clash between primitive and civilized peoples. In all parts of the world, in South Africa, New Zealand and North America, the penetration of white settlement into territories inhabited by native peoples has led to friction and war; Canadian expansion into the North-West led to a similar result. Both in Manitoba and in Saskatchewan the métis had their own primitive society and their own primitive economy. They hunted the buffalo, they trafficked in furs, they freighted goods for the Hudson's Bay Company, and they indifferently cultivated their long narrow farms along the banks of the rivers. Few of them were equipped by education or experience to compete with the whites, or to share with them the political responsibilities of citizenship. When faced with the invasion of civilization they drew together; they did not want to be civilized; they wanted only to survive. Their fears and bewilderment drove them into resistance which, when reduced to armed conflict, held small chance of success.

Fundamentally there was little difference between the métis and the Indian problems. Even less than the mixed-bloods were the native Indians prepared to take a place in the highly competitive civilization of the white men. To the Indian and métis alike, civilization meant the destruction of their culture, with assimilation or extinction as their ultimate fate. The Riel risings were not, as the politicians said and believed, a war between French and English, but between plough and prairie. But these facts were hidden from the Canadian public by the timidity and prejudices of politicians; and the visionary defender of an obsolete cultural epoch in Western Canadian history became the martyr of a race.

The dates of the two risings associated with the name of Louis Riel are not without significance. The first, 1869–70, coincided with the passing of the Hudson's Bay Company as the governing power of the North-West. The second, 1885, coincided with the completion of the Canadian Pacific Railway, an event which definitely marked the end of the old order in the North-West. With the suppression of the last effort on the part of Canada's primitive peoples to withstand the inexorable march of civilization, and the execution of Riel, the domination of the white man was forever

83

assured. Henceforth the history of Western Canada was to be that of the white man, not that of the red man or of the half-breed.

Simple as are the conflicts of 1869 and 1885 when viewed as episodes in the history of the cultural frontier, they have always been complicated by the enigmatic personality of their leader. A man with a real popular appeal and considerable organizing ability, Riel was able to give unity and corporate courage to his followers. In him the self-assertive tendencies of the métis were liberated; to him they owed that self-confidence which they had never previously possessed and were never to possess again. Whether Riel was mad will ever remain a matter of debate. Medical opinion inclines to the view that his grandiose visions, his obsessional neurosis, his intense egotism, his intolerance of opposition, were all symptoms of a paranoid condition. It must be remembered that primitive aggressiveness and hostility lurk deep in the minds of all of us. Unless these tendencies can get adequate sublimation they reveal themselves in strong self-assertion, ruthless desire for power, delusions of persecution, irrational fixations and megalomania. That Louis Riel fits into this pattern there seems little real doubt. Perhaps the psychologist has the final answer to the problem of Riel's personality when he suggests that a repressed primitive aggressiveness explains, in part at least, Riel's behaviour in 1869 and in 1885.

The Basic Cause of the Red River Rising

The half-breeds of the Hudson's Bay Company Territories were a remarkable people. Children of the fur traders and the Indian women of the plains, they combined many of the best qualities of both races. Physically they excited the admiration of visitors. They were as much at home on the prairie as any Indian tribesmen and in their elaborate organization for the buffalo hunt they had a self-made military organization as efficient for its own purpose as the Boer Commando. Despite their semi-nomadic life and their mixed blood they were not savages. They were religious and reasonably honest; and in the golden days of the Red River Settlement serious crime was unknown. The authority of the Hudson's Bay Company was almost entirely moral; and when left to themselves the métis got on well with the Indians, with each other and with their rulers.

The serpent in this Eden was progress. For a long time the menace came from the south. American settlement proceeded faster than Canadian, and while there was still an empty wilderness between Fort Garry and Western Ontario there were fast growing settlements in the United States. Developments south of the frontier made it difficult if not impossible to enforce the fur monopoly; and developments south of the frontier meant the end of the buffalo and the demoralization of the Indians.

The newly created federation of Canada, fearful — and with ample justification — of American expansion northwards and of the intrigues of Senator Alexander Ramsey and the Minnesota party, finally concluded an agreement with the Hudson's Bay Company for the transfer of the Company's territories to Canada. To Canada and to the Canadians the acquisition of

84

the North-West was a logical and necessary corollary to confederation; but to the people of Red River it meant their transfer to a "foreign" government whose interests were very different from their own. Evidence of these differences was soon afforded by the arrival in Red River of a party of Canadian surveyors who proceeded to lay out the land in a symmetrical pattern, taking little or no heed of the irregularities of the métis holdings, and precursing, in any event, close settlement, the destruction of the buffalo and the end of the wandering life of the prairie. The sons of Isaac were advancing on the lands of the sons of Ishmael. A clash was inevitable.

Louis Riel Organizes the Métis

Louis Riel, the man who organized the resistance of the Red River métis, was born in St. Boniface, October 22nd, 1844. His mother, Julie Lagimodière, was the daughter of the first white woman in the North-West, and his father, a métis, had been the leader of the "free trade in furs" movement in the forties. A serious, somewhat introspective boy, Louis Riel was selected by Bishop Taché of St. Boniface with several other métis boys, to be educated in Eastern Canada. As a scholar at the Collège de Montréal his studies were satisfactory, particularly in rhetoric, although his lack of humility in the eyes of his ecclesiastical tutors unfitted him for a religious vocation. He remained, as he always was, aloof, egotistical, without real friends among his comrades. These were years of intense political activity in the Canadas, years of constitutional deadlock, of "Rep by Pop", "No Popery", "Double Majority", and "Confederation". Riel's patrons, the Masson family, were well known in Canadian political circles and it is not surprising that young Louis Riel should have shown a greater interest in politics than in religion. He worked for a brief time as a student-at-law; then in 1867 he went back to the west, to St. Paul, where he remained until his return to Red River a year later.

85

Riel did not stir up the métis to the insurrection that occurred in 1869. He only assumed the leadership of an already existing discontent, moulded it, and gave it form according to his judgment or his impulse. His education, his eloquence, his knowledge both of the English and French languages, and his genuine belief in the justice of the métis cause marked him out at once as the obvious leader of his people, and to him the frightened, confused métis turned. Their obvious need for leadership gave young Louis confidence, and he was able, in turn, to inspire them with a sense of national destiny. Small secret meetings developed into large political gatherings, and when news reached the Settlement that a Canadian Lieutenant-Governor, William McDougall, with a ready-made government and several cases of rifles, was approaching Red River by way of Pembina, the aroused métis met at the house of the abbé Ritchot in St. Norbert determined to organize their resistance. John Bruce, a man of little consequence, was elected president of the métis "National Committee"; Louis Riel, the real leader, was named secretary. A barricade was then erected across the road and on October 21st a warning was sent to

McDougall not to attempt to enter the country without the express permission of the "National Committee". Having taken the first step towards armed resistance, the second came easily enough. The Hudson's Bay Governor, William McTavish, mortally ill, had virtually abdicated all authority and Riel's organization was able not only to cut McDougall off from the small but noisy group in Winnipeg favouring annexation to Canada, but to intercept all mails and parties entering the Settlement.

The day of decision for Riel was November 2nd. On that day he and a band of armed métis occupied Fort Garry without opposition. It was a daring and decisive act. Situated at the junction of the Red and Assiniboine rivers, with ample stores of food and munitions, and defended by stone walls, Fort Garry was both the geographical and strategic centre of the Red River Settlement. Whoever controlled the fort controlled the colony.

Meanwhile McDougall, much to the delight of the Americans who continually poked unkind fun at him in their newspapers, fretted and fumed at Pembina. He had been told to proceed with all convenient speed to Fort Garry and there to make arrangements for the completion of the transfer which had been fixed for December 1st, 1869. His line of duty to him was clear. Unaware of the fact that the Canadian government had at the last moment postponed the date of transfer, McDougall issued, on December 1st, in the name of Queen Victoria, a proclamation announcing the transfer of the North-West to Canada with his own appointment as Lieutenant-Governor, and he commissioned Colonel J. S. Dennis to raise a force to deal with the insurgents.

To proclaim a transfer which had not been effected was meaningless; but to propose to overcome by armed force the people whom he expected to govern, was dangerous both for McDougall and for the country he represented. It was fortunate that the response to McDougall's appeal fell far short of what he had hoped for. Henry Prince and a few Saulteaux Indians turned out, ready to fight the métis or anyone else, and the Canadians who had settled in the vicinity of Winnipeg displayed a genuine eagerness to enlist; but the great body of settlers, both mixed-blood and white, held back. Dennis soon realized the folly of any attempt to overthrow the Riel movement by force of arms and told McDougall so. But the enlisted Canadians, forty-five of them, led by Dr. John Schultz, believed themselves stronger than they were, and ignoring Dennis's advice they occupied a fortified house in Winnipeg. When, however, they found themselves faced with the muskets of six hundred métis even Schultz could see the force of the argument; they therefore emerged from "Fort Schultz" and dragged themselves between the files of Riel's ragged soldiery towards the cells of Fort Garry.

The First Convention, November 1869

Meanwhile Louis Riel had been seeking to broaden the basis of his support. Hitherto his movement had been limited to the French-speaking métis. Almost equal in number to the métis were the English-speaking half-breeds, whose interests, while differing in detail, were ultimately the same as those of their French-speaking kindred. It was thus Riel's aim, not to fight Canada, but to unite the whole body of mixed-blood settlers who formed over eighty per cent of the population of Red River, in a demand that Canada negotiate with them the terms of their entry into the Canadian federation. It was with this end in view that he invited the several parishes of the colony to send representatives to meet in convention at Fort Garry on November 16th.

From Riel's standpoint the convention was only a partial success. He had prepared no agenda; his supporters, most of them unschooled buffalo hunters, lacked any real knowledge of parliamentary procedure, and the English-speaking half-breeds to whom he was appealing, had no clear cut ideas as to what their role should be. Much time was wasted in fruitless disagreement over the question of forming a "Provisional Government" to take over the authority previously exercised by the Hudson's Bay Company. The English half-breeds were inclined to suspect the nature of Riel's motives although the continued presence of the Union Jack above the walls of Fort Garry and the moderation which characterized the "List of Rights" which Riel submitted for discussion, did much to minimize the disagreements between the two half-breed groups. However, McDougall's proclamation renewed the doubts of the English-speaking members of the convention, and, intolerant of any further delay, Riel, on December 8th, issued a "Declaration of the People of Rupert's Land and the North West" to the effect that, since the Hudson's Bay Company had, without the consent of the settlers, sold the country to a "foreign power", the people of Red River were, in the absence of any legal authority, free to establish their own government "and hold it to be the only and lawful authority now in existence in Rupert's Land and the North-West, which claims the obedience and respect of the people". In other words, the métis National Committee was the only "lawful" as well as the only "effective" government in Red River. The Declaration continued, however, by expressing the willingness of the people to "enter into such negotiations with the Canadian government as may be favourable for the good government and prosperity of this people". On December 23rd, John Bruce resigned and Louis Riel became the titular president of the National Committee. He was now complete master of the Red River Settlement.

87

The Canadian Government Attempts to Placate the Métis

Five days previously McDougall had quitted the inhospitable village of Pembina. In Ottawa the Prime Minister, Sir John A. Macdonald, wrote to one of his colleagues, "McDougall is now at St. Paul's and leaves this morning for Ottawa. He has the redoubtable Stoughton Dennis with him. The two together have done their utmost to destroy our chance of an amicable settlement with these wild people." Sir John A. Macdonald and the others completely misunderstood the real nature of the métis grievances. They viewed the troubles in Red River primarily as an expression of French-Canadian particularism, and so they sent as peace messengers to Red River a French-Canadian priest and a French-Canadian soldier from Eastern Canada. Neither Grand Vicar Thibault nor Colonel de Salaberry accomplished anything. Riel quickly found that the Canadian emissaries possessed no real authority to treat with the National Committee, and he would not, therefore, permit them to carry out their intended role of spreading propaganda on behalf of Canada.

Of far greater significance was the appearance in the Settlement towards the end of December 1869 of Donald A. Smith, the chief representative of the Hudson's Bay Company in Canada. Smith had offered his services to the Canadian Government in November, and his offer had been accepted. Smith was a man of drive, ambition and resource, a cold and unemotional master of business. He had distinguished himself as administrator of the Company's Labrador District and was, at this time, manager of the Montreal District. Although fifty years of age, he was just crossing the threshold of that remarkable career which saw him enter parliament, make possible the building of the Canadian Pacific Railway, receive a peerage, and become High Commissioner for Canada in London. He had never before visited the North-West, but he had married a Red River girl and his name was well known to Company servants and métis alike.

As representative of the Company, Smith found little difficulty in entering the Settlement. Although his freedom of movement was circumscribed by a suspicious Riel, he had frequent visits from "some of the most influential and most reliable men in the Settlement", who not only made known to the people generally "the liberal intentions of the Canadian Government", but who helped Smith distribute no less than £500 among the French métis in those quarters where it would be most to the advantage of Canada. He had taken care to leave his official papers at Pembina in order to prevent their seizure, and by spreading word of their existence and implying that he possessed the power to negotiate, Smith finally compelled Riel to call a general meeting of the inhabitants of Red River to hear a public statement of Canada's position.

The Second Convention and the Establishment of the Provisional Government, January-February 1870

Despite the cold — the temperature was near to twenty degrees below zero [−29°C] — upwards of a thousand men, French métis, English half-breeds and Scotch settlers, assembled in the snow-packed square of Fort Garry on January 19th and 20th. The chairman of the meetings was Thomas Bunn, an English half-breed who was nominated for the position by Louis Riel. Riel himself acted as interpreter. At first it seemed as though the mature, experienced Scot had gained the upper hand, but by the second day it became clear that the young and inexperienced métis still retained his ascendancy over the people of Red River. His proposal that another convention should meet at Fort Garry to consider "the subject of Mr. Smith's commission and to decide what would be best for the welfare of the country" was seconded by A. G. B. Bannatyne, a white settler, and carried unanimously. The unity which Riel had sought before Christmas without achieving it now appeared to be on the point of realization; and the métis leader's suggestion that the proposed convention should include both French and English in equal numbers was a popular one. The fact is that on fundamental problems the mixed-blood population thought alike. Despite the failure of the first convention there had been no real difference of opinion over the proposed "List of Rights". The only real division was between the half-breeds and the "Canadians", who were cordially disliked by the old settlers of Red River, both French and English-speaking.

The convention met on January 25th. For seventeen days the representatives discussed the "rights" which they should claim from Canada. On several occasions Riel's proposals were rejected, much to his indignation and annoyance. In the end a new "List of Rights" was drawn up, delegates were appointed to carry it to Ottawa, and a Provisional Government was established under the presidency of Louis Riel. Towards midnight on February 9th the cannon of Fort Garry belched forth a salute and fireworks, which the Canadians had purchased to celebrate the arrival of McDougall, were exploded in honour of Riel and his associates. The métis leader's star was at its zenith.

89

The Execution of Thomas Scott, March 1870

There was, however, a cloud upon the horizon. Even while the members of the convention were still sitting at Fort Garry, the Canadians at Portage la Prairie had started a second counter-Riel movement. It was largely the work of one Thomas Scott, a Canadian who had been taken prisoner in December and who had succeeded in escaping from Fort Garry. A small band of these Canadians marched towards Kildonan where Dr Schultz, who had likewise escaped from Riel's hands, was doing his best to enlist the sympathies and persons of the Scottish settlers; but they decided against armed resistance. Unfortunately the métis, believing an attack to be imminent, began to round up the Canadians as they were marching back to Portage la Prairie. The latter quietly submitted to being taken to the Fort and thrust into the prison rooms from which the first group of prisoners had only recently been freed.

The outcome of the Canadian action — which Macdonald called both "foolish" and "criminal" — was the trial and execution of Thomas Scott. The métis court martial which condemned him was no judicial tribunal; and the execution was both senseless and cruel. "Consider the circumstances. Let the motives be weighed," pleaded Riel at a later date. The métis leader justified the execution of Scott by declaring that he had been guilty of disorderly conduct the previous autumn, that he had twice been involved in offensive actions against the Provisional Government, and that he had been abusive to his guards and incited the other prisoners to insubordination; but these were hardly offences calling for the death penalty. A more honest explanation may be found in Riel's words to Donald A. Smith: "We must make Canada respect us." Both Riel and the métis, despite their swagger and apparent self-assurance, felt inadequate to the situation in which they found themselves. Fundamentally they were suffering from an inferiority complex and from it they sought to escape by a deliberate act of self-assertion.

The Despatch of Delegates to Ottawa, March 1870

Five days after the death of Scott, on March 9th, Bishop Taché, who had been absent during this critical period in the history of the North-West while attending the Oecumenical Council at Rome, arrived back in the Settlement. He had answered the urgent appeal of the Canadian government to lend his influence towards restoring peace and order to the country. There was little, however, at this point, that Taché could do. The death of Scott had occasioned but small excitement in the colony, and both English-speaking half-breeds and French-speaking métis continued to work together in the Convention and in the Provisional Government. Final discussions on the demands to be sent to Ottawa and preparations for the despatch of the delegates to Canada occupied the energies of the Convention. The last-minute addition of a demand for separate schools to the already familiar requests for provincial status, a general amnesty, the protection of local customs, the equality of French and English languages, treaties with the native Indian tribes and federal financial concessions, was, however, doubtless the Bishop's work.

The Manitoba Act, May 1870

On March 23rd, the delegates set out. On May 2nd, 1870, a bill called the Manitoba Bill, incorporating most of the features of the métis "List of Rights", was introduced into the Canadian House of Commons by Sir John A. Macdonald. Ten days later, it received the royal assent. When the news reached Fort Garry, a twenty-one gun salute was fired, and a special session of the Provincial Legislature, upon the motion of the métis Louis Schmidt, unanimously agreed to accept the terms of entry of Red River into the Dominion of Canada. With the troubles now virtually at an end the completion of the transfer could be effected, and on July 15th, 1870, the North-West territories formally became part of Canada, with that small portion of which Red River was the centre being admitted as the fifth province of the Canadian federation.

Were this the whole story, the question whether Riel may be looked upon as a patriot or a rebel would be a simple one. Unfortunately, however, as the excitement in Red River waned, that in Canada waxed in-

90

creasing great. The execution of Thomas Scott had ramifications beyond anything anticipated by Louis Riel and his colleagues. Admittedly Scott was not a popular figure, even among the Canàdians in Red River. He was hot-headed and aggressive. Donald A. Smith called him a "rash, thoughtless young man whom none cared to have anything to do with." But he was from Ontario; and he was an Orangeman. As the news of his death became known in Ontario, the latent hatreds of race and religion burst forth. A storm of indignation swept over the province. Schultz and other "refugees" from Red River, screamed for "justice" for Scott; the Orange lodges loudly demanded that no truck be had with the "rebels", no treaty with the "traitors", and no negotiations with the "murderers". Riel's delegates had no sooner arrived in Ontario than they were arrested for complicity in the "murder" of Scott on a warrant sworn out by Scott's brother, but lacking evidence to support the charge they had been discharged. The negotiations had gone ahead to a successful conclusion, but the rancour remained.

91

Wolseley's Red River Expedition, May-August 1870

Partly to assist public opinion in Ontario and partly to provide armed support for the new Canadian administration, which was to be set up under the new Lieutenant-Governor, A. G. Archibald, the Canadian government decided to send a military force to Red River. Early in May this force, under the command of Sir Garnet Wolseley, and comprising two battalions of Canadian militia in addition to a force of British regulars, set out over the rocky waterways which led from Lake Superior to Fort Garry. On August 24th, Wolseley and the troops entered the Fort. Despite the assurances of pacific intent upon the part of the federal authorities, Louis Riel had been warned that the troops, particularly the militia, were hostile, and together with several companions he fled across the river. Thus, when Wolseley's soldiers, who had spent ninety-six gruelling days forcing their way through a wilderness of forests, rivers, lakes and portages, entered the stone gate of Fort Garry, they were greeted, not by armed métis but only by "a half-naked Indian, very drunk" who stood by to watch the rain-drenched British regulars form up on the empty square. Not far away Riel muttered bitterly, "he who ruled in Fort Garry only yesterday is now a homeless wanderer with nothing to eat but two dried fishes."

Louis Riel's Achievement in Red River

But for the execution of Scott, Louis Riel today would probably be looked upon by English and French, white and métis, as the father of the province of Manitoba. The "rebellion" would have passed for a patriotic demonstration in arms of the unwillingness of the people of Red River to be sold like a piece of landed property.

Wherever our sympathies lie, we cannot with justice deny the achievement of the métis leader. That Manitoba should have achieved provincial status and responsible government in 1870 — for good or for ill — was the work of Louis Riel. A glance over the subsequent history of the North-West Territories is enough to set aside any fond belief that the federal government would willingly have conceded provincial status to the infant half-breed colony at the time of the transfer of the territories to Canada, had it not been for Riel's protest.

Even more important was the part played by Louis Riel in preserving the western plains for Canada. The northern states were keenly interested in the acquisition of that area, and in 1868 the Minnesota legislature protested formally against the proposed transfer of the Hudson's Bay Company territories to the new Dominion. In 1869, J. W. Taylor, who had inspired this protest, was appointed by the State Department as United States Secret Agent in the Red River Settlement. From the outset the small but aggressive American party within the colony did everything it could to direct the Riel movement towards annexation. H. N. Robinson, in the pro-Riel newspaper, the *New Nation*, at Fort Garry, wrote vigorously in favour of "independence" and full union with the United States; Oscar Malmros, the American consul at Winnipeg, asked the State Department to give financial support to the métis resistance to Canada — a demand which was backed up by Senator Ramsey's appeal to President Grant. The Fenian, W. B. O'Donoghue, who was one of Riel's councillors, consistently intrigued for annexation. At first Riel was disposed to welcome American support. Encouragement from every source was grist to the métis mill: but with the strengthening of the métis position and the appointment of delegates to Ottawa, Riel's attitude towards the United States underwent a change. The *New Nation* dropped its pro-American tone, and under the editorship of a Canadian, became very British. On April 23rd the Union Jack was raised over Fort Garry on Riel's orders. When O'Donoghue endeavoured to tear it down, a métis guard was stationed beneath the flag with strict orders to shoot anyone who should endeavour to remove it. There is little doubt that, for several months, the fate of Red River hung precariously in the balance. Weaker men than Riel would, under the circumstances, the provocations and irritations, have yielded to the blandishments and intrigues of the Americans and become the tool rather than the master of the Yankee wirepullers at Fort Garry, Pembina and St. Paul.

The Political Aftermath, 1870–1875

One of the terms of the métis "List of Rights" had been a general amnesty to all who had participated in the troublous events of 1869–70. No statement with regard to an amnesty had been inserted in the Manitoba Act, but verbal assurances of an amnesty had been given both to Bishop Taché, while in Ottawa on his way back to Red River, and to the métis delegates who had been sent to negotiate the terms of federation in 1870. That undertakings committing the government to secure an amnesty were actually given there seems little doubt, after a review of the evidence which was subsequently made public in 1874 by the Select Committee appointed to inquire into the causes of the Riel insurrection: that the Canadian government could not, in view of the intensity of public opinion in Ontario, give immediate effect to these undertakings is equally clear. Therein is to be found the dilemma of the next five years.

As the rumours of an amnesty began to circulate through the country, the anti-Riel agitation grew more and more violent. Ontario was ablaze with fury and Liberal party politicians welcomed what to them was a heaven-sent opportunity to turn the popular indignation to political account and capture the normally Conservative Orange vote. As the anti-French, anti-Catholic, agitation developed in Ontario, so too did an anti-English, anti-Orange agitation develop in Quebec. The attacks upon the métis "rebels" were interpreted as an attack upon French Canada and Roman Catholicism. What Ontario regarded as a criminal act, Quebec began to look upon as a patriotic deed. The virulence of the Ontario press was matched by that of the Quebec press, and Sir John found himself between the upper and nether millstone of racial and religious conflict. For promising an amnesty he was denounced in Ontario; for neglecting to proclaim it he was denounced in Quebec.

93

But Macdonald had ridden out political storms before and reasoned that no action at all was often better than one which might permanently impair the future of the new political union which he had done so much to bring about. Yet Riel seemed to be an ever-present nemesis for past sins of omission and commission in the North-West. In the autumn of 1871 he opened old wounds by returning to Red River and offering the services of himself and several companies of métis horsemen to defend the province against a filibustering raid inspired by the ex-Fenian, ex-Provisional Government treasurer, ex-American agent, O'Donoghue. It was embarrassing to Macdonald that the Lieutenant-Governor of Manitoba should publicly have thanked Riel for this offer. It was even more embarrassing when the Liberal government in Ontario proceeded to offer $5000 reward for the apprehension of the métis leader. To avoid the crisis which an arrest would bring, Macdonald forwarded secret service funds to Bishop Taché to induce Riel to go to the United States; and then, to appease a wrathful Ontario, he righteously said, "Where is Riel? God knows: I wish I could lay my hands on him!"

Had Riel been content to remain quietly in the United States, at least until the political storm had blown itself out, it is possible that the problem might have yielded to Macdonald's solution. He had, however, developed within himself a strong sense of grievance at the continued postponement of the promised amnesty. He returned to Manitoba to stand for the constituency of Provencher, but on receiving assurances regarding the promulgation of his amnesty he temporarily withdrew in favour of Sir George Cartier. Following the latter's sudden death he came forward again and was elected both in the by-election of 1873 and in the general election of 1874. Then, once more, he was forced to flee across the border when an ambitious lawyer, Henry J. Clarke, anxious to cultivate the growing Orange vote in the province, obtained a warrant for his arrest.

In March 1874 Riel went to Ottawa, where he succeeded in signing the members' register, thus qualifying to take his seat. After a heated debate in the House of Commons, however, a motion for his expulsion was carried by a majority of 56 votes on a division along racial and not party lines.

Twelve months later, in 1875, five years after the Red River troubles, a general amnesty was proclaimed by the Governor-General entirely upon his own authority. It was a qualified amnesty, one hedged in with the condition that Riel remain in exile for five years.

Riel's Period of Exile, 1875–1884

Always introspective by nature, Louis Riel brooded over the events of 1869–70 and the years of persecution, as he viewed them, which followed. It was a period of strong religious feeling, this period of the struggle between Catholic liberalism and resurgent Ultramontanism, and Riel in his moments of heightened religious experience began to dream of a vast new Catholic state on the prairies with Bishop Ignace Bourget of Montreal as the Pope of the New World. The idea of a religious mission, casually mentioned by Mgr. Bourget in a letter, became an obsession or mental fixation with Riel. He adopted the name of "David", and, in the eyes of his French-speaking friends in the United States, he became more and more irrational both in his actions and in his views. As a result, he was committed, early in 1876, to the St. Jean de Dieu asylum at Longue Pointe, and several months later to the asylum at Beauport near Quebec under fictitious names.

In January 1878 Riel was discharged from Beauport and certified as cured, but he was warned to avoid excitement. For several months he followed this advice. He lived quietly at Keeseville, N.Y., where he became engaged to marry one Evelina Barnabé; but there was nothing there for him to do. Thus it was that he turned his eyes once more towards the west, where alone he was at home.

From St. Paul he went to St. Joseph near Pembina and then to the métis country in the upper Missouri. He tried his hand at trading, at interpreting for Indians and whites, and, according to the North-West Mounted Police, at selling liquor to the Indians. He lived with and like the métis. Within a few years his name became well-known in the territory of Montana. He threw in his lot with the Republicans and sought to deliver the métis vote for that party. He forgot his British allegiance — after all what had it done for him? — and became a United States citizen. He even forgot Evelina and married a métisse. One thing he could not forget; it was always somewhere in the background of his mind, the idea of his "mission".

In 1883 Riel paid a brief visit to Manitoba. Here he learned from the disconsolate and distressed métis the full story of their failure to adapt

94

themselves to the new civilization which had descended upon Red River in the wake of the Manitoba Act. Then came appeals to the old days of the Provisional Government, to his patriotism, and to his egotism. He returned to Montana and met the old Fenian leader, J. J. Donnelly. There was talk of freeing the métis from the baneful yoke of Ottawa, of petitions, and of arms. Then on June 4th, 1884, four men rode into the little settlement in Sun River County where Riel was teaching at the Jesuit mission school. They were Gabriel Dumont, Michel Dumas, Moïse Ouellette and James Isbister. They had ridden over 600 miles and with them they carried an urgent invitation to the former president of the Provisional Government to return to the North-West to lead another protest movement against the government of Canada.

Discontent in Saskatchewan, 1870–1884

Although Riel had achieved many of his objectives during the Manitoba rising, the sad fact was that no legislative safeguards or grants of scrip for lands could really enable the métis to compete with the new settlers who poured into Manitoba after the formation of the province. Within a few years the métis were outnumbered and their homeland remade into something alien to their culture and to their inclination. Sullen, suspicious, embittered over the failure to adapt themselves and estranged from the civilization of the new settlers, many métis sold their scrip for a small portion of its value and sought new homes. Westward they moved, like the buffalo; and in the valley of the Saskatchewan they founded new settlements: St. Laurent, St. Louis and St. Antoine (Batoche). Here, once more, they were able to live for a few short years the old life of the plains, the semi-primitive existence which they had enjoyed before the arrival of the Canadians in Red River.

But the civilization they feared was close upon their heels. As early as 1873, only three years after the transfer of the North-West to Canada, a bill was introduced into the Canadian House of Commons to found a semi-military police force called the North-West Mounted Police. In 1874 three hundred policemen in scarlet tunics and pill box caps set out across the plains towards the hilly country of what was to become southern Alberta. They were the forerunners of civilization, with its surveyors, its colonization companies and its railway. Civilization meant the end, both for the Indians and the métis, of the old way of life in the North-West: it meant the end of the hunt and the chase, and the end of the buffalo; it meant the establishment of Indian reserves; it meant the filling up of the country with immigrants.

There may have been excuses for Sir John A. Macdonald in 1869; there could be none in 1885. For the problem which faced the Prime Minister was the same one which had faced him earlier; the problem of conflicting cultures, of reconciling a small primitive population with a new complex civilization. But Sir John had other things upon his mind — he was building the Canadian Pacific Railway — and the Ministry of the Interior, Sir John's own ministry, starved the Indian services and failed to allay the fears and suspicions of the métis that they would lose their rights as the original holders of the soil. And to add to the bewilderment of the native peoples came the subtle suggestions of those white settlers, who, beggared by early frosts, poor crops and low prices for grain, were prepared to use the métis grievances as a means of belabouring an apparently indifferent government. Thus it was that the settlers of the North Saskatchewan, mixed-blood and white, English and French-speaking, joined together to invite Louis Riel to take charge of their campaign for the redress of western grievances.

96 Riel's Agitation in Saskatchewan, 1884–5

Riel was nervous when he began his agitation in the North Saskatchewan valley in the summer of 1884. He felt unsure of himself when addressing white settlers and the recollections of his past relations with Canadians were not very happy. But as the weeks passed he acquired more confidence. His programme was a moderate one. It was directed towards the white settlers as well as to the half-breeds, and his secretary, Henry Jackson, was Ontario-born. Under Riel's direction a petition was drafted; on December 16th it was sent to Ottawa. This petition embodied the grievances of all the elements then supporting Riel. It demanded more liberal treatment for the Indians, scrip and land patents for the half-breeds; responsible government, representation at Ottawa, reduction in the tariff, modification of the homestead laws and construction of a railway to Hudson's Bay for the white settlers. It also contained a lengthy statement of Riel's personal grievances against Ottawa. Receipt of the petition was acknowledged and in January it was announced that a commission would be appointed to investigate and report upon western problems.

It would be an error to suppose that Riel's agitation was carried on with the whole-hearted support of all western people. The Riel movement began to acquire a definite party colour with the support of such well-known Liberals, as the Jacksons; and the adherents of Macdonald, even those, who, like the editor of the Prince Albert *Times*, had formerly expressed their sympathies with the métis, condemned Riel's leadership in no uncertain terms. The old feelings engendered by the execution of Scott in 1870 had never subsided and there were many who disliked and distrusted Riel for no other reason. From the clergy, however, came the greatest opposition. They were suspicious of the métis leader and feared that the North-West reform movement, under his leadership, might well get out of control. Riel's eccentricities troubled them and they doubted whether on matters of faith and politics he was really quite sane.

That a serious situation was developing in the North-West was by no means unknown to the Canadian government. Police, government officials and private individuals appealed unceasingly to Ottawa. Admittedly the appointment of a commission to look into the complaints from the North-West had been promised, but Macdonald's delays were notorious and the mere promise of a commission of inquiry seemed to hold out but small hope of early redress. In any event it was not until March 30th that the government finally decided to name the members. By that time it was too late.

Originally Riel had not intended to stay long in Canada, but as his enthusiasm for the political agitation waxed, his desire to return to Montana waned. Late in February 1885 he went as far as to propose that, should his supporters desire it, he should turn the leadership over to someone else; but it is doubtful whether he really expected or desired that his offer of resignation should be accepted. He turned towards a more active and more dangerous course of action. Ordinary constitutional methods were too slow, too ineffective. Bold action, the policy of 1869-70 would arouse the government out of its lethargy. Riel therefore decided to follow the same formula which had been successful on the previous occasion. He would form a Provisional Government, put his supporters under arms, and compel the federal authorities to negotiate a revision of the terms which had brought the North-West into Confederation. It was the scheme of a mad man. The methods which had succeeded, in part at least, in Manitoba could never succeed again. There was now a military force in the country to support the government where formerly there had been none in 1869 to assist the Hudson's Bay Company; there was now a railway to bring men and arms from Eastern Canada. Riel ignored the changed conditions and embarked upon the desperate gamble which was to take him to the scaffold.

97

From Agitation to Rebellion, March 1885

The decisive day was March 19th, the feast of St. Joseph, the patron saint of the métis, and it was to be celebrated by the baptism of Henry Jackson. Métis from nearby settlements flocked into Batoche, carrying their rifles with them. The moment was opportune and Riel took advantage of it. With all the fire and spirit which he could command in his speech, he told the assembled gathering that the Mounted Police were preparing to attack them and suppress their movement. Alarm spread like panic and preparations were made for defence. A Provisional Government was immediately proclaimed, Riel nominating the members and the métis signifying their approval. Pierre Parenteau was elected president; but the real leaders were Gabriel Dumont, who was appointed "adjutant-general", and Louis Riel himself. With a group of excited followers Riel rushed towards the church, thrust aside the protesting priest and took possession of the building as his headquarters. "Rome has fallen" cried Riel. The rebellion had begun.

Riel was in no way disturbed by the alienation of the clergy — he had, after all, his own ideas of a religious organization for the métis — but he was disturbed by his failure to retain the support of the English half-breeds. The whites may have been willing to use him for their own purposes, and the English half-breeds to support him in a constitutional agitation, but they would not follow him as far as taking up arms or forming a Provisional Government. Several times he appealed to their old loyalties. "Gentlemen, please do not remain neutral. For the love of God help us to save the Saskatchewan," he wrote. "A strong union between the French and English half-breeds is the only guarantee that there will be no bloodshed." His appeals met with no response. Riel would have to go on alone — except perhaps for the Indians.

The Indians had found themselves in an even more desperate condition than the métis as a result of the white immigration, and many of them were in an ugly mood owing to the indifference displayed by the government towards their appeals for help. The summer of 1884 had almost seen an Indian outbreak, and during the autumn of that year a number of Indians turned to Louis Riel for advice and leadership. At first he restrained them but as his temper changed so too did theirs. From them at least he might hope for support in arms.

The Military Events, March-June 1885

The fighting began on March 26th at Duck Lake. Here Gabriel Dumont and the métis ambushed a force of Mounted Police, compelling them to abandon Fort Carlton and to retire to the principal settlement of Prince Albert. Further west Cree Indians from the Poundmaker and Little Pine Reserves broke into and pillaged the Hudson's Bay Company store and other buildings in the town of Battleford. They do not appear to have had in mind an attack upon the town, probably nothing more than a demonstration in force to obtain concessions and supplies; but the Stonies from the Eagle Hills, who joined them, murdered their Farm Instructor and a white settler and set up a "soldiers' lodge". Even the Stonies, however, did not propose to attack a fortified position and the Indians contented themselves, during the next few weeks, with prowling around the neighbourhood while the police and settlers watched with anxious eyes from the barricaded Mounted Police barracks. Further up the Saskatchewan the Crees of Big Bear murdered several men at Frog Lake, including the Indian agent and two missionaries, then descending the Saskatchewan river they terrified the inhabitants of Fort Pitt into surrender.

Thus the situation stood at the end of April. Everywhere the métis and Indians had met with surprising success. They had defeated the white men in pitched battle. Fort Carlton and Fort Pitt had fallen without even a fight. The white men had been driven into the narrow confines of Prince Albert and Battleford. These successes had not been the result of any concerted plan; they were entirely spontaneous and fortuitous. The métis were in no position to carry on a long war. They lacked numbers, supplies and wholehearted support. The Indians, held together by no strong principle of cooperation and with no central authority to combine their strength, were likewise incapable of sustained effort. Moreover, by far the greater number of Indian nations were prepared to wait and watch, while accepting and enjoying the gifts so freely handed out by the Indian Department to ensure their neutrality.

Meanwhile the Canadian government had taken prompt action. A military force numbering nearly 8000 men was mobilized and despatched to the North-West under the command of General Frederick Middleton. Three columns of troops were sent against the three principal centres of disaffection. The first, under the command of Middleton himself, was directed against Riel's capital at Batoche. It fought an indecisive action with the métis at Fish Creek on April 24th and was held up there for two weeks. The second, under the impetuous Colonel Otter, speedily relieved Battleford. The third, under Major-General Strange, moved against Big Bear marching from Calgary by way of Edmonton and the North Saskatchewan river. In none of these operations did the commanding officers distinguish themselves. Middleton's movements in particular were slow and his dispositions questionable. Little use was made of cavalry in a country made to order for mounted warfare. Much of the responsibility for the ponderous conduct of the campaign must rest upon the shoulders of an uninspired commander-in-chief; but part, too, must be attributed to the lack of training on the part of the troops and their inexperience in warfare.

In the face of these developments Riel made desperate efforts to concentrate all his forces. He had been disappointed that the Indians of Alberta, in particular the associated Blackfoot tribes, had yielded to the persuasions of Father Lacombe, and sought anxiously to persuade Big Bear and Poundmaker to join the métis at Batoche without delay. But the Indians could not arrive at a rapid decision, and before any concentration was achieved both Poundmaker and Big Bear were attacked separately by Otter and by Strange. Marching at night from Battleford Otter almost caught the Indians unawares. As the troops rushed to seize the high ground known as Cut Knife Hill the Indians spread out through the coulées surrounding it, taking full advantage of the only cover available. All day militia and Indians fought at full rifle range, until Otter, realizing that his unprotected situation would be particularly precarious when night should fall, cleared his line of retreat with a charge and made his way back to Battleford. His retirement might have become a rout had not Poundmaker held back his warriors and prevented them from cutting the retreating column to pieces.

Meanwhile, on May 7th, Middleton began to move from Fish Creek towards Riel's capital. He had with him about 850 men; his opponents could probably muster at the most about 350. On May 9th the attack began. An attempt to use the steamer *Northcote* as an armed vessel to attack simultaneously with the land troops proved to be a fiasco, and the

99

land attack was halted by the métis riflemen in trenches which Dumont had constructed in the reverse slope leading down to Batoche. Middleton himself declared, on inspecting the field after the action was over, "I was astonished at the strength of the position and at the ingenuity and care displayed in the construction of the rifle pits". These pits or trenches were Dumont's work; for Riel was no military leader. He had not been present at Fish Creek, and at Duck Lake he had watched the fighting armed only with a crucifix.

For three days the fighting at Batoche continued. By May 12 the métis' supplies of ammunition were almost exhausted; so too was the patience of Middleton's troops who, exasperated at the general's cautious tactics, took matters into their own hands and charged the enemy. With gathering momentum the Canadian militia dashed through the métis lines and down the hill towards Batoche. The métis fled to the woods. On May 15th Riel gave himself up. Dumont and several others fled on horseback towards the United States.

There still remained the Indians. Poundmaker surrendered to Middleton on May 23rd, after learning of Riel's defeat; but Big Bear was at large up the North Saskatchewan with his mixed force of Plains and Wood Crees. His band was split on the issue of continued resistance, and it was while the chiefs were endeavouring to heal the rupture that they were attacked by General Strange at Frenchman's Butte, on May 28th. After offering stout opposition the Indians finally fled from the field, just as Strange called off the attack. The heavy guns had taken the edge off their fighting enthusiasm. With their prisoners and their loot they began a disorderly retirement northwards through the woods.

Strange made no real effort to follow his retreating foe. He had no intention, as he often said, of "committing Custer", and it was not until the arrival of Middleton that the troops were once more sent into action. Steele's mounted scouts had proved their worth in keeping in touch with the Indians, but Middleton continued to rely upon his infantry. He ignored offers of assistance from the Mounted Police and set out with his wagons and his soldiers through a country which even light-burdened Indians found difficult to traverse. On June 9th the commander abandoned the pursuit. The Indians, however, did not continue together as a fighting force. They released their prisoners and broke up into small bands. On July 2nd Big Bear himself surrendered to a surprised police sergeant at Fort Carlton. The rebellion was at an end.

The sequel was a bitter one. The métis were not only defeated, as a politically cohesive group they were practically destroyed. Their homes were burned and their property looted or destroyed. Those who had taken part in the Provisional Government were sentenced to terms of imprisonment. A number of métis were compelled to seek entrance to the Indian treaties by virtue of their Indian blood; others moved westwards, towards Northern Alberta, to escape the merciless pressure of civilization. Those who did not join the rebellion received the scrip and patents which Louis Riel had demanded — tacit admission of the justice of the métis grievances. But just as the Manitoba half-breeds had done so too the Saskatchewan métis disposed of their scrip to eager and unscrupulous buyers. They lived only for the present and forgot about the future. What did it hold for them? Destitute and disillusioned, unable to compete with the white men either as traders or farmers, they gradually sank further and further in the social scale, their life, society and spirit crushed and destroyed.

The Indians suffered less from the rebellion than did the métis. Of the leaders some went to the gallows, others, including Big Bear and Poundmaker, went to prison. The rebels were deprived of their annuities until the destruction wrought by the rising had been made good and their horses and rifles were taken from them. However, in 1886 a general amnesty was declared for all who were not actually under sentence, and in the following year Big Bear and Poundmaker were released from prison. Several years later negotiations were undertaken with the United States for the return to Canada of those Indians who had sought refuge in Montana after the collapse of the rebellion.

101

The Trial and Execution of Louis Riel

On July 6th, 1885, a formal charge of treason was laid against Louis Riel, then in gaol at Regina. This was the beginning of that trial which was to have such drastic consequences, not only for Riel himself, but for the whole of Canada. The jury was entirely Anglo-Saxon and Protestant, the defendant French and, by training at least, Catholic. Here were the old familiar elements of discord. And into the little courtroom stalked the ghost of Tom Scott, whose memory his Orange brethren had never permitted to rest. As the howl for vengeance grew louder in Orange Ontario so too did the cry for clemency in Catholic Quebec. A madman, a heretic, a métis he might be, to the people of Quebec Louis Riel was nevertheless a French Canadian, a victim of Anglo-Saxon persecution. Even while shots were still being fired at Canadian soldiers on the plains, Quebeckers had expressed admiration for Riel's heroic battle for the rights of his people, and when he surrendered they sprang to his defence and provided him with eminent counsel.

The argument adopted by the defence lawyers was that Riel was insane. It was pointed out that he had twice been in asylums, that he had committed the folly of attacking the church, that he had planned the establishment of a Canadian Pope and spent valuable time during the actual rising changing the names of the days of the week. But Riel would not accept this defence. He repudiated the plea of insanity. "I cannot abandon my dignity!" he cried. "Here I have to defend myself against the accusation of high treason, or I have to consent to the animal life of an asylum. I don't care much about animal life if I am not allowed to carry with it the moral existence of an intellectual being . . . " Twice he addressed the court in long rambling speeches; but the jury was only bored, and after one hour and twenty minutes deliberation they declared him guilty. Henry Jackson, despite similar denials of insanity and an expressed desire to share the fate of his leader, was acquitted within a few minutes. To an English-speaking jury the English-speaking Jackson must obviously have been insane to have taken part in the rebellion. There was much truth in the statement made by one of the jurors fifty years later: "We tried Riel for treason, and he was hanged for the murder of Scott."

As the date set for Riel's execution approached feelings throughout Canada became more and more intense. Efforts to save the métis leader were redoubled in Quebec; efforts to ensure his death never slackened in Ontario. The Prime Minister temporized. He was uncertain what course to follow. The execution was postponed, and then put off again while a medical commission examined the question of Riel's sanity. But the terms of reference of the commission limited it to a determination of Riel's capacity to distinguish right from wrong and did not allow an investigation of his delusions; and when the report of the commission was published it was published in a truncated form. Throughout the autumn months petitions and letters from all parts of the world poured into Ottawa. Sir John had not a jot of sympathy for Riel, but he had to balance the political consequences of death or reprieve. There was danger of political disaster if Riel were hanged, but perhaps Sir John could trust to the loyalty of his French Canadian colleagues, Hector Langevin, Adolphe Caron and Adolphe Chapleau, and to the support of a Catholic hierarchy offended at Riel's apostasy. There might be still greater danger of political disaster if Riel were not hanged with every Orangeman in Ontario baying for his death. So Riel was hanged. On November 16th, once more a son of the church, the métis, Louis Riel, mounted the gibbet of Regina. The madman became a martyr.

The Political Consequences of Riel's Death

It is hard to escape the conclusion that Riel's execution, to some extent at least, was determined by political expediency, that, in the final analysis, it represented the careful assessment by the Canadian government of the relative voting strengths and political loyalties of the two racial groups in Canada. If this were so then, for the moment, Macdonald's choice was not unsound. Admittedly the "nationalists" in Quebec, led by Honoré Mercier, succeeded in 1886 in overthrowing the provincial Conservative government in an election fought largely on the Riel issue; but in the federal election of 1887 Macdonald, with the support of his French Canadian ministers, still retained a sufficient number of Quebec seats to keep in power.

Yet he had lost ground. And even if he did not recognize it, the election results were an ominous warning of the fate which awaited the Conservative party in Quebec. In the long run the trial and execution of Louis Riel and the racial bitterness which it engendered led to a profound revolution in Canadian politics. As a result of the crisis of 1885 the most conservative province in Canada swung over to the Liberal party, a change in political allegiance which was cemented by the selection of a French Canadian, Wilfrid Laurier, as leader of that party. This shift in the political weight in Quebec, not as the result of any fundamental change in political outlook, but under the stress of a racial emotion, brought about a new orientation in Liberal policy. The old radical tradition of Clear Grittism and Rougeism was swamped by a basic rural conservatism; and for over seventy years the paradox endured of the backbone of the Liberal party being provided by rural Quebec.

Conclusion

Louis Riel was not a great man; he was not even what Carlyle would call a near great. Nevertheless he became, in death, one of the decisive figures of our history. By historical accident rather than by design he became the symbol of divisions as old as the Franco-British struggle for the control of northern North America. It is this historical accident which has obscured the fundamental character of the two risings which bear Riel's name; for the Riel "rebellions" were not what the politicians argued and what the people believed, a continuation on the banks of the Red and the Saskatchewan of the traditional hostilities of old Canada. They were, instead, the typical, even inevitable results of the advance of the frontier, the last organized attempts on the part of Canada's primitive peoples to withstand what, for want of a better word, may be termed progress, and to preserve their culture and their identity against the encroachments of civilization. To present-day Canadians Riel appears, no longer as the wilful "rebel" or "murderer" of Thomas Scott, but as a sad, pathetic, unstable man, who led his followers in a suicidal crusade and whose brief glory rests upon a distortion of history. To the métis, the people whom he loved, he will always be, mad or sane, the voice of an inarticulate race and the prophet of a doomed cause.

103

Canada's Subjugation of the Plains Cree, 1879–1885 *

JOHN L. TOBIAS

One of the most persistent myths that Canadian historians perpetuate is that of the honourable and just policy Canada followed in dealing with the Plains Indians. First enunciated in the Canadian expansionist literature of the 1870s as a means to emphasize the distinctive Canadian approach to and

*From *Canadian Historical Review*, LXIV (December 1983): 519-548. Reprinted by permission of the author and the University of Toronto Press.

the unique character of the Canadian west,[1] it has been given credence by G.F.G. Stanley in his classic *The Birth of Western Canada*,[2] and by all those who use Stanley's work as the standard interpretation of Canada's relationship with the Plains Indians in the period 1870-85. Thus students are taught that the Canadian government was paternalistic and far-sighted in offering the Indians a means to become civilized and assimilated into white society by the reserve system, and honest and fair-minded in honouring legal commitments made in the treaties.[3] The Plains Indians, and particularly the Plains Cree, are said to be a primitive people adhering to an inflexible system of tradition and custom, seeking to protect themselves against the advance of civilization, and taking up arms in rejection of the reserve system and an agricultural way of life.[4] This traditional interpretation distorts the roles of both the Cree and the Canadian government, for the Cree were both flexible and active in promoting their own interests, and willing to accommodate themselves to a new way of life, while the Canadian government was neither as far-sighted nor as just as tradition maintains. Canada's principal concern in its relationship with the Plains Cree was to establish control over them, and Canadian authorities were willing to and did wage war upon the Cree in order to achieve this control.

104

Those who propagate the myth would have us believe that Canada began to negotiate treaties with the Indians of the West in 1871 as part of an overall plan to develop the agricultural potential of the West, open the land for railway construction, and bind the prairies to Canada in a network of commercial and economic ties. Although there is an element of truth to these statements, the fact remains that in 1871 Canada had no plan on how to deal with the Indians and the negotiation of treaties was not at the initiative of the Canadian government, but at the insistence of the Ojibwa Indians of the North-West Angle and the Saulteaux of the tiny province of Manitoba. What is ignored by the traditional interpretation is that the treaty process only started after Yellow Quill's band of Saulteaux turned back settlers who tried to go west of Portage la Prairie, and after other Saulteaux leaders insisted upon enforcement of the Selkirk Treaty or, more often, insisted upon making a new treaty. Also ignored is the fact that the Ojibwa of the North-West Angle demanded rents, and created the fear of violence against prospective settlers who crossed their land or made use of their territory, if Ojibwa rights to their lands were not recognized. This pressure and fear of resulting violence is what motivated the government to begin the treaty-making process.[5]

Canada's initial offer to the Saulteaux and Ojibwa Indians consisted only of reserves and a small cash annuity. This proposal was rejected by the Ojibwa in 1871 and again in 1872, while the Saulteaux demanded, much to Treaty Commissioner Wemyss Simpson's chagrin, farm animals, horses, wagons, and farm tools and equipment. Simpson did not include these demands in the written treaty, for he had no authority to do so, but he wrote them down in the form of a memorandum that he entitled 'outside promises' and which he failed to send to Ottawa. Thus, the original Treaties 1 and 2 did not include those items the Saulteaux said had to be part of a treaty before they would agree to surrender their lands. Only in 1874, after the Indian leaders of Manitoba became irate over non-receipt of the goods that Simpson had promised them, was an inquiry launched, and Simpson's list of 'outside promises' discovered and incorporated in renegotiated treaties in 1875.[6] It was only in 1873, after the Ojibwa of the North-West Angle had twice refused treaties that only included reserves and annuities, that the government agreed to include the domestic animals, farm tools, and equipment that the Ojibwa demanded. After this experience Canada made such goods a standard part of late treaties.[7]

Just as it was pressure from the Indians of Manitoba that forced the government of Canada to initiate the treaty process, it was pressure from the Plains Cree in the period 1872-5 that compelled the government of Canada to continue the process with the Indians of the Qu'Appelle and Saskatchewan districts. The Plains Cree had interfered with the geological survey and prevented the construction of telegraph lines through their territory to emphasize that Canada had to deal with the Cree for Cree lands.[8] The Cree had learned in 1870 about Canada's claim to their lands, and not wanting to experience what had happened to the Indians in the United States when those people were faced with an expansionist government, the Cree made clear that they would not allow settlement or use of their lands until Cree rights had been clearly recognized. They also made clear that part of any arrangement for Cree lands had to involve assistance to the Cree in developing a new agricultural way of life.[9]

In adopting this position, the Cree were simply demonstrating a skill that they had shown since their initial contact with Europeans in 1670. On numerous occasions during the fur trade era, they had adapted to changed environmental and economic circumstances, beginning first as hunters, then as provisioners and middlemen in the Hudson's Bay Company trading system, and finally adapting from a woodland to parkland-prairie buffalo hunting culture to retain their independence and their desired ties with the fur trade.[10] Having accommodated themselves to the Plains Indian culture after 1800, they expanded into territory formerly controlled by the Atsina, and as the buffalo herds began to decline after 1850, the Cree expanded into Blackfoot territory.[11] Expansion was one response to the threat posed by declining buffalo herds; another was that some Plains Cree bands began to turn to agriculture.[12] Thus, when the Cree learned that Canada claimed their lands, part of the arrangement they were determined to make and succeeded in making was to receive assistance in adapting to an agricultural way of life. So successful were they in negotiating such assistance that when the Mackenzie government received a copy of Treaty 6 in 1876 it accepted the treaty only after expressing a protest concerning the too-generous terms granted to the Cree.[13]

While willing to explore the alternative of agriculture, three Cree leaders in the 1870s sought means to guarantee preservation of the buffalo-hunting culture as long as possible. Piapot (leader of the Cree-Assiniboine of the region south of Qu'Appelle River), and Big Bear and Little Pine (leaders of

105

two of the largest Cree bands from the Saskatchewan River district) led what has been called an armed migration of the Cree into the Cypress Hills in the latter 1860s. All three men were noted warriors, and Big Bear and Piapot were noted religious leaders, but their prowess was not enough to prevent a Cree defeat at the Battle of the Belly River in 1870,[14] and as a result they explored the alternative of dealing with the government of Canada, but in a manner to extract guarantees for the preservation of Cree autonomy. They were determined to get the government to promise to limit the buffalo hunt to the Indians — a goal that Cree leaders had been advocating since the 1850s.[15] When Big Bear met with Treaty Commissioner Alexander Morris at Fort Pitt in September 1876, he extracted a promise from Morris that non-Indian hunting of the buffalo would be regulated.[16]

Big Bear refused to take treaty in 1876, despite receiving Morris's assurances about the regulation of the hunt. Little Pine and Piapot also did not take treaty when the treaty commissions first came to deal with the Cree.

106

Oral tradition among the Cree maintains that all three leaders wished to see how faithful the government would be in honouring treaties,[17] but equally important for all three leaders was their belief that the treaties were inadequate and that revisions were necessary. Piapot thought Treaty 4 (the Qu'Appelle Treaty) needed to be expanded to include increased farm equipment and tools, and to stipulate that the government had to provide mills, blacksmith and carpentry shops and tools, and instructors in farming and the trades. Only after receiving assurances that Ottawa would consider these requests did Piapot take treaty in 1875.[18] Big Bear and Little Pine objected to Treaty 6 (Fort Pitt and Carlton) because Commissioner Morris had made clear that in taking treaty the Cree would be bound to Canadian law. To accept the treaties would mean being subject to an external authority of which the Crees had little knowledge and upon which they had little influence. Neither Big Bear nor Little Pine would countenance such a loss of autonomy.

Big Bear had raised the matter of Cree autonomy at Fort Pitt in 1876 when he met Commissioner Morris. At that time Big Bear said: 'I will make a request that he [Morris] save me from what I most dread, that is the rope about my neck . . . It was not given to us to have the rope about our neck.'[19] Morris and most subsequent historians have interpreted Big Bear's statements to be a specific reference to hanging, but such an interpretation ignores the fact that Big Bear, like most Indian leaders, often used a metaphor to emphasize a point. In 1875, he had made the same point by using a different metaphor when he spoke to messengers informing him that a treaty commission was to meet with the Cree in 1876. At that time Big Bear said: 'We want none of the Queen's presents: when we set a foxtrap we scatter pieces of meat all around, but when the fox gets into the trap we knock him on the head; we want no bait . . .'[20] A more accurate interpretation of Big Bear's words to Morris in 1876 is that he feared being controlled or 'enslaved,' just as an animal is controlled when it has a rope around its neck.[21] In 1877, when meeting with Lieutenant-Governor David Laird, Little Pine also stated that he would not take treaty because he saw the treaties as a means by which the government could 'enslave' his people.[22]

The importance of these three leaders cannot be underestimated, for they had with them in the Cypress Hills more than fifty per cent of the total Indian population of the Treaty 4 and 6 areas. By concentrating in such numbers in the last buffalo ranges in Canadian territory, the Cree were free from all external interference, whether by other Indian nations or by the agents of the Canadian government — the North-West Mounted Police.[23] Recognizing that these men were bargaining from a position of strength, Laird recommended in 1878 that the government act quickly to establish reserves and honour the treaties. He was aware that the Cypress Hills leaders had the support of many of the Cree in treaty, and that many of the Cree leaders were complaining that the government was not providing the farming assistance promised. As the number of these complaints increased, so did Cree support for Big Bear and Little Pine.[24]

The Cree were concerned not only about the lack of assistance to farm, but when Canadian officials were slow to take action to regulate the buffalo hunt, Big Bear, Piapot, and Little Pine met with Blackfoot leaders and with Sitting Bull of the Teton Sioux in an attempt to reach agreement among the Indian nations on the need to regulate buffalo hunting.[25] These councils were also the forum where Indian leaders discussed the need to revise the treaties. On learning about the Indian council, the non-Indian populace of the West grew anxious, fearing establishment of an Indian confederacy which would wage war if Indian demands were rejected.[26] However, an Indian confederacy did not result from these meetings, nor was agreement reached on how the buffalo were to be preserved, because the Cree, Sioux, and Blackfoot could not overcome their old animosities towards one another.[27]

When in 1879 the buffalo disappeared from the Canadian prairies and Big Bear and Little Pine took their bands south to the buffalo ranges on the Milk and Missouri rivers, most of the other Cree and Assiniboine bands also went with them. The Cree who remained in Canada faced starvation while awaiting the survey of their reserves and the farming equipment that had been promised. Realizing that many of the Cree were dying, the government decided that those who had taken treaty should be given rations. As well, the government appointed Edgar Dewdney to the newly-created position of Commissioner of Indian Affairs for the North-West Territory; a farming policy for the western reserves was introduced; a survey of Cree reserves was begun; and twelve farming instructors were appointed to teach the Indians of the North-West.[28]

The new Indian Commissioner quickly sought to use rations as a means of getting control over the Cree. In the fall of 1879 he announced that rations were to be provided only to Indians who had taken treaty. To get the Cree into treaty more easily and to reduce the influence of recalcitrant leaders, Dewdney announced that he would adopt an old Hudson's Bay Company practice of recognizing any adult male Cree as chief of a new band if he could induce 100 or more persons to recognize him as leader. He expected

107

that the starving Cypress Hills Cree would desert their old leaders to get rations. As a means of demonstrating Canada's control over the Cree, Dewdney ordered that only the sick, aged, and orphans should receive rations without providing some service to one of the government agencies in the West.[29]

Dewdney's policies seemed to work, for when the Cree and Assiniboine who had gone to hunt in Montana returned starving, their resolve weakened. Little Pine's people convinced their chief to take treaty in 1879, but when Big Bear refused to do the same, almost half of his following joined Lucky Man or Thunderchild to form new bands in order to receive rations.[30]

Taking treaty to avoid starvation did not mean that the Cree had come to accept the treaties as written; rather they altered their tactics in seeking revisions. Believing that small reserves were more susceptible to the control of the Canadian government and its officials, Big Bear, Piapot, and Little Pine sought to effect a concentration of the Cree people in an Indian territory similar to the reservation system in the United States. In such a territory the Cree would be able to preserve their autonomy, or at least limit the ability of others to control them; they would be better able to take concerted action on matters of importance to them.[31]

Soon after taking treaty Little Pine applied for a reserve in the Cypress Hills, twenty-seven miles north-east of the North-West Mounted Police post of Fort Walsh. Piapot requested a reserve next to Little Pine's, while ten other bands, including most of the Assiniboine nation, selected reserve sites contiguous to either Little Pine's or Piapot's and to one another.[32] If all these reserve sites were granted, and if Big Bear were to take treaty and settle in the Cypress Hills, the result would be concentration of much of the Cree nation and the creation of an Indian territory that would comprise most of what is now south-western Saskatchewan.

Unaware of the intention of the Cree and Assiniboine leaders, Canadian officials in the spring of 1880 agreed to the establishment of a reserve for all the Canadian Assiniboine and reserves in the Cypress Hills for each of the Cree bands that wished them. In 1880, the Assiniboine reserve was surveyed, but the other Indian leaders were told that their reserves would not be surveyed until the following year.[33] In the interim, most of the Cree went to the buffalo ranges in Montana.

The Cree effort to exploit the remaining American buffalo ranges caused them much trouble. The Crow, the Peigan, and other Indian nations with reservations in Montana were upset by competition for the scarce food resource, and these people threatened to wage war on the Cree if the American authorities did not protect the Indian hunting ranges. These threats were renewed when the Cree began to steal horses from the Crow and Peigan. To add to their difficulties, American ranchers accused the Cree of killing range cattle. American officials, not wishing trouble with their Indians and wishing to placate the ranchers, informed the Cree that they would have to return to Canada. Most Cree bands, aware that if they did not leave voluntarily the American government would use troops to force them to move north, returned to the Cypress Hills.[34]

They returned to find that Canadian officials were now aware of the dangers to their authority posed by a concentration of the Cree. A riot at Fort Walsh in 1880, which the police were powerless to prevent or control, assaults on farming instructors who refused to provide rations to starving Indians, and rumours that the Cree were planning a grand Indian council to discuss treaty revisions in 1881 all caused the Indian Commissioner much concern.[35] To avoid further difficulties over rations, in late 1880 Dewdney ordered that all Indians requesting rations be given them, regardless of whether the supplicant was in treaty.[36] There was little that the government could do at this time about the proposed Indian council or the concentration of Cree in the Cypress Hills.

In the spring of 1881, Cree bands from all regions of the Canadian prairies left their reserves to go south to meet with Little Pine and Big Bear. Even the new bands Dewdney had created were going to the council in American territory. What was also disconcerting to Canadian officials were the reports that Big Bear and Little Pine, who had gone to Montana to prepare for the council, had reached an accommodation with the Blackfoot and had participated in a joint raid on the Crow. To all appearances the Blackfoot, the Indian confederacy the Canadian government most feared, would be part of the Indian council.[37]

The Indian council was not held because the raid on the Crow led American officials to intervene militarily to force the Cree to return to Canada. With Montana stockmen acting as militia units, the American army prevented most Cree and Assiniboine bands from entering the United States. As well, the American forces seized horses, guns, and carts, and escorted the Cree to Canada.[38] The Cree-Blackfoot alliance did not materialize, for soon after the raid on the Crow, young Cree warriors stole horses from the Blackfoot and thereby destroyed the accord that Little Pine and Big Bear were attempting to create.[39]

The actions of the American military in 1881 were extremely beneficial to Canada. Not only did the Americans prevent the holding of the Indian council, but by confiscating the guns and horses of the Cree, the Americans had dispossessed the Cree of the ability to resist whatever measures the Canadian authorities wished to take against them. The Canadian authorities also benefited from Governor-General Lorne's tour of the West in 1881, for many of the Cree bands that had gone to the Cypress Hills in the spring went north in late summer to meet Lorne to impress upon him the inadequacy of the treaties and the need to revise them.[40] Thus, Lorne's tour prevented the concentration of most of the Cree nation in the Cypress Hills.

The threat posed to Canadian authority in the North-West by concentration of the Cree was clearly recognized by Dewdney and other Canadian officials in late 1881. They saw how the Cree had forced officials to placate them and to ignore their orders in 1880 and 1881. This convinced both Dewdney and Ottawa that the Cree request for contiguous reserves in the Cypress Hills could not be granted. Dewdney recognized that to grant the Cree requests would be to create an Indian territory, for most of the Cree who had reserves further north would come to the Cypress Hills and request reserves contiguous to those of the Cypress Hills Cree. This would result in so large a concentration of Cree that the only way Canada could enforce its laws on them would be via a military campaign. To prevent this, Dewdney recommended a sizeable expansion of the Mounted Police force and the closure of Fort Walsh and all government facilities in the Cypress Hills. This action would remove all sources of sustenance from the Cree in the Cypress Hills. Dewdney hoped that starvation would drive them from the Fort Walsh area and thus end the concentration of their force.[41]

Dewdney decided to take these steps fully aware that what he was doing was a violation not only of the promises made to the Cypress Hills Indians in 1880 and 1881, but also that by refusing to grant reserves on the sites the Indians had selected, he was violating the promises made to the Cree by the Treaty Commissions in 1874 and 1876, and in the written treaties. Nevertheless, Dewdney believed that to accede to the Cree requests would be to grant the Cree de facto autonomy from Canadian control, which would result in the perpetuation and heightening of the 1880-1 crisis. Rather than see that situation continue, Dewdney wanted to exploit the opportunity presented to him by the hunger crisis and disarmament of the Cree to bring them under the government's control, even if it meant violating the treaties.[42]

In the spring of 1882 the Cree and Assiniboine were told that no further rations would be issued to them while they remained in the Cypress Hills. Only if the Indians moved north to Qu'Appelle, Battleford, and Fort Pitt were they to be given assistance, and at those locations only treaty Indians were to be aided. The Mounted Police were ordered to stop issuing rations at Fort Walsh and the Indian Department farm that had been located near Fort Walsh was closed. Faced with the prospect of starvation, without weapons or transport to get to the Montana buffalo ranges, and knowing that if they were to try to go south the Mounted Police would inform the American military authorities, many Cree and all the Assiniboine decided to go north.[43] Even Big Bear discovered that his people wanted him to take treaty and move north. In 1882, after taking treaty, he, along with Piapot and Little Pine, promised to leave the Cypress Hills.[44]

Only Piapot kept his promise and even he did not remain long at Fort Qu'Appelle. By late summer of 1882, Piapot was back in the Cypress Hills complaining about how he had been mistreated at Qu'Appelle, and making the Cree aware of how they could lose their autonomy if the government could deal with them as individual bands.[45] On hearing this report, the other Cree leaders refused to leave the Fort Walsh region and insisted upon receiving the reserves promised them in 1880 and 1881. North-West Mounted Police Commissioner Irvine feared a repetition of the incidents of 1880 if he refused to feed the Cree and believed that the hungry Cree would harass the construction crews of the Canadian Pacific Railway for food, which would lead to a confrontation between whites and Indians which the police would be unable to handle and which in turn might lead to an Indian war. Therefore Irvine decided to feed the Cree.[46]

Dewdney and Ottawa were upset by Irvine's actions. Ottawa gave specific instructions to close Fort Walsh in the spring of 1883. When Irvine closed the fort, the Cree faced starvation. As it was quite evident that they could not go to the United States, and as they would not receive reserves in the Cypress Hills, the Cree moved north. Piapot moved to Indian Head and selected a reserve site next to the huge reserve set aside for the Assiniboine. Little Pine and Lucky Man moved to Battleford and selected reserve sites next to Poundmaker's reserve. Big Bear went to Fort Pitt.

The move to the north was not a sign of the Cree acceptance of the treaties as written, nor of their acceptance of the authority of the Canadian government. Big Bear, Little Pine, and Piapot were aware that the other Cree chiefs were dissatisfied with the treaties, and were also aware that if they could effect concentration of the Cree in the north they would be able to preserve their autonomy, just as they had done in the Cypress Hills in the 1879-81 period. Therefore, the move to the north was simply a tactical move, for no sooner were these chiefs in the north than they once again sought to effect a concentration of their people.

111

By moving to Indian Head, Piapot had effected a concentration of more than 2,000 Indians. This number threatened to grow larger if the council he planned to hold with all the Treaty 4 bands to discuss treaty revisions were successful. Commissioner Dewdney, fearing the results of such a meeting in 1883, was able to thwart Piapot by threatening to cut off rations to any Indians attending Piapot's council and by threatening to arrest Piapot and depose any chiefs who did meet with him. Although Dewdney, in 1883, prevented Piapot holding a large council by such actions, Piapot was able to get the Treaty 4 chiefs to agree to meet in the late spring of 1884 for a thirst dance and council on Pasquah's Reserve, near Fort Qu'Appelle.

While Piapot was organizing an Indian council in the Treaty 4 area, Big Bear and Little Pine were doing the same for the Treaty 6 region. Little Pine and Lucky Man attempted to effect a concentration of more than 2,000 Cree on contiguous reserves in the Battleford district, by requesting reserves next to Poundmaker, whose reserve was next to three other Cree reserves, which in turn were only a short distance from three Assiniboine reserves. Another 500 Cree would have been located in the Battleford area if Big Bear's request for a reserve next to Little Pine's site had been granted. Only with difficulty was Dewdney able to get Big Bear to move to Fort Pitt.[48] However, he was unable to prevent Big Bear and Little Pine from sending messengers to the Cree leaders of the Edmonton, Carlton, and Duck Lake districts to enlist their support for the movement to concentrate the Cree.[49]

Dewdney was convinced that the activities of Big Bear, Piapot, and Little Pine were a prelude to a major project the Cree planned for the following year, 1884. He was also aware that his ability to deal with the impending problem was severely limited by decisions taken in Ottawa. The Deputy Superintendent-General of Indian Affairs, Lawrence Vankoughnet, was concerned about the cost of administering Dewdney's policies, and he ordered reductions in the level of assistance provided to the Cree and in the number of employees working with the Cree.[50] In making these decisions, Ottawa effectively deprived Dewdney of his major sources of intelligence about the Cree and their plans. It also deprived Dewdney of a major instrument in placating the Cree — the distribution of rations to those bands which co-operated.

Vankoughnet's economy measures led to further alienation of the Cree. In some areas, notably in the Fort Pitt, Edmonton, and Crooked Lakes regions, farming instructors were assaulted and government storehouses broken into when Indians were denied rations. The incident on the Sakemay Reserve in the Crooked Lakes area was quite serious, for when the police were called upon to arrest those guilty of the assault, they were surrounded and threatened with death if they carried out their orders. Only after Assistant Indian Commissioner Hayter Reed had agreed to restore assistance to the Sakemay band to the 1883 level and had promised not to imprison the accused were the police allowed to leave with their prisoners.[51]

112   The violence that followed the reductions in rations convinced Dewdney that starving the Cree into submission was not the means to control them. He wanted to use coercion, but this required an expansion of the number of police in the West. Therefore, he recommended that more men be recruited for the Mounted Police. In addition, Dewdney wanted to ensure that jail sentences were given to arrested Indians so that they would cause no further problems. Having seen the effects of incarceration on Indians, Dewdney was convinced that this was the means to bring the Cree leaders under control. However, what was needed in his opinion were trial judges who 'understood' Indian nature at first hand and who would take effective action to keep the Indians under control. Therefore, Dewdney wanted all Indian Department officials in the West to be appointed stipendiary magistrates in order that all Indian troublemakers could be brought to 'justice' quickly. As Dewdney stated in his letter to Prime Minister John A. Macdonald: 'The only effective course with the great proportion [of Indian bands] to adopt is one of sheer compulsion . . .'[52]

Dewdney used the policy of 'sheer compulsion' for only a few months in 1884. He found that his efforts to use the Mounted Police to break up the Indian councils and to arrest Indian leaders only led to confrontations between the Cree and the police. In these confrontations the police were shown to be ineffectual because they were placed in situations in which, if the Cree had been desirous of initiating hostilities, large numbers of Mounted Police would have been massacred.

The first incident which called the policy of compulsion into question was the attempt to prevent Piapot from holding his thirst dance and council in May 1884. Assistant Commissioner Hayter Reed, fearing that the council would result in a concentration of all the Treaty 4 bands, ordered Police Commissioner Irvine to prevent Piapot from attending the council. Irvine was to arrest the chief at the first sign of any violation of even the most minor law. To be certain that Piapot broke a law, Reed promised to have an individual from Pasquah's reserve object to the council being held on that reserve in order that the accusation of trespass could be used to break up the meeting, which all the bands from Treaty 4 were attending.[53]

With a force of fifty-six men and a seven-pounder gun, Irvine caught up with Piapot shortly before the chief reached Pasquah's reserve. Irvine and the police entered the Indian camp at 2 A.M., hoping to arrest Piapot and remove him from the camp before his band was aware of what happened. However, when they entered the camp, the police found themselves surrounded by armed warriors. Realizing that any attempt to arrest the chief would result in a battle, Irvine decided to hold his own council with Piapot and Reed. This impromptu council agreed that Piapot should receive a new reserve next to Pasquah, in return for which Piapot would return to Indian Head temporarily.[54]

The agreement reached between Piapot and Irvine and Reed was a victory for Piapot. By getting a reserve at Qu'Appelle again, Piapot had approximately 2,000 Cree concentrated on the Qu'Appelle River, and he was able to hold his council and thirst dance, for after going to Indian Head, he immediately turned around and went to Pasquah's. Reed and Irvine were aware of Piapot's ruse, but did nothing to prevent his holding the council, for they were aware that the Cree at Qu'Appelle were prepared to protect Piapot from what the Indians regarded as an attack on their leader. Realizing the effect that an Indian war would have on possible settlement, and that the police were inadequate for such a clash, the Canadian officials wished to avoid giving cause for violent reaction by the Cree.[55] Piapot acted as he did because he realized that if any blood were shed the Cree would experience a fate similar to that of the Nez Percés, Blackfoot, and Dakota Sioux in those peoples' conflicts with the United States.

113

Dewdney and the police were to have a similar experience when they attempted to prevent Big Bear from holding a thirst dance and council at Poundmaker's reserve in June 1884. Dewdney feared that Big Bear's council, to which the old chief had invited the Blackfoot and all the Indians from Treaty 6, would result in a larger concentration of Cree than Little Pine had already effected at Battleford. Dewdney also believed that he had to undo what Little Pine had accomplished, and refused to grant Little Pine and Lucky Man the reserve sites they had requested next to Poundmaker. Big Bear was again told that he would not be granted a reserve in the Battleford district. Dewdney believed that the Cree chiefs would ignore his order to select reserve sites at some distance from Battleford, and that this could be used as a reason for arresting them. To legitimize such actions on his part, Dewdney asked the government to pass an order-in-council to make it a criminal offence for a band to refuse to move to a reserve site the Commissioner suggested.[56] In order to avoid violence when he attempted to prevent Big Bear's council and ordered the arrests of Lucky Man and Little Pine, Dewdney instructed the Indian agents at Battleford and Fort Pitt to purchase all the horses, guns, and cartridges the Cree possessed. He increased the size of the police garrison at Battleford and ordered the police to prevent Big Bear from reaching Battleford.[57]

All Dewdney's efforts had little effect, for Big Bear and his band eluded the police, reached Battleford, and held their thirst dance. The Cree refused to sell their arms, and even the effort to break up the gathering by refusing to provide rations had no result other than to provoke another assault on a farm instructor on 17 June 1884. When the police sought to arrest the farm instructor's assailant, they were intimidated into leaving without a prisoner. When a larger police detachment went to the reserve on 18 June, the police were still unable to make an arrest for fear of provoking armed hostilities. Only on 20 June, when the thirst dance had concluded, were the police able to arrest the accused and only then by forcibly removing him from the Cree camp. This was done with the greatest difficulty for the police were jostled and provoked in an effort to get them to fire on the Cree. That no violence occurred, Superintendent Crozier, in charge of the police detachment, attributed to the discipline of his men and to the actions of Little Pine and Big Bear, who did all that was humanly possible to discourage any attack on the police.[58]

114

The events at Battleford frightened all parties involved in the confrontation. Big Bear was very much disturbed by them, for he did not want war, as he had made abundantly clear to Dewdney in March 1884, and again to the Indian agent at Battleford, J.A. Rae, in June. However, he did want the treaties revised and establishment of an Indian territory.[59] Agent Rae was thoroughly frightened and wanted Dewdney and Ottawa to adopt a more coercive policy designed to subjugate the Cree. Superintendent Crozier argued for a less coercive policy, for unless some accommodation were reached with the Cree, Crozier believed that out of desperation they would resort to violence.[60]

On hearing of the events of May and June 1884, Ottawa decided that Dewdney, who was now Lieutenant-Governor in addition to being Indian Commissioner, was to have complete control over Indian affairs in the North-West Territories. As well, the Prime Minister informed Dewdney that more police were being recruited for duty in the West and that the Indian Act was being amended to permit Dewdney to arrest any Indian who was on another band's reserve without the permission of the local Indian Department official.[61] Dewdney was thus being given the instruments to make this policy of compulsion effective.

Dewdney did not, however, immediately make use of his new powers. He still intended to prevent concentration of the Cree, and rejected the requests Big Bear, Poundmaker, Lucky Man, and others made for a reserve at Buffalo Lake, and later rejected Big Bear's, Little Pine's, and Lucky Man's renewed requests for reserves next to Poundmaker's.[62] However, rather than following a purely coercive policy, Dewdney adopted a policy of rewards and punishments. He provided more rations, farming equipment, oxen, ammunition, and twine, and arranged for selected Cree chiefs to visit Winnipeg and other large centres of Canadian settlement. If the Cree were not satisfied with his new approach, he would use force against them. To implement this new policy, Dewdney increased the number of Indian Department employees working on the Cree reserves, for he wanted to monitor closely the behaviour of the Indians, and, if necessary, to arrest troublesome leaders.[63]

While Dewdney was implementing his new policy, the Cree leaders continued their efforts to concentrate the Cree in an exclusively Indian territory. Little Pine went south to seek Blackfoot support for the movement.[64] Big Bear, Lucky Man, and Poundmaker went to Duck Lake for a council with the Cree leaders of the Lower Saskatchewan district. The Duck Lake council, attended by twelve bands, was initiated by Beardy and the chiefs of the Carlton District. Beardy, who acted as spokesman for the Carlton chiefs, had been relatively inactive in the Cree movements in the 1881-3 period. He, however, had been the most vehement critic of the government's failure to deliver the farm materials promised by the treaty commissioners. In the 1877-81 period, Beardy was a man of little influence in the Carlton area, but when Mistawasis and Ahtahkakoop, the principal Cree chiefs of the Carlton District came to share his views, Beardy's standing among the Carlton Cree rose dramatically.[65]

115

The Duck Lake Council, called by Cree leaders who Dewdney thought were loyal and docile, and of which the Commissioner had no foreknowledge, was a cause of much concern. Especially vexing was the detailed list of violations of the treaty for which the Cree demanded redress from the government. The Cree charged that the treaty commissioners lied to them when they said that the Cree would be able to make a living from agriculture with the equipment provided for in the treaties. However, rather than provide all the farming goods, what the government did, according to the Cree, was to withhold many of the cattle and oxen; send inferior quality wagons, farm tools, and equipment; and provide insufficient rations and clothes, and no medicine chest. The petition closed with the statement expressing the Cree sentiment that they had been deceived by 'sweet promises' designed to cheat them of their heritage, and that unless their grievances were remedied by the summer of 1885, they would take whatever measures necessary, short of war, to get redress.[66]

Dewdney originally assumed, as did some newspapers across the West, that the Duck Lake Council was part of a plot by Louis Riel to foment an Indian and Metis rebellion. Dewdney's assumption was based on the fact that the Duck Lake Council was held a short time after Riel had returned to Canada. It was also known that Riel had attended it, and that he had advocated such an alliance and a resort to violence when he had met the Cree in Montana in 1880.[67] Further investigation, however, made quite clear that Riel had little influence on the Cree. To allay the growing concern about the possibility of an Indian war, Dewdney had Hayter Reed issue a statement that nothing untoward was happening and that there was less danger of an Indian war in 1884 than there had been in 1881. Privately Dewdney admitted to Ottawa and his subordinates in the West that the situation was very serious.[68] After both he and Dewdney had met with Cree leaders throughout the West and after carefully assessing the situation, Hayter Reed stated that the government had nothing to fear from the Cree until the summer of 1885. What Reed and Dewdney expected at that time was a united Cree demand to renegotiate treaties.[69]

What Reed and Dewdney had learned on their tours of the Battleford, Edmonton, Carlton, and Qu'Appelle districts in the fall of 1884 was that Big Bear, Piapot, and Little Pine were on the verge of uniting the Cree to call for new treaties in which an Indian territory and greater autonomy for the Cree would be major provisions. In fact, throughout the summer and fall of 1884 Little Pine attempted, with limited success, to interest the leaders of the Blackfoot in joining the Cree movement for treaty revision. Little Pine had invited the Blackfoot to a joint council with the Cree leaders on Little Pine's reserve scheduled for the spring of 1885.[70] If the Blackfoot joined the Cree, Ottawa's ability to govern the Indians and control the West would be seriously jeopardized.

At the moment that the Cree movement seemed on the verge of success, Big Bear was losing control of his band. As he told the assembled chiefs at Duck Lake in the summer of 1884, his young men were listening to the warrior chief, Little Poplar, who was advocating killing government officials and Indian agents as a means of restoring Cree independence. Big Bear feared that if Little Poplar's course of action were adopted the Cree would fight an Indian war that they were certain to lose.[71]

Dewdney was aware of Little Poplar's growing influence on the young men of Big Bear's and the Battleford Assiniboine bands; however, he wished to wait until after January 1885 before taking any action, because after that date the new amendments to the Indian Act would be in effect. These amendments could be used to arrest and imprison Little Pine, Little Poplar, Big Bear, and Piapot, and thereby, Dewdney hoped, destroy the movements these chiefs led.[72] In anticipation of confrontations in 1885, Dewdney ordered that the guns and ammunition normally allotted to the Cree so they could hunt for food be withheld. In addition, Indian councils were prohibited, including the one scheduled for Duck Lake in the summer of 1885, to which all the Cree in Treaty 6 had been invited. Arrangements were made to place the Mounted Police at Battleford under Dewdney's command, and serious consideration was given to placing an artillery unit there also.[73]

To get improved intelligence, Dewdney hired more men to work as Indian agents with the Cree. These men were given broad discretionary powers and were to keep the Commissioner informed on Cree activities. As well, English-speaking mixed-bloods, many of whom had worked for the Hudson's Bay Company and had the confidence of the Cree, were hired as farm instructors. There would now be a farm instructor on each Cree reserve, with explicit instructions to keep the Indian Agent informed of what was happening on his reserve. Staff who had personality conflicts with any of the Cree leaders were either transferred or fired. Only Thomas Quinn, Indian Agent at Fort Pitt and his farming instructor, John Delaney, were not removed before March 1885, although both were slated for transfer.[74]

Dewdney found that his most important staffing move was the employ-

116

ment of Peter Ballendine, a former Hudson's Bay Company trader much trusted by the principal Cree leaders. Ballendine's job was to ingratiate himself with Big Bear and report on that chief's comings and goings. Ballendine won the confidence of Big Bear and reported upon how wrong Dewdney's earlier efforts to break up Big Bear's band had been. Because so many of Big Bear's original followers either joined Lucky Man, Thunderchild, or Little Pine's bands, Big Bear by 1884 was left with only the most recalcitrant opponents of the treaty. These individuals were only lukewarm in support of their chief's non-violent efforts to get the treaty revised. They favoured instead the course of action advocated by Little Poplar. Ballendine believed that the government could expect trouble from the Big Bear and Little Poplar bands. However, Ballendine emphasized that there was little danger of a Cree-Metis alliance, for the Cree were refusing to meet with the Metis, and were rejecting all entreaties from the Metis suggesting the two should make common cause. Instead the Cree, under the leadership of Big Bear, Beardy, and Little Pine, were planning their own council for the summer of 1885.[75]   *117*

Ballendine also developed a new source of information in Poundmaker, who was also acting as a police informer. It was from Poundmaker that Dewdney and the police learned that Little Pine was attempting to involve the Blackfoot in the summer of 1884, and wanted to do so in January 1885, but was prevented from doing so because of temporary blindness—a possible sign of malnutrition from the hunger that most Cree experienced in the extremely harsh winter of 1884-5. Little Pine had sought to get Poundmaker to encourage Crowfoot to join the Cree movement but Poundmaker refused to aid Little Pine, and when Little Pine recovered from his blindness, he went south to meet with Crowfoot.[76]

While Little Pine met with Crowfoot, Big Bear was being challenged for the leadership of his band by his son Imases, also called Curly, and by one of his headsmen, Wandering Spirit. These two men were spokesmen for the younger men of Big Bear's Band, and wanted to work with Little Poplar. In the winter of 1885, Little Poplar was journeying constantly between Pitt and Battleford enlisting support for his plan of action. Although Ballendine could not get precise information on Little Poplar's plans, he did report that by March 1885 Big Bear had asserted himself and that the influence of Imases and Wandering Spirit had seemed to wane.[77]

On the basis of these and similar reports, Dewdney and the police were convinced that, although a number of councils were expected in 1885, no violence was to be anticipated from the Cree. Nevertheless, Dewdney wished to prevent the Cree from holding their councils. His strategy was to make the Cree satisfied with the treaties. He therefore admitted in February 1885 that the government had violated the treaties and ordered delivery to the Cree of all goods the treaties had stipulated. In addition, he ordered a dramatic increase in their rations. If this failed to placate them he planned to arrest their leaders, use the police to keep the Cree on their reserves, and to depose any chief who attempted to attend an Indian council.[78]

Dewdney had the full support of Ottawa for his policy of arresting Cree leaders. The only reservations the Prime Minister expressed were that Dewdney have sufficient forces to make the arrests and that he provide enough evidence to justify the charges of incitement to an insurrection. Macdonald also volunteered to communicate with the stipendiary magistrates to assure their co-operation in imposing long prison terms for any Cree leader convicted of incitement.[79] Macdonald was willing to provide his assistance because Dewdney had earlier complained that he could not use preventive detention of Indian leaders because the magistrates 'only look at the evidence and the crime committed when giving out sentences,' rather than taking into consideration the nature of the man and the harm that he might do if he were released at an inopportune time.[80] All these preparations were complete when word reached Dewdney of the Metis clash with the Mounted Police at Duck Lake in March 1885.

The Riel Rebellion of 1885 provided Dewdney with a new instrument to make his coercive policy effective. The troops sent into the North-West to suppress the Rebellion could be used to destroy the Cree movement for an Indian territory. The Cree themselves would provide the excuse Dewdney needed virtually to declare war on the bands and leaders who had led the Cree movement for treaty revision. During March 1885, the Cree did engage in some acts of violence that Dewdney chose to label acts of rebellion.

These acts were unrelated to the Cree movement for treaty revision. In fact, these acts that led to the subjugation of the Cree were committed by persons not involved with the Cree movement for autonomy. It is one of the ironic quirks of history that the leaders of the Cree movement had little or nothing to do with the events which would destory that movement to which they had devoted ten years of their lives. Nevertheless, they would be held responsible for the actions of their desperate and hungry people. To heighten the irony, it was the Metis movement, from which the Cree had held aloof, which would give Dewdney the excuse to use military force to subjugate the Cree.

The Duck Lake clash coincided with a Cree Council on Sweetgrass Reserve. The council of the Battleford area Cree had been called to consider how they could press for increased rations. When word reached the Cree at Sweetgrass of the clash at Duck Lake, they felt that circumstances would make Indian Agent Rae willing to grant them more rations. Thus the Cree, taking their women and children with them to demonstrate their peaceful intent, set out for Battleford. Fear and panic prevailed at Battleford, for on learning of the Crees' approach, the town's citizens assumed that the Cree had thrown in their lot with the Metis. The town was evacuated; most townspeople took refuge in the Mounted Police post.[81]

When the Cree arrived at Battleford they found the town abandoned. They sent word to the police that they wished to speak to the Indian Agent, who refused to leave the safety of the post. The Cree women, seeing the abandoned stores and houses filled with food, began to help themselves. Then, fearing arrest by the police, the Cree left town. On the way back to their reserves, as well as on their way to town, the Cree assisted a number of Indian Department employees and settlers to cross the Battle River to get to the police post, thus demonstrating the pacific nature of their intentions.[82]

Rather than returning to their individual reserves, the Cree went to Poundmaker's, for as the leader in the Battleford district to whom the government had shown much favour in the past, Poundmaker was seen as the man best able to explain to the government what had happened at Battleford. A second significant reason was the deaths of two prominent Cree leaders: Red Pheasant, the night before the Cree left for Battleford, and Little Pine, the night they returned. As it was the practice for the Cree to leave the place where their leaders had expired, both bands left their reserves and went to Poundmaker's, who, given the fears the whites had concerning a Cree and Metis alliance, might possibly defuse any crisis. Thus, in March 1885, Poundmaker became the spokesman of the Battleford Cree.[83]

No sooner were the Cree at Poundmaker's than they were joined by the local Assiniboine, who insisted that a soldier's (war) tent be erected, for events at the Assiniboine reserves convinced them that an attack on the Indian camp was imminent. The Assiniboine explained that when word had reached them of the Duck Lake fight, a few of their young men sought revenge on farming instructor James Payne, who was blamed for the death of a girl. The girl's male relatives killed Payne and murdered farmer Barney Tremont. The Assiniboine now assumed that the Canadian authorities would behave in a similar manner to the Americans and blame all Indians for the actions of a few individuals.[84]

Erection of the soldier's tent meant that the warriors were in control of the camp and that Poundmaker and the civil authorities had to defer to them. It was at this time that the Metis appeal for aid was received. The Cree refused to assist the Metis, although they expected an attack on their camp. Watches were set on the roads, and protection was offered to the Metis at Bresaylor for the settlers there had earned the enmity of the Batoche Metis. As long as no military or police forces came towards the Cree camp, the Cree remained on their reserves and did not interfere with anyone going to or leaving Battleford. The Mounted Police detachment from Fort Pitt and Colonel Otter's military unit arrived in Battleford without encountering any Indians. Nevertheless, reports from the police and local officials maintained that the town was under siege.[85]

While the Battleford Cree were preparing their defences, Big Bear's band was making trouble for itself. Big Bear was absent from his camp when the members of his band heard about the fight at Duck Lake. Wandering Spirit and Imases sought to use the opportunity presented by the Metis uprising, to seek revenge for the insults and abuses perpetrated against the Cree by Indian Agent Thomas Quinn and Farming Instructor Delaney. Quinn had physically abused some of the Indian men, while Delaney had cuckolded others before he brought a white bride to Frog Lake in late 1884. Big Bear's headmen demanded that the two officials open the storehouse to the Cree, and when they refused to do so, they were murdered. This set off further acts of violence that resulted in the murder of all the white men in the camp save one.[86]

On his return to camp Big Bear ended further acts of violence. Although

119

unable to prevent a minor skirmish between his young men and a small police patrol, he convinced his warriors to allow the police detachment at Fort Pitt to withdraw from the post without being attacked and to guarantee safety to the civilian residents of the Frog Lake and Fort Pitt regions. Big Bear then led his people north, where he hoped they would be out of harm's way and not engage in further acts of violence.[87]

Beardy also lost control of his band. He and the neighbouring One Arrow band had reserves next to Batoche. Before the clash with the police, the Metis had come to the One Arrow Reserve, captured Farming Instructor Peter Tompkins, and threatened the Cree band with destruction unless the Cree aided the Metis. Some of the younger men of One Arrow's band agreed to do so.[88] The Metis made the same threat against Beardy and his band, and although a few of his young men joined the Metis, Beardy and most of his people remained neutral.[89] It is doubtful that the Cree would have aided the Metis without the threat of violence. Earlier, the Cree of the Duck Lake region had threatened hostilities against the Metis, for the Metis had settled on One Arrow's Reserve and demanded that the government turn over to them some of One Arrow's Reserve. Ottawa, fearing the Metis more than the Cree in 1880, acquiesced. Over the next four years, one task of the local Indian Agent and the police was to reconcile the Cree with the Metis of the Batoche region.[90]

The Cree acts of violence in March 1885 were the excuse Dewdney needed to justify the use of troops against them. He maintained that the Battleford, Fort Pitt, and Duck Lake Cree were part of the Riel Rebellion. Privately, Dewdney reported to Ottawa that he saw the events at Battleford and Frog Lake as the acts of a desperate, starving people and unrelated to what the Metis were doing.[91] In fact, Dewdney had sought in late March to open negotiations with the Battleford Cree, but Rae refused to meet the Cree leaders. Subsequent efforts to open negotiations ended in failure because there was no way to get a message to Poundmaker, and after Colonel Otter's attack on the Cree camp any thought of negotiations was dropped.[92]

Publicly Dewdney proclaimed that the Cree were part of the Metis uprising. He issued a proclamation that any Indian who left his reserve was to be regarded as a rebel.[93] As well, to intimidate Piapot and the Treaty 4 Cree, Dewdney stationed troops on their reserves. To prevent an alliance of Blackfoot and Cree, Dewdney announced that he was stationing troops at Swift Current and Medicine Hat. Dewdney took these steps, as he confided to Macdonald, because he feared that the Cree might still attempt to take action on their own cause, and he was concerned because in the previous year the Cree had attempted to enlist the Blackfoot in the movement to revise the treaties.[94]

The military commander in the North-West, General F.D. Middleton, was not as concerned about the problems with the Cree. He wanted to concentrate his attention on the Metis. Although he did send troops under Colonel William Otter to Swift Current, he refused to order them to Battleford to lift the alleged siege until he received word of the Frog Lake massacre.

Otter was then ordered to lift the 'siege' and protect Battleford from Indian attack, but he was not to take the offensive. At the same time General Thomas Strange was ordered to bring Big Bear under control.

Otter reached Battleford without seeing an Indian. He was upset that he and his troops would not see action. He therefore proposed that he attack the Indian camp at Poundmaker's Reserve. Middleton vetoed the plan, but Dewdney welcomed it as a means to bring the Cree under government control. Taking the Lieutenant-Governor's approval to be paramount to Middleton's veto, Otter launched his attack. The engagement, known as the Battle of Cut Knife Hill, almost ended in total disaster for Otter's force. Only the Cree fear that they would suffer the same fate as Sitting Bull after the Battle of the Little Big Horn saved Otter's troops from total annihilation.[95]

The tale of the subsequent military campaigns against the Cree by Strange and Middleton and the voluntary surrenders of Poundmaker and Big Bear is found in detail in Stanley's *Birth of Western Canada* and Desmond Morton's *The Last War Drum*. With Big Bear and Poundmaker in custody, Dewdney prepared to use the courts in the manner he had planned before the Riel Rebellion. Both Cree leaders were charged with treason-felony, despite Dewdney's knowledge that neither man had engaged in an act of rebellion. Eyewitnesses to the events at Fort Pitt, Frog Lake, and Battleford all made clear that neither chief was involved in the murders and looting that had occurred. In fact, many of these people served as defence witnesses.[96] As Dewdney informed the Prime Minister, the diaries and letters of the murdered officials at Frog Lake showed that until the day of the 'massacre' there was 'no reason to believe that our Indians were even dissatisfied much less contemplated violence.'[97] Ballendine's reports indicated that there were no plans for violence, that the Cree were not involved with the Metis, and that they planned no rebellion. Dewdney believed that the Cree had not 'even thought, intended or wished that the uprising would reach the proportion it has . . . Things just got out of control.'[98] As Dewdney related to the Prime Minister, had the people living in the region not been new settlers from the East, and had they not fled in panic, much of the 'raiding' and looting would not have occurred. In regions where people had not abandoned their homes no raiding occurred.[99] Therefore, the charges against Big Bear and Poundmaker were designed to remove the leadership of the Cree movement for revision of the treaties. They were charged to elicit prison sentences that would have the effect of coercing the Cree to accept government control. The trials were conducted to have the desired result, and both Big Bear and Poundmaker were convicted and sentenced to three years in Stoney Mountain Penitentiary.[100] Neither man served his full term, and both died a short time after their release from prison.

By the end of 1885, Dewdney had succeeded in subjugating the Cree. Big Bear was in prison, Little Pine was dead, and Piapot was intimidated by having troops stationed on his reserve. Dewdney had deprived the Cree of their principal leaders and of their autonomy. He used the military to disarm and impoverish the Cree by confiscating their horses and carts; he increased the size of the Mounted Police force, and used the police to arrest the Cree leaders who protested against his policies; he broke up Cree bands, deposed Cree leaders, and forbade any Indian to be off his reserve without permission from the Indian Agent.[101] By 1890, through vigorous implementation of the Indian Act, Dewdney and his successor, Hayter Reed, had begun the process of making the Cree an administered people.

The record of the Canadian government in dealing with the Cree is thus not one of honourable fair-mindedness and justice as the traditional interpretation portrays. As Dewdney admitted in 1885, the treaties' promises and provisions were not being fulfilled, and Dewdney himself had taken steps to assure Canadian control over the Cree, which were themselves violations of the treaties. Thus, he had refused to grant the Cree the reserve sites they selected; he had refused to distribute the ammunition and twine the treaties required. His plans for dealing with the Cree leaders were based on a political use of the legal and judicial system, and ultimately he made use of the military, the police, and the courts in a political manner to achieve his goals of subjugating the Cree. Only by ignoring these facts can one continue to perpetuate the myth of Canada's just and honourable Indian policy from 1870 to 1885.

122

Notes

1. Doug Owram, *Promise of Eden: The Canadian Expansionist Movement and the Idea of the West, 1856–1900* (Toronto 1980), 131–4.
2. G.F.G. Stanley, *The Birth of Western Canada: A History of the Riel Rebellions* (Toronto 1960)
3 Ibid., 206–15
4. Ibid., vii–viii, 196, 216–36. It should be noted that the traditional interpretation of a Cree rebellion in association with the Metis has been challenged by R. Allen, 'Big Bear,' *Saskatchewan History*, xxv (1972); W.B. Fraser, 'Big Bear, Indian Patriot,' *Alberta Historical Review*, xiv (1966), 1–13; Rudy Wiebe in his fictional biography, *The Temptations of Big Bear* (Toronto 1973) and in his biography of Big Bear in the *Dictionary of Canadian Biography* [DCB], xi, 1881–90 (Toronto 1982), 597–601; and Norma Sluman, *Poundmaker* (Toronto 1967). However, none of these authors deals with Canada's Indian policy, and none examines what the Cree were doing in the period 1876–85.
5. Alexander Morris, *The Treaties of Canada with the Indians of Manitoba and the North-West Territories* (Toronto 1880), 37; Public Archives of Manitoba, Adams G. Archibald Papers (hereafter cited as PAM Archibald Papers, letters)
6. Public Archives of Canada, Record Group 10 Indian Affairs Files, vol. 3571, file 124–2, also vol. 3603, file 2036 (hereafter cited as PAC, RG 10, vol. file). See also Morris, *Treaties of Canada*, 25–43 and 126–7, for a printed account of the negotiations and the texts of the original and renegotiated treaties, pp 313–20, 338–42. Two articles by John Taylor, 'Canada's Northwest Indian Policy in the 1870's: Traditional Premises and Necessary Innovations' and 'Two Views on the Meaning of Treaties Six and Seven' in *The Spirit of Alberta Indian Treaties* (Montreal 1980), 3–7 and 9–45 respectively, provide a good account of the Indian contribution and attitude towards the treaties.
7. Morris, *Treaties of Canada*, 44–76; on pp 120–3 Morris demonstrates how he had to make Treaty 3 the model for the Qu'Appelle Treaty to get the Saulteaux and Cree of the Qu'Appelle River region to accept what he originally offered them. Compare Treaties 1–6 to see what the government was forced to concede. Also see Taylor's 'Traditional Premises' for Indian contributions to the negotiation process.
8. PAC, RG 10, vol. 3586, file 1137, Lieutenant-Governor Morris to Secretary of State for the Provinces, 13 Sept. 1872; PAC, RG 10, vol. 3576, file 378 entire file; vol. 3609, file 3229; vol. 3604, file 2543; vol. 3636, 6694-1
9. PAC, RG 10, vol. 3612, file 4012, entire file; PAM Archibald Papers, W.J. Christie to George W. Hill, 26 Apr. 1871; Archibald to Secretary of State for the Provinces, 5 Jan. 1872; also letters in note 15; William Francis Butler, *The Great Lone Land* (Rutland, VT 1970), 360–2, 368; PAC, Manuscript Group 26A, John A. Macdonald Papers, vol. 104, entire volume (hereafter cited as PAC, MG 26A, letters),

PAM, Archibald Papers, Joseph Howe to Archibald, 30 June 1872; PAM, Alexander Morris Papers, Lt Governor's Collection, Morris to Minister of the Interior 7 July 1873 (hereafter cited as PAM, Morris Papers, letter); PAC, RG 10, vol. 3625, file 5366, Morris to Minister of the Interior, David Laird, 22 July and 4 August 1875; RG 10 vol. 3624, file 5152, Colonel French, Commissioner of the NWMP to the Minister of Justice, 6 and 19 August 1875; Morris, 170-1, RG 10 vol. 3612, file 4012, entire file; Adams G. Archibald Papers, Petition of James Seenum to Archibald, 9 Jan. 1871, and attached letters of Kehewin, Little Hunter, and Kiskion; Archibald to Secretary of State for the Provinces, 5 Jan. 1872

10. Two excellent studies of the Cree in the pre-1870 era are those by Arthur J. Ray, *Indians in the Fur Trade: Their Role as Hunters, Trappers, and Middlemen in the Lands Southwest of Hudson Bay 1660–1870* (Toronto 1974), and David G. Mandelbaum, *The Plains Cree*, xxxvii, Part II of Anthropological Papers of the American Museum of Natural History (New York 1940).

11. Ibid. An excellent study of the Cree expansion is the unpublished MA thesis by John S. Milloy, 'The Plains Cree: A Preliminary Trade and Military Chronology, 1670-1870' (Carlton University 1972); also Henry John Moberly and William B. Cameron, *When Fur Was King* (Toronto 1929), 208-12, describes part of the last phase of this movement. The shrinking range of buffalo and how the Cree reacted are also discussed in Frank Gilbert Roe, *The North American Buffalo: A Critical Study of the Species in Its Wild State* (Toronto 1951), 282-333.

12. Henry Youle Hind, *Narrative of the Canadian Red River Exploring Expedition of 1857 and of the Assiniboine and Saskatchewan Exploring Expedition of 1858* (Edmonton 1971), vol. i, p. 334; Irene Spry, *The Palliser Expedition: An Account of John Palliser's British North American Expedition, 1857-1860* (London 1964), 59-60; Viscount Milton and W.B. Cheadle, *The Northwest Passage by Land, Being the Narrative of an Expedition from the Atlantic to the Pacific* (Toronto 1970), 66-7; Edwin Thompson Perry, *Five Indian Tribes of the Upper Missouri: Sioux, Arickaras, Assiniboine, Crees, Crow* (Norman, OK 1969), 99-137; J. Hines, *The Red Indians of the Plains; Thirty Years' Missionary Experience in Saskatchewan* (Toronto 1916), 78-80, 88-91.

13. Morris, *Treaties of Canada*, 77-123 and 168-239, discusses the negotiations of Treaties 4 and 6 with the Cree and how he was forced to modify his offer. Also described is the Cree concern about their land. The reaction of the Mackenzie government is detailed in PAC, RG 10 vol. 3636, file 6694-2 and in particular, Minister of the Interior Report to Privy Council, 31 Jan. 1877 and order-in-council, 10 Feb. 1877.

14. Milloy, 'The Plains Cree' 250-62; Alexander Johnson, *The Battle at Belly River: Stories of the Last Great Indian Battle* (Lethbridge 1966).

15. Henry Youle Hind, vol. 1, pp 334, 360-1, carries reports of Mistickoos or Short Stick's comments on a council of Cree leaders that resolved to limit white and Metis hunting privileges. Viscount Milton and W.B. Cheadle, *The Northwest Passage by Land, Being the Narrative of an Expedition from the Atlantic to the Pacific*, 66, 67, contains comments on the Cree determination to limit non-Indian involvement in the hunt. PAM, E. Adams Archibald papers, letter #200, Macdonald to Archibald, 14 Feb. 1871; letter #170, English halfbreeds to Archibald, 10 Jan. 1871, all stress that Cree were taking action to limit non-Indian involvement in the buffalo hunt.

16. Morris, *Treaties of Canada*, 241

17. Interview with Walter Gordon, Director of the Indian Rights and Treaties Program, Federation of Saskatchewan Indians, Mar. 1974. Poundmaker made a similar statement in an interview quoted in 'Indian Affairs,' *Saskatchewan Herald*, 2 Aug. 1880. The importance of Big Bear, Piapot, and Little Pine cannot be underestimated, for those Cree chiefs who took treaty only Sweetgrass had the standing of these men, and Sweetgrass died within a few months of taking treaty.

18. Morris, *Treaties of Canada*, 85-7. More detailed information on the adhesions of Piapot and Checkuk is to be found in PAC, RG 10, vol. 3625, file 5489; W.J. Christie to Laird, 7 Oct. 1875

19. Morris, *Treaties of Canada*, 240 for the quotation. See p. 355 for the clauses in Treaty 6 respecting acceptance of Canadian laws.

20. Ibid., 174.

21. Fraser, 'Big Bear, Indian Patriot,' 76-7 agrees that Big Bear was not referring specifically to hanging but to the effect the treaty would have on the Cree.

22. PAC, RG 10, vol. 3656, file 9093, Agent Dickieson to Lt-Gov. Laird, 14 Sept. 1877

23. PAC, RG 10, vol. 3648,file 8380; vol. 3655, file 9000, Laird to Minister of the Interior, 9 May 1878

24. PAC, RG 10, vol. 3655, file 9000, Laird to Minister of the Interior, 9 May 1878; vol. 3636, file 9092, Laird to Superintendent-General, 19 Nov. 1877; PAC, RG 10, vol. 3670, file 10,771 Laird to Minister of the Interior, 12 Nov. 1878. PAC, RG 10, vol. 3672, file 10,853, Dickieson to Meredith, 2 Apr. 1878; vol. 3656, file 9092, Inspector James Walker to Laird, 5 Sept. 1877. Department of Indian Affairs and Northern Development, Ottawa, file 1/1-11-3, Laird to Minister of the Interior, 30 Dec. 1878; Dickieson to Laird, 9 Oct. 1878; Walker to Laird, 4 and 26 Feb. 1879 (hereafter cited as DIAND, file, letter)

25. PAC, RG 10, vol. 3655, file 1002, Laird to Minister of the Interior, 9 May 1878; vol. 3672, file 19,853, Dickieson to Vankoughnet, 26 July 1878; PAC, MG 26A, E.D. Clark to Fred White, 16 July 1879

26. 'News from the Plains,' *Saskatchewan Herald*, 18 Nov. 1878; 'From the Plains,' *Saskatchewan Herald*, 5 May 1879; 'Contradictory News from the West,' *Fort Benton Record*, 31 Jan. 1879.

27. PAC, RG 10, vol. 3672, file 10,853, M.G. Dickieson to Vankoughnet, 26 July 1878; *Opening Up the West: Being the Official Reports to Parliament of the North-West Mounted Police from 1874–1881*) Toronto 1973), Report for 1878, p.21

28. PAC, RG 10, vol, 3704, file 17,858, entire file; vol. 3648, file 162–2, entire file. *Ibid.*, vol. 3699, file 16,580, order-in-council, 9 Oct. 1879; vol. 3766, file 22,541; E.T. Galt to Superintendent-General of Indian Affairs, 27 July 1880; vol. 3730, file 26,279, entire file; vol. 3757, file 21,397, entire file.

29. House of Commons, Ottawa, *Sessional Papers*, xvii (1885), Report No. 3, 157 (hereafter cited as CSP, vol., year, report); Edward Ahenakew, *Voices of the Plains Cree*, Ruth Buck, ed. (Toronto 1973), 26. Dewdney in adopting this tactic simply copied what the fur-trading companies had done in the past. The Cree tolerated such practises because they improved the opportunities to have better access to European goods. See Arthur J. Ray and Donald Freeman, *'Give Us Good Measure': An Economic Analysis of Relations between the Indians and the Hudson's Bay Company before 1763* (Toronto 1978), passim. Ray, *Indians in the Fur Trade*, passim, deals with the same practice in the post-1763 period. Mandelbaum, *The Plains Cree*, 105–10 discusses the nature of Cree political organization and leadership that explains their acceptance of such practices.

30. Morris, *Treaties of Canada*, 366–7. DIAND, Treaty Annuity Pay Sheets for 1879. More than 1,000 Plains Cree took treaty for the first time in 1879 under Little Pine, Thunderchild, and Lucky Man. Others from Little Pine's and Big Bear's bands had already taken treaty a year earlier as part of Thunder Companion's band, while others joined Poundmaker, and the three Cree bands settled in the Peace Hills. A portion of the Assiniboine also took treaty under Mosquito in 1878, while many of the northern Saulteaux who had followed Yellow Sky took treaty in 1878 under the leadership of Moosomin.

31. PAC, RG 10, vol. 3745, file 29506-4, vol. 2. Ray to Reed, 23 Apr. 1883; vol. 3668, file 9644, Reed to Commissioner, 23 Dec. 1883. Although these materials refer to events in the Battleford district, as will be demonstrated, the tactics in 1883–4 were similar, if not exactly the same as those used in the Cypress Hills between 1879 and 1882. That they were not better recorded for the earlier period is due to the fact that the government had fewer men working with the Indians, and did not have as effective supervision in 1879–82 period as it did at Battleford. Also much of the police and Indian Affairs material relating to this region in the 1879–82 period have been lost or destroyed.

32. PAC, RG 10, vol. 3730, file 36,279, entire file; vol. 3668, file 10,440, Agent Allen to L. Vankoughnet, 11 Nov. 1878, CSP, vol. xvi (1883), Paper no. 5, p. 197. *Settlers and Rebels: Being the Reports to Parliament of the Activities of the Royal North-West Mounted Police Force from 1882–1885* (Toronto 1973), Report for 1882, pp 4–6 (hereafter cited as *Settlers and Rebels*)

33. PAC, RG 10, vol. 3730, file 26,219, Report of surveyor Patrick to Superintendent-General, 16 Dec. 1880; vol. 3716, file 22,546, Assistant Commissioner E.T. Galt to Superintendent-General, 27 July 1880; vol. 3757, files 31,393 and 31,333; vol. 3757, file 20,034. PAC, MG 26A, vol. 210, Dewdney to Macdonald, 3 Oct. 1880

34. RG 10, vol. 3652, file 8589, parts 1 and 2, entire file; vol. 3691, file 13,893, entire file. The *Benton Weekly Record* throughout the spring and summer of 1880 carried reports of Cree and Assiniboine horse-stealing raids, and reports of what the Cree were doing in Montana. On 7 May 1880, the paper carried an article entitled 'Starving Indians,' which was a strong denunciation of Canada's Indian policy and the effect it had on the Cree.

35. PAC, MG 26A, vol. 210, Dewdney to Macdonald, 29 Oct. 1880; *Saskatchewan Herald*, 14 Feb. 1881

36. PAC, MG 26A, vol. 210, Dewdney to Macdonald, 26 Oct. 1880 and 23 Apr. 1880; *Saskatchewan Herald*, 14, 28 Feb. 1881

37. PAC, MG 26A, vol. 210, Dewdney to MacPherson, 4 July 1881; vol. 247, Galt to MacPherson, 14 July 1881; 'Edmonton,' *Saskatchewan Herald*, 12 Nov. 1881

38. Ibid., also PAC, MG 26A, vol. 210, Dewdney to Macdonald, 19 June 1881; vol. 247, Galt to Vankoughnet, 16 July 1881. PAC, RG 10, vol. 3739, file 28, 748-1, Dewdney to Macdonald, 3 Apr. 1882; Fred White to Minister of the Interior, 9 June 1882; Freylinghausen to Sackville-West, 9 June 1882. *Saskatchewan Herald*, 1 Aug. 1881; 'Starving Indians,' *Benton Weekly Record*, 14 July 1881; 25 Aug., 1 Sept., and 13 Oct. 1881

39. PAC, RG 10. vol. 3739, file 28,478-1, C.G. Denny to Commissioner, 24 Oct. 1881; vol. 3768, file 33,642; vol. 3603, file 20,141, McIlree to Dewdney, 21 June 1882. Glenbow Institute, Calgary, Edgar Dewdney Papers, v, file 57, Irvine to Dewdney, 24 June 1882 (hereafter cited as Dewdney Papers, vol., file, letter). *Saskatchewan Herald*, 24 June 1882; *Edmonton Bulletin*, 17 June 1882

40. PAC, RG 10, vol. 3768, file 33,642, entire file

41. PAC, MG 26A, vol. 210, Dewdney to Macdonald, 19 June 1881; vol. 247, Galt to Vankoughnet, 16 July 1881. *Saskatchewan Herald*, 1 Aug. 1881. 'Starving Indians,' *Benton Weekly Record*, 14 July 1881. See also *Benton Weekly Record*, 25 Aug., 1 Sept., and 13 Oct. 1881

42. Morris, *Treaties of Canada*, 205, 218, 352–3

43. PAC, RG 10, vol. 3604, file 2589, entire file. See also *Settlers and Rebels*, 1882 Report. See also Dewdney Papers, v, file 57, White to Irvine, 29 Aug. 1882, RG 10, vol. 3604, file 2589. 'The Repatriated Indians,' *Saskatchewan Herald*, 5 Aug. 1882. 'From the South,' *Saskatchewan Herald*, 21 May 1882; 'Back on the Grub Pile,' *Saskatchewan Herald*, 24 June 1882

44. Dewdney Papers, v, file 57, Irvine to Dewdney, 24 June 1882 and 25 Sept. 1882. *Settlers and Rebels*, 1882 Report, pp. 4, 5. CSP, xvi (1883), Paper no. 5, p 197, RG 10, vol. 3604, file 2589. 'Repatriated Indians,' *Saskatchewan Herald*, 5 Aug. 1882

45. Ibid.; Dewdney Papers, iv, file 45, White to Dewdney, 12 Oct. 1882, *Saskatchewan Herald*, 14 Oct. 1882. 'Big Bear and Others,' and the 'I.D.,' *Edmonton Bulletin*, 21 Oct. 1882

46. Dewdney Papers, iv, file 45, White to Dewdney, 17 Oct. 1882, PAC, MG 26A, vol. 289, Vankoughnet to Macdonald, 2 Nov. 1882

47. PAC, MG 26A, xi, Dewdney to J.A. Macdonald, 2 Sept. 1883. PAC, RG 10, vol. 3682, file 12,667, Dewdney to Superintendent-General, 28 Apr. 1884

48. PAC, RG 10, vol. 3668, file 10,644, Reed to Commissioner, 23 Dec. 1883. Robert Jefferson, *Fifty Years on the Saskatchewan* (Battleford 1929), 103

49. PAC, RG 10, vol. 3668, file 10,644, Reed to Commissioner, 23 Dec. 1883. *Edmonton Bulletin*, 9 Feb. 1884; *Saskatchewan Herald*, 24 Nov. 1883

50. PAC, MG 26A, vol. 289 Vankoughnet to Macdonald, 4, 10 Dec. 1883; vol. 104, Deputy Superintendent-General to T. Quinn, 21 Sept. 1883; Dewdney to Superintendent-General, 27 Sept. 1883; Deputy Superintendent-General to Reed, 10 Apr. 1884; vol. 212, Dewdney to Macdonald, 2 Jan. 1883 [sic! Given the contents of the letter, it is obvious Dewdney forgot that a new year had begun the previous day], vol. 91, Dewdney to Macdonald, 24 July 1884, another letter but without a date, which was probably written in the first week of Aug. 1884; vol. 107, entire file. PAC, RG 10, vol. 3664, file 9843, entire file

51. PAC, RG 10, vol. 3616, file 10,131. Burton Deane, *Mounted Police Life in Canada: A Record of Thirty-One Years in Service, 1883–1914* (Toronto 1973), 140–53. Isabell Andrews, 'Indian Protest Against Starvation: The Yellow Calf Incident of 1884,' *Saskatchewan History*, xxviii (1975), 4–52. *Edmonton Bulletin*, 7 Jan., 3 Feb., 7, 28 July, and 4 Aug. 1884

52. Dewdney Papers, v, file 58, Dewdney to Superintendent-General, 29 Feb. 1884; PAC, MG 26A, vol. 211, Dewdney to Macdonald, 6 Oct. 1883; vol. 212, Reed to Dewdney, 15 Feb. 1884; Dewdney to Macdonald, 16 Feb. and 9 Apr. 1884

53. PAC, RG 10, vol. 3682, file 12,667, Dewdney to Superintendent-General, 28 Apr. 1884; vol. 3686, file 13,168, entire file; vol. 3745, file 29,506-4(2), Reed to Colonel Irvine, 18 May 1884

54. Ibid., vol. 3745, file 29,506-4(2), Reed to Irvine, 18 May 1884; Irvine to Comptroller Fred White, 27 May 1884; White to Vankoughnet, 19 May 1884

55. Ibid., Agent Macdonald to Commissioner, 29 May 1884; vol. 3655, file 9026, Dewdney to Superintendent-General, 13 June 1884

56. PAC, RG 10, vol. 3745, file 29,506-4(2), Reed to Superintendent-General, 19 Apr. 1884. Similar report in vol. 3576, file 309B, PAC, MG 26A, file 37, Dewdney to Macdonald, 3 May 1884. Dewdney's request and actions were contrary to what the Cree had been told about how reserve sites could be chosen, as were the government's actions in denying the Cree reserves in the Cypress Hills and forcing them to move north. See Morris, *Treaties of Canada*, passim. PAC, RG 10, vol. 3576, file 309B, Vankoughnet to Dewdney, 10 May 1884; MG 26A, vol. 104, Dewdney to Superintendent-General, 14 June 1884. Campbell Innes, *The Cree Rebellion of 1884: Sidelights of Indian Conditions Subsequent to 1876* (Battleford 1926), 'Fineday Interview,' 13-15. *Saskatchewan Herald*, 19 Apr. and 17 May 1884

57. PAC, RG 10, vol. 3576, file 309B, Reed to Superintendent-General, 19 Apr. 1884. Reed to Vankoughnet, 19 Apr. 1884; Ray to Commissioner, 23 Apr. 1884; Reed to Superintendent-General, 20 May 1884. Dewdney Papers, iii, file 36, Dewdney to Macdonald, 12 June 1884

58. PAC, RG 10, vol. 3576, file 309B, Ray to Commissioner, 19, 21 June 1884; Crozier to Dewdney, 22 June 1884. Jefferson, 108-9, Innes, *The Cree Rebellion of 1884*, 13-17, 28.

59. PAC, RG 10, vol. 3576, file 309B, Ray to Commissioner, 28 June 1884; see also Rae to Dewdney, 9 June 1884, Innes 'McKay Interview,' 44. PAC, RG 10, vol. 3576, file 309B, Dewdney to Ray, 5 July 1884

60. PAC, RG 10, vol. 3576, file 309B, Ray to Dewdney, 23 June 1884; Crozier to Dewdney, 23 June 1884.

61. Dewdney Papers, iii, file 37, Macdonald to Dewdney, 18 July 1884, 11 Aug. 1884, and 2 Sept. 1884; iv, file 45, Macdonald to White, 15 Sept. 1884. PAC, RG 10, vol. 3576, file 309A, Vankoughnet to Dewdney, 27 July 1884

62. PAC, RG 10, vol. 3576, file 309B, Ray to Commissioner, 30 June 1884; file 309A, Ray to Commissioner, 24, 29 July 1884. PAC, MG 26A, vol. 212, Dewdney to Macdonald, 14 July 1884; J.A. MacRae to Commissioner, 7 Aug. 1884; vol. 107, Ray to Commissioner, 29 July 1884

63. PAC, RG 10, vol. 3745, file 29,506-4(2), Dewdney to Superintendent-General, 7 Aug. 1884; vol. 3576, file 309A, Ray to Dewdney, 19 July 1884. PAC, MG 26A, vol. 104, Dewdney to Department, 19 July 1884

64. PAC, RG 10, vol. 3576, file 309B, Ray to Commissioner, 30 June 1884; file 309A, Ray to Commissioner, 24, 29 July 1884. PAC, MG 26A, vol. 212, Dewdney to Macdonald, 14 July 1884; J.A. MacRae to Commissioner, 7 Aug. 1884; vol. 107, Ray to Commissioner, 29 July 1884

65. PAC, MG 26A, vol. 107, Ray to Commissioner, 29 July and 2 Aug. 1884; J.A. MacRae to Commissioner, 29 July 1884

66. PAC, RG 10, vol. 3697, file 15,423, J.A. MacRae to Dewdney, 25 Aug. 1884

67. Ibid., Reed to Superintendent-General, 23 Jan. 1885; Reed to Dewdney, 22, 25 Aug. 1884. PAC, MG 26A, vol. 107, J.A. MacRae to Commissioner, 29 July 1884; J.M. Ray to Commisioner, 2 Aug. 1884; MacRae to Commissioner, 5 Aug. 1884; vol. 212, MacRae to Commissioner, 7 Aug. 1884. PAC, RG 10, vol. 1756, file 309A, J.M. Ray to Commissioner, 24, 25 July 1884. 'Big Bear Rises to Speak,' *Saskatchewan Herald*, 5 Aug. 1882. *Saskatchewan Herald*, 25 July and 9 Aug. 1884

68. Ibid., PAC, RG 10, vol. 3576, file 309A, Commissioner to Ray, 7 Aug. 1884. Ray to Commissioner, 29 July 1884; see also in PAC, MG 26A, vol. 107. Dewdney Papers, vi, file 69, Crozier to Comptroller, NWMP, 27 July 1884. PAC, MG 26A, vol. 212, Dewdney to Macdonald, 8 Aug. 1884

69. PAC, MG 26A, vol. 107, Reed to Dewdney, 23, 24, 25 Aug., 4 Sept. 1884; Dewdney to Macdonald, 5 Sept. 1884

70. PAC, RG 10, vol. 3576, file 309A, Begg to Commissioner, 20 Feb. 1885; 'Indian Affairs,' *Saskatchewan Herald*, 31 Oct. 1884

71. Dewdney Papers, vi, file 66, Reed to Dewdney, 4 Sept. 1884

72. Statutes of Canada, 43 Vict. i, cap. 27, 'An Act to Amend the Indian Act, 1880,' 12 Apr. 1884. PAC, MG 26A, vol. 107, Dewdney to Macdonald, 24 Aug. 1884

73. PAC, MG 26A, vol. 212, Reed to Dewdney, 7 Sept. 1884; vol. 107, Dewdney to Macdonald, 24 Aug. 1884

74. PAC, RG 10, vol. 3576, file 309A, Reed to Dewdney, 12 Sept. 1884; vol. 3745, file 29,506-4(2), Reed to Dewdney, 14 Sept. 1884; vol. 3704, file 17,799, entire file; vol. 3664, file 9834 and 9843; vol. 3761, file 30,836, entire file; Dewdney Papers, iv, file 45, Reed to Dewdney, 12 Sept. 1884; vol. iv, file 47, Crozier to Comptroller NWMP, 4 Nov. 1884; v, file 57, Crozier to Dewdney, 30 Jan. 1885

75. PAC, RG 10, vol. 3582, file 749, Ballendine to Reed, 8 Nov. and 26 Dec. 1884

76. PAC, RG 10, vol. 3582, file 949, P. Ballendine to Reed, 20 Nov., 26 Dec., 2 Jan., 1885: J.M. Ray to Commissioner, 27 Dec. 1884; Crozier to Commissioner, NWMP, 14 Jan. 1885; vol. 3576, file 309A, Magnus Begg to Dewdney, 20 Feb. 1885. PAC, MG 26A, extract of Ray to Dewdney, 24 Jan. 1885, Ray, Ballendine, and Crozier when they reported on Little Pine mentioned that their principal source of information was Poundmaker, although Ballendine did get some of his information directly from Little Pine himself.

77. PAC, RG 10, vol. 3582, file 949, Ballendine to Reed, 10 Oct. and 26 Dec. 1884, and 2 Jan. and 16 Mar. 1885: Ballendine to Dewdney, 19 Mar. 1885. PAC, MG 26A, vol. 107, extract of Ray to Dewdney, 24 Jan. 1885. PAC, Manuscript Group 27IC4, Edgar Dewdney Papers, ii, Francis Dickens to Officer Commanding, Battleford, 27 Oct. 1884 (hereafter cited as PAC, MG 27IC4, vol., letter)

78. PAC, MG 26A, vol. 177, Dewdney to Macdonald, 9 Feb. 1885. PAC, RG 10, vol. 3676, file 309A, Dewdney to Vankoughnet, 12 Feb. 1885

79. PAC, RG 10, vol. 3705, file 17,193, Vankoughnet to Dewdney, 5 Feb. 1885; Vankoughnet to Macdonald, 31 Jan. 1885; vol. 3582, file 949, Vankoughnet to Reed, 28 Jan. 1885. Dewdney Papers, iii, file 38, Macdonald to Dewdney, 23 Feb. 1885

80. PAC, RG 10, vol. 3576, file 309A, Dewdney to Vankoughnet, 12 Feb. 1885

81. Jefferson, *Fifty Years on the Saskatchewan* 125

82. Ibid., 126-8. PAC, MG 26A, deposition, William Lightfoot to J.A. MacKay, 31 May 1885

83. Jefferson, *Fifty Years on the Saskatchewan* 127, 130, 138

84. Innes, 'Fine Day Interview,' 185. Sluman, *Poundmaker*, 199-200, 184-5. Jefferson, *Fifty Years on the Saskatchewan*, 130-8

85. Desmond Morton, *The Last War Drum* (Toronto 1972), 98-102. Jefferson, *Fifty Years on the Saskatchewan*, 125-40

86. PAC, RG 10, vol. 3755, file 30,973, Reed to Commissioner, 18 June 1881; see also material cited in note 72 above. William B. Cameron, *Blood Red the Sun* (Edmonton 1977), 33-61, vividly describes the slaughter at Frog Lake.

87. Cameron, passim

88. Charles Mulvaney, *The History of the North-West Rebellion of 1885* (Toronto 1885), 212-16. *Settlers and Rebels*, 1882 Report, pp 22, 26-7. PAC, RG 10, vol. 3584, file 1130, p. 1, Superintendent Herchmer to Dewdney, 5 Apr. 1885

89. Ibid.

90. PAC, RG 10, vol. 3697, file 15, 446, entire file; vol. 3598, file 1411, entire file; vol. 7768, file 2109-2; vol. 3794, file 46,584

91. PAC, MG 27IC4, vol. 7, letters, Dewdney to White, Mar.–Apr. 1885. This correspondence reveals that in early Apr. Dewdney believed that he had to deal with an Indian uprising. However, he did not admit that this impression was based on scanty and often faulty or false information. By mid-Apr., Dewdney makes clear to White, the NWMP Comptroller, that he did not believe that he was dealing with either an Indian uprising or a rebellion.

92. PAC, MG 27IC4, vol. 1, Dewdney to Begg, 3 May 1885; vol. 4, Dewdney to Middleton, 30 Mar. 1885. RG 10, vol. 3584, file 1130, Dewdney to Ray, 7 May 1885 Jefferson, *Fifty Years on the Saskatchewan*, 128-33

93. PAC, RG 10, vol. 3584, file 1120. Proclamation of 6 May 1885
94. MG 26A, vol. 107, Dewdney to Macdonald, 6 Apr. 1885
95. Morton, *The Last War Drum* 96-110
96. Cameron, *Blood Red the Sun*, 195-204. Sandra Estlin Bingman, 'The Trials of Poundmaker and Big Bear,' *Saskatchewan History*, xxviii (1975), 81-95, gives an account of the conduct of the trials and raises questions about their conduct, particularly the trial of Big Bear. However, Bingman apparently was unaware of Dewdney and Macdonald's efforts to use the courts and whatever other means possible to remove Cree leaders.
97. PAC, MG 26A, vol. 107, Dewdney to Macdonald, 3 June 1885
98. Ibid.
99. Ibid.
100. Bingman, 'The Trials of Poundmaker and Big Bear,' 81-95
101. A very good account of Dewdney's actions to bring the Cree under government control after 1885 is to be found in Jean Lamour, 'Edgar Dewdney and the Aftermath of the Rebellion,' *Saskatchewan History*, xxiii (1970), 105-16. For a discussion of the use of the Indian Act as a means of destroying Indian cultural autonomy see John L. Tobias, 'Protection, Civilization, Assimilation: An Outline History of Canada's Indian Policy,' *The Western Canadian Journal of Anthropology*, vi (1976). For a discussion of specific use of this policy against the Cree, and how the Cree reacted see John L. Tobias, 'Indian Reserves in Western Canada: Indian Homelands or Devices for Assimilation,' in *Approaches to Native History in Canada: Papers of a Conference held at the National Museum of Man, October, 1975*, D.A. Muise, ed. (Ottawa 1977), 89-103.

Topic Four

Canadian Duality: The First Fifty Years

One of Canada's greatest challenges since Confederation has been to maintain unity between English- and French-speaking Canadians. During the immediate pre-Confederation period the future Ontario (Canada West), and the future Quebec (Canada East), had been joined together in the Union of the Canadas. In Canada West two political forces, John A. Macdonald's Conservatives and George Brown's Clear Grits (later to become the Liberals), had fought for power. Macdonald, who worked closely with George Etienne Cartier and the French Canadian Conservatives of Canada East, realized that his Party could only govern the Canadas by respecting the equality of English- and French-speaking Canadians. The Clear Grits, on the other hand, wanted to be free of what several of their leaders called "French domination." They resented the fact that the Conservatives in the legislature of the United Province of Canada had forced upon Canada West, overwhelmingly English-speaking and Protestant, a state-supported Roman Catholic school system, which most of the Canada West members had opposed. To bring about Confederation the Clear Grits had joined a coalition with the Conservatives; however, once it was achieved, they broke away and again insisted on local independence and provincial rights.

After Confederation, the question of duality ceased to be a concern only of the provinces of Ontario and Quebec (the United Canadas). Were the new Canadian provinces to have state-supported schools and dual language rights? New Brunswick and Manitoba became two critical test cases because of the large number (as a percentage of the province's total population) of French Canadians who resided in these two provinces. W.L. Morton in "Confederation, 1870–1896: The End of the Macdonaldian Constitution and the Return of Duality,"examines why Macdonald's original concept of a strong central government, one which would guarantee Canada's cultural duality, was not achieved. In his essay, "Unity/Diversity: The Canadian Experience, From Confederation to World War I," J.R. Miller explains how French Canadians came to reject Macdonald's and Cartier's original conception of what Canada should become. Ironically, in the 1890s they appropriated the Clear Grits' position of the 1860s. Instead of looking to the central government for the protection of their cultural rights — as a result of the linguistic clashes in the late nineteenth and early twentieth centuries — many French Canadians become strong advocates of provincial rights.

The literature on the question of Canadian duality is extensive. Perhaps the most complete overview of the major events in the first half century after Confederation appears in Volume I of Mason Wade's *The French Canadians* (Two volumes; Toronto: Macmillan, 1977). A short lively summary is also presented in Susan Mann Trofimenkoff's *The Dream of Nation: A Social and Intellectual History of Quebec* (Toronto: Gage, 1982), and a more detailed account can be found in P.B. Waite's *Canada 1874–1896: Arduous Destiny* (Toronto: McClelland and Stewart, 1971). The rise of a militant Anglo-Canadian Protestant movement agitating to make Canada into a unilingual country (and the French Canadian response) is contained in J.R. Miller, *Equal Rights: The Jesuits' Estate Act Controversy* (Montreal: McGill-Queen's University Press, 1979). Two of Miller's articles review the ideas and the activities of Dalton McCarthy, regarded as the leading advocate for the assimilation of the French Canadians: "D'Alton McCarthy, Equal Rights, and the Origins of the Manitoba School Question," *Canadian Historical Review*, 54 (December 1973): 369–392; and " 'As a Politician He is a Great Enigma'; The Social and Political Ideas of D'Alton McCarthy," *Canadian Historical Review*, 58 (December 1977): 399–422. The French-Canadian's changing outlook toward Confederation is presented by A.I. Silver in *The French-Canadian Idea of Confederation, 1864–1900* (Toronto: University of Toronto Press, 1982). Joseph Levitt reviews the ideas of Henri Bourassa, the important French Canadian spokesman, in *Henri Bourassa on Imperialism and Bi-culturalism, 1900–1918* (Toronto: Copp Clark, 1970). Ramsay Cook reviews the idea of Confederation as a compact of provinces or cultures in *Provincial Autonomy: Minority Rights and the Compact Theory, 1867–1921* (Ottawa: Queen's Printer, 1969).

129

Considerable attention has been given by historians to the rights of the French language in western Canada. Donald Creighton has argued that John A. Macdonald did not wish to protect French in Manitoba and the North West in "John A. Macdonald, Confederation and the Canadian West," *Historical and Scientific Society of Manitoba*, series 3, no. 23 (1966/67), and reprinted in D. Creighton, *Towards the Discovery of Canada: Selected Essays* (Toronto: Macmillan, 1972), pp. 229–237. Ralph Heintzman takes the contrary view in "The Spirit of Confederation: Professor Creighton, Biculturalism, and the Use of History," *Canadian Historical Review*, 52 (September 1971): 245–275. D.J. Hall enters into the debate, essentially on Professor Creighton's side in " 'The Spirit of Confederation': Ralph Heintzman, Professor Creighton and the Bicultural Theory," *Journal of Canadian Studies*, 9 (November 1974): 24–43. For specific information on the major issue of the Manitoba Schools Question in the 1890s, consult Lovell Clark, ed., *The Manitoba School Question: Majority Rule or Minority Rights?*

(Toronto: Copp Clark, 1968), and Paul Crunican, *Priests and Politicians*: *Manitoba Schools and the Election of 1896* (Toronto: University of Toronto Press, 1974). Cornelius Jaenen has completed a review of the language question in "The history of French in Manitoba: local initiative or external imposition?" *Language and Society*, no. 13 (Spring, 1984): 3–16.

Confederation, 1870–1896: The End of the Macdonaldian Constitution and the Return to Duality[1]*

W.L. MORTON

130

I

The Macdonaldian concept of the constitution was a compromise between what Macdonald, the British governors, and the Colonial Office had favoured, a legislative union under one government and one Parliament, and what was in fact necessary. That, as all but the most unrealistic admitted, was some acceptance of the federal principle.

Once this need was accepted, however, American example became relevant. And American example during the years of Confederation and the Civil War was that a central government insufficiently strong led to disruption and civil war. Any federation of British North America must therefore have a strong central government.[2]

A federation so like a legislative union Macdonald could accept, for he could hope that the same forces, the needs of defence and development, which had produced a confederation would continue to strengthen the central power. Cardwell, the colonial secretary, could accept it with good conscience as the best arrangement possible for the setting up of a practically independent state at a time when England proposed to withdraw from the St. Lawrence valley. The defenders of local powers, if they did not reject it, as Prince Edward Island did, could give reluctant assent because at least the principle was admitted of the existence in one system of both central and local powers. Like Macdonald, they too could hope for the future development of the constitution being favourable to their views.

The Confederation of 1870, then, was an extremely intricate and subtly poised combination of powers. Like the American Constitution after 1865, it rested on the explicit subordination of local powers to central, of the state, and of the province, to the nation. Unlike the American, which enjoyed the enormous advantage of having had the fundamentals on which it rested clari-

*From *Journal of Canadian Studies*, 1 (May 1966): 11-23. Reprinted by permission of Mrs. W.L. Morton.

fied by revolution, it did not rest on the principle of popular sovereignty. On the contrary, it rested on the traditional concept of allegiance to the Crown in which was vested the right and power to govern. The monarchical and imperial constitution of the United Kingdom was to be used for national ends in the Dominion of Canada. Yet, since the Crown was that of a constitutional and parliamentary monarchy, Confederation combined the legal authority of the Crown with the democratic power of the people. The Crown was meant to be, then, the centralizing element in the Confederation, and its principal government, the central one, was given all the great powers of government, with the former imperial powers to disallow provincial legislation, and to appoint provincial governors who were to correspond with Ottawa alone. To this was added the general power to legislate for "the peace, order, and good government of Canada." As if to stress its supremacy, the central legislature was given the power to tax "by any mode or system of taxation."

In contrast, the powers given to the provinces were merely local and private in nature; the powers of taxation were limited to the little used direct taxation of the day. The provinces were not, in fact, expected to be self-supporting as they were not thought sovereign even in their spheres of exclusive jurisdiction. They were subordinate governments in both appearance and in fact. They had no great tasks to perform and were given no great powers. *131*

Thus Confederation in its Macdonaldian conception was a strongly centralized government which made no more provision for local government than was necessary to obtain assent to Confederation from the colonial legislatures. The old colonies and new provinces were not, it is true, to be municipalities, but neither were they to be states. They were, perhaps, to be provinces like those of the New Zealand constitution of 1852, or even bodies like the English counties after 1888. Such subordination, it was hoped, would prove acceptable in the general expansion and prosperity which, it was also hoped, Confederation would bring.

The former was a hope, but it would be unjust to infer that it was a delusive hope. Macdonald, Galt, Cartier, Brown—all who accepted the Quebec Resolutions and even more those who, unlike Brown, accepted the Westminster Resolutions, knew how delicate were the compromises, how thin the paper over the cracks, of this constitution, at once traditional and innovating. One delicate subject was education, for example, which in Canada as in the United Kingdom meant religion also. An attempt had been made at Westminster to extend the Canadian compromise of separate schools to the whole Dominion in Section 93 of the *B.N.A. Act*. But the section did not make the Catholic schools of the other provinces separate; it guaranteed them only if they were established "by law" at the time of union, or established thereafter.

Another such subject was language, and the only language at issue then was French, which was necessarily involved with both religion and education. By the *B.N.A. Act* it was recognized only in the Province of Quebec, and the federal Parliament and courts. But denominational schools carried with them teaching in French as a matter of usage, and were thus a matter of language as well as religion in the Acadian districts of New Brunswick, the French settlements of Ontario, and later in Manitoba.

Confederation had the effect of creating the belief that the French province of Quebec had secured self-government in local and cultural matters, and that elsewhere the Roman Catholic religion and the French language were secured by the guarantee of separate schools in Section 93 of the *B.N.A. Act* of 1867.

That belief had, after all, been laid down by Cartier, who had declared emphatically: "Under this system of federation which places in the hands of the Central Government all matters of general interest, and to whom questions of race will be indifferent, religious or national rights will not be ignored."[3] The duality of French and English in United Canada was at once politically absorbed and culturally guaranteed in Confederation. It was the shattering of this delusion that by 1896 had made Quebec adhere to provincial rights secured by a federal system of coordinate powers and reject a national guarantee of cultural rights secured by the central government.[4]

And finally there was the matter, undefined but powerful, of local democracy. Two of the provinces, Nova Scotia and New Brunswick, were former self-governing colonies now diminished in power and stature and made subordinate to a government in majority Canadian. And Quebec had accepted a minority position in Confederation in return for local self-government at home. How could the question of the extent and powers of provincial government fail to arise?

For the moment, however, the Hercules who had carried Confederation seemed to have silenced these Hydra heads beneath the rock of the new Confederation. There they hoped they would remain securely buried, but they were not at all unaware that the heads were likely all to prove immortal.

II

Such were the basic elements of Confederation — a union that was imperial rather than federal, one that deliberately avoided American example, that required the most exquisite observance of practical religious toleration, that committed the national Parliament to the maintenance of separate schools; a union that left local matters, including education, and the language of instruction, to provincial jurisdiction.

That union meant, moreover, for Canada, division; for the other British North American colonies, diminished powers and subordination; for the united colonies expansion as the Dominion of Canada. Expansion was to reveal, however, that there was a French element outside Quebec: the *métis* of Red River. That fact was to introduce in another province of the Dominion the principle of ethnic duality, the duality that had been recognized in Quebec, and guaranteed by the national government, although on doubtful legal grounds and by implication with respect to language, in New Brunswick and Nova Scotia.

It was better, in the circumstances, to treat with Riel in the winter of 1869–70 than to fight with him in the summer of 1870. Out of those very tortuous and hurried negotiations came that curious result, the *Manitoba Act*. By that measure the Dominion acquired a new province, one not very much wanted by anyone and kept almost ludicrously small. It was only small territorially, however; in principle it was enormous, for it was in fact a little Quebec on Red River. It was bilingual; it had a dual system of confessional schools; it possessed a legislative council, like Quebec and unlike Ontario. It might even have adopted, had its legislature chosen, the Quebec civil code as its civil law. Thus the principle of duality, restricted to Quebec in old Canada, had reappeared in the West in the first province created by the Dominion.[5]

133

III

The *Manitoba Act* and the establishment of duality in the West did not affect the constitution of Confederation, except with respect to representation and that only temporarily. The West as far as the Rockies had merely been opened to settlement by both of the Canadian cultures. One other event did, however, like a puff of wind through curtains, reveal all the possibilities of constitutional change. That event was the *New Brunswick School Act* of 1871. It did so because it brought into the open one of the concealed contradictions of the B.N.A. Act of 1867. United Canada had developed two systems of public schools, schools supported by local taxes and open to all children up to the eighth grade. Each section had developed its own system, Quebec a denominational system of Catholic and Protestant schools, Ontario one of public schools with provision for separate schools. As long as the Union continued, the confessional minority of each section was in effect guaranteed by the confessional majority of the other. With Confederation each would pass under the jurisdiction of a majority to be given control of education in each of the two provinces. The question of how to preserve the former guarantee nearly wrecked the Confederation scheme in the last session of the Parliament of the old province of Canada. In consequence a guarantee of minority educational rights as they existed at the Union, or as they might be created thereafter, was devised, to become Section 93 of the B.N.A. Act. And at the Westminster Conference of 1866, as a result of the powerful lobbying of Archbishop Thomas Connolly of Halifax, who had done so much to carry Confederation in the Maritimes, the guarantee was extended to cover minority educational rights in all provinces of the Union. At the insistence of Alexander Galt, the representative of the Quebec Protestants, however, the right was qualified with the words, "by law". There can be no doubt, legally speaking, that this term defeated Connolly's purpose, as he himself thought, although Hector Langevin all too optimistically did not.[6]

The *New Brunswick School Act* of 1871 disrupted the situation glossed over by the *B. N. A. Act* of 1867 by establishing a system of tax-supported free and non-sectarian schools. Henceforth there were to be no grants made and no taxes paid to schools in which there was denominational teaching. As a result what the Roman Catholics of New Brunswick had in practice, state-supported denominational schools, were abolished despite the supposed guarantee of the *B. N. A. Act*. Moreover, as so often in Canada, the matter was not merely one of denominational teaching. Many of the Catholics of New Brunswick were Irish by nationality. But many were Acadian French. Their schools were therefore not only denominational; they were also French in language. Now education was to be non-sectarian, in English, and from textbooks prescribed by the province.

The *Act* therefore precipitated a contest which was, by implication at least, one of major constitutional significance. Certainly, it was of the first importance politically. Politics in Quebec revolved around the question for four years, and nothing in his last years gave more concern to Cartier. The province by Section 92 of the *B. N. A. Act* had control of education in the province. But a religious minority under Section 93 was guaranteed the possession of any right it had by law at the time of union (or that it might acquire thereafter). What rights, then, had the Roman Catholic minority of New Brunswick as against the new school act?

The answer came quickly when they requested the central government to disallow the measure under the powers given by the *B. N. A. Act*. The Minister of Justice, Prime Minister Sir John Macdonald, found that the act was within the competence of the provincial legislature, as Roman Catholics had lost no rights they had by law at the Union, or had acquired since.[7] There was no reason for disallowance, or for remedial action under Section 93. The opinion was to be upheld by the law officers of the United Kingdom and by the Judicial Committee.

For four years, however, a struggle against this decision was kept up by John Costigan, Irish Catholic member for Gloucester, a county of New Brunswick which was at least half Acadian. Costigan was supported by Timothy Anglin, also an Irish Catholic, and the member for Victoria, which was in the majority Acadian.[8] Even more significant was the steady and concerted support which they received from French Catholic members from Quebec. The nature of the support reveals how the school question, always nominally religious, was also usually, as in this instance, linguistic and cultural as well.

It was not the only support they received, of course; some came from English Protestants, and not only from Quebec. The question was in fact one of general interest as well as one of strong concern to Roman Catholics. It was so because it opened, in one of the most sensitive regions of Canadian life, the question of just what kind of constitution Canada had. And the debates on the question in the federal parliament raised all the issues that were settled by 1896, sectarian belief, local interest, Grit democracy.[9]

IV

The debates in Parliament began when in the spring of 1872 Auguste Renaud, the only Acadian member of the House of Commons, moved for the correspondence on the *New Brunswick School Act*. Macdonald defended his action in recommending that the act should not be disallowed. "It was known to everyone," he declared, "that the question of education had threatened Confederation at its very inception, and a proposition that education should be left to the General Legislature of the Dominion would have been enough to secure the repudiation of Confederation by the people of Lower Canada." The only grounds for disallowance, he said, were unconstitutionality or the detriment of the general interests of the Dominion. Neither ground existed in the present case. The federal power could not on other grounds be used to over-ride the powers given to the provinces, as was the control of education. "The constitution which had hitherto worked so easily and so well, could not survive the wrench that would be given if the Dominion Government assumed to dictate the policy or question the action of the Legislatures of the different Provinces on the subjects reserved by the *B.N.A. Act* to those Legislatures."[10]

135

This stand by the chief maker of the *B.N.A. Act* is surprising. It is to be explained by the fact that he had made his bargain with those who had insisted on a federation rather than a legislative union. By keeping that bargain he would help that growth of a sense of national union and general interest on which he counted. To use the central power in a clear case of provincial jurisdiction would hinder the growth for which he hoped. Cartier fully supported Macdonald. The Catholics of New Brunswick must get redress by political action within the province. But J. H. Bellerose, a Quebec member and an ultramontanist, protested that it was understood when the *Confederation Act* was passed that the rights of minorities in matters of education would be preserved.[11] The issue of the use of national power to defend minority rights against a provincial majority was clearly drawn.

The trouble was that in law there were no minority educational rights in New Brunswick. The next move by its opponents was a motion by Costigan requesting the government to disallow the *Act*, which was still possible as a month remained of the year following the passage of an *Act* during which disallowance was possible. The motion provoked an even stronger statement of the government's position from Cartier. The effect of disallowance, he asserted, would be to place the fate of the Roman Catholics of Canada in the hands of the Protestant majority. "The question of education rested entirely with the Local Legislature . . ." This he had insisted on when Confederation was formed; only existing legal rights were to be guaranteed. Again came a protest from a Quebec member, this time from the Rouge Leader, A. A. Dorion, who justly pointed out that ". . .the spirit of the Act of Confederation was to maintain all rights enjoyed at the time of the Union . . .", whether embodied in law or not.[12]

The debate waned to an anti-climax when J. H. Gray of St. John, moved in amendment that the *School Act* was constitutional, and P. J. O. Chauveau of Quebec in sub-amendment that the Queen be requested to use her influence on the government of New Brunswick.[13] The debate yielded little further light. Joly of Quebec, in support of the motion, declared in pregnant terms that "There might be national unity, but religious unity was impossible."[14] The amendment and sub-amendment were defeated, and then on May 29, an amendment by C. C. Colby of Quebec was carried. It was only an expression of regret by the House at a seeming injustice caused by the *Act*. More to the point was Alexander Mackenzie's motion, accepted with relief by the government, that the Dominion aid an appeal to the law officers of the United Kingdom and to the Judicial Committee of the Privy Council.[15]

The *New Brunswick School Act* had thus revealed the flaw in the *B.N.A. Act*, always known to those like Cartier, Langevin and Galt, that it had guaranteed no right in separate schools not established by provincial law. It had put Macdonald, the great centralizer of 1867, in the position of an unyielding defender of provincial powers. The deathless heads of sectarian belief and local rights were still writhing under the stones of the *B.N.A. Act*.

136

In 1873 the question arose once more with a motion by Honoré Mercier for correspondence following the resolution of 1872, and by an amendment to the motion to go into supply by Costigan, in which he asked for disallowance of the now amended *New Brunswick School Act*. Macdonald in debate said frankly that he regretted that the Quebec system had not been extended to New Brunswick. He himself had favoured a legislative union for Confederation, but a federal one had proved necessary, and must now be maintained as such. For ". . .the moment there was any attempt to coerce New Brunswick all hope for the Catholic minority was gone." To Macdonald thus speaking as the future Laurier, L. F. R. Masson replied that the Dominion Government must stand in the same over-riding relation to the local government as the imperial did to the Dominion. The *Act* should therefore be disallowed. He spoke as a supporter of Riel and the *Manitoba Act* in which the federal power had been used to create a denominational school system. It is interesting, and not wholly ironical, to see a Quebec ultramontanist demanding that the federal government be imperial and paramount. The ultramontanes were down to 1896 prepared to invoke the federal power to maintain the educational rights of minorities. Masson, however, failed to carry the support of his fellow French Canadians. Hector Langevin, for example, urged an appeal to the Privy Council, Dorion to the powers of remedial legislation in Section 93 of the *B.N.A. Act*. Each relied on the use of established procedures, without an explicit assertion of paramountcy by the central government. Then, despite Smith of Westmoreland's claim that New Brunswick was within its rights, and must not be interfered with, or Confederation would be a sham, Costigan's amendment was carried, Macdonald voting with the nays against most of his Quebec supporters.[16]

The law officers of the United Kingdom had already upheld Macdonald's opinion of the inadvisability of disallowance, and now did so again on this second reference. The appeal to the Judicial Committee, which was paid for by the central government, in turn upheld the validity of the *New Brunswick Act*.[17] The debates of 1874 are therefore silent on the subject except for a motion by Costigan for an address to the Imperial Government for an amendment to do what had been intended in 1867, he alleged, to provide for separate schools in New Brunswick. He, however, withdrew this logical, but daring, motion.[18]

Nevertheless in 1875 he made the motion again, and by doing so precipitated the most revealing of the debates on the underlying question of the nature and extent of central and local, federal and provincial powers, in Canada.[19] Appleby of Carleton strongly opposed the motion as an indefensible invasion of provincial powers. These, he declared, were absolute and could not be over-ridden. "He would lay down this principle that the Local Legislatures of this country on all subjects which came within their exclusive power, had equally with the Parliament of Canada, the quality of omnipotence."[20] Here was the language of the Judicial Committee in *Liquidators of the Maritime Bank vs. the Receiver-General of New Brunswick* in 1892, the declaration that the provinces were as sovereign in the exercise of their exclusive powers as the Dominion, or the Imperial governments, were in theirs.[21]

It was also the language of Edward Palmer in the debates of the Quebec Conference. Something of the sources of such thought was indicated by the member for Welland, W. A. Thomson, economist and author. "His political creed had always been Popular Sovereignty. He had given a good deal of study to the history of the United States during the last thirty or forty years, and that had led him to the belief that the only safety for the perpetuation of the institution of the United States was state sovereignty." This view the unreconstructed Mr. Thomson had upheld during the formation of Confederation, and still did.[22]

Cranky and a trifle archaic Thomson's views might be, but in substance they were held by most speakers. A. L. Palmer of St. John declared that, "The harmony of this Dominion, and the future working of the constitution depended on the strict observance of the powers conferred on each legislative body . . ."[23] And Mackenzie Bowell, one day to be prime minister in similar circumstances, opposed the motion on the ground that it would be improper for the House of Commons to do anything to interfere with the powers of the provincial legislature.[24] As Macdonald had already, he would have to reverse his views when faced with the conflict of local, general and sectarian interests of Canadian politics.

Costigan's motion was of course defeated; it was probably meant to embarrass the Liberals in the northern counties of New Brunswick by forcing a statement of their views on what were to be called "provincial rights." Amended to ask only to request the Queen to use her influence in New Brunswick, it was carried to no purpose.[25] The *New Brunswick School Act* had continued in operation, enforced on one occasion in early 1875 by the use of the militia.[26] Prompted perhaps by that outburst and its repression,

137

the government and the Roman Catholic Church reached in the same year a *modus vivendi* with respect to the question of the teaching of religion in the schools. With respect to the use of French in the schools, however, nothing was formally attempted until 1928, when even then the matter had to be dropped because of objection from English and Protestant opinion.[27]

The New Brunswick School Question had ceased to be a national political issue in a mere four years. Yet it was of first importance in the development of the Macdonaldian concept of the constitution. It had seen in the early years of its formation a seeming repudiation of the national character of that constitution by both Macdonald and Cartier. Those two astute politicians would not have taken that stand unless they both felt bound by the compromise between national and local interests on which Confederation rested, and by the threat of a conflict of national and provincial interests which in the circumstances would harm the cause of the national constitution. Cartier in particular was troubled by the question in Quebec. It was in many ways the chief issue in that province in the general election of 1872, and a powerful factor in Cartier's personal defeat in Montreal East. In Quebec indeed the question began that cleavage between Cartier's Bleus and clerical conservatism that was to aid the growth of the Rouge party, and prepare the cornerstone in Quebec of the dominance of the Liberal party in power in Canada after 1896. Most of all it forced on Quebec the choice between reliance on the national government for defence of minority rights in education, carrying with them in practice the use of the French language in French districts, or a reliance on the self-government of Quebec to preserve the French language and Roman Catholic schools in that province, if need be alone. In short, the trend towards provincial rights and the return to the institutionalized duality of the period of the *Act of Union* had begun.

V

Nothing so clear-cut was of course apparent in 1875. All the School Question had done was to make it clear how difficult it was to provide a general government, based on the principles of constitutional monarchy in a democracy, for communities as diverse within and among themselves as were those of Canada. The difficulty was now to be further illustrated by the history of temperance legislation in Canada between 1878 and 1896.

In 1878 the *Scott Act* became law for the whole Dominion. It thus extended legislation hitherto confined to Ontario to all the other provinces. It also bestowed the powers of local option on counties and cities, that is, on larger units than had the *Dunkin Act*. Finally, it tried to distinguish between the retail sale of liquor, which could be forbidden and the wholesale distribution of liquor which remained lawful for export and sale in those parts of the country not under local option: it refrained, of course, from trenching upon the provincial power to license taverns, etc., for the raising of a revenue. The *Act*, like Confederation itself, was a masterpiece of legal ingenuity. Its provisions were to come into operation only by a vote in a county or a city. Yet it was a Dominion statute based on the power to legislate for the peace, order and good government of Canada, and to regulate trade and commerce. A vast federal creation, it floated like a cloud castle over the country, but came to earth only in those parts of the land where a majority of the inhabitants called for it. Here perhaps was a piece of legislation which would, unlike the *B.N.A. Act* of 1867 in the instance of the *New Brunswick School Act*, uphold the exercise of a local democracy in the general interests of the Dominion.

At first it seemed that it might be so. Then in a bare three years, a gentleman of the name of Charles Russell of the city of Fredericton, New Brunswick, was fined in magistrate's court for selling intoxicating liquors contrary to the second part of the *Canada Temperance Act*. The Supreme Court of New Brunswick, and the Supreme Court of Canada had upheld the magistrate. Mr. Russell, presumably a publican of some wealth, and clearly a man of some determination, then carried his case to the Judicial Committee. That distinguished body, still the highest court of appeal for Canadian civil cases, also upheld the constitutionality of the *Temperance Act*, in perhaps the most famous of its Canadian decisions, *Russell vs. Regina*, 1882.[28] The power of the federal parliament to legislate in the general interest of the Dominion was vindicated and the Macdonaldian constitution was confirmed and reached the height of its growth.

139

VI

It was very natural to put the utmost interpretation on the decision in *Russell vs. Regina* in 1882. The whole Macdonaldian concept of Confederation was in full flower. The depression of the 1870s was behind, and prosperity had returned. The government of Mackenzie, prudent and penurious, had been defeated in 1878. The National Policy with the protective tariff of 1879 had freed Canadian industry from the fear of American and British dumping, and indeed of competition. The policy of building the Pacific Railway piecemeal as a public work and as the revenue of the country permitted, had been replaced by construction as a whole with all possible speed by a private company with government aid. The railway had linked Fort William with Winnipeg, and from the prairies and the Pacific was driving westward and eastward towards a junction in the Rockies. Even immigration was growing, as British farmers, at long last feeling the consequences of the abolition of the Corn Law, moved onto the fertile lands of the prairies. The development of the vast territories so recently united was going forward under Dominion powers and with federal support.

The new sweep of federal power and national prosperity had not, however, caused the provinces to wither away, or ended the strength of local sentiment in Canadian democracy. The next decade was to hear and see asserted in Canada and in London the new doctrine of "provincial rights."[29] The former colonies had not been abolished, or recreated, by Confederation. They had been united in Confederation, with diminished powers, but still with the essentials of responsible government, the Crown, the cabinet, and the legislature. There had come into being a tribe of provincial politicians who had not known Joseph and who sought, both for the sake of personal advancement and to serve their communities, to defend and add to provincial powers. And they were aided fortuitously by a curious paralleling of events. These were the return of depression in 1883, and the wish of the Judicial Committee to clarify the *B.N.A. Act* so as to make it a federal document as clear in federal principle as that of the United States. To this odd coupling of bad times and bad law, Judah B. Benjamin, late Attorney-General of the Confederate States of America and practising law in his London exile, was a macabre hedge priest. They were to be aided also by certain repercussions of the building of the Pacific Railway and the onset of depression in the West, the Saskatchewan Rebellion and the chartering of railways by the Province of Manitoba in defiance of the charter of the Canadian Pacific Railway.

140   The new trend towards provincial rights and the "federalisation" of the *B.N.A. Act* began innocently enough with the conviction by Magistrate G. T. Denison of a tavern keeper, Mr. Archibald G. Hodge, for having added a billiard room and table to the St. James Hotel on York Street, Toronto. The basis of the conviction was the *Ontario Licensing Act* of 1877. Hodge appealed on the ground that that Act was beyond the powers of the province. The appeal was refused in the Queen's Bench of Ontario, but upheld by the Ontario Court of Appeal. It was also upheld by the Judicial Committee of the Privy Council. *Russell vs. Regina*, it declared, was founded on the federal powers of Section 91, but these did not diminish or impair those of the provinces in Section 92. Nor were the provincial legislatures to be limited in the use of their powers. They had . . . "authority as plenary and as ample within the limits prescribed by Section 92 as the Imperial Parliament in the amplitude of its power possessed and could bestow. Within these limits of subjects and areas," the judgment continues, "the local legislature is supreme, and has the same authority as has the Imperial Parliament, or the Parliament of the Dominion, would have had under the circumstances . . ."[30] One can only hope that Mr. Appleby read this majestic confirmation of his oratory of 1872.

On Mr. Hodge's billiard table, then, the Macdonaldian concept of Confederation was baulked. The case was the point of turning away from the belief that in Parliament lay a general power which might in the national interest be used to legislate for the whole Dominion. From that point it was, legally speaking, only a step to the case of *Liquidators of the Maritime Bank vs. the Receiver-General of New Brunswick* of 1892. In that the Judicial Committee declared: "The object of the *B.N.A. Act* was neither to weld the provinces into one, nor to subordinate the provincial governments to a central one, but to create a federal government in which they should all be represented, entrusted with the exclusive administration of affairs in which they had a common interest, each province retaining its independence and autonomy." They, moreover, possessed, "powers, not of administration only, but of legislation, in the strictest sense of that word; and within the limits of Section 92 of the *Act* of 1867, these powers are exclusive and supreme."[31] The provinces, then, possessed powers not subordinate to, but co-ordinate with those of the Dominion, powers as sovereign in their spheres as it was in its own.

Any embarrassment that *Russell vs. Regina* might create was removed in the Local Prohibition Case of 1896. The Lords of the Privy Council neatly removed it from practical consideration by holding that the *Canada Prohibition Act* of 1886[32] rested only on the peace, order and good government clause of Section 91 and not on the power to regulate trade and commerce, thus reducing the former to the character of an emergency power.[33] The Macdonaldian concept of Confederation was ended in the law courts; and the premonitions of the *New Brunswick School Act* debates were firm law. And the judicial verdict was echoed in the political debates that marked the ending, also in 1896, of the controversy over the *Manitoba School Act* of 1890.

141

VII

That controversy reached its climax in the great debate, which became a filibuster, on Tupper's motion of March 3, 1896 for the second reading of the Remedial Bill to right the wrongs suffered by the Roman Catholics of Manitoba. Most of what was said had already been uttered in debate since 1892, especially in the debates of the session of 1893. Much was repetitious and political by-play within the debate itself. The real interest at the time lay in the forthcoming election. The main interest now lies in the statements of the Liberal opposition which spelled out the political constitutional theory which parallelled and confirmed the judicial interpretation of the constitution consummated by the Judicial Committee in the Local Prohibition Case of the same year.

Two Liberal voices may be cited as the clearest spoken examples of the constitutional position that the Manitoba School Question had brought to a head. One was the silver voice of Laurier, whose understanding of the constitution was as comprehensive as Macdonald's, although antithetic to it. The other was the ponderous voice of David Mills, the school inspector-lawyer expert of his party on constitutional matters. Laurier, having on March 3 moved in amendment that the Bill be given the six month's hoist, dealt with the awkward and undoubted power of the Dominion Parliament to pass remedial legislation, when a religious minority had demonstrated it had a grievance to remedy in matters of education. The power of disallowance, he said, was based on the Imperial power of vetoing and supervising colonial legislation. "This," he went on, "may be easily understood because colonies are dependencies. But the relations between the Dominion and the provinces are not the same. Between these there is no superiority and no inferiority; all are equal, with this exception, that the Dominion Parliament is invested with larger powers, that is, powers of a more extended and more important character than the local legislature.'' This, of course, is the doctrine of co-ordinate powers, with which there could be no paramountcy. But why should there be two sets of co-ordinate powers, why should provincial rights be as sovereign as federal powers? Laurier's answer is both curious and illuminating, because in making it he slipped from the legal to the political. ''Indeed,'' he went on at once, ''it must be accepted, and accepted as a truism, that under popular government the majority must rule,''[35] must rule, that is, in its exclusive jurisdiction in a federal system. This was Grit democracy speaking the language of the electoral mandate, not that of parliamentary authority.

It is not necessary to follow Laurier to his conclusion that the overriding powers of the constitution had been an error, and that now ''the power of interference . . . must be applied in such a way as not to provoke irritation . . .''

It is sufficient to note that, except with its explicit powers, the federal government and Parliament were powerless in the face of a provincial majority; a national majority in matters not explicitly federal had ceased to exist, except one must suppose, in emergency.

Thus was the Laurierian constitution proclaimed, the constitution as it was to be down to 1926.

The nails were now to be driven into the coffin of the Macdonaldian constitution by David Mills. Heavy, humourless and honest, Mills was the intellectual embodiment of that strain of Grit ideology which, held at bay by Macdonald at Confederation, by the creeks and inlets of provincial life had come flooding in during the post-Confederation generation. Facing on March 18 the same question as Laurier, how were the undoubted remedial powers of Parliament to be exercised, he was much more forthright and more profound. In using those powers, he warned, Parliament was not to treat the local legislatures as inferiors or with contempt. ''They are bound,'' he affirmed, ''to deal with the local legislature and government in this matter precisely as one state would deal with another. The whole of this proceeding from beginning to end is diplomatic in character, and there is a mode of procedure marked out in the law and each step must be taken in its turn''[37] — not necessarily a diplomatic procedure, one is bound to remark.

The massive Mills, however, ploughed on in his course like the Victorian ironclad he was. Of rigid intellectual honesty, he declined to take Laurier's course on the soft turf of political democracy; he stuck to the granite path of the law. ''The Federal Parliament and the Federal Administration,'' he asserted unequivocally, ''have their rights, duties and responsibilities under the constitution. These have been bestowed for general and for special purposes, for the peace, order and good government of Canada, and are not less entitled to be respected than those which, by the same instrument, are conferred on the provinces.''

Mills spoke as a declared federalist, and did not intend the seeming condescension implied when he placed federal powers on the same level as provincial powers. But having given the federal powers their due, he had also to define those of the provinces. This, with the same unbending honesty, he did in terms of "provincial rights." "What," he asked, "is meant by the doctrine of provincial rights in its true constitutional sense? Not rights beyond the law, but rights in conformity to the law, fairly and properly interpreted. It is this — that within the sphere of government and legislation assigned to the exclusive jurisdiction of the province the principle of parliamentary government shall be preserved, and the responsibility of the provincial ministry to the legislature, and of the legislature to the electorate of the province, shall not be interfered with. Within its own exclusive sphere it shall be sovereign. This is what I understand by provincial rights, and it is a constitutional doctrine of great importance in our federal system, for upon this doctrine rests the security of the provincial legislatures and government against federal encroachments."[38]

This was the end of the Macdonaldian constitution, the calm assertion that a national majority might not "encroach upon" or "coerce" a provincial government in its exclusive jurisdiction. It was the end of Macdonald's hope that in the growth of Confederation a national spirit might develop which would give the national government and parliament the practical power, and when not power, then the influence, to legislate when called in the national interest to do so by public opinion, for the peace, order and good government of Canada. It is of no avail now to protest that provincial rights may be minority, or national, wrongs. It was of no avail then to use weasel words with Tupper, and claim that Mills had substantiated the position of the government and justified remedial action as the remaining exception in an otherwise federal system.[39] Mills had ponderously capped the work of King of New Brunswick, Mowat of Ontario, and Greenway of Manitoba; of the Judicial Committee and Judah B. Benjamin, and affirmed that the constitution of Canada was all but a purely federal one in law, and practically should be applied as though it were.

143

VIII

Why such an outcome? And why did the two different and separate currents of political conflict and judicial interpretation which ran through this period move to the same conclusion of co-ordinate sovereignties in a federal system? Why did Macdonald's concept of a central government and a judicious paramountcy in all matters of national concern fail to become the dominant idea of the Canadian Confederation?

It is suggested in answer here that there were two chief reasons, one a failure of Macdonald conservatism, one a success of Grit democracy. The former was that the peace, order and good government clause was at once too sweeping and too imprecise to serve as the basis for a central, national government in all matters not strictly local and exclusive to the provinces, except in the most fortunate of economic and national circumstances. The Macdonaldian constitution rested on the hope that territorial expansion and national prosperity would allow a central government by Parliament to be come a national agent to which the provinces would be habitually and willingly subordinate. The frictions caused by national expansion and the failure to achieve national prosperity before 1896 led to a process of political conflict and judicial refinement in which the lawyers created, out of an imperial system remade for national purposes, a federal system of co-ordinate sovereignties based on popular sovereignty.

The triumph of Grit democracy was aided by the same factors of economic distress and the failure of the national ideal to flourish. Yet it was a powerful force in itself, and as such bound to affect the development of the constitution. By a process going back to the use of the historic county franchise and the grant of the vote to Roman Catholics in Canada in 1791 and in Nova Scotia in 1823, Canadian democracy was from the first widely extended, and representation in the colonial legislatures was widely popular. The democratic element in Canadian politics was always stronger than any other, including allegiance to the Crown. Under Grit influence after 1867 it was led to see the constitution as something based on popular will in both central and local jurisdiction, and that those jurisdictions were therefore equal and co-ordinate. Under Grit leadership in the provinces also Canadian democracy failed to become national; it remained what it had always tended to be, sectarian and local. And the lawyers, by recognizing the Crown in the provinces, gave a constitutional halo to the democratic image. Even the Crown became local, and failed to achieve the exclusive national role which Macdonald had hoped for it.

This (the monarchical idea) was the Canadian equivalent of the American "We the people" and "the supreme law" of the land. It carried with it the principle of centrality and paramountcy. But the monarchy in Canada was an idea and an ideal, at bottom the lawyer's abstraction of the Crown, a convention and a legal fiction. American democracy was a warm and living thing, and it was to make the American constitution such. But Canadian democracy, no less real than American, was not to be led to make the Confederation of 1867 a real and living thing as a monarchial form of government popularly inspired. Led by Grit democracy operating in the soreness of hard times, it was to insist on local independence and provincial rights. And in these circumstances the lawyers, set the intriguing problem of monarchial sovereignty operating in a federal system, used the fiction of the Crown to dissect the living organism of 1867 into two sets of co-ordinate sovereignties, equal in their various exclusive jurisdictions.

Thus the idea of centrality and paramountcy was reduced to that of a mere emergency power. A national majority could not operate in Canada except within the limits of the listed powers of Section 91, or in wartime.

Such was the curious outcome of the Macdonaldian attempt to use the constitution of the Empire for national ends. It is even difficult now, particularly in the light of his own stand on the *New Brunswick School Act*, to see how he could have hoped that it might succeed. Yet, if one recalls the circumstances of Confederation, and of Canada in the Empire and America at the time of Confederation, one can see that the shapers of the Canadian constitution had little choice except to use British institutions and conventions, and to accept the moral of the American Civil War, that states rights could lead to the disruption of a federal system. The explanation of the outcome of the replacement of the Macdonaldian constitution with its provision for an overriding national interest, by the Laurierian constitution of the co-ordinate powers of a Canadian federal system, is to be found in the failure of expansion and economic growth to give the new constitution a full tide for its launching, in the natural affinity of Grit democracy for local interests and provincial rights, and in the divisibility of the Crown among legislatures enjoying responsible government. Economic depression, Grit doctrinairism, and judicial legalism, had undone the hopes of 1867.

That explanation may explain; it does not justify. The destruction of the Macdonaldian constitution was surely a failure by Canadian politicians and British lawyers to grasp what had happened in the 1860s, that Britain in withdrawing her military power from North America had left behind a new state governed by British parliamentary institutions and not an American federal system, and that in the Civil War the American federal system had been destroyed and replaced by one essentially national. The Macdonaldian concept of Confederation was rejected as though the British Empire had never existed, and as though the American Civil War had never been fought.

The result was to make Quebec rely, not on national guarantees but on provincial rights, to safeguard the concern of French Canadians with religion and language. The duality of the Canadian Union, submerged and diffused in Confederation, re-appeared anew, armed with provincial powers, ingrowing and separatist in temper and in Quebec committed to a reliance on one party which has ever since thrust into Canadian politics the possibility of an English "backlash." And by a supreme irony the province, the interests of which would have benefited most by the carrying of remedial action, gave the Liberal party in the election of 1896 the victory which it failed to gain in English Canada. Quebec voted for provincial rights in a federal system by a majority of thirty-three; English Canada gave the Conservatives a majority of three over the Liberals, on the face of it for remedial action and justice to minorities in a national federation.

The result was that the Quebec reliance on provincial rights, itself the outcome of the failure before 1896 to maintain the Macdonaldian hope of a national spirit making a reserve paramountcy of the national government possible, was the revivial of the duality of French and English which had brought the Canadian Union to deadlock before 1864. Instead of a national guarantee, imperfect but practical, of the mutual rights of Catholics and Protestants, French and English, the provincial rights of the Province of Quebec became the guardian of the French in Canada. This prepared the way for a duality of French and English in Canada reminiscent of that in the United States before 1864. The redefining of the B.N.A. Act into a federal system of co-ordinate central and provincial powers prepared the way for separatism and the demand for special status, or even independence, for Quebec.

Notes

1. By the Macdonaldian constitution is meant a constitution preponderantly national in powers and interest, in which the national interests were safeguarded by disallowance, and in minority educational rights by the national power of remedial action under Section 93 of the B.N.A. Act.

By duality is meant political action by English Canada and French Canada as groups, or blocs. Such action happened most strikingly in the Canadian Union from 1841 to 1866; it has recurred to a large degree in Canada since 1896, and particularly since 1917.

'Dual' political action has, of course, never been absolute, nor has it even been institutionalized, even in the Canadian Union. It is a tendency in the Canadian political system, in the writer's opinion, much to be regretted and definitely to be opposed in any form.

2. This development may be supposed to explain why the plan of union was first usually called a "federation," and after the Westminster Conference of 1866 a "confederation," i.e. in its proper, but not historical sense, of a strongly centralized federation. This is presumably the meaning of the assertion in the preamble of the B.N.A. Act of 1867, that the provinces were to be "federally united."

3. A. D. Decelles, *Cartier (Makers of Canada, 1926)*, Vol. V, p. 75.

4. Two other factors greatly affected the development of the constitution after 1867. One was the fact, referred to in debate from time to time, that all the men active in carrying Confederation entered Dominion politics, or were given non-political office at or after 1867. Oliver Mowat significantly was the great exception. Thus provincial politicians were young men who had a necessity to make the most of their provincial positions.

The other factor, too little noted, was the ending of dual representation in all provinces by 1874. The practice was in many ways a continuation of the Union. After 1874 two separate kinds of politicians developed, the national and the provincial.

5. The same nationally sanctioned duality was extended to the Territories by Parliament in 1875, and developed by the Council of the North-West Territories before 1890.

6. W. L. Morton, *The Critical Years*, (Toronto, 1965), p. 208.

7. *Canada, Sessional Papers, 1872*, Vol. 7, No. 36, Macdonald's Report, Jan. 20, 1872.

8. H. G. Thorburn, *Politics in New Brunswick*, (Toronto, 1961), p. 38.

9. By Grit democracy is meant the Canadian version of democratic thought which was occupied with ending privilege and effecting popular sovereignty in Western Europe and North America in the nineteenth century. Most were, of course, members of the Liberal party, but the Conservative party was affected by this prevalent mode of political thought. The term is used without paritsan implication.

10. *Canada, Debates, 1872*, III, pp. 199–201.

11. *Ibid.*, pp. 201–202.

12. *Ibid.*, pp. 704–708.

13. *Ibid.*, pp. 760–764.

14. *Ibid.*, pp. 900.

15. *Ibid.*, pp. 899, 907, 909.

16. Canadian Library Association Microfilms, *Debates of Canadian House of Commons*, May 14, 1873, pp. 188–190.

17. W. E. Hodgins, *Reports of Ministers of Justice and Orders in Council Upon the Subject of Dominion and Provincial Legislation* (Ottawa, 1896), pp 693–94.

18. C.L.A., *Debates, 1874*, May 18, 1874.

19. *Canada, Debates, 1875*, I, p. 555.

20. *Ibid.*, p. 564.

21. E. R. Cameron, *The Canadian Constitution*, (Winnipeg, 1915), p. 418.

22. *Canada, Debates, 1875*, I, p. 576.

23. *Ibid.*, p. 579.

24. *Ibid.*, p. 616.

25. *Ibid.*, pp. 611 and 634.

26. James Hannay, *History of New Brunswick*, (St. John, 1909), II, p. 320.

27. Thorburn, *Politics in New Brunswick*, pp. 33 and 38.

28. Cameron, *The Canadian Constitution*, pp. 310–22.

29. The term seems not to have been used in the 1870s, but was widely used in the 1880s. Its usage indicates how both the Grit democracy of Canada and the justices of the Judicial Committee had come to interpret the Canadian constitution, framed to be as little like that of the United States as possible, in terms relevant to that document.

30. Cameron, *The Canadian Constitution*, p. 346.

31. *Ibid.*, p. 419.

32. Successor to the Scott Act.

33. Cameron, *The Canadian Constitution*, pp. 492–94.

34. The best account of the politics of these years is J. T. Saywell's Introduction to *The Canadian Journal*

146

of Lady Aberdeen, 1893–1898, (Toronto, Champlain Society, 1960).
35. *Canada, Debates, 1896*, I, p. 2741.
36. *Ibid.*, p. 2742.
37. *Canada, Debates, 1896*, II, p. 3821.
38. *Ibid.*, pp. 3833–34.
39. *Ibid.*, p., 3879.
40. The Liberals had a majority of thirty-three in Quebec; the Conservatives a plurality in the other provinces as a whole, a majority of seventy-two to sixty-nine. Seven other candidates were elected in those provinces.
   I am indebted to Mr. Lovell Clark, whose work of the 1890s changes the usual account of that decade, for pointing out the above.

Unity/Diversity: The Canadian Experience; From Confederation to the First World War.*

J.R. MILLER

147

I

While everyone conceded in the 1860's that the object of the Fathers of Confederation was to produce the bases of one political entity, no one anticipated that this task would be performed by imposing uniformity on the diverse peoples and regions of British North America. Indeed, had such a goal been sought, it would have proved impossible of attainment. The various colonies, with their unique historical development, their different religious denominations, and their distinct nationalities, could not have been homogenized culturally as they were joined politically. The peculiarities of language, creed, and regional identity had to be maintained, for several good and compelling reasons.

Diversity was both desirable and unavoidable, first, because the existing differences were simply too strong to be dismissed. This was true not just in the case of the French Canadians, but even with the local autonomists of Ontario, the Grits, and, most especially, in the Maritimes. The *Acadian Recorder* lamented: " 'We don't know each other. We have no trade with each other. We have no facilities or resources or incentives to mingle with each other. We are shut off from each other by a wilderness, geographically, commercially, politically and socially. We always cross the United States to shake hands.' " Joseph Howe, as usual, put it more pungently: " 'Take a Nova Scotian to Ottawa, away above tidewater, freeze him up for five months, where he cannot view the Atlantic, smell salt water, or see the sail of a ship, and the man will pine and die.' "[3] Diversity was a force too powerful to be exorcised.

Even were it possible to assimilate all British North Americans, to what would you assimilate them? Unlike the United States, a community created

*From *The Dalhousie Review* LV, 1, (Spring, 1975): 63–81. Reprinted by permission

by revolution and compact, the proposed Canada was to be produced as the result of an evolutionary process by an act of an external authority, the United Kingdom. Rather than a society of revolution and consensus, Canada was to be a community of evolution and allegiance. The society of allegiance did not require conformity to any one model; the Canadians had no object of assimilation.[4] If they copied anything at all, it was the British pattern, which, since the days of imperial expansion and Catholic Emancipation, meant not something monolithic, Protestant, and Anglo-Saxon, but a number of things more diversified. Canadians could not, at Quebec and Charlottetown, have sought unity at the expense of diversity because there was nothing to which they could conform, and no imperative of revolution to force them to make such a compact.

Finally, Canadian unity was not purchased at the price of homogenization because the colonial politicians who produced it had no intention of creating problems for themselves by debating something as abstract and theoretical as the cultural basis of the new state. These were practical politicians with painfully real problems. Their attention was devoted to solving the difficulties created by deadlock, acquisition of the Northwest, inadequate defences, and promotion of intercolonial commerce, not to searching for new ones. They were, as Donald Creighton has observed, "as far away from the dogmas of the eighteenth-century Enlightenment as they were from twentieth-century obsession with race, and with racial and cultural separatism." These men "saw no merit in setting out on a highly unreal voyage of discovery for first principles."[5] In short, the delegates at Quebec were not about to open a new can of worms by debating the place of various cultural and religious groups in Canada. Such a discussion was as undesirable as it was unnecessary.

These were the reasons why the British North American colonies, as Arthur Lower pointed out, "were carpentered together, not smelted."[6] Or, as G.F.G. Stanley observed: "The Canadian Confederation came into being not to crush but to reconcile regional diversities. . . . Union, not unity, was the result."[7] As one might expect, it was the French-Canadian leader, George-Etienne Cartier who expressed the idea of unity in diversity most clearly:

> In our own Federation we should have Catholic and Protestant, English, French, Irish and Scotch, and each by his efforts and his success would increase the prosperity and glory of the new Confederacy. . . . They were placed like great families beside each other, and their contact produced a healthy spirit of emulation. It was a benefit rather than otherwise that we had a diversity of races. . . .
> Now, when we were united together, . . . we would form a political nationality with which neither the national origin, nor the religion of any individual, would interfere. It was lamented by some that we had this diversity of races, and hopes were expressed that this distinctive feature would cease. The idea of unity of races was utopian—it was impossible. Distinctions of this kind would always exist. Dissimilarity, in fact, appeared to be the order of the physical world and of the moral world, as well as of the political world.[8]

The key words were "a political nationality": the unity that Confederation was to produce was union at the political level, not cultural. While "carpentering" political unity, British North Americans would retain regional, religious, and cultural diversity; Canada was founded on unity in diversity. And, in passing, one might note the type of diversity intended — "Catholic and Protestant, English, French, Irish and Scotch". This was a very Britannic mosaic.

II

Of course, the formula "Unity in diversity" raised as many questions as it answered. What did the concept mean? How did you hold a diverse country together? Specifically, what were the rights and privileges of the most distinctive minority, the French Canadians? More specifically still, what was to become of the principle of cultural and political *duality* that had evolved in the Province of Canada (the future Ontario and Quebec) between 1841 and 1867? It would take a decade and more to work out the first set of answers to these riddles; and, then, the first essay at a resolution of them would come under attack and be modified substantially.

The first question dealt with was the fate of the duality of the Canadian union. Here the answer was starkly simple: duality would be eliminated. This did not mean any tampering with the official status of the French language that was protected by Section 133 of the British North America Act in the courts and Parliament of Canada, as well as in the courts and Legislature of Quebec. However, in succeeding years it was evident that Canadians were not prepared to foster the expansion of this limited, pragmatic recognition of French into a great principle of *duality* throughout the land. Although French was officially countenanced in Manitoba and the Northwest Territories, under special and pressing circumstances, it was not enshrined in the other new provinces of British Columbia and Prince Edward Island. Indeed, in New Brunswick, the Acadian minority suffered the loss of an important cultural bulwark in the 1870's, when their Legislature deprived them of public support for their denominational schools. In short, the first generation of Canadian politicians was prepared to grant French culture official status where temporary exigencies and local pressures made it politically expedient to do so, and nowhere else. They certainly were not about to erect linguistic duality into a great principle of the federation.

Moreover, other aspects of dualism, the double political and administrative institutions that had developed in the United Province, were deliberately removed. Governor General Monck's invitation to John A. Macdonald to form the first Dominion Cabinet explicitly forbade the continuation of the dual premiership. Sectional equality in the Cabinet was replaced by a careful balancing of regional, economic, religious, and cultural interests in Macdonald's first ministry, and in almost all that have succeeded. Duality of administrative posts was also abolished, essentially because the unsatisfactory quasi-federalism of the Union was replaced by a real federation and division of powers between levels of government. There were for example no longer two Superintendents of Education because the schools were now the responsibility of the provinces. Similarly, two Attorneys-General were not needed because French Canada's peculiar civil law was to be controlled by Quebec. And so it went. Institutional duality, whether at the political or civil service level, was eradicated because it was unnecessary and unwanted.

Whatever else the first decade demonstrated, it proved that unity in diversity did not mean the retention of any more duality than was essential. There still remained the more difficult question: if unity in diversity did not mean duality, what did it mean? How was it to be formalized, embodied, made concrete? How did you tack together "a political nationality" out of diverse elements?

The first indication of the means that would be used to hold the country together came in 1868, in Minister of Justice Macdonald's memorandum on the federal power of disallowance. Macdonald laid down guidelines for the federal veto of provincial legislation that were sweeping. They were so general as almost to be unqualified, as was suggested by the provision that provincial statutes "as affecting the interests of the Dominion generally" could be struck down if Ottawa wished.[9] This was Macdonald's instinctive reversion to the eighteenth-century Tory tradition of centralized governmental power. Under his leadership, the first government after Confederation followed a highly centralist policy, one suspects because he regarded such centralization as being as essential to the well-being of the fragile union as it was congenial to his Conservative temperament.

Gradually during the 1870's the rest of the apparatus for ensuring the unity of the state was put into place. The policy of pushing the Indians out of the arable lands of the prairie West and replacing them with white, agricultural settlers was one such project. The gargantuan task of binding the newly-acquired and sparsely-populated West to the rest of the country with a transcontinental railroad was another. And the policy of forcing economic diversification and regional specialisation of economic function through the imposition of the protective tariff was the final means chosen to produce enduring unity out of diversity and distance. The objective of these national policies of expansion and development was to provide an economic *raison d'être* for the political state; or, if you prefer, it was the means of putting the flesh of economic self-interest on the bare bones of the constitutional skeleton. The West, once filled, would produce agricultural products for export and would serve as a captive market for Canadian manufacturers. Central Canada would manufacture goods, protected and encouraged by the tariff; would fuel her industries with Nova Scotian coal; and would sell her products to Maritimers and Westerners alike. The whole scheme would be facilitated by the network of railways that was so essential to the Canadian federation: the Grand Trunk, Intercolonial, and Canadian Pacific. And, finally, the scheme of economic nationalism — the encouragement of a transcontinental economy of diverse, but integrated economic regions — would be supervised and protected by a powerful central government.

Now, the formulation of these policies was undoubtedly much more accidental than the foregoing sketch suggests. The steps toward adoption of the various pieces were often hesitant, taken out of a sense of constitutional obligation (the promise of a railway to B.C.), and motivated more by partisan political calculations than nation-building ambitions. And, yet, what seems striking is the fact that the pieces fit, that they made up a coherent, compelling, and politically appealing programme of national self-defence through economic expansion and integration. Furthermore, when the pieces are put together, they provide an answer to the question of how unity could be maintained amidst diversity. The answer was that diverse regions, religious groups and nationalities could stay united politically while remaining different culturally because they had a programme of economic development from which they could all benefit. And, moreover, these policies meant that the focus of political life at the federal level would not be on sensitive issues of religion and nationality, but on economic issues that cut across regional, religious, and cultural lines. Macdonald's nationalism would make unity in diversity possible by concentrating on those things that united Canadians, or, at least, did not divide them according to religion and language. The recipe was: diversity locally, but political unity in pursuit of common economic objectives.

Not the least significant feature of this concoction is the fact that, to a large extent, it succeeded. The French Canadians participated in the scheme as enthusiastically as anyone else. There were no more fervent Protectionists than Quebec's leaders, who saw the industrialization of the Townships as the alternative to the continuing hemorrhage of French-Canadian youth to the detested United States. Ontario was satisfied, for the key to Macdonald's scheme was the realisation of Ontario's traditional dream of opening and developing the West in Ontario's image and for Toronto's pecuniary benefit. The national policies embodied Ontario imperialism. And the Maritimes benefited too, although the advantages were offset by the general deterioration of the Atlantic economy in the waning years of wind and wood transportation. There was substantial growth in the Nova Scotian coal industry, as the industrialization encouraged by the tariff created markets for the fuel in urban Quebec.[10] The only region that did not benefit very much from the scheme was the West. There the response to centralization and the national policies was protest: formation of the Manitoba and Northwest Farmers' Union, Riel's second Rebellion, the provincial autonomy campaign in Manitoba, and the steady intonation on the litany of grievances (freight rates, elevators, and tariffs) that was to become so familiar. But, frankly, no one worried much about western complaints, for colonies were only supposed to produce wealth, not be happy. Western grievances aside, however, the Tory scheme of unity through economic expansion was quite successful.

III

This unity based on pursuit of common economic goals under the direction of a strong central government began to erode in the 1880's as the result of three corrosive influences. Political opportunism inspired an attack on cen-

151

tralization by the Liberal parties at the federal and provincial levels. The economic stagnation that returned after 1883 destroyed the rosy dreams of prosperity and unity. As is normally the case in difficult times, economic discontent led to internal bickering: the provinces *versus* Ottawa; and Ontario against the rest, especially Quebec, when the provinces succeeded in extorting "better terms" from the Conservative federal government. Finally, the desired unity within the country was eroded by the influence in Canada of radically new theories of national unity that focused upon language and culture, rather than economic cooperation, as essential criteria for unification.

The new theories which sought unity at the expense of cultural diversity were represented in the 1880's and 1890's by such men as D'Alton McCarthy and Goldwin Smith. McCarthy, an Anglo-Saxon supremacist, imperialist, and tariff reformer, was worried about the lack of cohesion in Canada and anxious about the declining power of the central government. To him the villain of the piece seemed to be the French Canadian who insisted on having his own way, thereby preventing fusion:

152

> My own conviction is that it is not religion which is at the bottom of the matter but that it is a race feeling. There is no feeling so strong — no feeling which all history proves so strong — as the feeling of race. Don't we find the French today in the province of Quebec more French than when they were conquered by Wolfe upon the plains of Abraham? Do they mix with us, assimilate with us, intermarry with us? Do they read our literature or learn our laws? No, everything with them is conducted on a French model; and while we may admire members of that race as individuals, yet as members of the body politic I say that they are the great danger to the Confederacy.[11]

In McCarthy's view, "It was the language of a people that moulded its nationality."[12] The "science of language" demonstrated "that there is no factor equal to language to band people together, and . . . as is demonstrated in our own case, that nothing is more calculated to keep people asunder."[13] If McCarthy's analysis was correct, then it followed that Canadian unity could be achieved only through the imposition on Canada of one language: unity was to be achieved, not through diversity, but through cultural uniformity brought about by assimilation. His programme for national unity was summarized in his resolution calling for the abolition of the official use of French in the Northwest Territories: that it was " 'expedient in the interest of national unity that there should be community of language among the people of Canada.' "[14]

Goldwin Smith, free trader, continentalist, and Anglo-Saxon racist, advocated a slightly different programme to achieve the same end. He believed that French Canada was an obstacle to unity not just because of its language, but also because of its obscurantism and economic backwardness, both of which were the results of clerical domination:

> Quebec is a theocracy. While Rome has been losing her hold on Old France and on all the European nations, she has retained, nay tightened, it here. The people are the sheep of the priest. He is their political as well as their spiritual chief and nominates the politician, who serves the interest of the Church at Quebec or at Ottawa. . . . Not only have the clergy been the spiritual guides and masters of the French Canadians, they have been the preservers and champions of his nationality, and they have thus combined the influence of the tribune with that of the priest.[15]

The French province, the people of which live on the produce of their own farms and clothe themselves with the produce of their spinning, is uncommercial, and lies a non-conductor between the more commercial members of the Confederation.[16]

Unlike McCarthy, Smith did not seek a solution to this problem in Canada, because he believed the political parties were totally and irrevocably the tools of the Quebec clergy. To Smith it was "perfectly clear that the forces of Canada alone are not sufficient to assimilate the French element or even to prevent the indefinite consolidation and growth of a French nation."[17] The answer, then, was obvious: "French Canada may be ultimately absorbed in the English-speaking population of a vast Continent; amalgamate with British Canada so as to form a united nation it apparently never can."[18] Canada should join the Americans to form an Anglo-Saxon republic of North America in which the French Canadians would drown.

There is a two-fold significance in the emergence of such advocates of Anglo-Saxon cultural uniformity as McCarthy and Smith. The first is that they are evidence that in English Canada, for a variety of reasons, many people had by the 1890's rejected the pursuit of unity in diversity. The second is that the country as a whole rejected the extreme prescriptions put forward by continentalists and cultural assimilationists alike for coercive uniformity. Parliament's response to McCarthy's call for linguistic uniformity was a compromise resolution that said that nothing had happened since Confederation to justify taking from the French Canadians the guarantees they received at the time of union, while allowing the populace of the Northwest Territories itself to decide the fate of the official use of French on the prairies.[19] And in the 1890's such annexationist schemes as Smith's Continental Union Association were rejected by the electorate.

153

Though McCarthy and Smith failed, they were not without lingering influence. French Canadians, seeing assimilationist movements such as the Equal Rights Association, Equal Rights League, Protestant Protective Association, and Continental Union Association, found renewed cause for anxiety about their future as a distinct cultural entity within the Canadian "political nationality". This disquiet was aggravated by a new phenomenon of the late 1890's and early 1900's, massive European immigration to the Canadian West. As French-Canadian leaders quickly perceived, this demographic change made Cartier's doctrine of diversity a source of danger.

IV

The problem arose because of Engish-Canadian reaction to the immigration of the Laurier period. As thousands of Poles, Russians, Germans, Italians, Scandinavians, and Ukrainians flooded the West, middle-class, Anglo-Saxon Canadians began to join working-class critics of extensive immigration. Whereas the old trade union criticism of immigration was essentially economic in character,[20] the new critique was fundamentally concerned with the cultural effects of immigration. Stephen Leacock observed disapprovingly that the new immigration was "from the Slavonic and Mediterannean peoples of a lower industrial and moral status", and consisted of "herds of the proletariat of Europe, the lowest class of industrial society".[21] Principal Sparling of Wesley College, Winnipeg, warned that Canadians "must see to it that the civilization and ideals of Southeastern Europe are not transplanted to and perpetuated on our virgin soil".[22] While Ralph Connor fictionalized Sparling's injunction in *The Foreigner*,[23] a poet, of sorts, expressed similar ideas in verse:

They are haggard, huddled, homeless, frightened at — they know not what:
With a few unique exceptions they're a disappointing lot;
But I take'em as I get'em, soldier, sailor, saint and clown
And I turn'em out Canadians — all but the yellow and brown.[24]

In the era of the Laurier Boom many Canadians recoiled from the tidal wave of immigration, sorrowfully concluding that they could not make a nation by holding a basket at the hopper of an immigration chute."[25]

The English-Canadian answer to these cultural dangers was a drive to assimilate the "foreigner" by inculcating in him the values of British-Canadian civilization. What precisely that meant, and the danger it portended, manifested itself in the prescriptions critics of immigration put forward for the solution of the problem. "One of the best ways of Canadianizing, nationalizing, and turning all into intelligent citizens," said one Protestant clergyman in 1913, "is by means of a good English education. . . ."[26] When J.S. Woodsworth asked himself how "are we to break down the walls which separate these foreigners from us?", his conclusion was that first and foremost was "the Public School. Too great emphasis cannot be placed upon the work that has been accomplished and may — yes, must — be accomplished by our National Schools."[27] Linguistic uniformity imposed by the schools was the answer:

If Canada is to become in any real sense a nation, if our people are to become one, we must have one language. . . . Hence the necessity of national schools where the teaching of English — our national language — is compulsory.

The public school system was "the most important factor in transforming the foreigners into Canadians."[28]

French Canada, not unnaturally, took alarm at such programmes, which drew no distinction between the worthy French Canadian and the despised "Galician". The emerging champion of French-Canadian nationalism, Henri Bourassa, protested that the Fathers of Confederation had never intended "to change a providential condition of our partly French and partly English country to make it a land of refuge for the scum of all nations."[29] Bourassa's complaint was that diversity, by which Canadians had meant a mixture of English, French, and Scot, now seemed to mean Ukrainian, German and Italian; and that English Canadians, in reacting to this new form of diversity, attacked French-Canadian rights as well as the pretensions of the European "scum". Bourassa knew whereof he spoke, for, in the early years of the twentieth century, Woodsworth's prescription (and Bourassa's nightmare) was realized. In 1901 and 1905 on the prairies, and in 1912 in Ontario, unilingual education was imposed in an effort to assimilate all minorities, including the French Canadians. In the era of massive European immigration Cartier's "multicultural argument could only accelerate, not retard the unilingual process."[30]

Bourassa's, and French Canada's, response to this danger was to work out a new theory of Canadian unity that protected rather than jeopardized French-Canadian cultural rights. The new spokesman of French Canada found his justification of his culture in Providence and History. God, he argued, had placed the Latin culture of French Canada in North America as a spiritual beacon in the materialistic, Anglo-Saxon darkness. And what God planted, not even the Canadian Parliament ought to root out. Furthermore, he insisted, Canadian history was the record of the preservation of cultural duality. The Royal Proclamation of 1763 and Quebec Act of 1774 had ensured the survival of the primary agency of French Canada, the Roman Catholic Church. A political process stretching from the Constitutional Act of 1791 to the struggle over responsible government of the 1840's had expanded the limited eighteenth-century guarantees into semi-official recognition of duality. Confederation, in Bourassa's historical recitation, became the adoption by the new Dominion of Canada of biculturalism and bilingualism. Hence, French Canada should be respected because it was a co-ordinate partner with a special providential mission to perform. Not even the infringements of the Confederation compact in the West and Ontario between 1890 and 1912 could alter that fact. "The Canadian nation", Bourassa argued, "will attain its ultimate destiny, indeed it will exist, only on the condition of being biethnic and bilingual, and by remaining faithful to the concept of the Fathers of Confederation: the free and voluntary association of two peoples, enjoying equal rights in all matters."[31] In other words, in flight from the vulnerability of diversity, Bourassa had erected duality as a new line of defence. Bourassa and biculturalism had replaced Cartier and diversity as the theoretical justification of French Canada's right to exist.

In the first half-century of Confederation, then, Canadians' concept of their political community as a unity in diversity had come under attack on two fronts. English assimilationists had argued for cultural homogenization as an answer to disunity, and French-Canadian nationalists had responded with a messianic and historical defence of cultural duality. The two conflicting viewpoints were the subject of much public discussion in the early years of the twentieth century, as each struggled for mastery. As it turned out, with the coming of the Great War the English-Canadian assimilationist model triumphed. Several provinces terminated the official use of French; Ontario refused to soften the assimilationist thrust of its 1912 policy; and Quebec, as a result of the language issue and the conscription crisis, was politically isolated and alienated.

Notes

1. J.S. Woodsworth, "Some Aspects of Immigration", *The University Magazine*, XIII (1914), 191.
2. *Viewpoint* by Vancouver reporter Doug Collins, CBKST-TV, 18 November, 1974.
3. *Acadian Recorder*, quoted in Ricker, Saywell and Cook, *Canada, a Modern Study* (Toronto, 1963), 101; J. Howe quoted in J.M. Beck, *Joseph Howe, Anti-Confederate* (Ottawa, 1956), 15.
4. W.L. Morton, *The Canadian Identity* (Madison and Toronto, 1961), 100-7, 110-12.
5. D.G. Creighton, *The Road to Confederation* (Toronto, 1964), 141-2.
6. A.R.M. Lower, *Canadians in the Making* (Don Mills, 1958), 289.
7. G.F.G. Stanley, "Regionalism in Canadian History", *Ontario History*, LI (1959), 167.
8. P.B. Waite (ed, *Confederation Debates in the Province of Canada/1865* (Carleton Library edition, Toronto, 1963), 51 and 50.
9. Quoted in J.M. Beck (ed.), *The Shaping of Canadian Federalism* (Toronto, 1971), 159.
10. P.B. Waite, *Canada, 1874-1896: Arduous Destiny* (Toronto, 1971), 184.
11. Quoted in F. Landon, "D'Alton McCarthy and the Politics of the Later Eighties", Canadian Historical Association, *Report of the Annual Meeting 1932*, 46.
12. Stayner Speech, 12 July, 1889, *Toronto Daily Mail*, 13 July, 1889.
13. *Speech of Mr. D'Alton McCarthy delivered on Thursday, 12 December, 1889 at Ottawa*, (n.p., n.d.), 9-10.
14. *Debates of the House of Commons*, Fourth Session, Sixth Parliament, XXIX (1890), columns 674-5.
15. G. Smith, *Canada and the Canadian Question* (Toronto, 1891), 5-6.
16. *Ibid.*, 206-7.
17. *Ibid.*, 275.
18. *Ibid.*, 215.
19. *Debates of the House of Commons*, 1890, columns 881-2 and 1017-8.
20. With the exception, of course, of British Columbia, where the objections had been based on both economic and racial arguments. See J.A. Munro, "British Columbia and the 'Chinese Evil': Canada's First Anti-Asiatic Immigration Law", *Journal of Canadian Studies*, VI (1971), 42-9.
21. S. Leacock, "Canada and the Immigration Problem", *The National Review*, LII (1911), 317 and 323.
22. Principal Sparling, "Introduction" to J.S. Woodsworth, *Strangers Within our Gates, or Coming Canadians* (Toronto, 1909).
23. R. Connor [C.W. Gordon], *The Foreigner. A Tale of Saskatchewan* (Toronto, 1909), especially 23-5 and 37-41. This theme in Connor's work has been analysed carefully in J.L. Thompson and J.H. Thompson, "Ralph Connor and the Canadian Identity", *Queen's Quarterly*, LXXIX (1972), 166-9.
24. R.J.C. Stead, "The Mixer" (1905), quoted in R.C. Brown and R. Cook, *Canada 1896-1921: a Nation Transformed* (Toronto, 1974), 73.
25. Leacock, "Canada and the Immigration Problem", 318.
26. Rev. W.D. Reid, in R.C. Brown and M.E. Prang (eds.), *Confederation to 1949* (Scarborough, 1966), 84.
27. J.S. Woodsworth, *Strangers Within Our Gates*, 281.
28. J.S. Woodsworth (1905), quoted in Brown and Cook, *Canada 1896-1921*, 73.
29. H. Bourassa (1904), quoted *ibid.*, 74.
30. A. Smith, "Metaphor and Nationality in North America", *Canadian Historical Review*, LI (1970), 268. This paper owes far more than this isolated quotation to Professor Smith's stimulating analysis, as students of the topic will realize.
31. H. Bourassa (1917), quoted in R. Cook, *Canada and the French-Canadian Question* (Toronto, 1966), 51.

Topic Five:
Immigration and Western Settlement

Between 1896 and 1914 over two million immigrants arrived in Canada, the majority of them settling in the West. A large proportion of those came from Britain and the United States and assimilated relatively easily into Canadian society. A significant number, however, arrived from continental Europe and found it more difficult to adjust because of cultural and linguistic differences.

Changed world conditions partially explain the expansion of immigration to Canada. With the best homestead land in the American West settled by the 1890's, immigrants began considering the Canadian prairies — "the last best West" — as a viable alternative. The world-wide prosperity of the turn of the century enabled more immigrants to come to Canada. The efforts of the Liberal government of Wilfrid Laurier, elected in 1896, also helped to settle the West. Under the leadership of Clifford Sifton, the minister of the interior, the Liberals vigorously recruited immigrants. Sifton doubled, then redoubled, the expenditures of the Immigration Branch. He sent government agents to Britain, the United States, and various European countries armed with propagandist literature on Western Canada. In Europe the Canadian government offered special bonuses to steamship agents booking immigrants to Canada. Immigration officials assured various ethnic and sectarian groups that they could establish bloc settlements, and retain their customs in the new world.

Gerald Friesen provides an overview of immigration to, and ethnic settlements in, the Canadian prairies in "Immigration Communities 1870–1940." Howard Palmer examines the negative response of the dominant Anglo-Canadian community to these "foreign" immigrants in "Reluctant Hosts: Anglo-Canadian Views of Multiculturalism in the Twentieth Century."

For an overview of immigration to Western Canada, see the chapter "Opening Up the Land of Opportunity," in R.C. Brown and R. Cook's *Canada: 1896–1921: A Nation Transformed* (Toronto: McClelland and Stewart, 1974), pp. 49–82. Pierre Berton's *The Promised Land: Settling the West, 1896–1914*

(Toronto: McClelland and Stewart, 1984) is a popular treatment. *Immigration and the Rise of Multiculturalism*, edited by H. Palmer (Toronto: Copp Clark, 1975), contains a good selection of primary readings on the subject of immigration. An important study is Donald Avery's *Dangerous Foreigners: European Immigrant Workers and Labour Radicalism in Canada, 1896-1932* (Toronto: McClelland and Stewart, 1979). Howard Palmer reviews the Anglo-Albertans' reaction to "foreign" immigrants in *Patterns of Prejudices: A History of Nativism in Alberta* (Toronto: McClelland and Stewart, 1982). The immigrant's viewpoint appears in John Marlyn's novel *Under the Ribs of Death* (Toronto: McClelland and Stewart, 1971) and in R.F. Harney and H. Troper's *Immigrants: A Portrait of the Urban Experience: 1890-1930* (Toronto: Van Nostrand Reinhold, 1975). The Department of the Secretary of State is currently publishing individual histories of some thirty ethnic groups in Canada. On Clifford Sifton's role in promoting immigration to the West see D.J. Hall's two volume biography: *Clifford Sifton*, I: *The Young Napoleon 1861-1900* (Vancouver: University of British Columbia Press, 1981) II: *A Lonely Eminence 1901-1929* (Vancouver: University of British Columbia Press, 1985), and his "Clifford Sifton: Immigration and Settlement Policy, 1896-1905," in *The Settlement of the West*, edited by H. Palmer (Calgary: University of Calgary Comprint Publishing Co., 1977), pp. 60-85. Two articles provide an overview of work in Canadian immigration and ethnic history: H. Palmer, "Canadian Immigration and Ethnic History in the 1970's and 1980's," *Journal of Canadian Studies*, 17 (Spring, 1982): pp. 35-50; and Roberto Perin, "Clio as Ethnic: The Third Force in Canadian Historiography," *Canadian Historical Review*, 64 (December 1983): pp. 441-467.

158

Immigrant Communities 1870-1940: The Struggle for Cultural Survival*
G. FRIESEN

The prairie west adopted recognizably 'modern' institutions in the half-century after 1840. By the end of the 1890s, its residents simply assumed that a capitalistic labour market, private property, and individualism were part of the environment, like the plains and the river valleys. But there were further surprises in store. In the next three decades, prairie society changed almost as drastically as it had in the preceding three generations. Its population increased sixfold from just over 400,000 in 1901 to 2.4 million in 1931, and its ethnic composition, as a result of an influx of hundreds of thousands of Britons, Americans, and Europeans, was altered forever. Its major cities

*Chapter 11 from *The Canadian Prairies: A History*, by Gerald Friesen. Copyright 1984 by the University of Calgary Press. Reprinted by permission of the University of Calgary Press.

grew rapidly and, like their counterparts in other developed nations, endured increasing tension among social classes. A vast rural community was built on a foundation of thousands of schools and railway sidings, villages and churches. New solutions to the eternal human issues of freedom, order, justice, and equality were made the subjects of economic and political debate. New political parties contested elections. Around the turn of the twentieth century, in brief, the prairie west entered a new phase in its evolution as a region.

Cultural diversity was one striking feature of prairie society in the opening decades of this century according to visitors from eastern Canada and Great Britain. To descend from the train at the CPR station in Winnipeg was to enter an international bazaar: the noise of thousands of voices and a dozen tongues circled the high marble pillars and drifted out into the street, there to mingle with the sounds of construction, delivery wagons, perambulatory vendors, and labour recuiters. The crowds were equally dense on Main Street, just a block away, where shops displayed their wares in a fashion more European than British North American: fruits and vegetables, books and newspapers, coats and jackets stood on sidewalk tables and racks; even on the outer walls of buildings when weather permitted. The smell of fresh earth at an excavation site, of concrete being poured and lumber being stacked, reminded the visitor of the newness and vitality of the place. But the smells were mixed with beer and whisky and sweat and horse manure to remind one, too that this was not a polite and ordered society but rather was customarily described as Little Europe, Babel, New Jerusalem, or the Chicago of the North.

159

Prairie society was much more than cosmopolitan Winnipeg. Visitors who travelled further west might have chanced on quite different scenes: at the southeastern edge of the plains, where the rough wooded terrain of the parkland stretched to the international border, they would have discovered an English parish church identical to those in Surrey or Sussex except that it was constructed of wood rather than stone. In this district, now known as Manor, Saskatchewan, there were indeed, manor houses; near the church there was, if not a high street, at least the makings of one. On special occasions, visitors might have seen mounted huntsmen assemble at the sound of a horn to assault the unsuspecting coyote or might have watched neighbours congregate in the library for a reading evening. The observer could then have taken the new train service north through Saskatoon and alighted at Hague, to be greeted by utter silence. A buggy might move slowly past the single row of stores behind the station, dark-skirted women might avert their eyes, and a murmur of phrases in low German would identify the distinctiveness of a Mennonite village. The examples could be multiplied many times: Mormons at Cardston, Alberta, where the great white temple dominated the district; Ukrainians near Wakaw, Saskatchewan, where the small onion dome of their frame church transported one to the steppes of Russia; Jews at Bender Hamlet, where the rows of houses suggested yet another settlement on the steppes; Hungarians at Esterhazy, Doukhobors at Verigin,

Swedes at Erickson; the map of the southern half of the western interior was a giant checker-board of culturally and linguistically distinctive settlements.

The population of the western interior had been overwhelmingly Canadian by birth and British by national origin in the late nineteenth century, but within one generation the cultural composition changed dramatically. Almost half of all prairie residents at the start of the First World War had been born in another country, and the proportion was still one in three as late as 1931. Those who were British by 'origin' (a census term defined by the ancestral roots of a family's male line) had similarly declined to about 50 per cent of the prairie total (of this group, half were English, one-quarter Scots), while the various eastern European groups (Ukrainian, Austro-Hungarian, Polish, and Russian) numbered about 20 per cent, and western Europeans (German, Dutch, French, including French Canadians) also numbered about 20 per cent.[1]

160
As a community of immigrants was created in the opening decades of the twentieth century, phrases such as 'New Canadians,' 'strangers within our gates,' 'foreigners,' and 'ethnic groups' gradually became part of the Canadian vocabulary. Even today, westerners use the term 'ethnic' in everyday language and make broad generalizations about ethnic behaviour, tell crude stories known as ethnic jokes, and celebrate the changing seasons with ethnic festivals.

Definitions of the term 'ethnic' or of its many close relatives, from 'immigrant' to 'New Canadian' and 'displaced person,' are vague. According to popular convention, however, the term 'ethnic group' does not apply to Canada's aboriginal peoples and founding nationalities but does include all other minority groups whose identity is derived from racial origin, national origin, language, religion, and historical or contemporary consciousness.[2] To exclude the British and the French in a discussion of ethnic groups in the western interior would be a mistake. Their unique status in the west derives more from linguistic and historical precedence — for French and English are Canada's 'official' languages — than from officially sanctioned cultural privileges. In other ways, the English and French, like all other peoples, were immigrants to western Canada and behaved as members of ethnic groups.

The western interior has experienced five significant infusions of immigrants in its history. The first, a product of the fur trade, resulted in the establishment of a fur post society and in the birth of the most numerous new element in the area, English- and French-speaking métis. The second occurred in the decades after Confederation and, because it was composed largely of British Canadians, resulted in the establishment of a new, Ontario-like agricultural community; despite the apparent homogeneity of this society it is well to underline that it contained pockets of a quite different nature, including British ranchers and artisans, non-British agricultural settlements of Mennonites and Icelanders and Jews and, of course, continuing communities of Indians and métis. The third infusion of immigrants, and by far the largest, occurred between 1897 and 1913, and was comprised in equal parts of British, Canadian, American, and continental European arrivals, with a sprinkling of others from around the globe. The fourth, an extension of the third in terms of national origin, took place in the 1920s. And the fifth significant addition occurred in the decades after the Second World War. The subject of our immediate concern is the extraordinary burst of immigration in the 1897–1929 era. The implications of this multinational migration for the host society, whether local, provincial, or regional, were undoubtedly important, just as the new environment was an important factor in the life of the immigrants. We are only now coming to unravel the two threads of this story — the adjustments of the larger society and of the immigrants who composed it.

Canadian immigration policy was, according to the BNA Act of 1867, a subject of concurrent jurisdiction between the federal and provincial governments (section 95), but the central government retained paramountcy in case of conflict. In practice, however, the federal government took the lead in the establishment of policy with its act of 1869 which established immigration offices in Britain and Europe, quarantine stations at the three ports of importance (Halifax, Saint John, and Grosse Isle, Quebec), and domestic branches of the service in a number of Canadian cities. Restrictions were few: the entry of immigrants who were destitute, or physically or mentally unfit, and thus likely to become a public charge, was permitted only on payment of a bond; and criminals could be denied admission. This unusually open policy was limited once in the following three decades: as of 1885, most Chinese immigrants were required to pay a tax.[3] Policy was established by regulation as well as by statute, however, and with the appointment of Clifford Sifton as minister of the interior in 1897, clear but informal guide-lines worked to encourage some immigrant groups and to discourage others. Sifton was young, pragmatic, a westerner, convinced of 'the potential of the West, and its centrality to the future development and prosperity of Canada.' Thus the promotion of immigration and settlement was, he believed, a crucial 'national enterprise' akin to the construction of the transcontinental railway or the passage of the BNA Act itself. He worked to encourage the immigration of experienced farmers by spending considerable sums in the agricultural districts of the United States, Britain, and Europe, and he tried to discourage others, such as blacks, Italians, Jews, Orientals, and urban Englishmen, who would not, he believed, succeed on farms and would thus end up in the cities. These informal recruitment and entry qualifications were based more on occupational than race criteria, therefore, and worked to encourage such diverse groups as Ukrainians and Doukhobors while also discouraging English mechanics. Sifton was aware of and not immune to criticism of this policy; moreover, like his critics, he believed in assimilation of the immigrants to a British-Canadian norm. But he was in the business of building a bigger, better Canada, and, as a 'long-term investment,' farmers, British or non-British, constituted blue-chip stock.[4]

Immigration policy changed course slightly when Sifton was replaced by

161

Frank Oliver in 1905. A vigorous defender of western Canada's interests, Oliver was also staunchly British in an era when national reaction to 'foreign' newcomers was increasing. He was more inclined to reduce the recruiting activity in central and eastern Europe and to increase it in Great Britain, including its cities, in order to preserve the 'national fabric' of Canada. The official effect of Oliver's tenure was a series of revisions to the Immigration Act between 1906 and 1910 which prohibited entry to those deemed medically or morally unfit, to those who were likely to become public charges, to criminals, to those not on a continuous journey from their country of origin (immigrants originally from India were thus virtually excluded), and to those who advocated the violent overthrow of constituted authority. But the unofficial consequence of Oliver's rule was to permit and even encourage the immigration of many more British subjects, including thousands of paupers who were assisted by charitable organizations, and virtually to deny entry to blacks and orientals. Despite his preference for agriculturalists, Oliver was less successful than Sifton in resisting the pressure of business leaders and cabinet colleagues to recruit 'alien navvies.' As railway construction activity increased after 1907, the demand for unsophisticated labourers also multiplied because the railway builders wanted nothing to do with workers who expected 'high wages, a feather bed and a bath tub' in their construction camps.[5] The result was free entry for 'foreign' navvies in 1910–11. Because Robert Borden's new Conservative government was equally sensitive to the demands of contractors, mine owners, and lumber entrepreneurs, the policy was continued until the outbreak of war in 1914. Untold thousands of immigrants in this era belonged to this category of foreign navvy, to the dismay of observers such as Clifford Sifton.

162

The hiatus in immigration caused by the war was extended into the early 1920s by the prohibition of Doukhobors, Hutterites, Mennonites, and 'enemy aliens,' including Ukrainians and Germans, two especially favoured groups of Sifton's days. The government also reimposed monetary requirements on all newcomers except those destined for farm or domestic work. But, in 1923, in the face of mounting pressure from such European peoples as Mennonites, who faced very difficult times in the Soviet Union, the ban on enemy aliens was lifted. The failure of British population sources and mounting Canadian emigration to the United States may also have had a bearing on this decision. And, in 1925, in an even more important policy change, Mackenzie King's government decided to permit the two Canadian railway companies, the Canadian National Railway (CNR) and the CPR to embark on an expensive recruitment campaign in central and eastern Europe among those very farmers who for almost five years had been viewed as 'non-preferred' classes. Nearly 370,000 continental citizens left for Canada in the next six years, half of them under the terms of the railway agreement.[6]

The tide of immigrants was simply too great to be absorbed easily into the Canadian economy during the late 1920s. As hostility to foreigners and demands for restriction increased, the federal government moved to reduce

the numbers of new arrivals in 1929. In accordance with an election promise, King's successor, R.B. Bennett, cancelled the railway agreement in 1930.
The gates of Canada were esentially closed to immigration for the next decade. Immigrants of Asian origin found it virtually impossible to enter, and
from 1931 only certain British subjects and American citizens, wives and
children of legal Canadian residents, or agriculturists 'having sufficient means
to farm in Canada' were permitted to enter the country. Where 1.8 million
immigrants arrived in Canada between 1911 and 1921, and 1.2 million
immigrants arrived in 1921-31, only 140,000 arrived between 1931 and
1941.[7]

In view of the wide variation in immigration during Canada's first sixty
years as a nation (see Table 1), one might wonder why the government had
not acted to implement a system that regulated the intake more effectively.
The short answer is that the government seemed to have little control over
immigration totals. Canadian recruitment of immigrants in the generations
around Confederation had been something of a disaster. In every decade
from the 1860s to the 1890s, Canada lost more citizens through emigration
to the United States that it gained through immigration. In the face of significant western settlement difficulties, the weakness of the national economy in the 1880s and early 1890s, and the overwhelming presence of the
American competitor, not to mention Australia, Argentina, and Brazil, western Canada failed to make an impact on the popular imagination in Britain
and Europe. The well-tried tactics of immigration pamphlets, recruiting
offices, assisted passages, and free tours for delegates of various communities were employed consistently throughout these decades, but the results
were meagre. The best results came as a consequence of negotiations with
particular groups, especially those facing straitened circumstances or political oppression. These talks led to colony migrations of Mennonites, Icelanders, French Canadians from New England, Hungarians, Scandinavians,
Jews, and others. But each of these many colonies was established as the

163

TABLE 1
Canada's population record (in thousands) 1861-1941

	Natural increase	Immigration	Emigration	Net migration	Population at end of decade
1861					3,230
1861-71	650	186	376	-191	3,689
1871-81	720	353	438	- 85	4,325
1881-91	714	903	1,108	-205	4,833
1891-1901	719	326	507	-181	5,371
1901-11	1,120	1,782	1,066	715	7,207
1911-21	1,349	1,592	1,360	233	8,788
1921-31	1,486	1,198	1,095	103	10,377
1931-41	1,242	149	262	-112	11,507

Source: David C. Corbett *Canada's Immigration Policy: A Critique* (Toronto 1957) 121

result of special circumstances rather than popular response to an advertising campaign. Canada was just too small and too little-known in the late nineteenth century to win an international reputation as an immigrant destination.[8]

What happened to change the circumstances in the late 1890s? The question has sparked much scholarly debate and a wide range of answers. First, the Canadian government established a more serious and much more effective recruiting campaign. Second, circumstances in the United States, Britain, and Europe all had changed in ways that favoured Canada's recruiters. Third, the situation of the prairie agricultural frontier was more attractive as a result of important breakthroughs in farm technology and farm practice. And, fourth, the agricultural boom stimulated booms in coal, lumber, and railway construction that offered the prospect of abundant jobs to international migrants who might, in time, become immigrants; whether they stayed in Canada or returned home, however, they swelled the entry rolls.

164

Traditional Canadian interpretations of the immigration boom have paid great attention to the role of Clifford Sifton, minister of the interior 1897–1905, in stimulating Canada's recruitment efforts. There can be no question of Sifton's effectiveness as an administrator and as a leader of the nation's search for new citizens. He simplified the homestead procedures, promoted vast irrigation schemes in the arid areas of southern Alberta, eliminated the so-called land-lock by forcing the railways to select and patent their grants, and imparted new life to the immigration branch, where previously 'the pall of death seemed to have fallen over the officials.' New employees, a larger budget, millions more of advertising pamphlets, dozens of displays at regional exhibitions in the United States and Great Britain, numerous tours for visiting journalists, and provision for many more colony migrations were products of his tenure. He enlarged the immigration service in the United States from 6 agents to 300 and asked them to pursue recruits rather than wait for inquiries. He ensured that a similarly aggressive campaign was undertaken in the rural areas of England and Scotland. Finally, in Europe, where immigration propaganda was declared illegal by a number of governments, Sifton expanded a secret bonusing system through the North Atlantic Trading Company whereby recruiters would receive a money grant for every adult dispatched to Canada. Between 1899 and 1906, when the system was halted, nearly 71,000 immigrants arrived in Canada by this system and over $350,000 was paid to recruiters.[9] That Sifton and his department's activity brought Canada to the attention of the world is undeniable; whether it convinced reluctant people to emigrate is unlikely.

Canadian economic historians have recently taken a different tack in their analysis of western agricultural expansion. In the past, their response had been to cite a 'conjuncture of favourable circumstances' in the 1890s: a rise in wheat prices caused by European and American industrialization, falling wheat transport costs as railway and ocean shipping became more efficient, the end of available free land in the United States, the resumption of international circulation of labour and capital after a prolonged depression, and scientific and technological breakthroughs in the production of wheat and flour. Recent analysis has suggested, however, that some of these factors were more important than others. Sub-humid land in central North America was always preferable to semi-arid land, and thus the eastern American plains inevitably were developed first. The filling in of these preferred sites, the development of appropriate dry-land farming techniques, the movements in relative real wages in the North Atlantic community, which made Canadian wages seem vastly higher than those in Europe, and the rise of world wheat prices are thus seen to be important and interrelated factors. By contrast, the extension of the prairie rail network and the increase in government advertising played a small role in the determination of the rate of settlement, chiefly by hastening the process that was under way, but were not of pivotal importance.[10]

Another avenue of explanation of the Canadian immigration boom juxtaposes the 'pull' factors — the attractions in North America that might persuade immigrants to try their luck in a new land — with the 'push' factors — reasons that brought immigrants to the conclusion that life in the home country was no longer acceptable or that it could be made agreeable only by visiting the new land for a period. Here the stories of departures were as diverse as the communities that contributed to the stream of emigrants. Great Britain, Scandinavia, Italy, the Austro-Hungarian Empire, Russia, the small nations of southeastern Europe, and the United States were the chief contributors to the growth of western Canada's population. Each had specific circumstances that encouraged thoughts of escape.

The extraordinary migration from Europe must be seen as a product of vast changes in the continent's society and economy. Without the revolution in industry that began in England in the eighteenth century and spread across Europe in the nineteenth century, this world-shaking phenomenon would not have commenced. The growth of industry was associated, in ways that are still debated by scholars, with amazing changes in population: birth rates rose and death rates plummeted, first in western Europe and, after 1870, in southern and eastern Europe. The resultant natural increases in population were unprecedented; local opportunities were never sufficient to provide adequate employment for the numbers of young adults who were ready and eager to leave their homes. Cities burst at the seams as the rural exodus gathered speed, and when European investment stimulated overseas development people began to take ship for the 'new world' — South Africa, Argentina, Brazil, Australia, and North America. Two waves of emigrants can be distinguished. The first, between 1820 and 1890, was drawn almost exclusively from northwestern Europe — Great Britain and Ireland, Germany, and Scandinavia — and was directed principally to the United States. The second, between 1890 and 1930, was dominated by emigrants from southern and eastern Europe and had many destinations.

What pushed this second wave? In Britain, rural poverty and the unending reminders of deadening class restrictions went far to explain the exodus. Skilled workers, farmers, and unskilled servants and labourers were the components of the emigration, and, except in the years just before the First World War, the skilled labourers were in a decided minority. Pauper emigration schemes also pulled residents from city slums and sent them across the Atlantic. One poignant part of this story was the fact that 80,000 slum children were exported — alone — to Canada between 1869 and 1925, some of them to the west.[11] The situation in Austria-Hungary was slightly different. There, population growth had fragmented rural land holdings and, because of rapid economic development and the continuance of class rule, had created vast numbers of landless or nearly landless peasants. Farms of one, three, or eight acres were common; in the most notorious case, the province of Galicia, over 1 million farms were smaller than eight acres and only 1,500 farms were larger than fifty acres. Tiny holdings could not sustain a family. Moreover, ethnic or linguistic tensions complicated the lives of many citizens in the Hungarian part of the empire; the national revival of the Magyars brought with it discrimination against other ethnic groups and the repression of other languages: Croats, Slovaks, Ukrainians, Germans, and Jews bore the brunt of these measures. In Russia, a similar revival brought comparable problems. The Jews suffered great pain as a result; and Mennonites, Doukhobors, German Lutherans, and German Catholics, though not subject to such overt physical attacks, also feared for their survival as religious and ethnic communities. The American exodus to Canada, when placed beside the European emigration, is unusual: in a few cases, such as the Hutterites, religious liberty was an issue, but in most the wish for greater economic opportunity was the motivation that caused families to move north of the border.

The migration of navvies was a special case. They were males, usually young, many of whom planned to return to their European villages after a season or two in North American construction, mine, or lumber camps. A common feature of the Canadian working classes from the days of the mid-nineteenth century Irish canal-labourer, these workers appeared first in western Canada as the builders of the CPR. Ten thousand Chinese were said to have been employed in the mountain sections of the railway, and numbers followed them into mines and other enterprises, almost exclusively in British Columbia, until the influx was more or less halted by anti-oriental riots and political pressure in 1907-8. The need to find disciplined obedient workers who were willing to accept rough conditions and low wages led the railway entrepreneurs next to the *padrones* who trafficked in Italian labourers. Despite the objections of the ministers of labour and the interior, business leaders were able to win cabinet support for the importation of navvies from Italy and the Balkans between 1908 and 1914. In these years the proportion of unskilled immigrants in the total of male immigrants rose from 31 per cent to 43 per cent, and the proportion of central and southern Europeans rose from 29 per cent to 48 per cent. Many of these men did return to their European homes, if not within a season or two then certainly within a decade. But others, more often the victims of fraud than fecklessness, stayed on and became members of the Canadian community.[12]

The journey to the western interior of Canada included, for many immigrants, an ocean voyage. Not for them, however, the indescribable chaos of the timber ships of the early nineteenth century. Rather, the post-1896 emigrants, whether embarking from Hamburg or Bremen, Liverpool or Trieste, voyaged on steamships constructed for the purpose of Atlantic passenger traffic. The entire system of emigration was similarly more efficient by this time. As families of Ukrainians left their villages in Galicia or Bukowina, a dance or parade and a church blessing would mark their departure. A cart ride would take them to the city and the railway. As they passed through Germany in fourth-class train carriages, buttons or ribbons affixed to their coats to distinguish their shipping line, they found hawkers on the station platforms selling sandwiches and drinks. When they arrived at Hamburg, they learned that entire streets of lodging-houses were ready to provide shelter in exchange for their scarce cash. Bags roped shut, children clutched firmly by the hand, the families endured the line-ups for medical inspection, vaccination certificates, baggage fumigation, and steamship places, and then, finally, they were shepherded up the gangway to the ship.

The vessels of the Atlantic varied from 5,000-ton antiques to 30,000- or even 50,000-ton palaces such as Cunard's *Mauretania* and Hamburg-America's *Imperator*, but the typical ship was perhaps 15,000–20,000 tons, about 700 feet long, and 70 feet wide, carrying 400 first-class, 300 second-class, and 1,000 or 1,500 steerage passengers. The crossings were ten or twelve days and, unlike the era of sail, occasioned few deaths at sea.

Early passenger vessels (1870–90) housed the steerage passengers in bunks that lined the walls of the large lower-deck dormitories; long tables down the centre of these spaces served as eating and public areas. Later vessels had compartments for single men and women and family cabins and also provided separate dining and public rooms. Washing and toilet facilities were generally primitive and, because few, of an unsavoury character. Food was plain but, despite the lumpy slices of bread, gristly beef, and cold potatoes complained of by one passenger, usually adequate on the North Atlantic runs. Steerage class out of a northern European port may have been cramped, smelly, and crowded, but it was tolerable. The southern ports offered less attractive sailing prospects: food, cleanliness, sleeping accommodation, washing facilities, and the amount of space in which to move and to find some peace all were inferior to the better ships in the British and German ports. Naturally, those who travelled first or second class might have been living on a different planet: their restaurants offered linen and silver on the tables, as well as painted ceilings and mahogany panelling; they listened to string orchestras in the lounges; their staterooms, each equipped with a steward, featured carpet on the floor, double beds, easy chairs, and discreet lighting; but, of course, such accommodation was available only to a limited number of wealthy travellers, few of whom were likely to be emigrants.[13]

Arrival was exciting for everyone. Passengers pushed forward to the rails to catch the first sight of land, cheered as the port came into view, rushed to

167

collect their belongings and children, to put on their best clothes, or to have a last wash or shave as the horns and whistles sounded to announce arrival at the dock. What followed was bedlam: the noise, the confusion, the strangeness of the place and the language or the accent, the difficulty of ascertaining where to go and what to do; hawkers' cries, children's talk, officials' orders, baggage handlers' oaths; medical inspection followed by immigration review followed by money changing, food purchases, a search for baggage, and, finally, release from the immigration sheds and into the streets. If one was fortunate, one purchased without undue strain a ticket on a 'colonist car' to western Canada, but there were stories of cheats and sharpies who would offer a ticket to Edmonton but provide instead a taxi fare to Quebec's city centre. If fortune smiled, the family's belongings would remain intact. Inevitably, however, some people lost items of value, as did the two little Danish girls whose prized dolls were left behind.[14]

168   The colonist cars became little communities in themselves. The wooden seats could be made up into berths: James Minifie, the journalist, remembers as a young traveller sharing an upper with his mother and brother, while a family of four slept beneath them. At the end of their car was a tiny kitchen for the preparation of simple meals. Armed with 'yard of tickets' and a few supplies, the immigrants embarked upon the rough and, even for romantics, seemingly endless train journey through the trees and lakes of the Shield. The ride was interrupted by quick sorties to railside stores in the northern Ontario bush and by long waits on sidings for priority trains to roar through. Inevitably, talk turned to the future and to inquiries about 'what it was like.' Everyone had a calculation about how to start anew, but chance as much as plan must have affected many of those early decisions. Minifie's father had a ticket to Calgary but, on the strength of conversations with a seat mate and the train conductor—who assured him there was no good land left in Alberta (this was 1909) and that farm labour was needed in the parts they were traversing—grabbed his bags and jumped off the train at Sintaluta, on the endless plains of southern Saskatchewan.[15] Other new arrivals were met by husbands, brothers, and cousins; but how many times was this moment of family reunion associated with a sinking heart? Mrs Johanne Frederiksen arrived at Ellis Island in New York harbour on 13 May 1911, and a week later she and her six children alighted from the train at Nokomis, Saskatchewan, to be met by her husband who had preceded them by a year: 'You must excuse me [she wrote to her family in Denmark] . . . I haven't managed to write but we were all so exhausted . . . It has been difficult just to get food ready three times a day . . . When we were set out in the middle of the night in the cold at the last station in a driving snowstorm, we all cried but then my husband was there . . . Here it's still so desolate and frightening on the wild prairie. It is like the ocean. We are a tiny midpoint in a circle . . . You will . . . understand that it looks terrifying, more than you can imagine.'[16]

For others, the first home was a government-run immigration hall in one of the larger cities. In a noisy 'family room' or a large dormitory for single

men or women, troubles and ambitions were the currency of exchange as
the arrivals sought a place to live, a job, a niche in the new environment.
The hall would soon be replaced by a more permanent home, a room in a
lodging-house in a poorer part of the city or, in the case of single men, a
boarding-house. Here, strands that knit together a community would quickly
be extended and knotted: a church, a social club, or a language-based association would be a place of meeting; the street, the shops, and the job, too,
would provide instruction in the ways of the economy; and, most of all, the
family — nuclear, extended, adopted, perhaps only spiritually present by
means of letters and messages from the Old Country—would exert its influence as a source of stability and standards. The members of a boarding-
house might be drawn from the same village or region and thus might re-
establish a familiar outlook and behaviour with scarcely a misstep. But,
too, the newcomer might soon leave the circle of children and women and
old folk to take a job in a work camp or resource town. There, he would face
the brutalizing possibilities that accompanied hard labour and coarse life in
'the bush.'[17]

169

Adjustment to new circumstances was never automatic, as anyone who
has ever changed residences or cities will attest. But was immigration a traumatic crisis, an event burned into the mind that left a numbness for months
and even years?[18] Surely the impact of the move varied with the individual;
but it would be useful to remember the resilience of youth and the willingness implied in the original departure to make a new start. If adjustment
was difficult, it was none the less a task most were able to master. As the
Frederiksens learned, it was a battle 'against nature's fury, the unyielding
soil, the harsh climate.' But, in another letter home, one of the family extended the list of difficulties when she described their life as 'a struggle for
existence, a struggle against the loss of culture's benefits: church, school,
parish, community. How deep roots a man has in his fatherland he may
never know himself, until he loses them.' And therein lay the heart of the
matter: adjustment meant both economic survival and cultural accommodation. Material rewards came, in some degree, to almost everyone; western Canada was soon a viable community insofar as food and shelter and
health services could make it comfortable. But what about the cultural arrangements? On what terms was one to re-establish faith, learning, traditional customs, and the family? These matters were just as important as
food. Should the Frederiksens allow their older girls to hire out? Was the
boy big enough to work in the neighbour's fields? Dare they risk a winter
with father away in a lumber or construction camp? Could the family and
its ideals survive even the shortest separations? 'It is Sunday. We have just
arranged ourselves around the table to have afternoon coffee and read your
letter; thank you so much for it, it brings us great joy. This is the way it goes
here. On Sunday, when we assemble, we read the weekly letter, the gospel,
or some other reading . . . It makes the day a holy one for us and I hope,
gives the children something to remember.' But on another day the eldest
son, Henning, then sixteen, was delayed at the neighbours where he was

working from 5 a.m. to after 9 p.m.: 'Yesterday was Ellen's birthday (her seventh) and Henning was supposed to come over in the afternoon for hot chocolate and cake. He didn't come until eight in the evening and I told him at once that that was wrong. Still, we set the table, brought out the Danish flag and tried to look happy. But it happened as it has with so many others who have tried to have a celebration far, far from everyone — we couldn't do it . . . Henning put his arms on the table and burst into tears. Marie . . . and Ellen . . . cried too . . . That day Henning had been loading hay since early morning, the same the previous day . . . It's a hard school he is in.'[19]

English-speaking newcomers also had to adjust to the strange ways of the west. The appearance of a dictionary of the western Canadian 'language' in 1912 was one small indication of the distance between the prairies and other English-speaking communities. The definitions were both social commentaries and linguistic aids. The definition of 'All aboard' was 'the train conductor's call to passengers when the train is about to pull out. At such a moment in the Old Country, the railway officials smilingly invite the first-class passengers and deadheads to "take your seats, gentlemen, please," and bang the doors on the third-class passengers' fingers.'[20]

The important adjustments for English immigrants were not in the realm of linguistic novelties, of course, for it was a simple matter to pick up the slang, if one chose, and even to moderate one's accent to meet the flat intonation and lazy rhythms of local speech. The greater challenge was to make one's way and to maintain 'standards.' Within weeks of his arrival in Saskatchewan, Philip Minifie learned to harness horses western-style, to plough a straight furrow, to exchange his tweeds for denim, and to purchase horsehide gloves and rawhide boots. Within a year, he had joined a group of Ontario men who were planning to homestead a new district in southwestern Saskatchewan. In two years, he was joined by his family. And within three — a measure of his acceptance in the wider community — he had added to his responsibilities as pioneer farmer those of secretary-treasurer of the local school board (District 717, Malvern Link, named after the Malvern Hills near his Shropshire home) and of the local branch of the Grain Growers' Association. Mrs. Minifie was the organist at the Anglican church, a much more sedate institution than the hot gospel fellowship church that met at nearby Turkey Track school. And by 1916, seven years after Philip's arrival in Canada, his eldest son, sixteen-year-old James, was off to fight in the First World War. In 1919, James, who had returned from English army camps without ever seeing shots fired in anger, went to Regina College, and in 1920 he went to the University of Saskatchewan at Saskatoon. Two years later he travelled to Oxford as the province's Rhodes Scholar.[21]

The Minifies were not a typical English family, and yet their fortune was representative of a theme that recurs in prairie history. The Minifie children found it easier than their European-born contemporaries to be loyal to the empire and to make their way in the world through education. Like members of other ethnic groups, the English tended to marry their own, to locate in boarding-houses run by their countrymen, to congregate in certain areas of the cities, and to support their own football teams, music halls, and fish and chip shops. One bastion of their community was the Church of England, the prairie wing of which was dominated by English immigrants after 1900. The familiar liturgy and accents were significant aspects of the transition to the new land. As a labourer said: 'When we are at church it seems much like home, and one feels the new life enter in him, after the toils of the week.' The strength of the Sons of England, a cultural society that presented social evenings on the model of the music hall, including rousing patriotic hymns and familiar anecdotes and even English refreshments, was another index to the solidarity of the group. The function of such rituals as the church service and social evening was economic as well as psychological. The newcomers wanted jobs and a secure income; they disdained their competitors, especially the strangers from southern Europe, and attempted to control jobs through their ethnic networks. To assert their ethnic superiority, they contrasted their language and manner with that of other newcomers: as one English maid explained, 'To tell the truth, I didn't bother with any foreign people. I was too English for that.' They sponsored their own when openings came up in mine or plant, and they dominated the hiring system in such companies as the T. Eaton Company department stores and the CPR shops.[22] The English were indeed different from western Canadians when they arrived and were often disliked for their superior airs and alleged 'softness.' But they spoke English, the public language of the prairies, they knew the rules of politics and social intercourse, and they were a repository of wisdom when the institutions of the new society — trade unions, school districts, political parties — were created.

171

French-speaking immigrants had a more difficult transition. They spoke Canada's other 'official' language, insofar as the British North America Act permitted the use of French in federal courts and Parliament, but their numbers in the west were never sufficient to entrench the bilingual promise of the Manitoba Act and the North-West Territories Act into daily usage in public life. Immigration was the central difficulty. From the earliest days of the west's existence in Confederation, French-speaking citizens of Quebec had not responded as had Ontarians to the call of the west. The reasons for this apparent lack of interest in a promising investment frontier are numerous. Québécois had their own 'frontier,' the Shield, which was promoted by church colonization societies and seemed much closer to home. Other restless Québécois would be attracted by the prospect of industrial jobs just a few miles to the south of the St Lawrence, in the mills and factories of New England. Fainter hearts would be deterred from western migration by Quebec newspaper attacks on 'Ontario fanaticism' which allegedly resulted in assaults on French rights during the 1869–70 troubles, the 1874–5 debates concerning Riel's amnesty, the 1879 Norquay ministerial crisis, the 1885 Territorial uprising, and the Manitoba school and language legislation of 1890. And, finally, if one scholar is correct, French-Canadian culture itself was inimical to adventure: according to Arthur Silver, Québécois were less likely to try their luck in an unknown land, preferring instead the familiar ambiance of their province or the niche already created for them by their compatriots in the eastern United States. The prairies were just too far away and too strange for Québécois.[23]

The failure to establish significant French-Canadian immigration in the first generation of settlement was fatal to the French cause in the west during the post-1900 boom. With only 23,000 French-speaking settlers in the region in 1901, there was little hope that chain migration — the links that encouraged residents of a community to join friends in a new land — would offset the tide of non-French arrivals. Moreover, the citizens of the prairie region, recognizing that the French and Roman Catholic element — the two loyalties were not synonymous but were closely linked — was small and weak, proceeded to cancel the institutional guarantees of a continued French-Canadian presence. The use of the French language in the Manitoba courts and legislature was ended by an enactment of the Manitoba government in 1890. The territorial assembly followed suit in 1892. The use of French as a language of instruction in the schools rather than merely a subject of study was cancelled by the Manitoba government in 1890, restored in 1897 as part of a 'bilingual' program in which English had primacy, and abolished again in 1916. The Territories eliminated French as a language of instruction except in the primary grades in 1892 but restored it in the upper grades for one hour per day at the end of the school day in 1901. In 1918, Saskatchewan reduced the use of French to the first year of school only, though the optional hour at the end of the school day was retained. In 1931, after continuing debates about papal influence and foreign subversion, the government of Premier J.T.M. Anderson virtually eliminated French as a language of instruction in Saskatchewan schools. Alberta permitted only limited use of languages other than English after a crackdown on abuses of the school regulations in 1913. The loss of official status for the French language in government and schools was another blow to the French-speaking peoples of the western provinces.[24] The result was that Canada's newest regional community did not provide the bilingual compromises of Canada's federal government, and did not appear to be a congenial destination to French-speaking immigrants in the years of prairie growth after 1900.

The pattern of French settlement in the west illustrated the meagre input of French immigration agencies. In the 1870s and 1880s, when recruitment fell largely to the Roman Catholic church and its Manitoba leader, Mgr Alexandre Taché, archbishop of St Boniface, the French were encouraged to settle in the Red River valley on lands vacated by the métis. However, the plan to concentrate the French in a homogeneous bloc was undercut by the rapid dispossession of the métis, by the relative failure of church efforts to win migrants in Quebec and New England, and by the weakness of the attempts to secure colonists in the French-speaking lands of Europe. Insofar as French, Belgian, and Swiss recruits did arrive in the following decades, they destroyed plans for a single bloc by setting up homes wherever larger groups could be accommodated. Thus, at St Albert under Bishop

Grandin and Abbé Morin, at Grande Clairière under Abbé Gaire, at Montmartre, St Brieux, and Gravelbourg, French communities were created. In the end, the French had established something more important than a homogeneous bloc. Their communities constituted a chain of parishes across the west from the Red River to the Rockies, the spine as well as the creation of the Roman Catholic church in the region. French influence in culture and politics was to be important in the politics of cultural development for the next three decades.[25]

The English and the French were not ethnic groups like the others. They represented the two officially recognized languages of the country and the two largest national groups in Confederation; moreover they were the tacitly acknowledged leaders of the two dominant religious groups in Canada, the Roman Catholics and the Protestants.[26] Thus, the two collectives derived their influence from much more than simply their roots in a single nation of origin, their religious identity, or their common tongue. Each represented an alternate vision of Canada. One, Protestant, English-speaking, and pan-Anglo Saxon in cultural tone, was in the ascendant. The other, Roman Catholic and French-speaking, was on the defensive, having lost important institutional guarantees in the preceding decades. Neither was prepared for the influx of strangers that changed the very nature of prairie society in the three decades after 1900.

Some of the newcomers accepted voluntarily and with few apparent reservations the principle that they should accommodate themselves to the standards and customs of the dominant English-Canadian culture. The Icelanders can be taken as representative of this outlook. This is not to suggest that they willingly abandoned their language and culture, for they did not, but rather that they wished to be seen as good citizens and to conform to the conventions of their new home. A few Icelanders had left their island in the North Atlantic in the mid-nineteenth century because of economic depression, but their numbers grew in the 1870s. About 2,000 Icelanders emigrated to Canada, first to the Muskoka district of Ontario and later, in 1875, to the western shore of Lake Winnipeg. There, in the district of Gimli ('Paradise'), just north of the province of Manitoba, they secured exclusive rights to a bloc of land and created a large self-governing settlement, the Republic of New Iceland. They immediately founded a school, churches, and an Icelandic-language newspaper. Despite some very dark days, the community survived. The hardest chapter of its early days occurred in 1876-7, just after the colony was founded, when a devastating smallpox epidemic struck. During this disastrous winter, the province of Manitoba provided no relief beyond the dispatch of three doctors and the imposition of an armed quarantine upon the entire settlement that lasted for seven months. Over 100 citizens, mainly the very young, died. A second crisis occurred in 1877-9 when settlers debated whether the broad-minded Church of Iceland or the conservative German Lutherans of the American Missouri Synod should lead them. This conflict exacerbated tensions created by floods in 1879 and 1880 and drove many settlers out of the settlement, some to the Dakotas and others to southern Manitoba. Nevertheless, the settlement grew and even prospered. It was integrated within the municipal system of Manitoba government, and with the rest of the province acquired community halls, farmers' institutes, debating clubs, and sports events. The Icelanders retained a newspaper in their own language and founded a national festival (*Islendingadagurinn*), but they used English as the language of instruction in their schools, even after the 1897 Laurier-Greenway compromise would have permitted the addition of Icelandic on a bilingual basis. In 1897, they acquiesced, too, in the federal government's decision to open the Icelandic reserve to 'any class of settlers.' In the next decade, as Icelanders became a part of Winnipeg and Manitoba society, and members of other cultures, particularly Ukrainians, moved into the former New Iceland, an identifiable Icelandic community ceased to exist. Aside from its clubs and magazines and the August festival, the 5,000 Icelanders had few means of public expression. But pride in nationality remained. The Icelandic ideal was a combination of public conformity to English-Canadian cultural norms and private, family-centred efforts to retain their language and culture and to instil in their children an awareness of and pride in their national heritage.[27]

174

The situation of the German community in western Canada was different, yet in many respects it led to a conclusion akin to the Icelandic example. The Germans who arrived in western Canada during the immigration boom came principally from the Austro-Hungarian and Russian empires rather than from Germany. Roman Catholic and Protestant, urban and rural, Low and High German-speaking, they were numerous in total but divided into so many parts and so affected by the events of world politics that they never achieved a pan-German identity in Canada. Eventually, they too accommodated to the British-Canadian norm.[28]

Jews began to arrive in numbers in western Canada as a direct result of the pogroms in tsarist Russia in the early 1880s. Similar pressures drove other Jews out of Poland, Austria-Hungary, and Germany in the following decades. Differences of national origin and form of worship, though important, were transcended by the things they shared, including their faith, their language, and, most of all, their history as a people apart. They gathered in Winnipeg, where employment could be obtained, friends of one's faith found, and a religious congregation established, but they were also to be found in the rural west, both in agricultural colonies such as those near Wapella, Hirsch, Cupar, Lipton, and Sonnenfeld in Saskatchewan; Rumsey, Alberta; and Bender Hamlet, Manitoba; and in the little towns of the agricultural region where the Jewish general store — at one time there were over 100 in Manitoba — was as common as the Chinese café.[29]

The Jewish agricultural settlements knew mixed fortunes. The first, New Jerusalem, near Moosomin, North-West Territories, met a succession of disasters from the time of its foundation in 1884, including early frost and fire. Others, such as the Wapella colony, which was established in 1888 over the protests of some district residents, flourished for many years. But, whether success or failure, the settlements were homes for several thousand new Canadians. In Bender Hamlet, in the Interlake district of Manitoba, a European-style village was set out. Its half-mile of main street was lined on one side by houses with spruce logs chinked with a mixture of mud, straw and manure; fields were laid out, cropping routines established, animals purchased, gardens planted. Income was earned by hauling timber, cutting pulpwood, gathering seneca root, selling eggs, and, of course, attempting to raise grain on land that was better suited to raising rocks. Each spring the frost pushed a new crop of limestone boulders to the surface. The colony endured for twenty-five years and then collapsed, a victim of the children's need to find a wider world and, when they embarked on that search, of their refusal to return to poverty. The last individual to leave the Hamlet, Jack Lavitt's father, sold out, after a quarter-century of steady labour, for $700 in 1926. Like most of his contemporaries, young Jack had obtained only eight years of schooling, and yet, for all its poverty, he still recalls the riches of the community; he and his friends knew everyone, played pranks, attended *shul* on Saturday and Hebrew lessons after school, went to all the parties, picnics, bar mitzvahs, and weddings, and, eventually, moved to Winnipeg and started again. 'But we could work. We could get by. When everyone was out here at Bender, it was a happy place. A healthy place. It was a different world. You worked, you ate, you lived. And, you came out of there with . . . something.'[30]

175

The life of a small-town Jewish merchant was uncertain for different reasons. He was a businessman in a society that distrusted 'middlemen,' and he was a Jew in a world where Protestant and Catholic alike might object to his presence. He never would be accepted unreservedly. His children, though part of the town concert and team and club, might feel the same distance during Christmas celebrations or high holidays. One never knew whether a debtor would renounce his obligation and start a new account across the street, all the while condemning 'the Jew store' in a loud voice; one never knew, either, whether one's contribution to the grade 3 bake sale would be accepted without a fuss. Novelist Adele Wiseman described it best:

So there was I, overly sensitive, terribly high strung, a regular little bleeder. What could I do to protect myself, delicate little artist in the bud, against, for instance, my teachers?
We had a celebration in school and all the kids were supposed to bring stuff to eat. We didn't happen to have any weekday ordinary bread in the house, so Mom made my contribution, fancy little sandwiches, out of the Holy Sabbath egg bread. They were the only ones left on the plate one teacher was holding, and both teachers looked down at the plate and then at each other as though the plate had worms on it.
Honest to God Historic Dialogue:
Mama: You're still crying? Why are you still crying? You've been crying for hours.
Me: I'll cry until I stop.[31]

There were quotas to restrict Jewish entrants to Manitoba's medical and law schools. A tacit covenant excluded them from a summer resort. But they made their way and found their salvation despite the slights.

In Winnipeg, Jews began as unskilled labourers and small businessmen. At the turn of the twentieth century, they congregated in the city's north end, in the slum area known to them as Mitzrayim (Egypt) and to the press as New Jerusalem. They were itinerant pedlars, draymen, scrap and rag collectors, garment workers, tailors, and storekeepers. And, with the exception of a few who quickly perceived the lay of the land, they were socialists: Zionist, Marxist, or democratic, almost all of them espoused some kind of socialist reform for Canadian and international society. As the years passed and prosperity favoured their community, politics and religion and even dwelling place changed. By the mid-1920s, Jews were leaving the city centre for the more spacious lots on the northern edge of the city and even for the British Canadian bastions south of the Assiniboine River. They were more likely to become Liberal or Conservative in politics, too, and to have exchanged the traditional for the reform branch of their faith.[32] But their group exclusiveness remained. They were still Jews in the census report, they were probably still described as members of a synagogue, and, to a degree unmatched by almost any other group, they still married within the faith. History and religion ensured their active rejection of Anglo-conformity but, as their place in school and business and politics demonstrated, in most other respects they conformed to the standards and the institutions of British Canada.

176

The migration to Canada of thousands of peasants from the Hapsburg provinces of Galicia (Halychyna) and Bukovina — Ruthenians to their contemporaries, Ukrainians in modern-day terms — created an ethnic group whose internal politics were complex and whose impact on the larger society is still being felt. The Ukrainians were not, in general, content to join Icelanders and Germans in passive accommodation to the British-Canadian norm, but they were not sufficiently united to join Hutterites and Doukhobors in active rejection of or isolation from the culture of the charter group. As much as any other single ethnic group, the Ukrainians were responsible for the official adoption of today's bilingual-multicultural definition of Canadian society. And the origins of this important departure lay in the internal battles of prairie Ukrainian-Canadian people in the four decades after 1900. Their tenacity and cultural loyalty overcame myriad divisions and eventually led to their establishment of a Canada-wide, pan-Ukrainian voice and thence to national ethnic assertiveness.

Ukrainians were the most visible of all the southeastern European peasant cultures that came to the prairie west. They numbered at least 200,000 by 1931, and their striking characteristics—language, clothing, and housing—were obvious and distinctive features of the prairie environment.[33] Their sheepskin jackets, embroidered shirts, and baggy trousers were a common sight in rural districts for a generation; their two- or three-bedroom log houses, whitewashed, thatched, and dominated inside by a large clay stove,' dotted the countryside.[34] And their numerical strength imparted considerable importance to their internecine conflicts, and to their eventual unity.

Like other European peasant migrants, the Ukrainians left behind a world of poverty and carried with them little material wealth and few acquired skills. They were experienced farmers, however, and were prepared to work and to endure privation. They left regions where most citizens were illiterate, where most farms were too small for subsistence operations, where agricultural technology was primitive, and where drunkenness and indices of ill-health were proof of social crisis. Their two dominant religious institutions, the Greek Catholic church (the Uniates, product of a union between the Roman Catholic and Greek Orthodox churches in Poland in 1596) in Galicia and the Romanian-based Greek Orthodox church in Bukovina, were little inclined to press for social change. As a result, socialist and Protestant ideas had already taken root among their 'intelligentsia' — groups of literate reformers — in the late nineteenth century. These ideas came to Canada with the migrants. By the second decade of the twentieth century, the Ukrainian community was divided into four prominent factions and a number of smaller ones: the Protestants migrated into a Presbyterian-sponsored Greek independent church; the Marxists had joined the Ukrainian-language locals of the Social Democratic party or even the locals of the ideologically strict Socialist Party of Canada and eventually found their way into the Communist party and the Ukrainian Labour — Farmer Temple Association; the nationalists adhered to the reinvigorated Ukrainian (Greek) Orthodox church, which acquired a following after 1918; and the religious loyalists were members of the French-led Roman Catholic or Austrian-run Greek Catholic community.[35]

177

The impact on Canadian Ukrainians of the Russian revolution and the subsequent Ukrainian uprising in the steppes of southern Europe was considerable. Not only did it result in the emergence of a communist party but it also spawned monarchist and republican parties in Canada dedicated to the eventual creation of an independent Ukraine. One common thread can be discerned in this bewildering multiplicity of leagues and churches: the peasant culture was adapting to industrial capitalism. The oppressive conformity of the village, the brutal brawls of the drunken spree, the magic and superstition, and the proverbs that declared, for example, that 'an unbeaten wife is like an unsharpened scythe' were not mere figments of Protestant social workers' imaginations. They constituted centuries old habits of a peasant society and were sources of tension when this society was re-established. What was especially significant in the Canadian setting was that, after the initial decades of hardship on pioneer farms, new ideas were debated and new courses of action were decided on. The world of the peasant was being transformed into the world of ethnic politician. By 1940, under the pressure of war, the factions merged into the Ukrainian Canadian Committee, a loose coalition dedicated to democratic principles and British institutions, to promotion of Ukrainian cultural objects in Canada, and naturally, to support of the aspirations of Ukrainians in Europe.[36] Four decades on the prairies had created Ukrainian Canadians; their accommodation to North American technology was accompanied by religious and, to a greater degree than with the Jews, cultural community. They had been acculturated but not fully assimilated.

The Mennonites were even slower to adapt to British-Canadian ways, but in their case adjustment was delayed by their determination to remain separate from the materialism and godlessness that they associated with the larger prairie community. Mennonites first came to western North America in the years after 1874. They had sought large blocs of land where they might have freedom of religion, German-language schools, and exemption from military service and in 1874 were granted two exclusive tracts of land in southern Manitoba. The migration of about 7,000 souls from southern Russia was composed of Dutch-North German Anabaptists, descendants of the sixteenth-century left wing of the Reformation who had moved eastward in Europe in order to retain their group identity and religious freedoms. The increasing pan-Slav nationalism of the tsars had caused the most conservative among them, after a century of prosperity and expansion, to fear for their separate identity and thus to move once again.[37]

178

The Manitoba Mennonite colonies of the 1870s and their Saskatchewan descendants of the 1890s adapted their Russian agricultural pattern to the North American square survey. The basic unit of Mennonite settlement was the village rather than the homestead, and the units of cultivation were small strips of land rather than quarter-sections owned by individual farmers. To satisfy the homestead regulations individual Mennonites entered patents for 160 acres, but these formal requirements bore little relationship to their village-based farm system. The community itself determined the allocation of plots and the rotation of crops. The village, too, hired a herdsman who every morning walked the length of the single elm-shaded street to collect the cows at every gate and to lead them to the community pasture. The village had its own government, its own insurance or social security fund, and its own religious community. About 100 such villages functioned in Manitoba in the late nineteenth century, and others were established in Saskatchewan offshoots. With their own schools, churches, and agricultural systems, the villages seemed remote from the Canadian society that surrounded them.

The Mennonites themselves were also distant from other settlers on the prairies. They dressed austerely, they stayed largely among their own kind and married within their community, and they conversed almost entirely in Low German. Their domestic architecture, unvarying in pattern and yet quite different from house to house, was a distinctive variation on the peasant home: the neat front room was used only on formal occasions, and two or three bedrooms and kitchen completed the square. The focus of all such houses was the large stove and oven that heated the entire dwelling. What startled Canadians (though it was common in central Europe) was a passageway that linked house to barn, thus creating a single unit where the proper Anglo-Saxon assumed there should be no association. Despite their exclusiveness and the unusual aspects of their culture, the Mennonites were prosperous farmers who were interested in trade and accustomed to business dealings, and so their relations with neighbouring service towns were good.

If it seemed to some that the Mennonite commonwealth might flourish for generations, others recognized that the prairie environment was imposing new and different pressures on the group. Significant changes in theology and worship were affecting Christians around the world in the late nineteenth century, and several aspects of this change, including the rise of evangelical 'brethren' and the inevitable conflicts between conservatives and progressives over styles of worship, affected prairie Mennonites. So too did disagreements between ambitious expansion-minded farmers and the lazy, of whom every community has one or two: the nucleated village system held back the hard worker and bred resentment. Thus, by the late 1880s farmers were beginning to risk excommunication because they preferred to live and farm their own quarter-sections.

The construction of a railway through the West Reserve, the largest bloc of arable land in the Mennonite community, and its inevitable accompaniment of service centres complete with elevators and stores, altered the Mennonite situation again. The towns served as 'the bridgeheads for the assimilation of Mennonites into prairie society' because they enabled the individual farmer to survive outside the village system.[38] And the pressures of the provincial educational system began to affect the villages too. Schools have always been the crucial battleground for cultural ideals in western Canada and were the scene of a concerted Mennonite defence against the uniform English-language public education system. The most determined of the Mennonite idealists could not accept the unilingual and compulsory features of Manitoba's 1916 school law and within a decade had moved on to new promised lands in Mexico and Paraguay. In one of history's ironies, their lands in Manitoba were taken up by a second wave of Mennonite migrants fleeing the civil war in the Soviet Ukraine. Whether a 'Canadian' of the 1870s migration or a 'Russian' of the 1920s exodus, however, all the prairie Mennonites were learning to adapt to a wider Canadian environment in the inter-war decades. Radios and young people's groups, co-operatives and trunk highways were symbols of their rapid integration into the communications web of the 'modern' world. The village agricultural system and the separate school were things of the past; the language and the faith remained.[39]

179

Mennonites were often confused with two other groups of pacifists who settled in Canada, Doukhobors and Hutterites, but they were quite distinct from either. Doukhobors, the most famous of the three, were Russian rather than German-speaking; their faith developed out of eighteenth-century dissent within the Russian Orthodox church and was based on the rejection of formal church organization and of a mediatory priesthood. Their doctrine and history were preserved in hymns — 'The Living Book' — and were associated at some points in their history with a degree of Christian 'communism.' They fled Russian persecution in the 1890s and through the intervention of Tolstoy and Kropotkin, among others, eventually established three colonies in what became Saskatchewan. These 7,400 souls were mainly followers of the visionary Peter Verigin who accepted his insistence upon village-centred agriculture, communal labour, and collective ownership of property. But some did not, and soon conflicts arose over whether to acquiesce to the demands of 'the state' — in this case, Canadian government regulations that homesteads be patented and that births and deaths be recorded — and whether to maintain the communes. The most vehement Verigin loyalists, the fervent Sons of Freedom, in order to demonstrate their opposition to worldly wealth, began in 1902–3 to destroy their belongings and to embark on nude demonstrations as visible expressions of their faith. The colony survived these disruptions and even prospered in the next several years, but in 1906–7 Canada's new minister of the interior, Frank Oliver, began to revise his predecessor's rulings on Doukhobor lands, thus forcing them to conform to a strict reading of the law or lose their reserved blocs. In the ensuing conflict, over one-third of the community opted for individualism and the customary homestead. Under the leadership of Peter Makaroff of Blaine Lake, they ceased to practice communalism but retained their religious beliefs and pacifist principles as the Society of Independent Doukhobors. The larger fraction of the community joined Verigin in the creation of a new communal utopia in the interior of British Columbia where the familiar cycle of prosperity, collapse, and eventual migration occurred. The prairie Doukhobors were still a distinct community in the inter-war years. They spoke Russian, they lived in close proximity to each other in the districts of the three original blocs of land, and they continued to practise their religion. Not for them the excesses of the Sons of Freedom, or even the commune of the Veriginites, but rather the combination of faith, language, and community by which they were distinguished, like the Ukrainians and Mennonites, from the larger prairie society.[40]

Hutterites alone maintained the utopian communal ideal over several generations. They came late to the prairie west, having left Russia for the United States in the 1870s and then, in reaction to the overheated patriotism of South Dakota in 1917–19, negotiated entry into Canada, chiefly Manitoba and Alberta, between 1918 and 1922. Like the Mennonites, they were pacifists and descendants of the Anabaptist wing of the Reformation. They originated in the south Tyrol and Moravia and followed Jacob Hutter and a succession of others across central Europe in the sixteenth and seventeenth centuries. At each colony, they re-established their communal specialization of labour, with children's nursery, women's spinning hall, and a common dining-room, as well as dormitories with individual apartments for couples and their unmarried children. This was the pattern they re-created on the prairies. They retained the dress — black and white were predominant colours — and customs and simple manner of living of their ancestors and, though they spoke English and German, continued to communicate in an almost-extinct Tyrolean dialect. Their colonies would attain a population of 100 to 200 before a new branch community was established and, as exemplary social and economic democracies, were remarkably successful at meeting the material and spiritual needs of their members. Children were trained in the colonies' own schools to prepare for adult responsibilities within the faith; adults were taught to accept their roles, to suppress carnal desires, and to prepare for death. The communities prospered and the families multiplied. Aside from minor skirmishes with governments in their purchases of land for new colonies, they were left to live in peace. By the end of the 1920s, just as three centuries earlier, the Hutterian brethran remained self-sufficient, autonomous, and remote from the society in which they dwelt. Could they resist the assimilative pressures that had altered Mennonite and Ukrainian life? Could the state avoid intervention in colony affairs, especially during the creation of new communities? The answers remained to be given.[41]

One group of prairie Canadians remained almost as distant from its fellow citizens as did the Hutterites, though it lived in daily contact with the larger society. About 3,500 Chinese lived in Canada in 1880, and, in the five years of CPR construction, 1880–5, the Chinese population rose sharply to about 15,000 because of the recruitment of railway labourers. In the boom after 1900 it reached nearly 30,000 again because of the Canadian quest for hardy workers. Thus, several thousand Chinese resided in each prairie province in the first half of the twentieth century. Theirs was an unusual community not only because of its cultural roots but also because it was overwhelmingly male and apparently restricted in occupation. The ratio of Chinese women to men was 1:25 in prairie cities in 1921, for example, and about 80 per cent of the prairie Chinese work-force in 1931 was employed in two types of business — restaurants and laundries. The social life was narrow; they established their own political and benevolent associations but had only limited contact with Canadian institutions. From the 1890s, the Chinese were subject to hostility from the larger prairie community. There was a riot in Calgary in 1892 when a Chinese laundry worker was discovered to be a smallpox carrier, Saskatchewan disenfranchised the Chinese in 1903, and later both Saskatchewan and Manitoba enacted laws forbidding the employment of white women in Chinese restaurants. When the federal Chinese Immigration Act of 1923 ended further immigration to Canada, the growth of the community was effectively halted. Aging single men clustered in Chinatowns in the larger cities, victims of racist taunts and otherwise cut off from white society. In the prairie villages, however, the restaurant owner sometimes found a niche: 'When the hotel closed down, he started his own restaurant and a store as well . . . He always put in a bag of candy for the children with an order . . . He acted as a banker on Saturday nights . . . He kept many people from starving during the Depression.'[42] It was a lonely life, none the less, and must have offered little to those who spent their declining years in such isolation.

What metaphor will crystallize the social and cultural composition of prairie society in the first four decades of this century? Perhaps one should think in terms not of melting pots or mosaics but of stews. Simmered long enough, the ingredients might indeed assume a uniform consistency as in a melting pot, but, in the period that concerns us, between 1900 and the 1930s, that process had not occurred. Ethnic identity remained, in this period, unmistakeable.

To extend the metaphor, many of the stew's ingredients were imported.

Prairie population growth, from 400,000 in 1901 to 2 million in 1921 to 2.4 million in 1941 (a ratio of 1:5:6), was fuelled by immigration. This prairie 'stew' relied not only on imported ingredients but also on constant replenishment as it was drained off by other, chiefly American and European, consumers. The prairie population was always changing. We must beware the convenient assumption that individuals descended from an immigrant car, selected a home in city or country, and there remained to raise a family and grow old. This is certainly wrong. Prairie people were on the move, from farm to city, construction camp to coal mine to homestead, southern prairie to northern parkland, and, most of all, out of the region entirely. They migrated to the Pacific, to the United States, or back to Europe. If one estimate of this migration is accurate, as few as 800,000 of the original 2 million immigrants (two of five) remained in the prairies by 1931.[43]

One significant characteristic of these unassimilated elements was their 'foreign' character. By 1940, five prairie residents in ten acknowledged paternal origins other than British, two of these in eastern Europe and another two in western Europe. One more would be from England rather than British Canadian. And, to a degree that is difficult to imagine today, these ethnic peoples lived in discrete blocs. Whether the result of organized group settlement (Icelandic, Mennonite, Hutterite, Doukhobor), of chain settlements (links in the place of origin that were re-established in the new home as in the Hungarian case), or of gravitation group settlement (migrants who arrived independently but were drawn together by mutual attractions, as with Ukrainians and Germans), ethnic groups peopled vast areas of the prairies. Some of the nearly exclusive enclaves included up to thirty towns and villages within a single district. The enclaves were isolated from each other and, to a remarkable degree, from the larger prairie community. They retained such localisms as the dialect, customs, and traditions peculiar to their home districts in Europe, and they possessed an amazing institutional completeness. In matters as small as cuisine and as large as choice of marriage partner, the blocs remained relatively distinct in the 1920s and 1930s. A rough calculation based on the federal census suggests that at least 6 in 10 Scandinavians, 7 in 10 French and Germans, 8 in 10 Slavs, including 9.4 of 10 Ukrainians, in north-central Saskatchewan still spoke their mother tongue at home in 1941; other statistics suggest that this underestimated the persistence of languages other than English.[44] Ethnic identity remained a real and important factor in the life of many prairie Canadians in the 1930s.

When Stephen Leacock undertook his famous speaking tour through western Canada in the 1930s he learned quickly enough that the talk of 'balkanization' and 'bohemianization' and 'ruthenization' of the prairies that had filtered into eastern Canadian circles did not convey an accurate picture of the region. He concluded that one of his fondest assumptions about racial character seemed to be borne out in the west as in every other advanced society: give Scotsmen the smallest opening, he loved to say, and they would soon rule the roost. His conclusion was pure Leacock, but it was perceptive: after three decades of European immigration, the cultural standards of prairie society remained British; social and economic leadership rested firmly in the hands of the British Canadian; and, even in politics, where notions such as socialism and social credit were bandied about, British institutions and principles were as yet unshaken. But we must not assume that the mix of ingredients in this community was so diverse that each sample drawn from the whole was different in composition from every other: there was, I am certain, a consistency in prairie society, as in the stock of a stew, that was obvious in its dominant flavour if subtle in its variations.

Notes

1. Canada *Census* 1901, 1911, 1921, 1931; A.S. Whiteley, 'The Peopling of the Prairie Provinces of Canada; *American Journal of Sociology*, 38 (1932-3), pp. 240-52.
2. Joseph R. Manyoni 'Ethnics and Non-Ethnics: Facts and Fads in the Study of Intergroup Relations' in Martin L. Kovacs, ed., *Ethnic Canadians: Culture and Education* (Regina 1978), pp. 27-42.
3. Warren E. Kalbach, *The Impact of Immigration on Canada's Population* (Ottawa 1970), pp. 12-13. The 1885 Chinese 'head tax' was $50; in 1903 it was raised to $500.
4. D.J. Hall, 'Clifford Sifton: Immigration and Settlement Policy, 1896-1905' in Howard Palmer ed. *The Settlement of the West* (Calgary 1977), pp. 62, 68.
5. The statement was made by President Thomas Shaughnessy of the CPR. The navvy issue is discussed in Donald Avery, *'Dangerous Foreigners': European Immigrant Workers and Labour Radicalism in Canada 1896-1932* (Toronto 1979), pp. 25-37.
6. Ibid., pp. 90-112.
7. Canada, Royal Commission on Bilingualism and Biculturalism, cited in Howard Palmer, ed. *Immigration and the Rise of Multiculturalism* (Toronto 1975), p. 12.
8. Vernon C. Fowke *Canadian Agricultural Policy: The Historical Pattern* (Toronto 1946), pp. 161-77; the quotation on homestead policy is from pp. 179-80.
9. Hall, 'Sifton' pp. 68, 71-2.
10. Kenneth H. Norrie, 'The National Policy and the Rate of Prairie Settlement: A Review, *Journal of Canadian Studies*, 14, no. 3 (fall 1979), pp. 65-72.
11. Joy Parr *Labouring Children: British Immigrant Apprentices to Canada, 1869-1924* (London 1980).
12. Donald Avery, 'Canadian Immigration Policy and the "Foreign" Navvy 1896-1914,' Canadian Historical Association, *Historical Papers* (1972), pp. 143-5.
13 Philip Taylor, *The Distant Magnet: European Emigration to the U.S.A.* (New York 1971).
14. Jorgen Dahlie, 'Scandinavian Experiences on the Prairies, 1890-1920: The Frederiksens of Nokomis,' in Howard Palmer, ed. *The Settlement of the West* (Calgary 1977), p. 257 n.
15. James M. Minifie, *Homesteader: A Prairie Boyhood Recalled* (Toronto 1972), pp. 30-1.
16. Dahlie, 'Scandinavian,' pp. 106-7.
17 Robert Harney, 'Men without Women: Italian Migrants in Canada, 1885-1930' *Canadian Ethnic Studies*, 11 no. 1 (1979), pp. 29-47.
18. Oscar Handlin, *The Uprooted: The Epic Story of the Great Migrations That Made the American People* (New York 1951), provides one American perspective on dislocation. Another view is presented in Timothy L. Smith 'New Approaches to the History of Immigration in Twentieth-Century America,' *American Historical Review*, 71, no. 4 (July 1966), pp. 1265-79.
19. Dahlie 'Scandinavian,' pp. 109, 111.
20. John Sandilands, ed. *Western Canadian Dictionary and Phrase-Book: Things a Newcomer Wants to Know*, first pub. Winnipeg 1913 (facsimile edition Edmonton 1977), p. 3.
21. Minifie, *Homesteader*.
22. Ross McCormack, 'Cloth Caps and Jobs: The Ethnicity of English Immigrants in Canada, 1900-1914,' in Jorgen Dahlie and Tissa Fernando, ed. *Ethnicity, Power and Politics in Canada* (Toronto 1981), pp. 38-55.
23. A.I. Silver, 'French Canada and the Prairie Frontier, 1870-90', *Canadian Historical Review*, 50, no. 1 (March 1969), pp. 11-36; Robert Painchaud 'French Canadian Historiography and Franco-Canadian Settlement in Western Canada, 1870-1915,' *Canadian Historical Review*, 54, no. 4 (1978), pp. 447-66.
24. Keith A. McLeod, 'Politics, Schools and the French Language, 1881-1931' in Norman Ward and Duff Spafford, eds. *Politics in Saskatchewan* (Don Mills, 1968), pp. 124-50; John Herd Thompson, *The Harvests of War: The Prairie West, 1914-1918* (Toronto 1978), pp 87-94; Raymond Huel, 'French Language Education in Saskatchewan' in Susan Mann Trofimenkoff, ed. *The Twenties in Western Canada* (Ottawa 1972), pp. 230-42; the 'French' population of the prairies was 136,000 in 1931.

25. Robert Painchaud, 'Les exigences linguistiques dans le recrutement d'un clergé pour l'ouest canadien, 1818–1920,' and Gilbert-Louis Comeault, 'Les rapports de Mgr L.-P.-A. Langevin avec les groupes ethniques minoritaires et leurs répercussions sur le statut de la langue francaise au Manitoba, 1895–1916,' both in La Societé canadienne d'histoire de l'église catholique Sessions d'étude (1975), pp. 43–64, pp. 65–85.

26. Canada, Census, 1901, 1911, 1921, 1931. The Anglicans, Presbyterians, and Methodists together included 45 per cent of Canada's population between 1900 and 1925.

27. W. Kristjanson, The Icelandic People in Manitoba: A Manitoba Saga (Winnipeg 1965); Laura Goodman Salverson, The Viking Heart, first pub. 1947 (Toronto 1975), and Confessions of an Immigrant's Daughter, first pub. 1939 (Toronto 1981).

28. Arthur Grenke, 'The Formation and Early Development of an Urban Ethnic Community: A Case Study of the Germans in Winnipeg, 1872–1919,' PhD. dissertation, University of Manitoba, 1975.

29. Arthur A. Chiel, The Jews in Manitoba: A Social History (Toronto 1961).

30. Ted Allan, 'New Jerusalem Just a Memory,' Winnipeg Free Press, 10 December 1980, p. 57.

31. Adele Wiseman, 'A Brief Anatomy of an Honest Attempt at a Pithy Statement about the Impact of the Manitoba Environment on My Development as an Artist,' Mosaic, 3, no. 3 (spring 1970), 101. Another fascinating perspective is Fredelle Bruser Maynard, Raisins and Almonds (Don Mills 1964).

32. R. Usiskin, 'Toward a Theoretical Reformulation of the Relationship between Political Ideology, Class and Ethnicity: A Case Study of the Winnipeg Jewish Radical Community 1905–1920,' MA thesis, University of Manitoba, 1978.

33. Canada, Census, 1931.

34. John C. Lehr, 'The Government and the Immigrant: Perspectives on Ukrainian Block Settlement in the Canadian West,' Canadian Ethnic Studies, 11, no. 2 (1977), pp. 42–52, and John C. Lehr, Ukrainian Vernacular Architecture in Alberta, Alberta Historic Sites Service Occasional Paper no. 1 (1976).

35. Orest T. Martynowycz, 'Village Radicals and Peasant Immigrants: The Social Roots of Factionalism among Ukrainian Immigrants in Canada 1896–1918,' MA thesis, University of Manitoba, 1978; John Marlyn, Under the Ribs of Death, first pub. 1957 (Toronto 1964).

36. Oleh W. Gerus, 'The Ukrainian Canadian Committee,' In Manoly R. Lupul ed. A Heritage in Transition: Essays in the History of Ukrainians in Canada (Toronto 1982), pp. 195–214.

37. Frank H. Epp, Mennonites in Canada, 1786–1920: The History of a Separate People (Toronto 1974). The Mennonite immigrants to western Canada were distinct from the various Swiss-German Mennonites who joined William Penn's colony and then migrated north to Upper Canada with the Loyalist in the late eighteenth and early nineteenth centuries.

38. John H. Warkentin, 'The Mennonite Settlements of Southern Manitoba,' PhD. dissertation, University of Toronto, 1960, p. 147.

39. E.K. Francis, In Search of Utopia: The Mennonites in Manitoba (Altona, Manitoba, 1955), and Frank H. Epp, Mennonites in Canada, 1920–1940: A People's Struggle for Survival (Toronto 1982).

40. George Woodcock and Ivan Avakumovic, The Doukhobors (Toronto 1968).

41. Victor Peters, All Things Common: The Hutterian Way of Life, first pub. 1965 (New York 1971), and John Ryan, The Agricultural Economy of Manitoba Hutterite Colonies (Toronto 1977).

42. J. Brian Dawson, 'The Chinese Experience in Frontier Calgary: 1885–1910,' in Rasporich and Klassen, eds. Frontier Calgary; Harry Con, et. al., From China to Canada: A History of the Chinese Communities in Canada (Toronto 1982).

43. J.H. Richards, 'Retrospect and Prospect,' in P.J. Smith ed. The Prairie Provinces (Toronto 1972), p. 131.

44. Alan B. Anderson, 'Linguistic Trends among Saskatchewan Ethnic Groups,' in Martin L. Kovacs, ed., Ethnic Canadians: Culture and Education (Regina 1978), pp. 63–86.

Reluctant Hosts:
Anglo-Canadian Views of Multiculturalism in the Twentieth Century*
HOWARD PALMER

Introduction

The way in which Anglo-Canadians have reacted to immigration during the twentieth century has not simply been a function of the numbers of immigrants or the state of the nation's economy. The immigration of significant numbers of non-British and non-French people raised fundamental questions about the type of society which would emerge in English-speaking Canada; hence, considerable public debate has always surrounded the issue of immigration in Canada. The questions which have repeatedly been raised include the following: Were the values and institutions of Anglo-Canadian society modelled exclusively on a British mold and should immigrants be compelled to conform to that mold? Or, would a distinctive identity emerge from the biological and cultural mingling of Anglo Canadians with new immigrant groups? Would cultural pluralism itself give English-speaking Canada a distinctive identity? These three questions reflect the three theories of assimilation which have dominated the twentieth century debate over immigrant adjustment.

185

The assimilation theory which achieved early public acceptance was Anglo-conformity. This view demanded that immigrants renounce their ancestral culture and traditions in favour of the behaviour and values of Anglo-Canadians. Although predominant prior to World War II, Anglo-conformity fell into disrepute and was replaced in the popular mind by the "melting pot" theory of assimilation. This view envisaged a biological merging of settled communities with new immigrant groups and a blending of their cultures into a new Canadian type. Currently, a third theory of assimilation — "cultural pluralism" or "multiculturalism" — is vying for public acceptance. This view postulates the preservation of some aspects of immigrant culture and communal life within the context of Canadian citizenship and political and economic integration into Canadian society.[1]

There has been a recent burgeoning of historical and sociological research on Anglo-Canadian attitudes toward ethnic minorities. Much of this research contradicts the view which has been advanced by some Anglo-Canadian historians[2] and politicians that Anglo-Canadians have always adopted the "mosaic" as opposed to the American "melting pot"

* Revised by the author from an address to the Second Canadian Conference on Multiculturalism. First published in the conference report, *Multiculturalism as State Policy*, by the Canadian Consultative Council on Multiculturalism. Reprinted by permission of the Minister of Supply and Services Canada.

approach. Much of this rhetoric has simply been wishful thinking. Perhaps immigrant groups did not "melt" as much in Canada as in the United States, but this is not because Anglo-Canadians were more anxious to encourage the cultural survival of ethnic minorities. There has been a long history of racism and discrimination against ethnic minorities in English-speaking Canada, along with strong pressures for conformity to Anglo-Canadian ways.

The "Settlement" Period and the Predominance of Anglo-conformity: 1867-1920

Among the several objectives of the architects of the Canadian confederation in 1867, none was more important than the effort to accommodate the needs of the two main cultural communities. There was virtually no recognition of ethnic diversity aside from the British-French duality. This

186

is, of course, somewhat understandable since at the time of confederation, only eight percent of the population of three and one half million were of non-British[3] or Non-French ethnic origin. There were, however, significant numbers of people of German and Dutch origin, well-established black and Jewish communities as well as a few adventurers and entrepreneurs from most European ethnic groups now in Canada.

The proportion of people of other than British, French, or native origin in Canada remained small until nearly the turn of the century; the United States proved more attractive for most European emigrants. In fact it was attractive for many Canadians as well, and the Dominion barely maintained its population. But with the closing of the American frontier which coincided with improving economic conditions in Canada and an active immigration promotion campaign by Wilfrid Laurier's Liberal government, many immigrants began to come to the newly opened land of western Canada in the late 1890's.[4] Immigration policy gave preference to farmers, and most non-British immigrants came to farm in western Canada. However, some immigrants ended up working in mines, laying railway track, or drifting into the urban working class.[5] During this first main wave of immigration between 1896 and 1914, three million immigrants, including large numbers of British laborers, American farmers, and eastern European peasants, came to Canada. Within the period of 1901 to 1911, Canada's population rocketed by 43 percent and the percentage of immigrants in the country as a whole topped 22 percent. In 1911, people of non-British and non-French origin formed 34 percent of the population of Manitoba, 40 percent of the population of Saskatchewan, and 33 percent of the population of Alberta.

Throughout the period of this first large influx of non-British, non-French immigrants, (indeed up until World War II), anglo-conformity was the predominant ideology of assimilation in English-speaking Canada.[6] For better or for worse, there were few proponents of either the melting pot or of cultural pluralism. Proponents of anglo-conformity argued that it was the obligation of new arrivals to conform to the values and institutions of Canadian society — which were already fixed. During this period when scarcely anyone questioned the verities of God, King, and country, there was virtually no thought given to the possibility that "WASP" values might not be the apex of civilization which all men should strive for.

Since at this time the British Empire was at its height, and the belief in "progress" and Anglo-Saxon and white superiority was taken for granted throughout the English-speaking world, a group's desirability as potential immigrants varied almost directly with its members physical and cultural distance from London, (England) and the degree to which their skin pigmentation conformed to Anglo-Saxon white. Anglo-Canadians regarded British and American immigrants as the most desirable.[7] Next came northern and western Europeans who were regarded as culturally similar and hence assimilable. They were followed by central and eastern Europeans, who in the eyes of Clifford Sifton and immigration agents, had a slight edge on Jews and southern Europeans, because they were more inclined to go to and remain on the land. These groups were followed in the ethnic pecking order by the "strange" religious sects, the Hutterites, Mennonites, and Doukhobors, who were invariably lumped together by public officials and the general public despite significant religious and cultural differences between them. Last, but not least (certainly not least in the eyes of those British Columbians and their sympathizers elsewhere in the country who worried about the "Asiatic" hordes) were the Asian immigrants — the Chinese, Japanese, and East Indians (the latter of whom were dubbed "Hindoos," despite the fact that most were Sikhs). Running somewhere close to last were black immigrants, who did not really arise as an issue because of the lack of aspiring candidates, except in 1911, when American blacks were turned back at the border by immigration officials because they allegedly could not adapt to the cold winters in Canada; a curious about-face for a department which was reassuring other American immigrants that Canadian winters were relatively mild.[8]

As might be expected, prevailing assumptions about the relative assimilability of these different groups were quickly transformed into public debate over whether immigrants whose assimilability was problematic should be allowed into the country. During this first wave of immigration, considerable opposition developed to the entry of central, southern and eastern European immigrants, Orientals, and to the three pacifist sects. Opposition to these groups came from a variety of sources, for a variety of reasons. But one of the most pervasive fears of opinion leaders was that central, southern and eastern Europeans, and Orientals would wash away Anglo-Saxon traditions of self-government in a sea of illiteracy and inexperience with "free institutions."[9] Many English-Canadian intellectuals, like many American writers at the time, thought that North America's greatness was ensured so long as its Anglo-Saxon character was preserved. Writers emphasized an Anglo-Saxon tradition of political freedom and self-government and the "white man's" mission to spread Anglo-

Saxon blessings.[10] Many intellectuals and some politicians viewed Orientals and central southern and eastern European immigrants as a threat to this tradition and concluded that since they could not be assimilated they would have to be excluded. The introduction in Canada of a head tax on Chinese immigrants, a "gentlemen's agreement" with Japan which restricted the number of Japanese immigrants, the passing of orders-in-council which restricted immigration from India, the gradual introduction of restrictive immigration laws in 1906, 1910, and 1919 relative to European immigration and the tightening of naturalization laws was based in considerable part on the assumptions of anglo-conformity — immigrants who were culturally or racially inferior and incapable of being assimilated either culturally or biologically, would have to be excluded.[11] Those who rose to the immigrants' defence argued almost entirely from economic grounds: immigration from non-British sources was needed to aid in economic development, not because it might add anything to Canada's social or cultural life.

188

Although the trend toward restrictionism during the early 1900s seemed to indicate a government trend toward anglo-conformity in response to public pressure, for the most part between 1867 and 1945, there was no explicit federal government policy with regard to the role of non-British and non-French ethnic groups in Canadian society. It was generally assumed, however, that immigrants would eventually be assimilated into either English-Canadian or French-Canadian society. A recent careful study of Clifford Sifton's attitudes toward immigrant groups in Canadian society concludes Sifton assumed that central and eastern Europeans ". . . would be 'nationalized' in the long run through their experience on the land . . .".[12] The federal government's concern was tied to the economic consequences of immigration, while schools, the primary agents of assimilation, were under provincial jurisdiction. The federal government had encouraged Mennonites and Icelanders to settle in blocks in Manitoba during the 1870's and had given them special concessions (including local autonomy for both and military exemptions for the Mennonites) to entice them to stay in Canada rather than move to the United States.[13] But this was not because of any conscious desire to make Canada a cultural mosaic, nor was it out of any belief in the value of cultural diversity. Block settlements, by providing social and economic stability, were simply a way of getting immigrants to settle in the west and remain there.[14] The government policy was pragmatic and concerned primarily with economic growth and "nation building;" there was little rhetoric in immigration propaganda picturing Canada as a home for oppressed minorities who would be able to pursue their identities in Canada.

Provincial governments were faced with the problems of assimilation more directly than the federal government since the provinces maintained jurisdiction over the educational systems. The whole question of the varying attitudes of provincial authorities toward assimilation is much too complex to outline in this article; suffice it to say that with some notable exceptions (like the bilingual school system in Manitoba between 1896 and 1916, and the school system which was established for Hutterites in Alberta), anglo-conformity was the predominant aim of the public school system and was an underlying theme in the textbooks.

Anglo-conformity was most pronounced during World War I as nationalism precipitated insistent hostility to "hyphenated Canadianism" and demanded an unswerving loyalty. For many Anglo-Canadians during the war, loyalty and cultural and linguistic uniformity were synonymous. During the war, western provincial governments acted to abolish the bilingual schools which had previously been allowed.[15] The formation of the Union government of Conservatives and Liberals during the first World War was an attempt to create an Anglo-Saxon party, dedicated to "unhyphenated Canadianism" and the winning of the war; even if this meant trampling on the rights of immigrants through press censorship and the imposition of the War Time Elections Act which disfranchised "enemy aliens" who had become Canadian citizens after March 21, 1902.[16] Various voluntary associations like the YMCA, IODE, National Council of Women, Canadian Girls in Training, Girl Guides, Big Brothers and Big Sisters Organizations and Frontier College, as well as the major Protestant denominations also intensified their efforts to "Canadianize" the immigrants, particularly at the close of the war when immigrant support for radical organizations brought on anti-radical nativist fears of the "menace of the alien."[17] The pressures for conformity were certainly real, even if English-Canadians could not always agree completely on the exact nature of the norm to which immigrants were to be assimilated.

189

All the major books on immigration prior to 1920, including J. S. Woodsworth's *Strangers Within Our Gates*, J. T. M. Anderson's *The Education of the new Canadian*, Ralph Connor's *The Foreigner*, Alfred Fitzpatrick's *Handbook for New Canadians*, C. A. Magrath's *Canada's Growth and Some Problems Affecting It*, C. B. Sissons, *Bilingual Schools in Canada*, and W. G. Smith, *A Study in Canadian Immigration*, were based on the assumptions of anglo-conformity. To lump all these books together is of course to oversimplify since they approached the question of immigration with varying degrees of nativism (or anti-foreign sentiment), and humanitarianism. Nor were all of the voluntary organizations' attempted "Canadianization" work among immigrants motivated solely by the fear that immigrants would undermine the cultural homogeneity of English-speaking Canada. Many of these writers and organizations saw their work with the immigrants as a means of fighting social problems and helping immigrants achieve a basic level of political, social, and economic integration into Canadian society. But it cannot be denied that their basic assumption was that of anglo-conformity. Cultural diversity was either positively dangerous, or was something that would and should disappear with time, and with the help of Anglo-Canadians.

Perhaps it should be emphasized that the individuals advocating anglo-conformity were not just the reactionaries of their day. Protestant Social

Gospellers (including J. S. Woodsworth, later one of the founders of the CCF) who played such a prominent role in virtually all the reform movements of the pre-World War I period (including women's rights, temperance, and labor, farm, and penal reform) believed that immigrants needed to be assimilated to Anglo-Canadian Protestant values as part of the effort to establish a truly Christian society in English-speaking Canada.[18] Women's groups pushing for the franchise argued that certainly they deserved the vote if "ignorant foreigners" had it, and joined in the campaign to Canadianize the immigrants who "must be educated to high standards or our whole national life will be lowered by their presence among us."[19]

But there was a central contradiction in Anglo-Canadian attitudes toward ethnic minorities. Non-Anglo-Saxon immigrants were needed to open the west and to do the heavy jobs of industry. This meant not only the introduction of culturally distinctive groups, but groups which would occupy the lower rungs of the socio-economic system. The pre-1920 period was the period of the formation of, and the most acute expression of what was later called the "vertical mosaic." Anglo-Canadians were not used to the idea of cultural diversity, nor the degree of class stratification which developed during this period of rapid settlement and industrialization. The answer to all the problems of social diversity which the immigrants posed was assimilation. The difficulty however with achieving this goal of assimilation was not only the large numbers of immigrants, or the fact that not all (or even a majority) of them wanted to be assimilated. One of the major factors preventing assimilation was discrimination by the Anglo-Canadian majority.

The basic contradiction, then, of Anglo-Canadian attitudes as expressed through the "Canadianization" drives was the tension between the twin motives of humanitarianism and nativism — between the desire to include non-British immigrants within a community and eliminate cultural differences and the desire to stay as far away from them as possible because of their presumed "undesirability." This contradiction was graphically revealed at the national conference of the IODE in 1919. The women passed one resolution advocating a "Canadianization campaign" to "propagate British ideals and institutions", to "banish old world points of view, old world prejudices, old world rivalries and suspicion" and to make new Canadians 100 percent British in language, thought, feeling and impulse." Yet they also passed another resolution protesting "foreigners" taking British names.[20]

It does not appear that this was simply a case of the Anglo-Canadian majority being divided between those who wanted to pursue a strategy of assimilation, and those who wanted to pursue a strategy of subordination and segregation. Certainly there was some division along these lines, but as suggested by the IODE resolutions, discrimination and anglo-conformity were often simply two different sides of the same coin — the coin being the assumption of the inferiority of non-Anglo-Saxons.

What developed throughout English-speaking Canada during this period was a vicious circle of discrimination. Non-Anglo-Saxons were discrimi-

190

nated against because they were not assimilated, either culturally or socially, but one of the reasons they were not assimilated was because of discrimination against them. As one researcher noted in a 1917 report on "Social Conditions in Rural Communities in the Prairie Provinces," the group "clannishness" of immigrants which was so widely deplored by the public was caused as much by the prejudice of the "English" as it was by the groups' desire to remain different.[21]

There is no need to catalogue here the extensive patterns of social, economic and political discrimination which developed against non-Anglo-Saxons.[22] Patterns of discrimination parallelled preferences of immigrant sources with northern and western Europeans encountering relatively little discrimination, central and southern Europeans and Jews encountering more discrimination and non-whites encountering an all pervasive pattern of discrimination which extended to almost all aspects of their lives. Discrimination was one of the main factors which led to the transference (with only a few exceptions) of the same ethnic "pecking order" which existed in immigration policy to the place each group occupied in the "vertical mosaic," with the British (especially the Scots) on top, and so on down to the Chinese and blacks who occupied the most menial jobs.[23] Non-British and non-French groups not only had very little economic power; they also would not even significantly occupy the middle echelons of politics, education or the civil service until after World War II. *191*

The ethnic stereotypes which developed for eastern European and Oriental groups emphasized their peasant origins. These stereotypes played a role in determining the job opportunities for new immigrants and functioned to disparage those who would climb out of their place. Opprobrious names such as "Wops," "Bohunks" and especially "foreigner" indicated class as well as ethnic origin and these terms were used as weapons in the struggle for status. The very word "ethnic" carried, for many people, such an aura of opprobrium that even recently there have been attempts to expurgate the use of the word. Ethnic food and folklore were regarded by most Anglo-Canadians as not only "foreign," but "backward" and lower class. Folklorist Carole Henderson has aptly described the views of Anglo-Canadians toward folklore, (views which continue to the present day): "Except for members of some delimited regional and usually ethnic, subcultures such as Newfoundlanders or Nova Scotian Scots, most Anglo-Canadians simply fail to identify folklore with themselves, and tend to consider such materials to be the . . . unimportant possessions of the strange, foreign or 'backward people in their midst'."[24]

The 1920s and the Emergence of "Melting Pot" Ideas

The 1920s brought the second main wave of non-British and non-French immigrants to Canada and saw the emergence of the second ideology of assimilation, the "melting pot." During the early 1920s both Canada and the United States had acted to further restrict immigration from southern, central and eastern Europe and from the Orient. Chinese were virtually excluded from Canada, and central, southern and eastern Europeans were classified among the "non-preferred" and restricted category of immigrants. But by the mid-1920s several powerful sectors of Canadian society, including transportation companies, boards of trade, newspapers and politicians of various political persuasions, as well as ethnic groups, applied pressure on the King government to open the immigration doors.[25] These groups believed that only a limited immigration could be expected from the "preferred" countries and that probably only central and eastern Europeans would do the rugged work of clearing marginal land. The railways continued to seek immigrants to guarantee revenue for their steamship lines, traffic for their railways and settlers for their land. With improving economic conditions in the mid-twenties, the Federal government responded to this pressure and changed its policy with respect to immigrants from central and eastern Europe.

192

While continuing to emphasize its efforts to secure British immigrants, in September 1925, the Liberal government of Mackenzie King entered into the "Railways Agreement" with the CPR and CNR which brought an increased number of central and eastern Europeans. The Government authorized the railways to encourage potential immigrants of the "non-preferred" countries to emigrate to Canada and to settle as "agriculturalists, agricultural workers and domestic servants."[26]

Through this agreement, the railways brought to Canada 165 000 central and eastern Europeans and 20 000 Mennonites. They represented a variety of ethnic groups and a diversity of reasons for emigrating. Most of the Ukrainian immigrants were political refugees. Poles, Slovaks, and Hungarians were escaping poor economic conditions. German-Russians and Mennonites were fleeing civil war, economic disaster, and the spectre of cultural annihilation in Russia.[27] Often they chose Canada since they could no longer get into the United States because of its quota system and the Canadian route was the only way they could get to North America. With this new wave of immigration, the proportion of the Canadian population that was not of British, French, or native origin, rose to more than 18 percent by 1931.

In responding to this new wave of immigration, many opinion leaders held to an earlier belief that Canada should be patterned exclusively on the British model, and continued to advocate anglo-conformity. In national periodicals and newspapers during the 1920s, the emphasis which was placed on the need to attract British immigrants was related to this assumption that anglo-conformity was essential to the successful development of Canadian society. "Foreign" immigrants had to be assimilated and there needed to be enough Britishers to maintain "Anglo-Saxon" traditions.[28] R. B. Bennett, later to become the Conservative prime minister during the early 1930s, attacked melting pot ideas in the House of Commons and argued "These people [continental Europeans] have made excellent settlers: . . . but it cannot be that we must draw upon them to shape our civilization. We must still maintain that measure of British civilization which will enable us to assimilate these people to British institutions, rather than assimilate our civilization to theirs . . .".[29]

The influx of new immigrants from central and eastern Europe during the mid and late twenties also aroused protests from a number of nativist organizations such as the Ku Klux Klan, The Native Sons of Canada, and The Orange Order who were convinced that Canada should "remain Anglo-Saxon."[30] Nativist sentiment in western Canada was most pronounced in Saskatchewan where one of its leading spokesmen was George Exton Lloyd, an Anglican bishop and one of the founders of the Barr colony at Lloydminster.

In a torrent of newspaper articles and speeches, Lloyd repeated the warning that Canada was in danger of becoming a "mongrel" nation: "The essential question before Canadians today is this: Shall Canada develop as a British nation within the empire, or will she drift apart by the introduction of so much alien blood that her British instincts will be paralyzed?"[31] According to Lloyd, Canada had but two alternatives: it could either be a homogeneous nation or a heterogeneous one. The heterogeneous or "melting pot" idea had not worked in the United States (as evidenced by large numbers of unassimilated immigrants at the outbreak of World War I), and could not, he argued, work in Canada. With Lloyd, as with other individuals and organizations promoting anglo-conformity at this time, one gets the distinctive feeling that they were on the defensive. Like other English-speaking Canadians who had a strong attachment to Britain and the Empire, Lloyd saw a threat to Canada's "British" identity, not only in the increasing numbers of "continental" immigrants, but also in the declining status of things British as Canadians moved towards a North American based nationalism which did not include loyalty to the British Empire as its primary article of faith.[32]

During the late 1920s, a new view of assimilation, the melting pot, developed greater prominence. This view of assimilation, which arose partly as a means of defending immigrants against nativist attacks from people like Lloyd, envisioned a biological merging of Anglo-Canadians with immigrants and a blending of their cultures into a new Canadian type. Whereas Lloyd and other nativists argued that since immigrants could not conform to Anglo-Canadian ideals they should be excluded, a new generation of writers argued that assimilation was indeed occurring, but to a new Canadian type.[33] Since assimilation was occurring, nativist fears were unwarranted. Indeed, immigrants would make some valuable cultural contributions to Canada during the process of assimilation. Although these writers did not all use the "melting pot" symbol when discussing their view of assimilation, one can lump their ideas together under the rubric of the "melting pot" because they did envisage the emergence of a new society which would contain "contributions" from the various immigrant groups.

Most of these writers who defended "continental" European immigra-

193

tion did not seriously question the desirability of assimilation. Robert England, a writer and educator who worked for the CNR had read widely enough in anthropological sources to be influenced by the cultural relativism of Franz Boas and other anthropologists and did in his writing question the desirability of assimilation.[34] But most of these writers were concerned primarily with attempting to promote tolerance toward ethnic minorities by encouraging their assimilation, and many became involved in programs to facilitate this assimilation.

Advocates of anglo-conformity and the melting pot both believed that uniformity was ultimately necessary for unity, but they differed on what should provide the basis of that uniformity. Advocates of the melting pot, unlike the promoters of anglo-conformity, saw assimilation as a relatively slow process, and saw some cultural advantages in the mixing that would occur.

194   There was not, however, always a clear distinction between anglo-conformity and the melting pot. Rhetoric indicating that immigrants might have something more to offer Canada than their physical labor was sometimes only a thinly veiled version of anglo-conformity; the melting pot often turned out to be an Anglo-Saxon melting pot. For example John Blue, a prominent Edmonton promoter and historian, wrote in his history of Alberta in 1924 that the fears about foreign immigration destroying Canadian laws and institutions had proved groundless. "There is enough Anglo-Saxon blood in Alberta to dilute the foreign blood and complete the process of assimilation to the mutual advantage of both elements."[35]

There were a variety of reasons for the development of melting pot ideas during the 1920s.[36] The growth during the 1920s of an autonomous Canadian nationalism helped the spread of melting pot ideas. Some English-Canadian opinion leaders began to discuss the need for conformity to an exclusively Canadian norm rather than a "British" norm. One of the arguments that John W. Dafoe, the influential editor of the *Winnipeg Free Press* and J. S. Ewart, a constitutional lawyer, used in support of their view of Canadian nationalism was that non-British immigrants could not be expected to feel loyalty to the British Empire.[37]

Melting pot advocates tended to be people who had some personal experience with immigrants, and recognized both the intense pride that immigrants had in their cultural backgrounds as well as the rich cultural sources of those traditions. But they also lived in a time when recognition of ethnicity meant mostly Anglo-Canadian use of ethnicity as a basis of discrimination or exploitation. It was also a time when some ethnic groups were still close enough to their rural peasant roots that ethnic solidarity was often not conducive to upward mobility. The view of most melting pot advocates that the disappearance of ethnicity as a basis of social organization would increase the mobility opportunities of the second generation was based on a sound grasp of the realities of the day. The life-long campaign of John Diefenbaker for "unhyphenated Canadianism" and "one Canada" grew out of this experience with ethnicity as something that could be used to hinder opportunities, and was consistent with his emphasis on human rights, rather than group rights.[38]

The 1930s

Although immigration was severely cut back during the depression of the 1930s, the role of ethnic minorities in English-speaking Canada continued to be a major public concern. Paradoxically, although the depression witnessed the high point of discrimination against non-Anglo-Saxons, it was also during the 1930s that the first major advocates of cultural pluralism in English-speaking Canada began to be heard.

The depression affected non-Anglo-Saxon immigrants more than most other groups in the society. These immigrants because of their language problems and lack of specialized skills, were concentrated in the most insecure and therefore most vulnerable segments of the economy. Since immigrants were the last hired and the first fired, a large proportion were forced onto relief. Government officials were gravely concerned about the way immigrants seemed to complicate the relief problem. Calls by some officials for deportation as the solution to the relief problem were heeded by the federal government; sections 40 and 41 of the Immigration Act (still essentially the same act as the one which existed in 1919) provided for deportation of non-Canadian citizens on relief and government officials took advantage of the law to reduce their relief rolls.

While there was some continuing concern over the assimilation of non-British and non-French immigrants during the 1930s, most Anglo-Canadians were more concerned about protecting their jobs.[39]

Prior to the depression, most Anglo-Saxons were content to have the "foreigners" do all the heavy work of construction, and the dirty work of the janitors and street sweepers. But as the economy slowed down, these jobs became attractive. Whereas the pre-depression attitude was "let the foreigners do the dirty work," the depression attitude became "how come these foreigners have all of our jobs?" The 1930s also saw the high point of anti-semitism in English-speaking Canada as the patterns of discrimination which had hindered the desires of second generation Jews for entry into the professions, were extended into a vicious and virulent anti-semitism by fascist groups.[40]

Barry Broadfoot's book *Ten Lost Years* also makes it very clear that discrimination and prejudice flourished during the depression. In the transcripts of his interviews with the "survivors" of the depression, one is struck by the all-pervasiveness of derogatory ethnic epithets in interviewees' recollections of their contact with immigrants. One does not read of Italians, Chinese or Poles. One reads of "Dagos," "Wops," "Chinks," "Polacks," "Hunyaks."[41] One "survivor" of the depression, waxing philosophical, gives explicit expression to the prevailing attitudes of the time. He compares how the depression affected people from R. B. Bennett down to "the lowest of the low," "some bohunk smelling of garlic and not knowing a word of English. . . ."[42] Another "survivor" recalls that her boy had great difficulty finding work during the depression, and went berserk because of the blow to his self-esteem when the only job he could find was "working with a bunch of Chinks . . ."[43]

The vicious circle of discrimination became perhaps even more vicious during the 1930s as non-Anglo-Saxons' political response to the depression further poisoned attitudes toward them. The discrimination and unemployment which non-Anglo-Saxons faced was an important factor in promoting the support of many for radical political solutions to the depression, in either communist or fascist movements. Indeed the vast majority of the support for the communists throughout Canada, and for the fascists in western Canada came from non-Anglo-Saxons.[44] Ethnic support for these two movements, and the conflict between left and right within most central and eastern European groups and the Finns was seen as further evidence of the undesirability of non-Anglo-Saxons. The existence of

fascist and communist movements in Canada was not of course due simply to the presence of immigrants bringing "old world" ideas. The leaders in both movements were predominantly of British origin,[45] and their "ethnic" support came more from immigrants reacting to depression conditions than from immigrants bringing to Canada "old world" ideas. But the depression gave further support to the notion of non-Anglo-Saxons being unstable politically; one more proof along with immigrant drinking, garlic eating and the legendary violence at Slavic weddings, that non-Anglo-Saxons were in dire need of baptism by assimilation. Deporting immigrant radicals was seen as one alternative to assimilation and the federal government did not hesitate to use this weapon.[46]

The relationship in the public mind between ethnicity, lower social class origins, and political "unsoundness" explains why during the late 1920s so many second generation non-Anglo-Saxons who were anxious to improve their lot economically made deliberate attempts to hide their ethnic background, such as changing their names. Ethnic ties were clearly disadvantageous for those non-Anglo-Saxons seeking economic security or social acceptance. The experience of the second generation in English-speaking Canada was similar to the second generation experience as described by a historian writing about ethnic groups in the United States. "Culturally estranged from their parents by their American education, and wanting nothing so much as to become and to be accepted as Americans, many second generation immigrants made deliberate efforts to rid themselves of their heritage. The adoption of American clothes, speech, and interests, often accompanied by the shedding of an exotic surname, were all part of a process whereby antecedents were repudiated as a means of improving status."[47]

Despite the continuing dominance of the old stereotypes concerning non-Anglo-Saxons and the continuing dominance of assimilationist assumptions, the 1930s also saw the emergence of the first full blown pluralist ideas in somewhat ambiguous form in John Murray Gibbon's book, *The Canadian Mosaic* and in the writings of Watson Kirkconnell, then an English professor at the University of Manitoba. These writers were much more familiar than earlier writers with the historical backgrounds of the ethnic groups coming to Canada, and they were influenced by a liberalism which rejected the assumptions of Anglo-Saxon superiority. Gibbon, a publicity agent for the Canadian Pacific Railway, wrote his book as an expansion of a series of CBC radio talks on the different ethnic groups of Canada. He traced the history of each group and related their "contributions" to Canadian society. Although he was concerned with the preservation of folk arts and music, he also went out of his way to alleviate fears of unassimilability by discussing individuals' assimilation as well as the "cement" of common institutions which bound the Canadian mosaic together. Although Gibbon was not the first writer to use the mosaic symbol, he was the first to attempt to explore its meaning in any significant way.

Kirkconnell was an essayist, poet, and prolific translator of European *197* verse from a number of European languages. His writing on ethnic groups was based on a different approach than Gibbon's. He tried to promote tolerance toward "European Canadians" by sympathetically portraying the cultural background of the countries where the immigrants originated and by demonstrating the cultural creativity of European immigrants in Canada through translating and publishing their creative writing.[48] In his writing he attacked the assumptions of anglo-conformity, and advocated a multicultural society which would allow immigrants to maintain pride in their past.

". . . it would be tragic if there should be a clumsy stripping-away of all those spiritual associations with the past that help to give depth and beauty to life . . . If . . . we accept with Wilhelm von Humboldt 'the absolute and essential importance of human development in its richest diversity,' then we shall welcome every opportunity to save for our country every previous element of individuality that is available."[49]

Kirkconnell was not advocating complete separation of ethnic groups so that they might be preserved. He believed that assimilation needed to occur in the realm of political and economic values and institutions but he hoped that some of the conservative values and folk-culture of immigrants could be preserved.

Kirkconnell did not ignore the political differences within ethnic groups. Indeed, with the outbreak of World War II he wrote a book in which he attempted to expose and combat both fascist and communist elements in different ethnic groups.[50] But he was also active in attempts to bring various other factions of eastern European groups together in order to alleviate public criticism of divisions within ethnic groups.[51]

These advocates of pluralism believed that ethnic diversity was not incompatible with national unity. Unity need not mean uniformity. They believed that recognition of the cultural contributions of non-Anglo-Saxon groups would heighten the groups' feeling that they belonged to Canada and thus strengthen Canadian unity. But Gibbon and Kirkconnell were voices crying in the wilderness — a wilderness of discrimination and racism.

After World War II: The Emergence of Multiculturalism

The war period and early post-war period was a transitional time with respect to attitudes toward immigration and ethnicity. Although the war brought renewed hostility toward enemy aliens, a number of developments during the war eventually worked to undermine ethnic prejudice. During the arrival of the third wave of immigration in the late 1940s and 1950s, many pre-war prejudices lingered, and ethnic minorities encountered considerable pressures for conformity. But for a variety of intellectual, social, and demographic reasons, the ideology of cultural pluralism has been increasingly accepted in the post-World War II period. The post-war decline of racism and the growing influence of theories about cultural relativism opened the way for the emergence of pluralist ideas. The arrival of many intellectuals among the post-war political refugees from eastern Europe and the growth in the number of upwardly mobile second- and third-generation non-Anglo-Canadians, some of whom felt that they were not being fully accepted into Canadian society, increased the political pressures at both federal and provincial levels for greater recognition of Canada's ethnic diversity. Some suggested that this could be achieved through the appointment of senators of a particular ethnic origin, or through the introduction into the school curriculum of ethnic content and of ethnic languages as courses (and sometimes as languages of instruction).[52]

These demands for greater government recognition of "other ethnic groups" increased during the 1960s in response to the French-Canadian assertion of equal rights and the Pearson government's measures to assess and ensure the status of the French language and culture. In 1963 the Royal Commission on Bilingualism and Biculturalism was appointed to "inquire into and report upon the existing state of bilingualism and biculturalism in Canada and to recommend what steps should be taken to develop the Canadian Confederation on the basis of an equal partnership between the two founding races, taking into account the contribution made by the other ethnic groups to the cultural enrichment of Canada." Many non-British, non-French groups, but particularly Ukrainians, opposed the view that Canada was bicultural. By 1961, 26 percent of the Canadian population was of other than British or French ethnic origin; over two hundred newspapers were being published in languages other than French and English; there were fairly well-defined Italian, Jewish, Slavic and Chinese neighbourhoods in large Canadian cities, and there were visible rural concentrations of Ukrainians, Doukhobors, Hutterites and Mennonites scattered across the western provinces: thus, how was it possible for a royal commission to speak of Canada as a *bi*cultural country?

This feeling that biculturalism relegated all ethnic groups who were

198

other than British or French to the status of second-class citizens helps explain the resistance some of these groups expressed to the policies and programs that were introduced to secure the status of the French language in Canada. The place of the so-called "other" ethnic groups in a bicultural society became a vexing question for federal politicians, who had originally hoped that steps to ensure French-Canadian rights would go a long way towards improving inter-ethnic relations in Canada. The partial resolution of this dilemma was the assertion in October 1971 by Prime Minister Trudeau that, in fact, Canada is a *multi*cultural country and that steps would be taken by the federal government to give public recognition to ethnic diversity through the introduction of a policy of multiculturalism. Several provinces with large numbers of non-Anglo Canadians have also initiated their own policies of multiculturalism.

Although most political leaders in English-speaking Canada have accepted and proclaimed the desirability of Canada's ethnic diversity, the Canadian public has not given unanimous support to pluralism. The debate over the place of ethnic groups in Canadian life continues, focusing on such questions as: Does the encouragement of pluralism only serve to perpetuate the vertical mosaic, in which class lines coincide with ethnic lines, or does it help break down class barriers by promoting acceptance of the legitimacy of cultural differences? Are the goals of current government policy — cultural pluralism and equality of opportunity — mutually compatible? Does the encouragement of ethnic group solidarity threaten the freedom of individuals in these groups, or can ethnic groups provide a liberating, rather than a restricting, context for identity? Does the encouragement of cultural diversity serve to perpetuate old-world rivalries, or will the recognition of the contributions of Canada's ethnic groups heighten their feeling that they belong in Canada and thus strengthen Canadian unity? Is government talk of multiculturalism just a way to attract the "ethnic vote," or is positive action necessary to preserve cultural pluralism when cultural diversity throughout the world is being eroded by the impact of industrial technology, mass communication and urbanization? Does the encouragement of multiculturalism simply heighten the visibility of the growing numbers of non-whites in the country and hinder their chances of full acceptance as individuals into Canadian life, or is a public policy of multiculturalism essential to an effective campaign against racism? The nature of these arguments suggest that the prevailing assumptions about immigration and ethnicity have changed over time in English-speaking Canada. They also suggest that the discussion about the role of immigration and ethnic groups in Canadian life is still an important, and unfinished, debate.

Notes

1. For a discussion of these three ideologies of assimilation in the United States, see Milton Gordon. *Assimilation in American Life* (New York, 1964).

2. L. G. Thomas, "The Umbrella and the Mosaic: The French-English Presence and the Settlement of the Canadian Prairie West," in J. A. Carroll ed., *Reflections of Western Historians*, (Tucson, Arizona, 1969) pp. 135–52; Allan Smith, "Metaphor and Nationality in North America," *Canadian Historical Review*, Vol. 51 #3, September, 1970.

3. The Canadian census has consistently classed the Irish as part of the "British" group.

4. Howard Palmer, *Land of the Second Chance: A History of Ethnic Groups in Southern Alberta*, Lethbridge, 1972; Norman Macdonald, *Canada Immigration and Colonization, 1841–1903*, Toronto, 1967; Harold Troper *Only Farmers Need Apply*, Toronto, 1972.

5. Donald, Avery, "Canadian Immigration Policy and the Foreign Navvy", *Canadian Historical Association Reports*, 1972; Edmund Bradwin, *Bunkhouse Man*, New York, 1928, H. Troper and R. Harney, *Immigrants*, Toronto, 1975.

6. Donald Avery, "Canadian Immigration Policy, 1896–1919: The Anglo-Canadian Perspective," Unpublished Ph.D., University of Western Ontario, 1973. Cornelius Jaenen, "Federal Policy Vis-à-Vis Ethnic Groups", unpublished paper, Ottawa, 1971; Howard Palmer, "Nativism and Ethnic Tolerance in Alberta, 1880–1920", unpublished M.A., University of Alberta, 1971; "Nativism and Ethnic Tolerance in Alberta, 1920–1972, unpublished Ph.D., York University, 1973.

7. H. Palmer, "Nativism and Ethnic Tolerance in Alberta, 1880–1920", unpublished M.A. University of Alberta, 1971, Chapters 1 and 2; H. Troper *Only Farmers Need Apply* (Toronto, 1972); D. J. Hall, "Clifford Sifton: Immigration and Settlement Policy, 1896–1905" in H. Palmer, ed., *The Settlement of the West* (Calgary, 1977), pp. 60-85.

8. H. Troper, "The Creek Negroes of Oklahoma and Canadian Immigration, 1909–11". *Canadian Historical Review*, September, 1972, p. 272–288.

9. Rev. George Bryce, "Past and Future of Our Race", *Proceedings*, Canadian Club of Toronto, 1911, p. 6–7; C. A. Magrath, *Canada's Growth and Problems Affecting It*, (Ottawa, 1910); Goldwin Smith in *Weekly Sun*, Feb. 1, 1899, Sept. 17, 1902, Sept. 23, 1903, May 18, 1904, Aug. 16, 1905; W. A. Griesbach, *I Remember*, Toronto, 1946, pp. 214–217, 220–221.

10. Carl Berger, *Sense of Power*, Toronto, 1970, p. 117–188.

11. Morton, *In A Sea of Sterile Mountains*, Vancouver, 1974; W. P. Ward, "The Oriental Immigrant and Canada's Protestant Clergy, 1858–1925", *B.C. Studies*, Summer, 1974 p. 40–55; Ted Ferguson, *A White Man's Country*, Toronto, 1975.

12. D. J. Hall, "Clifford Sifton: Immigration and Settlement Policy: 1896–1905", in H. Palmer, ed., *The Settlement of the West* (Calgary, 1977), pp. 79–80.

13. W. L. Morton, *Manitoba*, A History, Toronto, 1957, p. 161, 162.

14. J. B. Hedges. *Building the Canadian West*, New York, 1939; Frank Epp, *Mennonites in Canada*, 1786–1920, Toronto, 1974.

15. Cornelius J. Jaenen, "Ruthenian Schools in Western Canada 1897–1919" *Paedagogica Historica*, International Journal of the History of Education, X.3; 1970, pp. 517–541. Donald Avery, "Canadian Immigration Policy", pp. 374–420.

16. Avery, Ibid. p. 408.

17. Kate Foster, *Our Canadian Mosaic*, Toronto, 1926; J. T. M. Anderson, *The Education of the New Canadian*, Toronto, 1918; C. B. Sissons, *Bi-Lingual Schools in Canada*, Toronto, 1917; W. G. Smith, *Building the Nation*, Toronto, 1922. For a discussion of some of the concrete activities involved in these "Canadianization" programs, see R. Harney and H. Troper, *Immigrants* Chapter 4.

18. J. S. Woodsworth, *Strangers Within our Gates*, Winnipeg, 1909; Marilyn Barber, "Nationalism, Nativism and the Social Gospel: The Protestant Church Response to Foreign Immigrants in Western Canada, 1897–1914" in Richard Allen ed. *The Social Gospel in Canada*, Ottawa, 1975, pp. 186–226.

19. Quoted in Barbara Nicholson, "Feminism in the Prairie Provinces to 1916", unpublished M.A. University of Calgary, 1974, p. 71. For the views of womens' groups on immigration and the role of immigrants in Canada society, see Ibid. pp. 83–85, 86, 114, 121, 133, 165–169, 186–187.

20. Reported in *Lethbridge Herald* May 29, 1919.

21. J. S. Woodsworth, "Social Conditions in Rural Communities in the Prairie Provinces", Winnipeg, 1917, p. 38.

22. For a fairly extensive chronicling of patterns of discrimination against a number of minority groups see Morris Davis and J. F. Krauter, *The Other Canadians*, Toronto, 1971.

23. For an analysis of the various causes of ethnic stratification (settlement patterns, time of arrival, immigrant and ethnic occupations, ethnic values, language barriers and discrimination and exploitation) see Book IV, *Report of the Royal Commission on Bilingualism and Biculturalism*, Ottawa, 1969, Chapter 2.

24. Carole Henderson, "The Ethnicity Factor in Anglo-Canadian Folkloristics", *Canadian Ethnic Studies*, Vol. VII No. 2, forthcoming.

25. *Canadian Annual Review,* 1923, p. 264–265; 1924–25, p. 190–192.

26. *Canada Year Book,* 1941, p. 733.

27. Olha Woycenko, *The Ukrainians in Canada* (Winnipeg, 1967); Victor Turek, *Poles in Manitoba* (Toronto, 1967), p. 43; J. M. Kirschbaum, *Slovaks in Canada* (Toronto, 1967), p. 101; Edmund Heier, "A Study of German Lutheran and Catholic Immigrants in Canada formerly residing in Czarist and Soviet Russia", unpublished M.A. (University of British Columbia, 1955) Chapter 3.

28. R. B. Bennett, House of Commons *Debates,* June 7, 1929, p. 3925-7.

29. Ibid.

30. H. Palmer, "Nativism in Alberta," 1925–1930, *Canadian Historical Association Reports,* 1974, pp. 191–199.

31. G. E. Lloyd, "National Building", *Banff Crag and Canyon,* Aug. 17, 1928.

32. A. R. M. Lower, *Canadians in the Making,* Don Mills Ontario, 1958. Chapter 22, 27.

33. J. S. Woodsworth, "Nation Building," *University Magazine,* 1917 pp. 85–99. F. W. Baumgartner, "Central European Immigration", *Queen's Quarterly* (Winter, 1930), p. 183–192; Walter Murray, "Continental Europeans in Western Canada", *Queen's Quarterly,* 1931; P. M. Bryce, *The Value of the Continental Immigrant to Canada* (Ottawa, 1928), E. L. Chicanot, "Homesteading the Citizen: Canadian Festivals Promote Cultural Exchange", *Commonwealth,* May, 1929, pp. 94–95; E. K. Chicanot, "Moulding a Nation", *Dalhousie Review,* July, 1929, pp. 232–237. J. H. Haslam, "Canadianization of the Immigrant Settler", *Annals,* May, 1923, pp. 45–49; E. H. Oliver, "The Settlement of Saskatchewan to 1914" *Transactions of the Royal Society,* 1926, pp. 63–87; Agnes Laut, "Comparing the Canadian and American Melting Pots", *Current Opinion,* Vol. 70, April, 1921, pp. 458–462; Kate Foster *Our Canadian Mosaic* (Toronto, 1926). Robert England, "Continental Europeans in Western Canada", *Queen's Quarterly,* 1931.

34. Robert England, *The Central European Immigrant in Canada* (Toronto, 1929).

35. John Blue, *Alberta Past and Present* (Chicago, 1924), p. 210.

36. There were some advocates of the melting pot prior to 1920, but it did not gain widespread acceptance until the 1920's. See H. Palmer, "Nativism in Alberta, 1880–1920" Chapter 1. Marilyn Barber, "Nationalism, Nativism, and the Social Gospel".

37. Douglas Cole, "John S. Ewart and Canadian Nationalism", *Canadian Historical Association Report,* 1969, p. 66.

38. John Diefenbaker, *One Canada,* Toronto, 1975, p. 140, 141, 218–19, 274.

39. H. Palmer, "Nativism in Alberta, 1920–1972" Chapter 3.

40. James Gray, *The Roar of the Twenties,* (Toronto, 1975) Chapter 11; Lita-Rose Betcherman, *The Swastika and the Maple Leaf.* (Don Mills, Ontario) 1975.

41. Barry Broadfoot, *Ten Lost Years,* p. 25, 70, 76, 132, 156–164, 186, 279.

42. Ibid p. 132.

43. Ibid p. 186.

44. Ivan Avakumovic, *The Communist Party in Canada: A History,* (Toronto, 1975) p. 66–67; Lita-Rose Betcherman, *The Swastika and the Maple Leaf,* Chapter 5.

45. Ibid.

46. H. Palmer, "Nativism in Alberta, 1920–1972" Chapter 3.

47. M. A. Jones, *American Immigration,* (Chicago, 1960) p. 298. For fictional treatments of the second generation's repudiation of the ethnic past in an attempt to become accepted see John Marlyn, *Under the Ribs of Death,* (Toronto, 1951) and Magdelana Eggleston: *Mountain Shadows,* (New York, 1955) p. 122. See also *Change of Name,* Toronto: Canadian Institute of Cultural Research, 1965.

48. Watson Kirkconnell, *The European Heritage, A Synopsis of European Cultural Achievement,* London, 1930; *Canadian Overtones,* Winnipeg, 1935. For a complete listing of Kirkconnell's work, see the list in his memoirs, *A Slice of Canada* (Toronto, 1967) p. 374–375. For an assessment of his work see J. R. C. Perkin ed. *The Undoing of Babel.* (Toronto, 1975).

49. W. Kirkconnell, Trans., *Canadian Overtones,* preface.

50. Watson Kirkconnell, *Canada Europe and Hitler,* (Toronto, 1939).

51. W. Kirkconnell, *A Slice of Canada.*

52. For documentary evidence of changing ethnic attitudes in the post-war era and the emergence of multiculturalism as an idea and as a governmental policy, see H. Palmer, *Immigration and the Rise of Multiculturalism* (Toronto, 1975), chapter 3.

Topic Six
Industrialization and Responses To It

202   At the turn of the century Canada underwent its industrial revolution. A unique combination of events brought about rapid industrial growth: the end of a prolonged depression; the increased world-wide demand for our agricultural and mineral resources; and an increased private and public investment. At last the economy was expanding, and the structures set in place by the National Policy could be put in effect. Western settlement became a reality, as did large-scale industrialization in southern Ontario and Quebec.

   Between 1890 and 1920, Canada's population doubled. To serve the larger domestic market, factories and businesses, owned and/or managed by wealthy entrepreneurs, expanded across the country, particularly in the urban centres of Central Canada. Many have claimed that this was "the Golden Age of Canadian business enterprise," a period in which businessmen (in alliance with politicians) created an idyllic commercial atmosphere. Yet according to Michael Bliss in " 'Dyspepsia of the Mind': The Canadian Businessman and His Enemies, 1880–1914," businessmen felt they were operating in a "hostile environment," rather than in ideal conditions.

   Conditions remained far from ideal for the working class at this time. Workers became the "urban poor" living in congested and filthy slums, exposed to disease and impure water. They worked long hours at monotonous jobs in cramped and poorly ventilated factories for low wages. If laid off or unable to work as a result of sickness or disability, these individuals had to depend on charitable organizations. In "The Condition of the Working Class in Montreal, 1897–1920," Terry Copp describes the urban poor in what was then Canada's largest and most populous Canadian city.

   The predicament of many working women was worse than that of men: they received lower wages and often worked longer hours; and they laboured without unions that could act as agencies of identification and solidarity to pressure employers to improve conditions. Why did working women fail to form unions to combat their intolerable situation? Traditionally, students of women and labour history have explained this shortcoming in terms of "feminine psychology", a lack of self-assertiveness. (Two of the readings in Topic 8 examine feminist attitudes at the turn of the century.) Wayne Roberts offers an alternative explanation in "Honest Womanhood: Feminism, Femininity and Class Consciousness among Toronto Working Women, 1893 to 1914."

Michael Bliss has examined the attitude of Canadian businessmen in *A Living Profit: Studies in the Social History of Canadian Business, 1883–1911* (Toronto: McClelland and Stewart, 1974). For a fine study of one notable Canadian businessman see Bliss, *A Canadian Millionaire* (Toronto: Macmillan, 1978). For a good overview of the rise of business at the turn of the century in English- and French-speaking Canada respectively see "The Triumph of Enterprise," and "French Canada and the New Industrial Order," in R.C. Brown and R. Cook, *Canada, 1896–1921: A Nation Transformed* (Toronto: McClelland and Stewart, 1974).

Three excellent primary sources exist for a study of the impact of indus- 203 trial growth in Canada at the turn of the century. The first is *The Royal Commission on the Relations of Labour and Capital, 1889.* An abridged version has been published, *Canada Investigates Industrialism*, edited and with an introduction by Greg Kealey (Toronto: University of Toronto Press, 1973). The other two sources are collections of documents: *The Workingman in the Nineteenth Century*, edited by M.S. Cross (Toronto: Oxford University Press, 1974), and *The Canadian Worker in the Twentieth Century*, edited by I. Abella and D. Millar (Toronto: Oxford University Press, 1978). A worthwhile collection is *Essays on Canadian Working Class History*, edited by G. Kealey and P. Warrian (Toronto: McClelland and Stewart, 1976). Terry Copp has studied in depth working-class life in Montreal in his *The Anatomy of Poverty: The Conditions of the Working Class in Montreal, 1897–1929* (Toronto: McClelland and Stewart, 1974). A counterpart to Copp's work is Greg Kealey's *Toronto Workers Respond to Industrial Capitalism, 1867–1892* (Toronto: University of Toronto Press, 1980). A second valuable study on Toronto is Michael Piva, *The Conditions of the Working Class in Toronto, 1900–1921* (Ottawa: University of Ottawa Press, 1979). For a discussion of working class culture see Bryan Palmer's *A Culture in Conflict: Skilled Workers and Industrial Capitalism in Hamilton, Ontario, 1860–1914* (Montreal: McGill-Queen's University Press, 1979), and his *Working-Class Experience: The Rise and Reconstitution of Canadian Labour, 1800–1980* (Toronto: Butterworth and Co., 1983).

On working women see selected essays in the following anthologies: Janice Acton et al., ed., *Women at Work: Ontario 1850–1930* (Toronto: Women's Educational Press, 1974); L. Kealey, ed., *A Not Unreasonable Claim: Women and Reform in Canada, 1880s–1920s* (Toronto: Women's Educational Press, 1979); G. Matheson, ed., *Women in the Canadian Mosaic* (Toronto: Peter Martin, 1976); and S.M. Trofimenkoff and A. Prentice, eds., *The Neglected Majority* (Toronto: McClelland and Stewart, 1977).

"Dyspepsia of the Mind": The Canadian Businessman and His Enemies, 1880-1914*
MICHAEL BLISS

The late nineteenth and early twentieth centuries were the Golden Age of Canadian business enterprise. Or, for those not impressed with unrestrained capitalism, they were the years of the Great Barbecue in Canada. The close class linkages between businessmen and politicians, the numerical insignificance of the Canadian labour movement, the subsidization of entrepreneurship in Canadian national tariff and transport policies, miniscule taxation and the eagerness with which Canadian resources were doled out to capitalists native and foreign, all suggest an environment promoting the maximum business opportunity while providing minimum social regulation of profitmaking. It was the age of the Canadian Captain of Industry, the age when businessmen seemed to be the national class in Canadian life and an enthusiastic editor could put everyone in his place with the following:

204

The development of the last few years has been magnificent; the development of the next few years depends on our having confidence. The country is rich, immigration is proceeding apace, the Government is doing its duty, and the rest lies with the people — the capitalists, the bankers, the businessmen, and the other classes.[1]

But one of the more unexpected conclusions that emerges from a study of business rhetoric and action during this period is that the business class on the whole perceived itself to be operating in a hostile environment. In many instances businessmen felt themselves to be under severe pressure from competing social groups, sometimes at the mercy of these groups. More important, they also felt at the mercy of one another because of the competitiveness of the Canadian economy, so much so that doing business at times seemed an almost unbearable strain. The Captains of Industry, it turns out, often thought their ships were sailing through exceedingly stormy seas.

From a contemporary perspective the relations between businessmen and Canadian governments after Confederation seem almost idyllic. To take the two most obvious examples, the tariff seemed to exist in large part as the repayment of subsidies given by the manufacturing interest to the Conservative Party. Similarly the Canadian Pacific Railway was what John A. Macdonald called the "sleeping partner" of the Conservative government in the 1880's (though it could be remarkably awake and active at election time). Actually neither the manufacturers nor the C.P.R. were ever particularly satisfied with this apparently happy political relationship. At the best of times their spokesmen were haunted by doubt and uncertainty as to the reliability of their political allies.

*From *Canadian Business History: Selected Studies, 1497-1971* pp. 175-191. Copyright 1971 by McClelland and Stewart Ltd. Reprinted by permission.

Even in the heydays of the National Policy in the 1880's the federal government appears to have made clear to the Canadian Manufacturers' Association that it would not accept manufacturers' demands for Chinese Wall protectionism.[2] Then in the later years of the Conservative regime manufacturers had first grudgingly to accept tariff readjustments to mollify public opinion, and almost immediately afterward watched and fretted helplessly as racial and religious issues wrecked "the only party which is prepared to protect the manufacturer."[3] Actually the Liberal party turned out to be sound on the broad principle of protection by 1896 (though the C.M.A. officially panicked at the thought of a Liberal victory), but the Laurier Government's introduction of preferential tariff schedules, its refusal to bow to the heavily financed protectionist campaign of 1902-6, above all its reversion to reciprocity in 1911, all frustrated manufacturers who found that the government was by no means in their pocket. The members of the C.M.A.'s important Tariff Committee satisfied themselves in December 1910 that reciprocity was a dead issue:[4] the agreement with the United States was announced a month later. Such were the uncertainties of mixing business with politics. It cost an annoying amount of money and time to help overthrow the government and preserve the *status quo*.

The alliance between the Canadian Pacific Railway and the Canadian Government, personified respectively by George Stephen and Sir John A. Macdonald, was one of the closest political-business friendships in North American history. Nevertheless it had ups and downs. A great many of the eight hundred or so letters Stephen wrote to Macdonald contain bitter complaints about the failure of the government to safeguard properly the interests of the railroad. "The Company has never had a transaction with the Government to which there was not, in the end, some mischievous condition attached, which largely lessened the benefit which would otherwise have come to the Company,"[5] Stephen wrote in 1889 in a fairly typical letter. The next year he summed up a decade of frustration in a remarkable outburst:

> It is positively heartbreaking the way we are treated and I am tired of beseeching & begging for fair treatment, & have resolved on giving up all further efforts to secure it, as useless, . . . in almost every transaction we have had with the Govt arising out of the contract we have been taken advantage of and duped and deceived in the most cruel manner. Had I been the worst enemy of the Govt politically I could not have been worse treated than I have been by the Dept of Railways.[6]

The government's disregard of his railway so depressed Stephen that for the only time in the entire correspondence he reminded Macdonald in this letter of his contribution of one million dollars to the Conservative cause since 1882, adding that he would not ask anything of the government "but what is right and fair, and which ought to be granted even had I never done a thing or spent a dollar for it politically." Macdonald's replies to these and similar criticisms involved chastising the C.P.R. for asking too much ("You C.P.R. folk are forgetful and I fear rather too ungrateful"), arguing that the Government had to respond to other pressures ("We are closely watched

205

by the opposition who are lying in wait for us at every turn''), and urging the Company to involve itself still more deeply in political manipulation (''The C.P.R. might get control of the legislature of Manitoba for the next four years if it chose, and those would be four years of comfort'').[7] This was very far from an alliance of two equal colleagues smoothly dividing the reins of power — the alliance that contemporary Liberals as well as later critics have thought existed, the alliance that George Stephen always hoped would exist.

In addition to having to worry about the refusal of governments to bend totally to their will, businessmen could not help but be anxious about any question that was an issue of partisan politics. What happened when the other side won? Both the C.P.R. and the Canadian Manufacturers' Association had to intervene directly in politics in the 1880's because they were convinced a Liberal victory would have had a catastrophic effect on their interests. In their ideal world both political parties would have recognized that high tariffs and railways were always and utterly in the national interest, thereby removing the issues from politics entirely and relieving interested businessmen from the need to go electioneering. A typical protectionist editorial in 1882 was entitled ''Let Us Have Peace'' and read in part:

> It is for the country's interest that the trade question should be taken out of politics . . . as long as it continues to be a political issue there continues also the element of doubt and uncertainty as to the future, which is a prime hindrance to the country's development . . . For want of complete assurance as to the permanence of the National Policy the country is losing millions annually . . . Capitalists require certainty, they want the assurance that the conditions upon which they embark their capital will be permanent. Something hinders this assurance from being as complete and as satisfactory as it ought to be, and what is it? Everyone knows that it is the interference of *political* contingencies with the question whether the investment of capital in this or the other industry would be safe.[8]

Of course the trade question was not taken out of politics, and throughout the last quarter of the century there were frequent complaints that almost no business was done during election campaigns while everyone waited until the settlement of ''political contingencies'' also settled the future course of business.[9]

(Complaints about political interference with business may have been more justified in the late nineteenth century than they are now. From about 1911 a combination of shifting public concerns, Parliament's devolution of responsibility for many areas of government-business contact into the hands of administrative bodies, and the professionalization of the civil service seem to have made many issues such as transport regulation and tariffs less politically volatile. Certainly neither of Canada's two major political parties has recently frightened leading business interests as much as the Liberal Party did in the 1880's and 1890's. Except for the somewhat shadowy presence of the C.C.F.-N.D.P. the Canadian political system seems to have provided a much more certain environment for business activities than it did in what is thought to have been the period of greatest business-government cooperation. Alternatively it may be that private business has simply learned to expect less from government and roll with the political punches with rather more good grace than formerly. Still, the only election since the depression that has frightened the Canadian business community as much as those of 1878, 1882, 1887, 1891, 1896, and 1911 was the Quebec provincial election of 1970.)

Provincial governments during the period were also acting with less docility than we would expect from John Porter's model of them as guardians of vested business interests.[10] The corporation tax, for example, came to Canada in 1882 in the Province of Quebec. When companies refused *en masse* to pay the new imposition, the government coolly laid four hundred charges for non-payment of taxes, causing the organ of Montreal's business community to doubt "if any similar instance of oppression can be cited in modern history."[11] A test case carried to the Privy Council was finally decided in favour of the Quebec government in 1887; the Mercier administration, ignoring deputations of the leading businessmen of the province, proceeded to collect five years' back taxes. This was a government which the same year had been hailed as one that would give the "skillful protection and encouragement" to the business community "which their importance warrants."[12]

207

Almost simultaneously the citizens of Manitoba were winning their great struggle against the monopoly clause of the C.P.R. charter, a remarkable victory over both the greatest corporation in the Dominion and the federal government. Later the private telephone interests and the grain elevator owners in western Canada would be unable to prevent the growth of government ownership and regulation in their industries. In general, for all their complaints against eastern business oppression, Western Canadians were remarkably successful in passing legislation to limit the powers of private corporations.[13]

The most sensational struggle of the period in the provinces was the Whitney-Beck crusade to create Ontario Hydro against the determined opposition of the private power interests. The turning point in an otherwise typical conflict between the "people" of Ontario and a few large power corporations came with Whitney's Power Commission Amendment Act of 1909 by which all municipal contracts with the Ontario Hydro Commission were declared valid by act of the legislature and all pending and future court actions testing that validity were void.[14] The investment community exploded in anger over what the *Financial Post* called "one of the most tyran nous acts that has ever been committed", an Act which violated all basic declarations of right from the Mosaic Code to Magna Carta. Such legislation, accompanied by judicial decisions upholding a province's absolute constitutional power to override civil and property rights (as the federal Minister of Justice admitted, proved provincial legislatures really could repeal Magna Carta), brought home to businessmen for the first time the fragility of property rights in a British parliamentary system. Disallowance petitions and political pressure flowed to Ottawa to stop the renegade province, more court cases were launched, amendments to the B.N.A. Act were suggested, and concerted efforts were made at home and abroad to ruin Ontario's credit.

All failed. For the *Financial Post* Whitney became "the Socialist Premier now masquerading under the title of a Conservative"[15] and the public ownership movement marched on. Indeed the hydro fight was only the most spectacular instance of the nation-wide expansion of municipal ownership of utilities from about 1890 to 1914, always carried out against the opposition of private companies.

These political frustrations of the business classes — and there were many more of them — were simply the consequence of the Canadian political system's responsiveness to the desires of a plurality of interest groups. In the early years the most powerful group opposing businessmen was the agricultural interest — permeated with free trade ideas, stoutly opposed to insolvency laws that would limit the freedom of debtors (commercial interests failed for twenty years to have a federal insolvency law passed), anti-railroad, anti-corporation, and often anti-urban. The Quebec corporation tax was a clear instance of the use of agrarian power against companies — what the *Journal of Commerce* alternately called "hayseed" and "class' legislation foisted upon the province by rural assemblymen of "bovine" simplicity.[16] Similarly the agrarians provided the voting base for anti-protectionist campaigns and it was the revival of agrarian power with the opening of the West in the Laurier years that swung the Liberal party back to reciprocity in 1911. The manufacturers fully realized this; the C.M.A.'s closed strategy sessions — when businessmen were talking to themselves and not for public consumption — resounded with denunciations of a government that sacrificed manufacturing interests for farmers. Significantly, the manufacturers thought that the best way to apply political pressure to the government against reciprocity would be to sponsor delegations of farmers and workingmen to protest the agreement.[17]

But by 1911 delegations of workingmen were used to going to Ottawa for distinctly different purposes than supporting the political aims of the C.M.A. The direct power that organized labour could mobilize for either industrial disputes or independent political action was still comparatively insignificant; the indirect influence it exercised on politics and business was not. This influence was not sufficiently hostile to the interests of employers that the business community already had a healthy sense of being harassed by organized labour.

For one thing the agitations of the unions seemed to bear political fruit. From the initial legalization of trade unions in 1872 through the Factory Act legislation of the 1880's and 1890's, down to Ontario's model revision of workmen's compensation legislation in 1915, the advances in labour legislation in Canada were surprisingly rapid in the context of both the late development of Canadian industrialism and what the business community would have liked to concede.[18] In terms of what organized labour thought it should get, of course, the pace of legislation was agonizingly slow. But business organizations made exactly the same complaints about the reluctance of government to legislate in their interests. In fact, promoters of associational activities by businessmen consciously and enviously took trade unions as their model. "Labor, in particular, is becoming so effectively organized that it wields a power and influence that is astonishing," the C.M.A.'s Secretary told the annual meeting in 1887, going on to add, "the manner in which they have perfected their organization affords a lesson, not without significance to those to whom this paper is addressed."[19] Businessmen thought it particularly unjust in 1888 that business combinations designed to achieve a "living profit" should be the subject of a Parliamentary inquiry, while labour combinations for the same purpose were being ignored.[20] The 1889 legislation following the combines inquiry did not, as some historians have believed, place all combinations in restraint of trade on the same footing. Trade unions were guaranteed exemption from the laws governing business "unions," a fact that caused bitter complaints about "class legislation" from big businessmen in the Senate.[21] The further clarification of labour's right to strike in 1890 seems to have been a deliberate reaction against prosecutions sponsored by the C.M.A.[22] And Sir John Thompson's amendment to the Criminal Code in the same year protecting female factory employees from seduction by their employers was considered a pernicious and humiliating example of the "Minister of Injustice" courting the "beslobberment of the Knights of Labor."[23] In the Laurier years businessmen called repeatedly for measures to force unions to become legally responsible corporate bodies in the same way that business organizations were. They did not succeed, and always resented the special status labor organizations seemed to them to enjoy in law and practice.[24]

209

Secondly, even though serious industrial disputes in Canada were comparatively rare — though by no means non-existent — the spectre of open industrial or class warfare began to haunt Canadian business from at least the 1880's. There was the United States — the country of Haymarket, Homestead, Pullman, et al— providing the model of what real industrial strife in a society could mean. There were the socialists—Anarchists, Nihilists, Communists, Single Taxers, et al— causing trouble in all the other countries of the world and posing the ultimate threat of social cataclysm. Canada was virgin land still; but these things had a way of spreading, say through the organizers of international unions. Businessmen were not sure whether repression or concession would be the most appropriate response to large scale labour troubles when they finally came to Canada. The significant point is that they perceived foreign social unrest as a model of what could be in store for Canada, and they worried about it.[25] In the 1960's, one of the happiest decades in their history, Canadians did exactly the same thing.

The business community's sense of weakness in the face of labour was reflected in any number of ways. Editors of business journals marvelled at political, public, and newspaper pandering to the prejudices of labour leaders from the mid-1880's. They worried incessantly about the "Labour Question" as the great issue of the day, and used an endless stock of arguments to convince the "fair-minded" worker that his "interests lay with his employer" rather than with the "walking delegates" and "jawsmiths" of the union.[26] In a more positive way business journals discussed such schemes for industrial reconciliation as profit-sharing from the 1880's and always encouraged the firm picnics, dances and excursions that were commonplace in the period. By the Laurier years there was a significant industrial welfare movement in Canada, urging concessions to labour for both humanitarian and strategic reasons.[27] The Canadian Manufacturers' Association was much less eager to engage in all-out struggles against organized labour than its American counterpart, the National Association of Manufacturers. Its minutebooks show a surprising caution and regard for public opinion on such issues as recruiting skilled labour, engaging in strike-breaking, and overt resistance to the more reasonable legislative requests of unions.[28] In addition, the *cris de coeur* that rang out against unions in private meetings of C.M.A. committees ("Mr. Harris . . . quoted from his own experience with the unions to show that the union leader had no soul, that the union man had to do what he was told and that generosity and fair treatment counted for nothing"),[29] belie the supposition that public anti-unionism was merely a cynical tactical ploy. There was something almost pathetic about the 1910 decision of the Executive of the Toronto Branch of the C.M.A. to send an anti-labour journal, *The Square Deal*, for one year to two hundred prominent Canadians as a means of counteracting what they thought was labour's political strength.[30]

210

When political decisions were taken in the interests of labour or other groups in Canadian society, businessmen held legislators responsible for their actions. In their frustration they singled out and defined "professional politicians" as a distinct and disreputable social class. Most of them were lawyers or doctors, what J.B. Maclean called "the sediment of the learned professions," who went to Parliament because "it is the best paying job their mediocrity will allow them to obtain."[31] To preserve their comfortable incomes professional politicians became abject slaves of their political parties, the machines that existed solely to capture and divide the spoils of office. Concepts of patriotism, independent public service, and the national interest, were sacrificed to the whims of men "who care nothing for the country so long as . . . it affords for them a sure means of extorting from a long suffering people a living for which they never worked."[32]

The antidote to the professional politician was the businessman in politics— the practical, honest, patriotic man who knew that the business of Canada was business and was also wealthy enough not to be influenced by mere pecuniary considerations. Everyone who meditated on business matters called for more business representation in politics. No one knew how to encourage a most reluctant business community to dirty its hands with the muck of electioneering.[33] The trouble, explained the *Journal of Commerce*, was that the extension of the suffrage had confided the future of the country "to the hands of the poorest and most ignorant, and therefore most numerous" class of its population. It had set up "the rule of a brute majority over an educated and intelligent minority," resulting in that minority withdrawing from political life.[34] Control had been given over by default to the professional politician. This idea of an ignorant majority manipulated by an unprincipled, self-seeking elite was as dear to the hearts of Canadian businessmen in the 1880's and 1890's as it was to the Left in the 1960's. The businessmen may at least have had the virtue of originality.

Businessmen saw the Manitoba Schools issue as a prime example of how professional politicians neglected the real needs of the nation to pander to groups organized according to race and religion. By 1895 business interests found request after request ignored by a government totally preoccupied with education, religion and its own survival. Their frustration welled up in the columns of the *Canadian Grocer*, the country's largest trade journal:

. . . For three months the House has been in session; and what for? Merely to keep boiling the pot of race and creed; dividing race against race and creed against creed; creating food for sharpening the appetite of fanatics, who in the name of religion would tear each other to pieces. While this is going on not only are the business interests of the country dying of neglect, but the Dominion is retrograding . . .

Goodness knows when this race and religious war in the hearts of the people will give place to peace. But one thing is certain: every year it continues it throws the country and the business interests of the country back a decade. If this thing goes on we shall ere long be back into the middle ages . . .

Had the politicians at Ottawa — we cannot call them statesmen; we have no statesmen, or, at least, enough to act as pallbearers to a light-weight corpse — passed the three months in discussing ways and means of hoeing corn they would have done more good than they have done in discussing the question they have; they would not, at any rate, have done as much harm.[35]

Complaints like these with their overtones of resentment at priority being given to the interests of religious groups reflected a more general business resentment at the role of the professional classes in Canadian society. In the early 1890's the *Canadian Manufacturer*, official organ of the C.M.A., carried on a prolonged campaign against the professional classes. It objected vigorously, for example, to the exemptions of religious institutions from taxation. Pointing out that the extra tax burden fell on manufacturers and workers alike, the journal assumed a common cause with labour against the power of organized religion:

The lofty cathedral with its spire and bells, its expensive organ and its cushioned pews, costing thousands and thousands of dollars, and used almost exclusively by wealthy people, goes untaxed, while perhaps across the street, or within the shadows of its walls, is the small factory where the poor man works for his daily bread, and the humble cottage that shelters him and his family, and which are taxed, a part of the tax money going to support the rich man's church.[36]

The tax question opened up the whole issue of higher education, which at the post-primary level seemed directed almost solely towards producing more professional people — doctors, lawyers, and ministers. In an age before businessmen, their sons, or their employees felt they had any particular need for higher education, public subsidization of high schools and universities seemed to be an institutionalization of class privilege. As the *Canadian Manufacturer* put it:

It has became (*sic*) painfully evident that society is divided into a privileged class, and a class who not only have to bear their own burdens, but are outrageously taxed to help support the

211

others. As in days when the Israelites were in bondage in Egypt, there are taskmasters, and there are servants who labor for them. If a parent desires to give a son a collegiate education, let him pay for it out of his own resources, and not compel others to do it for him. The system that allows this to be done is inherently wrong.[37]

Moreover, businessmen complained that a social structure which gave the highest status to learned professionals led to an overcrowding of these professions at the expense of businessmen and farmers who suffered from labour shortages. "Hundreds of young men," the *Canadian Manufacturer* argued, "who might make good farmers, or blacksmiths, or coal heavers, or scavengers, or stablemen, are ruined for all useful purposes by a system which draws them away from the occupation for which they are best fitted, and at the expense of the public galvanized into professionals for which the country has no possible use."[38] The problem, it suggested, was the "glamour" with which the professional men artificially surrounded their occupations, "knowing that if this glamour is dispelled and their importance measured according to its true worth and intrinsic merit, a much larger percentage of them *(sic)* who are now unemployed would be forced to earn their bread by honest toil."[39] "Honest toil" was thought to characterize the businessman, the worker, and the farmer, but not the professional. He was too often "a caterpillar on the leaf of commerce."

By the twentieth century simple resistance to subsidizing education for professionals gave way in business circles to demands that the educational system be adjusted to include technical or vocational training; in other words that the state bear the expense of training workers just as it did the expense of training professionals. At the university level the transition came fairly easily because of the pressure that would–be philanthropists could apply, and also because the new scientific and technical courses could be tacked on to liberal arts programs without eliminating them.[40] The struggle to achieve technical education in the primary and secondary schools, though, was long and difficult. It took a decade of organized agitation by the Canadian Manufacturers' Association before the Dominion government appointed a Royal Commission on the subject and the provinces began making serious efforts in that direction. This was not the fault of a conservative, cautious business class—which in fact was more united and aggressive on this than any other single issue. Rather it was partly due to the rigidity of the constitution, partly to the conservatism of the professional elites in Canada who resisted challenges to their vested interest in an archaic educational establishment.[41]

It is unclear whether business distaste for professionals was objectively rooted in the Canadian class and power structure or whether many of the protests reflect business envy of the high social status accorded to professionals. In presenting a Board of Trade brief to the Royal Commission on Industrial Training and Technical Education in 1912, a Toronto manufacturer complained of the element growing up in Canadian universities "that looks down upon our commercial and industrial courses." Although the world had now become "a great arena for commerce," too much of the teaching in the schools emphasized the heroes of war, literature, art, and history.

"Industry and commerce will never be put on its proper plane," he said, "until we have the idea from the beginning that the heroes and the great men and the industrious men in those two channels are just as great in the sight of Providence and in the sight of the nation as men in some of the professions."[42] Technical education would have improved the skills of this man's employees; honour to the heroes of industry would have uplifted his ego.

All the prestige-inflated professions, professional politicians, union agitators, and ignorant voters put together could not equal the threat to the businessman's well-being posed by members of his own class. Business disunity is the key factor explaining most of the problems bedevilling Canadian businessmen during the period. One main reason the C.P.R. could not feel secure in its partnership with the Conservative government was the Grand Trunk's active partnership with the Liberal Opposition. Then again, neither giant railway could be secure in its relations with any government after shippers began their campaign against soulless, irresponsible railway corporations in the 1880's.[43] The C.M.A. proudly took credit for the eventual establishment of formal public control over railways when the Board of Railway Commissioners was founded in 1902 and went on to sponsor many of the anti-railway charges brought before the Commission.[44] In turn, though, on the issue of protection the lumbering, mining, and importing interests formed a powerful Fifth Column in the business community working hand in glove with the farmer against the manufacturers (who always had great difficulty agreeing among themselves on desirable rates of duty). Businessmen also divided on questions of public ownership: Ontario's public power crusade was almost entirely a struggle within the business community, the nature of which was camouflaged only because for campaign purposes manufacturers equated their desire for cheap electricity with populist anti-corporation sentiment. Throughout the period honest businessmen who wanted to put business-government relations on a business-like basis were thwarted by the grafting and boodling section of the business community allied with the grafting and boodling section of the political community.[45] There was always an enterprising businessman to break a common front against labour; alternatively the problem of competing with non-union firms stifled many prospects for mutual cooperation between well meaning employers and their unions. Small businessmen initiated most of the critique of big business usually identified with populism and progressivism in North America, largely because big business thrived on the wreckage of small business. Finally, organized in their local and regional Boards of Trade, businessmen engaged in endless struggles against one another for local and sectional profit, thus generating most of the sound and fury of Canadian regional disunity.

The associational activities of the business classes—usually organizations and combines to fix prices, control production, and limit access—were the clearest expression of a thrust towards class consciousness and unity. In most ways they were the exact analogues of labour unions, particularly in their vulnerability to that peculiar form of scabbing known in the business world as competition. Virtually every combine put together during the 1880's and 1890's was broken by business disunity. The government's fairly feeble antitrust activities of the late 1880's were also directly sponsored by businessmen, though at this stage it was hardly necessary for the government to supplement the operations of the free market with legislation.[46] The very operation of the free market was both a symptom of the business disunity that existed and a guarantee that it would continue to exist.

The very real anxieties felt by businessmen operating in a harshly competitive environment were expressed in many ways. Dozens of articles in trade journals condemned unfair competitive methods, such as price-cutting, slaughter sales of bankrupt stocks, and the use of extended credits. There was even a wistful "Psalm for the Trade" printed in several trade journals of the 1880's:

> Shun this reckless competition.
> Look beyond the moment's gain,
> Learn that honest coalition
> Is far better in the main.[47]

"Demoralizing" was the standard word used to describe fierce competition in any trade. It carries endless connotations. Other writers condemned unrelenting business competition as a misapplication of the analogy of war to commerce, and blamed its practitioners for bringing the morality of war to business life.[48] Men who opposed any kind of limitation of competition were asked to consider "the heartbreaking anxiety of men who can only do business at a loss" and then they would appreciate the problem in a new light.[49] Images of business brotherhood and cooperation, the concept of strength through unity, permeated the rhetoric of trade association banquets and journals.[50] The very idea of competition was dismissed as "too destructive to be permitted to exist," "too destructive to be tolerated"[51] (business historians, the worst "whig" historians of all, too often ignore the long failure lists published in every trade journal, mute evidence of the validity of the complaint). Businessmen frequently complained about too many men chasing too little business, suggesting now and then that a return to the farm would be the best thing that could happen to ease the crush of competition.[52] Looking into the future in 1894 a Canadian banker foresaw that competition was approaching the period of its old age, that individualism in material affairs would soon come to an end, and the "commissariat department of society" would soon be organized entirely "collectively." The insecurity of competitive business life would be banished forever, as the young man on leaving school or college "will be drafted into the service of one or other of the great industrial corporations of the country, which he will never leave during the period of his working life." That would be a wonderfully beneficial development.[53]

Feeling himself harassed and set upon by enemies and competitors, it is not surprising that the Canadian businessman worried about the state of his health. George Stephen constantly teetered on the brink of a nervous breakdown. Joseph Flavelle enjoyed good health himself, but repeatedly advised friends that they were making impossibly large drains on their stock of nervous force. A doctor advised businessmen through the *Monetary Times* that the constant overpressure they endured in modern business life was sure to lead to the destruction of the nervous system. And when Erastus Wiman was arrested on charges of embezzlement the same doctor argued that he had finally broken down under the strain and become completely insane.[54] The employee had a very easy time of life compared with his employer, claimed an article in the *Canadian Grocer*.

His hours of labor are fixed, and his work is of a routine nature, requiring very little thought or care, except that necessary to the faithful performance of his duties. He knows just how much he is making, and when his day's work is done he can lay aside all care without fret or worry.

But with his employer it is quite different. With him it is constant, unceasing work, and his mind can never be entirely free from his business cares. He has to meet and overcome competition. He must watch the markets, both as a purchaser and a seller of goods. He must plan and devise, control and direct . . . Not for a moment can he rest.

The life of a successful business man is one constant round of work from morning till night, . . .[55]

Worry, it appeared, was the everyday state of mind of the man in business. It was a condition that the Winnipeg *Commercial* labelled "dyspepsia of the mind."[56]

This evidence should sustain the one proposition under examination: that in the formative years of Canadian industrialism the business class perceived itself to be operating in a hostile environment. Accepting that, many questions remain: Are these expressions of frustration and resentment, this basic business insecurity, simply self-pitying shudders at the approach of an imaginary wolf? Were these businessmen simply members of a simpering, paranoic elite, unaware of their overpoweringly dominant role in Canadian society — captains of industry raging through limpid pools? Or will future analyses of Canadian social structure in the late nineteenth and early twentieth centuries (at the moment of writing we have none) verify some of the business complaints? Perhaps Canadian politicians were an order unto themselves, juggling competing religious, racial, regional and economic interests to no purpose beyond being able to go on juggling. Possibly the liberal professions in Canada did enjoy a disproportionate share of social and political power. Similarly it may be that the Canadian working classes, benefiting from battles won abroad, in fact gained social and political influence in Canada relative to their employers more rapidly than workingmen had in other countries during the early years of industrialism.

Further, what are the entrepreneurial implications of this kind of insecurity on the part of a business community? Did we have in Canada a spiritually decapitated bourgeoisie, too timid and uncertain to provide us with the kind of solid national economic base that true Schumpeterian entrepre-

215

neurs would have created?[57] Does this in turn help to explain the ensuing decades of American takeovers of Canadian enterprises? Alternatively, it may well be that constant anxiety has always been the silent partner of businessmen operating in any society (when you have to rely on the future for returns on your investment how can you avoid anxiety?), particularly in fiercely competitive capitalist societies. Perhaps this very anxiety has in many cases driven entrepreneurs on to build great industrial empires, thus forestalling all future anxieties incident to competition (monopoly being the obvious answer to the parenthetical question).

Perhaps some variation of the Polanyi thesis applies to Canada: the social consequences of unrestrained capitalism were too much for actors in society to bear. They created an immediate and massive reaction against *laissez-faire* throughout the western world leading to social arrangements guaranteeing the individual a measure of relief from the strains of life in an unregulated, uncertain society.[58] Robert Wiebe and others have provided some evidence that this process did operate in late nineteenth century America, and that it was in part led by businessmen fleeing from the chaos of adolescent industrialism.[59] The simple generalization implied in this interpretation — that open competition in a dynamic society makes all its participants anxious — provides the broadest covering explanation of the evidence presented here. Further research will flesh out some of the details.

216

Notes

1. *Canadian Magazine*, March, 1905, p. 487.
2. Canadian Manufacturers' Association, *Scrapbook, 1883–1888*; General letter to members of the Ontario Manufacturers' and Industrial Association, signed by A.W. Wright (Secretary), Nov. 14, 1883; General letter to members of the O.M.A. signed by Frederic Nicholls (Secretary), Nov. 1885.
3. *Canadian Manufacturer*, Jan. 17, 1896, "The Fiscal Outlook." The article continues, "It is an unpleasant thing to say but it is one which every thinking man knows — we cannot, dare not, trust the Liberal party."
4. C.M.A. Tariff Committee, *Minutebook*, Dec. 5, 1910.
5. Public Archives of Canada, *Macdonald Papers*, Stephen to Macdonald, Sept. 3, 1889.
*It is significant for the general argument of this essay that the C.M.A. launched its campaign for more tariff protection at the peak of the first round of Laurier prosperity, arguing that depression would soon come again and Americans would breach our industrial fortresses. So much for the infant industries developing the confidence of adolescence.
6. *Ibid.*, Stephen to Macdonald, July 29, 1890.
7. P.A.C., *Stephen Papers*, Macdonald to Stephen, April 28, 1889; Oct. 6, 1887; June 15, 1888.
8. *Canadian Manufacturer*, May 12, 1882, p. 169. The C.M.A. would later advocate a Tariff Commission for the same reason.
9. *Canadian Manufacturer*, May 26, 1882, p. 192; "The Elections," *Canadian Journal of Commerce*, Jan. 21, 1887, p. 152; "The Coming Election," *Ibid.*, March 6, 1891, p. 454; "The Results of the Elections," *Monetary Times*, June 5, 1896, p. 1560.
10. John Porter, *The Vertical Mosaic*, pp. 379–485.
11. *Canadian Journal of Commerce*, Dec. 29, 1882, pp. 621-2. "The Business Tax."
12. *Ibid.*, Feb 4, 1887, pp. 272-3, "The Quebec Cabinet." See also J.H. Parry, *Taxes. Tariffs and Subsidies*, (Toronto, 1955) V.1, pp. 77-8.
13. V.K. Fowke, *The National Policy and the Wheat Economy* (Toronto, 1957) pp.93, 153 ff.
14. Merrill Denison, *The People's Power* (Toronto, 1960), Ch. 9; *Canadian Annual Review*, 1909, pp. 371-383.
15. *Financial Post*, June 5, 1909; July 31, 1909.
16. *Canadian Journal of Commerce*, July 9, 1887, p. 20; "The Tax on Corporations," July 13, 1888, pp. 67-8, "The Tax on Corporations."

17. C.M.A. Tariff Committee, *Minutebook*, Dec. 5, 1910; C.M.A. Executive Council, *Minutebooks*, May 5, 1910; Feb. 16, 1911.
18. Margaret Evens, "Oliver Mowat and Ontario, 1872–1896: A Study in Political Success" (unpublished Ph.D. Thesis, University of Toronto, 1967), ch. III. For the integration of the early labour movement into the existing political system see Martin Robin, *Radical Politics and Canadian Labour, 1880–1930* (Kingston, 1968), pp. 1–18 (esp. pp. 17–18: "The spread of trade unionism in Canada testified to the ability of the organized skilled stratum of artisans to win concessions under the prevailing system; its very success guaranteed that drastic solutions would not be sought"). For the striking success of the Provincial Workingman's Association in achieving legislative concessions in Nova Scotia in the 1880's and 1890's see H.A. Logan, *Trade Unions in Canada* (Toronto, 1948), pp. 172–3: "In 1896 the grand secretary declared that the miners of Nova Scotia were in advance of those of any English-speaking country with regard to legislation."
19. From a paper on "Organization" read at the 1887 annual meeting of the C.M.A. by its Secretary, Frederic Nicholls, *Canadian Manufacturer*, March 18, 1887, p. 176. See also the call for a "union" by a small jeweller in *The Trader*, June 1884; also *Canadian Grocer*, April 12, 1895, p. 8, "Where Do We Come In"?
20. *Report of the Select Committee to Investigate and Report Upon Alleged Combinations in Manufactures, Trade and Insurance in Canada* (Ottawa, 1888), pp. 516–7, 519; *Canadian Manufacturer*, March 16, 1888, p. 184, "The Trades Union 'Combine' ".
21. The Liberals claimed that the new statute took away the right to strike that had been granted to labour in 1872. This interpretation was accepted and popularized by Bernard Ostry in "Conservatives, Liberals and Labour in the 1880's," *Canadian Journal of Economics and Political Science*, XXVII, p. 2, (May, 1961). In fact the Government assured unions that the bill did not apply to combinations of workingmen, promised to appeal any successful action against unions under the Act to the highest court, and, as is noted in the text, strengthened the right to strike in the following year. See Thompson's speech to the House of Commons, April 30, 1889, *Debates*, p. 1690, and the report of his promise to Montreal printers in the *Toronto Mail*, Sept. 4, 1890. See also the exchange on the subject between Senators Power and Sanford, Senate *Debates*, April 29, 1889, p. 650. Also the speech of Senator Ogilvie, *Ibid.*, p. 643.
22. House of Commons, *Debates*, April 10, 1890, pp 3163, 3372–9; *Canadian Manufacturer*, June 21, 1889, p. 392, "Justice Versus Trade Unions."
23. *Canadian Manufacturer*, May 2, 1890, p. 292, "Pernicious Legislation."
24. *Industrial Canada*, Oct. 1907, p. 211 (Report of Parliamentary Committee to C.M.A. annual Convention).
25. One of many examples of this perception is "Undesirable Emigrants," *Canadian Journal of Commerce*, Aug. 6, 1886, p. 385: "The United States is already suffering from the Bohemian and other foreign Anarchists who have chosen it for their temporary home, and though as yet, the solid common sense and sturdy industry of the Canadian has swamped their incendiary efforts on this side of the line, the increasing number of idle and unemployed of the vicious classes in our cities must eventually form a fruitful ground for their mischievous and vicious doctrines."
26. For example, *Canadian Journal of Commerce*, June 3, 1881, "The Labor Question"; April 28, 1882, p. 335, "The Labor Question," May 22, 1886, p. 1342, "The Labor Question"; *Canadian Manufacturer*, Feb. 5, 1886, p. 80, "The Relations of Capital to Labor," Feb. 18, 1887, p. 115, "The Labor Candidate."
27. On profit-sharing see *Canadian Manufacturer*, Sept. 24, 1886, p. 549; for the industrial welfare movement see *Industrial Canada*, Nov. 1909, pp. 424–7, "Welfare Work in Factories"; Feb. 1910, pp. 693–6, "How Efficiency in Workmen is Improved."
28. For recruiting labour see C.M.A. British Office Committee, *Minutebook* (1906–08); on strike-breaking, C.M.A., Executive Council, *Minutebooks*, Sept. 18, 1902 (resolved "that no active part should be taken by the Association in organizing Employers' Protective Associations"); manufacturers' resistance to workmen's compensation was minimal.
29. C.M.A., Executive Council, *Minutebooks*, June 20, 1907.
30. C.M.A., Toronto Branch Executive, *Minutebooks*, July 14, 1910.
31. *Canadian Grocer*, June 19, 1896, p. 15.
32. *The Trader*, Oct. 1885, "Commercial Union."
33. See, for example, the complaints expressed in the C.M.A., Toronto Branch Executive, *Minutebook*, Dec. 9, 1909.
34. *Journal of Commerce*, May 23, 1890, pp. 978–9, "Political Morality"; *Industrial Canada*, Jan. 1908, p. 471, "Misleading the Masses."
35. April 13, 1896. See also *Canadian Manufacturer*, Jan. 3, 1896: "Is it possible that the manufacturing industries of Canada are to be sacrificed to propitiate kickers who have no substantial grievances, or to enable the Government to hold to them those who would make the best interests of the country subservient to the demands of cranks who place religious prejudices above everything else?"
36. Dec. 2, 1887, p. 364. See also *Canadian Journal of Commerce*, Oct. 21, 1887, pp. 754–5, "The Civic Debt": "The existence of a law allowing exemption of property from taxation simply on the grounds of its belonging to a religious body is a relic of feudalism that is simply an anachronism in a civilized city in the nineteenth century."

37. Nov. 17, 1893, pp. 402-3, "Student Pranks."
38. *Ibid.*
39. March 26, 1891, p. 188, "Unemployed Churchmen." See also *Canadian Manufacturer*, Jan. 19, 1894, p. 51, "Over-Production of Professional Men"; July 17, 1891, p. 78, "The Education of Doctors"; *Canadian Journal of Commerce*, Dec. 12, 1890, p. 1125, "Our Boys."
40. See *Report of the Royal Commission on the University of Toronto* (Toronto, 1906), passim.
41. For technical education see the annual reports of the C.M.A. Technical Education Committee, reprinted in *Industrial Canada*; for professional resistance see *Canadian Annual Review*, 1904, pp. 579-80.
42. Royal Commission on Industrial Training and Technical Education, *Report of the Commissioners*, (Toronto, 1913), Part IV, pp. 2102-3.
43. See *The Trader, Canadian Manufacturer, Canadian Journal of Commerce*, pp. 1882-3, passim.
44. *Industrial Canada*, Oct. 1903, p. 117.
45. The problem greatly worried Joseph Flavelle. See Flavelle to J. Willison, Nov. 11, 1913, *Flavelle Papers*, Douglas Library, Queen's University.
46. *Report of the Select Committee to Investigate and Report Upon Alleged Combinations in Manufactures, Trade and Insurance in Canada* (Ottawa, 1888), *passim*. All of the witnesses against combines were businessmen. Chairman of the Committee and initiator of the first anti-combines bill, Clarke Wallace, was a small businessman.
47. *The Trader*, Feb. 1885.
48. *Canadian Grocer*, July 8, 1892, p. 1.
49. *Monetary Times*, Feb. 22, 1895, p. 1091.
50. *Canadian Grocer*, Jan. 29, 1892, p. 26; "Modern Industrialism," *Financial Post*, July 1, 1911.
51. See any issue of the *Retail Merchant's Journal of Canada*, 1903-07.
52. Speech of Geo. Hague at annual meeting of the Merchant's Bank, *Monetary Times*, June 18, 1886, p. 1447.
53. Thomas Fyshe, "The Growth of Corporations," *Journal of the Canadian Bankers' Association*, II, 2 Dec. 1894, pp. 197-203.
54. *Flavelle Papers*, Flavelle to J.S. Willison, Nov. 28, 1902; Jan. 22, 1903; *Monetary Times*, Dec. 23, 1887, "The Health of Businessmen," 790; June 29, 1894, 1651, "The Case of Erastus Wiman."
55. *Canadian Grocer*, March 18, 1892, p. 8, "Attention to Business."
56. *Ibid.*, July 31, 1883, p. 928, "Business Worry."
57. As Melville Watkins has argued. See his "A New National Policy." in Trevor Lloyd and Jack McLeod, eds., *Agenda 70: Proposals for a Creative Politics* (Toronto, 1968).
58. Karl Polanyi, *The Great Transformation* (Boston, 1944).
59. Robert Wiebe, *Businessmen and Reform*, (Cambridge, Mass., 1962); *The Search for Order* (New York, 1967); Thomas C. Cochran, *Railroad Leaders, 1845-1890* (Cambridge, Mass., 1953); Gabriel Kolko, *The Triumph of Conservatism* (New York 1963); E.C. Kirkland, *Dream and Thought in the Business Community, 1868-1900* (Ithaca, 1956).

The Condition of the Working Class in Montreal, 1897-1920[1] *

J.T. COPP

I

During the autumn of 1896 a young Montreal businessman, Herbert Brown Ames, employed a number of "enumerators" to undertake "A Sociological Study of a portion of the City of Montreal, Canada". Ames assembled the results of the questionnaires into a short book called "*The City Below the Hill*", which was published in 1897.[2] The district surveyed, portions of the

*From Canadian Historical Association *Historical Papers* (1972): 157-180. Reprinted by permission.

St. Antoine and St. Anne's wards, contained 38,000 people, of whom only fifteen percent earned enough to be classified as "well to do". The residents were "evenly divided as to nationality: one third French Canadian, one third English, and one third Irish." So it was, wrote Ames, "an opportunity to study a class rather than a race".

The "City Below the Hill" was not a completely typical working class area. Its northwestern boundary was the main line of the C.P.R. leading into Windsor Station and just a block to the southeast, the Grand Trunk right-of-way to Bonaventure Station cut through the area. Two blocks further south the Lachine Canal, focal point of an earlier phase of industrialization, created a third axis of development. As a consequence the district contained more than its share of relatively high wage industries including iron and steel, machine shops and the railways.

There are other indications that much of the district was one of the better-off working class areas. With the exception of Griffintown, the "Poor Irish" ghetto, the density per acre figures and the mortality rate, particularly infant mortality, were much more favourable than in the central and eastern wards of the city. Using Ames' statistics as the basis for a descriptive account of working class life in Montreal in the 1890's may lead to underestimating the extent of poverty in the city but no material of comparable value is available for the city as a whole.

The 1890's were a period of slow economic growth in Montreal as in all of Canada. The city's population grew by only 18 percent in the decade, the smallest decennial increase since the 1860's.[1] The total value of manufacturing production increased by a mere 5.09 percent,[4] prices were at their lowest point since Confederation and contemporary observers complained of difficult business conditions. The Montreal *Real Estate Guide* noted that there were an "abundance of dwellings for rent and that tenants were displaying a marked independence."[5]

Ames' study allows us to examine the working class areas of the city at a point in time when the first tremors of the great "boom" of the early years of the twentieth century were still a full year off in the future.

II

Rue Notre Dame bisected "The City Below the Hill" and the axis of all the *old quartiers* of the city. By 1897 it was paved for most of its length with a mixture of cobblestones and tamarack blocks.[6] Like the other main streets it was festooned with the overhead wires of the Montreal Street Railway Company. At night the glare of arc lamps and the glow of the remaining gas lights cast dark shadows over most of the street. Notre Dame was lined, except in the financial district, with one and two storey structures; the solid brick and stone buildings intermingled with flimsy wooden houses. The side streets were frequently unpaved (only 27 of the city's 178 miles of streets were paved in 1897)[7] and according to the City Surveyor "dust in the autumn is very bad and the mud wears out the streets quicker than the traffic

219

does".[8] Elzéar Pelletier, the Secretary of the Quebec Board of Health, described the streets of Montreal as "intolerable though tolerated" and claimed the lanes resembled "refuse dumps".[9] The presence of 3000 horse stables and 500 cow sheds[10] within the narrow city limits added colour and aroma to the streets.

The lofty tenements of New York and Chicago were absent in Montreal. Instead, "the typical home was a *five room flat in the terrace of duplexes*." Ten percent of the total housing stock in the area surveyed by Ames consisted of "rear tenements", "either an ancient wooden cottage of the rural habitant type or a two-storey building encased in refuse bricks and reached by rickety wooden stairs or galleries".

Sewer and water lines reached most parts of the city but despite the municipal by-law of 1887 which had forbidden the further construction of houses served by the outdoor "pit privy", over 5000 privies remained in existence within city limits in 1898.[11] Over half the households in the "City Below the Hill" were "dependent entirely on such accommodation". Communal outdoor water taps were common.

Little attention had been paid to city planning in Montreal and the working class wards were densely populated, with narrow streets and few open spaces or parks. The 38,000 inhabitants of the western section of the lower city shared two formal public squares, Richmond and St. Patricks. The 26,000 residents of St. Louis Ward could utilize Viger Square while in St. Laurent Ward there was the two acres of Dufferin Square.[12] Montreal did possess a "Great Park", Mount Royal, designed by Frederick Law Olmstead who considered it to be one of the best in North America.[13] But Mount Royal, like St. Helen's Island which could be reached by ferry, was remote from the everyday life of the city. Lafontaine Park, located just to the north of some of the more congested areas of the city, had more potential as a people's park. In the late 1890's it was undergoing extensive landscaping and the serpentine, the park's feature attraction, was under construction.[14] The playground movement which was spreading across North America from the "sand garden" and "outdoor gymnasium" created in Boston in the 1880's had not yet reached Montreal.

The local bar was the focal point of the neighborhood. Ames counted 105 licensed saloons and 87 liquor selling groceries in the area and concluded that even if one eliminated those outlets adjacent to the railway stations there was a licensed liquor outlet, "goodness knows how many unlicensed", for every forty-five families. Forty-three percent of the arrests made in the city during the year Ames undertook his survey were for drunkenness.[15]

Six mornings a week the narrow, damp, smoky streets filled with workers headed for shop or factory. A work week of 58–60 hours meant being on the job at seven or seven-thirty if a full ten hours was to be put in. Twenty percent of the labour force in the "City Below the Hill" was composed of women and approximately five percent of children.[16] Women and children were not permitted to work more than ten hours a day unless a special permit had been obtained for a period not exceeding six weeks.[17] This regula-

220

tion, as well as the other rules laid down in the Industrial Establishments Act (1893) and the By-laws of the Quebec Board of Health Relating to Sanitary Conditions of Industrial Establishments (1895), did not apply to retail stores, home workshops or the many other forms of casual employment which absorbed the energies of working children.[18]

Something of the nature of working conditions in the factories of Montreal can be learned from the reports of the Factory Inspectors. The inspectors had the theoretical power to enforce rules concerning cubic feet of air space per worker, separate sanitary accommodation for men and women, cleanliness and appropriate fire escape mechanisms. Employers who offended against these regulations could be fined $200 for each contravention of the Act and $6 per day until the fault was remedied. In practice, since the inspector was required to institute court proceedings himself, a mixture of persuasion and threats were used to reform the more obvious abuses of the code. References to evasion of specific parts of the code, such as failure to provide fire escapes, were frequent and the inspectors returned each year to *221* the theme of the "ugly, dirty, dingy buildings redolent with the odours of old age and decrepitude".[19] The inspectors tended to concentrate on the two most serious problems confronting them, the prevalence of child labour and the frequency of industrial accidents.

In his *Report* for 1897 Louis Guyon, who was to become Chief Factory Inspector in 1900, focused in on these issues;

There have been very few infractions to note in regard to the employment of children under age; the limit of 12 years for boys being so low that there is hardly any desire among manufacturers to employ them younger . . .
From the standpoint of the prevention of accidents . . . inspection is very important. It is impossible not to feel a profound sense of pity for these poor victims of labour. For the inspector, it is part of his duty which calls for the most effort and perseverance, to find in the first place the means of protection best suited to the circumstances and next to convince employers that such improvements form part of well understood progress, and that in protecting their employees against accidents they are protecting themselves from an economical point of view.[20]

With twelve as the minimum age for boys and fourteen for girls child labour was not only common but legal. Workers who were injured, or the family of those who were killed were required to institute legal proceedings against the employer and had to prove negligence, if compensation was to be obtained.

Guyon devoted much of his career to a campaign to abolish child labour and secure a Workmen's Compensation Act. One of his colleagues, James Mitchell, was more cautious about the child labour question:

What of the ordinary labourer receiving $1.50 a day. Could he support a large family if deprived of the right of sending his children to work until they are fifteen? . . .[21]

The answer was clearly no, the ordinary labourer could not support his family on the basis of his own earnings. Ames found that the average family in 1897 had 1.4 wage earners and his statistics on family income suggest the importance of a second breadwinner.

Ames acquired information on 7671 families and found that their average income was $11.00 per week. He eliminated "the well to do" who earned more than $20.00 a week (15%) and the "submerged tenth" (11%) who received less than $5.00 a week. The remaining 74 percent which he called "the real industrial class" had an average income of $10.00 to $10.25 per week composed of some combination of wage earners earning an average of $8.25 per week, for a man, $4.50 for a woman and $3.00 for a boy. These figures cannot be translated into annual earnings by multiplying by 52. Ames himself noted that unemployment was the major cause of the poverty of the "submerged tenth" and that among families belonging to the "real industrial class" 23 percent had incomes "which could not be counted on as constant and regular throughout the year".

Ames sought to define the meaning of wages by establishing a "point below which comfort ends and poverty commences". He did this by deciding that since unskilled labourers earned a dollar a day but worked irregularly the sum of $260 per year could be used as the minimum necessary for "decent subsistence". Ames had never heard of the "working poor" and was unable to develop the concept. He avoided setting out the details of the style of life that might be enjoyed on $260 a year.

222

If the method of calculating a "theoretical weekly budget for a workingman's family of five" used by the Dominion Department of Labour after 1915[22] is applied as a "poverty line", then a family of five would have required a weekly income of $11.23 in 1902 to reach the level of a "typical family".[23] Very few working class families in Montreal could aspire to this level of expenditure unless there was more than one wage earner and work was available fifty-two weeks a year.

The Department of Labour's family budget is used as a "poverty line" throughout this study. It would be noted that the concept is not a new one. Robert Hunter, the author of one of the first estimates of the extent of poverty in the United States, argued in 1904 that only the most miserable of the needy were destitute and that the real poor in a community consisted of those who had "too little of the common necessities to keep themselves at their best . . . the large class in any industrial nation who are on the verge of distress".[24] The majority of the population of Montreal at the turn of the century fit this description and were, in the words of Jacob Hollender, "in constant danger, even with the exercise of care and foresight of falling or of slipping or of being crowded off the treacherous path encircling the morass of pauperism".[25]

There were other constant dangers confronting the residents of the working class wards. Montreal's death rate was generally recognized as among the highest in the civilized world. In 1898 Montreal's rate was 22.9 deaths per thousand, compared to 19.0 for New York city and 15.2 for Toronto.[26] The death rate in Ames' "City Below the Hill" was 22.47, in St. Jean Baptiste Ward it reached 35.31 and in St. Marie 33.2,[27] the upper section of St. Antoine Ward. "The City Above the Hill", to use Ames' phrase, had a death rate of 13 per thousand.

The key factor in Montreal's high death rate was infant mortality, which accounted for more than half of the total deaths. Montreal was the most dangerous city in the western world to be born in. Between 1899 and 1901 26.76 percent of all new born children died before they were one year old. This was more than double the figure for New York and was customarily cited as being lower than only one larger city — Calcutta.[28] These statistics were largely the result of unsafe water, impure milk and the limited use of vaccination against smallpox and diptheria. The Secretary of the Provincial Health Board commented that:

... the thought of having little angels in heaven can only afford consolation when one is satisfied that everything possible was done ... there should be no misconception on the subject, the use of antidiptheric serum has not yet become general in our province.[29]

In Montreal vaccination had indeed not become general. City health officials estimated that they had performed primary vaccinations on only one-fifth of the children born in the city during 1899.[30] The water supply was described by the Superintendent of the Water Works as "pure during ordinary times ... (but) dangerous during spring and fall". He noted that the main reservoir leaked badly and that the boom which blocked floating refuse at the entrance was in a "state of decay".[31] Milk was of course unpasteurized and civic inspection and distributing facilities were completely inadequate.

223

Eighteen hundred and ninety-seven is frequently seen as the pivotal year in the history of education in the province of Quebec. The newly formed Liberal administration was determined to fulfill the *rouge* dream of a Ministry of Public Instruction and the rejection of the bill in the *bleu* dominated Legislative Council postponed the creation of an education ministry for sixty-five years. For the resident of working-class Montreal the great debates over the control of education must have seemed of little interest. Primary education was neither compulsory nor free and although the school inspectors and the Superintendent of Public Instruction insisted that the city's schools were generally excellent[32] there is little evidence that supports their view and much which contradicts it.

The Provincial Board of Health was a trenchant critic of the sanitary and safety conditions in the schools of the city. It noted that while ideal standards called for 250 cubic feet of space per pupil and Quebec law required 150 cubic feet, the average in Montreal was only 75 cubic feet. The Board noted that little attention was paid to siting, orientation, ventilation or heating and that many schools lacked fire escapes.[33] Ninety percent of the teachers had less than eleven years of schooling and salaries in the Roman Catholic sector were among the lowest in North America. Over eighty percent of the total enrollment was in grades one to three and less than three percent of the total was in grade six.[34] Public expenditure on education was at the lowest point in the province's history having declined in absolute terms from $155,000 (1883) to $153,000 (1901) and from 75 cents per student to 56 cents per student over the same period.[35] The frequent comments of the factory Inspectors on the illiteracy of children in the work forces add to the picture of an educational system which had little positive impact on working class children. Even the goals pursued by the Superintendent of Public Instruction, the teaching of ". . . great respect for paternal, civil and religious authority . . . warn against intemperance and extravagance that impoverish our country . . . avoid quarrels and law suits . . . show the benefits conferred by agriculture . . ."[36] could not have been very adequately fulfilled in such a system.

The years between 1897 and 1920 were, with the single serious exception of the recession of 1913–15, a time of rapid growth in the city's population and productivity. It is not possible in a paper of this length to analyze developments in all aspects of working class life and the problems discussed in this section can only provide an impressionistic picture. However, the general thesis put forward here, that the conditions of life for the city's working class deteriorated during this era of "national prosperity", can be argued on the basis of this evidence alone.

Housing Conditions

The accelerated growth of Montreal's population which began at the end of the 19th century placed a severe strain on the housing supply available to the working class. Contemporary observers were well aware of the shortages and the consequent necessity for subdividing flats, converting cellars into dwellings and the multiplication of what was called the "lodger evil". *Le Canada*, one of the most progressive voices on civic questions, reminded its readers in 1904 that the lack of housing in the city was an index of progress.[37] It is apparent that "progress" continued. The Federal Government's *Board of Inquiry into the Cost of Living* reported in 1915 that:

Housing conditions (in Montreal) have degenerated and there is a decided lack of workingman's dwellings with proper conveniences at low rental. Rents have increased by fifty percent in the last seven years leading to a doubling up of families in the same apartment or house causing over-crowding and ill-health.[38]

The city's chief sanitary inspector felt that the situation had further deteriorated by 1920. "The inspection dwellings" he wrote,

has become more difficult since a few years. The high cost of materials and labour are the main factors of this difficulty. The number of dwellings of low rent no longer meets the demand and attempts are being made to meet the scarcity by transforming existing houses built for one or two families into several small dwellings . . . much discernment and circumspection must be used in the revision of building plans and specifications in order to assure all possible protection to public health without hindering the progress of construction.[39]

Public health standards had certainly not been allowed to hinder the "progress of construction" in the years before 1920. Montreal's housing regulations, like those of most North American cities, had not been consolidated into a clear concise code which could be rigorously enforced. Instead vague bylaws empowering the sanitary inspectors "to prevent overcrowding" and require "proper sanitary conditions" were in force throughout the period.[40] The sanitary inspectors of the city's Health Department devoted their energies to "correcting nuisances" and attempting to persuade proprietors to improve dwellings classified as "damp", "dirty and overcrowded" or containing "dark rooms" (Rooms without any direct means of ventilation). In 1905 the inspectors reported 223 dwellings in the first category, and 261 in the second. In 1918, 1868 homes were included in this classification.[41] No valid statistical inference can be drawn from such figures but the observer cannot help but be struck by the size of the problem confronting the sanitary inspectors.

Elzéar Pelletier, the Secretary of the Provincial Health Board, was the leading crusader for housing reform. His attitudes and specific ideas were derived from careful study of the European and American experience. Like Lawrence Veiller, the American housing reformer, Pelletier believed that the enforcement of adequate regulatory legislation was the first priority. Pelletier was responsible in 1906 for drafting a set of by-laws to the Quebec Public Health Act which "if enforced by the municipalities, would prevent the construction of unhealthy dwellings".[42] He urged municipalities in the province to control building operations by giving "the Municipal Architect the power to reject plans that do not conform to (provincial) health laws" and to expropriate existing structures on the ground of unhealthiness, basing compensation on the "sanitary value and not on the revenue the owner receives".[43]

225

The following year Pelletier focused his attentions on Montreal.

As the city spreads the streets and lots are arranged to suit the speculator . . . the city must plan with reserves for parks. . . . It must avoid the population density in the new wards such as exists in the old . . .[44]

The attempts to secure adequate housing legislation met with slight success. The city did eventually forbid the occupation of dark rooms but not their construction.[45] In 1916 the Montreal Board of Health reported that, "by-laws concerning construction regulate only the strength of buildings".[46] That was still the case in 1921.

No survey comparable to the one undertaken by Ames is available for the early 1920's but one study of post-war housing conditions suggests that the average number of persons to a room in Montreal had increased from 1 (Ames' figure) to 1.4 in 1921.[47] The author of the 1921 study, Arthur St. Pierre, a professor at the University of Montreal, maintained that though his estimate of 100,000 persons living in overcrowded dwellings indicated a grave problem it was not the most serious aspect of the Montreal situation. For St. Pierre the distinguishing feature of Montreal was, "la densité des logements sur une surface donnée, et non pas la densité de la population dans les logements" (italics in the original). St. Pierre estimated that eighty percent of the city's population were tenants and suggested that only New York city had a comparable ratio.

Chez nous, sauf dans deux ou trois petits districts privilégiés, auxquels la voracité des speculateurs en immeubles n'accorde qu'une existence précaire les maisons s'entassent et s'agglutinent, les logements s'écrasent et se superposent dévorant l'espace dans ses . . . trois, j'allais dire dans ses quatre dimensions.[48]

Montreal had not been a very pleasant place for the working class in 1897. By 1921, with a population growth to 750,000 conditions were considerably worse. There had been some "progress"; the paving of streets, and the construction of a new adqueduct were examples of limited municipal action, but the list of such achievements is a very short one.

The Working-Class Child

The campaign to end child labour in the factories of the province received occasional support from newspapers and voluntarist organizations, but the key figure was unquestionably Louis Guyon. Guyon and his associates led an indirect attack on the province's failure to impose compulsory education. In 1901 he described himself as a "convinced advocate of admitting children to factories on the basis of education and physical condition and reported that in a personal investigation of a large Montreal cotton mill . . . out of 65 girls 13 were illiterate and 18 wrote with difficulty. Out of 65 boys 21 were illiterate and 11 could hardly sign their names".[49]

The minimum age for boys in the factory work force was raised to 13 in 1903, then in 1907 the I.E.A. was amended to set 14 as the minimum age and require a test of literacy. Children between 14 and 16 who were unable to pass the test were required to attend night school. Guyon's reaction to the amendments is worth quoting at length:

The obligation for children between 14 and 16 to be literate or attend night school is a very difficult one to fulfill . . . in the first place because in many cases there are no night schools, or at best for boys only . . .
If I have fully seized the legislators' idea, the obligation for children to attend night school could only have been preparatory to a general law compelling children between 14 and 16 to fulfill the requirements regarding elementary education. Is it very practical to compel a child fatigued by ten hours of assiduous labour to spend even an hour and a half at school?[50]

A general law compelling children to fulfill the requirements of elementary education was not forthcoming. The inspectors' reports continued to advocate a literacy requirement or an elementary school certificate as a condition of entry into the factory labour force and urged that the provisions of the I.E.A. be extended to cover all working children. "There are" he wrote in 1912, "thousands of children over whom the factory inspectors have no control".[51] As the war continued the number of underage children in factories grew rapidly[52] and the problem of illiteracy among adolescent workers remained unresolved. By 1920 Guyon, who had become Deputy Minister of Labour, estimated that there were between eleven and twelve thousand children between 14 and 16 working in Montreal alone.[53] The Labour Department supervised a literacy exam for 6912 children in this age category and reported that 3081 were of the class of pupils at night school . . . some of them who could write in a fairly good hand their names, their address and the name of the company employing them, could read only hesitatingly while others who could read very well could write only with difficulty.[54]

In 1916 Louis Guyon had, in a moment of despair, complained that "child labour remains the same unsolvable problem we have encountered since 1888".[55] The problem remained "unsolvable" in 1921.

Working Class Women

The working class woman did not wait for the typewriter and the switch-board to "emancipate" her from domestic drudgery. Ames found that twenty percent of the labour force was composed of women in 1897, by 1921, one quarter of those gainfully employed were women.[56]

Women workers were viciously exploited receiving on the average just half of what men earned throughout the period under review.[57] Part of this discrepancy can be explained by the concentration of women workers in retail trade and the garment, textile and food processing industries which paid unusually low wages to all employees, but simple discrimination between men and women doing the same job was a major factor.

Intellectuals who studied "social questions" believed that working women were earning supplementary income and the question of wage differentials was seldom raised. In 1918 the provincial government introduced a Minimum Wage Act for women in Industrial Establishments but four years passed before the regulatory commission required to enforce the Act was appointed. The minimum set out in the Act followed the pattern of most such legislation by setting a floor low enough to avoid interference with all but the smallest and most inefficient firms.

The Quebec Department of Labour did appoint several women to the provincial factory inspectorate and they were charged with special responsibility towards women workers. Louisa King and Louise Provencher, the first two appointees, campaigned vigorously for "seats for shop girls who stand from eight in the morning to six at night", separate sanitary facilities, factory cleanliness and cheerful lunch rooms. They paid particular attention to home workshops and garment lofts. Madame Provencher's report for 1899–1900 included the following description of the practices of the garment industry.

. . . ready made clothing houses are actually offering to poor women compelled to earn their living with their needle, prices so low that they cannot earn their daily bread. To give 75 cents for a dozen morning gowns, 20 cents a dozen for undergarments and 5 to 15 cents (never more) for a dozen of neckties, is it not taking undue advantage of the ignorance and poverty and painful circumstances under which an unfortunate woman may labour?[58]

The factory inspectresses could do little to effect change in wage rates but they were convinced that their efforts won improvements for women workers with regard to the physical conditions under which work was undertaken. Miss Louisa King described her role in the following terms:

227

Like bounteous dew falling noiselessly on thirsty plants and revivifying them, like the sun's rays that spread joy and life, whenever they shine, thus does the inspectress fulfill her mission.[59]

Workman's Compensation

Louis Guyon and his fellow inspectors won their greatest success in convincing the provincial government of the need for a Workman's Compensation Act. The Industrial Establishment's Act contained a clause which required employers to notify the factory inspectors of accidents and the inspectors were required to undertake an investigation and to appear in court to offer testimony should litigation follow. The Civil Code required the victim of an industrial accident to prove that the accident was due to the employer's negligence. Winning such court cases was not easy as Guyon testified in his 1897 report.

228

There have been fewer suits this year on account of accidents, and a great many cases won in the lower courts were dismissed in the Supreme Court. In fact decisions favourable to workmen are becoming rarer and rarer.[60]

Accidents however, were becoming more and more common. Guyon quoted "the eminent Italian sociologist Mr. Lugattis" description of modern industry as "a real battlefield with its dead and wounded" and added that "each new invention, each increase in the rapidity of the means of production seems to carry in its wake a new train of dangers".[61]

During the year 1899–1900, in one textile mill in Montreal, 23 accidents were reported most of them involving the loss of a finger or hand. Between 1890 and 1907 the factory inspectors investigated 4,608 accidents of which 263 were fatal. This figure quoted by the Commission on Labour Accidents represented only those accidents reported to the inspectorate. Many employers simply did not make reports and among the recalcitrant employers were the Grand Trunk Railway and most of the firms employing longshoremen. Guyon believed that at least one in every three industrial accidents went unreported.[62]

Guyon's views on industrial accidents were strongly influenced by his attendance at two conferences held in Paris in 1900. The sessions of fifth International Convention on Accident and Social Insurance and the First International Convention for the Legal Protection of Work People, provided Guyon with a detailed knowledge of European legislation.[63] His immediate preoccupation on returning from Paris was the development of a "Safety Museum" which included photographs, models and actual examples of safety devices. Guyon hoped that the museum would influence employers directly but in addition he was able to argue before the courts, with some success, that the absence of a safety device constituted negligence on the part of an employer.[64]

The factory inspectors continued to press for a Workman's Compensation Act. Guyon attempted to obtain the active support of organized labour in this campaign but the unions showed slight interest. When a compensation law was finally adopted in 1909, Guyon remarked that the law was "entirely due to the initiative of the government".[65] Most of that initiative came from Guyon himself.

Public hearings on workmen's compensation were held in 1907 under the auspices of a specially appointed Commission on Labour Accidents. While some employers were flatly opposed to any legislation (one employer complained "legislators should promote instead of fetter industrial interests")[66] the important business groups supported the principle of compensation. The Montreal branch of the Canadian Manufacturer's Association and the Builder's Exchange went so far as to favour the adoption of the "professional risk" principle. They were opposed to the existing trial by jury system because of the lack of limits on possible compensation and the cost of legal proceedings. Most of the spokesmen for organized labour supported the idea of compulsory insurance based on a concept of professional risk as well but the Commission accepted the argument of other business spokesmen who insisted that insurance based on the idea of professional risk would "place Quebec manufacturers in an unfair footing with other provinces".[67]

229

The Workman's Compensation Act of 1909 was the first such act to become law in North America. Pioneering, however, had its penalties. The Quebec law did not create an independent board or make insurance compulsory. It simply established a procedure for claims and a schedule of payments for partial and total disabilities as well as death benefits. If negligence or fault on the part of the employee could be proven, no compensation was payable. It was not until the mid 1930's that the law was amended to create a modern compensation system based on an independent board and compulsory insurance payments. In the interval seven Canadian provinces, beginning with Ontario in 1914, had passed Acts which were well in advance of the Quebec law.

The Real Income of Wage-Earners

The most important single measure of the consequences of a period of sustained growth is the effect of "national prosperity" on real income. The Department of Labour's index of wage rates in 13 Canadian cities, 1901–1920, indicates that wages moved steadily upwards for the 21 classes of labour examined. Average weekly wages increased by almost 33% — 1901 to 1911, a further 33% increase was obtained between 1911 and 1918 and in the following two years wage rates jumped by an unprecedented 38%.

The method of calculating changes in wages used by the Labour Department is open to a number of objections. The index is based on reported wage rates rather than actual income and the sample of occupations is heavily biased towards skilled and organized workers. The Census of 1921 notes that its figures on the percentage increase of income of heads of families in occupations comparable to those surveyed by the Department of Labour show a much smaller rate of increase (82.19 percent) 1911–1921 than the Labour Department's estimate (109.61 percent).[69]

Even if the Department of Labour's figures are used, a comparison of wage increases with the changes in the cost of living suggests that there was a slight decline in real income 1901–1920.

Index numbers of weekly wage rages for 21 classes of labour in 13 Canadian cities (1913 = 100)[70]		Index numbers of family budget 1913 = 100[71]	
1901	69.8	1900	69.7
1911	92.4	1911	92.7
1918	131.6	1918	147.2
1920	179.3	1920	184.7
1921	186.1[72]	1921	161.9

If figures on actual income rather than wage rates were generally available it would be possible to show that there was a significant decline in real income for most wage earners in Canada over the entire twenty year period. Certainly this was the case in Montreal.

The weekly income required by a family of five to reach the "typical expenditure" level in 1901 was $9.37 for the basic items of expenditure or $11.23 if these basic items are calculated at eighty percent of total family needs. How close to this figure could the average working man come in 1901? The primary income calculation used to establish this relationship was developed within the limitations of the material in the Census reports. For comparative purposes, it was necessary to eliminate those occupations which included significant numbers of women and child wage earners.

The average income for 6543 workers in those categories of "manufacturing" which did not have significant numbers of women and children workers was calculated.[73] This list excluded almost all of the classically low wage industries, yet the average income was only $405.00 per year or $7.78 per week. Average income for this group fell $3.45 below the sum required to meet the expenses of an ordinary family of five.

For 1911 the same method was used and the income of 9043 adult male workers averaged $549.00 a year or $10.55 a week.[74] The typical expenditure level in 1911 had risen to $15.68 a week. The figures for 1911 unlike the ones used in 1901 can be checked against the annual earnings of "Heads of Families in Specified Occupations" in Montreal.

Average income for the five categories of building trades craftsmen who were heads of families came to $711.00 per year or $13.70 a week. Labourers averaged $531.68 or slightly over $10.00 per week. Trainmen, traditionally one of the highest paid wage earners averaged $971.07 or $18.67 a week. They were the only category of wage earner in the Department of Labour sample who received an income high enough to place their families above the poverty line without the assistance of a second wage earner.[75]

The rapid rise in the cost of living during the years 1915–1920 is a well documented phenomena. For Montreal, it is possible to begin to use cost of living figures specific to the city thanks to the adjustments made by the

230

Quebec Statistical Yearbook. By 1920, the "basic" items of expenditure required a weekly income of $22.38[76] and the total family budget called for an outlay of $27.96 ($1,456 per year).

The Census of 1921 provides much more detailed information on incomes than any previous census and it is possible to calculate the average income of all adult male wage earners in Montreal. The average $1,100 dollars falls $356 below the typical expenditure level.[77]

There is a good deal of contemporary descriptive evidence of the plight of the working poor in Montreal during these years. The Committee which organized the Montreal Child Welfare Exhibit of 1912 tried to draw up a family budget on the basis of earnings of $10.50 a week[78] (which it suggested an unskilled labourer could hope to earn if continuously employed). The Committee noted that the budget made no provision for "sickness, recreation, church, house furnishing, lectures and savings". A family of five would with careful planning be able to allot .75 cents a day to food, but the Committee quoted its domestic science experts who suggested that a minimum of .25 cents a day was required for food for a growing child. The rent allowance in this budget came to $9.00 a month which the Committee noted could only pay for "unsanitary quarters, sometimes below street level".[79]

231

It seems necessary to conclude that as far as real income is concerned the average wage earner in Montreal was less well off during the period of economic expansion than during the "depression" of the late 19th C. There has been a general awareness that increases in the cost of living outstripped wage gains during the war and immediate post-war years but the overall trend of the first two decades has not been widely recognized. Given the small percentage of the labour force that was organized and the weakness of most components of organized labour the decline in real income should occasion no surprise.

It should be noted that the situation in Montreal was not unique, but part of a national pattern. However the Montreal wage earner's income remained at a substantially lower level than wage earners in Toronto and generally worked much longer hours throughout the period. Some improvement did develop with regard to hours of work. The average in 1897 was 58 hours per week and this had declined to between 50–55 hours per week by 1921.[80]

The overall pattern of decline in real income and only marginal reductions in the length of the work week did not hold for all segments of the working class. Significant gains were made by a few groups of skilled or strategically placed workers who were able to organize and sustain locals of national and international unions. The data on the organization of unions in the *Labour Gazette* and the *Quebec Statistical Yearbook* indicates an incredibly high mortality rate for union locals in Montreal. It also points to a strong will to organize among the city's workers.[81]

The obstacles to union organization and meaningful collective bargaining were not peculiar to Montreal. Stuart Jamieson sums up the problem in the following terms:

Labour in Canada and the United States has been especially difficult to organize for a number of reasons: high rates of immigration as well as mass migrations from rural areas to urban industrial centres; language and ethnic diversity of the labour force, the high mobility of the population, and the like. Employers, for the most part, presented an intense, and prolonged and at times violent opposition to unions. Up to the later 1930's generally less than 15% of the non-agricultural paid labour in either country was unionized.[82]

All of the factors noted by Jamieson applied in Montreal. The overwhelming majority of employers insisted on the "open shop", resisted use of the union label and opposed the principle of collective bargaining. Of the 287 strikes listed for the city by the Department of Labour between 1901 and 1921,[83] 115 resulted in the total rejection of employee demands, frequently accompanied by dismissal of the strikers and the employment of scab labour. Success in the sense of employer acceptance of the demands of the strikers, was obtained in only 49 strikes, most of them involving less than 100 workers in highly skilled craft unions. Some seventy strikes were identified as having ended in a compromise, but only detailed investigations of each one would reveal the meaning of that term to the employees.

232

It was not until 1916, when the demands of war production and army enlistments had created a labour shortage, that workers were able to bargain with some weight. Of the 21 strikes reported during the years 1916 and 1917, thirteen were described as "negotiations in favour of employees", two as "compromises" and two as under "arbitration". Close to 9000 workers were involved in strikes during this two year period. This pattern continued in 1918 though there were only six strikes unique to Montreal in that year reported in the *Labour Gazette*. The climate of labour relations during the three year period was determined by the demands of the war economy. Few employers could afford to allow their operations to be interrupted and they were ready to buy peace with substantial wage increases. The Department of Labour's index numbers for weekly wages illustrate this clearly. Averages for 21 classes of labour in 13 Canadian cities indicate unprecedented increases, 10 points in 1916, 4 points in 1917 and 15 points in 1918. These figures are representative of changes in wage rates in Montreal. Iron moulders in the city secured 10 cents an hour increases in 1917 and again in 1918. They also won a reduction of the work week from 60 to 54 hours. Machinists averaged 10 cents an hour gains in 1916 and a further 5 cents an hour in both 1917 and 1918. "Common Labour in Factories" obtained an average increase of 20% between 1915 and 1918.

These gains were however wiped out by the rise in the cost of living. The "typical family" that could be fed, clothed and sheltered for $14.15 in 1915 required $21.24 to maintain the same standard of living in 1918 — a 50% increase in the cost of living. In 1916 the Quebec Government's chief labour arbitrator described this problem and pointed to a popular solution:

. . . the cost of living continues to rise with a fearful rapidity . . . the average cost of mere necessities for a workman's family of five or six is $60.00 per month . . . the majority of workmen do not earn more than $15.00 per week. Consequently it is not so surprising to see children obliged to leave school and go to work at the age of fourteen or fifteen years. Their wages are very low but in many instances they are imperatively needed for the family's support.

In the presence of such a state of affairs, the earnest and sincere patriots are quite right in appealing to the people to attach themselves more and more to the soil and to seek from it not only subsistence but also sound and real freedom.[84]

Such solutions were popular amongst intellectuals; workers turned to organization and direct action to secure a just return for their labour. Nineteen-nineteen witnessed a wave of agitation and confrontation such as the city has never before experienced. Sixty-two strikes involving more than 30,000 workers occurred before the year was over. Felix Marois, the Commissioner of the Quebec Trade Disputes Act attempted to explain the mood of labour in his annual report.

Neither revolution nor socialism is arousing the working classes today. No doubt there are ardent theorists and partisans of these dangerous doctrines in our province but the masses are ignorant of them. What the working class wants is improvement in their lot, fair remuneration for work and, above all, that living may not be unjustly made too dear for them. They admit that one who has a fortune may increase it but they will not admit that he should do so at the expense of the whole nation.
Against this they rebel and protest; they find that food and clothing cost too dear. . . . They were told that the country's greatest interests were at stake and they were asked to consent to such a sacrifice, the better to ensure the Allies success. But the war has ended and there is no change. Far from dropping, the cost of living is soaring to heights more and more inaccessible to the masses.
The people seek a remedy for the evil . . . but nothing is done. They become irritated, for they rightly or wrongly suspect the authorities of having allowed a band of profiteers to make large fortunes out of labour. The authorities have had enquiry after enquiry made but they only show more clearly the gravity of the evil. The masses understand nothing, they are driven mad for no remedy comes from anywhere . . .[85]

233

Perhaps "driven mad" is an exaggeration but the situation in Montreal in 1919 might well have given birth to madness. A strike at Dominion Textiles involving 3200 workers serves to illustrate the frustration of the working class. The demands were: recognition of the United Textile Workers of America as bargaining agent, a 50% wage increase, 44 hours a week, time and one half for overtime, abolition of fines for bad work, pay for time lost when it is not the fault of the worker (i.e., other departments slow), 20% over day rates for night work and an increase in piece work rates. Marois had tried to arbitrate the dispute but the Company had contented itself with the flat refusal of all demands and the statement that there was nothing to arbitrate. It regretted the "ill-advised strike" and declared "the mill doors are open". Two months after the strike began the workers returned without having obtained a single concession from the Company.[86]

The pattern of confrontation continued through 1920 with 10,000 Montreal workers on strike during the year but rising unemployment and the abrupt break in the inflationary trends during 1920 cut into union membership and labour militancy. Unemployment statistics for trade union members in Quebec illustrate the trend clearly. In July 1920 trade unions reported that only 2.54 percent of their membership was unemployed, by November the rate was 13.83 percent and by May of 1921 it had reached 26.54 percent.[87] The cost of living had peaked in October of 1920 at an average of $26.46 for the family of five budget.[88] By October of 1921 declines in food prices had led the way to a reduction of $4.45 in basic costs. Expressed as index numbers the cost of living declined from 184.7 in 1920 to 161.9 in 1921 and it continued to decline a further 12 points in 1922.[89]

The vast majority of the working class in Montreal had to face the "lean years" of the 1920's with little prospect of any fundamental changes in their way of life. Stable prices if coupled with full employment might provide greater security temporarily, but the failure to develop viable working class institutions meant the vulnerability of the wage-earning population in times of trouble would remain. Most of the population of Montreal would continue to tread the "treacherous path encircling the morass of pauperism".

III

It has been suggested that the exclusion of the majority of Montreal's working class population from the benefits of a period of great "national" prosperity was in no way unique but simply part of the general national pattern. Wage-earners in Montreal may have been less well off than their counterparts in Toronto but average annual earnings in many occupations were above the national average. What then may be said about the peculiar cultural characteristics of French Canadian society which are so often alleged to have a determining influence on the structure of Quebec society? The answer is that for the working class as a class the "cultural" or "national" question was largely irrelevant.

The evidence on trade union activity and the data on strikes in Montreal points to only one conclusion. The working class in Montreal responded to the oppression of the industrial system with the same mixture of sporadic militancy and passive resignation which characterized industrial workers throughout North America.

It may well be that anglophone workers or their children found it easier to become upwardly mobile in society where business and industry was largely conducted in the English language but such mobility effected a small number of individuals and has little to do with the experience of the mass of the population. The crucial question for the working class was income distribution not upward mobility.

Income distribution refers not only to the proportion of national income placed directly in the hands of the working class through wage payments but also to expenditure in what is usually now called "the public sector". The evidence presented in this essay suggests that middle class Quebec society was little different than other North American societies in terms of ideological concern with "reforms" which would shift some percentage of national income from the private to the public sector.[90] In the early 20th century expenditure in the public sector meant increased funding of education and welfare services, the financing of public works designed to improve living conditions (parks, water systems, drainage etc.) and the creation or expansion of government regulatory agencies concerned with public health, factory conditions and other widely recognized social problems.

The Gouin government's attempt to raise teachers' salaries, establish tech-

234

nical schools and specialized institutions like the Ecole des Hautes Etudes Commercial may be judged as a modest response to a major problem but the same criticism may be leveled at all provincial governments. It was not ideology but tax resources which limited educational expenditure. The Loi d'assistance publique (1921) which channeled new tax revenues into hospitals and other welfare institutions met some opposition from social reactionaires like Henri Bourassa but the dominant Liberal party was not seriously threatened by such criticism.

The Quebec Trades Disputes Act (1901), the Workman's Compensation Act (1909), the Minimum Wage Act for Women in Industrial Establishments (1918), the numerous amendments to the Industrial Establishments Act and the Public Health Act, were typical examples of the kind of regulatory legislation passed in Canada. When the Gouin Government introduced legislation creating the Public Utilities Commission (1910) Gouin noted that the legislation was based on the system used in Wisconsin. This argument placed a very defective piece of legislation above criticism for everyone interested in public affairs believed that Wisconsin was the very model of a modern government.

235

The fact that these legislative initiatives appear to have had little real impact on the society is a comment on the history of regulatory legislation in North America not a critique of the peculiar characteristics of Quebec. Indeed it seems impossible to argue that the French Canadian middle class was in any way isolated from or hostile towards the ideas and techniques which were the common property of the nations of the western world. Louis Guyon and Elzéar Pelletier regularly attended international conferences and reported on developments in their fields. Since much of the pioneering work in social legislation originated in continental Europe, French Canadian reformers even enjoyed some advantages denied to their counterparts in English-speaking provinces.

To find evidence of the anti-statism so often attributed to the French Canadian elite the researcher must ignore the ideological center in French Canada and concentrate on the variable moods of a small number of not very influential *nationaliste* intellectuals. The press in French Canada consisted of more than *Le Devoir*, *Le Nationaliste* and *L'Action Sociale*. *Le Canada* and *La Presse*, for example, kept their readers informed of developments in social legislation in North America and Europe. Politicians could evoke graphic images by speaking of "les trusts" because their audiences knew about the Northern Securities affair and Standard Oil.

All of this is not to deny that there were problems which were different in detail because of the Quebec milieu. Education is the most obvious issue on which the case for "cultural determinism" might be made. Certainly resistance to compulsory education was much more powerful in Quebec than in other parts of Canada, though not more powerful than in other predominately Catholic societies. But compulsory education in Quebec was a political issue not a social issue. The idea of compulsion was so closely identified with the anti-clericism of the *rouge* element that otherwise reasonable men opposed or ignored the question while supporting other measures designed to accomplish the same purpose. Arthur St. Pierre for example, told the Canadian Conference on Child Welfare in 1923 that

> no law is harder to enforce than compulsory school attendance. It is the will of the parents, not the efforts of legislators, which will solve the problem. Underage workers seldom belong to well-to-do families, child labour is caused by low wages.[91]

Child labour was caused by low wages, and if the problem of child labour and indeed the problems of poverty and unemployment were more serious in Quebec than in some other parts of North America, the student will be well advised to ask questions about the special characteristics of the Quebec economy and the revenues available to provincial and city governments, rather than falling back on cliches about the weakness of Quebec's "social thought".

Arthur St. Pierre's 1923 address to the Canadian Conference on Child Welfare included a passage which dealt with the crux of the problem confronting wage-earners everywhere.

> . . . low wages are no more a necessary part of our social structure than the slavery of bygone days. They are, to a very large extent the product of ancient customs, of inherited habits, of ancestral fears that slowly but surely we are getting rid of. Wage rates are not fatally governed and kept down by any wage-fund law, but they are in a very large measure subjected to and limited by ways of thinking. . . .
> Today there are for a large minority of our workers, decent living conditions for themselves and family while there remains unfortunately a bare subsistence for millions of toilers. Tomorrow the minimum might be for all the salary of the well paid minority of today.[92]

Tomorrow has not yet arrived for Quebec or Canada.

Notes

1. This paper is based on sections of a work-in-progress of the same title. The author wishes to acknowledge the assistance provided by a research grant from the Centre de Recherche en Histoire Economique du Canada Français (C.H.E.).
2. H.B. Ames. *The City Below the Hill*, Bishop Printing, Montreal, 1897. All quotations in part one not otherwise footnoted are from *The City Below the Hill*. For a recent study of Ames' background and career in Montreal, see D. Russell, *H.B. Ames and Municipal Reform*. Unpublished M.A. thesis, McGill University 1971.
3. *Quebec Statistical Yearbook*, Vol. 3, 1914, p. 59.
4. Canada, Census of 1911, Vol. 2, p. XIX.
5. *The Real Estate Guide*, Spring 1897.
6. Montreal, Report of the City Surveyor, 1898, p. 4.
7. *Ibid.*, p. 4.
8. *Ibid.*, p. 2.
9. Quebec, "Report of the Provincial Board of Health" 1902 *Sessional Paper no.* 6 1903, p. 49, (afterwards RPBH).
10. Montreal, *Board of Health Report*, 1899, p. 7 (afterwards *B.H.R.*)
11. *B.H.R.* 1898, p. 13.
12. Jessie Di Paolo, *The Development of Parks and Playgrounds in Montreal 1900–1910* Unpublished B.A. Honours Essay, Loyola College, 1969, Appendix B.
13. F.L., Olmstead, *Mount Royal* (New York; 1881), p. 51.
14. Di Paolo, *op. cit.*, p. 27.
15. Montreal *Annual Report*, *Chief of Police*, 1896.
16. The estimate of the number of women in the work force is from Ames' survey. He made a distinction between "lads" and "children" without defining the difference.

17. The text of the *I.E.A.* is printed in Sessional Paper no. 7, 1896.
18. Louis Guyon, Chief Factory Inspector for the province claimed, "It must not be forgotten that the employees in the majority of our shops are chiefly children", Sessional Page no. 7, 1902–03 p. 193. *Reports of the Factory Inspectors.* (Afterwards R.F.I.).
19. *R.F.I.*, Sessional Paper no. 7, 1897, p. 208.
20. *Ibid.*, p. 41.
21. *R.F.I.*, Sessional Paper no. 7, 1902, p. 204.
22. This hypothetical family budget was constructed by R.H. Coats. Dominion Statistician, and published in Vol. II of the *Report of the Board of Inquiry into the Cost of Living*, Ottawa, 1915. It was intended to represent weekly consumption of food, fuel, lighting and rent of an urban working class family of five. These expenses were thought to constitute from 60 to 80 percent of ordinary expenditures.
23. Canada, *Labour Gazette*, March 1921, p. 432. The figures quoted for 1901, $9.37 for the four items analyzed by the Labour Department is eighty percent of $11.23.
24. Robert Hunter, *Poverty*, New York 1904, cited in Robert Bremner, *From the Depths*, N.Y., 1956, p. 125.
25. Jacob Hollender, *The Abolition of Poverty*, Boston, 1914, cited in Bremner, p. 125.
26. *B.H.R.*, 1898, p.6.
27. *Ibid.*, p. 93.
28. Joseph Gauvreau, *La Goutte de Lait. l'Ecole Sociale Populaire* No. 29, 1914, p. 5.
29. R.P.B.H., Sessional Paper no. 7, 1897, p. 36.
30. *B.H.R.*, 1899, p. 17.
31. Montreal, *Report of the Superintendent of the Montreal Waterworks*, 1897, p. 3.
32. By 1900 all Montreal Roman Catholic schools were graded "excellent" in all categories by the School Inspectors. See Sessional Paper no. 5 1901, *Report of the Superintendent of Public Instruction* "School Inspectors Reports".
33. "Memoir on School Hygiene", p. 25. RPBH Sessional Paper no. 6, 1900.
34. M.C. Urquhart and K. Buckley (eds.) *Historical Statistics of Canada*, p. 595.
35. *Report of the Superintendent of Public Instruction*, Sessional Paper no. 5, 1901, p. XXII.
36. *Report of the Superintendent of Public Instruction*, Sessional Paper no. 5, 1897. p. 323.
37. *Le Canada*, Oct. 30, 1904, p. 4.
38. Canada, *Board of Inquiry Into the Cost of Living*, Ottawa 1915, p. 483.
39. *B.H.R.*, 1921, p. 60.
40. *Charter of the City of Montreal, Corrected and Completed with all Amendments Adopted up to date 1908* (Montreal, A. Pigeon, 1908). Bylaw 63. The extensive revisions of 1909 which introduced a Board of Control into civic government under pressure from middle class groups determined to end corruption and promote "good government" did not modify the housing bylaws, nor it may be added make any other changes which could have affected conditions among the working class. See Montreal, *Amendments to the Charter 1909* (A. Pigeon, 1909) and *Amendments to the Charter 1924* (Montreal, 1924).
41. *B.H.R.*, 1906, 1919.
42. R.P.B.H., Sessional Paper no. 6, 1908–09, p. 10.
43. *Ibid.*, p. 79.
44. R.P.B.H., Sessional Paper no. 6, 1910, p. 49.
45. *B.H.R.*, 1911, p. 4.
46. *Ibid.*, 1916, p. 86.
47. Arthur St. Pierre, *Le Problème Social* (Montreal, 1925), p. 102.
48. *Ibid.*, p. 103.
49. *R.F.I.*, Sessional Paper no. 7, 1901, p. 193.
50. *R.F.I.*, Sessional Paper no. 7, 1908–09, p. 88.
51. *R.F.I.*, Sessional Paper no. 4, 1912, p. 37.
52. *R.F.I.*, Sessional Paper no. 4, 1917–18, p. 69.
53. *R.F.I.*, Sessional Paper no. 4, 1921, p. 73.
54. *Ibid.*, p. 72.
55. *R.F.I.*, Sessional Paper no. 4, 1916, p. 55.
56. Canada. *Census of 1921*, Vol. 4, p. 438.
57. Women earned an average of $185.00 per year in 1901, $286.60 in 1911 and $567.00 in 1921. (Figures are averages from information in respective Census Report).
58. *R.F.I.*, Sessional Paper no. 7, 1899–1900, p. 67.
59. *R.F.I.*, Sessional Paper no. 7, 1902–03, p. 186.
60. *R.F.I.*, Sessional Paper no. 7, 1897–98, p. 64.
61. *R.F.I.*, Sessional Paper no. 7, 1901–02, p. 64.
62. Quebec, *Report of the Commission on Labour Accidents* (appointed 1907) N.D. p. 11.
63. Guyon's Report on his experiences is included in *R.F.I.*, Sessional Paper no. 7, 1900–1901, p. 165.
64. *R.F.I.*, Sessional Paper no. 7, 1905–06, p. 183.
65. *R.F.I.*, Sessional Paper no. 7, 1909–10, p. 76.

237

66. *Report of the Commission on Labour Accidents*, p. 5.
67. *Ibid.*, p. 6.
68. *Labour Gazette*, March 1921, p. 3.
69. Canada, *Sixth Census of Canada, 1921*, Vol. III p. XXI.
70. *Labour Gazette*, March 1921, p. 3.
71. Urquhart & Buckley, *op, cit.*, p. 303.
72. Department of Labour, *Wages and Hours of Labour in Canada*, 1921-22, p. 2.
73. Canada, *Census of 1901*, Vol. IV Manufacturing, p. 313.
74. Canada, *Census of 1911*, Vol. III, p. 304-309, Vol. VI, p. 250-261.
75. All figures in this paragraph are from Table XI, p. XIX, Census of 1921, Vol. III.
76. Quebec, *Statistical Yearbook 1921*, p. 427.
77. Canada, *Census of 1921*, Vol. III, p. XIX.
78. Child Welfare Exhibition, Montreal, *Souvenir Handbook*, Montreal 1912, p. 31.
79. *Ibid.*, p. 32.
80. See Tables I-VI, *Wages and Hours of Labour in Canada, 1901-1920, op. cit.*
81. See Quebec, *Statistical Yearbook*, 1920, p. 414.
82. S. Jamieson, *Times of Trouble* (Ottawa, 1968), p. 39.
83. Michael Piva, a graduate student at Sir George Williams University, compiled the information on strikes in Montreal reported in the *Labour Gazette* for this study. All of the information on labour unrest in Montreal not otherwise cited is taken from this compilation except statements on wages and hours which are from *Wages and Hours of Labour in Canada 1901-1920, op. cit.*
84. *Report of the Commissioner of the Quebec Trades Disputes Act*, Sessional Paper no. 7, 1916, p. 109.
85. *Ibid.*, 1919, p. 146.
86. *Ibid.*, 1919, p. 149-151.
87. *Labour Gazette*, July 1921, p. 934.
88. *Ibid.*, Nov. 1921, p. 1329.
89. Urquhart & Buckley, *op. cit.*, p. 303.
90. See Michael Gauvin. *The Municipal Reform Movement in Montreal, 1886-1914* Unpublished M.A. thesis. University of Ottawa 1972 for further evidence of "reform" efforts at the municipal level.
91. *Report of the Canadian Conference on Child Welfare*, 1923, p. 123.
92. *Ibid.*, p. 123-124.

238

Honest Womanhood: Feminism, Femininity and Class Consciousness Among Toronto Working Women 1893-1914*

WAYNE ROBERTS

Passing through Toronto in 1913 as an accomplished trade unionist, Mrs. Nellie Wilson was disturbed to find that her native city had nothing like the Women's Trade Union League she boasted of in her adopted Los Angeles. Her grumbling echoed that of another American organizer, Miss Margaret Daly, when she had toured the city two years earlier as a staff member for the garment workers. "The greatest difficulty we have is to put fight into the Canadian women", she complained. "They are by nature and because of their customs, more timid than American women".[1]

These views were not just the product of uncommon Yankee arrogance. A chorus of Toronto critics of the woman worker dates back at least to Jean

*From *A Not Unreasonable Claim: Women and Reform in Canada, 1880's-1920's*, Linda Kealey (ed.). Women's Press, Toronto, 1979.

Scott's pioneering study of working women in Ontario, written in 1891. "Trades unions of women in Ontario have not been numerous or remarkably successful", she understated, noting that previous efforts of the Knights of Labor — a "Hope Assembly" especially for women workers, and a "Silver Fleece Assembly" for women tailors — had both wilted. She attributed this sorry record to the many disabilities confronted by working women, ranging from their inexperience in the work world to the social mobility which drained promising leadership from the movement. Moreover, their location in the labour market fostered a certain ambiguity toward unionism or even provisions enforcing equal pay for equal work: since the motivation for hiring women centred on the advantageous possibilities of super-exploiting a peculiarly vulnerable stratum of the workforce, employers usually reverted to male employees as soon as union organization boosted the conditions and wages of work. Thus, cautious women retained reservations "that it is not to their individual advantage to belong to the unions". Having conceded these objective difficulties, Scott proceeded to lay the burden of blame on women's consciousness itself. There did not exist that "class spirit . . . that is necessary to organized progress", Scott charged, "and men with reason complain that it is difficult to operate plans of any sort which require unselfish action among large bodies of women."[2]

Labour spokesman Tom Banton aired similar charges a few years later. Women "do not unite in demanding proper pay for their services", he accused. "They lack in ambition to get on in the world, being too often content to make a bare living. Then in too many cases they look to marriage as the door through which they will escape from toil, and not expecting to be permanently in the labour market, they do not insist on keeping it up to a high standard". The *Farmers Sun* editorial in the issue which reported Banton's speech agreed that "these impeachments are too true", but pleaded for understanding. "Our brothers must not expect us, all at once, to know what has taken them centuries to learn", Banton was reminded. "It is an impossibility for a woman who is driven into the labour market by poverty to stand aloof because offered less than a man would be for the same work. The only hope against this evil is in organization".[3]

The rebuke that underlay these hasty condemnations was in part provoked by frustration at the disappointing disparity between the enormity of working women's suffering and the apparent passivity that marked its endurance. Private agony haunted most women victims of oppression and exploitation. Its extent can only be suggested. One old Scotswoman was picked up off the streets, collapsed from starvation. Having given up laundry work as too heavy a month earlier, she was driven to selling shoelaces but was unable to earn enough to eat. Too weak to undergo surgery, she died a few hours later. A Mrs. Agnes Watson, who dwelled at the Gypsy camp in East Toronto, was arrested for shoplifting a can of salmon and other sundries. As she stood in the court dock with her young child, frantic at her forthcoming separation from her child, she had seven fits. On hearing of her thirty day sentence she broke down again, at which point the judge condescended to

239

allow the child to accompany her during her jail term. Many women were forced to abandon their children: there was scarcely a week in 1898 that abandoned live or dead babies were not reported. Maternity homes, probably used by unwed mothers, did little more than sanction child murders. Abortion, often resulting in the death of the mother, was frequent. And some women were jailed as lunatics, like one "white-haired old lady who has a delusion that she is possessed of great wealth and that she is owed a large sum of money for innumerable years' sewing".[4]

Suffering an even quieter desperation were those large numbers of women earning four to five dollars per week and hovering on the edge of subsistence. One secretary presented her yearly budget of $210 as the minimum required for "the neat appearance desired by my employer and keeping with my self-respect". Exceptionally low-priced accommodation kept her expenses low; yet her estimate did not include provision for books or amusement, illness or unemployment, vacation or travel money to see out-of-town parents, "all of which things every self-respecting girl should be entitled to indulge in." Wages earned frequently failed to purchase even those limited necessities, and women were driven to vagrancy and prostitution in certain periods merely to subsist. Subsistence, however, as one woman worker argued, should not have been the issue. In view of the fact that women "are building up fortunes for their employers", the "question should not be how much can a girl live on, but how much can she earn."[5]

Yet, in the face of this privation, which was considerably worse than that suffered by male workers, the ranks of Toronto's working women produced no major reform or labour leader, no major union or sustained organization reflecting their interests as women workers. They did not even enlist in union shops at anything like the rate of men. In 1900, they could only muster one representative to take part in a debate on equal pay for equal work.[6]

This inactivity extended to the political arena, despite the absence of crucial legislative protection. Inadequate safeguards endangered the legally regulated lunchhour as employers attempted to have the hour-lunch made optional. One woman worker complained of the obvious implications of this: "Now sir, you know what that would mean in many factories where they are completely at the mercy of the bosses. It is unnecessary to state that whenever an employer desired, the 'hands' would have to work, no matter what their objections might be — it would be as much as their situation was worth to openly complain against it." As late as 1913, factory legislation permitted women shop clerks to work 55 to 60 hours per week in normal seasons and 70 hours in rush seasons, hours that were not permitted for most men. Yet in the face of conditions such as these, working women contributed little to the political side of the labour movement. Nor did they play a marked role in the struggle for the suffrage.[7]

This gaping disparity between the oppression of working women and their lack of organization has been treated generally as the penalty for "feminine psychology". As some of the indictments above show, labour activists and commentators of the time laid the blame for working women's apparent passivity at the doorstep of a crippling femininity. Surprisingly, this approach has remained persuasive for modern feminists; even the essays in the otherwise pathbreaking and justly celebrated *Women at Work* subscribe to a modified form of this conception. It is strongly suggested that a self-deceptive sense of femininity eased working women's resignation to the quagmire of occupational oppression that the book focuses on. For instance, an article on school teachers explains that "women's role as hand-maiden to husband and family was from the outset easily adaptable to the ethic of uncomplaining work and service". This sense of femininity is seen as a crucial obstacle to collective action. "The failure of women to recognize the process of proletarianization stemmed from the influence of the domestic ideal on women's expectations", the press release for the book proclaims in summarizing a major motif of the book.[8]

In my own contribution to that book, I tried to argue in favour of discarding the prevailing personality-psychological model of working women's behaviour. In particular, I argued that the working women's sense of femininity was not a pacifying illusion or psychological sanction against collective action. Instead of assisting in the creation of a broad pro-capitalist consensus, it formed part of a separate working class identity which withstood the sermons of poorly-intentioned, "do-gooding" matrons and trade union patriarchs. "Hang-ups" on femininity or other allegedly false self-concepts, however much they may have hindered a full awakening of their consciousness, did not make working women spiritually inadequate for the challenge before them.[9]

241

If these arguments are correct, then we must set ourselves another course to explain the failure of working women in the 1896 to 1914 to respond to their problems in a more explicitly collective fashion. The framework for such an alternative explanation rests on a concrete understanding of the work-life and work-place ecology of working women. Reliance on pliable clichés and "momified" abstractions about feminine psychology has hindered a recognition of the strictures that demographic and occupational influences placed on the possibilities for concerted action. Combined with an appreciation of some of the activity and thoughts of working women, this approach should help us reevaluate both the objective constraints and the organizing capacities of the woman worker and the interplay of various aspects of her consciousness — particularly her feminism, her sense of femininity and her class consciousness.

Women in the Workforce

By 1900, wage work outside the home had become both an option and a necessity for large numbers of Canadian women. In 1891, 87 of 164 occupations listed in Toronto employed more than one woman. By 1898 Ontario factory inspector Margaret Carlyle marvelled at an occupational diffusion which found women in some 120 employments from bedspring to woolen factories. Carlyle attributed this to recent machinery, "almost human, needing directions only and a little manual strength''. These machines, often the same ones which displaced women from their traditional preserve of home handwork, ''opened up new and wide fields of labour for women'' in the factory. Two women could now tend machinery producing 240,000 screws a day, when a few years earlier twenty skilled men could turn out but 20,000.[10]

According to some contemporary enthusiasts, these technical innovations removed the disability of sex and erased the boundary line between the sexes in all but a few occupations, like bartending. But, far from heralding ''almost a complete break with the past'', many technical innovations merely legislated sexual discrimination in a new industrial setting. Even in cases where machinery was designed to eliminate bias against women based on their relative lack of brute strength, a legacy of profitable bias persisted. ''Curiously and unreasonably enough'', the *Globe* charged, the traditionally low wages that were supposed to correspond to feminine weakness had survived ''so that almost universally . . . women receive for performing the same labour from one-third to one-half less wages than men''. This pattern persisted throughout the period. Far from desexing the opportunity structure, the use of technical innovations capitalized on and reinforced the supposedly hereditary ''feminine'' virtues. It was said that while machines did not require muscular strength, they relied rather on ''alertness and exactness of attention and constant application.'' By a whimsical throw of the loaded dice of sexual stereotypes, long-recognized skills could be downgraded: the ''skilled'' work of the male linotyper became the ''nimble'' work of the female typist.[11]

In some cases the combination of technology and ''female dexterity'' led to a displacement of men that extended into both the white and blue collar world. As the work was light and required only nimbleness of finger, women were crowding men out even in the filthy brass and tin industry. But displacement of men was most marked in white collar occupations. In 1891 women had barely penetrated the fields of cashiering, bookkeeping, clerking, copying or sales. This quickly became the major area to experience substantial growth of female practitioners. The typewriter, among other factors, invited the invasion of women, again because of their vaunted nimbleness of finger.[12]

Quite often, women emigrated from the traditionally more self-sufficient household economy only to encounter occupational ghettoes designed to maximize the abilities of their domestic inheritance in a factory setting. In some cases the new division of labour and specialization degenerated into sweating, a form of production with which women's labour is closely identified. Subcontracting could place women back in the home where collectors would go from house to house picking up the products of the domestic sewing machine. Even in industries where women did not dominate the overall labour force, they came to dominate specific jobs. In one case, striking shoeworkers were replaced by women, ''as what they had been engaged in was girls' work''.[13]

Despite the exploitative quality of these arrangements, the conditions in which women entered the workforce inhibited their ability to organize. Although women were concentrated in certain industries like clothing, office, allied food industries, domestic service and teaching, the most striking characteristic of the feminine workforce was its fragmentation. Of 87 occupations employing more than one woman in 1891, a full 22 employed fewer than five. Because of the proliferation of establishments in occupations where women predominated, this pattern persisted even in occupations employing large numbers of women. Of eighteen trades hiring 25 to 100 women, only one was dominated by one establishment; the other women in the trade were dispersed over an average of fifteen establishments. Of those eighteen occupations hiring 100 to 500 women each, only one occupation had its workforce concentrated in two establishments; in the other occupations, the workforce was distributed over a wide number of establishments, sometimes as high as 98. This tendency was particularly pronounced in the clothing industry: nineteen establishments shared more than 500 women in shirt, collar and tie making; dressmaking and tailoring each employed more than 1000 women, who were spread over 402 and 216 establishments respectively.

243

Throughout the 1890's, when subcontracting in the clothing industry was still standard, the separation of workers in their homes precluded simple wage comparisons, not to mention union organization. Significantly, women workers did not take joy in being close to home and family. They "almost invariably" preferred the factory system, according to one investigation, reasoning that contractors, who made their money as middlemen, were more prone to super-exploit them. Occupations like personal service and cleaning similarly dispersed women over as many establishments as there were jobs. To the extent that these patterns persisted into the new century, it is unlikely that the concentration of women workers in centralized establishments and the experience of direct on-the-job collectivity — frequent preconditions for successful organizing among unskilled males — were normal.[14]

Lastly, recruitment of Toronto's 35,000 to 45,000 strong female workforce derived almost exclusively from one fraction of the population — young single women. Many of these were farm girls who left a hard country life which made no property provisions for them, preferring to work in the city "at starvation wages than live in the country at farmhouse work". Married women were common only in occupations such as domestic service and daycleaning. Their acceptance of these jobs was largely a reflection of the fact that they worked only under the pressure of extreme distress, and then only at part-time work.[15]

It was probably this limited labour pool which accounted for both the slow climb of the participation rate for women in the labour force — a mere two percent increase from 1901 to 1911 — and for the persistent pleas of Ontario manufacturers for up to 25,000 immigrant women workers. Generally speaking a simple cycle replenished the youthfulness of the workforce. "While it is true that many of these women marry after some years spent in the workforce", a study of Ontario's 175,000 women wage-earners pointed out, "their places are taken by other, generally younger women workers and thus this great total remains undiminished".[16]

Many a unionizing effort must have foundered in the shallowness of this demographic evolution. Although Toronto's working women came to number 35,000 to 45,000 mostly Canadian-born women, their entry into the workforce was not part of a normative transformation affecting women as a whole. Unlike working women of today who can evaluate their experiences in terms of widespread public discussion on the status of women and who can draw inspiration, clarity and legitimacy from a generalized movement, working women before 1914 operated in an ideological vacuum. They were restricted to one narrow age category of the population and represented only a temporary deviation from orthodox female standards. They were a small detachment who could not share in the process of reevaluating sexual standards with any substantial core of the population — not the middle class women reformers, not the male trade unionists and not even their elder sisters, all of whom had returned to the home upon marriage. Not only were they politically and socially isolated, the fact that they also left the workforce upon marriage meant that they were deprived of a continuity of experience that might have allowed them to come to grips with the political economy of their experience.[17]

Of course, the departure of working women from the workforce upon marriage conformed to one aspect of the behaviour expected of women. Nevertheless, the adoption of this new role as fulltime wife and crypto servant was more than a convenient social virtue; it was a necessity that corresponded to the primitive household and birth control technology of the time. It did not necessarily represent the fulfillment of a leisured fantasy that had deflected the working girls' aspirations away from collective struggle, nor was it acquiescence to the privatized and subordinate passivity of a feminine mystique. A working woman could not expect to experience wedded bliss free from the rigours of her class. Among other things, working class wives had to manage a household, control a family budget and take responsibility for purchases at working class levels. The control of the wife over these processes, although more suggestive of responsibility than power, was the unquestioned assumption of the labour movement's crusade to promote union label goods.

Women's entry into the workforce contained a cruel irony. A whirlpool of industrially imposed sexism dragged women down to the least rewarding depths of the economy at the same time that it tossed and pinned them to the sidelines of action. Dispersed and isolated, these young women workers responded as best they could to their exploitation. Their limited and tentative measures reflected the difficulties of responding to a truncated and distorted industrial existence. The absence of the structural preconditions that make collective action viable even for comparable male workers was decisive in their failure.

Rather than sit in judgment on the allegedly warped personality structure of their femininity — be it their illusions of the impropriety of struggle for passive females, for marriage as a release from wage work — we should celebrate the measures they did take as a tribute to their spirit and consciousness. Some of these responses, and the conditions that inspired them, can be explored as they developed in the various occupations and situations that working women confronted.

Feminism, Femininity and Class Consciousness

Among the limitations inherent in their objective conditions of work which consequently limited women workers' role in organized labour and reform movements, their stint, although short, was too long and miserable for that notion to be entertained by many for long; rather it dictated a lack of experience as well as a depleted fund of potential leadership. The continual renewal of the youthful female working force undermined the continuity and collective lessons and memory that may have been yielded had women worked longer. It is significant that "older girls" led the 1912 agitation for more pay and shorter hours at Bell Telephone. When they tried to induce the "younger centrals" to join them in a protest petition, they may well have been the only workers to recall the famous strike of 700 operatives over precisely the same issues.[18]

245

Women's experience in the workforce was historically as well as personally short-lived. Having entered the wage workforce in significant numbers so recently, they had been denied the work and life experience characteristic of the nineteenth century artisanal workman. Artisans exerted considerable power in the workplace based on a relative monopoly of skill, corresponding to a relatively underdeveloped level of standardized machine manufacture. This artisanal tradition was common to most workers who formed strong unions in the early twentieth century. These workers not only entered the twentieth century with strong unions; most had retained some sense of craft integrity and some forms of social solidarity that buttressed their union strength considerably.[19]

Women were denied this experience as a matter of course. Their entry into an occupation was the death knell of an artisanal trade. More, they were levers which destroyed its norms, habits and strengths. Their work lives typified the antithesis of artisanal modes. A good number of women factory workers were "floaters", drifting from job to job, staying only a short time. This of course offered no parallel to the habits of tramp artisans who used floating excursions to broaden their experiences, possibilities and loyalties within their chosen occupation. In the case of women, one observer found floating to be the standard technique for staving off the monotony of putting dabs of jelly on cookies or other assorted tasks. The proportion of floaters increased in the size of factories and led to chronic instability. These workers "may at any time be replaced by a younger girl, who may be trained satisfactorily in a few months at the utmost", one study reported.[20]

Employers preferred this raw workforce, which they trained in their own way, "saying that it is more trouble to have operatives unlearn what they have learned than to begin with an untrained applicant". The employer monopoly of training under this system was tied to the widespread use of fines. Although employers found this punishment impossible to impose on men, the practice of fining women workers for laughing, talking, using toilet-paper hair-curlers, or damaging work was common, especially in the early years of industrialism. In sharp contrast to the artisanal workman, trained under unionist auspices, this system forcefully alienated the command of the working girl over her work, ruptured any possibility for collectively shared work experiences and reinforced the atomization of the individual workers. In place of union rules, women found the regimentation of clocks, timed to the half second.[21]

The working woman's recreational life was equally inchoate and indiscriminate, lacking in any of the qualities common to artisanal patterns that could reinforce occupational solidarity. The widespread debate and concern over women's recreation in this period did not touch on this problem. Most reformers lamented the quality of the working girl's recreation, her penchant for cheap shows rather than church and settlement socials. In fact, the working woman had little time for recreation. Working at piece and time rates, many could not afford a holiday for five years. In order to have more free time in the evenings, working girls willfully violated legal regulations ensuring a long lunch-hour. Their need for recreation fractured workplace solidarity necessary to enforce certain minimum regulations. Time and money were so scarce that few alternatives were open for recreation, save for the short, cheap thrills like the popular five-cent shows that shocked reformers. These recreational habits unfortunately were as unsuited to the needs of unionism as they were to the gatherings of the holy.[22]

While leisure provided no bonds to reinforce occupational solidarity, it did have certain mechanisms for uniting working women as a whole against the hypocrisy of their critics. Their recreational needs did not permit them to languish in social passivity. One working girl wrote poignantly of the exhaustion of fellow workers on Saturday night, attacking both the enforcers of "blue" Sundays and the system of five and one-half working days. As it was, girls had to give up their "day of rest" in order to get some exercise and fresh air. "Or will some of the men in authority who have been easily defending the 'working classes' in these matters, do a harder thing . . . desist from handing out to the poor the Lord's 24 hours for amusement and recreation and give of their own six days at least one half day the year round for getting of 'God's pure air' of which they seem to think we've so much need."[23]

The attention reformers directed to the "degrading" entertainments of the working girl made recreation one of the ramparts under regular assault by those who would try to shape the self-definition and supervise the life of women workers. Several organizations began to specialize in serving the working girls. Ostensibly philanthropic groups were the first to do so under the guise of redeeming their women and girl inmates. The Industrial Department of the Fred Victor Mission, for instance, took charge of young girls by teaching them work songs, like

I'm called a good waitress,
A very good waitress
I'm sure you can always tell why.
I'm taught to step lightly
And have all things sightly
And watch every need to supply.

More ingenuity was required to reach women actually in the workforce. Believing that the way to a working girl's soul was through her stomach, churches provided cheap lunches in the downtown areas. A Canadian Working Women's Club was established in 1910 under the leadership of Miss Margaret Davidson, head of the Domestic Sciences and Art department at the Technical School. "The real object of the club is to fit us all for service", said one spokesperson. This later developed into the Canadian Business Women's Club, under the same Miss Davidson. "She seems to consider the Canadian girl her personal charge", one magazine respectfully reported. The club was open to any self-supporting woman, and was to provide social intercourse and unite "businesswomen". The main activity was Friday lectures on household science.[74]

The working woman's recreational experience was totally at odds with that of the artisanal workman. The artisanal pattern of recreation was closely integrated with unionism, re-inforced the command of workplace solidarity and expressed the norms of a craftsman's integrity and self-worth. When these bonds were dissolved for the male worker, the avenue was open for organizations like the Orange Order, whose ritual soothed alienation and gave the individual a place in return for adherence to a repugnant and reactionary ideology of bigotry. Something as controversial and partisan as Orangeism must have been unthinkable for those wishing to fill a vacuum in the working woman's life. They tried to fill it instead with the functionally equivalent anaesthetics of religious and feminine service for "business girls".

Despite the absence of preconditions that were basic to union organization before World War I, informal patterns expressing the working woman's independent solidarities were surprisingly common. Investigative reporter "Videre" found improvised social centres at the workplace, pressure on pieceworkers to restrain production to keep piece rates up, sacrifices made on behalf of workers in distress at the job, as well as frequent sororal assistance to the new worker. Similarly marked informal solidarity and social independence were marked by philanthropists. "The kindness of the poor to the poor has been brought to our notice very frequently", the Toronto Relief Society officers noted with mixed chagrin and awe. "One old woman and her little grandson have lived in a room all winter, rent-free, simply because the landlady, a poor charwoman, is too kindhearted to turn them out. For years the Society has helped to pay this old woman's rent, but refused to do so any longer as she really should be in the House of Industry, but she is one of the 'obstinates' and everyone knows how difficult they are to deal with". This informal occupational-class solidarity only received organized expression under specific circumstances, as has been shown.[25]

This latent consciousness merged with a melange of feminine and feminist sentiment. Although the feminist recognition of the special oppression of women provided the sharper edge to these concerns, the "feminine" side of the working women's consciousness should not be discounted. This phenomenon may be difficult to appreciate today because of the impact of the modern women's liberation movement. Betty Friedan's powerful indictment of the manipulative, self-destructive *Feminine Mystique* has led modern feminists and sympathisers to emphasize the negative impact on women's self-definition. Femininity has become the hallmark of traditionalist evils from privatization to passivity to self-denial of one's own interests.

The historiographical repercussions of this current awareness are best represented in William O'Neill's *Everyone Was Brave*, which largely explains the failure of the American suffrage movement to liberate women by referring to the suffragist internalization of the traditional stereotypes of womanhood. This kind of analysis reacts indiscriminately to the accentuation of certain virtues of motherhood by leading repressive reformers of the Progressive Era. The propaganda of the Progressive Era turned motherhood into the embodiment of policing virtues that would clean up the state and clean up the mob with the same ease these matrons once experienced in watching servants clean up their homes.

Working women did not appear to internalize these facets of femininity. They had antithetical definitions. Where the "womanly" reformers provided daycare to deserted mothers with the noble aim of securing the mothers' employment as servants, at the same time as their children were upgraded in the nursery, the working mother resented having to leave her children. Where matronly reformers safeguarded the preparation of working girls for motherhood, working girls defined their femininity as freedom to dress and look well in their own fashion and to enjoy themselves. Working women could even turn the Progressive concern for the rise in female crime to their own class advantage. If employers would pay the workers better instead of wasting money on ads, one woman bookbinder suggested, there would be fewer girls in the Mercer reformatory.[26]

Although the picture of women workers that this study had unveiled is far from totally clear, it reveals that the sense of feminine propriety or traditional feminine aspirations did not undermine their sense of oppression as workers or as women. Being self-respecting, they liked to dress well. Being "womanly", they did not want their children to work. As waitresses, they wanted the same treatment as wives and children. Liking "flirtation and dress", they could not stick with domestic servitude. Because women were good at coping with details, they deserved advancement. The contours of their sense of feminity could be stretched to accommodate the self-definitions and aspirations of women workers — what Joussaye referred to as "Honest Womanhood" or what the W.W.P.A. called "true womanhood" — as well as sanctimonious patriarchs. Working men had the same talent in dealing with beliefs often identified with false consciousness. While a banker had his own sense of what Jesus saved, many workers saw Jesus as a carpenter and God as a socialist. In terms of the relatively primitive body of ideas that widely prevailed at the turn of the century, it is not unusual that people expressed their aspirations in understandable and legitimized idioms.[27]

The working girls' consciousness and behaviour were circumscribed by certain firm boundaries, not often of their own choosing. Not only was their stay in the workworld short, their debut was proscribed to narrow channels of peripheral and atomized labour that were difficult to organize in the best of circumstances. Faced with these difficulties, the working girls responded with the means at their disposal. They left or switched jobs if necessary. When given some time, they would at least form an association. When given some leverage, they would organize into a union.

Judged by some standards, we should wonder at the absence of women from the organized labour and reform movements, though we should never lightly ascribe this to passivity or equanimity. Judged by the more relevant comparison with unskilled male workers, who did not organize successfully for some decades to come, women did not do so badly. Judged by the objective realities of their position, we must marvel at what they accomplished.

249

Notes

1. *Industrial Banner* (hereafter *IB*), October 10, 1913; *Lance*, August 26, 1911.
2. Jean Scott, *The Conditions of Female Labour in Ontario*, (Toronto, 1892) p. 27.
3. *Canada Farmers Sun*, November 13, 1895.
4. *Globe*, September 16, 1908; *Star*, March 16, 1911; See for example *Daily Mail and Empire* (hereafter *ME*), April 29, 1898, *Star*, March 17, 1898; The campaign around maternity homes can be traced in *Globe* November 3, 1897, *ibid.*, November 4, 1897, *ME* November 4, 1897, *Globe*, December 13, 1897, *ibid.*, December 14, 1897, *ME*, December 14, 1897, *ibid.*, December 31, 1897, *Star*, May 19, 1898, *Globe* October 28, 1898; *Weekly Sun*, August 19, 1914; *Star*, November 20, 1897.
5. *Star*, February 12, 1910; This can be intuited from the divergence in figures for prostitutes and vagrants and those lisitng themselves as such (naturally a very roughshod method, but the only one available to us) See for example Ontario, Inspector of Prisons and Public Charities, *Report*, 1896; *Star*, April 12, 1910.
6. For differential between male and female, see Ontario, Bureau of Labour, *Report*, 1903, p. 55, *ibid.*, 1905, p. 119, *ibid.*, 1913, p. 165; *Citizen and Country*, December 7, 1900.
7. *Brotherhood Era*, April 3, 1896, See also Ontario, Inspector of Factories, *Report*, 1898, p. 16; *ME*, March 12, 1913.
8. E. Graham, "Schoolmarms and early teaching in Ontario", *Women at Work* (Toronto, 1975) p. 203; press release, March 14, 1975. An article dealing with a later period, focusing on the 1931 dressmakers strike, is even more explicit in this regard: "Women were thought of and thought of themselves as transient workers. . . . Since the majority of women did not work, and those who did usually did so only until they were married, there was little contradiction between the prevalent ideology of the female role in society and the actual condition of women at that time." (p. 324) One reviewer correctly noted that "this is the pivotal statement of the book." *Canada. An Historical Magazine* Vol. 3 No. 3, March 1976, p. 63. For similar approaches in other countries, see E. Kaji, "The invisible proletariat: working women in Japan", *Social Praxis*, 1,4 (1973), P. Branca, "A new perspective on women's work: a comparative typology", *Journal of Social History*, IX, 2 (Winter, 1975) In seeming contrast (both views share the assumption that proletarian and feminine identities are historically contradictory) is K. Sacks, "Class roots of feminism", *Monthly Review*, XXVII, 9, February, 1976.
9. A. Klein and W. Roberts, "Besieged innocence: the 'problem' and problems of women workers", *Women at Work*.
10. This is derived from Canada, *Census of Canada*, 1890-91, III, pp. 4-379; Ontario Inspector of Factories, *Report*, 1898, p. 30; *ibid.*, 1907, p. 62.
11. *Globe*, June 25, 1897; *Star*, July 9, 1898; S. Ostry, "The female worker labour force", Women's Bureau, *Changing Patterns in Women's Employments*, (Ottawa, 1966), p. 5; *Globe*, June 25, 1897; Ontario, Bureau of Labour, *Report*, 1913, p. 162; *ibid.*, 1909, pp. 142-54; Ontario, Inspector of Factories, *Report*, 1896, p. 25.
12. *Star*, August 2, 1898; Canada, *Census*, 1890-91, II, pp. 163-9; F. Denton and S. Ostry, *Historical Estimates of the Canadian Labour Force*, (Ottawa, 1967), p. 50; *Star*, July 9, 1898.
13. *ME*, October 9, 1897; Ontario, Bureau of Labour, *Report*, 1911, p. 293.

14. This is based on the manufacturing census for 1891, *supra*, pp. 4–379; *Report Upon the Sweating System in Canada*, Canada, *Seasonal Papers*, 1896, pp. 6–7.

15. *Saturday Night*, August 2, 1913; M. MacMurchy, citing Peter MacArthur in *Canadian Courier*, May 18, 1912; Ontario, Bureau of Industry, *Report*, 1896, p. 125. Former farm girls also probably accounted for the high ratio of women who boarded out. For some idea of this proportion, see Unemp., p. 196; *ME*, February 3, 1914.

16. Denton and Ostry, *op cit*, p. 29; *Globe*, January 8, 1904; *Industrial Canada*, 1907, p. 899; Ont. Commission on Unemployment, 1916 (hereafter Unemp.), p. 71.

17. Canadian Reconstruction Association, *Women and Reconstruction*, (1919), p. 5.

18. *News*, March 2, 1912. The 1907 strike is discussed in Klein and Roberts, *loc cit*.

19. When women enjoyed this rich associational life, it deepened their unionism. See especially T. Dublin, "Women, work and protest in the early Lowell mills: 'the oppressing hand of avarice would enslave us' ", *Labour History*, 1975. See also D. Walkowitz, "Working class women in the Guilded Age: factory, community and family life among Cohoes New York cotton workers", *Journal of Social History*, Summer, 1972.

20. *Star*, June 1–4, 1912; Unemp. p. 171.

21. *Ibid.*, p. 172; cf. *Report of the Royal Commission on The Relations of Labour and Capital*, Ontario evidence (Ottawa, 1889), p. 91.

22. Cf. for example, the exchange in *Tribune*, October 28, 1905, *ibid.*, November 4, 1905, *ibid.*, November 11, 1905, *ibid.*, November 18, 1905; *Labour Gazette*, August 1913, pp. 150–1; J. Scott, *op cit*, p. 13.

23. *Star*, February 8, 1912, p.7 see also *ibid.*, June 17, 1912.

24. *Ibid.*, December 1, 1898; E. Lang, *Canadian Courier*, May 2, 1914, M. MacMurchy, *ibid.*, May 18, 1912; *Star*, February 5, 1910; E. Weaver et al, *The Canadian Womans Annual* (Toronto, 1915) p. 167. Employer provision of cheap lunches may have been part of the same phenomenon. Cf for example *ME*, January 22, 1904.

25. *Star*, June 1, 1912, *ibid.*, June 6, 1912, *ibid.*, June 22, 1912; Toronto Relief Society, *Annual Report*, 1899–1900 (Toronto, 1901), p. 14.

26. See the discussion of these issues in Klein and Roberts, *loc cit*.

27. For a dramatic look at a similar process of negotiation, reciprocity, modification and redefinition of expected behaviour among slaves in relation to the infinitely more self-damaging "Sambo" concepts inflicted by slaveowners, see E. Genovese, *Roll Jordan Roll: The World the Slaves Made*. Many radical scholars have so emphasized the hegemony of bourgeois ideology that they neglect the contradictory tensions and possibilities of development of working class movements, not to mention the possibilities of outgrowing and rupturing the dominant ideology in its totality. This essay is partially intended as a corrective to this tendency insofar as it relates to the history of women workers.

Topic Seven
Urbanization

Cities have had a profound influence on Canada's development, serving as focal points of identity, and as centres of growth in a sparsely populated nation. Among the most recent interpretations of Canadian history is metropolitanism — the study of the impact of cities on their respective hinterlands.

Urban communities have existed in Canada since the beginning of European settlement, but the rate of their growth has varied from region to region, and from one period to another. Urban historians generally agree that the "takeoff" period for the emergence of the modern city occurred between 1850 and 1914 — from the end of the mercantile system to the rise of the industrial city. By 1921, the census — for the first time — showed more Canadians living in urban centres than in rural areas.

The following readings discuss the evolution of cities in three different Canadian regions during this period. In "Aspects of Metropolitanism in Atlantic Canada," J.M.S. Careless analyses the metropolitan roles of Saint John, Halifax and Saint John's from the mid-nineteenth to the early twentieth century. In a chapter taken from their *Quebec: A History, 1867–1929*, P.-A. Linteau, R. Durocher, and J.-C. Robert explain the rise of the cities in Quebec in the late nineteenth century. Max Foran discusses the influential role that the Canadian Pacific Railway Company played in all facets of the West's urban development — townsite selection, differentiation between centres, and spatial development patterns — in "The CPR and the Urban West, 1881–1930."

J.M.S. Careless's *The Rise of Cities in Canada Before 1914* (Canadian Historical Association Booklet No. 32, Ottawa, 1978), presents a brief but informative overview of the history of cities in Canada. *The Canadian City: Essays in Urban History*, edited by G.A. Stelter and A.F.J. Artibise (Toronto: McClelland and Stewart, 1977, Second Edition, Carleton Library, 1984), provides an excellent anthology of articles in Canadian urban history and contains a good bibliography of recent publications organized according to regions. Two articles, in addition to Foran's, give an overview of urban development on the Canadian prairies: Paul Voisey's "The Urbanization of the Canadian Prairies, 1871–1916," *Histoire Sociale / Social History*, 8 (May 1975): 77–101; and Alan F.J. Artibise, "The Urban West: The Evolution of Prairie Towns and Cities to 1930," *Prairie Forum*, 4 (1979): 237–262. A major reference work is A.F.J. Artibise and G. Stelter, *Canada's Urban Past: A Bibliography to 1980 and Guides to Canadian Urban Studies*, (Vancouver: University of British Columbia Press, 1981). Also consult the journal *Urban History Review/Revue d'histoire urbane* (UHR/RHU), (Ottawa: National Museum of Man, 1972) for recent articles in urban history. The National Museum of Man in conjunction with the James Lorimer Company is currently publishing individual histories of some possible thirty Canadian cities.

---

252 # Aspects of Metropolitanism in Atlantic Canada*
J. M. S. CARELESS

I

Metropolitanism, the pattern of reciprocal relations whereby large urban communities focus broad areas on themselves, is intimately associated with regionalism. For regions usually centre on metropolitan communities, which largely organize them, focus their views, and deal with outside metropolitan forces on their behalf. Indeed, much of what is often called regionalism may be better expressed in terms of metropolitan relations and activities. In that belief, this discussion of metropolitanism in Atlantic Canada is offered. Because the subject is so large, it has been limited to the period from the mid-nineteenth to the early twentieth centuries, and to a selective consideration of the metropolitan roles of the three principal Atlantic cities, Saint John, Halifax, and St. John's during that period.

This time span is long enough to allow a considerable process of change to be examined, still highly significant today. Although its limits are inevitably imprecise, there is some validity in starting with the 1850's, after the end of the Navigation Acts and the old imperial system, and closing before the First World War brought striking new developments to the Maritimes and Newfoundland. As for the subject-matter, there seems no less validity in studying the three largest communities of the Atlantic region in themselves: both as regional leaders, and because we might well pay more regard to urban history in Canada.

The fact is that, land of vast frontiers and wilderness or not, urban communities long played a large part in Canadian development and this is no less true for the Atlantic region. Nor need the cities in question be huge and teeming by modern standards. It is far more the proportion of their population to the total in their regional community that has meaning. In

* From *Regionalism in the Canadian Community, 1867–1967*, Canadian Historical Association Centennial Seminars, edited by M. Wade. Copyright 1969 by University of Toronto Press. Reprinted by permission.

1861, for instance, Saint John had a population of 27 315 to 252 045 for all New Brunswick, or a proportion of close to 1 in 9; Halifax had 25 025 to 330 885 in Nova Scotia, or roughly 1 in 13; St. John's 30 475 to 122 635 in Newfoundland, or a remarkable proportion of almost 1 in 4. A century later, by the Canadian census of 1961, Saint John stood at something over 1 in 8, Halifax at about 1 in 8, St. John's around 1 in 9. Plainly then, even by present standards, each city has represented a decided concentration of population in its provincial community; not to mention a concentration of capital and labour that would enable it to fulfil metropolitan functions.

These functions or attributes of metropolitan stature have broadly been held to comprise, first, the provision of commercial facilities for the import and export trade of the city's dependent region or hinterland (on which, of course, it in turn depends); second, the establishment of industries to process products of, or imports for, the hinterland; third, the development of transport services to channel traffic to and from the urban centre; and fourth, the creation of financial facilities for investment and development in the region. All these attributes can be seen in greater or less degree within the three cities under inquiry. But to these economic characteristics might also be added those of political power or military authority often centred in the metropolis; and, quite as frequently, the exercise of religious, educational, and intellectual leadership for the regional community, along with press influence over its opinion.

Indeed, to a great extent a metropolitan system is inherently a system of communications, whether this carries goods, people or money, orders or ideas. As a result, it may be deeply affected by changes in technology; a point as true for the age that experienced the introduction of the steamship, railway, and telegraph as for that of automobility, jet transport, and television.

The effect of technological change on communications is notably clear in the case of Atlantic Canada. Although in assessing it, this general survey must to some extent put together material that is far from new, yet it is hoped that a restructuring in terms of metropolitan patterns and pulls will make the data more meaningful. And it is thought that a comparative analysis of the development of the three major Atlantic centres can promote new queries concerning their regional functions. The procedure will be to start with Saint John, then move out to sea, so to speak, in a properly Toronto-centred view of the globe.

II

In the mid-nineteenth century, Saint John held a prominent role in an Atlantic communications system extending to Liverpool and London in one direction, Boston and New York in another. It was the commercial metropolis for much of New Brunswick, exporting the timber wealth of the Saint John River from its position at the entrance to that long waterway, importing the British manufacturers or American provisions needed for a hinterland heavily based on forest production. It was a focus of

253

industry also, that utilized the chief product of its hinterland region in large-scale wooden shipbuilding. And through wealth acquired from the timber trade or the sale of Saint John ships in England, the city's business community was able to provide significant financial services, including by the later fifties three locally owned banks and four local marine, fire, or general insurance companies.

Yet Saint John's metropolitan stature had clear limits. First, although New Brunswick was past the frontier expansionist stage, the province was relatively poor and undiversified in depending on its forest staple. Second, since the whole region was largely composed of a series of separated river valleys, Saint John's sway over its own river and Bay of Fundy area by no means extended to the province's north shore. And third, since the city was not the seat of government, it could not enjoy the pervasive influence of a centre of political authority. Nor did it really exercise social or cultural headship, which remained with the genteel society of little Fredericton up-river.

254

Saint John's own leading elements composed a substantial, overlapping business élite of import merchants, timber traders, shipbuilders, and shipowners. The same individuals reoccurred in lists of the directors of banks, insurance firms, and other joint stock enterprises such as the Saint John Gas, Light, Electric, Telegraph or South Bay Boom Companies: men such as William Parks, President of the Commercial Bank, or shipbuilders and shipowners such as Wright, DeVeber, and Zebedee Ring.[1] Nor did this Saint John business community lack strong political ties. Out of its background came such major political figures as R. L. Hazen and R. D. Wilmot, W. H. Steeves, a father of Confederation, G. E. King, provincial premier of the seventies — or Samuel Leonard Tilley himself, partner in the prominent firm of Peters and Tilley, merchants.

The business élite of Saint John was perhaps more limited in its outlook than its counterparts in either Halifax or St. John's. The New Brunswick port's outside connections largely ran to Portland as an intermediary for Boston, or else focussed on Liverpool; hardly a city of light. A scion of the mid-century élite (son of the president of the Bank of New Brunswick) recalled that Saint John businessmen would cross to Liverpool and Manchester twenty times "without ever going on to London."[2] Yet the sober, workaday masters of Saint John were lively and enterprising enough when it came to the city's main industrial activity, shipbuilding.

In the prosperous fifties, stimulated by the gold rush to Australia, Saint John yards turned out a splendid succession of large sailing vessels for Liverpool owners. There was James Smith's famed *Marco Polo,* hailed as the fastest ship in the world, after her 68-day voyage from Liverpool to Melbourne in 1852; or the *Morning Light,* of over 2 300 tons, launched by William and Richard Wright in 1855, which remained for twenty years the largest ship constructed in British North America. By 1858, of 100 major vessels over 1 200 tons sailing out of Liverpool, 32 had been built in Saint John and the pace continued through the sixties.

Successful as it was in ocean transport, the city entered a whole new phase of problems when it looked to railways to improve its land communications in the prosperous mid-century years. Saint John interests were deeply involved in the scheme to build the European and North American Railway, which would link the Bay of Fundy port overland with the Atlantic shore at Shediac, and in the other direction with Portland, Maine, there connecting with the rails to Boston and with the Atlantic and St. Lawrence to Montreal, open since 1852. Saint John was thus to become the focus of a great international overland route between coasts close to Europe, New England, and Canada. It was a bright vision, often more appealing than the alternative Intercolonial Railway project from Nova Scotia through New Brunswick to Quebec — though, conceivably (in the brightest moments of vision) both lines might be built, and tied together at Saint John. Of course, John A. Poor, the Portland capitalist who expressed his own city's metropolitan ambitions, had other hopes as to the final focal point of the railway scheme he was promoting. But in any case it did not succeed.

255

Neither Portland nor Saint John could organize the capital for so large a design, and construction problems had been underestimated. The European and North American was completed only between Saint John and Shediac by 1860, and then as a publicly owned road. Moreover, Saint John was not really well placed to dominate overland routes to the interior of the continent, a fact of growing ominous significance in the spreading railway age. When again in 1865, an attempt by a new company under William Parks shortly failed to build the "Western Extension" from the city to Maine, it was no wonder that many in Saint John viewed with disdain the coming of Confederation, and its concomitant bargain to build the Intercolonial, but via New Brunswick's distant north shore. Indeed, they might sense that an oceanic metropolitan system in which their city had flourished was passing away, to be replaced by new continental patterns with which they were less equipped to deal.

Yet Confederation was more coincident than causal in regard to changes that affected the whole functioning of Saint John as a metropolis. In fact, the changes did not plainly reveal themselves until after the depression of 1873 began. Most vital was the shift from wood to iron technology in transport. It was not the steamship that drastically affected Saint John's shipping industry, but the iron-built vessel. British yards had begun turning out cheap, capacious iron and steel steamships in quantities. They doomed Saint John's Liverpool sales and attacked the lucrative charter business of wooden sailing craft, secure while the steamship itself had been limited to fairly small wooden hulls, carrying fuel as well as cargo on a relatively few high-cost ocean runs. And while it had once been economic to build wooden ships in New Brunswick instead of England, now the great British iron and steel capacity made it increasingly uneconomic to do so. The effects came gradually. A peak year for Saint John yards was 1873, and as late as 1888, 2 000 men were still employed there.[3] But through the seventies and eighties, the city's major industry inexorably declined.

One should recall, of course, that the sweep of technological change also affected wealthier adjacent American centres. Thus New England's magnificent but costly clippers could not compete, and the region failed to build an iron ship industry. This in part was because Boston capital had turned from marine to railway investment, in efforts to organize and dominate continental routes west that proved only somewhat less abortive than Saint John's hopes of the European and North American. Portland declined. Boston itself was not so well placed to collect the traffic from the ever growing continental hinterland. It could be the chief regional metropolis of New England, but not a great deal beyond.[4] Railways, which had made inland western development so much more feasible and valuable, had shifted the emphasis from ports chiefly well located for the exchange of water-borne coastal and ocean traffic to those which also offered the most effective land access to broad continental territories

256

All this was true for Saint John in the advancing railway age — itself another aspect of triumphant steel technology. Again the city was not in a position to benefit. Its own hinterland did not provide fuel or raw material for new heavy industry. And along with the relative down-grading of its timber resources went a decline in their quality, as the best pineries were cut over. Even in the 1860's it was becoming difficult to get good timber for large ships at Saint John yards.[5] Hence these underlying changes, affecting the commercial position, industrial enterprise, and even hinterland supply of the New Brunswick metropolis, were much more basic than any effects of Confederation, the National Policy of 1879, or the long depression of the later nineteenth century.

No doubt the lean depression years made the impact of change harder, especially for a city swept by the disastrous fire of 1877 that destroyed two-fifths of Saint John and $27 000 000 in property.[6] No doubt the protective tariff offered little to the business enterprises of a community largely geared to primary production, except for a declining industry tariffs could not protect. But world depression created none of Saint John's essential problems. And National Policy or not, the smaller business units of the Maritime centres would surely have faced powerful competition from much larger aggregations of capital and labour, once the age of overland communication by rail had tied them into major continental traffic systems. Here indeed lay the essential significance of the later nineteenth-century years for Saint John and its region; it was the difficult era when the old Atlantic system was failing and the New Brunswick metropolis had not yet adjusted to the new forces of continental dominance.

That adjustment came in the early twentieth century. It was, perhaps, only relatively successful, in that it could not restore all Saint John's vanished eminence, but it has largely endured to the present. Its effect was economic, yet it was achieved largely by political means for political reasons: not in spite of, but because of, the Atlantic region's membership in Canada. And it was built on the advantage the Atlantic region had to offer within that membership, year-round access to the ocean.

The Canadian federation had a political, national, need for winter ports of its own. In a sense, the process of developing them was a valid complement to the National Policy. For that programme, as Professor R. C. Brown has emphasized, must truly be seen as an expression of national aspirations, however much it might also enhance central Canadian metropolitan power.[7] If the federal state could pursue nation-building by tariffs, it could equally do so by railway and port development, by subsidies and preferential rail rates, to aid enterprises and areas disadvantaged by distance or tariffs. It was all a natural response to the problem of integrating regions within a Canadian continental entity.

The process of adjustment for Saint John really began when in 1887 business leaders in its Board of Trade opened a campaign to shift the winter terminus of the Dominion-subsidized mail steamers from Portland to the New Brunswick city. Then in 1890 the completion of the Canadian Pacific's Short Line from Montreal across Maine to Saint John meant that the Fundy port now had fairly direct access to central Canada, as well as by the more circuitous Intercolonial, intersected by the Saint John–Shediac line at Moncton. Now there indeed was hope that Canadian winter traffic still moving via Portland could be diverted to Saint John. Hence that city invested in building large ocean docks, to the extent of $1 000 000 by 1895.[8]

Late that year came the key political step. When city delegations repeatedly had failed to bring the federal government to grant a mail subsidy to a Saint John-based steamship line, the city's two MPS, J. D. Hazen and J. A. Cheslay, bluntly indicated they would resign their seats if nothing were done.[9] The Conservative cabinet, already in turmoil, and nearing highly doubtful elections, forthwith provided an annual subsidy of $25 000 to the Beaver Line for fortnightly service between Saint John and Liverpool. The Donaldson Line quickly followed in shifting its terminus from Portland; others soon did the same. Almost in months in 1896 Saint John emerged as a major winter port.

Thereafter, as the western Canadian boom developed, prairie grain flowed out of the port and imports for central Canada came in. Both the city and the CPR repeatedly enlarged the harbour facilities in a veritable race to keep up with cargoes. In 1910, the federal government entered directly into building ocean berths itself.[10] And though Saint John's old shipbuilding industry did not re-emerge, it gathered repair yards, railway shops, sugar refineries and lumber mills. Finally, another technological change benefited it and its provincial hinterland. The development of wood-pulp mills gave a new significance to forest resources, especially those that had been inferior, such as spruce.

By 1914, accordingly, the New Brunswick city had moved far in adjusting to continental pulls, and had succeeded in making connections inward to

257

share in western and central Canadian hinterlands. Its commercial future as a Canadian outlet and gateway would still largely depend on deliberate political policy, as in the provision of preferential railway rates. Industrial — and financial — pre-eminence had decisively moved to central Canadian metropolitan centres. Yet in the national continental system that had replaced the colonial and Atlantic one, Saint John clearly continued to play a metropolitan role within its own region.

III

Halifax and St. John's can be dealt with more briefly — not in any way as less significant, but as variations on a theme that has been established. The theme, of course, is the role of these communities in an Atlantic metropolitan system, and the effects technological change and continental pulls had upon them. However, there is more to say of Halifax during the period to be covered, since the changes in question affected St. John's later and more slowly.

258

The Nova Scotian city of the mid-nineteenth century did not have as full commercial control of an immediate hinterland area as did its New Brunswick neighbour. There was no long Saint John Valley to dominate; the open Atlantic coasts of the Nova Scotian peninsula enabled many lesser places to share in Halifax's importing or exporting functions, although at the same time no part of the province was wholly remote from its influence. Moreover, Halifax did not develop industry on the scale of Saint John; either wooden shipbuilding, or later enterprises. On the other hand, it was a notably larger focus of shipping interests and financial power. It was also political capital, intellectual centre — and perhaps social arbiter — as Saint John was not. Finally, Halifax, of course, was an imperial citadel and naval base: a transatlantic bastion of British metropolitan power that had strong ties to sustain and pounds sterling to spend. Still closely akin to Boston, despite the breach of the Revolution, the Haligonian descendants of Loyalist and pre-Loyalist New Englanders were happy to view London in their midst, in the fashionable society of the garrison.

As Saint John had grown with timber and the large shipbuilding it fostered, so Halifax had grown with the fishing staple and the schooners it required. The location of Halifax's superb harbour, at the corner of the continent adjacent to the main northwest Atlantic fishing grounds made it an excellent base for a fishing fleet. It was also well placed as a first mainland port of call for ships bringing imports on the great circle route from Europe to America; and for trading fish to the West Indies, in return for tropical products to be re-exported by coastal or transatlantic shipping. This extensive trading pattern, well settled by the mid-century, had made Halifax a major centre of shipping rather than shipbuilding, a commercial and financial emporium, and the wealthiest, most advanced metropolitan city in the British Atlantic provinces — focus of a fairly diversified regional society matured beyond the frontier phase.

The metropolitan stature of Halifax was evinced in the wealth and power of its merchants, notably its West Indies merchants, and in its banking institutions. In the 1850's and 1860's these included the long-established Halifax Banking Company, the Bank of Nova Scotia, the Union Bank, and the Merchants Bank, begun in 1864, which would become the Royal Bank of Canada. Again their directors and those of Halifax insurance, gas, and water companies formed a business élite interwoven with wholesale merchants, shipping magnates, and steamship operators.[11] Men such as Enos Collins, Samuel Cunard, W. A. Black, and M. B. Almon were prominent. Their political pedigree was evident also. Although the old days of the Halifax oligarchy and the Council of Twelve had vanished, other potent names like Uniacke, Fairbanks, Kenny and Tobin also revealed the strong connections of the Halifax business world with Nova Scotian politics. As for wealth, Collins died in 1871 worth $6 500 000; Cunard in 1865 worth $5 000 000; and many others amassed sizeable fortunes.[12]

259

Cunard might have moved to England to direct his burgeoning steamship line, but the foundations of his fortune had been laid in Halifax. He had no less benefited his native city by establishing his "ocean ferry" (steamships running to schedule as sailing ships could not), and making it the first port of call in the regular steam service from Liverpool to Boston, begun in 1840. Boston was thoroughly grateful for the Cunard Line, with good reason; Halifax had reason also.[13] At the same time Halifax and Cunard could thank the British metropolitan concern for improved Atlantic communications that produced the vitally needed imperial mail contract and subsidy. Still further, Cunard might thank the imperial dockyard at Halifax for a lucrative coal contract to supply steam warships.[14] And all the Halifax merchants could appreciate the dockyard contracts for provisions, or the imperial expenditures on Halifax defences which exceeded £170 000 in the later sixties.[15] These investments in steam communications or improved facilities at Halifax were aspects of British metropolitan influence wholly beneficial to the Nova Scotian centre.

Yet the wooden paddlewheeler was the forerunner of the iron screwsteamer, which in the seventies began to exert its effects on Halifax. No longer need the larger iron vessels call at the port for fuel after crossing the ocean; the tendency was to concentrate through runs at larger ports. Thus even in 1867 the main Cunard route ceased its stop at Halifax: an unfortunate coincidence with the inception of Confederation. And although Halifax had no major wooden ship industry to suffer, its functions as a wholesale centre did. For the ubiquitous iron tramp steamer could readily take cargoes direct to hinterland ports, instead of via Halifax warehouses. In fact, by the 1880's the ease of ordering goods direct by telegraph and the speed of steamship delivery was seriously affecting Halifax as an *entrepôt*.[16] Moreover, the decline in the West Indies sugar economy increasingly harmed Halifax shipping and fishing interests.

Again, the old oceanic trading pattern was failing, while the Nova

Scotian capital was being opened to rising continental influences. The Intercolonial was completed through to Halifax in 1876; the National Policy came three years after. Far from gaining the flow of western trade that had been hoped for, Halifax firms seemed chiefly to have acquired increasing competition from larger central Canadian firms — all this, and world depression, and the British government reducing expenditures on the Halifax base.

Nevertheless, the wealth and power of Halifax business were such that it was a case of slowed growth rather than absolute decline. New industries were started, some aided by tariff protection: cotton mills, shoe factories, sugar refineries.[17] But the important response was as that of Saint John: to make the city an effective part of the Canadian continental system as a winter port. The work began as early as 1882, when indeed the dominion government built a grain elevator at Halifax. But more important were the building of the big Halifax drydock in 1887–89, and the steady development of the Intercolonial's deep water terminus, which by 1899 could handle twelve large ocean steamers at once.[18]

With first-class port facilities and improving rail connections, Halifax was now equipped to take its own considerable share of the Canadian boom of the early twentieth century. It prospered vigorously, able to hold its own with Saint John — and hold as well the Atlantic margins of New Brunswick, more susceptible to its own rail connections. In fact, it made little difference when in 1905 a long era ended for Halifax, and Britain, concentrating her naval forces, gave up the Halifax naval base. Formal transfer of the naval dockyard to a largely store-keeping Canadian regime came in 1910, to mark another aspect of advancing continental dominance. Still another sign of that advance came in the financial field. In 1900 the general manager's office of the Bank of Nova Scotia was transferred to Toronto, in 1907 that of the Royal Bank to Montreal, and in 1903 the august Halifax Banking Company became part of Toronto's Bank of Commerce as it invaded the Maritimes.[19]

Still, if Halifax was thus being incorporated in the continent, it retained its essential strategic importance as a focal point for transatlantic communication. That was made abundantly plain only a few years thereafter, when the port was again called upon to prove its significance in naval war, as it had not been required to do since 1814. But that is another story.

IV

To conclude with St. John's: its metropolitan role might seem the least significant of the three Atlantic cities. Certainly its own hinterland was thinly populated and scarcely developed but for the fringe of fishing outports; it had virtually no industrial base apart from the cod and seal fisheries; and its financial services were limited by the backward state of the Newfoundland region in general. And yet, in other respects, St. John's had a decidedly powerful metropolitan role, as the great commercial and shipping *entrepôt* of the island. Its merchants and shipowners financed the fishing staple, marketed dried cod from the West Indies to the Mediterranean, imported and distributed foodstuffs and manufactures for the outports and through the use and abuse of the credit system tied the fishing population closely to the business houses of Water Street. Here was a compact urban élite, notably internationally minded, whose social predominance was unrivalled. One cannot doubt the enduring influence of the great dynasties of the St. John's business world, the Bowrings, Job Brothers, the Ayres, Newman and Company.[20] And one need scarcely assert the political ascendancy of St. John's figures like Charles Fox Bennett and Amrose Shea, Robert Thorburn and Robert Bond, when all the class and religious friction of the province found its focus in politics at the capital.

The city, moreover, was well integrated in the old Atlantic nineteenth-century system, traditionally linked with Liverpool, London, and Bristol, increasingly with the Maritimes and Boston. Yet it was still remote from the continent, buying supplies rather than selling there, and little affected by continental forces — as the flat rejection of Confederation with Canada might show. The state of the fishing and sealing catches also affected it far more immediately than the world process of technological change. Indeed, for much of the later nineteenth century St. John's was generally flourishing. It had four banks by the mid-seventies, direct steam service with England from 1869, the Atlantic cable since 1866, and regular steamship sailings to Halifax.[21] The eighties brought the beginning of railway building with the line to Harbor Grace and stimulated many small-scale industrial enterprises, of which Colonial Cordage survived.

But the well-being of St. John's continued to rest ultimately on the uncertain fortunes of the fisheries; its metropolitan ventures into industrial and transport development proved shaky and premature. After the Great Fire of 1892, that burned out most of the city's commercial firms and left 11 000 homeless, the whole strained overextended financial system was in deep trouble.[22] The bank crash of 1894 that followed, the failure of renewed Confederation negotiations with Canada the next year, left the city in financial chaos and considerable bitterness over apparent Canadian indifference to the gravity of the problem. When recovery came, with prosperous world trade in the new century, and a Newfoundland boom based on railway building and the development of pulpwood and mineral resources, it seemed that St. John's had again decisively turned its back on Canadian continental connections.

But had it? With hindsight, one could say that the connections had only been delayed; or rather, that they were so far premature for an island community which, in remoteness, had not yet felt the full impact of technological change in its communications system. The decline of the old-style Newfoundland fishery in face of modern big-ship operations would not become fully apparent until the bad years between the two world wars. Commission government might then be regarded as a final,

261

reluctant exercise of British metropolitanism; the establishment of American and Canadian bases on the island in the Second World War as a function of extending continental metropolitan dominance — to be consolidated politically in the Confederation settlement of 1949.

Furthermore, again with hindsight, one may note the growth of continental pulls upon St. John's even from the 1890's; above all, the fact that Canadian banks took over in the city after the collapse of its own financial institutions.[23] Also, the very Newfoundland railway boom was shaped, if not captured, by R. A. Reid, fresh from his building for the CPR. And the pulpwood and iron-mining developments that began at last to diversify the Newfoundland region were largely in accord with Canadian continental interests. The real point is that St. John's, like its sister cities of the Atlantic region, was going to join the continent; each in varying ways, perhaps, but decisively — with changes in metropolitan patterns of communications which involved them all. What remain are questions. There is no intention here to put forward technological change as a kind of simplified economic determinism — but how far did it relate to the decision-making processes both of business and of government? How far was it the factor that made urban business élite in the Atlantic metropolitan centres aware of their own need to respond to change and make adjustments? How far did they utilize political influence to do so, and what were the reactions in their own regional communities? We need a great deal more study of the role of these urban élites, in the Atlantic region as elsewhere in Canada: more urban history, more business history, more study of the political and social interweavings of these entrepreneurial elements — which will inevitably carry us further into regional socio-cultural history as well. In sum, the restructuring in this inevitably sketchy paper (that still leaves so much out) of things we already know, should only make us aware of how much we do not know, when we look at regionalism in terms of metropolitanism.

262

Notes

1. See *Saint John Business Directory and Almanac for 1857, et seq.* (Saint John 1857).
2. J. W. Millidge, "Reminiscences of Saint John from 1849 to 1860," *New Brunswick Historical Collections*, no. 10 (Saint John 1919), 135.
3. F. W. Wallace, *Wooden Ships and Iron Men* (London n.d.), 309.
4. A. P. Langtry, ed., *Metropolitan Boston* (New York 1929), 1067.
5. Millidge, *loc. cit.*, 131.
6. D. R. Jack, *Centennial Prize Essay on Saint John* (Saint John 1883), 151.
7. See R. C. Brown, "The Nationalism of the National Policy," in P. Russell, ed., *Nationalism in Canada* (Toronto 1966), 155–63.
8. F. W. Wallace and I. Sclanders, *The Romance of a Great Port* (Saint John 1935), 37.
9. *Ibid.*, 44.
10. *Ibid.*, 46.
11. See *Beecher's Farmers Almanack for 1850, et seq.* (Halifax 1850).
12. A. W. H. Eaton, *Chapters in the History of Halifax* (New York 1915), 839.
13. F. L. Babcock, *Spanning the Atlantic* (New York 1931), 48.
14. P. H. Watson, "The Two Hundredth Anniversary of the Halifax Dockyard," *Occasional Papers of the Maritime Museum* (Halifax 1959), 21.
15. *Ibid.*, 32.
16. P. R. Blakeley, *Glimpses of Halifax, 1867–1900* (Halifax 1949), 24.

17. *Ibid.*, 38–45.
18. *Ibid.*, 28.
19. See *McAlpine's Halifax City Directory for 1907–08* (Halifax 1907).
20. See *Year Book and Almanack of Newfoundland, 1913* (St. John's 1913); also C. R. Fay, *Life and Labour in Newfoundland* (Toronto 1956), 13–37.
21. P. Toque, *Newfoundland as it was and is* (London 1878), 76–87.
22. A. B. Perlin, "St. John's," *Atlantic Advocate* (June 1960), 47.
23. R. A. MacKay, ed., *Newfoundland* (Toronto 1946), 459.

Urbanization*

P.-A. LINTEAU,
R. DUROCHER,
J.-C. ROBERT

Because industrialization brings workers together in factories, the growth   *263*
of cities and changes in the living conditions of urban populations are among
its effects. In examining these effects, however, urbanization and industrialization should not be confused. Urbanization refers to a social process in
which people are grouped together in cities; in that sense it is a very old
phenomenon, but one whose characteristics change over time and vary from
one economic system to another. Industrialization does not create urbanization, but rather speeds up its pace and changes some of its characteristics.

General characteristics

To describe and explain the growth of cities, geographers have developed
the concept of urban function. An urban function is an economic activity
that distinguishes a city, employs a significant portion of its population, and
has a product that is intended for use outside the city. Until the middle of
the nineteenth century, the function of Quebec's cities was essentially commercial. They were trading posts with a double role, covering both international trade, as the major staples — furs, lumber and wheat — were brought
there to be shipped out, and internal distribution, as they provided goods
and services to a growing rural hinterland.

Quebec's dominant urban centres, Montreal and Quebec City, are also
among its oldest. The importance of these two cities, their control of economic activity and political power, and their attraction for a significant part
of the population have been evident from the seventeenth century to the
present day. As the area of Quebec under cultivation expanded in the late
eighteenth and early nineteenth centuries, a network of villages — points of
communication between city and country — appeared, forming the skeleton
of Quebec's future urban network. The dominant position of Montreal and

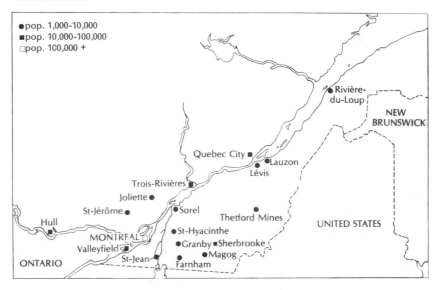

MAP 1: Quebec's Urban Network, 1901

Quebec City was not the only characteristic of the urban network that was already apparent in the commercial era; the geographer Louis Trotier has pointed out others as well. Urban centres grew up primarily along the banks of the St. Lawrence and its tributaries, and were most densely concentrated and most clearly organized into a hierarchy in the Montreal plain (Map 1).

The 1850s and 1860s were a transition period in several respects. In those decades, the first effects of industrialization began to be felt, especially in Montreal. Montreal's growth took off, and it definitively replaced Quebec City as the nerve centre of Quebec's economic life. The population gap between the two cities widened steadily from then on. In Quebec as a whole, the organization of the urban network was changed radically by the coming of the railway. The Grand Trunk main line became a second spinal column (after the St. Lawrence) through which part of Quebec's urban system was linked together. Thanks to the railway, some villages — Saint-Hyacinthe, Sherbrooke, Lévis, Rivière-du-Loup — became intermediate centres of regional significance and experienced a period of rapid growth. As urban areas grew, it became necessary to establish political structures on the local level. Between 1840 and 1870, a series of acts set up the municipal government system as it exists today.

After 1870, the industrial function clearly became the driving force behind urban growth in Quebec. Factories began to dot Quebec's territory, draining a portion of the surplus rural population towards the cities. The commercial function did not disappear, but rather remained a significant economic base for most of Quebec's urban centres. Its effects, however, were overshadowed by those of the new industrial establishments, which were generally built in already existing towns and villages, giving them a new impetus. Very few new towns were established in this period as a direct result of industry, and there was no radical change in the existing urban network. Rather, industrial centres were superimposed on commerical ones, and urban development became even more concentrated in the Montreal plain and its neighbouring region, the Eastern Townships.

The urban population

As a result of industrialization, the concentration of Quebec's population in cities increased, as can be seen by looking at the percentage of the population living in urban areas in a succession of census years (Table I). The census definition of an urban area is an incorporated municipality with a population of 1,000 or more; in 1851, a little under fifteen per cent of Quebecers lived in urban areas, while fifty years later the figure was more than a third. The growth of the urban population began to accelerate in the decade 1871–81.

The degree of urbanization in Quebec followed a similar pattern to that of Canada as a whole. Table I shows no evidence of a lag in the urbanization of Quebec in relation to that of Canada, and the percentage of Quebec's population living in urban areas was higher than the Canadian percentage for every census year except 1891. There is a clearer gap between Quebec and its neighbouring province, Ontario. In the middle of the nineteenth century the two provinces showed a similar level of urbanization, but after 1871 Ontario clearly outpaced Quebec as a result of its more favourable economic circumstances.

Table I shows that Quebec underwent a significant change in the second half of the nineteenth century. But in giving us snapshots at a succession of fixed points in time, these figures can be misleading and do not always do justice to the complexity of the real world. It could be argued, for instance, that Quebec's population also underwent another process of urbanization. Throughout this period, the surplus population of the countryside flowed to the cities. Some of those who left rural Quebec remained in agriculture, in the American mid-west or western Canada, but cities were

265

TABLE I Percentage of the Population Living in Urban Areas, Quebec, Ontario and Canada, 1851–1901

Year	Quebec	Ontario	Canada
1851	14.9	14.0	13.1
1861	16.6	18.5	15.8
1871	19.9	20.6	18.3
1881	23.8	27.1	23.3
1891	28.6	35.0	29.8
1901	36.1	40.3	34.9

Source: L.O. Stone, *Urban Development in Canada*, p. 29.

the destination for the largest part of Quebec's rural exodus. The weakness of Quebec's industrial structure relative to that of the United States made it impossible for Quebec cities to absorb all the surplus population. Those who were not absorbed within Quebec experienced urbanization outside Quebec, in the industrial towns of New England.

As was pointed out in chapter 2, migration was characteristic of North America as a whole in the second half of the nineteenth century, and it led to another phenomenon of continental significance. Much of the urban population of the time consisted of transients, either from overseas or from the rural hinterland, for whom the city was only a temporary place of residence. In a context of great geographical mobility, as people left, new arrivals came to take their place, so that the total number of people who lived in a city in a ten-year period was much larger than the population figure that showed up in a census. As major relay points in the continental communications network, Quebec City and Montreal saw part of their population periodically 266 replaced in this way. The scope of the phenomenon has not been measured, but the geographer Raoul Blanchard examined the case of the Irish of Quebec City. For a few decades in the middle of the nineteenth century, they represented a significant proportion of the population of the city. Around 1871, with Quebec City in a period of economic stagnation, they left en masse, some for Montreal, some for other parts of North America.

Urbanization was brought about by these population movements as well as by industrialization. In the last few decades of the nineteenth century, the process was clearly under way in Quebec and could not be reversed. All regions of the province were affected by it, but its pace and scope differed from one region to another.

The major cities

Montreal: At the time of Confederation, Montreal was unquestionably the metropolis not only of Quebec but of Canada as a whole, and it maintained its dominant position throughout succeeding decades. During the period, it registered a consistently high rate of population increase, with the most rapid growth occurring between 1881 and 1891 (Table II). In 1861, Montreal was a city of 90,000 people; adding the population of its still semi-rural suburbs gives a figure of almost exactly 100,000. At the end of the century Montreal proper, which now covered an expanded area, had a population of more than a quarter of a million, and adding the suburban municipalities brought the total to about 325,000, or half the urban population of Quebec.

As Raoul Blanchard pointed out, Montreal's rise was due to industry. A first period of industrial growth had occurred in the 1850s and 1860s, and was concentrated in the southwestern part of the city, especially along the Lachine Canal. Around 1867, Montreal's industrial structure was characterized by the presence of five major industries: sugar refining, flour milling, ironmaking, wood processing and shoemaking. In the 1880s, a second wave of manufacturing investment rounded out this early structure. Addi-

TABLE II Population of Major Urban Centres in Quebec, 1861–1901

Municipality	1861	1871	1881	1891	1901
Montreal Region					
City of Montreal	90,323	107,225	140,247	216,650	267,730
Montreal and suburbs[1]	100,723	126,314	170,745	250,165	324,880
Saint-Jérôme	—	1,159	2,032	2,868	3,619
Joliette	—	3,047	3,268	3,347	4,220
Sorel	4,778	5,636	5,791	6,669	7,057
Saint-Hyacinthe	3,695	3,746	5,321	7,016	9,210
Saint-Jean	3,317	3,022	4,314	4,722	4,030
Valleyfield	—	1,800	3,906	5,551	11,055
Quebec City Region					
City of Quebec	42,052	59,699	62,446	63,090	68,840
Lévis	—	6,691	5,597	7,301	7,783
Lauzon	—	—	3,556	3,551	3,416
Eastern Townships					
Sherbrooke	5,899	4,432	7,227	10,110	11,765
Magog	—	—	—	2,100	3,516
Granby	—	876	1,040	1,710	3,773
Thetford Mines	—	—	—	—	3,256
Coaticook	—	1,160	2,682	3,086	2,880
Farnham	—	1,317	1,880	2,822	3,114
Others					
Hull	—	3,800	6,890	11,264	13,993
Trois-Rivières	6,058	7,570	8,670	8,334	9,981
Chicoutimi	—	1,393	1,935	2,277	3,826
Rivière-du-Loup	—	1,541	2,291	4,175	4,569

1. A suburb is defined here as a town or village on Montreal Island bordering Montreal.
Source: Censuses of Canada

tional enterprises were founded in the existing sectors, while new ones such as meat curing, textiles, clothing, railway rolling stock and tobacco emerged. By the end of the nineteenth century Montreal had become an important industrial centre and accounted for half the value of Quebec's manufacturing production. Illustrations from the era show a landscape dominated by factory smoke in the southwestern and eastern parts of the city.

The advantages accruing to Montreal from its position at the centre of the transportation system were another factor in its growth. It benefited from the substantial investments in infrastructure made in the nineteenth century. The St. Lawrence River canals, the ship channel and the city's new harbour facilities made Montreal the focal point of water transportaton. It was also the base of operations for the two major railway systems, the Grand Trunk and the Canadian Pacific, which established their administrative offices and maintenance shops there, and the centre of a web of railway lines extending in many directions. Transportation was an essential factor in the marketing and distribution of the goods that were manufactured in the city. Because Montreal was so well endowed with means of transportation, the concentration of industry in the city increased and its status as a metropolis for all of Canada was enhanced.

Towards the end of the nineteenth century, Montreal's capitalist class clearly dominated the economic activity of Canada as a whole. The most visible symbol of this domination was the ascendant Bank of Montreal-Canadian Pacific tandem. These two companies seemed to be almost ubiquitous in Canada. They were controlled by a close-knit group consisting of Donald Smith, George Stephen, R.B. Angus, William C. Van Horne and others, whose interests extended to a large number of companies in the financial, commerical, industrial and transportation sectors.

Spatial extension was another aspect of Montreal's growth, as the area within the city limits was systematically occupied and the city began to overflow into the suburbs. Montreal's city limits had been officially designated in the late eighteenth century; within them were large areas that were not yet urbanized. These areas gradually became inhabited as the nineteenth century progressed; at the time of Confederation this progress was not yet completed. Three wards near the city limits grew substantially in the decades after Confederation— Saint-Antoine in the west end and Saint-Jacques and Sainte-Marie in the east (Map 2). By the late nineteenth century, occupation of the city's original territory was almost complete, and the overflow of population into the new suburban municipalities that had been established from the late 1860s on had begun. The most important of these new suburbs were the industrial towns of Saint-Gabriel, Sainte-Cunégonde and Saint-Henri on the banks of the Lachine Canal to the west; Saint-Jean-Baptiste and Saint-Louis to the north; and Hochelaga and Maisonneuve to the east. Between 1871 and 1901, the population of these newly urbanized areas on Montreal Island grew from 11,000 to 130,000, or from four per cent to twenty per cent of the urban population of Quebec. At the end of the century, the largest part of the population increase in the metropolitan region was occurring in these new areas.

Montreal's municipal authorities wanted to adjust the region's political structures to these new demographic and economic realities, and tried to extend the city's territory by annexing suburban towns. The process began in 1883 with the annexation of Hochelaga; in the subsequent years, three more municipalities met the same fate. The phenomenon took on new dimensions in the early twentieth century, when the annexation of nineteen suburban municipalities in twelve years brought about a spectacular increase in Montreal's territorial size.

These small municipalities were typically the creation of a handful of real estate promoters, who wanted to develop land that they owned. Towards this end, they would incorporate a small town, in which they would then control the town council. Through tax exemptions or cash subsidies, they attracted companies whose employees became residents of the new town. The promoters themselves also used tax exemptions to start development

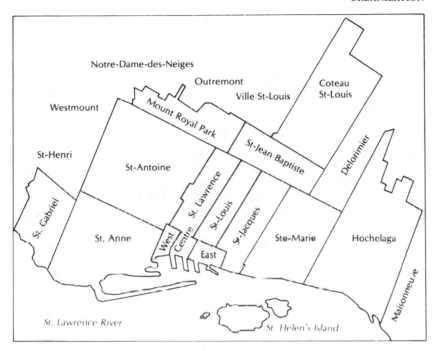

MAP 2: Montreal Wards in the Late Nineteenth Century

269

projects, which the municipality financed through borrowing, the burden of which was ultimately borne by small property owners and tenants. A few years or decades later, the municipality was heavily in debt, and annexation to Montreal seemed appealing as a solution to its financial problems.

The period was thus one of rapid growth and change for Montreal. One of the most significant changes was in the city's ethnic composition. Mid-nineteenth-century Montreal was culturally and politically a British city, with an English speaking majority between 1831 and 1865, the English-speaking proportion of the population reached a peak of fifty-seven per cent in 1844. This British preponderance was reflected in the city council, where decisions were made in the interests of the English-speaking majority. The appearance of the city also changed, and in the 1840s British-style architecture started to replace the old French architecture that had characterized the city until then, although French architecture was never completely eliminated. The situation began to be reversed around 1865, when a French-speaking majority was re-established in the city as rural French Canadians came to work in the factories and immigration from the United Kingdom slowed down. Annexation of suburban municipalities with large French-speaking majorities intensified the process. However, it was almost twenty years before the change in ethnic composition was felt on city council, and much longer before it was reflected in the city's appearance and major cultural institutions.

By 1896, Montreal had become not only a financial and commercial metropolis but also a great industrial city. However, as a result of its rapid growth, a number of problems of adjustment affected living conditions in the city: crowding, deficient sanitary conditions, a high death rate.

Quebec City: The evolution of Quebec City during this period was very different from that of Montreal. Founded in 1608, Quebec City was the oldest city in the province, and had been the principal centre of New France and later of British North America. However, it had gradually lost its political pre-eminence to Ottawa, and at the time of Confederation it was entering a period of relative stagnation that lasted until the end of the century.

270
Quebec City's population grew by forty-two per cent between 1861 and 1871 (Table I), but its growth in the three succeeding decades was very slow. A comparison between Quebec City and Montreal brings this slowdown into sharp focus. Throughout the first half of the nineteenth century, the population of the two cities was roughly the same. A clear gap began to appear in 1851, and by 1901, the Montreal urban area had a population five times as large as the Quebec City urban area. While twenty-two percent of Quebec's urban population lived in the Quebec City area in 1871, that figure had fallen to 10.5 per cent in 1901.

The transition from the commercial era to the industrial era was difficult for Quebec City. The difficulties the city experienced in the late 1860s were identified by Raoul Blanchard. Most significant was the decline of the timber trade. From the early nineteenth century, Quebec City was the port from which the largest part of Canadian lumber exports to England were shipped. But the replacement of squared timber by sawn lumber and the redirection of trade from Britain to the United States changed the lines of communication, so that Quebec City was no longer the pivot of wood exports. Ships built in Quebec City had carried Canadian timber to England, where the ships were resold; the slowdown in timber shipments thus adversely affected the city's shipbuilding industry. This industry was also hurt by changes in maritime technology, as the wooden vessel was replaced by the iron- or steel-hulled ship. From the 1870s on, Quebec City's shipyards declined rapidly. The port of Quebec City also experienced difficulties as a result of competition from Montreal. The dredging of the ship channel made it possible for ocean-going vessels to sail upriver as far as Montreal, and Quebec City gradually lost its importance as a terminus for transatlantic lines. Thus, as Blanchard pointed out, all of Quebec City's maritime activity was in decline, with thousands of workers losing their jobs and having to seek employment elsewhere.

Quebec City was also not well integrated into the railway system. With the Grand Trunk running along the south shore, it was the Lévis area rather than Quebec City that developed; it was not until the early twentieth century that the two banks of the river were linked by a bridge. It was only in 1879 that the North Shore Railway, connecting Quebec City with Montreal, was opened to traffic, and this long wait for railway service did not help the city get out of its slump. When the capital of Canada was established at Ottawa in 1867 there was an exodus of civil servants, which was followed by the departure of the British garrison in 1871.

While there were many unfavourable elements in Quebec City's situation, they were partly counterbalanced by the development of some compensating factors. Having lost its pre-eminence on a Canada-wide scale, Quebec City increasingly became a regional metropolis for eastern and central Quebec. Quebec City's immediate hinterland is fairly limited, so that new regions had to be brought under its influence and dominated, a task which occupied the Quebec City bourgeoisie during the last three decades of the century. Its main instrument was the railway. Thus, the Quebec and Lake St. John Railway allowed it to dominate the Saguenay region, the Lévis and Kennebec brought the Beauce within its orbit, and the North Shore Railway strengthened its links with the region to the west of the city. Also during this period, Quebec City attracted some industrial establishments, especially shoe factories. Some of the jobs lost through the decline of maritime activities were made up for by this industrial growth, but not enough to retain all the city's surplus population. An attempt was also made to breathe new life into the maritime sector by significantly enlarging the city's harbour facilities; this project was completed in 1890.

271

Thus, Quebec City's stagnation in the late nineteenth century was due to the decline of its traditional economic activities; their replacement by new activites did not occur quickly enough to stabilize its population.

This situation also had significant effects on the city's ethnic composition. In 1861, about forty per cent of its population was of British origin: by 1901 this figure had declined to fifteen per cent. The decline was just as dramatic in absolute numbers — from 23,000 to 10,000 in the same period. This population was mostly Irish and consisted primarily of labourers in the harbour or the shipyards; they were the first to feel the effects of the slowdown in economic activity and had no choice but to leave the city. Thus, Quebec City became increasingly French in the late nineteenth century. As Blanchard noted, this change affected the bourgeoisie as well, and there were a growing number of French Canadians among the owners of the major enterprises.

The growth of the population, limited as it was, nevertheless brought about an expansion of the city's inhabited area. This occured in the eastern part of the city, the population of which doubled between 1861 and 1901, especially in the neighbourhoods of Saint-Roch, Saint-Sauveur and Saint-Vallier, where new industries were established.

Other cities and towns: At the time of Confederation, Trois-Rivières was still the third largest city in Quebec, far behind Montreal and Quebec City; in the next three decades it was passed by Hull, Sherbrooke and Valleyfield in succession. Like Quebec City, Trois-Rivières was in a period of stagnation, and its population grew only from 6,098 to 9,981 in forty years; between 1881 and 1891, it even declined slightly. The reason for this situation was the decline of the timber trade in the last quarter of the century. The economy of Trois-Rivières' hinterland was essentially agricultural or agro-forest. It was not until the early twentieth century that hydroelectricity and the pulp and paper industry gave new impetus to the region's economy and brought about the development of an urban network (Cap-de-la-Madeleine, Shawinigan, Grand-Mère, La Tuque) for which Trois-Rivières was the bridgehead.

The situation was different in the Eastern Townships, where a relatively prosperous agricultural economy led to the growth of a network of villages. In the last quarter of the nineteenth century, factories were established in a number of these centres to make use of rural manpower, turning them into small towns, each with a population of barely 3,000 in 1901 — Magog, Granby, Coaticook, Farnham, Richmond, Windsor. Thetford Mines, whose growth was based on the asbestos-mining industry, was a special case. This little urban network was capped by a regional metropolis, Sherbrooke, which played a dominant role in the Eastern Townships during the period. Sherbrooke's location on the St. Francis River at its confluence with the Magog was advantageous, and it benefited further from being on the Grand Trunk Railway. It was both an industrial town and a service centre for the Eastern Townships as a whole.

272

There was also another regional network in Quebec, consisting of six satellite towns forming a ring around Montreal at a radius of about sixty kilometres — Saint-Jérôme, Joliette, Sorel, Saint-Hyacinthe, Saint-Jean and Valleyfield. Their combined population was more than 18,000 by 1871, and it was 40,000 in 1901. Industrial and commercial functions and a role as service centres all contributed to their growth. The town of Joliette is a representative case. Founded in 1824, it developed slowly until the middle of the century. It was the site of a large sawmill, and the forest industry was its main economic base. When neighbouring townships were opened to settlement, it quickly became a regional service centre, a development which brought new kinds of establishments to the town and introduced a form of economic activity that was both commercial and industrial. Typical of this process was the gradual evolution of a small ironworks into a plant where farm machinery was manufactured; another ironworks offered its customers a wide variety of iron goods, from machine parts to saucepans by way of *ferrures de moulin à laver* (iron parts for wood-frame washing machines). The population of Joliette at the turn of the century was 6,000; creation of a diocese of Joliette in 1904 was testimony to its importance.

At the end of the period, the process of urbanization in Quebec was well under way. Montreal's ascendancy had grown, while a network of small towns had developed primarily in the Montreal plain and the Eastern Townships.

The CPR and the Urban West, 1881-1930*
MAX FORAN

The pattern of urban development in western Canada was strongly influenced by the railway, first in determining the very sites of hundreds of communities along its various lines, and then in contributing markedly to these
centres' economic and spatial growth. The CPR's role in developing the urban west was not unusual in the sense that the pattern of urban growth in
frontier areas of this period generally occurred in tandem with the advance
of rail construction. The historical significance of the CPR lies here primarily
in the unique degree of its involvement in the process. No other railroad in
Canada, the United States or for that matter Australia, comes near it in
terms of exclusiveness or scope of operation. The Canadian road was also   *273*
consistent in its view of the importance of urbanization as linked with the
need to tap the resource potential of woodlands, prairies and mountains.
The CPR's urban role was a direct reflection of this view, and it was a manifestation as well of the more practical desire to increase company revenues
by judicious and large-scale involvement in the profitable townsite business.

As late as the 1870s, urban western Canada was virtually nonexistent.
The 1871 census gave the population of Manitoba and the North-West Territories as one-hundred-per-cent rural.[1] And the situation had not changed
dramatically by the end of the decade: Winnipeg was the only major centre,
incorporated as a city in 1873. The western prairies were empty apart from
a few scattered Mounted Police posts and a hamlet of sorts at Fort Calgary
on the Bow River. On the west coast, small established communities existed
at Victoria on Vancouver Island and on the mainland around present-day
New Westminster. Aside from the various Hudson's Bay Company posts
and missionary stations in the north, the only other settlement of note was
near Battleford in the valley of the North Saskatchewan River, where small
Métis communities pursued their traditional semi-nomadic life style.

The pattern of western Canada's urban growth was decided in 1880 with
the resolve of the reconstituted CPR Syndicate to push the belated transcontinental project to its completion. Within six years the ribbon of steel spanned
a continent, and along it had emerged the assorted townsites the company
deemed necessary to service surrounding agricultural areas. While the hoped-
for massive influx did not follow immediately, there was enough settlement
over the ensuing fifteen years to etch out the face of urban western Canada.
By 1901, Manitoba and the North-West Territories counted fifty-seven villages, twenty-five towns and three cities.[2] Equally significant was the fact
that fully twenty per cent of the 400,000 population lived in centres of a

*From *The CPR West: The Iron Road and the Making of a Nation*, edited by Hugh A. Dempsey
(Vancouver: Douglas & McIntyre, 1984).

thousand people or more.[3] Almost without exception, urban concentration was along the main line, or along branch lines under CPR control.[4]

The western settlement boom that began around 1900 and continued through 1912 meant a significant increase in the number of these urban centres. The population of the four western provinces rose from 598,168 in 1901 to 1,720,601 in 1911.[5] In the prairie west, the number of cities increased to seventeen, and incorporated towns and villages to 150 and 423 respectively.[6] By 1916, urban residents accounted for thirty-six per cent of the total population in the three prairie provinces.[7] This period also saw the construction of a series of branch lines which effectively tapped the agricultural and, to a lesser extent, mineral potential of the west.[8] Although its monopoly position was less dominant than it had been at the turn of the century,[9] the CPR was still the most important factor in defining the hierarchical network of villages, towns and cities that was evident by 1912. In the latter year, nine of the eleven largest metropolitan centres in Western Canada were located on CPR lines.[10]

By the outbreak of World War I, then, the face of urban western Canada had been fleshed out. Contributing factors included geography, federal government activity and the energies of private speculators and town developers. These forces were insignificant, however, compared with the role of the railroad. Urban western Canada was delineated by railroad policies. And in British Columbia, the southern prairies and large sections of the parkland belt, the railroad simply meant the CPR.

The years 1914–30 contrasted sharply with the previous era. Without the inflationary impact of immigration, western Canada experienced modest growth. While some rail construction occurred during these years,[11] the urban hierarchy established in the 1900–1914 period was not altered significantly. A glance at a map of western Canada in 1930 would show a configuration of urban places almost all created in large part by the CPR and, to a much lesser extent, its emergent rival, the Canadian National Railway system.

The specific contribution of the CPR manifested itself in three areas — townsite selection, differentiation between centres, and spatial development patterns. The company never wavered in its aggressive support of urban enterprises that complemented hinterland wealth. On a more practical level, however, it should not be forgotten that the CPR was a private-enterprise body dedicated to making money for its shareholders; many of its decisions that affected the development of individual places, as well as some general policy matters — especially in the twenties — were geared to immediate economic considerations.

Any discussion of the CPR's role in nineteenth-century townsite growth must take into account the presence of the Canada North-West Land Company. In 1882, this consortium of British and Canadian capitalists became a business ally of the CPR.[12] The coalition's prime responsibility was the advertising and disposal of lots in forty-seven townsites on the main line between Brandon and British Columbia. The railway was to receive half the net proceeds, with overall operations directed by a four-man Joint Townsite

Trustee Board.[13] The reasons for this partnership were the CPR's need for working capital, and ambivalence in the CPR's original charter about the company's legal right to get into the townsite business.[14] The Canada North-West Land Company was virtually an extension of the railway's land department until the anomoly was removed in 1908. The merits of this unique relationship were somewhat dubious from the viewpoint of the CPR, which found itself at a disadvantage in the first serious dispute with the towns it had created.

In 1880, a few months after the signing of the contract to build a railroad Pacific, the CPR Syndicate announced plans for the line from Winnipeg across the prairies. The sudden decision to abandon the formerly surveyed route along the North Saskatchewan was seen by many as unnecessary and ill advised.[15] The railway countered criticism by referring to the upward-revised assessments on the agricultural potential of the southern prairies and the need to forestall American competition to the south.[16] However, it was also true that the southern route across the empty prairie gave the CPR more arbitrary power over townsite selection than did the original survey, which traversed existing settlements. The choice of a southern route enabled the CPR almost literally to build urban western Canada from bald prairie, and primarily on its own terms. Site selection for major urban centres between the Lakehead and the Pacific showed how largely immediate economic considerations figured in company thinking. Similarly, the pattern of urban locations across the west generally revealed that the CPR expected the townsite business to be lucrative.

Under the terms of its contract, the CPR received 25 million acres of land in Manitoba and the North-West Territories. Whereas the deal gave the railway company every odd-numbered section to a depth of twenty four miles on both sides of the right of way, the company was not bound to adhere absolutely to this pattern. If the parcel chosen for a townsite was on Crown land, it was claimed as part of the company's land grant. The CPR also had the right to refuse land not suited for settlement; this option was exercised in southeastern Alberta,[17] which explains the absence of urban development between Medicine Hat and Calgary prior to the irrigation projects of the early twentieth century.

Company policy generally meant a townsite for each township traversed by the railway. During construction, prospective townsites were designated by siding numbers, and while the rudiments of business activity followed immediately, the railway often delayed actual site selection to forestall squatting and land speculators.[18] Once the decision was made, the company usually subdivided the land into four or more blocks, along with the necessary access to public road allowances. Interestingly, the locations of larger centres were decided by company requirements for divisional points. In these cases, the CPR simply increased the amount of subdivided acreage to provide for a more substantial business section as well as room for freight yards and switching terminals. The appearance of larger urban centres equidistant across the prairies was one obvious manifestation of this functional policy.

275

A survey of these sites, moreover, reveals that the railway was more interested in immediate profit than in using geographical advantages or envisaging any kind of popular consensus.

The CPR's decision in the early eighties to place a divisional point, steamer terminals and elevator sites at the Lakehead precipitated a bitter struggle between the neighbouring communities of Fort William and Port Arthur.[19] For several decades, the mining and forest hinterlands of northwestern Ontario had fed the modest growth of both centres, but especially Port Arthur, which by the eighties had clearly eclipsed its rival in population and commercial importance.[20] Certainly the residents of Port Arthur or the "Silver Gateway," as it fancifully called itself, had good reason to believe that their town would be the terminus and not Fort William, which was considerably smaller and, in their opinion, less progressive and hygienically inferior. At least one CPR engineer shared this view and advocated harbour preparations at Port Arthur.[21] The company's ultimate preference of Fort William was surprising to some, though not unexpected given the Hudson's Bay Company lands there and the influential presence of Donald A. Smith in the boardrooms of both the railway and the Bay company.[22]

276

Winnipeg is one metropolitan area that might not have been. Although incorporated as a city in 1873 and connected to the United States rail network by 1878,[23] bustling Winnipeg had a major setback when the CPR announced plans to cross the Red River at Selkirk, about twenty miles north of the city. The railway located its offices in Selkirk soon after the town's inception in 1875,[24] and increased building followed in anticipation of Selkirk becoming a major rail centre. Mindful of the implications of losing the transcontinental, Winnipeg fought back, wooing the company with lucrative incentives that included a bridge across the Red, a $200,000 subsidy, free land, and tax exemptions in perpetuity.[25] With these enticements, plus the presence of the ubiquitous Donald Smith who recognized the real-estate potential of some seventeen-hundred acres of Bay company land in Winnipeg, the railway decided to bypass geographically superior Selkirk and opt instead for flood-prone Winnipeg. That community's subsequent rise to the major metropolitan centre west of Toronto was due primarily to the CPR, but also indirectly to the energies of local residents who were able to convince the railroad company of practical realities.[26]

The pattern was similar in Vancouver. In 1885 Granville, as it was then known, was an isolated milling village with a population of less than three hundred. The prospects of neighbouring Port Moody were exceedingly bright by comparison: as the railway's designated coastal terminus, the town was experiencing considerable commercial growth and had initiated harbour and waterfront development. In 1886, however, the British Columbia government persuaded the CPR to use Vancouver by the promise of a land grant that eventually approximated 6500 acres.[27] When the five thousand ecstatic Vancouverites welcomed the first train in 1887, they probably cared little that about a fifth of their prime downtown and waterfront property belonged to the CPR.

In opting for townsites at Portage La Prairie and Brandon, the railway ignored the nuclei of existing settlements around the Hudson's Bay post and at Grand Valley respectively,[28] and chose sites offering maximum profits from company land sales. This situation was reproduced more dramatically at Calgary, where by 1881–82 a sizeable community had risen on the east bank of the Elbow River and around Fort Calgary at the confluence of the Bow and the Elbow. The company's later decision to place its townsite a mile to the west ignored topography as well as the strongly expressed feelings of the resident community.[29]

Events surrounding the choice of Regina as the new site of the territorial capital by the CPR and the federal government further indicated the importance of the profit motive in townsite selection. The Regina site had little to recommend it aesthetically or practically, located as it was on a featureless, treeless plain with an uncertain water supply. The railway had avoided the far more suitable Qu'Appelle Valley, ostensibly for engineering reasons.[30] It has been said that at that time the CPR needed to optimize land-sale profits to offset unforeseen construction costs on its Lake Superior section.[31] There was another interested party in the case; operating through Edgar Dewdney— lieutenant-governor of the North-West Territories and a more than occasional dabbler in real-estate speculation — the federal government chose land in Regina for legislative buildings, a government house and the new headquarters of the North-West Mounted Police.[32] The railway, however, located its station site half a mile east of the original townsite and began selling subdivided town lots there. The result was that Regina began its corporate history spread out unnecessarily over two miles and denied the cohesive advantages provided by permanent institutional facilities.

It is interesting to note that the CPR did not make Regina the headquarters for its Saskatchewan rail operations. In the wake of an acrimonious debate with federal authorities over the Regina site, the CPR opted instead for the town of Moose Jaw, some forty miles to the west. Like Regina, Moose Jaw was an instant community, and its designation as a divisional point was sealed by the construction of extensive freight-yard facilities and later several branch lines. Moose Jaw became the emergent industrial capital of Saskatchewan when that role could have fallen just as easily to Regina. The pattern was set solely by the CPR, partly in retaliation for an unpleasant experience and reduced land-sale profits in the capital.[33]

Unlike Moose Jaw, where the company had positive expectations of hinterland wealth, the town of Medicine Hat sprang up somewhat haphazardly. The semi-arid lands of southeastern Alberta held out little in the way of agricultural promise, though the railway was well aware of the area's natural gas potential and anxious to stimulate exploration. This did not require a major urban centre, however, and in fact, the CPR had been in Medicine Hat for two years before town lots were subdivided for sale; incorporation did not occur until 1889, fully six years after the arrival of rail.

The pattern of eclipse, dislocation and survival that typified the fates of pre-railroad communities offers further indication of the company's perva-

277

sive influence. Mention has already been made of Selkirk and Port Moody: Fort Qu'Appelle offers an even better example of what might have been. Situated in the beautiful and productive Qu'Appelle Valley, this historic fur-trading centre was also strategically located for access to water supply and wood for building materials. Its failure to get the railroad despite the early optimism of its largest landowner, the Hudson's Bay Company, put an effective damper on its economic future.[34] The Bay Company's gamble that the area's natural fertility would ensure the town's continued growth did not take account of the railroad's irresistible power.[35]

In other cases existing communities survived by deferring to the pull of the rails. The business community of Yorkton moved four miles in 1889 to be next to the newly constructed Manitoba and North-Western Railway.[36] In 1885, Nelsonville, Manitoba was an incorporated town with a courthouse, land titles office, weekly newspaper, grist and saw mills, a number of implement and carriage shops and more than sixty private residences. Denied a position on the new railroad, Nelsonville opted for its own demise and transferred itself to the new town of Morden, six miles away.[37] The story was somewhat different in Edmonton where the railway's will did not entirely prevail. When the line from Calgary reached the North Saskatchewan in 1891, the CPR did not cross the river as anticipated; instead, it built the small south-bank community of Strathcona into a sizeable town. Edmonton fought back, and drawing heavily on its more advantageous location for outfitting the new Klondike frontier, it was able to hold out until amalgamation with Strathcona in 1912 ended the contest largely in Edmonton's favour.[38]

The profit dimension also insinuated itself into the broader pattern of urban development throughout the west. During the period of prosperity in 1900–12, the CPR created hundreds of towns in the western provinces and generated land sales in excess of $16 million.[39] The profitability of town building was revealed not only in these substantial revenues, but also through the CPR's desire, expressed as late as 1912, to obtain townsite property wherever feasible.[40] Many of these eight hundred communities coincided with or anticipated rural development and did not emerge in response to hinterland needs. In this sense, the shaping of small-town western Canada in those years hinged primarily on the railway's perception of unproven agricultural potential, an opportunism associated with good business. In the sobering economic climate of the post-boom years, a chastened CPR was forced to admit that it might have spawned too many towns in western Canada.[41]

The CPR's role in the economic development of the towns it created took several forms. First, there were the automatic advantages of location on a railroad. In some centres, the CPR built facilities for its operation: towns so favoured quickly assumed positions of economic prominence and formed western Canada's upper urban echelon. The railway also contributed to economic growth by assisting civic corporations with direct aid. And together with various urban organizations, the company was extremely active, particularly in the twenties, in promoting industry and commercial growth

278

throughout the west. Although the CPR was generally a positive agent, its attitude in the early period towards payment of municipal taxes had the effect of retarding civic growth. Finally, it could be argued that the company's tremendous influence, together with its largesse, bred a disproportionate level of urban dependence, and to a degree supported the lingering chattel mentality of the many self-proclaimed CPR towns across the prairies.

The CPR fostered urban growth vicariously in that its mere presence guaranteed survival.[42] Once the railway had chosen its station site and subdivided some lots, every new town quickly attracted the rudiments of social, professional, institutional and commercial life. A typical western town was essentially a clearing house, serving the needs of surrounding residents and facilitating the delivery of farm produce to distant markets. Larger centres were differentiated by wholesale facilities, processing and manufacturing enterprises and a wider range of urban services. Moreover, railway-town residents viewed the steam locomotive as a harbinger of greatness. In the early period of settlement and rail construction, optimistic visions of new Chicagos, Torontos, Denvers and Pittsburghs were associated with small-town ambitions across the western plains.[43] The rail connection nourished an urban philosophy that saw prosperity and steady growth as virtually automatic. New arrivals were infected by this contagion, fuelling the boosterism typical of western towns between 1890 and 1912.[44]

CPR decisions about railroad facilities — whether freight yards, branch lines or maintenance and repair shops — had enormous implications for communities. In the period under discussion, they literally shaped the destinies of Winnipeg, Calgary, Moose Jaw and Vancouver. Winnipeg owed its rise to most important city in the west to its strategic position as a major transportation centre.[45] Its metropolitan hegemony over the rest of western Canada, as well as its growing importance as a grain-handling point, were made possible by the CPR's decision to locate major support facilities in the city. By 1930, the Winnipeg terminals accommodated 308.5 miles of trackage and counted twelve industrial yards covering fourteen miles. Daily shipments of grain through Winnipeg in the fall months exceeded 2.5 million bushels. Accustomed to handling up to seven thousand cars a day, and with some 270 private sidings with 847 local consignees, the CPR's Winnipeg terminals were considered to be the largest privately owned terminals in the world.[46] The Weston repair shops covered an area of 284 acres and contained the main locomotive and car repair facilities to western Canada. Employing up to 2500 men, the Weston shops were capable of handling as many as eight hundred repairs a month.[47] The centralization of CPR rail facilities in Winnipeg, bolstered by the routing of Canada's other transcontinental line and major terminus connections with American lines, made the city the unique focal point in Canadian continental trade.

Calgary's growth in the years 1885–1912, though not as significant as Winnipeg's, was still western Canada's second urban success story. As in Winnipeg's case, it was Calgary's role as a major transportation hub that gave it a decided edge over potential urban rivals in Alberta. By the turn of

279

the century, the CPR had consolidated Calgary's position as a rail centre with lines to Edmonton and the United States border.[48] Extensive freight facilities, begun in 1898 and extended in 1903 and again in 1910, made the city unquestionably the CPR headquarters west of Winnipeg. It was estimated in 1907 that the railway yards were worth over a million dollars annually to the city. On average, seven hundred cars were switched daily over twenty miles of track, while handling and maintenance gave employment to over three hundred men.[49] In 1912, the CPR chose Calgary as the site for its second repair and maintenance shops in the west. Construction of the Ogden shops was easily the biggest economic fillip the city received until the oil boom of the late forties. Covering 213 acres and offering continuous employment for twelve hundred men, the Ogden shops handled up to 525 locomotive and freight repairs monthly.[50] As the railway was Winnipeg's largest single employer, so it was Calgary's.

280

Moose Jaw's emergence as the industrial capital of Saskatchewan and a potential rival to Regina was due primarily to the CPR's decision to make it the headquarters of rail operations in that region. By 1927, no fewer than ten lines radiated from the city, while the CPR yards with their hundred miles of track were the third largest privately owned terminals in western Canada.[51] The presence of extensive stockyard and wholesale facilities further consolidated Moose Jaw's position as a major marketing and distributing centre for a rich rural hinterland.

Vancouver's rapid development after 1887 was almost entirely due to the CPR and its plan to make the city a major gateway for international trade. Between that year and 1890 the railway spent heavily on waterfront, freight handling and maintenance facilities. Almost $300,000 were spent on the last two categories in 1888 alone. It was estimated in the same year that ten per cent of the city's total population was in the CPR's employ, and three years later, the company was the source of about twelve per cent of all wages paid in Vancouver.[52] In this period, Vancouver had not yet begun to eclipse Victoria, and the frenzy of economic activity was all but completely the result of the heavy CPR building program.[53]

Vancouver's situation was repeated, though not so dramatically, at the Lakehead. In the early nineties the CPR is said to have spent a million dollars preparing Fort William as a major terminal point for switching grain from rail to steamer.[54] Similarly, the railway was instrumental in cementing Nanaimo's urban status. When the CPR took over the Esquimalt and Nanaimo railway in 1908, the latter community's location next to coal deposits coupled with Vancouver's energy demands enabled Nanaimo to expand significantly, becoming, according to one source "Vancouver's front door."[55] In southern Alberta, the CPR's arrival with rail acquisition and construction and irrigation transformed Lethbridge from a small coal town to the marketing and distribution centre for the area.[56]

Aside from consolidation of centralized rail facilities in favoured centres, the company aided towns' economic development directly in a variety of ways. Sometimes it was as simple as reduced rates on city and district goods headed out for exhibitions and fairs. Occasionally, special freight rate arrangements of a broader scope were conceded. Often, assistance came in the form of advice. The town of Cranbrook, for example, sought the railway's opinion on the disposal of some difficult waterworks bonds.[57] Medicine Hat and Calgary received free use of CPR equipment in their probes for natural gas during the nineties.[58] Bassano, Penticton and Medicine Hat were able to build hospitals because of company assistance.[59] Indeed, the railway's gifts of land to municipalities for needed facilities was an important, tangible way in which it came to the aid of financially strapped frontier towns. Swift Current's very survival was assured by the CPR, virtually the sole economic contributor to the community before 1903.[60] The centralization of irrigation management at Calgary in 1903 greatly helped that city in its quest for regional dominance in south and south-central Alberta. The St. Boniface markets were financed fifty per cent by the CPR. The company also kept the public schools open for a time in Laggan and Swift Current.[61]

While towns and cities welcomed all aid, their greatest plea was for revenue-generating enterprises. Beyond its rail services, the company spurred urban development by building stockyard facilities and hotels. Calgary offers an excellent example of the importance of the former type of installation. The establishment of stockyards there in 1886 signalled Calgary's displacement of Fort MacLeod as the headquarters of the burgeoning range-cattle industry. Within a few years, an assortment of related manufacturing enterprises had sprung up around the stockyards as Calgary exploited its first industrial base.[62] The same process occurred to a lesser extent in St. Boniface, Moose Jaw, Red Deer, Medicine Hat, Maple Creek and High River.

Hotels were extremely important in the urbanization process. They encouraged visitors, stimulated commerce and provided temporary residences as well as supplying vital focal points for society. Between 1886 and 1927, the CPR built splendid palaces in Vancouver, Victoria, Calgary, Winnipeg and Regina,[63] while aiding in the construction of smaller hotel facilities in Moose Jaw, Fort William, Sicamous and Penticton. The CPR hotels were dominant structures—usually architectural showpieces as well as the social centres of the cities they served.

The formation in 1912 of the company's natural resources department heralded a new era in land policy. With a mandate to develop the land grants profitably, the new department operated out of Calgary for reasons of centrality and had eight separate branches.[64] The industrial branch was vested with the promotion of urban development. Agents all over the west worked with private and public citizens' groups to foster economic growth in individual towns. The branch's main purpose was to attract viable commercial enterprises, preferably those which tapped regional resources. With this move, the CPR had transformed its role from that of direct benefactor to one of partnership with urban groups in the pursuit of mutually advantageous goals. Unchanged, however, was the railway's long-cherished vision of integrating urban growth with the development of hinterland resources.

Examples of the work of a CPR industrial agent in the twenties include the establishment of Imperial Oil warehouses at Manyberries, a McDonald jam factory at Nelson, an ore concentrator at Allenby, a brick and tile plant in Vancouver, a tire and rubber factory at Medicine Hat, fruit warehouses in Victoria, a hotel in Creston and a general store in Patricia.[65] The travelling agent usually met with the board of trade or town council to discuss specific needs and opportunities. He then tapped the company's extensive communication and information networks in Canada and the United States to find potential investors. Once he had made a contact, a meeting was arranged. Even when negotiations reached the practical stage of location, the railway remained involved with respect to site selection and extension of rail facilities when and if necessary. Beyond bringing industry to towns, the industrial branch was interested generally in new commercial prospects. A good example of this is the branch's work to develop a potato-flour industry in southern Alberta in the twenties.[66]

282

The company's efforts to promote urban development must be weighed against a corresponding retrograde or negative dimension. On occasion, CPR actions actually impeded urban growth. Moreover, the company's benevolence in terms of economic assistance to towns and cities must be balanced with the price these communities had to pay. As in site selection, the company was forever mindful of financial considerations.

The most flagrant example of the CPR impeding growth is the taxation controversy in the early period with Calgary, Regina, Moose Jaw and other towns under the control of the Canada North-West Land Company.[67] The company refused to pay municipal taxes on the grounds that it was exempt by contract. Since the Canada North-West Land Company was easily the largest landowner in all these towns,[68] the hard-pressed municipal administrations were in a serious dilemma. If they omitted the Canada North-West Land Company from the assessment rolls, they forced residents to bear an inordinately high mill rate, but its inclusion in assessment translated into a significant shortfall in tax collection. In any case, the result was delay in the provision of important urban services: Calgary had no fire department when a conflagration destroyed the business section in 1886, and lack of revenues severely delayed necessary water and sewer connections in Moose Jaw and Regina.[69] It took hard bargaining by municipal bodies, with threats of higher political intervention, litigation and cancellation of the railway's monopoly clause, to make the point. The conflict was settled eventually by a series of individual compromise agreements in which the Canada North-West Land Company agreed to a fractional payment of its taxes.[70]

Lethbridge's failure to develop into a major urban coal centre can be traced indirectly to unfavourable CPR policies. Although they were extensive, the coal deposits of southwest Alberta waited for a viable market that transcended regional demand. The CPR, a large user of this coal, chose not to develop the central Canadian market by the concession of lower freight rates.[71]

Towns and cities had to pay financially for CPR largesse. It cost Calgary a flat $25,000 grant to get freighting facilities in 1898.[72] Similarly, the Palliser Hotel was built subject to agreement on a fixed annual assessment of four thousand dollars, plus a provision that the city would never ask for further concessions or increases because of local improvements.[73] Property in the vicinity of the million-dollar Palliser was valued at about a thousand dollars a frontage foot at the time of this agreement, and in 1911, with land assessed at fair value and buildings at fifty per cent of actual value, the city was paying considerably for the coveted hotel. The Ogden shops cost Calgary dearly as well. Although the shops were fully three miles from the city limits, council agreed to construct a connecting road, bridge and street railway, furnish power at cost and, moreover, absolve the CPR of its obligations for construction of subways under its tracks.[73] The interesting point is that cities like Calgary were all too happy to meet the company's demands for such facilities. Indeed, the rivalry between western towns for the repair shops had been intense and at times bitter. It was only natural from the pragmatic CPR viewpoint that the lucky recipients should pay a price.

The importance of railway largesse, as evidenced by the frequent urban appeals for favours, was reflected publicly by the presence of so many self styled "CPR towns."[75] At one time or another, most towns across the main line manifested their enduring loyalty to the company.[76] Visiting CPR dignitaries were received royally by admiring town councils and boards of trade. In larger centres, resident senior rail officials were acknowledged leaders in local business circles, and in the early years sometimes wielded direct influence in municipal affairs. Although dependence on the company diminished in the cities as growth occurred in other sectors, the situation was different in smaller places, where the presence of the railway station was the sole pledge of continued existence. By the twenties the company was carefully assessing its interests in small-town western Canada, and in many instances its predilections were not for future development.[77]

The CPR played a major role in determining urban landscapes. Particularly in the early years, it operated arbitrarily in land-use designation, choice of transportation corridors and the placement of strategic facilities. These decisions were crucial in shaping the future growth patterns of towns and cities and were thus of vital significance in defining the physical face of urban western Canada.

If the company had a blueprint beyond site selection and the subdivision of townsite lots, it focussed on the location of the railway depot. A crucial deciding factor here was the placement of the station relative to the track. The direction of town growth would be decided by whether it was put on the north or south side of the rails. A familiar urban pattern across western Canada was a nucleus of commercial establishments and service facilities around the railway station. The railway usually reinforced this pattern by upgrading its station, with beautification and modernization of facilities,[78] and building hotels in larger communities. The station's commanding position in small towns simply emphasized in physical terms the dominance of the railroad, whereas in big centres it tended to pinpoint the heart of the business district.

Aside from the station, the physical presence of the rails themselves was an important ingredient in deciding land-use patterns. In Calgary, whole-sale facilities sprang up on one side of the tracks, effectively blocking retail expansion in that area and sandwiching Calgary's business district between the rails and the river.[79] In Winnipeg, the CPR rail facilities on the north side of the tracks attracted significant industrial activity. The result was the emergence of the North End as a clearly delineated district for the working man and the immigrant.[80] The original town of Regina was immediately south of its CPR station. The tracks acted as a buffer against northward expansion, with the result that Regina grew south and east, with its industrial concentration to the north.[81].

Another way in which the company influenced spatial development patterns was through its placement of important buildings and facilities. In new townsites, it usually donated land for churches, hospitals, post offices and civic buildings.[82] The choice of specific location was a company decision, however, and in many cases engendered debate and controversy. The location of these facilities was an important factor in deciding population growth and movement. In Calgary, for example, the CPR's insistence that the land for the town hall and police station be well to the east of the railway depot helped sustain growth in that area for several years.[83] In Vancouver, the CPR's choice of sites for its station, wharf, office and Hotel Vancouver along the Granville Street axis had the effect of moving urban development well to the west of the existing townsite.[84] Important recreational facilities like the exhibition grounds in Calgary and Regina tended to determine vehicular and even commercial and residential patterns. Both exhibition grounds owed their locations to the CPR. The same was true of schools: federal land allocations for school purposes in new townships were often inadequate, and the railway became actively involved in negotiations for additional land.[85]

As well as deciding street widths and subdivision locations, the CPR also influenced physical growth by its stipulations on residential and commercial lot sizes. Usually, residential lot frontages were kept small — forty feet or less — for maximum land-sale profits. Wealthier buyers who wished to live close to the business district did so simply by purchasing multiple lots and building on them. Since most were denied the luxury of this option, the CPR's penchant for narrow lot frontages led to the loosely concentrated, elongated pattern of residential land-use development so prevalent in prairie towns and cities.

The company was also largely responsible for the differentiation of residential districts in bigger centres. It achieved this by adjustments to land-sale policies in the new subdivisions that emerged during the period of rapid growth in the early years of the century. By varying lot sizes and changing the contours of street alignment, and through the imposition of stringent building restrictions, the CPR was able to preplan residential districts. The first exclusive residential suburbs in Vancouver and Calgary emerged as a direct result of these policies. The CPR developed Vancouver's Shaughnessy Heights as the city's most prestigious residential area.[86] Earlier, the CPR's variation on street layout had been a major factor in establishing West Vancouver as the premier residential district in the city.[87] In Calgary, the railway opened up the exclusive suburbs of Mount Royal and Sunalta in the southwest quarter. Their expansive lots and contoured streets, plus the ease of construction and the availability of utility services, were more than adequate compensation for the area's second-rate locality.[88] By 1912, the presence of huge, imposing edifices on the northern exposure of Mount Royal hill advertised Calgary's enclave of the privileged few. For similar practical reasons, the more remote high bluffs on the north side of the Bow River were set aside for modest development. Here, the CPR opened up the working-class suburb of Bridgeland.[89] The pattern thus established was reinforced over the years. Exclusive districts were contiguous to the Mount Royal area in the southwest, while north Calgary preserved its working-class orientation.

In smaller centres where the growth of separate subdivisions was less pronounced, the company contributed to differentiation on a much smaller scale by its policy of villa-lot reservation. Villa lots went on sale as large parcels of non-agricultural land and were usually located in areas of topographical excellence. Whether it were in Cranbrook, Lethbridge or Medicine Hat,[90] the CPR was able to adjust the focus of residential development.

It could be argued that the company's interest in urban land-sale profits had implications for physical growth patterns generally. This view emerged with special clarity in the period of rapid urban expansion between 1900 and 1912. With its extensive land holdings, the railway stood to profit handsomely from the speculation fever of these years. It welcomed municipal boundary extensions, and where possible, reserved land in anticipation of future development.[91] Whether in a burgeoning city like Calgary or a small town like Strathmore, the company seemed intent on playing the speculative game like everyone else.[92] The city of Calgary had no choice but to extend its corporate boundaries to include the railway's Ogden shops: it was an extension that added significantly to Calgary's gross area and contributed to the speculative rush touched off by CPR plans for adjacent communities.[93] Rampant urbanization was not restricted to Calgary; it was a phenomenon repeated across the prairie west. In this respect, the company's overt participation was in marked contrast to its long-standing operational strategy of coupling urban development with hinterland productivity.

The CPR contributed to the urbanization of western Canada in a number of other ways. The rise of several southeast Alberta towns was directly related to the company's extensive irrigation projects. The same was true with the mining towns of southwest Alberta and British Columbia. Indeed, the CPR's active role as coal merchant and its interest in natural gas potential had important repercussions for municipal policies in many towns and cities.[94] CPR employees played a vital role in the development of the western Canadian labour movement.[95] In some towns, the railway was directly involved in civic government.[96] And the rate structure it imposed had incalculable implications for the development of western Canadian industry:[97] the whole urban hierarchical structure of western Canada was underpinned to a large extent by the complicated system of freight rates.[98] Finally, there

285

were the trains themselves. For almost this entire period, they provided the only link with the outside world. As such, they were the harbingers of change, and agents for the metropolitanism of an emerging continental urban society.

That the profit motive figured prominently in the CPR's role in the urbanization of western Canada is revealed most clearly in the site selection process. It is probable that the CPR created too many small towns across the prairie, partly to make the townsite business as lucrative as possible. The opportunity of quick profits was also behind the CPR's participation in the pre-1914 speculative binge which led to the gross over-extension of most urban places in western Canada.

On the other hand, it is difficult to minimize the positive role played by the CPR in the urbanization of the west, and downright impossible to ignore the scope of its involvement. The origins and subsequent growth patterns of most towns and cities in western Canada were decided by the CPR. Within the economic parameters provided by its function as a private enterprise corporation, the railway generally acted practically and according to the temper of the times. Except for a brief aberration during the boom period, the CPR was consistent in its desire to build an urban west that complemented the needs and resources of a rural economy.

286

Notes

1. Alan F.J. Artibise, "Boosterism and the Development of Prairie Cities, 1871–1913," in Alan F. J. Artibise, ed., *Town and City: Aspects of Western Canadian Urban Development* (Regina: Canadian Plains Research Centre; University of Regina, 1981), p. 209.
2. For details as well as an excellent discussion on the origins of urban western Canada, see Alan F.J. Artibise, "The Urban West: The Evolution of Prairie Towns and Cities to 1930," *Prairie Forum* 4, no. 2 (Fall 1979): pp. 237–62.
3. *Ibid.*
4. Major branch-line acquisitions included the Manitoba South-Western Colonization Railway, the Manitoba and North-Western Railway of Canada, the Great North-West Central Railway, the Calgary and Edmonton Railway and the Alberta Railway and Irrigation Company.
5. Artibise, "The Urban West."
6. *Ibid.*
7. Artibise, "Boosterism," p. 209.
8. Especially the line through the Crowsnest Pass, which opened up the mining areas of the pass and the Kootenays.
9. By 1911 the rival transcontinental system of the Canadian Northern and the Grand Trunk Pacific had extended its influence into western Canada.
10. Winnipeg, Vancouver, Calgary, Regina, Moose Jaw, Brandon, Lethbridge, Medicine Hat and Portage la Prairie: only Edmonton and Saskatoon were not dependent on the CPR, but even these two cities were connected by CPR branch lines.
11. The main thrusts of new line construction in this period were in the northern regions of Alberta and Saskatchewan and the direction of Hudson Bay.
12. For a good discussion, see J. William Brennan, "Business-Government Co-operation in Townsite Promotion in Regina and Moose Jaw, 1882–1903," in Artibise, *Town and City*, p. 102.
13. Donald A. Smith and R.B. Angus represented the CPR: E.B. Osler and W.B. Scarth represented the Canada North-West Land Company.
14. "Outline of History of the Company's Land Grants," *CPR Report Calgary*, 1959, Glenbow-Alberta Institute (hereafter Glenbow), p. 12.
15. A good synopsis of the objection to the southern route appeared in the Toronto *Globe*, 3 March 1883.
16. G.P. de T. Glazebrook, *A History of Transportation in Canada* (Toronto: McClelland and Stewart, 1964), ii, p. 83.
17. "Outline of History," Glenbow, p. 4.

18. In Calgary, for example, the CPR changed its route plans repeatedly, and as late as March 1883, five months before the arrival of rail, rumours abounded that the line would bypass Calgary altogether.
19. Elizabeth Arthur, "Inter-urban Rivalry in Port Arthur and Fort William, 1870-1907," in Anthony W. Rasporich, ed., *Western Canada Past and Present* (Calgary: University of Calgary; McClelland and Stewart West, 1975), pp. 58-68.
20. *Ibid.*, p. 59.
21. *Ibid.*, p. 61.
22. *Ibid.*, p. 62.
23. This was the Pembina branch that provided an interim rail connection to the east by way of the American system.
24. R.C. Bellan, "Rails Across the Red-Selkirk-Winnipeg," *Papers Read Before the Historical and Scientific Society of Manitoba* ser. 3, no. 17 (1960–61), p. 71.
25. Alan F.J. Artibise, *Winnipeg, A Social History of Urban Growth, 1874–1914* (Montreal: McGill-Queen's University Press, 1975), p. 73.
26. *Ibid.*, p. 74.
27. For a good discussion of early Vancouver, see Robert A. McDonald, "City Building in the Canadian West: A Case Study of Economic Growth in Early Vancouver," *B.C. Studies* 43 (Autumn 1979): 3-28.
28. Paul Voisey, "The Urbanization of Western Canada, 1871–1916," *Histoire sociale/Social History* 8, no. 15 (May 1975): 80-81.
29. Max Foran, "Early Calgary, 1875–1895: The Controversy Surrounding the Townsite Location, and the Direction of Town Expansion," in R.A. McCormack and Ian MacPherson, eds., *Cities in the West: Papers of the Western Canada Urban History Conference — University of Winnipeg, October 1974* (Ottawa: National Museums of Man, Mercury Series, History Division Paper no. 10, 1975), pp. 26-45.
30. Brennan, "Business-Government Co-operation," p. 38.
31. W.A. Riddell, *Regina: From Pile o'Bones to Queen City of the Plains* (Burlington: Windsor Publications, 1981), p. 19.
32. Voisey, "The Urbanization of Western Canada," p. 81.
33. *Ibid.*
34. H. John Selwood, "The Hudson's Bay Company and Fort Qu'Appelle Townsite Development up to 1921," *Regina Geographical Studies* 3 (1980): 1–11.
35. *Ibid.*
36. J.W. McCracken, "Yorkton District During the Territorial Period, 1882-1905," *Saskatchewan History* 8, no. 3 (Autumn 1975): 95-109.
37. H.W. Winkler, "Early Manitoba Railroads," *Papers Read Before the Historical and Scientific Society of Manitoba* ser. 3, no. 10 (1953-54): 5.
38. John Gilpin, "Failed Metropolis: The City of Strathcona, 1891-1912," in Artibise, *Town and City*, pp. 259-88.
39. *Canadian Pacific Facts and Figures* (Montreal: Canadian Pacific Foundation Library, 1937), p. 156.
40. "Outline of History," Glenbow, p. 13.
41. Report prepared by Department of National Resources, 1916, Glenbow, CPR Papers, box 39, p. 459.
42. It was assumed that the presence of a railway siding necessarily meant townsite development.
43. For example, Calgary referred to itself at various times as the "Chicago of Canada," the "Denver of Canada" and the "Pittsburgh of Canada." Some may wonder at the latter comparison: it was made following a reputed iron-ore discovery in Alberta.
44. The best discussion of this is in Artibise, "Boosterism."
45. Artibise, *Winnipeg*, pp. 61-102.
46. *Factors in Railway and Steamship Operation* (Montreal: Canadian Pacific Foundation Library, 1937), pp. 68-70.
47. *Canadian Pacific Facts and Figures*, p. 135.
48. The line to Edmonton was completed in 1891 and taken over by the CPR. The extension to Fort Macleod, and later to the U.S. border via Lethbridge, was also undertaken in the nineties.
49. See Max Foran, *Calgary, Canada's Frontier Metropolis* (Burlington: Windsor Publications, 1982), p. 76.
50. *Canadian Pacific Facts and Figures*, page 135.
51. "Moose Jaw Diamond Jubilee Celebration, 1927," Glenbow.
52. Robert McDonald, "City building," p. 10.
53. Norbert McDonald, "The Canadian Pacific Railway and Vancouver's Development to 1900," *B.C. Studies* 35 (Autumn 1977): p. 21.
54. Arthur, "Inter-urban Rivalry," p. 62.
55. Norman Gidney, "From Coal to Forest Products: The Changing Resource Base of Nanaimo, B.C.," *Urban History Review* no. 1-78: 32.
56. For a good discussion of Lethbridge's early urban development, see A.A. den Otter, "Lethbridge: Outpost of a Commercial Empire, 1885-1906," in Artibise, *Town and City*, pp. 177-204.
57. Correspondence of P.L. Naismith to Col. J.S. Dennis, 20 April 1912, Glenbow, CPR Papers, box 1, p. 2.

287

58. Calgary *Tribune*, 11 April 1888; *Alberta Motorist*, March 1963.
59. James C. Bonar, "Canadian Pacific Railway Co. and Its Contributions Towards the Early Development and to the Continued Progress of Canada," vol. 4, "Transportation, Traffic, Citizenship, Educational and Departmental Construction," Glenbow.
60. Don C. McGowan, *Grassland Settlers* (Regina: Canadian Plains Research Centre; University of Regina, 1975), p. 19.
61. Bonar, "Canadian Pacific Railway Co."
62. For a fuller discussion, see M.L. Foran, "Urban Calgary 1884–1895," *Histoire sociale/Social History* 5 (May 1973): 61–76.
63. See Hardy D. Kalman, "The Railway Hotels and the Development of the Chateau Style in Canada" (University of Victoria, Maltwood Museum Studies in Architectural History, no. 1, 1948); also, *Canadian Pacific Facts and Figures*, pp. 87–100.
64. Executive, Agricultural and Animal Industry, Development, Engineering, Coal Mines, Forestry, Industrial and Accounting branches.
65. Letterbooks of travelling industrial agent, 1920–21, Glenbow, CPR Papers.
66. *Ibid.*
67. Brennan, "Business-Government Co-operation," 106–16; M.L. Foran, "Calgary Town Council 1884–1895: A Study of Local Government in a Frontier Environment" (master's thesis, University of Calgary, 1970), pp. 17–18.
68. In Calgary the NWLC's 1887 taxes amounted to approximately sixty per cent of the total levy.
69. Brennan, "Business-Government Co-operation," p. 112.
70. *Ibid.*; Calgary *Herald*, 21 August 1889.
71. A.A. den Otter, "Railways and Alberta's Coal Problem, 1880–1960," in Rasporich, *Western Canada Past and Present*, p. 97.
72. "City Agreement with the CPR" 23 August 1898, Glenbow, City Clerk Files, box 5, p. 410.
73. "Memorandum of Agreement between City of Calgary and the CPR, 1911," Glenbow, City Clerk Files, box 51, p. 408.
74. See city Clerk Files, box 48, p. 323; also, "Calgary Council Minutes,' 10–11 February, 21 June and 13 December 1911.
75. Particularly Vancouver and Calgary.
76. Usually these sentiments of loyalty were most strident when the town in question was asking a favour.
77. Glenbow, CPR Papers, box 14, p. 174. Referred to specifically is a 1933 comment by P.L. Naismith, land branch manager, that the CPR should unload all its townsite holdings since towns were "as big as they ever will be."
78. Gardens were a popular innovational feature, e.g. in Calgary and Victoria.
79. For a further discussion of this phenomenon, see Max Foran, "Land Development Patterns in Calgary 1884–1945," in Alan F.J. Artibise and G.A. Stelter, eds., *The Usable Urban Past: Planning and Politics in the Modern Canadian City* (Toronto: Macmillan of Canada, 1979), pp. 293–315.
80. Artibise, *Winnipeg*, pp. 158–59.
81. George A. Nader, *Cities of Canada*, vol. 2, *Profiles of Fifteen Metropolitan Centres* (Toronto: Macmillan of Canada, 1976), p. 302.
82. The company's generosity subsided somewhat with time: by the early twentieth century, it was charging fractional land values to religious and other institutions.
83. "Calgary Council Minutes," 11 March and 19 April 1885, Glenbow.
84. Norbert McDonald, "The Canadian Pacific Railway," p. 13.
85. *Canadian Pacific Facts and Figures*.
86. McDonald, "The Canadian Pacific Railway," p. 12.
87. *Ibid.*
88. See the Calgary *Optimist*, 18 December 1909. The CPR was able to enforce the building requirements inserted into land-sale agreements in the Mount Royal area.
89. In terms of site appeal, Bridgeland is far superior to Mount Royal, but its inaccessibility to roads and utilities made it a second-rate district in 1909.
90. For examples, see Glenbow, CPR Papers, box 1, p. 1, 2.
91. Correspondence of P.L. Naismith, 26 June 1912, Glenbow, CPR Papers, box 13, p. 165.
92. On Stratmore, for example, see correspondence of Naismith, e May 1912, Glenbow, CPR Papers, box 1, p. 1.
93. Land Branch correspondence, 5 December 1922, Glenbow, CPR Papers, box 13, p. 165.
94. For a good example of this involvement, see correspondence of Naismith re Lethbridge, 25 June 1912, Glenbow, CPR Papers, box 1, p. 2.
95. For instance, the radical element in the Calgary union movement was supplied by CPR employees. See E. Taraska, "The Calgary Craft Union Movement 1900–1920" (master's thesis, University of Calgary, 1975), pp. 51–69.
96. Norbert McDonald discusses this direct involvement in Vancouver in his "Canadian Pacific Railway."

97. For a good discussion, see Kenneth H. Norrie, "The National Policy and Prairie Economic Discrimination 1870-1930," in D.H. Akenson, ed., *Canadian Papers in Rural History* vol. 1 (Gananoque: Langdale Press, 1978); also, Voisey, "The Urbanization of Western Canada," p. 93.
98. See Donald Kerr, "Wholesale Trade on the Canadian Plains in the Late Nineteenth Century: Winnipeg and Its Competition," in Howard Palmer, ed., *The Settlement of the West* (Calgary: University of Calgary; Comprint Publishing Company, 1977), pp. 130-52.

289

Topic Eight

Women and Social Reform

Social reform was a logical by-product of the growth of urban-industrial Canada. As immigrants settled in cities more rapidly than they could be adequately accommodated, as industrial waste blighted the urban environment, and as factories created unhealthy working conditions, the cry for social reform became general.

Underlying the various reform movements — women's suffrage, prohibition, urban and agrarian reform — was a socially oriented approach to Christianity known as "the social gospel movement" which developed among the Protestant denominations. It provided much of the impetus and often the justification for other reform movements. In "The Social Gospel and the Reform Tradition in Canada," Richard Allen explains the historical context for the rise of the social gospel movement, analysing its major assumptions and its impact.

A group of middle-class women became active in social reform. These "new women" demanded a more prominent role in establishing the moral well-being of society, advocating a philosophy of "maternal feminism" to guard their home and family. "Maternal feminism" was premised on the following beliefs: that as procreators and nurturers, women had a moral obligation to create a strong and healthy race, that as "asexual beings" they had a responsibility to purify society of evils such as prostitution; and that as guardians of the family, they had a duty to rid society of alcoholism.

In "Race Regeneration and Social Purity: A Study of the Social Attitudes of Canada's English-Speaking Suffragists," Carol Bacchi examines the reasons why women social reformers concerned themselves with the issues of race regeneration and social purity. She shows how these ideas fitted into a traditional view of women. In "The WCTU: 'For God, Home and Native Land': A Study in Nineteenth-Century Feminism," Wendy Mitchinson analyses the ideas of the members of the Women's Christian Temperance Union. She outlines how they arrived at their positions towards prohibition, women's suffrage, and religion.

The social gospel is discussed in greater depth in Richard Allen's *The Social Passion: Religion and Social Reform in Canada, 1914-28* (Toronto: University of Toronto Press, 1971). John Thompson examines the social reform movements of the war years in " 'The Beginning of Our Regeneration': The Great War and Western Canadian Reform Movements," Canadian Historical Association *Historical Papers* (1972): 227-245, and his book-length study *The Harvests of War: The Prairie West, 1914-1918* (Toronto: McClelland and Stewart, 1978). R.C. Brown and R. Cook's *Canada, 1896-1921: A Nation Transformed* (Toronto: McClelland and Stewart, 1974), contains two chapters that give an excellent overview of social reform: "O Brave New World . . ." (Ch. 15) and ". . . That Has Such People In't" (Ch. 16).

Wayne Roberts's " 'Rocking the Cradle for the World': The New Woman and Maternal Feminism, Toronto 1877-1914," in *A Not Unreasonable Claim: Women and Reform in Canada 1880-1920*, edited by Linda Kealey (Toronto: Women's Press, 1979): 15-45, explains the origins, nature, and ultimate decline of the "new woman" who provided the impetus behind the social reform movements at the turn of the century. Carol Bacchi examines in greater depth the ideas and activities of the English-Canadian suffragettes in *Liberation Deferred? The Ideas of the English-Canadian Suffragists, 1877-1918* (Toronto: University of Toronto Press, 1983), while Deborah Gorham's "Singing Up the Hill," *Canadian Dimension*, 10 (June 1975): 25-38, traces the history of the Canadian woman's suffrage movement.

291

The period 1880 to 1920 witnessed the rise of a number of national women's organizations, which became forums for the women's social reform zeal. Wendy Mitchinson's study of the Women's Christian Temperance Union can be supplemented by her article, "The YWCA and Reform in the Nineteenth Century," *Histoire Sociale/Social History*, 12 (1979): 368-384; and Veronica Strong-Boag's "The Roots of Modern Canadian Feminism: The National Council of Women, 1893-1929," *Canada: An Historical Magazine*, 3 (December 1975): 22-33, and her " 'Setting the Stage': National Organization and the Women's Movement in the Late 19th Century," in *The Neglected Majority: Essays in Canadian Women's History*, edited by S.M. Trofimenkoff and A. Prentice (Toronto: McClelland and Stewart, 1977) pp. 87-103. A useful collection on women and social reform is *A Not Unreasonable Claim* (already cited and from which two of the articles in this section have been taken). A useful bibliography on women's history is B. Light and V. Strong-Boag, *True Daughters of the North: Canadian Women's History: An Annotated Bibliography* (Toronto: Ontario Institute for Studies in Education, 1980).

The Social Gospel and the Reform Tradition in Canada, 1890–1928*

RICHARD ALLEN

The literature of social reform has not been extensive in Canada even though a sizable movement of reform was abroad in the land from the 1890s through the 1930s, a movement that was found in church and in secular society, and at municipal, provincial, and, progressively, federal levels. In the last chapter of his *Progressive Party in Canada,* Morton sees the decline of that party as a result in part of the waning of the impulse towards reform in society as a whole. Underlying and accompanying the movement towards reform through the political system had been the social gospel, a movement of which the most important function was to forge links between proposed reforms and the religious heritage of the nation, thus endowing reform with an authority it could not otherwise command. At the same time it attempted to create the religious and social attitudes thought necessary for life in a world reformed. But the world proved too intractable for the realization of the movement's high socio-religious hopes, and in the wake of the frustrating experiences of the early 1920s, supporters of the social gospel, and other reform movements, took different paths; some withdrew from politics, some retreated to pragmatic politics, some transferred their enthusiasm to other causes (notably peace movements and personal religion), and others moved towards a new radicalism. The reform movement may be viewed from many standpoints, but only when it is looked at as a religious manifestation, a striving to embed ultimate human goals in the social, economic and political order, is its success and failure fully appreciated. The history of the social gospel in Canada is an account of that process.

The social gospel rested on the premise that Christianity was a social religion, concerned, when the misunderstanding of the ages was stripped away, with the quality of human relations on this earth. More dramatically, it was a call for men to find the meaning of their lives in seeking to realize the kingdom of God in the very fabric of society. It was a measure of the radicalism implicit in the Social Gospel that the Methodist church in 1918 called for complete social reconstruction by a transfer of the basis of society from competition to co-operation. It was a measure of the conservatism inevitably associated with such a call that even some of the most radical supporters of the social gospel believed that in the family as they knew it, and in the political democracy of their time, two essential elements of the society toward which Jesus pointed men were already in existence, or virtually so. Such a reduction was necessary to apply a pan-historical and transcendent concept to immediate needs. And without

*From *Canadian Historical Review*, XLIX (1968): 381–399. Reprinted by permission of the author and the University of Toronto Press.

292

such reduction the reform movement would have enjoyed considerably less power.

The Protestant background out of which the Canadian social gospel had to emerge was one dominated overwhelmingly by the Anglican, Methodist, and Presbyterian churches. The similarities and disparities in the social outlook of these churches prior to the onset of depression in the late nineteenth century may be suggested by their reactions to a strike of the Toronto Printers' Union in 1872. The Anglican *Church Herald* condemned the labourers for usurping the role of the employer and blamed the strike upon "the insidious whimperings of a foreign-born league." The *Presbyterian Witness* argued that labour's campaign "strikes at the very root of . . . personal independence and perpetuates their social demoralisation. . . . No man ever rose above a lowly condition who thought more of his class than of his individuality." The Methodist *Christian Guardian* declared a profound sympathy with all honest workingmen and a sincere desire for their betterment, but went on to say: "we seriously question the wisdom and advantage of this movement — especially the strikes to which it is likely to lead."[1] When news of Henry George's Anti-Poverty Society reached Toronto in 1887, the other two churches would probably have echoed the response of the *Christian Guardian* on 29 June: "We have no faith in the abolition of poverty by any laws that can be made in legislatures. . . . The best anti-poverty society is an association of men who would adopt as their governing principles in life, industry, sobriety, economy and intelligence." Such an individualistic ethic was unable, however, to withstand the combined onslaught of extended depression, the rapid growth of industrial urban centres, and the spread of new social conceptions.

It has been argued that the social gospel in Canada was an indigenous development.[2] Although it is possible that a Canadian social gospel might have developed simply in response to domestic urban and industrial problems, it did not in fact happen that way. To be sure, the earliest expressions of the social gospel in Canada may still lie in sources untouched by historians' hands. And in those sources, the rise of the social gospel may be obscured by the gradual nature of its separation from older forms of Christian social expression characterized by a concern for church-state relations, education, political corruption, and personal and social vice. But almost all evidence regarding the emergence of the social gospel from this tradition points to currents of thought and action which were sweeping the western world, none of which originated in Canada. To trace this "North Atlantic triangle" of culture and religion underlying the social gospel at large and its transmission to and development within Canada is a worthy but massive project. In this paper, only a description of some of its salient features can be attempted.

The inspiration of the pioneers of the social gospel in Canada and the origin of some of its prominent institutions reveal the extent of its indebtedness. W. A. Douglass in the 1880s expressed his disagreement with individualistic methods of social regeneration by tirelessly campaigning for Henry George's panacea of the single tax.[3] Salem Bland, later to become the philosopher and mentor of the movement, was an omnivorous reader, and in the decade of the 1890s when he seems to have first formulated a social gospel outlook, was especially influenced by Carlyle, Tennyson, Emerson, Channing and Thoreau, by the historical critics of scripture, and by Albert Ritschl, the great German theologian whose optimistic theology played a great role in the emergence of a social gospel theology. At least as significant for Bland was the literature of evolution.[4] The notes for his first socialist lecture, "Four Steps and a Vision," acknowledge various works of Darwin, Drummond's *Ascent of Man,* and Kidd's *Social Evolution,* as well as *Fabian Essays,* Arnold Toynbee, Edward Bellamy, and Henry George.[5] Canadians had attended the three great interdenominational conferences in the United States on social problems in 1887, 1889, and 1893, and one follow-up conference had been held in Montreal in the latter year.[6] Institutional vehicles and expressions of the social gospel such as the Brotherhoods, institutional churches, settlements and labour churches derived ultimately from British models, although American mediation and modification took place in some instances. This pattern of influence continued throughout the life of the social gospel in Canada.

294

The optimism of the social gospel drew on more than a generalized sense of progress, and even on more than the influence of evolutionary concepts. One of the more significant religious developments of the nineteenth century was the expansion of evangelicalism — expressed variously in German pietism, the Methodism of the English-speaking world, the missionary movement, and American revivalism. As against the reformed tradition of Calvinism, evangelicalism stressed free will, an immanent God, religious emotion, and a restrictive personal and social morality which made its followers formidably austere. Among its doctrines was a belief in the possibility of personal perfection beyond the temptation of sin. In the course of the nineteenth century it made an immense impact on all Christian traditions, especially in North America. As evangelicalism became more diffused in the latter half of the century and awareness of the social problem arose, the individualism of the evangelical way seemed to many to be less and less appropriate.[7] The demand "save this man, now" became "save this society, now," and the slogan "the evangelization of the world in our generation" became "the Christianization of the world in our generation."[8] The sense of an immanent God working in the movement of revival and awakening was easily transferred to social movements, and hence to the whole evolution of society. Thus Josiah Strong in the United States could speak of the "great social awakening," and many could come to view secular social action as a religious rite.

Such combinations of ideas and impulses were apparent in a sermon given to the first Brotherhood group in Canada on 14 April 1895. Speaking on "Social Resurrection," J. B. Silcox argued that Jesus' "resurrection means that humanity shall rise . . . into higher, nobler, diviner conditions of life." He joined several British thinkers, preachers, and writers, he said, in predicting a worldwide revolution for the people in the twentieth century. "This uprising of the people is divine in its source. . . . God is in the midst of it. . . . To the ecclesiastical and industrial Pharaohs of today, God is saying, 'Let my people go.'" He concluded by calling for "a political faith in Jesus" based on the charter of the Sermon on the Mount.[9] C. S. Eby in *The World Problem and the Divine Solution* (1914) was somewhat more philosophical in expression. Jesus Christ was the "type of coming man on this planet." The ultimate reality of which Christ was the revelation was in and through all things: "the universal spirit of Christ would reconstruct man and mankind." Trade unionism, socialism, and business organization were a work of this spirit developing a new social order.[10] On this basis Eby built his Socialist church in Toronto in 1909.[11] Many influences from the world of letters, science, religion, and reform were held in solution in the social gospel in various proportions. Few distilled the solution as did Douglass, Bland, Silcox, and Eby, and while they might be more radical than most, their thought represented the tendency of the movement as a whole.

295

The pressures of the last years of depression in the early 1890s precipitated a quickening interest in new forms of social thought and action among a growing group of Christian ministers and laymen. One of the most important centres of this interest was the Queen's Theological Alumni Conference, instituted by Principal G. M. Grant in 1893. At its annual meetings, the conference discussed papers on such topics as biblical criticism, economic development, the problems of poverty, socialistic schemes, the single tax, social evolution, interpretations of modern life by modern poets, studies of the prophets, Tolstoi, the relation of legislation and morality, and Christianity in its relation to human progress. As a Methodist minority among Presbyterians, Salem Bland was probably the most radical of the regular members.[12] At the beginning of the decade a pirated edition of General William Booth's *In Darkest England and the Way Out* was selling vigorously.[13] Booth's scheme, involving the establishment of labour exchanges, farm colonies and industrial towns, model suburban villages, paid holidays, and an intelligence service for processing useful social data, was branded by some as socialistic, but encouraged others to view social action as an essential part of true religion.[14] Two Canadian ministers, S. S. Craig and Herbert Casson, taking their cue from John Trevor in Manchester, attempted to found labour churches. Nothing more is known of Craig's venture in Toronto,[15] but Casson's attempt at Lynn, Massachusetts, lasted from 1893 to 1898, after which he became a well-known socialist lecturer in Canada as well as the United States.[16] The Congregationalist layman, T. B. Macaulay, in 1894 brought the Brotherhood movement from England to Montreal, whence its "brief, bright and brotherly" meetings, which mixed gospel songs with social reform, spread across the nation.[17]

Among social problems, those of slums and immigration prompted the larger part of the institutional response of the social gospel within the churches. Again, it was in the last decade of nineteenth century that the more ambitious innovations were undertaken with the establishment of St. Andrew's Institute in 1890 by the Presbyterian, D. J. Macdonnell, and the Fred Victor Mission in 1894 by a Methodist group under the impetus of the Massey family. Together providing facilities for night school, library, savings bank, nursery, clubrooms, gymnasium, medical centre, and restaurant, they reflected ventures pioneered in England, Scotland, and the United States in the previous decade.[18] Further institutional response to urban problems came after 1902 with the development of settlement houses by Miss Sara Libby Carson, working under the Presbyterian church. By 1920 there were at least thirteen settlements, in Canada, probably all of them formed under the impulse of the social gospel.[19] Where Miss Carson was not involved directly as organizer, she was often associated as consultant, as in the cases of the Toronto and McGill University settlements (1907 and 1909 respectively), which grew out of social concern in the student YMCAs. When the University of Toronto opened its Department of Social Service in 1914, the University Settlement provided the framework for practical work, and Miss Carson and the Rev. F. N. Stapleford of the Neighbourhood Workers' Association, among others, were recruited as lecturers.[20] Under J. S. Woodsworth, the settlement approach to the problems of north Winnipeg became a more potent spearhead of social reform, and the beginning, for Woodsworth, of an ever more radical formulation of the social gospel.[21]

In the 1890s, the churches were deeply involved in a mounting campaign against "drink." This was rationalized by leading figures such as F. S. Spence as part of the great gospel of liberty.[22] Significantly, however, a rude sort of environmentalism was creeping into the "ideology" of prohibition, placing it in the context of a reform programme based on the strategy of reform Darwinism: that the way to reform the individual was through alterations in his environment. As a wider array of social problems began to engage the minds of clergy and laymen alike, new committees and church structures were required. The Methodist Committee on Sociological Questions from 1894 to 1918 presented to general conference ever more progressive and comprehensive reports for church guidance. By 1914 committees or departments of temperance and moral reform had become full boards of social service and evangelism. The social task had been placed alongside that of evangelism in the official hierarchy of concerns of the Methodist and Presbyterian churches, and committees of social service were common in the other denominations. In 1913, when Methodists and Presbyterians combined in a programme of social surveys of major Canadian cities (and some rural areas), a systematic attack, chiefly upon the complex environment of the cities, was in the making.[23]

In the background of this escalation of social gospel enterprise was an ambitious effort at institutional consolidation. The Church Union movement, initiated in 1902, was making headway, and in 1907, an alliance of church and labour groups, having won the Lord's Day Act, blossomed into the Moral and Social Reform Council of Canada, jointly headed by J. G. Shearer and T. A. Moore, social service secretaries of the Presbyterian and Methodist churches respectively. Although until the middle of the second decade the provincial units of the council were largely engrossed in temperance campaigns, for several years thereafter they promoted a broad programme of social reform and community action that won the praise of young radicals like William Ivens and William Irvine.[24] In 1913 the national organization changed its name to the Social Service Council of Canada and further broadened its perspectives.[25]

These years were exciting ones for progressive churchmen. Not only were they advancing their campaign to win the churches to what they called sociological concepts, but they were also making significant progress in liberalizing the restrictive personal disciplines of their denominations and gaining ground for historical criticism and a reformation of theological curricula.[26] During and after 1908 a lively discussion on the relation of Christianity to socialism developed. The subject had been kept alive by a small group among whom were Bland, the Rev. Ben Spence, the socialist-prohibitionist who in 1904 managed A. W. Puttee's campaign to win a second term as a labour MP,[27] A. E. Smith, who endorsed labour candidates in successive pastorates at Nelson, B. C., and Winnipeg and Brandon, Manitoba,[28] and the Rev. W. E. S. James, who was general secretary from about 1905 of the Christian Socialist Fellowship in Ontario and organizer in 1914 of the Church of the Social Revolution in Toronto.[29] A wave of millennial socialism in Britain after the election of 1906, the controversy surrounding R. J. Campbell's New Theology,[30] and touring lecturers such as Keir Hardie (1908 and 1912) and the Rev. J. Stitt Wilson (1909 and 1910), who preached the message of socialism as applied to Christianity, undoubtedly spurred discussion in Canada.[31]

Both socialists and clerics picked up the theme. In 1909 W. A. Cotton, editor of the Canadian socialist journal, *Cotton's Weekly*, developed the notion that Jesus had been the original labour leader.[32] In 1910 a large meeting in Montreal heard an exposition of socialism based on the Bible, and the prominent socialist from British Columbia, E. T. Kingsley of the Socialist Party of Canada, declared Christianity and socialism to be identical. The current did not run all one way, of course. A group of Toronto socialists in November 1910 devoted at least one evening to the subject, "Why a Socialist Can Not Be a Christian."[33]

After 1908 professed socialists in the churches seem not to have been so isolated or so peripheral. In that year the Rev. Dr. D. M. Ramsey in Ottawa described socialism as "carrying into economic regions the Christian doctrine of human brotherhood."[34] The Rev. Elliott S. Rowe organized socialist leagues in Sandon and Victoria, B. C.[35] Bryce M. Stewart in his survey of Fort William in 1913 found a considerable number of Christians sympathetic to socialism, and observed: "It is beyond question that in purity of purpose, ethics, and scientific reasoning the socialist position is far beyond any other political organization, and should appeal especially to the Christian."[36] In the same year, the Rev. Thomas Voaden of Hamilton, in a series of lectures later published, presented the thesis that socialism was the effect of Christianity forced outside the churches.[37] But that socialism not entirely outside the churches was becoming more and more apparent. In a survey of London, Ontario, in 1913 by the Brotherhoods of that city, it was found to be common opinion in the churches that neither unions nor socialist groups threatened or interfered with the church's work, and further, men of both organizations were found among the church's workers.[38]

Given the groundswell that seemed to be building up for the social gospel as the twentieth century entered its second decade, it was not surprising that when the Social Service Council called a national congress on social problems for March 1914, the response was overwhelming. For three days over two hundred regular delegates from across the nation, representing welfare organizations, churches, farm and labour groups, municipalities, provinces, and the federal government, were subjected to a barrage of social statistics, social conditions, social challenges, and social exhortations.[39] Most of the forty Canadian speakers were from central Canada, and although the rural problem was considered, speakers overwhelmingly represented urban areas: social workers, city judges and politicians, city doctors, labour leaders, college professors, city clergy. Although city oriented, the world of business management and ownership was conspicuous by its absence.

This was primarily a professional man's conference. Its social sources lay outside and below the centres of power which were forging the new Canada. The lines of sympathy were clear in the enthusiastic response to the claim of a visiting speaker that "there is so much religion in the labor movement and so much social spirit in the Church, that someday it will become a question whether the Church will capture the labor movement or the labor movement will capture the Church."[40] Not all the speakers gave evidence of the social gospel, but when their concerns were related to other information about them, the inferences seemed clear: Dr. Charles Hastings, Toronto's medical health officer, was a Presbyterian elder, a past chairman of the Progressive Club, and a member of the Public Ownership League;[41] J. O. McCarthy, Toronto city controller, was a leading figure in the Canadian Brotherhood Federation and a member of the Methodist Board of Social Service and Evangelism;[42] James Simpson, vice-president of the Trades and Labor Congress, was a Methodist local preacher, a lecturer for the Dominion Prohibition Alliance, a vice-president of the Toronto branch of the Lord's Day Alliance, and a perennially successful socialist candidate for offices of city government in Toronto who was consistently supported in his campaigns by the Epworth League, the Methodist young people's organization.[43] In short, it seemed that to scratch a reformer at the congress was to find a social gospeller.

So popular were the evening open meetings that the *Ottawa Citizen* could not recall any recent visiting theatrical production to rival them and, when the tumult had subsided, concluded on 6 March that the congress had been "one of the greatest assemblages ever held in Canada to grapple with . . . social and economical problems." The congress represented the social gospel entering a crest of influence. C. W. Gordon (Ralph Connor), writing the introduction to the report, was excited by the challenge thrown down to the "economic and social conditions on which the fabric of our state is erected." He may not have been aware of the hint of incongruity in his conclusion that "there is in our nation so deep a sense of righteousness and brotherhood that it needs only that the light fall clear and white on evil to have it finally removed."[44] Was reform to be won so cheaply? An unevangelicalized Calvinist might have been pardoned his doubts.

During the generation of its ascent, from 1890 to 1914, the social gospel front had remained remarkably united. One could now discern three emphases or wings beginning to crystallize, however. The conservatives were closest to traditional evangelicalism, emphasizing personal ethical issues, tending to identify sin with individual acts, and taking as their social strategy legislative reform of the environment. The radicals viewed society in more organic terms. Evil was so endemic and pervasive in the social order that they concluded there could be no personal salvation without social salvation — or at least without bearing the cross of social struggle. Without belief in an immanent God working in the social process to bring his kingdom to birth, the plight of the radicals would surely have been desperate. Between conservatives and radicals was a broad "centre party" of progressives holding the tension between the two extremes, endorsing in considerable measure programmes of the other two, but transmuting them somewhat into a broad ameliorative programme of reform. The harmony of these wings was not to last. Between 1914 and 1928 the social gospel enjoyed and endured at one and the same time a period of crest and of crisis. Its growing differentiation in church, interdenominational, and secular organizations multiplied its impact on Canadian society, and at the same time initiated interaction between the various modes of its expression. These were the conditions of its potency. They were also the conditions of its crisis, for the encounter with social reality was the true test of social gospel concepts, and the very complexity of that reality and the conflict inherent within it inevitably set one wing of the social gospel in conflict with another. This involved process culminated in the years 1926–8, and the movement generally entered a period of weariness, reaction, and reconsideration.

The war of 1914–18 was the occasion, and in considerable measure the cause, of a crisis in relations between the radicals and the church. In the course of the war four radicals, then or later of some prominence, lost their professional posts: William Irvine, J. S. Woodsworth, Salem Bland, and William Ivens. The situation of each man was complex, but while they all believed their fate to be the result of increasing commercialism in the

299

church and growing reaction in the state, and while Professor McNaught adopts the radicals' arguments as to what happened to them, the thesis is hardly acceptable.[45] It can only be maintained by slighting a number of facts: the acceptance of their radicalism, either prior to their appointment or without protest during a considerable period before severance of employment; the obvious support all had in the courts of the church; the complicating factor of pacifism in two cases; a host of evidence that Bland was more likely a victim of retrenchment in Wesley Theological College; and most important, the growing progressivism of the churches throughout the war period.

The evidence of church progressivism, 1914 to 1918, is more than substantial. All churches were dismayed by the outbreak of war, and the Methodists and Presbyterians at least condemned the profiteering that accompanied it. The Methodist general conference in the fall adopted the strongest reform programme to date and promised a further instalment in four years.[46] The Presbyterian Department of Social Service in 1916 regarded with hope the increase of nationalization and social control of industry in allied countries, and took heart at new Canadian legislation on prohibition, female suffrage, workmen's compensation, and protective legislation, the beginnings of provincial departments of labour, government encouragement of fishermen's co-operative societies in Nova Scotia, and the establishment of a bureau of social research under Woodsworth by the prairie provinces.[47] The Social Service Council sponsored regional congresses carrying on the spirit of its Ottawa success, added several more secular affiliates to its roster, and just prior to the war's end established the first national social welfare publication.[48] The church declarations of social policy in 1918 were further left than the manifestos of any major Canadian party, and approximated the British Labour party's programme for national minimum standards.[49] The Methodist call for a complete social reconstruction received international circulation, and, stated the *New Republic*, placed that church in the vanguard of reform forces.[50]

Radical social gospellers like Ernest Thomas of Vancouver, Bland, and A. E. Smith,[51] had played an important role in the formation of these church resolutions, but for the radicals the most important consequence of their mid-war crisis with church and state was the impact of their association, and hence of the social gospel, on agrarian and labour movements. J. S. Woodsworth was to be found addressing meetings of the Federated Labour party in Vancouver, and writing in the *B. C. Federationist*. William Irvine had become a leading figure in the Non-Partisan League in Alberta, editor of its journal the *Alberta Non-Partisan*, and a key person in the Dominion Labour party in Calgary. William Ivens in 1918 undertook an organizing tour in the prairie region for the Dominion Labour party,[52] stepped into the high priesthood, as the *Voice* put it, of labour forces at Winnipeg by founding a thriving labour church, and became editor of the *Western Labor News*.[53] From 1917 to 1919, Salem Bland contributed a regular column to the *Grain Growers' Guide*, and during the summer of

1918 addressed tens of thousands of westerners (with Henry Wise Wood) from the Chautauqua platform. Adding their voices to the journalism of reform were two more radicals of the social gospel, A. E. Smith as editor of the *Confederate* in Brandon,[54] and James Simpson as editor of the *Industrial Banner* in Toronto.

Despite the wartime crisis, the progressive and radical social gospellers had by 1918–19 reached a position of considerable power and consequence in the Canadian reform movement. And in the conservative wing, the progress of prohibition was startling. The war economy aided the cause, and in 1918 a government order-in-council prohibited further manufacture and sale of liquor until a year after the war's end. But it must be admitted that the temperance forces had won a national consensus on the subject. By 1919 only Quebec held out as a province, and it was at least two-thirds dry by local option. The farm organizations for some time had officially endorsed the reform, and now labour was finding near prohibition a stimulus to union membership.[55] Anglican publications joined other church journals in declaring that if prohibition was good in wartime, it was good in peace as well.[56]

There can be no doubt that the unrest, and especially the great Winnipeg strike of 1919, dealt the social gospel a rude jolt — and yet the impact can be easily exaggerated. The radicals, of course, were in the midst of it, sometimes carried to enthusiastic excesses of rhetoric which could easily be misunderstood. Their social millenialism undoubtedly contributed to the élan and discipline of the strike, but also to an element of unreality in which it was shrouded.[57] The Labour church provided its focus and strove as eight continuing churches in Winnipeg to maintain the essential unity of the left and the religious sense of labour's purpose which had been generated.[58]

The critical question, however, was how the progressive social gospel at large reacted to the events of 1919. The problem was complicated not simply by the growth of conservative reaction inside and outside the churches, but by the complex of attitudes in progressive minds to employers, unions, and social conflict. Generally sympathetic to labour, and persuaded that the spirit of Jesus was in social unrest calling the church to her true function as a defender of the oppressed,[59] they nevertheless believed that the "day of club and bludgeon is gone by," as Creighton described it in the *Christian Guardian*.[60] Misreading the face of power in industry, they were often, as was H. Michel in the *Canadian Churchman*, as pleased with the ending of a strike with improved conditions and shop committees as with recognition of a union and bargaining rights.[61] Nevertheless, the social gospel position held remarkably firm. Of the church press inclined toward the social gospel only the *Presbyterian and Westminster* attacked the Winnipeg strike outright.[62] The *Western Methodist Recorder* sympathized with labour and strike action but attacked the most radical element of strike leadership.[63] The *Churchman* reluctantly conceded the case in the face of government charges of sedition.[64] But the *Christian*

Guardian and *Social Welfare* supported the strike throughout.[65] Clergy in and out of Winnipeg frequently spoke out on behalf of the strikers and questioned the government's interpretation and intervention. While the strike was on, numerous church conferences were in progress across the land, and it is difficult to find a case where social policies were modified in the face of unrest — quite the reverse.[66] S. D. Chown, superintendent of the Methodist church, in many addresses urged members to continue to cry out against injustice and to consider the social gospel the voice of prophecy in their time.[67] He has been charged with pronouncing a "ban" on the strikers.[68] He did not, but he was concerned that there was an indiscriminate injustice in the general strike weapon which he could not sanction, and believed that if labour continued such tactics the church might have to be more reserved in its support.[69]

302

Three events taken together served to heighten that reservation, however, to stalemate the progressives' programme for industrial peace and to perplex the social gospel. Even radicals of the social gospel had long argued that the very collective organization of industry bore out their arguments about the nature of society and hence the nature of the ethic required of modern man.[70] The businessman and industrial owner would surely come to recognize this. However, when in September 1919 the government gathered a national industrial conference with representatives from management, labour and the public, it was almost a total failure.[71] But when the churches conducted an immense Inter-Church Forward Campaign in the winter and spring to equip them for their enlarged social role in the new era, it was an immense success.[72] Some, like Chown, saw in the success a new alliance for progress — the socially minded clergyman and the "new businessman."[73] For some months, the Methodist social service officers had been aware of a small flood of enquiries from businessmen asking guidance as to how to apply the church's policies to their business operations.[74] J. G. Shearer in *Social Welfare* was astonished at the number of plants that had instituted joint industrial councils, although he was suspicious that some at least were intended to forestall unionization.[75]

The dilution of progressivism such developments entailed was completed for many by the printers' strike of 1921, in the course of which the church publishing houses, the Methodist in particular, experienced at first hand the hideous complexities of industrial conflict. The Methodist house encouraged union membership. Depressed business conditions of 1921 precluded meeting all union demands. Nevertheless, with most other printing establishments in Toronto, it was struck on 1 June. Its manager allowed himself to be drafted as chairman of the employers' anti-strike committee and soon found himself in the midst of an outright open shop campaign. The union on the other hand not only rejected reasonable offers, but turned on the Methodists with special fury because they seemed not to be living up to their progressive declarations of 1918. Despite an outcry from Methodist summer schools, and frantic negotiations by Ernest Thomas of the Social Service Department, there was little that could be done. Neither the church nor any other business could live now on the terms of the envisaged economic order of social gospel prophecy.[76] Creighton concluded that strikes were simply stupid, and had no constructive word for labour in the great British Empire Steel and Coal Company conflicts of the mid-decade.[77] The Social Service Council drifted from its celebration of the significance of labour in its Labour Day issues to its calm notices of the day at the decade's end.[78] The United Church's pronouncement on industry in 1926 simply launched the new church on a sea of ambiguities, which many recognized, but which none could chart more accurately.[79] The bright vision of the social gospel seemed to be going into eclipse.[80]

For a time the upward course of the agrarian revolt and the Progressive party offered new opportunities. From the earlier days of E. A. Partridge, the social gospel had had an intimate role in the theory and practice of the agrarian movements.[81] The churches had attempted to foster social life and community ideals through institutes, conferences, and summer schools.[82] The *Guide* promoted the notion of the church as a community centre.[83] Farm leaders like Drury, Good, Moyle, and Henders were prominent members of social service councils.[84] Bland and the Congregationalist, D. S. Hamilton, worked closely with S. J. Farmer and Fred Dixon in Winnipeg on behalf of the single tax and direct legislation.[85] Henry Wise Wood counselled his farmers to look to the church for a social saviour, for it was just now beginning to recognize Jesus as a social leader as well as a personal saviour.[86] Wood's whole programme of civilizational reform was built on the theological assumptions of the social gospel.[87] Since 1903, from Wesley College, Winnipeg, Salem Bland had been sending out young ministers of the social gospel who frequently became members of local units of the Grain Growers' Associations.[88] By 1919 the social gospel had become, in effect, the religion of the agrarian revolt,[89] and its continued involvement in the process of party and policy formation was such that Norman Lambert, secretary of the Canadian Council of Agriculture, observed that religion and social work were inextricably linked with the farmers.[90]

The victories of the Progressive party can, then, be viewed in part as victories of the social gospel. But equally, the failure of the Progressives in 1926 must be weighed on the social gospel scales. In brief, it must be conceded that the social gospel belief that in the rise of such movements true religion and genuine democracy were triumphing together in the modern world contributed to the Progressive party's sense of being something other than a traditional party, and of fulfilling something more than a political role. This non-politics of hope inevitably was ground to pieces in a parliamentary world where alliances were necessary, but compromising, where decisions were mandatory, but the better alternative seldom clear.

At mid-decade, although the great accomplishment of Church Union brightened the horizon, that victory had been won at some cost. The drive

303

to consolidate social service in the new church had worked to the disadvantage of other expressions of the social gospel. Support was withdrawn from the Brotherhood Federation, and the Social Service Council ran afoul of church financing and personal animosities. The former collapsed completely, and the latter, also hit by depression conditions, the counterattacks against prohibition, and the death of its secretary, G. J. Shearer, lived on in a maimed condition.[91] The campaign for a national church made church social service leaders more hostile than they would otherwise have been to the labour churches which had spread to at least ten other cities before collapsing in 1924–5.[92] T. A. Moore of the Methodist Social Service Department had for three critical years of their life played a dubious role with the RCMP in its investigation of the churches.[93] The labour churches, however, died chiefly of their own inadequacy as a religious institution. After 1924 they followed their logical course, with a transfer of religious commitment and zeal to the creation of a more radical reform party via Woodsworth's Ginger Group, and in A. E. Smith's case, one might observe, to the Communist party.[94] Not only did Church Union further drain progressive social gospel energies in the task of institutional reconstruction, but on the morrow of Union, the critical battle in defence of prohibition had to be fought. One by one after 1920 the provincial temperance acts had gone down to defeat. In 1926 the last main stronghold, Ontario, was under attack. The church which was to rally the forces of social righteousness was already fighting a rearguard battle.

At stake was the survival of the conservative social gospel. In the aftermath of defeat the temperance forces were shattered beyond repair.[95] "Old Ontario" has died, declared Ernest Thomas as he launched a careful critique of temperance strategy.[96] The consensus, carefully built up over the years, had disappeared, just as the association of social work and religion so long nurtured under the social service formula was now giving way to secular organizations quite outside, and often severely critical of, the churches.[97]

It was no coincidence that the crisis in the social gospel coincided so nearly with the crisis in Progressive politics and in the reform movement at large. The categories in which they all worked, and the divinities which moved them all, lay shattered. Nevertheless, the lessons of the encounter with reality were not easily absorbed, in part owing to the ease with which the social gospel could transfer its passion from one cause to another. Partly as a positive expression of the social gospel, but also, one suspects, as a sublimation of frustration, much progressive zeal in 1923 transferred itself to a resurgence of pacifism, and after 1926 to a more broadly conceived peace movement.[98] Only among a few individuals like Ernest Thomas and leaders in the Student Christian Movement were penetrating questions being asked about the adequacy of social gospel concepts.[99] Prosperous church expansion in the later 1920s was accompanied by an introversion religiously and by small fellowship groups.[100] But out of the latter, the reconsiderations of the more critically minded, the struggles

304

of the survivors of the political wreck of Progressivism, and a growing dialectic with more radical forms of socialist thought, was to come a new thrust of a reconstructed social gospel in the 1930s.

Notes

1. These reactions of the church press are cited in Stewart Crysdale, *The Industrial Struggle and Protestant Ethics in Canada* (Toronto, 1961), pp. 18–19. It is not unlikely that among the strikers and those who rallied to their support were some who were not prepared to accept the editors' opinions as to their Christian duty (See Doris French, *Faith, Sweat and Politics*, Toronto, 1962). For a fuller account of the social stance of Methodism and Presbyterianism in these years, see Marion Royce, "The Contribution of the Methodist Church to Social Welfare in Canada" (unpublished M.A. thesis, University of Toronto, 1940), and E. A. Christie, "The Presbyterian Church in Canada and Its Official Attitude Towards Public Affairs and Social Problems, 1875–1925" (unpublished M.A. thesis, University of Toronto, 1955).
2. Crysdale, *The Industrial Struggle and Protestant Ethics in Canada*, p. 22.
3. C. D. W. Goodwin, *Canadian Economic Thought* (Durham, N.C., 1961), pp. 32–8; *Toronto World*, 7 Feb. 1898, *Grain Growers' Guide*, 21 Nov. 1917, pp. 32–3.
4. United Church Archives, Toronto (UCA), reading lists in the Bland Papers.
5. Bland Papers.
6. C. H. Hopkins, *The Rise of the Social Gospel in American Protestantism, 1865–1915* (New Haven, 1940), pp. 110–15.
7. For an expression of this transition, see the introduction to General William Booth, *In Darkest England and the Way Out* (London: International Headquarters of the Salvation Army, 1890).
8. The distinction was between bringing the message and creating the social reality. For an illuminating discussion of this process, see Donald B. Meyer, *The Protestant Search for Political Realism, 1919–1941* (Los Angeles and Berkeley, 1960), chap. I.
9. UCA, J. B. Silcox, *Social Resurrection*.
10. C. S. Eby, *The World Problem and the Divine Solution* (Toronto: William Briggs, 1914).
11. W. S. Ryder, in a paper presented to the Pacific Coast Theology Conference, 1920; *Western Methodist Recorder*, Sept. 1920, pp. 4–5. See also David Summers, "The Labour Church" (unpublished Ph.D. thesis, University of Edinburgh, 1958).
12. Kingston *Daily News*, 14 Feb. 1894; 13 Feb. 1896; 20 Feb. 1896; 11 Feb. 1897; *Queen's Quarterly*, V (April 1898), 316–18; VI (April 1899), 314–16; VII (April 1900), 332; VIII (April 1901), 388.
13. Robert Sandall, *The History of the Salvation Army* (3 vols; London, 1955), III, *Social Reform and Welfare Work*, 80.
14. Alexander Sutherland, *The Kingdom of God and Problems of Today* (Toronto: William Briggs, 1898), p. xiii.
15. Bland Papers. Salem Bland, Sermon at St. James Bond United Church, 31 Oct. 1937.
16. Summers, "The Labour Church," pp. 427ff; Hopkins, *The Rise of the Social Gospel in American Protestantism, 1865–1915*, pp. 85–7; French, *Sweat and Politics*, pp. 129–30.
17. *Social Welfare*, Oct. 1923, pp. 14–15; W. Ward, *The Brotherhood in Canada* (London: The Brotherhood Publishing House, [1912]). See also F. D. Leete, *Christian Brotherhoods* (Cincinnati: Jennings and Graham, 1912).
18. J. F. McCurdy, *The Life and Work of D. J. Macdonnell* (Toronto: William Briggs, 1897), pp. 23–4, 289–309; Minutes of the Toronto City Missionary Society of the Methodist Church, 29 Dec. 1894. 10 Dec. 1895. For the less well-known Scottish side of the story, see Stewart Mechie, *The Church and Scottish Social Developments, 1780–1870* (London, 1960).
19. *Social Welfare*, Feb. 1929, p. 113; *The Social Service Congress of Canada, 1914* (Toronto: Social Service Council of Canada, 1914), pp. 134–6.
20. *Canadian Student*, Oct. 1919, pp. 16–20; *Social Welfare*, Feb. 1929, p. 113; Murray G. Ross, *The YMCA in Canada* (Toronto, 1951), pp. 215–32.
21. Kenneth McNaught, *A Prophet in Politics* (Toronto, 1959), chap. IV.
22. *Social Service Congress of Canada*, p. 307.
23. UCA, Methodist Church of Canada and Presbyterian Church in Canada, *Reports of Investigations of Social Conditions and Social Surveys*, 1913–14: Vancouver, Regina, Fort William, Port Arthur, London, Hamilton, Sydney.
24. *Voice*, 8 Dec. 1916, p. 8; *The Nutcracker*, 17 Nov. 1916, p. 8.
25. UCA, Moral and Social Reform Council, *Minutes of the Annual Meeting*. 5 Sept. 1913.
26. See H. H. Walsh, *The Christian Church in Canada* (Toronto, 1956).
27. A. E. Smith, *All My Life* (Toronto: Progress Publishing Co. 1949), p. 33.
28. *Ibid.*

29. W. E. S. James, "Notes on a Socialist Church," in Summers, "The Labour Church," pp. 690-6.

30. For an able discussion of these factors in their British context, see Stanley Pierson, "Socialism and Religion: A Study of their Interaction in Great Britain, 1889-1911" (unpublished Ph.D. thesis, Harvard University, 1957).

31. *Canadian Annual Review (CAR)*, 1908, p. 101; 1909, p. 307; 1910, p. 315; 1912, p. 277.

32. *Ibid.*, 1909, p. 306.

33. *Ibid.*, 1910, pp. 315-16.

34. *Ibid.*, 1908, p. 99.

35. Paul Fox, "Early Socialism in Canada," in J. H. Aitcheson, *The Political Process in Canada* (Toronto, 1963), p. 89.

36. Methodist and Presbyterian Churches, *Report of a Social Survey of Port Arthur* (n.p., 1913), p. 10.

37. Thomas Voaden, *Christianity and Socialism* (Toronto: Methodist Book Room, 1913).

38. Methodist and Presbyterian Churches, *Report of a Limited Survey of Educational, Social and Industrial Life in London, Ontario* n.p., 1913), p. 43.

39. *Ottawa Free Press*, 2 Mar. 1914; *Ottawa Evening Journal*, 3 Mar. 1914; and the record of the conference proceedings cited above, *Social Service Congress of Canada, 1914*.

40. Charles Stelzle, "Capturing the Labour Movement," *Social Service Congress of Canada*, pp. 35-8.

41. *Canadian Men and Women of the Time*, 1912.

42. UCA, Canadian Brotherhood Federation, *Constitution* [and list of officers and General Council], c. 1916.

43. *Canadian Men and Women of the Time*, 1912; *Canadian Forum*, Nov. 1938, p. 229; Summers, "The Labour Church," pp. 690-6.

44. *Social Service Congress of Canada, 1914*.

45. McNaught, *A Prophet in Politics*, pp. 79-85. For a detailed discussion from another point of view, see A. R. Allen, "The Crest and Crisis of the Social Gospel in Canada, 1916-1927" (unpublished Ph.D. thesis, Duke University, 1967), chap. II.

46. See for instance the early reactions of the Methodist Church, *Journal of Proceedings of the General Conference*, 1914, pp. 404-6; 1918, pp. 290-3.

47. Presbyterian Church in Canada, *Acts and Proceedings of the General Assembly*, 1916, Appendix, pp. 13-14.

48. *CAR*, 1918, p. 598. Social Service Council of Canada, *Minutes*, Annual Meeting. January 1918.

49. See the first issues of *Social Welfare*, beginning Oct., 1918; Methodist *Journal of Proceedings*, 1918, pp. 290-3; Statement of the Presbyterian Board of Home Missions and Social Service, *Presbyterian and Westminster*, 10 April 1919, p. 351.

50. *New Republic*, 8 Feb. 1919.

51. *Hamilton Spectator*, 12 Oct. 1918; *Western Methodist Recorder*, March 1919, pp. 5-6.

52. *Voice* (Winnipeg), 19 Apr. 1918.

53. *Ibid.*, 21 June 1918: 5 and 12 July 1918.

54. Summers, "The Labour Church," pp. 379-80.

55. *Edmonton Free Press*, 10 May 1919; *Industrial Banner*, 10 Oct. 1919; *Youth and Service*, Aug., 1919, pp. 114-15; *Western Methodist Recorder*, Oct., 1920, p. 3; *Alberta Labor News*, 25 Sept. 1920; *Christian Guardian*, 30 July 1919, p. 2, quoting John Queen of the Winnipeg strike committee.

56. *Canadian Churchman*, 28 Nov. 1918, p. 763.

57. See William Ivens' euphoric mixture of prophecy, platform rhetoric, and industrial tactics in *Western Labor News*, Special Strike Editions, e.g., No. 3, 19 May 1919.

58. For more extensive discussion of the Labour Churches in Canada, see McNaught, A *Prophet in Politics*, Allen, "The Crest and Crisis of the Social Gospel," Summers, "The Labour Church," and D. F. Pratt, "William Ivens and the Winnipeg Labor Church" (unpublished B.D. thesis, St. Andrew's College, Saskatoon, 1962).

59. Editorial, "I Was Hungry," *Christian Guardian*, 27 Nov. 1918, p. 6.

60. *Ibid.*, 5 Mar. 1919, p. 5.

61. *Canadian Churchman*, 27 Feb. 1919, p. 133; 10 Apr. 1919, pp. 234-5.

62. *Ibid.*, 29 May 1919, p. 344; 10 July 1919, p. 441.

63. *Western Methodist Recorder*, June 1919, p. 8.

64. *Presbyterian and Westminster*, 22 May 1919, p. 497; 29 May 1919, pp. 518-19; 5 June 1919, pp. 549-50.

65. *Social Welfare*, 1 Aug. 1919, pp. 266-70; *Christian Guardian*, 28 May 1919, p. 5; 4 June 1919, pp. 4-5; 11 June 1919, p. 3; 18 June 1919, p. 4; 25 June 1919, p. 4.

66. For a detailed discussion of the more general church reaction, see Allen, "The Crest and Crisis of the Social Gospel," chap. VI, VII.

67. *Western Methodist Recorder*, June 1919.

68. McNaught, *A Prophet in Politics*, p. 118.

69. *Christian Guardian*, 25 June 1919, p. 2; *Toronto Daily Star*, 12 June 1919, pp. 1, 8.

70. See for instance UCA, Bland Papers, Salem Bland, "Four Steps and a Vision."

71. *Social Welfare*, 1 Nov. 1919, p. 39; 1 Dec. 1919, p. 75; *Christian Guardian*, 1 Oct. 1919, p. 6.

72. *Canadian Baptist*, 1 May 1919, p. 4; 31 July 1919, p. 3; *Presbyterian and Westminster*, 19 June 1919, p. 603; 25 Dec. 1919, p. 594; *Christian Guardian*, 15 Oct. 1919, p. 22.

73. *Christian Guardian*, 30 June 1920, pp. 18–19.

74. *Western Methodist Recorder*, Oct. 1921, p. 4.

75. *Social Welfare*, 1 Sept. 1919, p. 287; 1 Aug. 1920, pp. 316–17; 1 Aug. 1922, p. 235.

76. See A. R. Allen, "The Crest and Crisis of the Social Gospel," chapter XI.

77. *Christian Guardian*, 25 Mar. 1925.

78. *Social Welfare*, Aug. 1927, p. 483; Aug. 1929, p. 242.

79. "The Christianization of Industry," *Social Welfare*, 1 Aug. 1927, pp. 488–9; see also, United Church, Department of Evangelism and Social Service, *Annual Report*, 1924–5, p. 10.

80. See Creighton's reflections on this possibility, *New Outlook*, 12 Jan. 1927, p. 19.

81. *Grain Growers' Guide*, 14 and 28 Aug. 1909; 30 Sept., 6 Oct. 1919.

82. McNaught, *A Prophet in Politics*, pp. 74, 74n.

83. *Grain Growers' Guide*, 7 June 1916; 20 Dec. 1916.

84. Moral and Social Reform Council, *Minutes*, 10 Sept. 1909; Social Service Council of Canada, *Minutes*, 5 Sept. 1913; Manitoba Conference of the United Church, *Minutes*, 1932, p. 42.

85. *CAR*, 1913, p. 578; Manitoba Conference, *Minutes*, 1929, p. 60; *The Single Taxer and Direct Legislation Bulletin* (Winnipeg), III, 8 (1916)

86. See his Circulars Nos. 9 and 10 for United Farmers of Alberta Sunday, 27 May 1917, Bland Papers, UCA.

87. *Grain Growers' Guide*, 29 Jan. 1917; 4 Dec. 1918.

88. *Christian Guardian*, 17 Mar. 1920, p. 25; 15 Dec. 1920, p. 14.

89. For further elaboration of this suggestion, see A. R. Allen, "Salem Bland and the Social Gospel in Canada" (unpublished M.A. thesis, University of Saskatchewan, 1961), chaps. V and VI.

90. *Presbyterian Witness*, 23 June 1921, pp. 10–11.

91. The documentation for this is too diffuse to be suggested through a few citations, but may be found in A. R. Allen, "The Crest and Crisis of the Social Gospel," chaps. XIV, XV, XVI.

92. *Ibid.*, chap. X.

93. See correspondence between Moore and Hamilton from 25 May 1920, to 25 April 1922, Papers on Methodist Industrial Relations, 1920–2, UCA.

94. A. E. Smith, *All My Life*, pp. 76–7.

95. United Church, Department of Evangelism and Social Service, *Annual Report*, 1927, pp. 24–5, 27–9; *New Outlook*, 21 Mar. 1928, p. 2; 8 Jan. 1930, p. 46; Dobson Papers, Union College Library, B.C., Hugh Dobson to L. C. McKinney, 30 April 1929.

96. *New Outlook*, 22 Dec. 1926, p. 5; 8 Jan. 1930, pp. 31, 44.

97. In 1926 the Canadian Association of Social Workers was formed, and in 1928 the Canadian Conference of Social Work held its first national meeting. The immediate shrinkage in size of the Social Service Council's annual meetings indicated the impact of these developments on the stature of the council. For an expression of the rationale upon which the council was founded, see *New Outlook*, 10 June 1925, p. 23. For expressions of the new social worker's outlook see J. D. Ketchum, "Judge and be Judged," *Canadian Student*, Nov. 1925; *Social Welfare*, June–July 1926, pp. 189–90; and for a warning about the dangers of a social work that had lost its sense of God, see United Church, Department of Evangelism and Social Service, *Annual Report*, 1927, p. 25. The social gospel stress upon the immanence of God of course abetted the very secularism about which some of them were now concerned.

98. See for instance, *Canadian Student*, Jan. 1924, p. 99; *Christian Guardian*, 20 Feb. 1924, and issues of subsequent months for discussion of the subject; *Social Welfare*, April 1923, pp. 137–9; *New Outlook*, issues of July through December 1925; *Canadian Churchman*, 21 Jan. 1926, p. 36.

99. *New Outlook*, 12 Aug. 1925, pp. 5–6; 12 Feb. 1930, p. 153; *Canadian Student*, March 1925, p. 163; March 1926, pp. 165–6. Student Christian Movement Archives, Minutes of the General Committee, 24–26 Sept. 1926.

100. [Ernest Thomas] *Fellowship Studies* (Toronto: United Church Department of Evangelism and Social Service [1927 or 1928]; *Canadian Student*, March 1926, p. 168; Dobson Papers, Dobson to Armstrong, 14 May 1928.

Race Regeneration and Social Purity. A Study of the Social Attitudes of Canada's English-Speaking Suffragists*

CAROL BACCHI

I

Feminist historians have recently pointed out that the female suffragists in Canada, Britain, the United States, and Australia had aims very different from today's liberation movement.[1] Attention has been drawn in particular to two facets of the women's ideology. First, the vast majority accepted that woman's most important contribution to society consisted of her role as wife and mother. As a result they usually assumed that a woman would stop working at marriage, to devote her full energy to her family. Second, rather than demanding sexual freedom for women, most upheld the Victorian idea that women stood above sex.

Though this synopsis of their social attitudes is accurate, little attempt has been made to understand why they held these views. This paper argues from the position that the women have to be understood within the context of the social group to which they belonged. Canada's English-speaking suffragists were members of a late nineteenth-century reform coalition drawn from the Anglo-Saxon Protestant middle classes.[2] Such middle-class reformers suggested only minor changes. The family, for instance, remained sacrosanct in their eyes. The suffragists did not want to challenge the accepted female role but only to raise its status.

This paper examines two parts of the reform ideology: the commitment to race regeneration and the crusade for social purity. It shows how both these goals depended on traditional views of women's virtues. The desire to create a strong and healthy race placed an emphasis on woman's role as procreator and nurturer. The crusade for purity, an attempt by the Protestant elite to reimpose its values on a deviant society, made a patriotic virtue of women's asexuality. Given the suffragists' Protestant Anglo-Saxon background it ought not to be surprising that they endorsed this programme. Their allegiance to their sex was not their sole allegiance. In fact, at times, the commitment to race, creed, and class superceded the commitment to sex.

II

Several studies of late Victorian and Edwardian society point to the fact that the English-speaking Anglo-Saxon community in Britain, its colonies, and

*From *Histoire sociale/Social History*, XI (November 1978): 460–474. Reprinted by permission.

the United States, felt defensive in this period.[3] Britain faced the particular trauma of declining imperial supremacy. The number of recruits for the Boer War who were rejected on the grounds of physical incapacity seemed to indicate that the British were becoming a race of weaklings. Bernard Semmel has labelled the reforms advanced in this period to upgrade the health of the population "social imperialism".[4]

The "race suicide" scare, the suggestion that Anglo-Saxon numbers were declining while "inferior" races proliferated, aroused particular concern. The old Malthusian fear that too many people were being born gave way to the idea that the English population had stopped growing. The problem was not simply numbers, though it was frequently expressed in this way. The real problem was that the best stock were being outbred by the unfit. Studies, for example, revealed an increasing number of feeble-minded in the population.

Canada's middle-class reformers came from sound Anglo-Saxon stock and were well aware of the warnings about the degeneration of the race. Social gospel leaders S.D. Chown and W.W. Andrews viewed with alarm "the diminishing birth rate in some sections of our population". They considered it a great national evil "that some of the best strains in our country are becoming extinct".[5] The large influx of eastern and southern European immigrants between 1896 and World War I increased their anxiety. Much of the reform programme aimed at finding ways to improve the calibre of tomorrow's citizens. A commitment to race-regeneration and nation-building dominated the movement.

The idea of evolution aroused interest since it seemed to suggest that the race was moving forward. All they had to do was harness this process. Unfortunately, scientists could not agree upon the mechanism by which evolution took place. Two contrary theories developed. Environmentalism, traceable to Jean-Baptiste de Lamarck, maintained that a modification in the environment produced in a person visible physical and mental changes which were transmittable to the next generation. The opposing school of thought, labelled "eugenics" by its founder, Francis Galton, placed emphasis on nature (i.e. heredity) rather than nurture.[6]

The two schools of heredity offered different solutions to the race-degeneration and race-suicide problems. Lamarckians and neo-Lamarckians believed in the inheritance of acquired characteristics and recommended ameliorative legislation to improve the living and working conditions of underprivileged groups. According to their hypothesis this would produce higher types in the future. The simple answer to the birthrate dilemma lay in reducing the infant death rate by upgrading the standard of living generally. Discounting the impact of environment, eugenists insisted that the only way to improve the race was through selective breeding. They advocated legislation to prevent the unfit from multiplying and to encourage the fit to have more children.

The middle-class reformers tended to be humanists who defended the need for environmental change. Environmentalism (or "euthenics" as it came to be called in contradistinction to eugenics[7]) provided them with a

309

raison d'être since it suggested that people living today could build for the future. But eugenics seemed to make social reform unnecessary. Worse still, it implied that reformers were actually contributing to the deterioration of the race by preserving weak specimens.[8]

Some reformers rejected eugenics outright since it seemed to deny their effectiveness. The Rev. A.E. Smith, a Methodist minister from Brandon, Manitoba, and an exponent of the social gospel, felt uncomfortable with the new creed: "We do not believe in the survival of the fittest. We do not believe in the brushing on one side of the weak and the helpless."[9] Others took up those parts of eugenics which retained environmental overtones, for example restricting the propagation of those with hereditary defects. Beyond this, they retained their faith in the benefits of environmental change.

Dr. Peter Bryce, the President of the Canadian Purity-Education Association, provides a good example of this ability to integrate some eugenic arguments without abandoning a basically environmental approach. To control the spread of hereditary weakness he recommended stricter government regulation of marriage and the removal of the feeble-minded to state-supported homes. In the field of euthenics he called for a "sanitary environment," improved housing, lessening of overcrowding, a reduction in local taxation and child labour, and lower costs for food and land. Bryce coined his own terms for the complementary processes. The "Law of Heredity" doomed men and women to carry their ancestral physical structure and character with them. But the "Gospel of Heredity" mitigated the doom, providing in environment the "potentialities of almost infinite improvement".[10]

Because of their reform orientation the suffragists also placed more faith in environment than in genes. Emily Stowe, the founder of Canada's first woman suffrage society, for example, blamed the environment, not heredity, for the production of the criminal.[11] Most reforms in the suffrage platform (factory legislation, compulsory education, city planning, health and hygiene, temperance, prison reform, pure food laws) were euthenist and aimed at improving the living and working conditions of the poor.[12]

As with the reformers, however, the suffragists could not ignore the discoveries of genetics. Ethel Hurlbatt, a vocal member of the Montreal Suffrage Association and Warden of McGill's Royal Victoria College in 1907, explained clearly the dilemma posed by eugenics and the way in which it challenged the basic assumption of reform:

Is degeneracy in every form to be attributed to poverty bad housing, unhealthy trades, drinking, industrial occupations of women and other direct and indirect environmental influences on offspring? Can we, by education, by legislation, by social effort change the environmental conditions and raise the race to a markedly higher standard of physique and mentality? Or is social reform really incapable of effecting any substantial change, nay by lessening the selection death rate, may it not contribute to emphasizing the very evils it was intended to lessen? . . .

Through investigations they [eugenists] show that improvement in social conditions will not compensate for bad hereditary influences; that the problem of physical and mental degeneration cannot be solved by preventing mothers from working, by closing public houses, by erecting model dwellings; that the only way to keep a nation strong mentally and physically is to see that each new generation is derived from the fitter members of the generation before.[13]

Placed on the defensive the suffragists also proposed a compromise. They accepted that environmental reform could not affect mental capacity and therefore agreed upon the need to control strictly the breeding of the retarded. One Western woman wanted special industrial farms, segregation of the sexes, and in some cases sterilization to keep the feeble-minded from multiplying.[14] In the East, Constance Hamilton, the President of the National Equal Franchise Union, included drunkards among the unsalvageable. She recommended keeping them under restraint rather than leaving alcoholic mothers "free to fill cradles with degenerate babies".[15]

Beyond the regulation of the feeble-minded, however, most suffragists were unwilling to go. Strict eugenists were few. Only Carrie Derick, a student in McGill's Botanical Department between 1887 and 1890, and later a Professor of Evolution and Genetics, championed the direct application of scientific principles to human conditions. That is, she believed that the struggle for existence ought to be allowed to proceed unrestrained, so that the truly fittest would survive. She preferred a "spirit of indifference" to the "happy feeling" that education, pure air, good housing, proper food, and short hours of work may bring about a permanent improvement in people.[16] To justify her activities as a reformer and a suffragist, she argued that "If men and women were taught to be chaste, clean living and high thinking, there would be an uplifting of the race without any special legislation."[17] The higher education of women and the freeing of women from conventional ideas, Derick maintained, would help achieve this aim.

311

Generally, the application of theories of evolution, be they eugenist or environmental, tended to reinforce traditional sex roles. The obsession with the numbers and quality of the next generation accentuated woman's maternal function. The particular reforms one espoused depended on the school of heredity to which one belonged. The environmentalists concentrated on two things: improving the health and fitness of women on the grounds that their children would benefit and bettering the home environment in which those children would spend the first crucial formative years. The eugenists tried to popularize the idea of controlled breeding. The suffragists almost invariably favoured the Lamarckian programme, firstly because they were environmentalists, and secondly because it allowed greater scope for women to contribute actively to the creation of a new race.

Eugenics reduced the maternal function to a mere biological capacity. The main concern for the future of the race, according to eugenic theory, was that those with hereditary defects were multiplying faster than those with desirable traits. The source of this problem was traced partly to the reluctance of intelligent women to stay home and have babies. Statistics revealed a lower marriage and birth rate among college women, proving to eugenists that these women were neglecting their duty.[18] Francis Galton, the well-known founder of the movement, was willing to force this duty upon them: "If child-bearing women must be intellectually handicapped," he

explained, "then the penalty to be paid for race predominance is the sub-
jection of women."[19]

This conclusion raised a real dilemma for the suffragists. Since most were
well-educated and since they shared the concern for the future of the race,
what could they say to those who accused them of not doing their share?
Ethel Hurlbatt did some soul-searching over the issue:

> If the philanthropists are right, there is no doubt that college women are contributing their
> share to movements which will secure better physical and moral conditions for the race. If the
> eugenists are right, are college women? Do college women maintain the same standard of
> physical efficiency as their less educated sisters? Do they as readily marry? Do they bring into
> the world as many children?[20]

She could only hope that the "philanthropists" (or environmentalists) were
right since that made women's contribution to the reform effort as important as their breeding function. Hurlbatt is not suggesting that female reformers might want to abandon the domestic sphere but that the improved
environment they were helping to create was of more value than the simple
multiplication of offspring. Environmental theory thus allowed a greater
scope for activity, albeit within a restricted domain.

In a similar fashion the environmental approach to bettering the race
was partly responsible for altering the traditional image of the Victorian
woman. A belief in the inheritance of acquired characteristics produced a
new concern for both woman's physical and mental fitness. The "frail vessel" fell into disrepute. Dr. Edward Playter, an Ottawa reformer, announced
that "the age for regarding as fashionable and popular delicate women and
girls is past."[21] It had become "a woman's duty to be well."[22]

The dress-reform movement received a real fillip from this idea. Many
medical men approved looser-fitting garments on the grounds that the "corset
curse" might damage the womb and/or its occupant.[23] More and more educators began to press for physical education facilities for girls in order to
improve the health of future mothers. All the new women's colleges in the
period, such as the Royal Victoria College in Montreal, had large recreation
rooms where women learned calisthenics.

Environmentalism could also be used to justify women's higher education. Many people, including many clerics, had begun to criticize the traditional academy education, which concentrated on needlework, dancing, and
languages, on the grounds that it produced a flighty and frivolous woman.
According to one champion of women's higher education, McGill's Principal William Dawson, the mental discipline of future wives and mothers had
to be improved since the children were in their care all day.[24] This logic
made university-level courses in moral philosophy, history, and Christian
doctrine quite acceptable. But the education was still essentially education
for motherhood. There was no suggestion that better educated women move
into the job market.

While the environmental approach encouraged women to break free from
certain parts of Victorian convention, on balance the Lamarckian school

reinforced traditional sex roles. Women were simply allowed the liberty to become better mothers. This is aptly demonstrated by the reformers' enthusiastic support for domestic science education for women. Since the home life was crucial to the physical and mental development of an individual, they wanted more attention paid to the training of the homemaker. J.W. Dafoe, editor of the *Grain Growers' Guide*, believed that the health of the nation depended upon "the proper balancing of foods in the bill of fare" and that, upon its health depended its achievements in commerce, arts, and science. In brief, "the gastric organs are the hub of the wheel."[25] Consequently, above all else, women needed instruction in physiology, hygiene, and nutrition.

The idea of domestic science training fitted in nicely with developments in education theory. Towards the end of the nineteenth century many educators began promoting a practical over a general liberal arts programme.[26] It was argued that the strength of the nation required that boys receive technical education in industrial schools. On the same grounds and given the traditional assumptions about the sexual division of labour it was decided that girls needed training in the skills of household management. Between 1893 and 1908 home economics classes were established in the public schools of thirty-two Canadian cities.[27] In 1894 the Hamilton School of Domestic Science opened and in 1900 a Hamilton Normal School for training teachers of domestic science was established, with government aid.[28]

The reaction of the suffragists to domestic science provides a good example of the way in which they accepted and worked within the reform ideology. Because of their enthusiasm for improving the race, the majority warmly approved the new education. In 1889 Emily Stowe asked for the incorporation of one grand Normal School for domestic instruction in every city.[29] The Manitoba suffragist and journalist, Lillian Beynon Thomas, wanted girls in public schools to receive a thorough training in domestic science because, in her words, "the health of the nation is largely in their hands."[30] Only a small feminist minority realized that home economics restricted women to a purely domestic function: Carrie Derick saw the danger in the new trend. She pointed out that centring a woman's education around cooking and sewing restricted her choice of career.[31] The majority accepted this restriction.

The general acceptance of domestic science ought not to be surprising. The suffragists shared the concern for the race which made it necessary that the home life of the masses be improved. Also, the idea of scientific training for motherhood provided a new status for a role most of them accepted. In the eyes of the Manitoba suffragist Mrs. Frances Graham, home economics had dignified the old-time "kitchen drudgery" into a delightful and controlled science.[32] Moreover, few suffragists did their own housework and domestic science education promised to replenish the ever-diminishing supply of domestic servants.

Other parts of the suffrage programme illustrate the priority placed on racial improvement. Their arguments in favour of factory legislation were essentially racial, that is, that women had to be kept healthy to protect their offspring. The Toronto Suffrage Association, for example, included among its list of reasons why women needed the vote ". . . because millions of women are wage workers and their health and that *of our future citizens* are often endangered by evil working conditions that can only be remedied by legislation."[33] In the early days of sweatshop labour some safeguards were necessary, but the suffragists failed to consider that protective legislation burdened a working woman with a handicap which made her less employable. Only a very few suffragists, notably Carrie Derick, argued the modern feminist position that restrictive legislation tended to drive women out of work they were well able to perform.[34] Ideally, the majority of the suffragists wanted women out of the factories altogether because of the threat such work posed to their health.

314

This is not to say that the suffragists allowed the male reformers to define their programme but that they accepted the need for racial improvement and hence had no intention of challenging the importance of woman as mother. The motto adopted by the Child Welfare Exhibition, sponsored by the Montreal Suffrage Association in 1912, could well stand as the motto for the suffrage movement: "If we are to become a great nation, the well-being of our children must be our first care."[35]

Within this framework the women demanded the esteem they deserved as the "mothers of the race". To justify their enfranchisement, they put forward the simple plea that they needed a vote to protect their homes and children properly. Industrialization, they argued, had intruded into woman's sphere and transferred many of her functions to distant, impersonal, collective enterprises.[36] Factories made the food and clothing; schools educated the children; governments controlled the environment which affected her family's health. To guarantee that these tasks, which were actually her responsibilities, were performed well, woman needed to intrude into the world. Government had become housekeeping on a grand scale and women were still the most natural housekeepers.

The suffragists were thus able to capitalize on the paranoia over the deterioration of the race to raise their status. They sensibly aligned themelves with the environmentalists who at least promoted women above the level of breeding stock. But the obsession with racial perfection made woman's maternal and nurturant functions far more important than any contribution she could make outside the home. This helps explain why very few suffragists suggested a serious restructuring of sex roles.

III

Social purity formed one of the most persistent themes running through both the suffrage and the general reform movements. According to David Pivar, it provided "the moral cement that gave cohesiveness to otherwise disassociated reforms".[37] Its central role tells us a great deal about the reform ideology and helps us understand the suffragists' prudery.

As with race regeneration, social purity was essentially defensive. The style of city living, brought on by the rapid urbanization of the end of the century, challenged the standards of the Protestant middle class. The numbers of foreigners who congregated in urban slums increased the feeling that they had lost control of the nation's character. Richard Hofstadter's "status anxiety" still best describes their attitude.[38]

The most visible signs of disregard for the Christian way of life were the bar-rooms and the brothels. Numerous studies of the temperance campaign describe the reaction to the first of these and show how it aided the suffrage movement.[39] Only a few historians have examined the second.

Social purity crusaders concentrated predominantly upon the problem of prostitution which seemed to embody the challenge to Christian morality. Social gospel preachers and civic leaders complained ceaselessly about the degree of "social vice" rampant in Canada. In 1894 Rev. W.J. Hunter reported that Montreal with a population of 220,000 supported 228 "houses of shame".[40] J.S. Woodsworth drew attention to the problem in the West where, in 1911, Winnipeg had one hundred and fifty houses of ill-fame.[41]

Prostitution raised an additional problem for reformers dedicated to improving the race: venereal disease. Syphilis and gonorrhea reportedly had reached staggering proportions. Dr. Charles Hastings, Toronto's public health inspector, quoted the ominous findings of the 1901 New York State Commission of Seven which concluded that one New Yorker in five had venereal disease.[42] (Canadian reformers often looked to the United States to forecast their future.) The Alberta reformer, Emily Murphy, indicated the deteriorating situation in Canada. She found that one in three prisoners in Alberta's Provincial jail had to be treated for syphilis and gonorrhea.[43]

The impact on future generations magnified the seriousness of these diseases. In 1905 Fritz Schaudinn and Erich Hoffman discovered the spirochete which caused syphilis and proved that it could be transmitted from an infected mother to an unborn baby.[44] Subsequent studies claimed that syphilis produced other afflictions including insanity, paralysis, blindness, deformity, and sterility in the victim and the victim's offspring. Lillian Beynon Thomas blamed syphilis for 50% of all mental deficiency.[45] Dr. Hastings attributed to gonorrheal infection 20 to 25% of all blindness, 17 to 25% of all sterility, and 60 to 80% of all miscarriages.[46]

Science proved no more helpful than in the heredity debate for, while it could list all the deplorable side-effects of venereal disease, it could offer no cure. One treatment for syphilis, doses of mercury, used as early as 1497, killed many patients and made the medicine as dangerous as the disease. Arsphenamine or salvarsen, a derivative of arsenic, developed in 1910, proved more successful but a clinical cure still required repeated injections over a period of one and a half years.[47] Some stages of later syphilis proved refractory to all forms of therapy. Although Albert Neisser discovered the organism which caused gonorrhea in 1879, no effective treatment was developed until the 1940s.[48] Municipal authorities in Europe, Britain, and in some American cities tried to control the problem by segregating prostitutes and subjecting them to compulsory medical inspection. The British Contagious Diseases Acts, introduced between 1864 and 1869, constituted a test case of social supervision.[49] But the Puritan reformers would not support this technique which they interpreted as state sanctioning of moral evil. In any case the idea of regulation was doomed to failure for a far more practical reason: it failed to work. Prostitution simply went underground and venereal disease statistics rose.[50]

The reformers decided to attack the problem at its source and launched a crusade for the general reformation of the nation's morals. Several Canadian reform organizations joined in the purity crusade. Between 1906 and 1915 a Purity-Education Association, staffed mainly by doctors, operated out of Toronto.[51] A second group, the National Committee for the Suppression of the White Slave Traffic, founded in 1912, fought against the international trade in prostitutes. Social purity also operated as a subsidiary theme in associations committed to other causes. The Women's Christian Temperance Union, for example, had committees for press and literature censorship, as well as those dedicated to eliminating white slavery and the "social evil."[52]

The reformers adopted several types of tactics. For the "fallen" they could only suggest that they be prevented from transmitting the disease to others. In 1912 the Methodist Church demanded that all cases of venereal disease be reported to Medical Health officers and that no one be granted a marriage licence until he or she could produce a medical certificate that established freedom from venereal disease.[53] Dr. Hastings suggested the provision of public laboratories where Wasserman tests (discovered in 1906) could be carried out.[54] In 1918 Mary McCallum, then woman's editor for the *Grain Growers' Guide*, recommended the strictest and closest quarantine of venereal disease patients.[55] For those yet to fall, the strategy included censorship and sex education. The logic behind the latter was that, if more people were aware of the frightening consequences of "loose morals," they would reform. A *Self and Sex* series, consisting of eight volumes and published in the United States between 1900 and 1915, became very popular among Canadian reformers. One volume, entitled *What a Young Man Ought to Know*, contained a sixty-page lecture on the frightful effects of venereal disease. Purity lecturers, notably Beatrice Brigden, William Lund Clark, and Arthur W. Beall, hired by the W.C.T.U. and the evangelical Churches, toured the country, imparting the secrets of life to the young.[56] The instruction they offered was filled with threats and warnings, encouraged continence and discouraged sexual activity.

Victorian vitalist physiology, which maintained that the body contained a limited amount of energy, strengthened the reformers' contention that sexual activity ought to be discouraged for the sake of the race. The Rev. W.J. Hunter explained that sex depleted the body's working power, shortened human life, and burdened it with infirmities and diseases. He defended sexual abstinence on the grounds that the vigour of the race demanded it. Masturbation or the "solitary evil" also stood condemned since "loss of semen is loss of blood".[57]

The reformers' underlying strategy was to raise the status and influence of good Christian women. The Victorian female was popularly believed to be asexual. Moreover, it was obvious that male promiscuity was primarily to blame for the degree of prostitution. The simplest answer, therefore, was to enlist the asexual females to help impose a higher standard of morality upon men. The double standard which allowed a man to "sow his wild oats" had to be demolished. Dr. Hastings felt it most important to blot out the "physiological fallacy of sexual necessity for men".[58]

The revelation of police compliance in prostitution convinced many reformers that women needed a ballot in order to be effective in altering men's moral standards. Almost every reformer who supported woman suffrage believed that women would help improve the nation's morals. This involved no real change in woman's role or function. It merely meant capitalizing on woman's traditional perceived virtues: her conservatism and her chastity.

Canada's suffragists confirmed the reformers' faith in woman's purity and removed any hesitation they may have had to give women a vote. Almost without exception the women upheld a strict Victorian code of morality. Emily Stowe approved of the "anti-sex" sex education which taught the young "all the consequences of the transgression".[59] In a similar vein, Dr. Amelia Youmans, founder of the Manitoba Equal Suffrage Club in 1894, issued a foreboding pamphlet entitled "Warning Words," which recounted all the dire effects of venereal disease. Lillian Beynon Thomas advised women to wear modest dress in order to curb "animal desire".[60] Alice Chown, a Toronto feminist, wished to limit sex relations to purposes of reproduction.[61]

The campaigns against prostitution and white slavery attracted enthusiastic suffrage support. Dr. Margaret Gordon, President of the Toronto Suffrage Association, called white slavery the strongest reason which made her a suffragist.[62] In 1908, Flora Macdonald Denison, the President of the National Suffrage Association, was even willing to violate cherished civil liberties to end the trade. She wanted the city to be divided into districts each having an officer with the power to go into any home and find out about its inmates.[63] The suffragists tried to protect young girls from the white slave traders by raising the age of consent to twenty-one. Every suffrage society also demanded that proprietors be held responsible for the order and respectability of their houses, an attack aimed directly at the brothel keepers.[64]

The purity problem seems to have been the main issue over which the suffragists displayed sex antagonism, uniting in a sisterhood of sorts against the men. It angered them that the prostitute consistently played the villain while the man got off with a nominal fine.[65] In their opinion the prostitute was less guilty since she often fell through hunger or was driven into sin because "some man" paid her starvation wages.[66] Conversely the client always went through choice. Flora Macdonald Denison bemoaned the fact that "hundreds of our sisters are forced to live lives of shame to keep body and soul together."[67] Lillian Beynon Thomas wished to subject the men to equal mortification by having the names of those found in houses in the red light district published in newspapers.[68]

The unwed mother, considered another victim of male licentiousness, also aroused sympathy. Agnes Chesley, women's editor for the *Montreal Star*, recommended that she be treated with infinite compassion: "If a girl goes astray, the fault must be looked for in her heritage from her parents, her environment and, above all, in her upbringing."[69] Existing parental custody laws made the father the sole legal guardian of legitimate offspring but left the illegitimate child the sole responsibility of its mother. The well-known Manitoba suffragist, Nellie McClung, pointed to the injustice of this situation: "If a child is a treasure in a married happy home and clouds arise and a separation follows, who gets the child? The father! But who gets the illegitimate child that bears the brand of shame? The poor unfortunate mother. . . ."[70] Equal parental rights over legitimate and illegitimate children became a popular cause among the suffragists.

The move to liberalize divorce laws also aimed at freeing women from sexual exploitation. The suffragists objected most strongly to the clause which allowed a man a divorce on the grounds of adultery but which denied such a right to a woman unless she was forced to cohabit with her husband's mistress.[71] The option of divorce meant a woman no longer had to tolerate her husband's sexual whims, his brutality, or his promiscuity.

According to John and Robin Haller, Victorian feminists used purity reform to try to achieve a kind of sexual freedom.[72] Since contemporary social values would not countenance female promiscuity, the women went the other way and denied their sexuality, in an effort to keep from being considered or treated as sex objects. Their prudery was a mask that conveniently hid the more "radical" effort to achieve freedom of person. Michael Bliss also links the movement for sexual repression to the movement to liberate women — "often, indeed, to liberate them from male sexual tyranny."[73]

Canada's suffragists definitely tried to play down the physical side of relationships. They constantly exhorted women to become friends and companions to men rather than sexual toys or dolls.[74] They seemed to feel that physical strength still played a prominent role in work and in defence and that in order to claim equality women must emphasize the spiritual and the intellectual side of human nature. It could be argued then that they feared sex because it accentuated physical needs and kept the weaker woman in a subservient relationship. As Alice Chown explained, "So long as woman accepts indiscriminate sex relations, so long will she be subject to man."[75] For the same reason the suffragists were unable to assess the value to women of artificial birth control devices which they interpreted simply as one more means of facilitating male licentiousness.[76]

Purity reform was offensive as well as defensive. In a period plagued by revelations of corruption and disease, the claim to represent a higher morality became a very powerful weapon in the suffragists' arsenal. With a ballot in their hands they could bring their moral pressure to bear upon deviant males and become the moral arbiters for the nation. Their strength rested in the respect they gained by presenting themselves as upholders of conventional female virtues.

IV

In order to understand the suffragists' social attitudes we have to understand the values of the group with which they identified. As Anglo-Saxon, Protestant middle class, such women shared the anxieties and expectations of this group. They saw women's problems through glasses tinted with values shaped by this allegiance.

As demonstrated in the first section, the Anglo-Saxon elite in this period were attempting to preserve or regain racial predominance. Two schools advocated different means towards this end. Eugenists concentrated upon applying lessons in animal breeding to humans while a group of environmental reformers argued for the need to improve the living and health standards of the population. Both approaches stressed the importance of woman's role as mother. The suffragists wished to participate in the re-creation of the race and therefore accepted the priority of woman's maternal function. Environmentalists themselves, they found within this theory a justification for their activities in the reform movement. Environmentalism also promised women greater freedom of movement and more diverse activities. Finally, the approval of domestic science training raised the status of homemaker. These factors together satisfied the suffragists' longing for recognition.

319

The same Anglo-Saxon Protestant elite faced another challenge in the growth of large cities, city slums, and resultant intemperance and social vice. The campaign to reinstate Protestant standards of chastity and sobriety naturally attracted the women since it glorified their particular virtues.

With an understanding of the suffragists' background their social attitudes become predictable. It would have been inconceivable to most of these women to suggest serious restructuring of sex roles or to suggest that women imitate male immorality. Rather, they took advantage of the new dignity bestowed on women to achieve certain victories. The vote and the acquisition of higher education facilities, less restricting garments, and a wider range of physical activities ought to be counted among these.

Notes

1. Aileen Kraditor, *The Ideas of the Woman Suffrage Movement, 1890–1920* (New York: Anchor Books, 1971); Anne Summers, *Damned Whores and God's Police* (Victoria: Penguin Books, 1975); C. Rover, *Women's Suffrage and Party Politics in Britain, 1866–1914* (London: Routledge and Kegan Paul, 1967); R. Dalziel, "The Colonial Helpmeet: Women's Role and the Vote in Nineteenth-Century New Zealand," *New Zealand Journal of History* (October 1977).
2. Carol Bacchi, "Liberation Deferred: The Ideas of the English-Canadian Suffragists, 1877–1918" (Ph.D. thesis, McGill University, 1976). In the thesis the instigators of the suffrage societies and some of their followers are described as more feminist than social reformers. This paper is not concerned with these since they were a distinct minority.
3. Ronald Hyam, *Britain's Imperial Century, 1815–1914* (London: B.T. Batsford, 1976); G.R. Searle, *The Quest for National Efficiency* (Longon: Oxford University Press, 1971).
4. Bernard Semmel, *Imperialism and Social Reform* (Massachusetts: Harvard University Press, 1960).
5. Graeme Decarie, "The Prohibition Movement in Ontario, 1894–1916" (Ph.D. dissertation, Queen's University, 1972), p. 261.

6. The theory of acquired characteristics had been unchallenged until the middle of the nineteenth century. In 1869 Galton published *Hereditary Genius* which stressed the hereditary aspects of human existence and society. In 1883 the German embryologist and geneticist, August Weissman, developed his "germ-plasm" theory which completely denied the impact of environment. The rediscovery of Mendel in 1900 strengthened the allegiance to hereditary determinism. Donald K. Pickens, *Eugenics and the Progressives* (Nashville: Vanderbilt University Press, 1968), p. 26; Hans Stubbe, *History of Genetics* (Massachusetts: M.I.T. Press, 1972), p. 176; A.H. Sturtevant, *A History of Genetics* (New York: Harper and Row, 1965), Chapter 3.

7. Mark H. Haller, *Eugenics: Hereditarian Attitudes in American Thought* (New Jersey: Rutgers University Press, 1963), p. 82.

8. Kenneth M. Ludmerer, *Genetics and American Society: A Historical Appraisal* (Baltimore: Johns Hopkins University Press, 1972), p. 10.

9. Rev. A.E. Smith, "Cutting Down an Evil Tree" in SOCIAL SERVICE CONGRESS OF CANADA, *Report of the Proceedings and Addresses* (Toronto, 1914), p. 204.

10. Peter H. Bryce, M.D., "The Ethical Problems Underlying the Social Evil," reprinted from the *Journal of Preventive Medicine and Sociology*, Toronto (March 1914), p. 13. Bryce was also the Chief Medical Officer for the Department of Immigration, Ottawa.

11. Waterloo Lutheran University Archives, Emily Stowe Papers, Scrapbook III, undated (c. 1897) letter from Stowe to the editor of the *Toronto Mail*.

12. Bacchi, *op. cit.*, pp. 234–37.

13. *Montreal Witness*, 12 Oct. 1910.

14. Archives of Saskatchewan, Mrs. S.V. Haight Papers, Drafts of Speeches, undated speech on feeble-minded.

15. NATIONAL COUNCIL OF WOMEN OF CANADA, *Annual Report* (1912), p. 29.

16. *Montreal Witness*, 23 Feb. 1912.

17. *Montreal Star*, 24 Oct. 1914.

18. Mark Haller, *op. cit.*, p. 81.

19. Semmel, *op. cit.*, p. 46.

20. *Montreal Witness*, 12 Oct. 1910.

21. Edward Playter, M.D., "The Physical Culture of Women," in *Woman; her Character, Culture and Calling*, ed. Rev. B.F. Austin (Ontario: Book and Bible House, 1890), p. 225.

22. DOMINION WOMEN'S CHRISTIAN TEMPERANCE UNION (W.C.T.U.), *Annual Report* (1891), Department of Heredity and Hygiene, p. 88.

23. John S. and Robin M. Haller, *The Physician and Sexuality in Victorian America* (Urbana: University of Illinois Press, 1974), p. 146.

24. Suse Woolf, "Women at McGill: the Ladies' Education Association of Montreal" McGill University, 1971, p. 9, (mimeographed).

25. *Grain Growers' Guide*, 14 Oct. 1914.

26. R.J.W. Selleck, *The New Education, 1870–1914* (London: Isaac Putnam and Sons, 1978).

27. Mary Q. Innis, *The Clear Spirit* (Toronto: University of Toronto Press, 1966), p. 109.

28. NATIONAL COUNCIL OF WOMEN OF CANADA, *Women of Canada: Their Life and Their Work*, ed. Ishbel Aberdeen, (Paris International Exhibition, 1900), p. 110.

29. Emily Stowe Papers, *op. cit.* Scrapbook IV, article entitled "Housewifery", (May, 1889).

30. *Winnipeg Free Press*, 8 Apr. 1916.

31. NATIONAL COUNCIL OF WOMEN, *Report* (1904), p. 121.

32. *Grain Growers' Guide*, 27 Sept. 1911.

33. Victoria College Library, Emily Stowe Papers, Scrapbook VI, Printer flier, "Votes for Women! The Woman's Reason."

34. *Montreal Gazette*, 27 March 1912.

35. Child Welfare Exhibition, *Souvenir Handbook*, 8–22 Oct. 1912.

36. Bacchi, *op. cit.*, p. 167.

37. David J. Pivar, "The New Abolitionism: The Quest for Social Purity" (Ph.D. dissertation, University of Pennsylvania, 1965).

38. Richard Hofstadter, *The Age of Reform* (New York: Vintage Books, 1955).

39. Decarie, *op. cit.*, John H. Thompson; "The Prohibition Question in Manitoba" (M.A. Dissertation, University of Manitoba, 1969); Robert Irwin Maclean, "A 'Most Effectual' Remedy: Temperance and Prohibition in Alberta, 1875-1915" (M.A. dissertation, University of Calgary, 1969); Albert J. Hiebert, "Prohibition in British Columbia" (M.A. dissertation, Simon Fraser University, 1969).

40. Rev. W.J. Hunter, *Manhood Wrecked and Rescued* (Toronto: William Briggs, 1894), p. 71.

41. J.S. Woodsworth, *My Neighbour* (Toronto: University of Toronto Press Reprint, 1972), Chapter 8.

42. SOCIAL SERVICE CONGRESS, *op. cit.*, p. 208.

43. Emily Murphy, *The Black Candle* (Toronto: Thomas Allen, 1922), p. 307.

44. William J. Brown, M.D., *Syphilis: A Synopsis* (Washington: Public Health Service Publications, 1968), pp. 9–11.

320

45. *Winnipeg Free Press*, 3 July 1915.
46. SOCIAL SERVICE CONGRESS, *op. cit.*
47. Brown, *op. cit.*
48. D. Llewellyn-Jones, *Sex and Venereal Disease* (London: Faber and Faber, 1974), p. 42.
49. Glen Petrie, *A Singular Iniquity: The Campaigns of Josephine Butler* (New York: Viking Press, 1971).
50. Haller and Haller, *op. cit.*, p. 243.
51. Michael Bliss, "Pure Books on Avoided Subjects: Pre-Freudian Sexual Ideas in Canada," Canadian Historical Association, *Historical Papers* (1970), p. 104.
52. W.C.T.U., *Annual Reports*.
53. Methodist Church, Department of Evangelism and Social Service, *Annual Report* (1912–1913), p. 10.
54. SOCIAL SERVICE CONGRESS, *op. cit.*, p. 208.
55. *Grain Growers' Guide*, 16 Jan. 1918.
56. Beatrice Brigden and William Lund Clark were hired by the Canadian Methodist Church. Arthur W. Beall lectured to the schoolboys of Ontario on behalf of the W.C.T.U. Methodist Church; Board of Evangelical and Social Service, Correspondence between Beatrice Brigden and Dr. Albert Moore; United Church Archives, Beatrice Brigden and William Lund Clark Papers.
57. Hunter, *op. cit.*
58. Social Service Congress, *op. cit.*, p. 213.
59. Waterloo Lutheran University Archives, Emily Stowe Papers, *op. cit.*, Scrapbook IV, undated (c. 1877) newspaper clipping.
60. *Winnipeg Free Press*, 19 Aug. 1916.
61. Alice A Chown; The Stairway (Boston, Cornhill Co., 1921), p. 114.
62. University of Toronto Archives, Flora Macdonald Denison Papers, collection of newspaper clippings, *Star Weekly*, Toronto, 23 March 1913.
63. *Ibid.*, unpub. typescript, "The White Slave Traffic", n.d.
64. SASKATCHEWAN PROVINCIAL EQUAL FRANCHISE BOARD, *Minutes of Meetings*, 18 Feb. 1916.
65. *Montreal Herald*, Woman's Edition, 26 Nov. 1913, p. 24.
66. *B.C. Federationist*, 17 Oct. 1916. A quote from a B.C. suffragist.
67. *Toronto World*, 15 Jan. 1911.
68. *Winnipeg Free Press*, 7 Oct. 1916.
69. *Montreal Herald*, 24 Sept. 1913.
70. *Grain Growers' Guide*, 26 Feb. 1913.
71. Helen Gregory Macgill, *Daughters, Wives, and Mothers in British Columbia: Some Laws Regarding Them* (Vancouver, 1913), p. 31.
72. Haller and Haller, *op. cit.*, p. xii.
73. Bliss, *op. cit.*, p. 103.
74. *Grain Growers' Guide*, 14 Aug. 1912; *Winnipeg Free Press*, 28 Aug. 1915; *Toronto World*, 31 Oct. 1909; *Montreal Herald*, Woman's Edition, 26 Nov. 1913, p. 17.
75. Chown, *op. cit.*, p. 114.
76. C. Rover, *Love, Morals and the Feminists* (London. Routledge and Kegan Paul, 1970).

The WCTU: 'For God, Home and Native Land': A Study in Nineteenth-Century Feminism*

WENDY MITCHINSON

The organizational woman is a familiar phenomenon today whether she belongs to a feminist group, a church society or one of a myriad of other women's organizations. But this was not always the case. In the early part of the nineteenth century women were seldom organized, prevented by distance, poor transportation facilities and lack of time. Only the more privileged could overcome these obstacles and those who did tended to form local church and benevolent societies. By 1900, however, this situation had altered greatly. Women's organizations had increased in number: many continued the work of the church and benevolent societies which had formed earlier in the century; others formed to provide new expressive outlets for women; still others organized to reform what women saw as problems in society. All represented the ability and desire of many Canadian women to become active outside the domestic sphere.[1]

322

Several reasons account for this extraordinary expansion of women's activities: transportation had improved, making it easier for groups of women to meet together; towns and cities were growing in size, thus enlarging the membership potential of women's groups; and the increasing affluence of Canadian society meant that more middle-class women had leisure time to devote to women's organizations. In 1871, 81.2 per cent of the Canadian population lived in areas classed as rural. By 1901 this had declined to 62.5 per cent. The greater population density of cities heightened the need for institutional responses on the part of society — orphanages, refuge homes and hospitals — philanthropic areas in which women had long been involved. Cities also accentuated the problems of poverty, crime and intemperance. Many Canadian women realized such problems could not be offset through traditional benevolent activities and responded by searching for the causes of these problems. The result was the formation of reform organizations designed to eradicate the source of a specific social ill and not simply to ameliorate its symptoms. The willingness of many women to become so involved reflected an important change that was occurring in their lives.[2]

Throughout the latter half of the nineteenth century, Canada was slowly emerging from a commercial to an industrialized society. At the same time it was becoming more urbanized. As both these processes occurred, the workplace became separated from the home, where women were increasingly isolated. The domestic isolation of women was complemented by what

*From *A Not Unreasonable Claim: Women and Reform in Canada, 1880s–1920s*, ed. by Linda Kealy. Copyright 1979 by Women's Press. Reprinted by permission.

historians have referred to as the 'cult of domesticity', the dominating image of which was 'woman as mother'. Ironically, as woman's prestige in society was being enhanced by her maternal role, the actual fertility of women was declining. In 1871 the registered legitimate fertility rate in Canada was similar to what it had been in the eighteenth century, 378 births per 1,000 women aged 15 to 49 years. By 1891, however, it had declined by 24 per cent to 285 births per 1,000 women aged 15 to 49 years. This decline was especially extreme in urban areas. Although women were having fewer children than had been the case in the earlier century this did not necessarily lessen women's commitment to the domestic sphere; indeed, through an intensification of the mother-child relationship it may have increased it. Women were becoming, in fact as well as in ideal, the emotional centre of the home and family.[3]

Women may have had influence within the home but the ideal of domesticity certainly limited them outside it. The emergence of women from the domestic sphere through women's organizations was a response to their dissatisfaction with this situation. Many women wanted to preserve their status within and control of the family by becoming active in society. As well, the seeming increase in power and prestige that women had gained through the rise of the domestic ideal led to a desire to publicly assert and extend that power outside the home. The easiest way to accomplish this, given the context of Canadian society at the time, was to rationalize it by an appeal to domesticity.[4]

Women's reform organizations were one way in which Canadian women hoped to protect the family and assert themselves in an acceptable way. Each organization was initially formed to right a specific wrong, but once formed, each tended to involve itself in a number of reform enterprises. The Woman's Christian Temperance Union was such an organization. It provides an example of the emergence of women from the domestic sphere to an active participation in society.

Formation and Platform

The first local WCTU was formed in Ontario in 1874, the first provincial union in 1877 in Ontario and the Dominion Union in 1883. By 1900, the Woman's Christian Temperance Union had approximately 10,000 members. This made the WCTU one of the largest women's organizations of the time and certainly much larger than any of the suffrage societies. As well, the WCTU was a truly national organization and was located in both small towns and urban centres across Canada, whereas the Dominion Women's Enfranchisement Association, the one national suffrage organization, was essentially based in Toronto.

The Union very early adopted prohibition as its main platform. While most reform organizations in the nineteenth century emphasized the importance of adjusting the individual to the existing norms of society, temperance organizations emphasized the adjustment of society to create an atmosphere of temperance for the individual. By mid-century, temperance advocates had concluded that voluntary appeal did not work. When the state of Maine introduced a compulsory temperance law—that is, prohibition — Canadian temperance advoates quickly followed its lead. Consequently, by the time the WCTU was formed in 1874, prohibition had become *the* weapon against intemperance. But because it depended on government support, its adoption by the WCTU paved the way to an eventual confrontation between the temperance union and the elected representatives of male society, if and when the latter refused to adopt prohibition.[5]

The WCTU had few qualms about supporting prohibition. Its members believed it to be a radical reform but an essential one. The atrocities of war were negligible beside the atrocities of the liquor trade. As a foe of morality 'it turns men into demons, and makes women an easy prey to lust.' Because the majority of convicted criminals were known to drink, the WCTU concluded that alcohol caused crime and argued that supporting such a criminal population was uneconomical. Intemperance was ruining the physical health of Canadians as well, one member of the WCTU even linking the spread of cholera with the consumption of alcohol. The statistics of alcohol consumption served only to increase these fears. In 1871 the total alcohol consumption per capita, 15 years of age and older, was 1.19 imperial gallons, rising to 1.29 in 1873 and in 1874, the year in which the WCTU formed, to 1.42. WCTU members were convinced something had to be done to prevent the terrible toll in human suffering that this increase represented to them.[6]

They believed women, as innocent victims of an invasion of alcohol into their homes, suffered most from the liquor trade, and they exploited this appeal to the fullest. 'How can Christian women sit still and be quiet while women's cries for help are in their ears?' they asked. Children's cries were also heard. The Children's Aid Society in Vancouver noted in its first annual report that, with one exception, 'Every case which has been brought before us had been brought about through drink.' Temperance women felt they had a special duty as women to protect these children. Certainly men did not seem willing to do anything about alcohol abuse, perhaps because they were the main consumers of alcohol and profiteers from the liquor trade. The WCTU believed most women did not drink. Where men were seemingly unable to act, then, women could and would. A social ill such as intemperance could not be kept isolated; it reached out and affected temperate and intemperate alike. It had to be stopped.[7]

The WCTU was not particularly concerned about the individual inebriate — the union had neither the resources nor the time to help individuals. They were more concerned with the effects of intemperance on society, the way in which the inebriate hurt innocent people such as his wife and children, and the way in which he undermined the strength of society.

Blaming alcohol for society's ills was a comfortable belief. It did not threaten the economic status of the temperance women or their families because they did not talk about intemperance in personal terms. In fact, their belief in prohibition was a reflection of their class status. Most execu-

324

tive members of the WCTU were married to lawyers, businessmen, doctors, journalists and clergymen. Considering the connection temperance women made between intemperance, crime and sexual immorality, it is not surprising that they saw in intemperance a challenge to their middle-class way of life. It was the foreign element in an otherwise ordered society.[8]

The Politicization Process

Only the state, through legislation, could ensure a temperate society. To persuade the various levels of government to respond, the WCTU became actively involved in the public sphere. Its members believed they had a responsibility as *women* to protect not only their own but all homes.[9]

One of the WCTU's methods was the use of petitions. They were circulated for signatures, then forwarded to the appropriate level of government in the hope that once officials realized there was a good deal of support for prohibition, they would act. This naive view of the democratic process assumed a common morality for all and, in fact, the existence of an absolute 'right' in society, a notion which derived from a fundamentalist interpretation of Christian morality and the members' own political inexperience.[10]

325

These petitions did have limited success. Through them, governments became aware of the demand for prohibition, and usually responded by granting a plebiscite on the question. The plebiscite was a good tactic, for it allowed Canadians to inform the government of their views on a controversial problem on which the government was hesitant to act. If supported by an overwhelming majority, plebiscites permitted the government to act with few fears of political reprisals. Prohibition was undoubtedly a controversial question. It not only attracted opposition from the liquor interests, but also from those opposed to government intervention in the day-to-day lives of individuals, especially in a practice that was as widespread as drinking was in the nineteenth century.

Petitions and plebiscites were the high points in the preventive public work of the WCTU. They both legitimized temperance work and forced Canadians to consider the question of control. Generally the WCTU's activity was more mundane. Members painstakingly distributed literature and called on electors to vote for temperance advocates. They appealed to 'their fathers, husbands, brothers, sons and friends who possessed the right of suffrage to exercise this right in the interest of temperance and total abstinence'. The WCTU approached clergymen, church members, teachers of Sunday schools and public schools and heads of organizations such as the Knights of Labor, requesting them to use their influence to dissuade people from drinking. It asked doctors to stop prescribing liquor as medicine. Members tried to persuade anyone in a position of prestige to recognize their work, or any part of it, thus using their influence as women in a very traditional way, that is, through moral suasion.[11]

Yet they did not limit themselves to this tactic. The WCTU was so determined to achieve prohibition that it even gave guarded support to a new political party. In March 1888, through the efforts of male temperance organizations, Canada's New Party was formed. Soon afterwards, in the WCTU publication, the *Woman's Journal*, Mrs. Rockwell, a prominent member of the union, appealed to her readers to use their 'influence with husbands, fathers and brothers, for the first and only Political Party committed to the accomplishment of the prohibition of the liquor traffic'. The Dominion WCTU resolved to give 'individual support to the party which will unequivocally put the plan of Prohibition in its platform'. This resolution could only apply to the New Party; however, the party floundered. Old party loyalties remained entrenched and, as the corresponding secretary of the Ontario WCTU reported, 'Politics first, politics last, politics everytime, each party afraid of the temperance question.'[12]

This was proven again and again. In provincial plebiscites in Manitoba, Prince Edward Island, Ontario and Nova Scotia, prohibition seemed, to the WCTU, overwhelmingly endorsed; yet the respective governments did nothing. Unfortunately for the temperance women, greater disillusionment lay ahead.

In 1896 the Liberal Party under Wilfrid Laurier promised a national plebiscite on prohibition. Great excitement pervaded the temperance forces. As the president of the Nova Scotia WCTU declared,

The question of Prohibition is at last a Political issue. Not as a weak, struggling Third Party, but a live question with which both parties feel that they must deal whether they will or not. . . . The world is turning to our country today, with great interest for a solution of the Liquor Question. It is nearer a solution with us than anywhere else on earth.[13]

The women naturally felt they should be able to vote in the plebiscite. When this was refused, even the Nova Scotia WCTU, usually more quiescent than others about the enfranchisement of women, showed its exasperation.

Dear women, are we free and intelligent citizens of a civilized country, or are we the irresponsible nonentities that our government reckons us? If the former in the name of all that is just and right in the name of all that is pure and lovely and of good report; in the name of God and home and humanity, let us rise and claim the citizen's heritage — the right of self-government! If the latter then may we write 'failure,' not only of the cause of prohibition, but of every other righteous reform for the stream never rises above the mothers of men. If they be 'small, slight . . . miserable,' how shall we grow?

Once again the women argued that they should be allowed to enter society in order to protect their homes; moreover, as the domestic force in society they should be encouraged to do so. Many of these women were becoming increasingly frustrated and bitter about being dependent on men to determine the nature of the society in which they lived. They used all the power they had as women to obtain a favourable result, but in the end they could only watch while men voted. The plebiscite took place on September 28, 1898. Every province with the exception of Quebec voted for prohibition, for a net majority of 13,687. The temperance forces felt this was a victory; the government, whose support lay in the province of Quebec, did not.[14]

With this defeat the women of the WCTU lost their faith that governments act in the best interests of the people. In their eyes, prohibition was never a question of individual rights but of moral rights, and it believed no government had the power to make what was morally wrong a legal right. The state was an active agent in society and as such had a responsibility to do 'not what shall punish wrong-doing so much as what shall tend to right doing'. The Canadian government legalized the liquor trade and, 'for a price, for revenue, makes the whole nation, women and all, party to its own degradation.' The only solution was for temperance women to have representation at all levels of government.[15]

One reform essential to this process was the enfranchisement of women. Appealing to the good will of men in power had failed. The alternative, then, was for women to represent themselves. By supporting a controversial reform, the WCTU women had confronted their own lack of power as women. With their espousal of suffrage they went on record as supporting two of the most controversial reforms of nineteenth-century Canada. From a desire to protect their homes through the protection of society, these Canadian temperance women had come far. One way in which they met the challenge was to hold fast to the traditional concept of themselves as women, that is, they did not support suffrage as a right owed to them as individuals, but as a useful means by which to meet their feminine responsibility — the care of the family.

327

The WCTU, Women's Suffrage and a Sense of Identity

The WCTU had not always supported the enfranchisement of women. In the early years of organization Letitia Youmans, WCTU president, deliberately avoided the issue of women's rights and stressed the protection of home and children. In this way she hoped to gain support for the union.

So strong was the opposition in Canada to what was commonly termed 'women's rights', that I had good reason to believe that should I advocate the ballot for women in connection with my temperance work, it would most effectively block the way, and it was already uphill work for a woman to appear on a public platform.[16]

In the 1870s, the suffrage question had been a divisive issue. By the 1890s, after the WCTU had come face to face with government intransigence, it was acknowledged as *the* weapon against the liquor interests.

The WCTU stressed the good that would result if women were given the vote. Mrs. Jacob Spence, first superintendent of the Ontario WCTU's Franchise Department and mother of Canadian temperance leader F.S. Spence, explained the reasons best:

It is not the clamor of ambition, ignorance or frivolity trying to gain position. It is the prayer of earnest, thoughtful, Christian women in behalf of their children and their children's children. It is in the interest of our homes, our divinely-appointed place, to protect the home against the licensed evil which is the enemy of the home, and also to aid in our efforts to advance God's kingdom beyond the bounds of our homes.

It is only by legislation that the roots of great evils can be touched, and for want of the ballot we stand powerless in face of our most terrible foe, the legalized liquor traffic. The liquor sellers are not afraid of our conventions, but they are afraid of our ballots.

The appeal to woman's maternal role attracted many women who might otherwise have rejected such a reform. Home and family were the cornerstones of society; an attack on one was an attack on the other.[17]

The connection between prohibition and votes for women was made clear. Where it was not, support for the franchise was weakened. In the Maritimes, for example, there seemed to be little concern over the ballot except among the WCTU unions, and even this was negligible when compared to other provincial unions. One reason was that the Maritimes, more than the other provinces, took advantage of the *Scott Act*, the local option law, with the result that they had the lowest per capita alcohol consumption in Canada. Because of this virtual prohibition in the Maritimes, the connection between temperance and the enfranchisement of women could not be easily made. There, only the justice argument for suffrage remained. It was a political appeal, one that suggested a challenge to the established order that would force women out from behind their concerns of home and family into the world. Few women in the nineteenth century identified with this concept, for it negated the altruism which was seen as the source of their influence in Canadian society.

The struggle for the franchise was the epitome of the temperance women's confidence in themselves, a confidence which had emerged only slowly. In the early years they were very hesistant, even to the point of discussing whether a woman should lead a public prayer unless careful scrutiny of the audience revealed the absence of men. Such timidity was understandable. The WCTU had formed at a time when women were not used to speaking in public, and although this timidity lessened as the women learned to run meetings and publicly express themselves, it never disappeared. Certainly their attitude toward working with men remained ambivalent. On the one hand, they encouraged men's support through honorary memberships and the occasional men's auxiliaries. On the other hand, men were not allowed to vote in their meetings. There were other men's-only and mixed temperance organizations, but there was only one *Woman's* Christian Temperance Union. Its members formed a wholly female society in which they were comfortable and in which their individual efforts were recognized.[18]

The campaign for prohibition was a significant one for the temperance women. The liquor interests represented 'the heaviest monied monopoly on the continent. It has an outpost in every town. It cows legislation. Its grip is upon the throttle valve of all political enginery.' To counter such evil, the women of the WCTU had to be strong. Their special mission allowed no compromise, even to attract new members.

I have heard it hinted by some, by both within and without our fold, that our burning need was an influx of the upper tendom, 'to give tone to the movement', to popularize it. If the money and influence secured in this way were not counter-balanced by some shrinkage of our principles, to accommodate the less rigid notions of those educated to a polite tolerance of wrong, we would doubtless be the gainers. Yet, the 'if' is a large and serious one. It is to be feared that the Dons would have more to get than to give. The common people have ever been the bond and sinew of successful revolutions, whether in morals or estates.[19]

The revolution they wanted was one of morals and attitudes. It was a world where their position as leaders would be recognized and where they would receive the accolades which normally went to 'society' women. As one member explained, 'While we believe there are many good women leading a social life, yet we believe no true woman whose spiritual sensibilities have not been benumbed by habit and custom, finds in this a satisfying portion.' A woman was to be admired for what she did herself and not for her husband or family connections. This belief provided these organizational women with a feeling of unity and devotion to one another and to their leaders.[20]

This feeling of solidarity is evident in the following description of Frances Willard, president of the American and World WCTU. One member of the Canadian WCTU recalled with quiet reverence her first contact with Miss Willard.

329

At the first appearance of her calm sweet face, I was enraptured and before she had closed, her thrilling words and the spirit within her had so filled my heart that I too would have been more than willing to have left all and followed her. . . . As I look back through the vista of years to this first knowledge of Miss Willard, I think I have a dim realization of the feelings of the disciples when our Master and Saviour stood revealed to them in all purity and truth of His manhood and called to them 'come and follow me.'

Feminine friendships were particularly strong in the nineteenth century because women were expected to remain within their own, separate sphere. In the rarefied atmosphere of women's organizations, women could find congenial company and develop friendships which, as revealed by the love shown to Frances Willard, were very deep. Such devotion and trust in one another and their leaders was also necessary. WCTU members faced great opposition to their advocacy of prohibition and suffrage and they undoubtedly found needed support in these friendships.[21]

The Struggle for a Moral Society

Support for women's suffrage did not negate the belief in separate spheres for men and women. Temperance women made it clear that their espousal of suffrage did not make them 'new' women. 'A man is to a woman and a woman is to a man, a stronghold; a completeness such as no two women or two men ever can be to one another,' they declared. Mothers were urged to train their daughters in the duties of housekeeping. The Union stressed the adoption of manual training in schools to ensure that children received the practical skills requisite for their future careers; in the case of girls this meant domestic science. Better fulfilment of the domestic role even justified support for higher education. The WCTU also advocated the appointment of female school trustees, factory inspectors, physicians at girls' reformatories, matrons, bailiffs and police matrons. The limited acceptance of these demands resulted in the creation of new work roles that extended women's participation and involvement in society and did so on a premise which most could accept, that is, the domestic ideal of woman.[22]

The women of the WCTU also wanted to protect children. The British Columbia WCTU endeavoured to secure a Children's Protection Act similar to the one in Ontario; the Dominion WCTU supported the establishment of cottage homes as reformatories for boys and girls so that juvenile offenders could be reformed in a home atmosphere; and several provincial WCTUs tried to institute curfew bells which would ring at a certain hour, usually nine o'clock, after which time no child was to be on the street unless accompanied by parent or guardian. The WCTU hoped a curfew would prevent late hours, 'that most subtle of stimulants', and thus lessen the number of children who would be tempted to drink. It began to realize, however, that curfew bells only controlled the actions of children to a limited extent, whereas education encouraged them to voluntarily restrain their actions, and in 1896 the women of the New Brunswick WCTU supported compulsory education for this reason. Education for its own sake was not their goal, but it could offset a bad home influence and teach children to be well-behaved.[23]

The WCTU was equally concerned about young girls and women. Its members felt that all girls did not have the advantages of a decent home life and a loving and protecting mother, and as mothers themselves they wanted to help them. They believed that young girls kept ignorant about the beginnings of life were especially vulnerable and urged that mothers and educators be honest about sex, arguing that ignorance was not a protector of purity but a weapon against it. Society was seen by them as dangerous to women; man was the seducer, woman his victim, and unfortunately, the law favoured the former. The WCTU of British Columbia pointed out that the law did not appear concerned with the protection of girls since it allowed them to give sexual consent at the age of sixteen, yet did not prosecute the seducer until the age of twenty-one. The WCTU protested that when police raided houses of ill fame only the names of the prostitutes were published. It demanded that the names of the men be published as well, so that respectable women would know which men to shun.[24]

In many areas the WCTU was over-zealous, its members responding in a drastic way to what appeared harmless to most Canadians at the time. Concern for the moral health of society led them to condemn certain styles of evening dress, round dances, nude art, gambling, theatre, prize fights and the use of women as bar maids. For members of the WCTU these were serious problems which had dire consequences.

What has produced the almost numberless bands of young thieves, murderers, and train-wreckers, of whom we read in every day's paper? Dime novels, indiscriminately sold. . . .

Why are there so many divorces among young married people, now-a-days, where they have not the Bible ground of excuse to plead. Distorted views of life gathered from the trashy novel, where the heroes are all strong, tender and wealthy, and the heroines are beautiful, pure, and loving. Real life proves a different thing, and there is no strength of character to meet and bear the common discipline of plain human nature.

The WCTU invited confrontation in its advocacy of prohibition and suffrage.

Because of the continued rejection by the majority of Canadians of their two central reforms, WCTU members developed a siege mentality. They saw the foundations of their world — that is, the sanctity of the home — attacked on all sides. As a result, they became more entrenched in their own principles.[25]

Any compromise in the struggle for a moral society was unthinkable. The WCTU protested vehemently when the British government reintroduced the *Contagious Diseases Act*, whereby brothels were legally licenced. When Isabella Somerset, vice-president of the World WCTU, apparently approved of the Act, she was criticized severely. At the quarterly meeting on February 4, 1898, the Stanstead County WCTU resolved, 'That we have no sympathy with the propositions of Lady Henry Somerset in relation to the C.D. Act and we reaffirm that the first plank in our platform is no compromise with sin.' Dr. Amelia Yeomans, a vice-president of the Dominion WCTU, condemned the re-election of Somerset by the World WCTU and urged the Canadian union to resign from the international body. By this time, however, Somerset had recanted and the Dominion executive, with the exception of Dr. Yeomans, voted full confidence in her.[26]

331

The WCTU accepted the view that woman was and should be the moral guardian of society and so took a particular interest in the campaign for purity. Its campaign emphasized a single standard of sexual morality for both men and women, the standard being that dictated to women — control. This standard would not only help individuals, but would safeguard the future of the race. 'Impure living', whether represented in sexual promiscuity, reading licentious novels (any novels) or the 'secret vice' (masturbation) had, the WCTU believed, horrendous results on subsequent generations. The WCTU held that a mother's thoughts could influence her child before birth, warning that 'sensuality may be transmitted to the yet unborn child by . . . want of care in this respect.' The new science of eugenics confirmed it. Heredity was important physically and morally and therefore men and women had a responsibility to choose their spouses wisely. Intemperance itself was hereditary, they thought, and its consequences reached out to maim the innocent, as the 1892 Report of the Department of Heredity and Hygiene was meant to illustrate.

Recently a friend of mine was urging a little boy two years of age to join the Band of Hope, when he startled her by saying, 'You don't know what you are asking of me. *Never drink any more liquor?* I love it better than my life, I could not live without it.' Think you that was an acquired taste with that child? No, no; his parents are responsible for it. 'A corrupt tree cannot bring forth good fruit.'

The purpose of this obviously fantastic story is clear.[27]

The belief in heredity created a problem. If intemperance was inherited, the WCTU could do little to prevent it, and this would mean defeat, a negation of its entire educational and preventive program. Fortunately, the members of the WCTU had a strong belief in the spiritual power of man. As upholders of morality they were upholders of the Christian faith. The two were inseparable in their eyes and so to fully understand their determination it is important to understand the source of it.

The WCTU and the Church

The WCTU wanted a Protestant Christian society. For most of its members, faith and temperance went hand in hand. The fight for prohibition was part of a religious battle, and one which women were determined to win. In the early years of its existence this religious strain probably did much to attract the initial WCTU membership and make it a respectable organization. Certainly the WCTU was closely aligned with those churches which endorsed prohibition, as revealed by the religious affiliation of its executive. Forty-three per cent of its executive were Methodist, 18 per cent were Presbyterians and only 10 per cent were adherents to the Church of England. Methodists had long disapproved of the consumption of alcohol and had been active in condemning it, although Presbyterians had not. Except for the more evangelical among them, Church of England supporters were uncomfortable in an organization which disapproved strongly of their church's use of wine as part of its religious service. The WCTU, then, was aligned to the church most active in its social involvement and strongest in its encouragement to women to become involved, to accept personal responsibility and to follow Christ's teachings.[28]

The Union patterned itself after the church. Its meetings opened with a prayer and a hymn and ended with a benediction. During the meeting there was more hymn singing, a collection and often an address by a minister. The WCTU believed that religious faith was the cornerstone of a temperate society and supported anything which strengthened the church. It firmly endorsed the movement to maintain Sabbath Observance and devoted a department to this end. Sunday law allowed families to be united by granting workers one day of rest, but Sunday laws also made it difficult for the working man and his family to have outings together. In the same way that curfew bells limited the freedom of children, Sunday laws limited the freedom of working men on the one day they had to call their own.[29]

The WCTU's religious faith was strong. Uppermost in its members' minds was the spiritual welfare of the people they were trying to help, for although they rejected the denominational exclusiveness of missionary societies, they still retained the 'spirit of Faith and Prayer' which characterized them. They believed that they could help men stop drinking if they could only bring them back to the Christian faith. They did not advocate temperance as simply a rational economic philsophy, but as a moral ethical one which was necessary if man was to live through Christ. Because reform of men's temporal state came only through Christ, the WCTU wanted 'to carry the Gospel cure to the drinking classes.' Its only approach to the individual inebriate, then, came through an evangelical commitment.[30]

Many work departments reflected this evangelical tendency: Flower Mission, Work Among Sailors (Immigrants, Lumbermen, Railwaymen), Sabbath Observance and Sabbath Schools, and Work in Jails. The women attempted to comfort those in need with the solace of religion. They often visited the inmates of prisons, hoping to win these men and women away

332

from their former intemperate habits by bringing them the word of God. Yet when faced with prison conditions, they were led to demand prison reform. They became the advocates of prisoner classification, work for the incarcerated, the indeterminate sentence (an open-ended sentence which would terminate only when the individual had reformed), the parole system and schoolrooms within the jail. However, the women of the WCTU were worried that prison reform might take the spotlight away from their evangelical work and so continually stressed the need to remember the power of prayer and maintained a vigilance over their own spiritual well-being.

The church was the one institution in which women had been permitted and encouraged to work, even if only in a subordinate role. More importantly, the women of the WCTU believed a common Christianity bound them together as women, allowing them the freedom to think and act. They were convinced that Christianity and its handmaiden, the Protestant church, recognized women as being equal to men. Believing this, their involvement in public agitation to support prohibition and suffrage was not a denial of their proper sphere but a fulfilment of it. Their activism was justified by faith.

WCTU members were part of a movement to rectify wrong. As individuals they counted for little; as part of a great crusade they believed they became worthy of Christ.

The Woman's Christian Temperance Union is no accident, but one of God's special creations. Throughout the ages since the fall of man Divine Love has been raising up instrumentalities for the restoration of our race to its original standard of moral rectitude.[31]

Conclusion

The Woman's Christian Temperance Union played a significant role in the lives of many Canadian women in the nineteenth century. Its advocacy of prohibition necessitated state intervention, which meant the WCTU was forced to appeal to the public in order to persuade the government to implement such a controversial policy. This made the union much more visible than most other women's organizations and hastened the time when its members would be faced with their own powerlessness as women. Through this politicization process the members of the WCTU confronted the reality of their lives in nineteenth-century Canada — they had little concrete power. As a solution they advocated women's suffrage, not so they could represent themselves as individuals, but so they could extend their domestic power as women in their effort to protect their homes by protecting society from the problems within it that could undermine both. They did not reject society's view of women, but argued that what made them different from men and what made them the centre of domestic life necessitated their involvement in temporal society. Their belief in an active Christianity supported them in this endeavour. That their actions and beliefs might appear contradictory did not concern them. They were practical women; they did what they felt had to be done and rationalized it by any means possible.

The rationales they used were the domestic ideal of woman and Christian duty. These were successful because the members really believed in them and these were also two supports which could not be attacked by those disapproving of women's activism. There were limits to what women could do using the ideal of domesticity to justify their actions. It meant an acknowledgement that woman's role was to care for the home. However, few Canadian women in the nineteenth century perceived this as a limitation. For them there was no contradiction between their actions and belief. Their interpretation of the domestic ideal of womanhood was a dynamic one, one that could and did encompass the women's rights movement. They were social feminists, not feminists.

As a precursor for the experience of other women's groups the WCTU's significance is great. It exposed the importance of the domestic ideal and Christian duty for women in the nineteenth century and demonstrated how Canadian women were able to use what some historians have seen as restrictive concepts to extend and exert their power in society.[32]

Notes

1. The following is only a partial list of the women's clubs which were formed in the latter part of the last century: the Woman's Auxiliary to the Board of the Domestic and Foreign Missionary Society of the Church of England in Canada, (1885); The Woman's Baptist Missionary Union of the Martime Provinces, (1885); The Woman's Foreign Missionary Society of the Presbyterian Church in Canada, Eastern and Western Division, (1876); The Woman's Missionary Society of the Methodist Church, (1881); The Woman's Art Association of Canada, (1890); the National Council of Women, (1893); the Woman's Christian Temperance Union of Canada, (1885); the Young Women's Christian Association, (1893); the Dominion Order of the King's Daughters, (1891); the Victorian Order of Nurses, (1898); the National Home Reading Union, (1895); the Aberdeen Association, (1897); the Girls' Friendly Society of Canada, (1882); the Imperial Order of the Daughters of the Empire, (1900); the Dominion Women's Enfranchisement Association, (1889); plus numerous local musical clubs, historical societies, literary societies, dramatic, athletic and charitable associations.

2. In Ontario and Quebec, the most populated provinces, 22.8 per cent of the population lived in centres classed as urban in 1881. By 1891 this had increased to 33.2 per cent and 29.2 per cent respectively. No province, however, matched British Columbia, whose urban population increased by 30.6 per cent between 1881 and 1891. *Census of Canada 1890-1891*, Vol. 4, p. 401; *Sixth Census of Canada*, 1921, Vol. 1, p. 346.

3. Barbara Welter, 'The Cult of True Womanhood 1820-1860,' *American Quarterly*, Vol. 18 (Summer 1966), pp. 258-71; Jacques Henripin, *Trends and Factors of Fertility in Canada* (Ottawa: Statistics Canada, 1972) pp. 39, 36. See Ann D. Gordon and Mari Jo Buhle, 'Sex and Class in Colonial and Nineteenth-Century America,' in ed. Bernice Carroll, *Liberating Women's History* (Chicago: University of Illinois Press, 1976), p. 286, for a discussion of the intensification of the mother-child relationship in the American context.

4. The second hypothesis has been suggested by Daniel Scott Smith's concept of domestic feminism. See Daniel Scott Smith, 'Family Limitation, Sexual Control, and Domestic Feminism in Victorian America,' in eds. Mary Hartman, Lois W. Banner, *Clio's Consciousness Raised* (New York: Harper & Row, 1974), pp. 119-37.

5. For a discussion of the early temperance movement in Canada and the way in which it was influenced by the American, see J. K. Chapman, 'The Mid-19th Century Temperance Movements in New Brunswick and Maine,' *Canadian Historical Review*, XXXV (1954), pp. 43-60. The confrontation with government was experienced by other women's organizations much later since few advocated such controversial reforms. Eventually, however, most women's groups were faced with government reluctance to implement their reforms.

6. Annual Report, Woman's Christian Temperance Union of Ontario, 1898, p. 96; ibid., 1899, pp. 50-51; Robert Popham, Wolfgang Schmidt, *Statistics of Alcohol Use and Alcoholism in Canada 1871-1956* (Toronto: University of Toronto Press, 1958), pp. 15-25.

7. Annual Report, WCTU, Ontario, 1882, pp. 5-6; Anne Angus, *Children's Aid Society of Vancouver 1901-1951* (Vancouver: Children's Aid Society, 1951), p. 5.

8. The percentage of the WCTU executive who were traceable was small, only 38 per cent.

WCTU *Executive 1890-1901; Occupation of Husband:*

	Traceable	%
Business	8	19
Law	6	14
Ministry	9	21
Medicine	4	9.5
Journalism	5	12

9. State intervention was gradually adopted by most women's reform organizations. It was the method by which they could cope with an increasingly complex society.

10. The importance of religious faith for the WCTU will be examined later.

11. Annual Report, WCTU, Ontario, Oct. 24, 1878, Resolutions; Annual Report, Woman's Christian Temperance Union of British Columbia, 1889, p. 18.

12. Ruth Spence, *Prohibition in Canada* (Toronto: Ontario Branch of the Dominion Alliance, 1919), p. 144; Annual Report, WCTU of the Dominion of Canada, 1889, p. 3; ibid., p. 18; ibid., 1891, p. 43.

13. Annual Report, WCTU, Nova Scotia, 1896, p. 27.

14. Ibid., 1897, p. 3; Rev. W. Peck, *A Short History of the Liquor Traffic* (n.p., 1929), p. 14.

15. Annual Report, WCTU N.S., 1897, p. 24; Annual Report, WCTU Canada, 1892, p. 53.

16. Letitia Youmans, *Campaign Echoes* (Toronto: William Briggs, 1893), pp. 206-207.

17. Annual Report, WCTU Ontario, 1880, p. 10. For further information on the suffrage movement in Canada and the role the WCTU played, see Catherine Cleverdon, *The Woman Suffrage Movement in Canada*, 2nd ed. (Toronto: University of Toronto Press, 1974).

18. *The Templar Quarterly*, (Aug. 1897), p. 28.

19. Annual Report, WCTU New Brunswick, 1899. p. 26; Annual Report, WCTU Ontario, 1898, p. 66.

20. Annual Report, WCTU Manitoba, 1890-91, pp. 43-44; Scott Smith, op. cit., p. 125. There is a suggestion in Alison Prentice, 'Education and the Metaphor of the Family: the Upper Canadian Example,' *History of Education Quarterly*, XII, No. 3 (1972), p. 286, that the family as a source of identification in mid-nineteenth-century Canadian society was declining, due to the discredit brought upon the concept by the Family Compact.

21. Scrapbook, WCTU, 1898, lent to the author by Mrs. Harris Magog, Quebec. For information on feminine friendships in the United States, see Carroll Smith-Rosenberg, 'The Female World of Love and Ritual: Relations Between Women in Nineteenth-Century America,' *Signs* I (Autumn 1975), pp. 1-31.

22. Annual Report, WCTU of the Maritime Provinces, 1890, p. 43.

23. Annual Report, WCTU Ontario, 1893, p. 117; Annual Report, WCTU B.C., 1899, p. 58.

24. Annual Report, WCTU B.C., 1897, p. 32; Annual Report, WCTU Ontario, 1894, p. 140.

25. Annual Report, WCTU Maritimes, 1890, p. 49.

26. Scrapbook, Stanstead County WCTU, 1898.

27. Annual Report, WCTU B.C., 1899, p. 60; Annual Report, WCTU Canada, 1892, p. 76. This emphasis on heredity was common in the latter nineteenth century. See Michael Bliss, 'Pure Books on Avoided Subjects,' Canadian Historical Association, *Historical Papers*, 1970, pp. 89-108.

28. WCTU *Executive*:

	Number	%
Presbyterian	7	18
Church of England	4	10
Catholic	—	—
Methodist	17	43-44
Baptist	6	15
Congregational	5	13

29. Annual Report, WCTU Canada, 1891, p. 93.

30. Annual Report, WCTU Ontario, Oct. 23, 1878, Resolutions; Annual Report, WCTU Quebec, 1884-85, p. 70.

31. Annual Report, WCTU B.C., 1893, p. 23.

32. See Jill Conway, 'Women Reformers and American Culture,' *Journal of Social History*, 5, No. 2 (Winter 1971-73), pp. 164-77, for an expression of this phenomenon in the American context.

Topic Nine
World War I

When World War I broke out in August 1914, most Canadians agreed with the Conservative government's decision to support Britain. Even anti-imperialists, like Henri Bourassa, initially agreed as long as the government did not introduce conscription. Canadians from every province volunteered. But as the fighting continued on from months to years, volunteer enlistment declined, and enthusiasm for Canadian involvement waned. In particular, French Canadians questioned the rationale for fighting in a European war under the direction of Britain. After living 300 years in North America, French Canadians did not have the same emotional link with Britain and Europe that English Canadians had. The Borden government, pressured by British leaders and by enthusiastic supporters in English Canada, decided to increase Canada's manpower contribution to the war effort. In "Conscription," John English outlines the political developments leading up to the implementation of conscription in 1917, and discusses its impact on the future development of Canadian political parties.

The strongest resistance to conscription occurred in French Canada. Part of this opposition arose from a long-standing distrust of Britain, but it was also due to the Canadian government's mismanagement of the war effort. For one thing, the government handled recruiting badly, obliging many francophones to serve under English-speaking officers in English-speaking regiments. Secondly, the educational policies of two English-speaking provinces did not help. At the very moment the federal government pressured French Canadians to fight for democracy in Europe, the provincial governments of Ontario and Manitoba eliminated what French Canadians considered a democratic right in Canada — publicly-supported French-language schools. As a result, recruitment in Quebec declined drastically, much to the annoyance of English Canadians. Two different French-Canadian viewpoints of the war are presented in "An Open Letter from Capt. Talbot Papineau to Mr. Henri Bourassa" and in "Mr. Bourassa's reply."

Others opposed the introduction of conscription: farm groups, labour organizations, and Canadian pacifists. Some were sectarian pacifists such as the Quakers, Mennonites and Hutterites who opposed fighting on religious grounds. Others represented the liberal peace movement who wanted to achieve order and stability in the world through the use of international arbitration and courts. The outbreak of war fractured this liberal pacifist movement. Some attempted the contradictory position of sympathizing with the war effort while adhering to their pacifist ideals; others saw the war as a crucible in which Christianity and the ideals of Christian peace could be achieved; while still others consistently opposed war and the existing social and economic order which they believed produced war in the first place. Thomas Socknat examines and analyses these various pacifist positions in "Canada's Liberal Pacifists and the Great War."

For an overview of the war years, see the relevant chapters in R.C. Brown and R. Cook's *Canada, 1896–1921: A Nation Transformed* (Toronto: McClelland and Stewart, 1974) and D. Morton's *Canada and War: A Military and Political History* (Toronto: Butterworth, 1981). A number of biographies of key politicians during the First World War touch on the war years. The most important are R.C. Brown's *Robert Laird Borden: A Biography*, Vol. II, 1914–1937 (Toronto: Macmillan, 1980); J. Schull's *Laurier: The First Canadian* (Toronto: Macmillan, 1965); Robert Rumilly's *Henri Bourassa* (Montréal: Chantecler, 1953); and R. Graham's *Arthur Meighen*, Vol. I: *The Door of Opportunity* (Toronto: Clarke Irwin, 1960).

    On the issue of conscription, see Elizabeth Armstrong's *The Crisis of Quebec, 1914–1918* (New York: Columbia University Press, 1937), J.L. Granatstein and J.M. Hitsman's *Broken Promises: A History of Conscription in Canada* (Toronto: Oxford University Press, 1977; new edition, 1984), and Brian Cameron, "The Bonne Entente Movement, 1916–17: From Cooperation to Conscription," *Journal of Canadian Studies*, 13 (Summer 1978): pp. 42–55. Henri Bourassa's views are presented in Joseph Levitt, ed., *Henri Bourassa on Imperialism and Bi-culturalism, 1900–1918* (Toronto: Copp Clark, 1970).

337

Conscription*
JOHN ENGLISH

In December 1916 David Lloyd George, the 'Welsh Wizard' who 'in some vague and inspired manner . . . represented all those forces of national energy which were determined on a complete victory,' became prime minister of Great Britain.[1] If September 1914 represented the baptism of the British war effort, December 1916 was its confirmation, its sacred rededication to an earlier commitment made almost unknowingly. To Canadians concerned about their nation's flagging resolve, the British change of leader served as both an omen and a model. Would Canada rededicate itself to the war, or would Canada's contribution continue to dwindle until, in a final moment of national agony, it collapsed? Patriotic groups were unwilling to let events take their course, and in December 1916 they began an intensive campaign to shape the future.

One of the leaders of this movement was the Toronto businessman and Sir Robert Borden's long-time confidant, Joseph Flavelle. As chairman of the Imperial Munitions Board he should, properly, have refrained from direct political action, but the war was not a question of politics for Flavelle: 'I return from England deeply impressed with the absence of party spirit, in the conduct of public business in Great Britain. This results not only from the gravity of the issues which have caused men to rise above party, but because the Government is made up of men from both parties.' On 16 December 1916, at the Ottawa Canadian Club, Flavelle, ignoring Borden's strenuous objections, urged the formation of a 'non-partisan' government for Canada, a coalition comprised of the 'best elements' of both parties.[2] Because Borden's close relationship with Flavelle was well known and because the Conservative party had been identified with men of his type since 1911, the speech had unusual significance and Borden was forced to respond to the growing agitation of which it was a part.[3]

Borden shared with Flavelle the perception of the war as the paramount concern of the nation, and he had also shown himself to be a leader who was willing to embark upon unconventional political adventures. Yet he distrusted Flavelle's motives, and perhaps correctly — we cannot be certain — he saw in the speech and the 'national government' agitation an implicit threat to his leadership. He knew that national government would likely mean conscription and, inevitably, a dangerous domestic situation. Moreover, Australia's popular rejection of conscription had shown the perils of moving too quickly.[4] In Canada, a nation with much greater heterogeneity, conscription would surely meet even stronger opposition. Thus Borden moved hesitantly, leaving his options open.

In December 1916 for the first time he publicly refused to reiterate his promise that there would be no conscription.[5] Then, in a letter to his former mentor, Sir Charles Hibbert Tupper, at the beginning of the new year, he outlined the great difficulties involved in introducing conscription, but expressed a willingness to consider it if the voluntary system completely broke down:

I do not know that I can say more as to the question of enforced military service than was expressed at our personal interview in Ottawa. We have more than two and a half millions of French Canadians in Canada and I realize that the feeling between them and the English people is intensely bitter at present. The vision of the French Canadian is very limited. He is not well informed and he is in a condition of extreme exasperation by reason of fancied wrongs supposed to be inflicted upon his compatriots in other provinces, especially Ontario. It may be necessary to resort to compulsion. I hope not; but if the necessity arises I shall not hesitate to act accordingly.[6]

Borden made clear in another letter that the necessity had not yet arisen and

338

that a coalition would be of more advantage 'in solution of the railway situation,' which was of extreme 'urgency,' than in the conduct of the war.[7] But he knew that a decision could not be long postponed. An invitation to join in 'special and continuous meetings' of the Imperial War Cabinet gave him a few extra months, but with an election virtually a certainty, 1917 loomed as a crucial year.[8]

No event so magnified the potential dangers of a general election as a by-election in the Quebec constituency of Dorchester in January 1917. By-elections had been one of the few casualties of the Canadian party truce:[9] Dorchester was to be an exception because of the unusually bitter personal feelings involved. The Conservative candidate was the newly appointed minister of inland revenue, Albert Sévigny, who had been elected in 1911 as a 'Nationalist-Conservative.' Unlike Frederick Monk, Sévigny had accepted the Conservative naval policy in 1912 and 1913, disavowing by this action his stand on the issue in the 1911 election. Because of this background he was detested by Quebec Liberals and *nationalistes* who thirsted for revenge for what they regarded as the hypocritical Conservative campaign in 1911. The choice of the Dorchester Liberals and the Quebec provincial party was the fiery young Lucien Cannon. Sir Wilfrid Laurier, sensing the dangers inherent in such a contest, saw nothing to gain and much to lose in a Quebec by-election fought on the war issue. Nevertheless, local sentiment and the decisive voice of Premier Sir Lomer Gouin forced the national leader to capitulate. On 16 January, a scant eleven days before the election, a local convention nominated Cannon.[10] Two days later, an 'assemblée contradictoire' brought Cannon and Sévigny face to face.

Cannon immediately denounced Sévigny's support of the Borden government as a betrayal of the principles upon which he had been elected in 1911. More controversially, he claimed that a Sévigny victory would be interpreted by the government as a mandate for conscription. The latter, in Cannon's view, would 'ruin the country from the point of view of men and wealth and everything else for England.' The frankness of his remarks astonished not only Sévigny but also the English-Canadian Liberal press, which immediately disavowed him and asked Laurier to do the same. But his willingness to raise the fundamental issue of conscription nevertheless won him the support of Le Nationaliste and of the vituperative pen of Georges Pelletier of Le Devoir.[11] Sévigny, however, had abundant resources with which to meet the attack. He pointed out the patronage which his election in 1911 had brought to the constituency and which his re-election would bring in the future. More significantly, he brought in his two French-Canadian cabinet colleagues, P. E. Blondin and E. L. Patenaude, and argued that only their presence in the cabinet would provide the electors with a guarantee against conscription.[12] This argument was as decisive in Dorchester in 1917 as it was in 1939 in all of Quebec when federal Liberal cabinet members employed the same plea to defeat Maurice Duplessis.[13] The effect outside Quebec was also remarkably similar. English Canadians tended to interpret the Sévigny win as an indicator of support for the war effort in Quebec, and

339

as a firm rebuke to the *nationalistes*. The possibility that Sévigny's victory resulted from the belief that he would act as a deterrent to a more intensive war effort from within the cabinet was apparently not considered.[14]

The Dorchester victory came as a breath of fresh air to a federal Conservative party on the brink of suffocation. Borden noted in his diary the 'great excitement' produced by the event. Little did he appreciate the irony of his analysis which saw the victory as leading to 'a better understanding between the two races.'[15] It was, perhaps, the exhilaration caused by Dorchester which inspired him to discuss the formation of a coalition with his cabinet. After a long series of setbacks, the Tories at last could bargain from strength. In the cabinet discussion of 3 February 1917 several ministers expressed themselves 'apparently in favour of' coalition.[16] But Borden's 12 February departure for the Imperial War Conference was approaching too rapidly for fuller consideration of the question. Furthermore, the full effect of national registration was still unknown, and the new year stirred fresh hopes that the war would end.[17] For Liberals and Conservatives, for patriotic agitators and pacifists, Borden's impending journey created an uncomfortable hiatus. All knew that no action could be taken until his return; all hoped that a favourable verdict in the trenches of France would make a decision unnecessary. Not for the last time in 1917, fate was malevolent.

On 14 February Borden embarked for England from Halifax. The days before he left were filled with discussions on the three major problems facing the government: the railway situation, recruitment, and government reorganization. The railway question awaited the report of a commission, and therefore nothing was done. On recruitment, the cabinet decided that the voluntary system should be continued.[18] No decision was made on government reorganization. To those seeking a definite direction, the government offered none.

The three months of Borden's absence from Canada were probably the most significant months of the war. In March the abdication of the Czar astonished Canadians and left Russia's future role in the war uncertain. One month later, in April, Woodrow Wilson, whose Autumn 1916 campaign slogan 'he kept us out of war' had angered so many Canadians, led the 'great peaceful people' of the United States into 'the most terrible and disastrous of all wars.'[19] At that precise moment in the war, the impact of these two remarkable events was unknown. Ultimately, the resources of America could assure Allied victory, but would there be sufficient time for American soldiers to set foot upon French soil? Lloyd George's determination to launch a great offensive in the spring and summer of 1917 made this question particularly meaningful for Canadians.[20] The Nivelle offensive, as it was termed, required extensive participation by the Canadian troops, who were already facing manpower difficulties. The Canadians nevertheless participated, and the capture of Vimy Ridge in early April was the one notable success of a generally calamitous operation. But the Canadian laurels were blood-red — 3598 Canadians died at Vimy.[21]

The Vimy triumph had an important side-effect; Borden, visiting Britain at the time, shared the praise lavished upon the Canadian soldiers,[22] and the infectious war enthusiasm was too much for the Canadian leader to resist. Suddenly, the preoccupations of Ottawa became as distant emotionally as they were geographically. Thus, he completely ignored the pleas of his secretary, A. E. Blount, who urged him to return to Canada to retrieve a desperate political situation.[23] When a nervous Sir Thomas White, the acting prime minister, cabled to Borden his view that the 'absolute necessity' of the railway problem compelled his presence, an angry Borden replied that no 'distraction' should interfere with Canada's commitment and, by implication, his own activities in London, during 'the most critical and terrible period of the war.'[24]

Having learned the perilous Allied position, Borden cabled to his militia minister, Sir Edward Demp, on 5 April: 'It is believed that Germany stakes everything on this Summer[']s operations and the demand for men is therefore very urgent. What success are you having in proposal for home defence force and how is recruiting progressing for Expeditionary Force?' Borden had apparently decided that the Americans would be too late; the supreme test would come in 1917 before they arrived. Kemp had also reached such a decision; he replied promptly and pessimistically: '. . . General feeling large number of recruits will not be forthcoming under the voluntary system. Publicity campaign for Home defence force also covers necessity for enlistment overseas forces. Hoped it would be productive of results but voluntary enlistment has about reached its limit. Enlistment overseas for March seven thousand and sixty three . . . Thirty five thousand will be shipped during April.' Conscription was inevitable.[25]

On 17 May 1917, three days after his return from Europe, Borden announced to the cabinet his intention to introduce conscription in Canada. The discussion revealed the dangers but nevertheless produced agreement. He wrote in his diary: 'All agreed that conscription necessary. Patenaude and Blondin said they [were] prepared to stand by us but that it will kill them politically and the party for 25 years.' The next day Borden announced conscription to the House of Commons. To conscriptionists, the justifications were unassailable. With the Americans adopting a selective draft, Canada would be disgraced if she refused to follow. Her honour and her new voice in the Empire symbolized by her prime minister's participation in the Imperial War Cabinet would perish. To Borden and to hundreds of thousands of others in English Canada, such a prospect was unthinkable.[26]

It seemed that a failure of leadership and the weakness of national institutions had made compulsory military service necessary. Conscription accordingly inspired in its advocates the desire to alter and strengthen these national institutions and the leadership. During the 17 May cabinet discussion, some had raised the 'question of coalition government.' The majority, Borden recorded in his diary, seemed to be in favour although there was 'considerable divergence of opinion' on the matter. Still, nothing was said about coalition when conscription was announced. A few days after the announcement, however, Arthur Ford, the exceedingly well-informed Tory journalist, reported that a movement for coalition had arisen in the Conservative caucus, 'largely among the Ontario members.' These members were urging Borden to form a coalition with what Ford termed the 'patriotic wing' of the Liberal party.[27] Of course, not all Conservatives favoured a coalition, particularly when conscription sprang open a profound fissure in the Liberal party. The movement, however, soon won the support of Borden himself, who had been impressed by the widespread endorsement of conscription.

On 18 May Edward Brown, the provincial treasurer of Manitoba, had announced his personal and his government's belief in conscription. The following day the Toronto *Globe*, whose readership was largely drawn from Liberal supporters in Ontario, defended 'the compulsory organization of all the military resources of the country.' After Borden's conscription speech, N. W. Rowell publicly and privately declared that there was 'only one course open to Liberals . . . to support the principle of the government's proposals.'[28] Public rallies were held throughout English Canada where Liberals nervously shared the same platform with lifelong Tory enemies. Letter after letter from Laurier's oldest political friends in English Canada — W. S. Fielding, George Gibbons, W. E. Rundle, Hartley Dewart, Levi Thomson, and J. H. Sinclair — told the veteran Liberal leader that he must not oppose conscription.[29] Most Liberals, however, knew that Laurier would surely denounce the measure, and would therefore create for them their most difficult dilemma. Frank Carvell, a New Brunswick Liberal often mentioned as Laurier's successor, has left an excellent description of his own confusion at this time: 'There is something within me which abhors the idea of throwing up my hands when others are fighting my battles and not being willing to do everything possible to stand by the men who are doing this for me voluntarily. I do not know where I am going to land. I am going home this afternoon to consult with my constituents, and I may as well tell you frankly, especially with my family, because after all there comes a time in the life of every man when he and his own must do some hard thinking for themselves.'

Carvell's constituents did nothing to resolve his problem: they unanimously supported coalition, but were split along religious lines on conscription. And, indeed, other proponents of conscription found less enthusiasm than they had expected at the 'grass roots.' George Gibbons told Laurier that western Ontario farmers were hostile to compulsion. The public attacks upon conscription by two well-known agrarian spokesmen, Peter McArthur and W. L. Smith, seemed to confirm this interpretation. The increasingly influential United Farmers of Ontario, while hesitant to openly denounce the Military Service Act, called for a referendum on the subject.[30] The *Weekly Sun*, the most spirited and candid of all Ontario farm organs, showed no such diffidence, and boldly asserted on 23 May that Canada owed her allies no more men. One of the shrewdest observers of Canadian politics, O. D. Skelton of Queen's University, warned Laurier not to be deluded by the widespread press support for conscription, especially in Toronto.

'The voice of Toronto,' Skelton declared, 'is not the voice of God,' nor even of Ontario, nor of the nation as a whole. In the circumstances, the Liberals must not despair, must maintain cool heads, and await the unfolding of events. Never should they help the Tories 'in pulling the chestnuts out of the fire.'[31]

A cabinet meeting on 24 May revealed that the political chestnuts were as hot as Skelton had suggested. Unanimity disappeared when several Conservative ministers blamed Borden for a situation from which there was no apparent escape. In any election, these ministers argued, a combination of the French Canadians, farmers, and 'slackers' would defeat the government.[32] Borden shared these fears more than he admitted; time alone could afford a solution, and to this end he engaged Laurier in a masterful political minuet.

Borden took the lead and proposed on 25 May that the two leaders join with their parties to carry through conscription. There would be an equal number of Liberals and Conservatives in a new government, apart from the position of prime minister.[33] Laurier was equally nimble: while expressing his adamant opposition to conscription, he took refuge in ambiguity and agreed to consider Borden's proposition. He, too, needed time. Probably neither was serious in this political flirtation. Borden knew that Laurier could not accept any coalition for which the price was support of conscription, and Laurier certainly would never have accepted a role as Borden's deputy when an election promised a strong possibility of a Liberal victory. Both, however, were performing for the benefit of others, in particular, the members of their respective parties.

Conservative dissent from Borden's course arose in two quarters: the French-Canadian Tories and those Conservatives closely associated with Robert Rogers. Borden's adoption of conscription and coalition flabbergasted Rogers. For five years the prime minister had neglected his party; now he proposed to sacrifice it. Rogers knew very well that he would be the first to be cast off if any coalition was formed. Also, the party machine which Rogers had so lovingly constructed would crumble under any coalition government.[34] He moved quickly to assemble allies to block Borden's apparent path, and he found sympathizers among the machine politicians and among those Tories whose inveterate and even phobic hatred of Liberals made them regard coalition as an outrage. Unfortunately for Rogers, this group, which was centred mainly in Ontario and Manitoba, lacked sufficient numbers to withstand the public pressure favouring coalition in their own political bailiwicks. Yet their presence, if not an insuperable barrier to coalition, was certainly a major irritant, and was bound to become a problem whenever a coalition was formed.

The French-Canadian Conservatives raised questions of a different order for Borden. Their constituency meant, of course, that for them support for conscription was tantamount to political suicide; but, on the other hand, opposition to conscription offered no political reward either. The strength of the French-Canadian Conservatives lay, paradoxically, in their weakness.

343

Realizing that the French-Canadian Liberals would never enter a coalition, Borden and the French-Canadian Conservatives knew that the government must retain the support of some French Canadians in order to give the appearance of national representation. Borden, to whom Quebec Conservatism was a curious mixture of the politics of Ruritania and Mahagonny, with the delightful incompetency of the former and the sordid battles for spoils of the latter, had little choice. His best French-Canadian minister, E. L. Patenaude, resigned on 5 June and denounced conscription as a threat to national unity.[35] This left only two French-Canadian ministers: Albert Sévigny, whose Dorchester victory was tarnished by the discovery of some furniture 'borrowed' from the burnt-out Speaker's Chamber in his own home, and P. E. Blondin, the postmaster-general, who devoted his energies in 1917 to a largely futile attempt at recruiting a French-Canadian battalion.[36] Both these ministers agreed to remain in the government after considerable argument and, when the Union government was finally formed, they were the sole French-Canadian members of the cabinet.

Laurier's task was a much more difficult one than Borden's, one which required singular political deftness. Indeed, the skill of Laurier was so great that Borden and future historians have frequently failed to note it. Looking back at the Liberal leader's actions in 1917, Borden attributed his hesitation on coalition to weakness and his advanced years. A close examination of his actions does not sustain that interpretation. On closer scrutiny, one finds that Laurier had lost little of his brilliance or his guile, and, in the end, by his evasiveness, his extraordinary ability to manage individuals, and his sure knowledge of the sources of his political strength, he not only survived the political crisis of 1917 but, unlike most aged political leaders, assured the future effectiveness of his political testament.

When Borden spoke to him about coalition on 25 May, Laurier had already decided upon a stance from which he would never waver.[37] W. L. Mackenzie King, a supporter of conscription himself but nevertheless a close adviser and eager student of Laurier in May and June 1917, had outlined the Laurier formula on 15 May, three days before conscription was announced: 'How I hope a general election may be avoided. Were Borden to bring in conscription, as we hear he is likely to, I think that the Liberal Party should extend the life of parliament at least 6 months. It will be a difficult measure to enforce and may cost his party its life. If the Liberals are wise they will put the responsibility on [Borden] and leave him the consequences.'[38] While Laurier disagreed with King on the questions of extension and conscription, he nevertheless concurred with his analysis of the political impact of conscription and with his recommendation for future Liberal policy.

In the conscription crisis, Laurier saw a great opportunity: Laurier Liberalism had been challenged before 1917 by the aggressive Anglo-Saxon reform Liberalism of the western provinces and Ontario. Step by step, these 'new Liberals' had won concessions from the national leader, such as the National Liberal Advisory Committee which was created in 1915 to develop a policy for the party. The 1916 report of that committee had recommended an advanced social programme which included old age pensions, mothers' allowances, unemployment insurance, and other similar measures.[39] Such a platform, especially when linked with such reform Liberal planks as prohibition and female suffrage, promised to be most unpopular in conservative Quebec and among the non-Anglo-Saxon immigrants who had flooded the country after 1896 and who had generally voted Liberal. Such men, as fanatic in their different way as the Catholic bishops whom Laurier fought in the 1870s, threatened to impose an exclusive mould upon the national Liberal party that would almost certainly seal its fate. The confrontation between 'new' and 'old' Liberalism was widely expected to occur during the search for Laurier's successor. With conscription, it came in the spring of 1917 with the 'new Liberals' not yet in control of the party.

Thus, when Borden offered coalition and Liberals such as J. W. Dafoe, Rowell, and Joseph Atkinson of the *Toronto Star* urged Laurier to accept, Laurier used the carrot and stick to force the combative conscriptionist Liberals on the defensive. He first marshalled his forces, notably the unbroken phalanx of opponents of conscription in Quebec led by Sir Lomer Gouin. Even the rebel Henri Bourassa could rally behind this Liberal standard.[40] Laurier then waited for reinforcements, which came in the form of the hesitation and, in some cases, antagonism expressed towards conscription in rural areas of English Canada, areas, particularly in Ontario and the West, which had long been Liberal party strongholds. Having received encouragement, he told Borden on 6 June that he totally rejected both coalition and conscription.[41] This was the 'stick' which forced conscriptionist Liberals into the open; there was also a 'carrot.'

On 5 June, the day before he met Borden for the final meeting of the negotiations, Laurier tested his proposal for compromise on Mackenzie King, who was used during this period as political litmus paper for determining English-Canadian opinion: Laurier would permit conscriptionist Liberals to run as 'official Liberals' provided that they agreed to a referendum on conscription. King indicated that he found the position quite acceptable; but others, Laurier knew, would not. Those Liberals who rejected a referendum must therefore be driven out of the party and, in going, give up their right to determine the future course of the party and to choose Laurier's successor. For those prominent English-Canadian Liberals like King who stayed with the old leader, their decision was made easier by Laurier's shrewd declaration that the next Liberal leader must be an English Canadian and a Protestant.[42]

By rejecting Borden's offer, Laurier assured a Liberal Quebec, not only in the next election but for many elections thereafter. By proposing a referendum, Laurier made the decision to defy the Liberal whip more difficult for English Canadians who favoured conscription. The vote on the Military Service Act was not on a black and white issue, but one which involved considerable shades of grey and therefore safety.[43] Laurier forced the English-Canadian Liberals on the defensive in 1917 and for the future. After 1917, any English-Canadian Liberal leader had to be acceptable to Quebec, which more than ever was the heart of the Liberal party of Canada. Most of all, Laurier's negotiation, hesitation, and manipulation broke the powerful impetus behind the conscription-coalition movement, and afforded him the time to assemble a strong political base in Quebec and among non-British elements in Canada. Many Liberals whom Borden had thought might cross the floor of the Commons hesitated. The Conservative leader was thereby forced to move outside Parliament to find Liberal allies for his enterprise, and there the terrain was almost unknown.

Notes

1. Lord Beaverbrook, *Politicians and the War, 1914-1916* (London, 1928, 1932; 1960), 408-9.

2. Flavelle to Borden, 13 Dec. 1916, PAC, Borden Papers (BP), v. 63. An account of this incident is found in Henry Borden, ed., *Robert Laird Borden: His Memoirs* (Toronto, 1938), II, 617-19. Borden recalls that his finance minister, Thomas White, was most outraged by Flavelle's action. White's anger may have arisen from his knowledge that Flavelle and many of his friends favoured the former Toronto banker for the leadership.

3. O. D. Skelton, in *Life and Letters of Sir Wilfrid Laurier* (London, 1922), interpreted the Toronto speech as part of a Toronto conspiracy to take over the government, an interpretation supported by some evidence. See, for example, G. M. Wrong to C. Sifton, 2 March 1917, PAC, Sifton Papers, v. 206; and J. W. Dafoe to Wrong, 12 Dec. 1916, Dafoe Papers, microfilm copy. When Flavelle read Skelton's account he wrote to him denying that his promotion of 'national government' represented 'the views of a distinctive body of opinion,' but admitting that he reflected and often inspired the political actions of a close group of Toronto friends in 1916 and 1917. Flavelle to Skelton, 5 June 1922, Queen's University Archives, Douglas Library, Flavelle Papers, box 9, folder S-U.

4. Conscription was defeated twice in Australian plebiscites, first in 1916 and again in 1917.

5. Borden and R. B. Bennett, national service director, refused to rule out conscription when meeting a labour delegation. For an account of this meeting, see Martin Robin, *Radical Politics and Canadian Labour 1880-1930* (Kingston, 1968), 122.

6. Borden to Tupper, 2 Jan. 1917, BP, v. 16.

7. Willison to Borden, 26 Jan., and Borden to Willison, 2 Feb. 1917, BP, v. 78.

8. Walter Long, colonial secretary, to Borden, cited in Borden, *Memoirs*, II, 625. This journey would also allow Borden to learn British opinions on the length of the war, crucial information for a politician.

9. No writs were issued for twenty constituencies which became vacant between March 1915 and July 1917. See A. M. Willms, 'Conscription, 1917: A Brief for the Defence,' *Canadian Historical Review*, XXXVII (Dec. 1956), 339.

10. Laurier wrote to the party organizer: '. . . ce ne serait pas un gain politique: ce serait simplement un argument de plus dans la campagne sourde qui se fait dans les autres provinces contre Québec. Réservons nos forces pour la bataille générale.' Gouin certainly appears to have had the final word in federal as well as provincial party matters; in the case of Dorchester he believed that if the Liberals did not run the *nationalistes* would. Laurier to Philippe Paradis, 8 Jan., Paradis to Laurier, 15 Jan. 1917, PAC, Laurier Papers, v. 705. See also J. C. Hopkins, *The Canadian Annual Review, 1917* (Toronto, 1918), 483.

11. Cannon was cited in the Toronto *Globe*, 20 Jan. 1917; he finally issued a weak retraction. For the reaction among English-Canadian Liberals, see Frank Carrel to Laurier, 20 Jan. 1917, Laurier Papers, v. 705. For Cannon's support see Robert Rumilly, *Henri Bourassa* (Montreal, 1953), 572; and *Le Devoir*, 20 Jan. 1917.

12. An excellent description of the campaign which illustrates this point is Renaud Lavergne, *Histoire de la famille Lavergne*, ed. B. C. Payette (Montreal, 1968), 105-6. Lavergne campaigned for Sévigny in this election and felt he was a traitor when he later supported conscription.

13. See J. L. Granatstein, *The Politics of Survival* (Toronto, 1967), 34-5.

14. See, for example, the *Globe*, Toronto, 30 Jan. 1917; Hopkins, *Canadian Annual Review, 1917*, 482-6; and Elizabeth Armstrong, *The Crisis of Quebec: 1914-1918* (New York, 1937), 159. Dorchester was an overwhelmingly French-speaking constituency with French Canadians numbering 42,983 in an overall population of 44,823. *Sixth Census of Canada, 1921* (Ottawa, 1924), I, 364.

15. BP, Borden Diary, 27 Jan. 1917.

16. *Ibid.*, 3 Feb. 1917.

17. Good news to Canadians in Jan. 1917 was the enlistment of 9194 men and the 'wastage' of only 4396. Hopkins, *Canadian Annual Review, 1917*, 307. Borden himself regarded Germany as 'relatively weaker' in 1917 compared to 1916 and thought the war might well end that year. Borden Diary, 13 Jan. 1917. In this period the German army was on the defensive and the food shortage in Germany was acute. See Arthur Rosenberg, *Imperial Germany* (1928, Boston, 1964), 153–90.

18. Borden Diary, 7–11 Feb. The railway commission, composed of Sir Henry Drayton, W. M. Acworth of Great Britain, and A. H. Smith of the New York Central, reported in April 1917.

19. Arthur S. Link, *Woodrow Wilson and the Progressive Era, 1910–1917* (New York, 1954), 282.

20. Many of Lloyd George's reasons had little to do with military strategy. See P. Guinn, *British Strategy and Politics* (Oxford, 1965), 211–17.

21. J. Swettenham, *To Seize the Victory* (Toronto, 1965), 161.

22. Borden Diary, 10 April 1917. Borden was most disturbed by the failure of *The Times* to comment editorially on the Vimy capture. See also 'Domino' (Augustus Bridle), *The Masques of Ottawa* (Toronto, 1921), 35.

23. Blount to Borden, 28 March 1917, PAC, Blount Papers, v. 1. Blount was troubled by the lack of leadership in the government and by the stridency of public criticism. According to him there was no one in Ottawa 'to take a leading hand.'

24. White to Borden, 27 and 28 March, Borden to White, 30 March, White to Borden 2 April 1917, BP, v. 31.

25. Borden to Kemp, 5 April, and Kemp to Borden, 10 April 1917, PAC, Kemp Papers, v. 53, file 8; Borden, *Memoirs*, II, 698. Sir George Foster wrote: 'Only compulsory service can meet the situation and though it is full of grave difficulties come it must.' Foster Diary, 7 May 1917. PAC, Foster Papers, v. 1.

26. Even Laurier felt the intense pressure when three of his former Ontario ministers urged that conscription become Liberal policy in order to pre-empt the Tories. Sir Allen Bristol Aylesworth to Laurier, 10 May, and Sir William Mulock to Laurier, 11 May 1917, Laurier Papers, v. 708. Mackenzie King also supported conscription at this time. See R. M. Dawson, *William Lyon Mackenzie King* (Toronto, 1958), 260. Premier W. M. Martin of Saskatchewan also urged that the Liberals should adopt conscription. Martin to Laurier, 17 May 1917, Laurier Papers, v. 708.

27. Ford to Willison, 23 May 1917, PAC, Willison Papers, v. 30.

28. Rowell to A. K. Maclean, 19 May, and Rowell to R. Lemieux, 21 May 1917, PAC, Rowell Papers, v. 3.

29. In a letter to Laurier on 31 May Fielding favoured the acceptance of the bill, but urged that a referendum be taken before the law took effect. This is, perhaps, the origin of Laurier's own proposal for a referendum. See also Bruce Fergusson, *Hon. W.S. Fielding: Mr. Minister of Finance* (Windsor, NS, 1971), 171–3. Dr. Fergusson seems to have overlooked that letter cited here. Gibbons to Laurier, 27 May, Rinfret to Laurier, 27 May, Dewart to Laurier, 25 May (Dewart later became an opponent of conscription), Thomson to Laurier, 19 May, Sinclair to Laurier, 22 May 1917, Laurier Papers, v. 708 and 709.

30. Carvell to A. K. Cameron, 1 June 1917, PAC, Cameron Papers, v. 2; Carvell to Laurier, 4 June, Gibbons to Laurier, 27 May 1917, Laurier Papers, v. 709 (Gibbons pointed out the 'articulate opinion' in western Ontario was for conscription); Hopkins, *Canadian Annual Review, 1917*, 340.

31. Skelton to Laurier, 30 May 1917, Laurier Papers, v. 709.

32. Borden Diary, 25 May 1917.

33. Borden, *Memoirs*, II, 720–1.

34. Rogers reportedly opposed conscription as well as coalition, seeing in the former the death-knell of the Conservative party in Quebec and in non-Anglo-Saxon areas of western Canada. He was already most concerned about the state of the party in these areas. See Rogers to Borden, 10 April 1917, BP, v. 32; Arthur Ford, *As the World Wags On* (Toronto, 1950), 29; and Ford to Willison, 27 May 1917, Willison Papers, v. 30.

35. *Globe*, Toronto, 6 June 1917. For the Quebec Conservative press the conscription issue was especially difficult: to support conscription was to risk the loss of the party subsidy and government advertising; to oppose it meant the loss of subscribers. They therefore tried to straddle a middle position. See Armstrong, *The Crisis of Quebec*, 177.

36. Hopkins, *Canadian Annual Review, 1917*, 318.

37. Laurier's firm position was outlined in Laurier to Martin, 21 May 1917, Laurier Papers, v. 708.

38. PAC, King Papers, King Diary, 15 May 1917.

39. The committee and its report are covered in Dawson, *Mackenzie King*, 259, 300–3.

40. Bourassa, however, did not do this immediately. See Rumilly, *Henri Bourassa*, chap. 28.

41. Cited in Borden, *Memoirs*, II, 724–5.

42. King Diary, 5 June 1917.

43. Rowell recognized the tempting escape which Laurier's offer created and pleaded with George Graham to resist it. Rowell Papers, v. 3, contains the correspondence.

347

An Open Letter from Capt. Talbot Papineau to Mr. Henri Bourassa*

(A copy of this letter was sent to Mr. Bourassa by Mr. Andrew-R. McMaster, K.C., on the 18th of July, 1916. It was published, on the 28th of July, in most of Montreal, Quebec, Ottawa and Toronto papers, English and French).

In the Field,
France, March 21, 1916.

To Monsieur Henri Bourassa,
    Editor of Le Devoir,
        Montreal.

348

My dear Cousin Henri, —

I was sorry before leaving Quebec in 1914 not to have had an opportunity of discussing with you the momentous issues which were raised in Canada by the outbreak of this war.

You and I have had some discussions in the past, and although we have not agreed upon all points, yet I am happy to think that our pleasant friendship, which indeed dates from the time of my birth, has hitherto continued uninjured by our differences of opinion. Nor would I be the first to make it otherwise, for however I may deplore the character of your views, I have always considered that you held them honestly and sincerely and that you were singularly free from purely selfish or personal ambitions.

Very possibly nothing that I could have said in August 1914 would have caused you to change your opinions, but I did hope that as events developed and as the great national opportunity of Canada became clearer to all her citizens, you would have been influenced to modify your views and to adopt a different attitude. In that hope I have been disappointed. Deeply involved as the honour and the very national existence of Canada has become, beautiful but terrible as her sacrifices have been, you and you alone of the leaders of Canadian thought appear to have remained unmoved, and your unhappy views unchanged.

Too occupied by immediate events in this country to formulate a protest or to frame a reasoned argument, I have nevertheless followed with intense feeling and deep regret the course of action which you have pursued. Consolation of course I have had in the fact that far from sharing in your views, the vast majority of Canadians, and even many of those who had formerly agreed with you, were now strongly and bitterly opposed to you. With this fact in mind, I would not take the time from my duties here

* From *Canadian Nationalism and the War*. Published in Montreal, 1916.

to write you this letter did I not fear that the influence to which your talent, energy and sincerity of purpose formerly entitled you, might still be exercised upon a small minority of your fellow countrymen, and that your attitude might still be considered by some as representative of the race to which we belong.

Nor can I altogether abandon the hope — presumptuous no doubt but friendly and well-intentioned — that I may so express myself here as to give you a new outlook and a different purpose, and perhaps even win you to the support of a principle which has been proved to be dearer to many Canadians than life itself.

I shall not consider the grounds upon which you base your opposition to Canadian participation in this more than European — in this World War. Rather I wish to begin by pointing out some reasons why on the contrary your whole-hearted support might have been expected.

And the first reason is this. By the declaration of war by Great Britain upon Germany, Canada became "ipso facto" a belligerent, subject to invasion and conquest, her property at sea subject to capture, her coasts subject to bombardment or attack, her citizens in enemy territory subject to imprisonment or detention. This is not a matter of opinion — it is a matter of fact — a question of international law. No arguments of yours at least could have persuaded the Kaiser to the contrary. Whatever your views or theories may be as to future constitutional development of Canada, and in those views I believe I coincide to a large extent, the fact remains that at the time of the outbreak of war Canada was a possession of the British Empire, and as such as much involved in the war as any country in England, and from the German point of view and the point of view of International Law equally subject to all its pains and penalties. Indeed proof may no doubt be made that one of the very purposes of Germany's aggression and German military preparedness was the ambition to secure a part if not the whole of the English possessions in North America.

That being so, surely it was idle and pernicious to continue an academic discussion as to whether the situation was a just one or not, as to whether Canada should or should not have had a voice in ante bellum English diplomacy or in the actual declaration of war. Such a discussion may very properly arise upon a successful conclusion of the war, but so long as national issues are being decided in Prussian fashion, that is, by an appeal to the Power of Might, the liberties of discussion which you enjoyed by virtue of British citizenship were necessarily curtailed and any resulting decisions utterly valueless. If ever there was a time for action and not for theories it was to be found in Canada upon the outbreak of war.

Let us presume for the sake of argument that your attitude had also been adopted by the Government and people of Canada and that we had declared our intention to abstain from active participation in the war until Canada herself was actually attacked. What would have resulted? One of two things. Either the Allies would have been defeated or they would not have been defeated. In the former case Canada would have been called upon either to surrender unconditionally to German domination or to have attempted a resistance against German arms.

You, I feel sure, would have preferred resistance, but as a proper corrective to such a preference I would prescribe a moderate dose of trench bombardment. I have known my own dogmas to be seriously disturbed in the midst of a German artillery concentration. I can assure you that the further you travel from Canada and the nearer you approach the great military power of Germany, the less do you value the unaided strength of Canada. By the time you are within fifteen yards of a German army and know yourself to be holding about one yard out of a line of five hundred miles or more, you are liable to be enquiring very anxiously about the presence and power of British and French forces. Your ideas about charging to Berlin or of ending the war would also have undergone some slight moderation.

350

No, my dear Cousin, I think you would shortly after the defeat of the Allies have been more worried over the mastery of the German consonants than you are even now over a conflict with the Ontario Anti-bi-linguists. Or I can imagine you an unhappy exile in Terra del Fuego eloquently comparing the wrongs of Quebec and Alsace.

But you will doubtless say we would have had the assistance of the Great American Republic! It is quite possible. I will admit that by the time the American fleet had been sunk and the principal buildings in New York destroyed the United States would have declared war upon Europe, but in the meantime Canada might very well have been paying tribute and learning to decline German verbs, probably the only thing German she *could* have declined.

I am, as you know, by descent even more American than I am French, and I am a sincere believer in the future of that magnificent Republic. I cannot forget that more than any other nation in the world's history — England not excepted — she has suffered war solely for the sake of some fine principle of nationality. In 1776 for the principle of national existence. In 1812 for the principle of the inviolability of American citizenship. In 1860 for the preservation of National unity and the suppression of slavery. In 1896 for the protection of her National pride and in sympathy for the wrongs of a neighbouring people.

Nor disappointed as I am at the present inactivity of the States will I ever waiver in my loyal belief that in time to come, perhaps less distant than we realise, her actions will correspond with the lofty expression of her national and international ideals.

I shall continue to anticipate the day when with a clear understanding and a mutual trust we shall by virtue of our united strength and our common purposes be prepared to defend the rights of humanity not only upon the American Continent but throughout the civilised world.

Nevertheless we are not dealing with what may occur in the future but with the actual facts of yesterday and to-day, and I would feign know if you still think that a power which without protest witnesses the ruthless spoliation of Belgium and Servia, and without effective action the murder of her own citizens, would have interfered to protect the property or the liberties of Canadians. Surely you must at least admit an element of doubt, and even if such interference had been attempted, have we not the admission of the Americans themselves that it could not have been successful against the great naval and military organisations of the Central Powers?

May I be permitted to conclude that had the Allies been defeated Canada must afterwards necessarily have suffered a similar fate.

But there was the other alternative, namely, that the Allies even without the assistance of Canada would *not* have been defeated. What then? Presumably French and English would still have been the official languages of Canada. You might still have edited untrammeled your version of Duty, and Colonel Lavergne might still, publicly and without the restraining fear of death or imprisonment, have spoken seditiously (I mean from the Prussian point of view of course). In fact Canada might still have retained her liberties and might with the same freedom from external influences have continued her progress to material and political strength.

But would you have been satisfied — you who have arrogated to yourself the high term of Nationalist? What of the Soul of Canada? Can a nation's pride or patriotism be built upon the blood and suffering of others or upon the wealth garnered from the coffers of those who in anguish and with blood-sweat are fighting the battles of freedom? If we accept our liberties, our national life, from the hands of the English soldiers, if without sacrifices of our own we profit by the sacrifices of the English citizen, can we hope to ever become a nation ourselves? How could we ever acquire that Soul or create that Pride without which a nation is a dead thing and doomed to speedy decay and disappearance.

If you were truly a Nationalist — if you loved our great country and without smallness longed to see her become the home of a good and united people — surely you would have recognised this as her moment of travail and tribulation. You would have felt that in the agony of her losses in Belgium and France, Canada was suffering the birth pains of her national life. There even more than in Canada herself, her citizens are being knit together into a new existence because when men stand side by side and endure a soldier's life and face together a soldier's death, they are united in bonds almost as strong as the closest of blood-ties.

There was the great opportunity for the true Nationalist! There was the great issue, the great sacrifice, which should have appealed equally to all true citizens of Canada, and should have served to cement them with indissoluble strength — Canada was at war! Canada was attacked! What mattered then internal dissentions and questions of home importance? What mattered the why and wherefore of the war, whether we owed anything to England or not, whether we were Imperialists or not, or

351

whether we were French or English? The one simple commending fact to govern our conduct was that Canada was at war, and Canada and Canadian liberties had to be protected.

To you as a "Nationalist" this fact should have appealed more than to any others. Englishmen, as was natural, returned to fight for England, just as Germans and Austrians and Belgians and Italians returned to fight for their native lands.

But we, Canadians, had we no call just as insistent, just as compelling to fight for Canada? Did not the *Leipzig* and the *Gneisnau* possibly menace Victoria and Vancouver, and did you not feel the patriotism to make sacrifices for the protection of British Columbia? How could you otherwise call yourself Canadian? It is true that Canada did not hear the roar of German guns nor were we visited at night by the murderous Zeppelins, but every shot that was fired in Belgium or France was aimed as much at the heart of Canada as at the bodies of our brave Allies. Could we then wait within the temporary safety of our distant shores until either the Central Powers flushed with victory should come to settle their account or until by the glorious death of millions of our fellowmen in Europe, Canada should remain in inglorious security and a shameful liberty?

352

I give thanks that that question has been answered not as you would have had it answered but as those Canadians who have already died or are about to die here in this gallant motherland of France have answered it.

It may have been difficult for you at first to have realised the full significance of the situation. You were steeped in your belief that Canada owed no debt to England, was merely a vassal state and entitled to protection without payment. You were deeply inbued with the principle that we should not partake in a war in the declaration of which we had had no say. You believed very sincerely that Canadian soldiers should not be called upon to fight beyond the frontier of Canada itself, and your vision was further obscured by your indignation at the apparent injustice to a French minority in Ontario.

It is conceivable that at first on account of this long held attitude of mind and because it seemed that Canadian aid was hardly necessary, for even we feared that the war would be over before the first Canadian regiment should land in France, you should have failed to adapt your mind to the new situation and should for a while have continued in your former views; — but now — now that Canada has pledged herself body and soul to the successful prosecution of this war — now that we know that only by the exercice of our full and united strength can we achieve a speedy and lasting victory — now that thousands of your fellow citizens have died, and alas! many more must yet be killed — how in the name of all that you hold most sacred can you still maintain your opposition? How can you refrain from using all your influence and your personal magnetism and eloquence to swell the great army of Canada and make it as representative of all classes of our citizens as possible?

Could you have been here yourself to witness in its horrible detail the cruelty of war — to have seen your comrades suddenly struck down in death and lie mangled at your side, even you could not have failed to wish to visit punishment upon those responsible. You too would now wish to see every ounce of our united strength instantly and relentlessly directed to that end. Afterwards, when that end has been accomplished, then and then only can there be honour or profit in the discussion of our domestic or imperial disputes.

And so my first reason for your support would be that you should assist in the defence of Canadian territory and Canadian liberties.

And my second would be this: —

Whatever criticism may to-day be properly directed against the Constitutional structure of the British Empire, we are compelled to admit that the *spiritual* union of the self governing portions of the Empire is a most necessary and desirable thing. Surely you will concede that the degree of civilisation which they represent and the standards of individual and national liberty for which they stand are the highest and noblest to which the human race has yet attained and jealously to be protected against destruction by less developed powers. All may not be perfection — grave and serious faults no doubt exist — vast progress must still be made — nevertheless that which has been achieved is good and must not be allowed to disappear. The bonds which unite us for certain great purposes and which have proved so powerful in this common struggle must not be loosened. They may indeed be readjusted, but the great communities which the British Empire has joined together must not be broken asunder. If I thought that the development of a national spirit in Canada meant antagonism to the "spirit" which unites the Empire today, I would utterly repudiate the idea of a Canadian nation and would gladly accept the most exacting of imperial organic unions.

Hitherto I have welcomed your nationalism because I thought it would only mean that you wished Canada to assume national responsibilities as well as to enjoy its privileges.

But your attitude in the present crisis will alienate and antagonise the support which you might otherwise have received. Can you not realise that if any worthy nationality is possible for Canada it must be sympathetic to and must co-operate with the fine spirit of imperial unity? That spirit was endangered by the outbreak of European war. It could only be preserved by loyal assistance from all those in whom that spirit dwelt.

And so I would also have had you support Canadian participation in the war, *not* in order to maintain a certain political organism of Empire, but to preserve and perpetuate that invaluable *spirit* which alone makes our union possible.

The third reason is this: You and I are so called French-Canadians. We belong to a race that began the conquest of this country long before the days of Wolfe. That race was in its turn conquered, but their personal liberties were not restricted. They were in fact increased. Ultimately as a minority in a great English speaking community we have preserved our

353

racial identity, and we have had freedom to speak or to worship as we wished. I may not be, like yourself, "un pur sang", for I am by birth even more English than French, but I am proud of my French ancestors, I love the French language, and I am as determined as you are that we shall have full liberty to remain French as long as we like. But if we are to preserve this liberty we must recognise that we do not belong entirely to ourselves, but to a mixed population, we must rather seek to find points of contact and of common interest than points of friction and separation. We must make concessions and certain sacrifices of our distinct individuality if we mean to live on amicable terms with our fellow citizens or if we are to expect them to make similar concessions to us. There, in this moment of crisis, was the greatest opportunity which could ever have presented itself for us to show unity of purpose and to prove to our English fellow citizens that, whatever our respective histories may have been, we were actuated by a common love for our country and a mutual wish that in the future we should unite our distinctive talents and energies to create a proud and happy nation.

354

That was an opportunity which you, my cousin, have failed to grasp, and unfortunately, despite the heroic and able manner in which French Canadian battalions have distinguished themselves here, and despite the whole-hearted support which so many leaders of French Canadian thought have given to the cause, yet the fact remains that the French in Canada have not responded in the same proportion as have other Canadian citizens, and the unhappy impression has been created that French Canadians are not bearing their full share in this great Canadian enterprise. For this fact and this impression you will be held largely responsible. Do you fully realise what such a responsibility will mean, not so much to you personally — for that I believe you would care little — but to the principles which you have advocated, and for many of which I have but the deepest regard. You will have brought them into a disrepute from which they may never recover. Already you have made the fine term of "Nationalist" to stink in the nostrils of our English fellow citizens. Have you caused them to respect your national views? Have you won their admiration or led them to consider with esteem, and toleration your ambitions for the French language? Have you shown yourself worthy of concessions or consideration?

After this war what influence will you enjoy — what good to your country will you be able to accomplish? Wherever you go you will stir up strife and enmity — you will bring disfavour and dishonour upon our race, so that whoever bears a French name in Canada will be an object of suspicion and possibly of hatred.

And so, in the third place, for the honour of French Canada and for the unity of our country, I would have had you favourable to our cause.

I have only two more reasons, and they but need to be mentioned, I think to be appreciated.

Here in this little French town I hear about all me the language I love so well and which recalls so vividly my happy childhood days in Montebello.

I see types and faces that are like old friends. I see farm houses like those at home. I notice that our French Canadian soldiers have easy friendships wherever they go.

Can you make me believe that there must not always be a bond of blood relationship between the Old France and the New?

And France — more glorious than in all her history — is now in agony straining fearlessly and proudly in a struggle for life or death.

For Old France and French civilisation I would have had your support.

And in the last place, all other considerations aside and even supposing Canada had been a neutral country, I would have had you decide that she should enter the struggle for no other reason than that it is a fight for the freedom of the world — a fight in the result of which like every other country she is herself vitally interested. I will not further speak of the causes of this war, but I should like to think that even if Canada had been an independent and neutral nation she of her own accord would have chosen to follow the same path of glory that she is following to-day.

Perhaps, my cousin, I have been overlong and tedious with my reasons, but I shall be shorter with my warning — and in closing I wish to say this to you.

Those of us in this great army, who may be so fortunate as to return to our Canada, will have faced the grimest and sincerest issues of life and death — we will have experienced the unhappy strength of brute force — we will have seen our loved comrades die in blood and suffering. Beware lest we return with revengeful feelings, for I say to you that for those who, while we fought and suffered here, remained in safety and comfort in Canada and failed to give us encouragement and support, as well as for those who grew fat with the wealth dishonourably gained by political graft and by dishonest business methods at our expense — we shall demand a heavy day of reckoning. We shall inflict upon them the punishment they deserve — not by physical violence — for we shall have had enough of that — nor by unconstitutional or illegal means — for we are fighting to protect not to destroy justice and freedom — but by the invincible power of our moral influence.

Can you ask us then for sympathy or concession? Will any listen when you speak of pride and patriotism? I think not.

Remember too that if Canada has become a nation respected and self-respecting she owes it to her citizens who have fought and died in this distant land and not to those self-styled Nationalists who have remained at home.

Can I hope that anything I have said here may influence you to consider the situation in a different light and that it is not yet too late for me to be made proud of our relationship?

At this moment, as I write, French and English-Canadians are fighting and dying side by side. Is their sacrifice to go for nothing or will it not cement a foundation for a true Canadian nation, a Canadian nation inde-

355

pendent in thought, independent in action, independent even in its political organisation — but in spirit united for high international and humane purposes to the two Motherlands of England and France?

I think that is an ideal in which we shall all equally share. Can we not all play an equal part in its realisation?

I am, as long as may be possible,

Your affectionate Cousin,

TALBOT M. PAPINEAU.

356

Mr. Bourassa's Reply to Capt. Talbot Papineau's Letter*

Montreal, August 2nd, 1916.

Andrew R. McMaster, Esq., K.C.,
189 St. James St.,
City.

Dear Sir,

On my return from an absence of several weeks, I found your letter of the 18th ult., and the copy of a letter apparently written to me by your partner, Capt. Talbot Papineau, on the 21st of March.

Capt. Papineau's letter, I am informed, appeared simultaneously, Friday last, in a number of papers, in Montreal, Quebec, Ottawa and elsewhere. You have thus turned it into a kind of political manifesto and constituted yourself its publisher. Allow me therefore to send you my reply, requesting you to have it transmitted to Capt. Papineau, granting that he is the real author of that document. I can hardly believe it. A brave and active officer as he is has seldom the time to prepare and write such long pieces of political eloquence. Then, why should Capt. Papineau, who writes and speaks French elegantly, who claims so highly his French origin and professes with such ardour his love of France, have written in English to his "*dear cousin Henri*"? How is it that a letter written on the 21st of March has reached me but four months later, through your medium? For what purpose did you keep it so long in portfolio? and why do you send me a copy, instead of the letter itself?

It is, you say, an "open letter". It was, nevertheless, meant to reach me. It opens and ends with forms of language bearing the touch of intimate relationship — more so even than could be expected from the rare intercourse which, in spite of our blood connection, had so far existed

* From *Canadian Nationalism and the War*. Published in Montreal, 1916.

between your partner and myself. The whole thing has the appearance of a political manoeuvre executed under the name of a young and gallant officer, who has the advantage or inconvenience of being my cousin. That Capt. Papineau has put his signature at the foot of that document, it is possible; but he would certainly not have written it in cool thought, after due reflexion. It not only expresses opinions radically opposed to those I heard from him before the war; it also contains inaccuracies of fact of which I believe him honourably incapable.

He mentions "some discussions in the past", "differences of opinion", which have left "uninjured" a "pleasant friendship", dating, he says, "from the time of [his] birth." From his childhood to his return from Oxford, I do not think we had ever met, and certainly never to exchange the slightest glimpse of thought or opinion. Of matters of national concern we talked but once in all my life. From that one conversation I gathered the impression that he was still more opposed than myself to any kind of imperial solidarity. He even seemed much disposed to hasten the day of the Independence of Canada. Since, I met him on two or three occasions. We talked of matters indifferent, totally foreign to the numerous questions treated with such eloquent profuseness and so little reasoning in his letter of the 21st of March.

How can he charge me with having expressed "unhappy views" "at the outstart of the war", in August 1914, and held them stubbornly "unchanged" till this day? In August 1914, I was abroad. My first pronouncement on the intervention of Canada in the war is dated September 8th, 1914. In that editorial, while repelling the principles of Imperial solidarity and their consequences, and maintaining the nationalist doctrine in which Capt. Papineau — and you as well — pretends to be still a believer, I pronounced myself in favour of the intervention of Canada, *as a nation*, for the defence of the superior interests uniting Canada with France and Britain. My "unhappy views" were thus analogous to those of your partner. It is but later, long after Capt. Papineau was gone, that my attitude was changed and brought me to condemn the participation of Canada in the war, — or rather the political inspiration of that participation and the many abuses which have resulted therefrom. The reasons of that change are well known to those who have read or heard with attention and good faith all my statements on the matter. To sum them up is now sufficient.

The free and independent participation of Canada — free for the nation and free for the individuals — I had accepted, provided it remained within reasonable bounds, in conformity with the conditions of the country. But the Government, the whole of Parliament, the press and politicians of both parties all applied themselves systematically to obliterate the free character of Canada's intervention. "Free" enlistment is now carried on by means of blackmailing, intimidation and threats of all sorts. Advantage has been taken of the emotion caused by the war to assert, with the utmost intensity and intolerance, the doctrine of Imperial solidarity, triumphantly

357

opposed in the past by our statesmen and the whole Canadian people, up to the days of the infamous South African War, concocted by Chamberlain, Rhodes and the British imperialists with the clear object of drawing the self-governing colonies into "the vortex of European militarism". That phrase of your political leader, Sir Wilfrid Laurier, is undoubtedly fresh in your mind. After having given way to the imperialistic current of 1899, Sir Wilfrid Laurier and the liberal party had come back to the nationalist doctrine. The naval scare of 1909 threw them again under the yoke of imperialism; the war has achieved their enslavement: they united with the tory-jingo-imperialists of all shades to make of the participation of Canada in the war an immense political manoeuvre and thus assure the triumph of British imperialism. You and your partner, like many others, have followed your party through its various evolutions. I have remained firmly attached to the principles I laid down at the time of the South African war and maintained unswervingly ever since.

358   As early as the month of March 1900, I pointed out the possibility of a conflict between Great Britain and Germany and the danger of laying down in South Africa a precedent, the fatal consequence of which would be to draw Canada in all the wars undertaken by the United Kingdom. Sir Wilfrid Laurier and the liberal leaders laughed at my apprehensions; against my warnings they quoted the childish safeguard of the "no predecent clause" inserted in the Order in Council of the 14th of October 1899. For many years after, till 1912, and 1913, they kept singing the praises of the Kaiser and extolling the peaceful virtues of Germany. They now try to regain time by denouncing vociferously the "barbarity" of the "Huns". To-day, as in 1900, in 1911, and always, I believe that all the nations of Europe are the victims of their own mistakes, of the complacent servility with which they submitted to the dominance of all Imperialists and traders in human flesh, who, in England as in Germany, in France as in Russia, have brought the peoples to slaughter in order to increase their reapings of cursed gold. German Imperialism and British Imperialism, French Militarism and Russian Tsarism, I hate with equal detestation; and I believe as firmly today as in 1899 that Canada, a nation of America, has a nobler mission to fulfil than to bind herself to the fate of the nations of Europe or to any spoliating Empire — whether it be the spoliators of Belgium, Alsace or Poland, or those of Ireland or the Transvaal, of Greece or the Balkans.

    Politicians of both parties, your liberal friends as well as their conservative opponents, feign to be much scandalised at my "treasonable disloyalty." I could well afford to look upon them as a pack of knaves and hypocrites. In 1896, your liberal leaders and friends stumped the whole province of Quebec with the cry "WHY SHOULD WE FIGHT FOR ENGLAND?" From 1902 to 1911, Sir Wilfrid Laurier was acclaimed by them as the indomitable champion of Canada's autonomy against British Imperialism. His resisting attitude at the Imperial Conferences of 1902 and 1907 was praised to the skies. His famous phrase on the "vortex of European militarism", and his determination to keep Canada far from it, became the party's by-word — always in the Province of Quebec, of course. His Canadian Navy scheme was presented as a step towards the independence of Canada.

Then came the turn of the Conservatives to tread in the footsteps of the Nationalists; they soon outstripped us. A future member of the conservative Cabinet, Mr. Blondin, brought back to life an old saying of Sir Adolphe Chapleau, and suggested to pierce the Union Jack with bullets in order to let pass the breeze of liberty. The tory leaders, Sir Robert Borden, Sir George Foster, the virtuous Bob Rogers, and even our national superKitchener, Sir Sam Hughes, while trumpeting the purity of their Imperialism, greeted with undisguised joy the anti-imperialist victory of Drummond-Arthabaska, and used it for all it was worth to win the general elections in 1911.

By what right should those people hold me as a "traitor", because I remain consequent with the principles that I have never ceased to uphold and which both parties have exploited alternately, as long as it suited their purpose and kept them in power or brought them to office?

Let it not be pretended that those principles are out of place, pending the war. To prevent Canada from participating in the war, then foreseen and predicted, was their very object and *raison d'être*. To throw them aside and deny them when the time of test came, would have required a lack of courage and sincerity, of which I feel totally incapable. If this is what they mean by "British loyalty" and "superior civilisation", they had better hang me at once. I will never obey such dictates and will ever hold in deepest contempt the acrobats who lend themselves to all currents of blind popular passion in order to serve their personal or political ends.

This, let it be well understood, does not apply to your partner. His deeds have shown the sincerity of his political turn. Without agreeing with his new opinions, I admired his silent courage in running to the front at the first call. His verbose political manifesto — supposing he is really responsible for it — adds nothing to his merits. Still less does it enhance the dignity and moral worth of the politicians and pressmen of all kinds, who, after having denounced war and imperialism, and while taking great care not to risk their precious body, have become the apostles of war and the upholders of imperialism.

I will not undertake to answer every point of the dithyrambic plea of my gallant cousin. When he says that I am too far away from the trenches to judge of the real meaning of this war, he may be right. On the other hand, his long and diffuse piece of eloquence proves that the excitement of warfare and the distance from home have obliterated in his mind the fundamental realities of his native country. I content myself with touching upon one point, on which he unhappily lends credit to the most mischievous of the many antinational opinions circulated by the jingo press. He takes the French-Canadians to task and challenges their patriotism, because they enlist in lesser number than the other elements of the population of Canada. Much could be said upon that. It is sufficient to signalise one patent fact: the number of recruits for the European war, in the various Provinces of Canada and from each component element of the population, is in inverse ratio of the enrootment in the soil and the traditional patriotism arising therefrom. The newcomers from the British Isles have enlisted in much larger proportion than English-speaking Canadians born in this country, while these have enlisted more than the French-Canadians. The Western Provinces have given more recruits than Ontario, and Ontario more than Quebec. In each Province, the floating population of the cities, the students, the labourers and clerks, either unemployed or threatened with dismissal, have supplied more soldiers than the farmers. Does it mean that the city dwellers are more patriotic than the country people? or that the newcomers from England are better Canadians than their fellow-citizens of British origin, born in Canada? No; it simply means that in Canada, as in every other country, at all times, the citizens of the oldest origin are the least disposed to be stampeded into distant ventures of no direct concern to their native land. It proves also that military service is more repugnant to the rural than the urban populations.

360

There is among the French-Canadians a larger proportion of farmers, fathers of large families, than among any other ethnical element in Canada. Above all, the French-Canadians are the only group exclusively Canadian, in its whole and by each of the individuals of which it is composed. They look upon the perturbations of Europe, even those of England or France, as foreign events. Their sympathies naturally go to France against Germany; but they do not think they have an obligation to fight for France, no more than the French of Europe would hold themselves bound to fight for Canada against the United States or Japan, or even against Germany, in case Germany should attack Canada without threatening France.

English Canada, not counting the *blokes*, contains a considerable proportion of people still in the first period of national incubation. Under the sway of imperialism, a fair number have not yet decided whether their allegiance is to Canada or to the Empire, whether the United Kingdom or the Canadian Confederacy is their country.

As to the newcomers from the United Kingdom, they are not Canadian in any sense. England or Scotland is their sole fatherland. They have enlisted for the European war as naturally as Canadians, either French or English, would take arms to defend Canada against an aggression on the American continent.

Thus it is rigorously correct to say that recruiting has gone in inverse ratio of the development of Canadian patriotism. If English-speaking Canadians have a right to blame the French Canadians for the small number of their recruits, the newcomers from the United Kingdom, who have supplied a much larger proportion of recruits than any other element of the population, would be equally justified in branding the Anglo-Canadians with disloyalty and treason. Enlistment for the European war is supposed to be absolutely free and voluntary. This has been stated right and left from beginning to end. If that statement is honest and sincere, all provocations from one part of the population against the other, and exclusive attacks against the French-Canadians, should cease. Instead of reviling unjustly one-third of the Canadian people — a population so remarkably characterised by its constant loyalty to national institutions and its respect for public order, — those men who claim a right to enlighten and lead public opinion should have enough good faith and intelligence to see facts as they are and to respect the motives of those who persist in their determination to remain more Canadian than English or French.

In short, English-speaking Canadians enlist in much smaller number than the newcomers from England, because they are more Canadian; French-Canadians enlist less than English-Canadians because they are totally and exclusively Canadian. To claim that their abstention is due to the "baneful" influence of the Nationalists is a pure nonsense. Should I give way to the suggestion of my gallant cousin, I would be just as powerless as Sir Wilfrid Laurier to induce the French-Canadians to enlist. *361* This is implicitly acknowledged in Capt. Papineau's letter: on the one hand, he asserts that my views on the participation of Canada in the war is denied by my own friends; on the other he charges the mass of the French-Canadian population with a refusal to answer the call of duty. The simple truth is, that the abstention of the French-Canadians is no more the result of the present attitude of the Nationalists than the consequence of the liberal campaign of 1896, or of the conservative appeals of 1911. It relates to deeper causes: hereditary instincts, social and economic conditions, a national tradition of three centuries. It is equally true, however, that those deep and far distant causes have been strengthened by the constant teaching of all our political and social leaders, from Lafontaine, Cartier, Macdonald, Mackenzie, to Laurier inclusively. The only virtue, or crime, of the Nationalists is to persist in believing and practising what they were taught by the men of the past, and even those of to-day. This is precisely what infuriates the politicians, either *blue* or *red*. To please the Imperialists, they have renounced all their traditions and undertaken to bring the French-Canadians under imperial command. Unable to succeed, they try to conceal their fruitless apostasy by denouncing to the hatred of the jingos the obtrusive witnesses of their past professions of faith.

The jingo press and politicians have also undertaken to persuade their gullible followers that the Nationalists hinder the work of recruiters *because* of the persecution meted out to the French minorities in Ontario and Manitoba. This is but another nonsense. My excellent cousin, I am sorry to say, — or his inspirer — has picked it up.

The two questions are essentially distinct, this we have never ceased to assert. One is purely internal; the other affects the international status of Canada and her relations with Great Britain. To the problem of the teaching of languages we ask for a solution in conformity with the spirit of the Federal agreement, the best interests of Confederation, and the principles of pedagogy as applied in civilised countries. Our attitude on the participation of Canada in the war is inspired exclusively by the constant tradition of the country and the agreements concluded half a century ago between Canada and Great Britain. Even if the irritating bilingual question was non existent, our views on the war would be what they are. The most that can be said is, that the backward and essentially Prussian policy of the rulers of Ontario and Manitoba gives us an additional argument against the intervention of Canada in the European conflict. To speak of fighting for the preservation of French civilisation in Europe while endeavouring to destroy it in America, appears to us as an absurd piece of inconsistency. To preach Holy War for the liberties of the peoples overseas, and to oppress the national minorities in Canada, is, in our opinion, nothing but odious hypocrisy.

Is it necessary to add that, in spite of his name, Capt. Papineau is utterly unqualified to judge of the feelings of the French-Canadians? For most part American, he has inherited, with a few drops of French blood, the most *denationalised* instincts of his French origin. From those he calls his compatriots he is separated by his religious belief and his maternal language. Of their traditions, he knows but what he has read in a few books. He was brought up far away from close contact with French-Canadians. His higher studies he pursued in England. His elements of French culture he acquired in France. The complexity of his origin and the diversity of his training would be sufficient to explain his mental hesitations and the contradictions which appear in his letter. Under the sway of his American origin, he glories in the Revolution of 1776; he calls it a war "for the principle of national existence". In good logic, he should approve highly of the tentative rebellion of the Sinn Feiners, and suggest that Canada should rise in arms to break the yoke of Great Britain. His American forefathers, whom he admires so much, fought against England and called upon France and Spain to help them against their mother-country, for lighter motives than those of the Dublin rebels. The Imperial burden they refused to bear was infinitely less ponderous than that which weighs today upon the people of Canada.

With the threat contained in the conclusion of his letter, I need not be concerned. Supposing always that he is truly responsible for that document, I make broad allowance for the excitement and perturbation resulting from his strenuous life. He and many of his comrades will have enough to do in order to help Canada to counteract the disastrous consequences of the war venture in which she has thrown herself headlong. To propagate systematically national discord by quarreling with all Canadians, either French or English, who hold different views as to the theory and practice of their national duty, would be a misuse of time. Moreover, it would be a singular denial of their professions of faith in favour of liberty and civilisation.

As to the scoundrels and bloodsuckers "who have grown fat with the wealth dishonourably gained" in war contracts, I give them up quite willingly to their just indignation. But those worthies are not to be found

362

in nationalist ranks: they are all recruited among the noisiest preachers of the Holy War waged for "civilisation" against "barbarity", for the "protection of small nations", for the "honour" of England and the "salvation" of France.

Yours truly,

Henri BOURASSA

P.S. — I hope this will reach you before you leave for the front: no doubt, you have been the first to respond to the pressing call of your partner.   H.B.

Canada's Liberal Pacifists and the Great War*

363

THOMAS P. SOCKNAT

On the eve of the Great War many Canadians vaguely thought of themselves as pacifists, causing that perennial observer of Canadian affairs, J. Castell Hopkins, to report that by 1914 "peace had become a habit of thought with many minds in Canada and, in some cases, was almost a religion."[1] Since pacifist rhetoric was "difficult to oppose and hard to discuss," explained Hopkins, it was "easy of presentment and popular acceptance."[2] Indeed, some Canadians expressed alarm that pacifism was actually "sweeping the country." Principal Maurice Hutton of Toronto's University College, for instance, warned a Toronto audience that "the air is so full of pacifism that it is necessary to urge upon the country the duty of national defense."[3]

Pacifists, on the other hand, were pleased with what they considered the "phenomenal advance" of the peace movement, but some were careful not to become complacent just because it appeared that pacifism had been "pretty generally accepted, in theory, at least, by the majority of thinking persons" in Canada. On the contrary, Arthur G. Dorland, Chairman of the Peace and Arbitration Committee of the Canada Yearly Meeting of the Society of Friends, emphasized that the position adopted by many of the liberal converts to pacifism differed fundamentally from that of Quakers. Although the former condemned the disastrous results of war, he argued, they still believed that, under certain circumstances, wars were justifiable and right, while true pacifists like the Friends believed that since war was inherently immoral it could never be right.[4]

In effect, Dorland was distinguishing between the two different but complementary traditions of pacifism in Canada. One was the historic religious adherence to non-resistance largely confined to sectarian pacifists such as the Quakers, Mennonites and Hutterites. Their exemption from military

*From *Journal of Canadian Studies*, 18 (4) (1983–84): 30–44. Reprinted by permission.

obligations had been specifically guaranteed by several Orders-in-Council during the late nineteenth century so that the tradition of religious pacifism was firmly entrenched in Canadian law and custom by 1914. Accordingly, the historic peace sects maintained their quiet pacifist witness throughout the war years.

The other tradition and that which was credited with popular appeal before 1914 was the movement for peace and world order motivated by the liberal reform impulse and the social gospel. By the late nineteenth century Quakers had become representative of both the historic and liberal pacifist traditions, but, as Dorland noted, the majority of liberal pacifists were preoccupied with the futility of war. The liberal peace movement, in other words, was largely representative of the progressive attempt to achieve order and stability within the world through the use of international arbitration and an international court. Moreover, it was elevated to a position of key importance since most reformers generally assumed that the success of their attempt to build a new social order depended upon a peaceful international climate. Political, church, farm and labour spokesmen, and women's groups such as the WCTU and the National Council of Women all endorsed the principle of international arbitration and the peace movement in general. But they gave little thought to the ethics of war and failed to penetrate the relationship between war and the economic order.[5] Rather than pursue the roots of war into the structure of society or formulate a proper response for pacifists in a time of war, the pre-war pacifists merely erected a superficial facade which quickly shattered upon impact with the Great War.

Although this rapid disruption of Canada's peace movement has been noted by historians in the context of other studies,[6] a close examination of the pacifist issue itself reveals that Canadian liberal pacifism ended up taking a radical new turn in its wartime evolution. For instance, rather than unanimously deserting pacifist ideals, the loose reform coalition of liberal pacifists actually splintered into various responses. Some attempted to maintain a moderate stance recognizing the necessity to support the war effort while, at the same time, striving towards pacifist ideals and a progressive post-war era. This was perhaps the most difficult, if not impossible, position to maintain. The majority gradually came to think of the war as the crucible in which Christianity and the ideal of Christian peace were in danger of extinction at the hands of the enemy forces and they joined in the crusade against German "barbarism." At the opposite extreme, however, was a small number who remained irrevocably opposed to war and militarism as antithetical to a Christian society. In addition, they broadened their attack to include not only war but the whole social and economic system which they believed had produced war in the first place. Contrary to earlier peace advocates of either the historic peace sects or the liberal reform movement, therefore, they began to associate peace with radical, non-violent, socio-economic change at home and abroad.

The general disintegration of the liberal peace movement occurred as the majority of its pre-war membership not only abandoned pacifism but helped build the war effort into a frenzied crusade. Almost all groups of liberal reformers reflected this transition one way or another. Women's groups, for instance, quickly redirected their energies towards more respectable pursuits. Indeed, it is ironic that the women who helped popularize the expectation that they would somehow react differently than men to war, because of their moral superiority, were the ones who substantially contributed to the disruption of this myth during the war through their Red Cross work and patriotic activities.

The most vocal expression of this moral transformation, however, was provided by the churches, especially the Methodist Church through its journal *The Christian Guardian*, previously a leading peace organ. Shortly after the outbreak of the war the editor, W. B. Creighton, still condemned war as foolish, costly and unchristian and reaffirmed his belief that Christian pacifism was still on its way.[7] On the other hand, he also supported the claim by the General Superintendent of the Methodist Church, S. D. Chown, that the war was "just, honorable and necessary" to really secure a durable peace. Stories of German atrocities in Belgium and government controlled war propaganda, however, eventually triggered a more emotional response and raised fears for the future of Christendom itself. As a result, the traditional concept of the just war was transformed into that of an apocalyptic crusade, an eschatological confrontation between good and evil, between Christianity and the anti-Christ epitomized by Germany.[9] Former pacifists who had found it difficult to rationalize support for a just war with their dedicated faith in the Christian gospel easily accepted the idea of a crusade to save Christianity and liberal democracy from the diabolical German menace.[10] As argued elsewhere, the result was a paradox: idealized Christian pacifism produced an extreme zeal for a holy war.[11] Furthermore, liberal reformers began to think of participation in the war as an act of "national regeneration."[12] The apocalyptic war hysteria demanded a concerted fight against all evil. The demon Hun, the demon rum, the scourge of venereal disease, and other vices affecting society became equal targets of this crusading zeal. Therefore, as the social and moral reform movement joined forces with the war effort, *The Christian Guardian* concluded that "theoretically the church knows no peace — she is always at war with evil."[13]

Given this redefinition of war, many of the pre-war pacifists went full circle and labelled pacifism itself as evil. The shifting perspective could be observed in November 1916, when W. B. Creighton, while praising pacifism as "one of the most hopeful signs of our time," claimed pacifists were guilty of "dull obstinacy," "bitter prejudice," and "plain stupidity" for the manner in which they attempted to apply pacifism to the war with Germany.[14] The conclusion to that line of thinking appeared in the April 3, 1918 issue of the *Guardian*. In a cover page editorial entitled "The vice of Pacifism" Creighton argued that, rather than a virtue, pacifism was "a vice revealing the terrible fact that the conscience has lost its sensitiveness and the soul has lost its courage."[15] The following month Creighton developed his assault further and declared in no uncertain terms that there was no

365

room in the Methodist Church for ministers with a pacifist conscience, even though the church had been pacifist in the past. "If a man cannot conscientiously declare himself a patriot," the editor asserted, "he has no business in any church which prides itself upon its patriotism."[16] Although such sentiments were echoed by the rest of the church press, the *Guardian* came to symbolize the wholesale desertion of the liberal peace movement during the war.[17] Its blanket condemnation of pacifism and denial of the right of conscience either silenced remaining pacifists or drove them further to the socialist camp.

Initially, however, some liberal pacifists tried to maintain moderate support for the war without condoning the extreme transformation of their earlier pacifist stand into a militant crusade. In effect, they attempted to unite a critical acquiescence in the war with a continuing opposition to militarism. Outright pacifist sentiments, on the other hand, were carefully aimed at future post-war society rather than the current conflict in order to avoid contradictions in such a tenuous position.

Two of Toronto's leading newspapermen had called themselves pacifists at the beginning of the war, but within a year both J. E. Atkinson, managing editor of the *Toronto Daily Star*, and J. A. Macdonald, managing editor of the Toronto *Globe*, had more or less succumbed to the patriotic fervor.[18] Macdonald, in particular, had been one of the leading spokesmen of the liberal peace movement in Canada before the war. He was the Canadian representative in various international peace organizations and was a director of the World Peace Foundation, the philanthropic peace research organization endowed by the American publisher, Edwin Ginn.[19] During the war Macdonald attempted to combine the call for patriotic duty with his familiar peace rhetoric, claiming that a time of war was also a time to prepare for peace and disarmament.[20] Following his lead, the *Globe* initially exercised a moderating influence on the public as its editorials protested against the effects of militarism upon society, warned against building anti-German sympathies in Canadian youth, and argued that "no Canadian cadet should be allowed to think of a German or any other man as a target for his marksmanship."[21] But given the circumstances, the two lines of thought were almost impossible to maintain for long and in 1915 Macdonald resigned as editor, thus freeing the *Globe* to assume a more ardent patriotic position. Macdonald himself began a series of patriotic addresses in which he urged young men to enlist. In the end, he joined those liberals who had accepted the war as a means to create a new democratic world order, but the idea of armed peace or preparedness he still denounced as "doomed to the rubbish heap of the world's barbarism."[22]

The underlying conflict within the liberal conscience was most clearly reflected by the Canadian Peace and Arbitration Society, the principal liberal peace organization in Canada, as it adjusted to wartime realities. Prior to the war the Society counted over a thousand members, including such prominent Canadian academics as Professor Adam Shortt of Queen's University, Professor J. McCurdy of the University of Toronto, Sir William

Mullock, Chief Justice of Ontario, and Lewis E. Horning, Professor of Classics at Victoria College.[23]

As the Society's wartime president, Horning spearheaded an effort to convince a dwindling audience to think "soberly, righteously and fairly" about the events occurring around them and thereby resist the growing war frenzy.[24] The aim of the Society was to combine support for Canada's war effort with some type of constructive action in line with their pacifist principles. As a start in that direction members of the Society made financial contributions, through the Canadian Society of Friends, to the Friends' Ambulance Corps organized in Europe by British Quakers.[25]

Although Horning accepted the war as a just struggle between democracy and militarism, his most perplexing problem was to reconcile it with Christianity. One solution, he proposed, was for peace-loving Christians to waste no time in building a new Christian spirit to supplant war.[26] Accordingly, he hoped the Canadian Peace and Arbitration Society, similar to the League for Democratic Control in Britain, would preserve clarity of thought during the war while working towards the post-war emergence of a new international system in accordance with liberal ideals.

Shortly after the outbreak of war, this position was articulated clearly by Horning in a letter to Dr. T. Albert Moore, Secretary of the General Conference of the Methodist Church. Horning appealed to the Church hierarchy for its "sympathy, whole-hearted co-operation and active support" in planning that coming generations think "more sanely and soundly than past and present generations."[27] As a course of action, he suggested combatting the martial spirit which had infiltrated daily lives and language by building a new vision of patriotism free from the taint of militarism and war. Horning argued that

. . . the old Patriotism is altogether too often associated with the soldiers' life. The language of our everyday life and of our past literature smacks very much of the martial, that is, it is a language based upon old ideals and old habits. "Patriotic fund". . . why not *Soldiers* fund?[28]

Conversely, the word patriotism was to be reserved for references to peace, self-sacrifice and brave service for one's fellow man. "The New Patriotism," claimed Horning, "calls for life and opportunity for life, not death and destruction, and vandalism and horrors." Pacifists, therefore, could also be viewed as patriots, contrary to the "fallacious arguments" of militarists.[29]

The Canadian Peace and Arbitration Society also maintained that its members and sympathetic friends had a special duty to perform regarding Canada's own peculiar problems, such as French-English relations, further complicated by the war, and the question of state ownership and control of the nation's productive wealth. "On all sides," Horning warned, "we need new light, new thought, a new spirit . . . we should believe in another destiny, that of the saving of the nations." In conclusion Horning made a final appeal to the Church:

Preachers of peace and believers in Goodwill, help us . . . by your heartfelt sympathy, cordial co-operation and willing openmindedness . . . we can be of great service to each other.[30]

367

Although the Church ignored Horning's appeal for a "New Patriotism," the Canadian Peace and Arbitration Society continued to sponsor peace meetings and addresses, at least as long as the United States remained neutral, but after 1917 its voice of moderation grew silent.[31] Even Horning ceased his attempt to organize a pacifist program of action and retreated to safer pursuits. In keeping with his personal desire to educate the public, for instance, he delivered a nation-wide series of lectures during the summer of 1918 concerning problems of war and Canadian citizenship.[32] Members of the Society and other frustrated liberals had tried in vain to prevent the development of an over-zealous war mentality but in the end they were not ready to go as far as to endorse radical dissent.

Once the majority of liberal pacifists accepted the war effort, one way or another, there remained only a small minority who maintained a pacifist opposition to the war. But these liberal reformers not only condemned war according to the Christian ethic, they also extended that analysis to social and economic questions, with the result that their views became more socially radical as well as pacifist. This blending of pacifism with social radicalism signified an important transition in the Canadian pacifist tradition: the pacifist initiative had passed from the old coalition of progressive reformers to a developing realignment of committed pacifists with the socialist ideal. The actual shift of some social reformers into more radical ranks was well underway before 1914, but the debate over the war and such measures as conscription further heightened their radicalism as it reinforced a growing awareness that socialists and pacifists shared many common objectives.

368

One of the earliest expressions of this new pacifist ethic came from a small group of radical feminists. Largely centred in Toronto, they worked through the Women's Social Democratic League and the Toronto Suffrage Association until the summer of 1915 when Elsie Charlton, Alice Chown, and Laura Hughes founded the Canadian Women's Peace Party.[33] Laura Hughes grasped the idea that spring while attending the International Congress of Women at The Hague. Once she learned that women around the world were organizing peace parties she became determined that Canadian women should not lag behind. The conspicuous involvement of Laura Hughes and Alice Chown in wartime pacifism proved to be a matter of some embarrassment to their uncles, S. D. Chown, General Superintendent of the Methodist Church, and Colonel Sam Hughes, the Canadian Minister of Militia, but the two women remained undeterred.[34]

The Canadian Women's Peace Party, later re-christened the Women's International League for Peace and Freedom (WILPF), endorsed the program outlined at The Hague for building a new international order through compulsory arbitration, universal disarmament and a league of democratic nations.[35] Upon closer examination, however, it appeared to be a "stop the war" movement and Laura Hughes actually admitted as much privately although in public she was more discreet in order to avoid the charge of treason.[36] Generally, Hughes moved to an increasingly radical outlook. With the WILPF she directed her wrath at the military capitalist complex behind the war effort and joined with labour-socialists in their attack on war profiteering by financial trusts and armament makers.

Alice Chown, another founding member, was also no newcomer to radical activities. Somewhat of a free spirit who usually appeared barefoot to emphasize her free will, Chown was active in furthering the cause of women's suffrage and women's trade unions.[37] By 1915 she turned her attention to the war, and, calling herself a "strenuous pacifist," she criticized all violent methods for settling disputes, whether they were strikes, anarchistic actions or wars, as too costly and only partially successful. Instead she suggested non-violent action was the best alternative and "the only right path for a nation to follow."[38]

Arguing that Christ was a better psychologist than man, Chown proposed that Germany be conquered through a new conception of brotherhood which included, first of all, eliminating injustice and selfishness within Canadian society. Such public declarations as "to conquer your enemy is to love him" insured Chown a hostile reception in a country at war, resulting in public abuse and demands that she be confined in an asylum or a jail.[39] Undaunted, Chown continued to work towards "the brotherhood of nations" and the "abolition of special privileges for individuals and states." "But for the people around me," she recalled, "the most heroic thing that they could do was to throw themselves disinterestedly into the war."[40] In a letter to her uncle, S. D. Chown, she explained how she had fought all through the war for a knowledge of facts, for justice to the enemy, and for the allies to refrain from acts of unrighteousness in Russia, while he and his associates in the Methodist Church hierarchy had allowed themselves to become "dupes" of the militarists. "I kept my faith in the sermon on the mount," she exlaimed, "and you have put your faith in force and have acquiesced in the lies of the censored press."[41]

369

Alice Chown also feared the war would have a brutal effect upon Canadian society in general. "I am positive," she wrote, "that the evils we go out to fight with violence we shall graft upon our own nation's life." She explained:

Starting with hatred of our enemy's cruelty, we shall end by being cruel ourselves; detesting the subservience of the German people to their state, we shall become indifferent to the subservience of our own people to our state. We shall lose our free institutions, free speech, free press, free assemblage, and have to struggle to regain them.[42]

Despite the work of the Toronto based WIL, the centre of pacifist activity was in Winnipeg where notable reformers like J. S. Woodsworth, William Ivens, F. J. Dixon, A. Vernon Thomas, and Francis Marion Beynon, some of whom were already known for their social radicalism, had begun to express radical pacifist sentiments as well. As early as the 1912 naval debate, for instance, Dixon had protested strenuously against what he called "creeping militarism" in Canada and during the war years he continued to air his pacifist views.[43] An independent member of the Manitoba legislature since 1914, Dixon was almost the only member of the House to speak out strongly against the war and its infringements on individual rights and freedoms.[44] In 1917 he withstood a movement to have him impeached and thereafter continued to voice anti-war sentiments, and particularly to publicize the position of radical labour on the war.[45]

It was no coincidence, therefore, that Winnipeg labour leaders were the most active in organizing an anti-conscription campaign. Although sympathetic to pacifism, labour opposition to the war, like that of farmers, was primarily a reaction against conscription and was based more upon economic than pacifist considerations.[46] Outside of a few violent protests and some isolated cases of resistance by western radicals, for instance, Canadian workers and farmers enthusiastically supported the war effort.[47] Nevertheless, what opposition there was had a doctrinal dimension which found suitable expression in the socially radical pacifism Dixon represented. Winnipeg's labour paper, *The Voice*, aired the full views of Dixon and other pacifists throughout the war and, although rejecting the principle of non-violence, urged tolerance for Canadians conscientiously opposed to the war for either socialist or religious reasons.[48]

One of the casualties of the anti-war campaign was the Winnipeg journalist, A. Vernon Thomas. Thomas had been attracted to the *Free Press* from the *Manchester Guardian* and he became involved in Winnipeg reform circles soon after his arrival. His wife, Lillian Beynon, was a prominent Winnipeg reformer and suffragist, as was her sister, Francis Marion Beynon. All three were radical pacifists. For a journalist to express such views publicly was dangerous, however, and in 1916 Thomas was quickly fired from his job at the *Free Press* after he walked onto the floor of the legislature to congratulate F. J. Dixon on one of his anti-war speeches.[49] Shortly afterward the Thomases, bitterly disappointed, left the country and spent the duration of the war in New York.

Writing to Woodsworth from his self-imposed exile, Thomas confessed that the sacrifice in their "little attempt at freedom" seemed contemptible compared to the personal vigil of Woodsworth and other pacifists in Canada.[50] Although Thomas continued to contribute anti-war, anti-racist articles to *The Voice*, he often wondered if he could not make a greater protest. "I don't think the pacifist note of my articles can be mistaken," he wrote. "But it ends there and my position is simply that I am not extolling the war in my daily work, which is a great satisfaction."[51] On the other hand, Thomas maintained there would be plenty to do once the war was over and "immediate fear is removed from the hearts of the people." He looked forward to the day when he could return to Canada and join Woodsworth in the work of "absolutely challenging the present constitution of society and its ideals."[52]

Despite his attempt to remain optimistic about the post-war era, Thomas became depressed over the increasing toll the war was having upon Canadian society. The evil fruits of war, he warned, were growing every day:

We cannot think the war out of existence. People are not what they were. Their minds have become militarized and we shall have to deal with people of that kind. The workers have not been spared. A good deal of the labor movement is now war. It is all a tragedy and we can only make the best of it.[53]

Thomas's sister-in-law, Francis Marion Beynon, stayed behind in Winnipeg for a time as the editor of the women's page of the *Grain Growers' Guide* and carried on the anti-war struggle. Social discontent was on the rise in wartime Winnipeg and Francis Beynon exemplifies the transition of pre-war liberal into radical. Like most liberals before 1914, Beynon subscribed to the usual anti-militarist, pacifist sentiments. But as Ramsay Cook has explained, the war raised serious questions about fundamental liberal intellectual assumptions, exposing a naive faith in moral progress.[54] Although she believed women had a greater interest in social and ethical questions than men, Beynon questioned the validity of feminist comments on the pacifist influence of women.[55] In a short time her growing skepticism seemed justified by the thorough involvement of women in various war activities and the intolerant, conformist attitude associated with patriotism. Consequently, Beynon accepted the diagnosis that there was something radically wrong with the whole social order that demanded correction.[56] Patriotism and nationalism merely defended the established order, she argued, while its intolerant, militaristic spirit was the same spirit that crucified Christ and continued to threaten those preaching His pacifist doctrine.[57]

The super-patriotic atmosphere of the country strengthened Beynon's individual resolve and her radical commitment to pacifism and social reconstruction. Initially, however, the popular association of dissent with subversion cautioned Beynon to restrain her pacifist sentiments in favour of safer demands like the conscription of wealth as well as men. But unlike those who associated this proposal with some form of graduated income tax, Beynon made it clear she favoured the actual "taking over by government of all real property."[58] As she became more outspoken she also echoed the familiar charge that the most fervent patriots were those getting rich from "seated labor and war profiteering."[59] Such regular anti-war statements and the whole radical tone of her column, she suspected, had aroused the wrath of the Press Censor and ultimately placed her at odds with her editor, George F. Chipman, who had moved towards support of conscription and Union government. Consequently, rather than restrain her pacifist and radical beliefs, Beynon resigned in the summer of 1917 and joined the Thomases in exile.[60]

Francis Beynon became convinced that the war was the result of capitalist, economic conflicts and a militant mentality and that it would create more problems than it would solve. Like other radical pacifists, for example, she feared that wartime mobilization was causing Canadian society to become increasingly insensitive to social injustice, as its treatment of enemy aliens testified.[61] The only way to solve world problems and prevent future military conflicts was through a social and intellectual revolution, the fear of which, she asserted, haunted Canadian capitalists by 1918.[62]

Before the war social reformers like Beynon had depended upon the theology of liberal Protestantism, but it now appeared the social gospel lacked the intellectual depth required to support a major movement of social and moral reconstruction.[63] What was necessary, according to socially conscious pacifists, was a synthesis of the ethical aspect of Christianity with a dynamic philosophy for radical change. A radicalized social gospel was partly an attempt in that direction.

Of the social gospel radicals, it was J. S. Woodsworth who most clearly represented the mixture of Christian pacifism and socialism.[64] Although Woodsworth ultimately became Canada's most famous pacifist, his pacifist convictions evolved slowly. It is not clear, for instance, if he was a confirmed pacifist before 1914. In fact, the first two years of the war were a time of confessed "heart searching" for Woodsworth but as he corresponded with numerous pacifists he became increasingly pacifist himself.[65] By June 1916, he was labelled a pacifist by the Manitoba press following an address to a young men's club in which he expressed doubt that moral issues could be settled by force, but it was not until conscription became the issue of the day that Woodsworth openly declared his pacifism.[66]

372

In a letter to the *Free Press* he condemned national registration as a prelude to conscription, a measure he could not conscientiously support.[67] As a result he was dismissed as director of the Bureau of Social Research and the agency itself, which supplied basic research for the social legislation of the three prairie governments, was closed.[68] For a time Woodsworth contemplated joining a Doukhobor community and even made active inquiries in that direction. The Doukhobors were sympathetic but wondered if he could really adapt to their ways.[69] Perhaps Woodsworth agreed, for he finally accepted a charge in Gibson's Landing, British Columbia. His outspoken pacifist views, however, proved to be no more welcome there than in Manitoba and the following year he was removed at the request of the congregation. In response and chagrined over Creighton's anti-pacifist editorial in the *Guardian*, Woodsworth resigned from the ministry entirely, citing the war policy of the Church and the issue of pacifism as his main reasons.[70] For the remainder of the war he worked as a longshoreman on the West Coast while his wife, Lucy, organized the Vancouver chapter of the Women's International League for Peace and Freedom.

Woodsworth's letter of resignation revealed a new socially radical pacifism — a synthesis of absolute Christian social ethics and the socialist critique. For instance, although he claimed war was the "inevitable outcome of the existing social organization with its undemocratic form of government and competitve system of industry," he emphasized that, above all, war was "absolutely irreconcilable" with the spirit and teachings of Jesus. "Christianity may be an impossible idealism," he declared, "but so long as I hold to it, ever so unworthily, I must refuse, as far as may be, to participate in or to influence others to participate in war."[71]

Woodsworth's brand of pacifism was also shared by William Ivens, another renegade in the Methodist Church. Although Ivens refrained from voicing pacifist views from the pulpit of Winnipeg's McDougall Methodist Church, he felt free to express himself on the outside. Consequently, he contributed regular anti-war articles to *The Voice* and became involved in trade union activities. Ivens' actions split his congregation and by the spring of 1918 an urgent appeal was made to the Manitoba Stationing Committee for his removal. Rather than be intimidated, however, Ivens immediately embarked on a speaking tour of the prairies.[72] Vernon Thomas wrote Woodsworth that it was "greatly encouraging" to see a pacifist such as Ivens speak out publicly and he praised him for fighting a tremendous fight and "winning his way into the hearts of people."[73]

Despite numerous letters and petitions in his support, Ivens was finally removed from McDougall, and, rather than accept a different charge, he assumed the editorship of the *Western Labor News*, the official organ of the Winnipeg Trades and Labor Council.[74] His old friend Vernon Thomas was quick to wish him luck in the new undertaking which, unlike the Methodist Church, might allow him to interpret Christ in his own way — as a pacifist.[75] But Ivens was soon under attack again when the Chief Press Censor, Ernest Chambers, threatened to outlaw the paper unless Ivens purged the publication of revolutionary and pacifist articles.[76] The most visible example of Ivens' radicalism, however, was his labor church founded in July 1918, as a creedless church dedicated to the "establishment of justice and righteousness on earth, among all men and nations."[77] Woodsworth later commented that "the Labor Church was born during the war, as a protest against war."[78]

By 1917, amid mounting casualties at the front and the enactment of the Military Service Act at home, anti-war sentiment in Canada reached its peak. As a catalyst, conscription not only resulted in the Quebec crisis and farm and labour protests but it necessitated pacifist resistance as well. Both Woodsworth and Ivens had begun to publicize their pacifism in response to the conscription issue and it remained the central stimulus to pacifist protests throughout the balance of the war. In the first instance, conscription brought conscientious objection into the open in a new way and exposed objectors to a new degree of maltreatment. The torture of Jehovah's Witnesses at the Minto Street Barracks in Winnipeg was a sensational example of this and fueled the protest of pacifist spokesmen.[79] F. J. Dixon raised the matter in the Manitoba legislature and demanded an immediate investigation, arguing that "the day of torture should be past."[80] Likewise, Ivens led a public outcry over the death of a conscientious objector in Stoney Mountain Penitentiary. Ivens used the incident to reiterate the radical pacifist demand that individual conscience be given full and proper respect rather than the type of maltreatment that led to the death of the young Pentecostal pacifist. "It may be that his death was necessary," Ivens argued, "to convince the Government that there are Conscientious Objectors in the Dominion outside of Pacifist Churches and Organizations who are prepared to die for their convictions rather than submit to perform military service."[81]

The young Canadians who conscientiously objected to military service were largely sectarian pacifists from the historic peace sects and the more recent pacifist groups like Jehovah's Witnesses. The majority of these religious pacifists, such as Mennonites and Hutterites, maintained an adamant isolation from war and society alike; nevertheless, their staunch resistance to compulsory military service reinforced the principle of conscientious objection and pacifist dissent in general within Canadian society.

The Society of Friends, on the other hand, had abandoned their old quietistic ways and had become an important part of the liberal reform movement. In effect, Quakers bridged the gap between traditional religious nonresistance and the liberal faith in social action. Accordingly, they attempted to maintain a program of pacifist activity, from assisting conscientious objectors to supporting war relief programs. It was the view of Friends that all pacifists should assume the role of reconcilers in the war and help suppress the feeling of bitterness and hatred intensified in society.[82]

Like other liberal pacifists during the war, Quakers also moved towards social radicalism. They began by examining the conditions that made for war and their own complicity in them. "Have we," Friends asked, "either as Christians or as responsible citizens of our respective countries, done all that we might or should to remove these conditions?"[83] Once they discovered the seeds of war sown within the established social order, the Quakers replaced their historic emphasis upon mercy in a static society with an increasingly radical commitment to change the social order.[84] Canadian Friends, for instance, began to endorse government control and possible ownership of all industries manufacturing war-related articles.[85] Furthermore, by the war's end they equated the causes of international war with those of the social struggle, something which was central to the new socially radical pacifism the war had bred.

J. S. Woodsworth was among the first to notice that Friends were "beginning to abandon their old rather negative and abstract position with regard to war and to attack the evils which are responsible for modern wars." Although expressing surprise to find Quakers advocating "scientific socialism," he was encouraged by their new line of thinking.[86] In 1919, for example, Friends warned that "the crime, the wickedness, the deceit, the hypocrisy that stood at the back of the conditions that produced the first war" remained, resulting in the post-war unrest which threatened to erupt in a violent social revolt, equal to the war in horror, unless there was a radical reconstruction of Canadian society. What was needed, they claimed, was a "revolution, not necessarily violent, and an edifice of new design" which would guarantee labour "shorter hours, more of the product it produces, larger opportunities, a different interpretation of justice."[87]

The Quakers and the other radical pacifists from feminist and social gospel ranks had moved a long way from the old progressive call for peace, order and stability. The war had changed that. It had confronted the liberal peace movement with an insurmountable challenge, resulting in its disruption and disintegration as the majority of its members deserted pacifism in favour of a new means to achieve their desired ends — a holy war. Even the few liberals who attempted to maintain a moderately realistic position were smothered in the process. Certainly, the ease and enthusiasm with which this reversal was made betrayed the rather ambiguous nature of pre-war pacifism.

374

But the death of the progressive peace movement early in the war was not the end of liberal pacifism in Canada. It would re-emerge in the post-war years among such groups as the League of Nations Society and, once again, attempt to ensure world peace without directly challenging the state. Amid the pressures of the escalating wartime crusade, however, liberal pacifism proved to be utterly untenable. Those who wished to maintain their pacifist protest found it necessary to adopt a radical critique of the social and economic roots of war and in doing so abandon their liberal reformism for some variant of the socialist creed. For some, that too became almost an eschatological warfare against the established social order, not entirely unlike their erstwhile colleagues who sought the reign of peace via the war to end war. Furthermore, just as the democratic socialist movement in the English-speaking world built upon and incorporated historic tenets of liberalism, so, too, the socially radical pacifism forged during the war retained a glimmer of its liberal past.

Although not fully articulated during the war, the new pacifist ethic would ultimately gain support in the post-war era and encourage a temporary alliance between a resurgent peace movement, democratic socialists, and elements of the far left. In 1919, however, socially radical pacifists failed to foresee a serious dilemma awaiting them beyond the horizon: their momentum towards radical reform and social change to secure peace and justice was on a long-term collision course with their pacifist rejection of the use of violence in any cause.

375

Notes

1. J. C. Hopkins, *The Canadian Annual Review*, 1914, p. 132.
2. *Ibid.*, p. 133.
3. *Ibid.*, p. 135.
4. Arthur G. Dorland, "Militarism in Canada," *The Canadian Friend*, July 1913, p. 14. Dorland was a history professor at the University of Western Ontario from 1920 to 1955.
5. Peter Brock, *Twentieth-Century Pacifism* (Toronto, 1970), p. 10. See also Michael Howard, *War and the Liberal Conscience* (Rutgers, 1978).
6. Those studies, by Richard Allen, J. M. Bliss, Ramsay Cook, Kenneth McNaught, Donald Page and John H. Thompson, are cited below.
7. *The Christian Guardian*, 19 August 1914, p. 5.
8. *Ibid.*, 26 August 1914, p. 5 and 16 September 1914.
9. J. M. Bliss, "The Methodist Church and World War I," *Canadian Historical Review*, September 1968, Reprinted in *Conscription 1917*, edited by Carl Berger (Toronto, 1969), p. 42; Albert Marrin, *The Last Crusade: The Church of England in the First World War* (Durham, North Carolina, 1974), pp. 124-25
10. *The Presbyterian Record*, June 1918.
11. Bliss, "The Methodist Church and World War I," p. 57.
12. John H. Thompson, " 'The Beginning of Our Regeneration': The Great War and Western Canadian Reform Movements," *Historical Papers*, Canadian Historical Association, 1972, pp. 238-39.
13. *The Christian Guardian*, 25 November 1914, p. 8.
14. *Ibid.*, 1 November 1916, p. 5.
15. *Ibid.*, 3 April 1918, p. 1.
16. *Ibid.*, 1 May 1918, p. 5.
17. The Presbyterian press, for instance, published very closely worded statements. See *The Presbyterian Record*, October 1914, p. 433; June 1918, p. 161; *The Presbyterian*, 12 November 1914, p. 436. Strong support for the war was also voiced by the Anglicans and Baptists. See Colm Brannigan, "The Anglican Church in Canada and the Great War," graduate seminar paper for Professor A. R. Allen, Department of History, McMaster University, 1978, and Steven R. Ramlochan, "The Baptists of Ontario and World War

I, 1914–1918,'' undergraduate paper for Professor C. M. Johnston, Department of History, McMaster University, 1973.

18. Atkinson finally claimed the war was a crusade to save Christianity itself. J. E. Atkinson, "The Aftermath of the War," *Canadian Club of Toronto, 1915–1916* (Toronto, 1916), pp. 60–61.

19. C. Roland Marchand, *The American Peace Movement and Social Reform 1898–1918* (Princeton, 1972), p. 19.

20. *The Globe* (Toronto), 21 August 1914, p. 4.

21. Hopkins, *Canadian Annual Review*, 1914, p. 136.

22. *Ibid.*, 1915, p. 351.

23. Henry James Morgan, ed., *The Canadian Men and Women of the Time* (Toronto, 1912), p. 833.

24. Victoria University Archives (VUA), Lewis E. Horning Papers, Lewis E. Horning, "The New Citizenship," unpublished manuscript.

25. *Minutes of the Genesee Yearly Meeting of the Society of Friends in Canada*, 1915 (Toronto, 1915), p. 25.

26. Horning, "The New Citizenship."

27. United Church Achives (UCA), The Methodist Church of Canada, General Conference Office, General Correspondence, 1914, Box 3 file 59, Lewis E. Horning to T. A. Moore, 26 September 1914.

28. *Ibid.*

29. *Ibid.*

30. *Ibid.*

31. Sometimes they sponsored well-known pacifist speakers such as the British pacifist, Chrystal MacMillan. Hopkins, *Canadian Annual Review*, 1915, p. 350.

32. VUA, Horning Papers, Vault, 12E. W566TP.

33. Saskatchewan Archives Board, Saskatoon (SAB), S. V. Haight, n.d.

34. Colonel Hughes even attempted to bribe his niece in order to remove the disgrace. Donald Page, "Canadians and the League of Nations before the Manchurian Crisis," Ph.D. Thesis, University of Toronto, 1972, p. 30.

35. *Ibid.*

36. *Ibid.*, p. 31.

37. Alice Chown, *The Stairway* (Boston, 1921), pp. 81, 103, 126. Chown's philosophy was heavily influenced by theosophy. See Michèle Lacombe, "Theosophy and the Canadian Idealist Tradition: A Preliminary Exploration," *Journal of Canadian Studies*, Vol. 17 (Summer 1982), pp. 100–18.

38. Chown, *The Stairway*, p. 294.

39. *Ibid.*, p. 260, 263.

40. *Ibid.*, p. 296.

41. UCA, S. D. Chown Papers, Box 10, file 214, Alice Chown to S. D. Chown, 17 December 1918.

42. Chown, *The Stairway*, p. 261.

43. Roy St. George Stubbs, *Prairie Portraits* (Toronto, 1965), p. 99.

44. *Manitoba Free Press*, 19 January 1917, p. 1.

45. *Ibid.*, p. 2; David J. Bercuson, *Confrontation at Winnipeg* (Montreal, 1974), p. 42.

46. A. Ross McCormack, *Reformers, Rebels, and Revolutionaries: The Western Canadian Radical Movement 1899–1919* (Toronto, 1977), p. 129.

47. *Ibid.*, p. 158; John H. Thompson, *The Harvest of War: The Prairie West 1914–1918* (Toronto, 1978), p. 117.

48. *The Voice*, 10 November 1916, p. 1; 19 January 1917, p. 13; 13 July 1917, p. 5; *Western Labor News*, 9 August 1918, p. 5. One pacifist later praised *The Voice* for its priceless wartime service of providing an open forum for the "bludgeoned minority," *Ibid.*

49. *Western Labor News*, 9 August 1918, p. 5; Ramsay Cook, "Francis Marion Beynon and the Crisis of Christian Reformism;" *The West and the Nation: Essays in Honour of W. L. Morton*, edited by Carl Berger and Ramsay Cook (Toronto, 1976), pp. 190–98.

50. Public Archives of Canada (PAC), J. S. Woodsworth Papers, Manuscript Group 27, Correspondence v. 2, A. V. Thomas to J. S. Woodsworth, 18 June 1981.

51. *Ibid.*

52. *Ibid.*, Thomas to Woodsworth, 24 April 1918.

53. *Ibid.*, Thomas to Woodsworth, 16 January 1919.

54. Cook, "Francis Marion Beynon," pp. 197–99.

55. *Grain Growers' Guide*, 24 November 1915, p. 10.

56. *Ibid.*, 3 March 1915, p. 10.

57. *Ibid.*, 7 March 1917, p. 10.

58. *Ibid.*, 2 July 1917, p. 9.

59. *Ibid.*, 13 June 1917, p. 10

60. *Ibid.*, 27 June 1917, p. 10; Cook, "Francis Marion Beynon," p. 200.

61. For Beynon's reaction to the treatment of enemy aliens see: *Grain Growers' Guide*, 6 June 1917, p. 9.

62. *Western Labor News*, 29 November 1918, p. 2.

63. Cook, "Francis Marion Beynon," p. 203.
64. I am in agreement with Kenneth McNaught, *A Prophet in Politics: A Biography of J. S. Woodsworth* (Toronto, 1959), p. 67.
65. J. S. Woodsworth, "My Convictions About War," *Vox*, December 1939, p. 5.
66. McNaught, *A Prophet in Politics*, p. 75.
67. *Manitoba Free Press*, 28 December 1916, p. 5.
68. I support Allen's assertion that Woodsworth's dismissal was due to his pacifism rather than to his social and economic radicalism. His pacifism represented an "unknown potential," especially since there was talk in labour circles of passive resistance to the registration scheme. See Richad Allen, *The Social Passion: Religion and Social Reform in Canada 1914–28* (Toronto, 1973), pp. 47–48.
69. I am indebted to Richard Allen for this information.
70. J. S. Woodsworth, *Following the Gleam* (Ottawa, 1926), p. 9.
71. *Ibid.*
72. Allen, *The Social Passion*, p. 51.
73. PAC, Woodworth Papers, Correspondence, v. 2, A. V. Thomas to J. S. Woodsworth, 24 April 1918; 18 June 1918.
74. Allen, *The Social Passion*, p. 53; McCormack, *Reformers, Rebels and Revolutionaries*, p. 153.
75. *Western Labor News*, 9 August 1918, p. 5.
76. McCormack, *Reformers, Rebels and Revolutionaries*, p. 153.
77. J. S. Woodsworth, *The First Story of the Labor Church* (Winnipeg, 1920), pp. 7–8.
78. *Ibid.*, pp. 12–13.
79. *The Voice*, 15 January 1918, p. 1. M. James Penton's *Jehovah's Witnesses in Canada* (Toronto, 1976) also provides a detailed account of the incident.
80. *Winnipeg Evening Tribune*, 24 January 1918, p. 1; PAC, Department of National Defense, Record Group 24, Vol. 2028, IIQ 1064 30-67, T. A. Crerar to Major-General S. C. Mewburn, 28 January 1918.
81. PAC, Sir Robert Borden Papers, RLB 2309, William Ivens to T. A. Crerar, 25 February 1918; *The Voice*, 1 March 1918, p. 1.
82. *Minutes of the Genesee Yearly Meeting of Friends*, 1915, pp. 24, 33.
83. *Ibid.*, p. 41.
84. Charles Chatfield, *For Peace and Justice: Pacifism in America 1914–1941* (Knoxville, 1971), p. 54.
85. *Minutes of the Genesee Yearly Meeting of Friends*, 1915, p. 33.
86. *Western Labor News*, 5 September 1919, p. 6.
87. *Minutes of the Genesee Yearly Meeting of Friends*, 1919, p. 21.

377

Topic Ten

Postwar Unrest

378 Labour, which had fought long and hard battles with business leaders before the war, quickly became unhappy with postwar conditions. During the war years they believed that they had made greater sacrifices than their opponents, and they now awaited their just reward. With their expectations unfulfilled, workers turned to radical action.

Western workers were particularly militant and disatisfied. High unemployment and inflation, and a tradition of radicalism made the West the most likely Canadian region for unrest. In 1919 Winnipeg, the largest and most economically advanced of the western cities, became the focal point of western labour strife. David Bercuson explains the historical context, the events, and the significance of 1919 in "The Winnipeg General Strike."

Western farmers joined labour in revolt. The farmers' protest had a history dating back to the time of the region's inclusion in the Canadian Confederation. The western farmers hated the high-tariff National Policy of 1879, which, they argued, favoured Eastern manufacturers and industrialists. In an effort to fight back, they formed co-operatives, which became effective economic organizations and also powerful political bodies. Western dissatisfaction emerged as a full-scale political protest movement, and a powerful third party in the early 1920s. From the beginning, however, this movement/party faced innumerable problems including serious internal dissension between two leading fractions. Walter Young discusses these tensions facing the Progressives and the lessons to be learned from their experiences in the "The Progressives."

The Maritimes also had a history of protest since Confederation. The postwar years proved a particularly disquieting period as Maritimers re-examined their position in Confederation, and compared their region's slow rate of growth to that of Central Canada and the West. Their complaints, like those of the western farmers, centered on the system of frieght rates. In "The Origins of the Maritime Rights Movement," E. R. Forbes analyses the motives of the different groups that participated in this effective protest group.

Labour radicalism in the West can be examined further in D. J. Bercuson's *Confrontation at Winnipeg: Labour, Industrial Relations and the General Strike* (Montreal: McGill-Queen's University Press, 1974), and his *Fools and Wise Men: The Rise and Fall of the One Big Union* (Toronto; McGraw-Hill Ryerson, 1978), as well as A. R. McCormack's *Reformers, Rebels, and Revolutionaries: The Western Canadian Radical Movement: 1899–1919* (Toronto: University of Toronto Press, 1977).

W. L. Morton's *The Progressive Party in Canada* (Toronto: University of Toronto Press, 1950), remains the definitive study of the farmer's protest movement. For background leading up to the rise of the Progressive party see Morton's "The Western Progressive Movement, 1919–1921," Canadian Historical Association *Report*, 1946: pp. 41–55. The link between the Progressive Movement and the social gospel movement is shown in R. Allen's "The Social Gospel as the Religion of the Agrarian Revolt," in *The West and the Nation: Essays in Honour of W.L. Morton*, edited by C. Berger and R. Cook (Toronto: McClelland and Stewart, 1976), pp. 174–186.   *379*

A more comprehensive treatment of the Maritimes' Rights Movement can be found in E. R. Forbes's *The Maritime Rights Movement 1919–27* (Montreal: McGill–Queen's University Press, 1979). Students will find the essays on the Maritimes in *Canada and the Burden of Unity*, edited by D. Bercuson (Toronto: Macmillan, 1977) of value in placing the Maritimes Rights movement in a wider perspective.

The Winnipeg General Strike*

DAVID BERCUSON

General strikes are cataclysmic events; they are, by their nature, unlikely to be created in a day. The first moments of a general strike take place against a background of many years of bitter relationships, class polarization, frustrated ambitions and real or imagined oppression. The Winnipeg General Strike of May and June 1919 fits snugly into this well-established pattern because its taproots may be found growing into the very bedrock of Winnipeg's development as a booming modern industrial centre. The attitudes and conditions that created the general strike were an integral part of the Winnipeg scene almost from its beginnings, although they were compounded by the effects of the Great War. Winnipeg was ripe for a general strike in the spring of 1919 because the division of the city into two separate and increasingly hostile camps had started so long before and had reached a point of no return.

*From *On Strike: Six Key Labour Struggles in Canada, 1919–1949*, ed. by I. Abella. Copyright 1974 by James Lorimer and Company. Reprinted by permission.

Winnipeg was destined to be a boom town, the new Chicago of North America. The analogy was to be used many times to describe the future of the city, particularly after civic leaders had succeeded in capturing the Canadian Pacific Railway route from the town of Selkirk in the early 1880s. Over the course of the next forty years, Winnipeg endured several periods of boom and bust, liberally watered by speculation dollars. This atmosphere of expected prosperity but realized chaos acted on the serious-minded men who had come to Manitoba to make their fortunes, and prompted them to assume leadership of the community, not only in business matters but in politics as well. They believed in the great future of their city but became convinced that it could only be realized if certain conditions prevailed: a rational and efficient city administration, a beneficent climate in which business could grow and prosper and the absence of any factor which could, if allowed to develop unchecked, disrupt the peace and prosperity of the business community. Unions fell within this last category.

Business in Winnipeg was anti-union from the beginning, but this was no different from the situation in other cities. What did make Winnipeg different was both the extent to which the business community ran the city — assuring the political powerlessness of the working class — and certain economic factors that affected Winnipeg to a greater extent than other cities. Winnipeg had the potential to become a great manufacturing and marketing centre, especially after all three Canadian transcontinental railroads established their repair shops, marshalling yards and roundhouses in and around the city, but it was distant from its sources of supply and its industrial markets. As long as the business community was content to allow Winnipeg to remain a trans-shipment point and distribution centre for the thousands of new prairie farmers who began to flood the plains after 1895, Winnipeg was not at any disadvantage. When they raised their sights to larger markets, however, they felt the pressures of higher transportation costs. When they began to think in terms of manufacturing for a national and even international market, they had to consider the price of bringing the raw materials in and shipping the finished goods out. To balance these higher costs they would try to keep other costs as low as possible, and this invariably affected wages.

There was yet another factor behind the long history of intransigent anti-unionism that developed early in Winnipeg's history: the myth of the self-made man.[1] Many of Winnipeg's political and industrial leaders were men of poor or humble origins who had made their way west to find their fortunes. They believed that they were destined to lead, having demonstrated their superior abilities by their rise through the social strata. Social Darwinism was a strong religion, diligently and consistently worshipped by many of the *nouveaux riches*, who were not yet confident or secure in their new-found wealth and station. These individualists scorned those whom they considered weaker than themselves — the men who were forced to resort to combination and organization to protect their jobs and living standards. Here workers and their unions stood indicted.

Trade unions did not play a passive role in this situation. Unions began to develop early in Winnipeg and grew quickly in the years prior to World War I. These organizations were led by strong-willed, tough-minded men, many of whom were immigrants from the industrial heartland of the British Isles and who had received their training in hard-knock schools such as Birmingham, Leeds, the Clydeside or the black mines of Wales.[2] They were fervent believers in the necessity of trade-union organization and many were followers of one socialist school or another, self-educated in the intricacies of Marxian analysis and rhetoric. These men were never timid in their assertion of labour's rights and challenged the power and prerogatives of management at every opportunity. Each victory confirmed them in their belief that theirs was the correct path; each defeat convinced them that society itself would have to be changed before the worker would ever receive his due.

Patterns of political and social separation developed early and were aggravated by physical separation. As new immigrants began to pour into Winnipeg they tended to settle in certain districts, usually together, seeking the security that new arrivals in a strange land crave. For the most part they gravitated to the area immediately north of the CPR mainline — the "north end."[3] This became Winnipeg's version of "the wrong side of the tracks," which it was in fact, clearly marked off from the new areas being opened up by Winnipeg's wealthier citizens. The rich and the aspiring to be rich settled along the river banks to the south, in locales such as River Heights and Wellington Crescent,[4] where they built magnificent mansions with long, broad driveways, well-manicured lawns and large stables or garages. The "south end" became as strongly symbolic in its own right of a bastion of privilege as the "north end" was of the home of the worker and the immigrant.

The results were almost predictable — Winnipeg was wracked by bitter strikes from the turn of the century, many involving the use of strikebreakers, court injunctions and even the armed militia on one occasion.[5] In most instances the issues were the same, the demand of workers that their unions be recognized and collective agreements entered into, and the absolute refusal of employers to allow unions in their plants or stores. The class polarization inherent in the city was heightened by these strikes because in most cases the very existence of the unions was at stake and courts and governments invariably sided with the employers. During the last boom period before World War I, some of the bitterness was dissipated as men with skills were able to wrench higher wages and better working conditions from their employers, but it never disappeared entirely because the basic attitudes creating it remained unchanged. By 1919, in addition to those attitudes, there was a history of bitterness, hatred and mistrust, and a martyrology to support it.

In August 1914 Canada entered the first large-scale war of her history ill-prepared for the hardships and trials that would test the national mettle in the next four years and three months. The effort involved in raising and equipping an army of over half a million men would have been monumental enough, but it was compounded by Canada's role as a breadbasket and arsenal for the allies. Within a short time the national economy began to suffer from manpower shortages, rapid cost-of-living increases, imbalances of supply and production and the machinations of unscrupulous men who tried to reap large and undeserved profits from munitions and war-supply contracts. Given these conditions, it is not surprising that labour-management relations began to break down on a national scale after 1917 and that deterioration greatly affected areas such as Winnipeg, where conditions were already ripe for industrial strife.

Inflation was, without doubt, the single most important factor causing industrial strife in the war and immediate postwar period. Though few reliable statistics are available to give an exact measurement of the increasing cost of living during the war, it is safe to estimate, on the basis of what data was collected by the federal Department of Labour and published monthly in *Labour Gazette*, that it increased from fifty to seventy-five per cent between 1914 and 1918–19.[6] Increased demands for all manner of manufactured and semi-manufactured commodities, as well as foodstuffs and raw materials, drove prices skyward. This was coupled with shortages of skilled manpower and, consequently, higher wages in certain industries, which furthered the inflationary trend. The net resulst was that tens of thousands of Canadians who were not in any position to earn substantial wage increases saw their already low standards of living further decline. The only worker groups able to stay ahead of the rising cost of living, and then only barely, were those in great demand for war industries and munitions production — machinists, tool and die makers, shipyard workers. The majority of workers in Winnipeg, however, did not fit into this category.

One group of workers in the city that was able to keep ahead of the rising cost of living was, at the same time, the most radical — the railway machinists. The machinists were in great demand throughout the war both in the maintenance and repair of railway equipment and in the manufacture of shells. They were irked, however, by a constant failure to organize their colleagues in the other machine shops and considered that the long hours of work and low wage scales in those shops posed a dangerous example for other metal workers in the city. They were frustrated also by the knowledge that their unions were strong enough to face Canada's powerful transcontinental railways across the bargaining table, but were still thwarted locally by the owners of three small contract shops which together employed fewer than five hundred men.[7]

In early 1917 the government of Prime Minister Robert Borden decided that conscription should be instituted to meet Canada's moral commitments to total support of the allied war effort. Labour leaders in western Canada were almost unanimous in their intense and unwavering opposition to this measure and led the forces inside the Trades and Labour Congress of Canada advocating a national general strike against compulsory military service.[8] In the end, they could not garner adequate support and the idea of a

382

strike was shelved, but the bitter anti-government feelings created by the campaign prompted many union men to decide that the government, rather than employers, was their greatest enemy. This, in turn, strengthened the influence of those labour leaders who were affiliated to one or another of the many socialist parties flourishing in the West at that time and resulted in a general shift to the left throughout the Prairies. The two main centres of this radical shift were Vancouver and Winnipeg.

War created labour shortages in hundreds of industries. Tens of thousands of skilled Canadians volunteered their services to the armed forces at the same time as the new war industries were exerting greater demands for manpower. Conditions for trade-union growth were better than they had been in many years and labour leaders were not slow to take advantage of them. In 1917 and 1918, vast organizing drives were launched throughout the country in almost every conceivable industry, and many new workers were brought into the fold. Even areas hitherto considered sacrosanct were entered: policemen, firemen, civic employees and provincial government employees, among others, became union members.[9] This growth process was bound to create industrial tensions as a byproduct.

In the days before the closed or union shop, automatic checkoff, labour-relations boards and certification votes, union organizing could be a hazardous business. In fact, union membership itself was sometimes hardly any safer. Unions were forced to battle tremendous odds, often including the forces of government and the judiciary, to sign members and thus had to demonstrate to prospective adherents the great advantages of affiliation. This could only be done by winning significant improvements in wage rates and working conditions, by demonstrating that the union was respected by employers and governments and by assuring prospective members that the union could protect them against arbitrary and unjust actions of management. This meant, in turn, that as the organizing campaign wore on, union leaders demanded more and were unwilling to settle for less — a situation creating militancy. When these unions confronted employers who were determined that workers and unions should not benefit from the labour situation created by the war, an irresistible force had met its immovable object.

Winnipeg was the scene of several such meetings in 1917. Three times in the year employers defeated strikes by applying for and receiving *ex parte* injunctions against picketing. In each case packinghouse workers, store clerks and contract-shop employees were unable to continue their respective strikes and suffered defeat.[10] The effect upon industrial relations in the city was traumatic; workers were forced to realize that very little had changed since the original use of injunctions in the city in 1906. All their organizing could come to naught if employers still had the ability to defeat recognition strikes by getting anti-picketing court orders and then bringing in scab labour. Labour leaders were forced to conclude that unions would have to band together and pool their resources if they hoped to force intransigent employers to the bargaining table. The formation of the Metal Trades Council in the spring of the following year was at least one result of the 1917 experiences.

383

In April 1918, three unions of civic employees struck for a new and higher wage schedule after having been offered a war bonus by city authorities. Almost immediately the straight dollars-and-cents issue was obscured by the question, posed by the *Free Press* and echoed by business leaders, of whether civic employees should have any right to strike. The atmosphere became further charged when sister unions rushed to the defence of the strikers and began to discuss the possibility of a sympathetic walkout of all civic workers. Even city firemen were in a fighting mood and issued an ultimatum threatening to strike unless their own pay demands were quickly met.

The city council reacted by appointing a committee of six, including the mayor and two Labour aldermen, to negotiate with the striking unions. The two sides settled down to serious bargaining and within a few days hammered out the rudiments of a settlement. On Monday, May 13, they presented the terms of the agreement to a full meeting of city council but were stunned when the council, led by Alderman F. O. Fowler, amended their proposal and added a proviso that all civic employees undertake to pledge that they would not strike at all in future but would have their grievances settled by arbitration. In effect this "Fowler Amendment," named after its sponsor, put the city council on record as opposing any right to strike for civic employees.

The new measure did not come out of the clear blue sky. It was clearly an accurate reflection of a new mood of toughness in business and city government circles and was strongly supported by the *Free Press* and the Winnipeg Board of Trade. It was a naked challenge to the Winnipeg Trades and Labour Council and was accepted as such. At this point, after the successful organizing drives and the frustrating strikes of 1917, labour was not about to turn from a fight on so fundamental an issue. The effects of the amendment were immediate and electrifying.

On Tuesday morning, May 14, city firemen walked off their jobs. Within the next ten days ten other unions joined the strike as the city government, supported by volunteer help supplied by the Board of Trade, attempted to continue the operation of civic services. By Friday, May 24, thirteen trades, totalling about seven thousand workers in government and industry, had met Fowler's challenge. Fire, water, light and power, public transportation, telephone service and railway maintenance were directly and drastically affected and there was every sign that the movement would continue to grow.

At this point the city government had become virtually paralyzed by indecision and passed responsibility for negotiations to a new, private body, formed for the purpose of helping to maintain essential services and bring about a settlement with the unions — the Citizens' Committee of One Hundred. On May 19 the first meeting between this group and the strikers took place and negotiations continued for the next few days. The two parties eventually succeeded in working out an agreement on almost all major points and were helped to the final solution by the intervention of Senator Gideon and Robertson, newly appointed to the upper House and, at the time, special assistant to the federal minister of Labour, who travelled to Winnipeg at the behest of Prime Minister Robert Borden. The agreement was essentially the same one that had been presented to the city council on May 13 but this time it was accepted by that council, largely because of Robertson's prodding. On Friday evening, May 24, the settlement was agreed to and the strike was over. The workers' victory was almost complete.[11]

The 1918 general strike strengthened the hand of the radicals in the city and pushed the labour movement further left. Labour leaders concluded that the combined power of the unions acting together was irresistible and was responsible for the crushing defeat inflicted upon the city government. Almost every commentator underlined the plain fact that the original striking unions would surely have been defeated if they had not been supported by the rest of the city's labour movement.[12] When this was contrasted, publicly and privately, with the events of the previous year, the lesson appeared to be obvious — individual unions could not face tough employers supported by governments and/or the courts, but a combination of unions could and had defeated an enemy just as powerful. From this point on labour men began to think of the general strike as a necessary adjunct to individual strikes, to be used when those individual strikes failed or showed signs of failure.

385

One concrete result of the metal workers' defeat in 1917 had been the creation of the Metal Trades Council. The reasoning was simple — since individual unions had no chance of defeating the contract-shop employers or forcing them to the bargaining table, perhaps a combination of unions could. A Metal Trades Council would bargain for all those workers in the plant and would, if necessary, have the authority to call all those workers out on strike. This was not industrial unionism, although many of the supporters of the Metal Trades Council clearly believed in industrial unionism as opposed to craft organization; it was, rather, modelled on the type of bargaining conducted by railway-shop craft workers in the United States and metal workers in other Canadian cities, such as Vancouver and Victoria shipyard workers.

In July of 1918 the Metal Trades Council struck the contract shops after failing to receive recognition following a long and apparently fruitless mediation procedure involving the federal government and a royal commission. The Winnipeg Trades and Labour Council threatened a general strike to support the contract-shop employees but did not act. By the end of September the strike had petered out and the workers had suffered yet another defeat. R. B. Russell bluntly attributed the failure to the fact that the rest of the city's workers did not back the Metal Trades Council adequately in its fight.[13]

The lesson of 1918 was now clearer than ever. Not only was it increasingly difficult for individual unions to win fights against intransigent employers; it was growing harder for combinations of unions in a single industry — such as the Metal Trades Council — to achieve victory. The civic workers, on the other hand, had achieved one of the most clear-cut victories in many years and only because they were promptly and adequately supported by workers in *every* industry. Where the workers had not been radical enough they had lost; where they had been, they had won. This finalized the trend towards the use of general strikes in industrial disputes and made the general strike in the spring of 1919 necessary in the eyes of many labour leaders in the city, radical or otherwise. The experiences of 1918 convinced them that a general strike was just like any other kind of strike, only larger, and that it enabled labour to bring its full power to bear in circumstances where that power was necessary. The Trades and Labour Council capped this process in December 1918 when it passed a motion giving itself the power to call out every union member in the city if a motion for a general strike was approved by a simple majority of all Winnipeg's union members.[14]

386

By the end of the war, labour leaders in the city were ready to reach for new objectives and were prepared to utilize new tactics in the effort. At the same time, the arrival of peace released the pent-up hope of many thousands of Canadians that the great sacrifices of the war would not have been in vain and that a new, more just, more equitable society would be fashioned out of the ruins of war. Men and women all over the country had worked ceaselessly to assure the victory while sixty thousand men, approximately one out of every ten Canadians in uniform, would never return. When it became increasingly apparent that there would be precious little forward movement and that the government's reconstruction efforts would, for the most part, be confined to dismantling the regulatory and managerial agencies established during the war, those who sought change grew more vociferous in their opposition to the status quo. By the end of 1918 the winds of change were already sweeping the rest of the world. Revolutions in Russia and Germany appeared to confirm that those who called for rapid social change were not isolated but, on the contrary, were the heralds of a great, globe-spanning move towards true reconstruction.

Western Canadian workers had always felt that their situation was somewhat different from that of their fellow labourers in central Canada and in the populous regions of the United States. They were numerically weaker, were, for the most part, engaged in extractive, resource industries, and were physically isolated from each other in small population centres scattered over the Prairies, in the British Columbia interior and on the Pacific Coast. These conditions, combined with the ideological leadership provided by former American progressives and British socialists who moved to Canada during the periods of great immigration, prompted western workers to call for trade-union participation in politics, organization of the tens of thousands of unorganized workers in extractive and mass industries all over the country and establishment of industrial unions which would group workers together on an industrial rather than a craft basis.[15] All these ambitions were in direct conflict with the ideological foundations of North American trade unionism, which was guided in thought and action by the principles of the founder of the American Federation of Labor, Samuel Gompers.

Gompers and his supporters believed that trade unions should not enter directly into politics, but should throw their support to the candidates or parties that favoured pro-labour principles. In addition, Gompers firmly believed in the necessity of keeping the labour movement relatively small and confined to the highly skilled, who had the best chance of wringing concessions from employers. Thus the principles of the AFL and its Canadian affiliate, the Trades and Labour Congress of Canada, contrasted sharply with the ideas held by western Canadian labour leaders, ideas which they believed had to be acted upon if the labour movement in the West was to survive.

These traditional points of contention had caused sharp disagreements in the TLC before the war — the numerically inferior West was almost always defeated. But three major inter-union squabbles during the war widened the gap between East and West and laid the groundwork for a western assault on the eastern bastions at the 1918 TLC convention. In the fight against conscription, westerners had been much more vociferous in their opposition and many believed they were being sold out by the congress's predominantly eastern leadership. This crisis in 1917 opened the first breach. The negotiations between Canada's railway-shop craft workers and the major Canadian railroads in 1918 made it almost permanent.

By the summer of 1918 negotiation procedures for railway-shop craft workers in Canada had been radically altered. The unions had joined in a loose bargaining federation known as Division 4 while management was combined into the Canadian Railway War Board. These two bodies met for the first time in late April 1918 to work out one contract to cover over fifty thousand railway workers. The unions demanded substantial wage increases, pointing to the greatly increased cost of living as justification, and threatened to pull every railway maintenance worker in Canada off the job if their demands were not met. Since this would eventually paralyze all national transportation, the government took a hand in the bargaining and prompted the railway managers to offer wage parity with American shop craft workers.

The move created a split in union ranks. Eastern labour leaders, heavily supported by the leadership of the AFL and the head offices of the shop craft unions in the United States, pressed for acceptance. They had no intention of forcing or risking a nation-wide rail strike against the opposition of the employers and the government, which was threatening to draft all railway maintenance workers and work them at military pay rates should they walk out. Western union leaders were disgusted at this attitude and, when they realized they could not prevail, called their negotiators home.[16] There was both anger and consternation directed not only at the government, but against the leadership of the international unions and their central Canadian supporters.

The third East-West split took place during Canada's first national postal strike in August. Once again eastern union leaders were prepared to order their men to accept compromise arrangements while westerners dissented. This time, however, the westerners continued their strike after the eastern

387

postal employees returned to work; they were not only able to wrench more concessions from the government, but also secured pay for the time they had been on strike.[17] Another Canadian union had split geographically because the westerners were more daring and perhaps more radical than the easterners.

Thus the stage was set for the September 1918 convention of the TLC in Quebec City. Westerners were sorely outnumbered but went ahead to present several resolutions demanding a reorganization of the TLC as an industrial congress, and the removal of civil-liberties restrictions imposed during the war — the release of political prisoners and the ending of government-imposed censorship. Each time they were defeated both on the floor of the convention and in committee rooms; when they appealed committee rulings they were defeated again. Recorded votes were called and they were defeated yet again; the eastern establishment controlled the steamroller and the westerners were flattened. To add insult to injury, the president of the TLC, James Watters, a westerner, was defeated in his bid for re-election by Tom Moore, a conservative and a friend and admirer of Samuel Gompers, in one of the very few contested presidential elections yet held by the congress. The West's defeat was total.[18]

The TLC convention was absolute proof that wars and industrial strife might come and go but things would never change for westerners within the congress. If their demands were to be satisfied, extraordinary measures would have to be taken. With this in mind several western delegates met in caucus at Quebec City and decided to hold a meeting of all western representatives prior to the next TLC convention to plan strategy and decide on a unified program. This was the objective of the man responsible for calling the meeting, Dave Rees, a United Mine Workers official from British Columbia and a TLC vice-president, but it was not shared by all.

The Socialist Party of Canada was a small, closely knit organization that proclaimed itself to be the only ideologically pure guardian of Marxist theory in Canada. Its members were dedicated, hard-working, and had met rather exacting standards before they were admitted to membership. The party was the most uncompromising of a plethora of socialist parties that had grown up in the West since before the turn of the century and it frequently ran candidates against other left-wing and labour politicial groups. Ordinarily it might not have achieved any significant influence in labour affairs but for the radical temper of the postwar period and the adherence of some of the best-known trade unionists in western Canada, including R. B. Russell, R. J. Johns, Victor Midgley and W. A. Pritchard.

SPC members were determined to seize the opportunity that now presented itself to build a new labour centre in Canada. Ostensibly they were interested in fulfilling the desires of western workers for industrial unionism and more intensified political action. These men had no intention of allowing the conference of western labour representatives to move in the direction Rees wished it to go, but prepared, instead, to begin a secessionist movement from the TLC and the AFL. They pressed for and were successful in securing a meeting not directly prior to the 1919 TLC convention, but in the very early spring in Calgary.

The Western Labour Conference opened in the foothills city on March 16, 1919. Rees reiterated his desire to forge a united policy for presentation to the next TLC convention, but at this point there was little possibility of the meeting following his suggestions. The British Columbia Federation of Labour, meeting the previous three days in the same city, had just opted for a program of unmitigated radicalism. Over some objections from moderate delegates, the federation had supported the idea of a new secessionist movement, attacked the federal government for allowing censorship and imprisonment of political dissenters to continue and sent greetings to the Bolshevik government in Moscow.

From the very beginning of the western conference, then, the moderates were outmanoeuvered. The meeting declared itself in favour of a nation-wide vote of all TLC-affiliated unionists on the question of secession and adherence to a new organization to be laid out along "industrial" lines. The policy committee, headed by Winnipeger R. J. Johns, suggested that the new body be called the One Big Union and that a five-man committee be elected to popularize the OBU, raise funds and organize the referendum. These men were subsequently chosen, along with provincial executives to act in conjunction with the new Central Committee.

The referendum decided upon was not to be a simple poll of all union members in Canada, since the ballots were to be divided between those from east of Port Arthur and those from the West. In addition, the question was to be decided by a majority vote of those organizations considered to be vital trades — transportation, metal trades, mining, etc. Locals of other trades were also to be polled with those members not voting to be counted in the affirmative. A second vote was to be taken in conjunction with the referendum to determine if Canadian workers favoured a nation-wide general strike on June 1 to institute the thirty-hour week.[19]

The Western Labour Conference did not actually launch the One Big Union; it was a declaration of intent to do so. But it reflected the mood of militancy that had been growing in the West for some time. Resolutions sending greetings to the new Soviet government in Russia, demanding Allied withdrawal from the Soviet Union and an end to government restrictions on civil liberties were only the outward manifestations of the new radicalism. The significant part of the three-day meeting was the delegates' decision to take secessionist action.

The One Big Union did not officially come into existence until the first week of June, when its founding convention was held in Calgary. By that time the Winnipeg strike was already over two weeks old and not a single member of the Winnipeg Trades and Labour Council was able to attend.[20] Nevertheless, the announced intention to found a radical Marxist labour union, industrial or syndicalist in nature and sympathetic to the aims and aspirations of the Bolsheviks, provided the enemies of the strike with a focal point for their deepest fears. Governments and employers asserted that the OBU was behind the strike, that the strike was a test of OBU tactics and that its defeat would prove to be a knockout blow against the One Big Union. In fact there was no connection between the events in Winnipeg and the One Big Union except that the Calgary convention formed part of the backdrop and contributed to the atmosphere in which events immediately leading to the strike took place.

The general strike was touched off by disputes in the metal and building trades that surfaced in April and May. The inability of the unions in these two industries to win concessions from management — higher wages in the case of the building trades, union recognition in the metal trades — prompted them to turn to the Trades and Labour Council for help. A sufficient number of workers believed the issues to be important enough to the welfare of all organized labour to enable the supporters of radical action to push a general strike vote through the Trades Council.

The Winnipeg Building Trades Council, uniting all the city's construction unions in one organization, had taken on a new task in the spring of 1919 — henceforth it would negotiate working agreements to cover all of its constituent trades directly with the employers' organization, the Winnipeg Builders' Exchange. This arrangement was welcomed by all since it meant that both sides would be unable to take advantage of disunity in their opponents, while the employers were particularly pleased since they would only have to negotiate one agreement to cover the entire industry. The discussions were difficult, because the unions were determined to win large wage increases to make up for the small gains they had made during the war. The employers, however, would not agree to anything better than half the amounts sought by the unions. They knew this was not sufficient and conceded the fairness of the unions' demands, but claimed it was all they could pay to avoid bankruptcy. Half a loaf was better than none, they pointed out, and a strike would only mean that no wages at all would go into their workers' pockets.

The workers' claim to large increases was buttressed by statistics showing they had been left behind in the race to keep wages ahead of the rising cost of living. This had increased by approximately seventy-five per cent since 1913, although the average wage in the building trades had only risen by about thirteen per cent. The employers, however, were actually in a real bind because the depression of 1913 had killed Winnipeg's construction boom while the war served to keep it dead. War priorities kept building at an all-time low and the builders were hard pressed to keep out of debt. Though many expected construction to pick up in the summer of 1919, these hopes had not yet been realized and the employers were no better off than they had been in the previous five years. These conditions created an impasse in the negotiations and prompted the Building Trades Council to call a strike for Thursday morning, May 1, 1919.[21]

While the crisis in the building trades was mounting, another impasse was developing in the city's metal trades. The Metal Trades Council, an amalgam of various metal craft unions whose members worked in the city's independent contract shops, automobile repair establishments and so on, had been formed in the spring of 1918 to increase the power of the individual unions in their attempt to gain recognition from the owners and managers of the contract shops. These unions had been trying to win recognition since 1906 and had fought and lost three bitter strikes in 1906, 1917 and July 1918, which saw the use of *ex parte* injunctions, damage suits and professional strikebreaking agencies. In April 1919, the Metal Trades Council prepared to do battle once again and sent letters to the contract-shop owners asking for a higher wage schedule and the forty-four-hour work week. It did not ask for recognition, since all parties realized that the acceptance or negotiation of the Metal Trades Council's demands would have amounted to *de facto* recognition. The contract-shop owners had successfully resisted the unions in the past, and again studiously ignored the letters from the Metal Trades Council.

One of the contract shops, Vulcan Iron Works, was owned and managed by E. G. and L. R. Barrett, brothers who had been in the forefront of opposition to union recognition for over thirteen years. In the third week of April they sent letters to each of their employees setting out their position on the question of union recognition; they claimed that although they would meet individual workers or a committee of workers they would not, under any circumstances, negotiate with the Metal Trades Council. They were running "an absolutely open shop" and would never bargain with any group or organization which contained members or representatives from other shops or factories. This letter was the only reply of any sort from the largest three of the contract shops; only three of the smaller establishments in the city signified their willingness to negotiate with the union.[22]

On the last night of April, metal-trade union members crowded into a room in the Labour Temple on James Street to hear the news that the council's approach to the contract shops had been spurned and that the executive was left with little choice but to turn matters over to the membership for some sort of decision. The meeting then voted overwhelmingly to begin a strike the next morning at eleven but was persuaded by the executive to postpone action for another twenty-four hours. The extra day of grace brought no response from the "Big Three" and on Friday, May 2, at eleven A.M., Winnipeg's third metal-trades strike in three years closed the factories down. The issues were familiar ones to this troubled industry: union recognition, a shorter work week and wage parity with metal workers in the city's railway repair and maintenance shops.

At this point many union members in Winnipeg were ripe to respond to a call of support for the two striking trades since several other unions were involved in disputes of their own. In the last week of April a strike of telephone operators was narrowly averted when the provincial government met demands for a pay increase scant days before the deadline ran out. At the same time, the policemen's union was also involved in negotiations and had a great deal of trouble squeezing higher wages out of the civic administration. The men had voted overwhelmingly to strike but received a new contract with higher wages in the last days of April. The street-railway employees had begun negotiations with their employer on April 21; after reaching an impasse, they had voted 900 to 79 in favour of strike action. They held off, however, until receiving the report of a conciliation commission appointed under the federal Industrial Disputes Investigation Act.[23]

Thus, when the metal-trades delegates entered the Labour Temple for the regular weekly Trades Council meeting of May 6, there was already widespread labour unrest in the city. Two trades were on strike, one was threatening to strike and two had just concluded bitter and protracted negotiations which had almost broken down. Metal-trades delegates were instructed by their locals to bring the matter of their own strike before the council and to ask for the council's support. They intended to tell the meeting that a defeat would now jeopardize the gains of the entire union movement and would set labour back many years.

The meeting hall in the temple was crowded to capacity as the Metal and Building Trades Councils reported on the lack of progress in their struggles. Delegate James Lovett told the meeting that union recognition had never before been an issue in the construction strike but that the Builders' Exchange was threatening to withdraw its recognition of the Building Trades Council unless the employers' offer was accepted. Lovett added the charge that the bankers were behind the current impasse since they would not allow the builders to increase wages to the levels sought by the workers. Lovett asked the Trades Council to help the construction trades because the Building Trades Council's strike had not been sanctioned by international union headquarters and the members were not receiving strike pay.

As the meeting progressed someone handed a note to Secretary Ernie Robertson informing him that a worker of German origin, who had been visiting metal-trades shops at the instruction of his local, had been arrested. A number of delegates immediately volunteered to go to the police station and returned shortly with the worker in tow. His impromptu speech, charging government support for the employers, was a sensation. It was nothing, however, to the one delivered by R. B. Russell, secretary and acknowledged leader of the Metal Trades Council. The fiery Scot was the centre of attention as he reviewed the dispute thus far and charged the Barretts with responsibility for the stiffening employer opposition. Winnipeg, he warned, must stand firm for the sake of labour everywhere. This strike was made necessary by the defeat of 1918, he claimed, and there must be no more defeats.

Finally Harry Veitch, former Trades Council president, told the delegates of the great progress that had been made in previous weeks in organizing non-union workers in the city, and claimed that a general strike would tie Winnipeg up completely. This was the final argument. The meeting voted to take a poll of every union member in the city and to make a final decision by May 13.[24] In accordance with action taken by the council the previous December, a simple majority of all union members in the city would suffice to instruct council delegates to call the walkout.

The next few days were feverish with activity as Robinson arranged the printing and distribution of eighteen thousand ballots. In a few cases, such as that of the letter carriers, the vote was taken by an open show of hands but in most instances ballots were simply filled out at work and returned to Robinson. Ballot boxes were rarely used and votes were added up as they came into the Labour Temple. The Typographical Union was the only organization affiliated with the Trades Council that refused to participate in the voting and it was bitterly attacked by other unions who charged that the typos were afraid to lose their funeral expenses and old-age homes.

On Tuesday evening, May 13, excited delegates gathered in the Labour Temple to hear further reports on the course of the building and metal-trades strikes and to receive the results of the general strike ballot. Lovett told the meeting that the Builders Exchange had carried out their threat and were now refusing to deal with the Building Trades Council. Delegates were also told that Premier Norris had met with the contract-shop employers and the Metal Trades Council earlier in the day in an attempt to work out a compromise. The Big Three told him they might form an employers' association in the future and would, at this point, consider union recognition, but discussions with the unions at the moment were definitely out. Undaunted, Norris appointed Russell and Trades Council solicitor T. J. Murray to an *ad hoc* conciliation committee. The union men ridiculed independent arbitration at this point, however, since their precondition for any settlement, union recognition, was not even being considered by management.

393

Robinson then read the results of the vote to the meeting. Union members in Winnipeg had demonstrated solid support for a general strike — over eleven thousand endorsed the idea while a mere five hundred were opposed. The council thus set Thursday, May 15, as the day and eleven A.M. the hour in which the general strike was to begin. In addition, Lovett, A. Scoble of the street railwaymen's union, Veitch, Russell and W. Logan of the machinists' union were appointed to act as the nucleus of the Strike Committee, which eventually consisted of three delegates from each of the unions represented on the council, to act on behalf of the strikers in all future negotiations.[25]

Several abortive attempts were made to avoid the strike in the seventy-two hours preceding the Thursday morning deadline. Both the premier and Mayor Gray tried unsuccessfully to bring the two sides together. In almost all cases it was apparent that the building trades workers and their employers were not far removed from an agreement, but the relative lack of disharmony here was overshadowed by the total absence of any spirit of compromise in the metal trades. The unions continued to demand recognition for the Metal Trades Council while the Big Three refused to recognize unions in any form.

On Wednesday night, May 14, Gray, Norris and the provincial attorney-general made an eleventh hour attempt to stop the strike. Gray telephoned James Winning, president of the Trades Council, and asked him if there was a chance of abandoning the strike should the ironmasters be persuaded to adopt a more reasonable approach. Winning, a moderate, was probably somewhat dazed by the rapidly developing events of the previous two weeks, but he was astute enough to realize that the movement towards a general strike had generated a momentum of its own. "It might help," he answered, "but it is too late to discuss that now."[26] The stage was set for the walkout to begin.

At precisely eleven o'clock the next morning, Winnipeg ceased to work. The strike was complete and overwhelming in its proportions as over twenty-two thousand workers answered the call within the first twenty-four hours. Ninety-four of ninety-six unions participated to a man. Firemen left their stations, telephones were shut down, the city's electrical workers left turbines and transmission equipment unattended; telegraphers and others responsible for keeping a modern city in touch with the world refused to work. At the waterworks a skeleton staff remained behind at the request of the Trades Council to provide a meagre thirty pounds pressure, sufficient for single-storey dwellings. Commercial establishments of every sort, from moving-picture houses to restaurants, were closed.[27]

The general strike was called in a moment of intense and hopeful enthusiasm amidst the certainty that labour would win this fight even more decisively than the strike of 1918. The duration of the strike and its completeness is only explained, however, by the fact that this was the culmination of over twenty years of struggle for the city's unions. This was to be the final battle in which nothing would be held in reserve. Years of despair and frustration fuelled the intense hostility of workers towards the employers and governments who had foiled their ambitions for so long. In this battle labour would win or lose all — the unions knew it, and so did the employers. This was a challenge to traditional ideas and methods that labour's opponents could not ignore and to which they responded in tough and decisive fashion.

From the first days of the walkout the strikers faced the powerful opposition of employers, governments and the Citizens' Committee of One Thousand. The last-named organization was loosely patterned after the Committee of One Hundred which had taken so active a role in the 1918 strike. Though it purportedly voiced the interests of the city's "neutral" citizens, it was strongly anti-strike, supported the employers, labelled the union leaders Bolsheviks and provided thousands of volunteers to run the services and equipment the strikers had abandoned. Citizens' Committee representatives sat in on secret government policy conferences and advised the contract-shop owners throughout the six-week period of the strike.

The new Citizens' Committee was an amalgamation of the old committee and individual members of organizations such as the Board of Trade, the Manufacturers' Association and the Winnipeg bar. Of several names that appeared most frequently, for example, H. B. Lyall was an official of Manitoba Bridge and a member of the Board of Trade. A. L. Crossin was a broker with Oldfield, Kirby and Gardner, a firm dealing in insurance and loans, and also a member of the Board of Trade. A. K. Godfrey, chairman of the

Citizens' Committee of One Thousand, was the 1917–18 president of the Board of Trade and an executive of the Canadian Elevator Company. J. E. Botterell was a senior partner in the grain- and stock-brokerage firm of Baird & Botterell and also a member of the Board of Trade. Isaac Pitblado, KC, was a senior partner in the law firm of Pitblado, Hoskin & Co., which handled the personal business of the Hon. Arthur Meighen, federal minister of the Interior.[28]

Direct anti-strike involvement by the Citizens' Committee added an element not present in the 1918 sympathetic walkout, but it was not as serious as the intervention by the federal and provincial governments. When the political leaders of the country and the province opted to intervene on the side of the employers, the strikers were faced with the choice of having the massive political, legal and military power of those governments levelled against them, or ending the strike. Though this was not immediately apparent, it became more evident as the strike dragged on that the governments were playing an active and interested role in events.

395

Within a week of the outbreak of the new strike, Gideon Robertson and Arthur Meighen were on their way to Winnipeg. Even before they reached the city they met with several members of the Citizens' Committee and heard biased accounts of what was going on in Winnipeg. Robertson, as a former labour man and an ardent supporter of the conservative craft-union status quo in the AFL and TLC, launched an immediate and all-out verbal assault against the OBU as soon as he arrived in the city, charging that the strike was a One Big Union affair aimed at revolution and the destruction of the international craft-union movement. Robertson and Meighen also decided to take post-office matters into hand and get the men back to work as quickly as possible. Robertson fixed a deadline for all post-office employees to return to work, under threat of dismissal if they did not show up. When the deadline passed, the vast majority of postal workers in the city were fired and replaced with volunteers.[29]

The ultimatum soon became the accepted method of dealing with government employees at every level. Robertson used it with great effect to end a one-day strike of railway mail clerks while the provincial government utilized it in an effort to force its telephone employees back to their jobs. Even the city got into the act and issued ultimatums to its firemen, clerks and waterworks employees. In most cases, employees did not heed their deadlines and lost their jobs.

Meighen and Robertson represented the government in body and in spirit. Their anti-strike views accurately reflected the beliefs and attitudes of the cabinet to which they belonged. From lesser luminaries such as C. C. Ballantyne, minister of Fisheries, up to Prime Minister Borden himself, the government was uniform in its condemnation of the strike, its assertion that the strike was revolutionary in origin and intent, and its firm resolve that the workers could not be allowed to win. Though they tried hard to convince some of the more hysterical voices, such as the New York *Times*, that Winnipeg was not in the midst of a revolution and that legitimate government authority still prevailed, they spoke in the House of Commons and to the newspapers of threats to constituted authority and of the strikers' desire to smash the traditional order of labour-management relations. Meighen revealed the innermost fears of the government when he attacked the general strike in the House in early June. If unions were going to be allowed to combine into larger unions, he asked, where was the logical end to the process going to be? Eventually there would be only one union capable of calling one tremendous strike which would bring anarchy to the country. This, he warned, could not and would not be allowed to happen.[30]

While talk of revolution surged and ebbed around their heads, the strike leaders bent every effort to keep the streets peaceful and to convince their followers to keep out of trouble. In most cases they even refused to grant permission for peaceful picketing. Though incidents involving strikebreakers did occur on occasion, they were usually initiated spontaneously by hotheads. The strike leaders had asked the police to remain at work and asked their followers to do nothing because they feared that the least provocation would bring the armed forces into the streets of Winnipeg, assuring defeat of the general strike.

What the strike leaders failed to realize was that the type of campaign they had embarked upon was different from any they had known before and was bound to present great difficulties which could not be easily resolved. An entire city had been paralyzed, but no one had taken the time to think about the ramifications of this beforehand. Workers too had families, let alone those people who sided neither with strikers or employers, and they also had to be fed and heated, their garbage collected and their milk, bread and ice delivered. The maintenance of essential services was of the utmost importance and was one of the most difficult problems wrestled with by the strikers.

On May 16 the intense and hostile public reaction to the termination of bread and milk deliveries forced the Strike Committee to begin to think about and attempt to find a solution to the problem of staples distribution. The strikers approached a sub-committee of the city council, a meeting also attended by A. J. Andrews, W. J. Botterell, representing the Committee of One Thousand, and J. W. Carruthers, owner of the Crescent Creamery Company. Carruthers suggested that the problem of staples distribution could be solved if special cards were issued to delivery wagons notifying the public that the man delivering bread and milk were not scabs. This was accepted by the meeting and approved by the Strike Committee, which soon issued cards reading "Permitted by authority of Strike Committee" to bakeries, dairies and other establishments.[31]

A degree of normalcy returned as businesses deemed essential to the well-being of the city reopened under the protection of the permits. The arrangement, however, made certain people uneasy. Mayor Gray was moved to point out that people should not think the necessities of life were now being supplied by an authority other than the legitimate elected government of the city. This did not stop the mounting criticism of those who charged that the administration of Winnipeg had now passed to the hands of the strikers. The strikers, for their part, claimed that they had no intention of assuming government authority and had merely issued the cards to protect their own men.

Pressure began to mount for the removal of the cards only a few days after their use had begun. Gray and Premier Norris told the strikers they objected to the cards, even though they knew why they had been issued in the first place. On Monday, May 20, Gray told the strikers that the permit cards would have to be removed before any effort could be made to solve the root causes of the walkout. The following day the mayor brought the issue before city council and demanded the removal of the permits since they had outlived their usefulness. Many people all over the country, he asserted, were under the false impression that their use signified the erosion of constitutional authority in Winnipeg. The result was a heated debate between the mayor's supporters and the Labour aldermen who claimed that the cards were absolutely necessary for the continuation of essential services. A. J. Andrews explained that, even though he too knew and understood why the permit cards had been decided upon, he believed that the city's necessities were being supplied by permission of the strikers and this was an erosion of constituted authority, whether intended as such or not. When the debate cooled, the council voted seven to four to have the cards taken down. The following day the Strike Committee complied.[32]

The permit episode cast a heavy shadow over the Strike Committee. Though the permits were not decided upon unilaterally and in fact were approved by two representatives of the Citizens' Committee and a subcommittee of city council, their wording created the impression that the strikers alone were responsible for the maintenance of essential services in the city. This naturally lead to a belief in some minds that the government of Winnipeg had passed to the Labour Temple, which now had the power to operate or shut down these facilities. From there it was but a small step to the assumption that the Labour Temple was now the "James Street Soviet." This cry reinforced the opinions and spurred the activities of those who claimed the strike was nothing but a revolutionary plot in the first place. Foremost among this group was the federal government.

The Borden administration led a coalition of forces which opposed the strike and could accept only two solutions — a total and complete collapse of the strike, or a compromise settlement that would leave little doubt that the strikers were accepting terms dictated by management. If the latter could not be accomplished, the former was necessary because in no way could the general strike be allowed to succeed or even to have the appearance of success. Agents of the federal government, in the persons of Robertson and Meighen, Brigadier-General H. D. B. Ketchen, officer commanding the Manitoba military district, Commissioner A. B. Perry of the RNWMP and A. J. Andrews, worked long and hard to see that the government's purpose

397

was accomplished. The federal government was thus deeply involved in each of the five major steps which led to the disintegration of the strike in the last week of June.

At the request of the Strike Committee, the members of the city police force had remained at their posts on May 15, but anti-strike forces, convinced that the police were either under the control of or were sympathetic to the strikers, found the situation intolerable. Anti-strike members of city council tried to rectify this by presenting the members of the force with an ultimatum: they were asked to sign a pledge dissociating themselves from the Trades and Labour Council and promising not to participate in any future sympathetic strikes. The police were nearly unanimous in their rejection of the ultimatum and the city council was left in the difficult position of having to ignore its own ultimatum or doing what the strikers had not dared to do — leave the city devoid of police protection.

The solution was provided by General Ketchen, who suggested the employment of an alternative force of "special police" to supplement or replace the regular constables. Supported by Ketchen and the Citizens' Committee, the city began to recruit special police, mostly from amongst anti-strike veterans and students, and paid them six dollars per day, a higher wage than that earned by the regular police. When a force of close to two thousand had been successfully recruited, the council repeated its earlier demands that members of the force sign the pledges. When they refused as they had on the first occasion, 240 of them, almost the entire force, were fired.[33] From June 10 the city was in the hands of a large group of men who were, with few exceptions and without pretence, hostile to the strike and the strikers. The fact that they were also inept was demonstrated on several occasions when fights and disturbances broke out due to the inability of these untrained men to conduct themselves properly.

The first afternoon of their service, a group of mounted specials rode down Main Street to a point near the junction with Portage where a crowd had gathered to hear a man speaking from a parked car. The specials, armed with clubs, attempted to disperse this group and rode up on the sidewalk. As they began to walk their horses slowly into the crowd, swinging their batons to force the group to scatter, one of their number was thrown from his horse and badly beaten. Sergeant Major F. G. Coppins, VC, was riding his horse slowly along the sidewalk when someone cupped his hands under Coppins's stirrup and heaved upward, unseating him. As this happened several men grabbed Coppins, helped pull him off the horse and began to beat him. Coppins, already injured, jumped to his feet swinging his club and had to be rescued from the crowd by other specials. He was subsequently taken to Tuxedo Military Hospital suffering from severe bruises.[34]

Ketchen was instrumental in setting up the force of special police, but he did not intend to rely solely on them should he have to use force to maintain order or put down the strike. From the beginning of the walkout he directed the buildup of a large military force in the Winnipeg area and, with the help of his superiors in Ottawa, the Mounted Police and the Citizens'

Committee, did it without bringing a single regular soldier to the city. By co-ordinating his activities with the Mounties and initiating a training program using newly recruited citizen volunteers for the miltia, Ketchen was able to build a large force in a relatively short time. To direct this group he called on former officers residing in the city, and to transport the militia he arranged for the use of trucks supplied by the Citizens' Committee to augment those already on hand. From outside the city a secret shipment of machine guns was forwarded by Ottawa, marked "regimental baggage" and included in the freight of the 27th Battalion, travelling to Winnipeg to demobilize. In addition he had an armoured car available which was regularly stationed in the city.

By Tuesday, June 17, Ketchen had a formidable group of Mounties, militia and civilian auxiliary volunteers at his disposal. At Fort Osborne Barracks an armoured car equipped with three machine guns and manned by three officers, two drivers and six riflemen was kept in readiness. The Citizens' Committee had completed the organization of an auxiliary motor-transport service and placed it under Ketchen's command. The Mounties, in addition to a reinforced complement of officers and men, had been issued four machine guns mounted on motor trucks and could put sixty men on horses into the streets in a matter of minutes. Two mobile militia groups had been placed in readiness, one stationed at Fort Osborne Barracks, the other at Minto Barracks. Each consisted of a troop of the Fort Garry Horse, one motor machine-gun section with two guns apiece, infantry escorts in motor trucks and one company of motorized infantry. The total force immediately available in an emergency numbered eight hundred and Ketchen had worked out special arrangements to call the rest of the militia into action at a moment's notice.[35] If necessary, the government had all the armed force it might require ready and available.

399

In the last few days of May a committee representing six railway running-trades unions approached the unions and the contract-shops employers with an offer to mediate the dispute. The offer was accepted and the committee got down to work inviting proposals from both sides. The Metal Trades Council and the contract-shop owners stuck close to their original positions, but the mediation committee saw nothing extraordinary about the unions' desire to gain recognition for a Metal Trades Council. They thus worked out what they believed was a compromise solution, which included recognition of the Metal Trades Council, and offered it to both sides. The unions accepted the settlement, the employers rejected it and the committee prepared to announce that its efforts had failed.[36]

At this point Senator Robertson arrived in the city once again. There were, at that point, ominous rumblings from the railway yards to the effect that train crews, including locomotive engineers, firemen and carmen, would join the general strike, paralyzing East-West rail transportation at its most vital point in the national communications network. Robertson could not let this happen and determined to find some immediate solution to the strike. The best opportunity appeared to be to use the offices of the mediation committee and to put pressure on the mediators to accept a solution, short of recognition of the Metal Trades Council, that they could bless. This task was relatively simple because Robertson was of the same ilk as the mediators, probably knew them all personally, and played on their fears of the rising power of the One Big Union.

On Sunday evening, June 15, Robertson finally succeeded in forcing the contract-shop employers to offer to recognize individual craft unions in their plants — there was no thought or mention of the recognition of the Metal Trades Council — and had the offer published in the newspapers the next morning.[37] He believed that this offer, containing part of the recognition the unions had sought for many years, might confuse the strikers and weaken their resolve to continue — the strike was already over four weeks old — and give the moderates on the Strike Committee a platform from which to advocate the end of the general strike. To insure that the radical hold on the Strike Committee was weakened at this crucial point, he ordered the arrest of Russell, Johns and the other radicals on Monday night.[38]

In the early hours of June 18, six Anglo-Saxon strike leaders along with a token handful of "enemy aliens" were arrested under authority of a new Immigration Act amendment which had been passed through Parliament in less than one hour on June 6.[39] They were taken straight to Stony Mountain penitentiary and placed in cells while the government decided their fate. Meighen wanted them deported immediately, while A. J. Andrews believed this would alienate the public and therefore argued for their release on bail. By early Friday, June 20, it was decided to release the men if they promised to take no further part in the strike.[40] By then deportation had become completely unnecessary since the moderates had taken Robertson's bait and were preparing to negotiate an end to the strike on the basis of the offer of June 16.

At this point control of events slipped from the Strike Committee's hands. Since the last days of May, several thousand veterans who supported the aims and tactics of the strikers had grown increasingly vocal and militant in their demonstrations of solidarity. On the final day of May, and for some days after, they had paraded in large numbers in the downtown streets of Winnipeg, to the city hall and legislative buildings and in front of Citizens' Committee headquarters. On days when they did not take to the streets they held boisterous meetings in Victoria Park, listening to speeches and reports from their leaders and members of the Strike Committee. To counter this new element, anti-strike veterans organized parades of their own; on one occasion the two groups narrowly missed each other while marching near the legislature. To avoid the possibility of a massive and violent confrontation the mayor issued a ban against parades and twice repeated the order during the course of the strike.[41] On June 20, however, the pro-strike veterans held a mass meeting in a park across from city hall and declared their intention to demonstrate the next day because of the arrests of the strike leaders and the resumption of streetcar service.

At 10:30 the next morning, a hurried meeting convened in Robertson's

400

suite in the Royal Alexandra Hotel. Three veterans' delegates had come to present their terms for cancellation of the planned parade to Robertson, Gray, Andrews and Commissioner A. B. Perry of the Mounted Police. The returned men planned to march from city hall to the Royal Alexandra, where they hoped to be addressed by Senator Robertson, return down Main Street and take possession of the Industrial Bureau, headquarters of the Citizens' Committee. Government and city officials could avert the demonstration, the veterans claimed, if the streetcars were removed from the streets, the strike settled within the next four hours and Robertson agreed to speak to the men in the Industrial Bureau. Gray retorted that it would be impossible to bring about a negotiated end to the strike within the time limit indicated and he had no intention of sending the streetcars back to their barns. They would, however, try to fulfil the third of the conditions and, at that point, Andrews left immediately for the bureau to line up meeting space for the afternoon. By the time he was able to report back to the hotel, events had already passed him by.

The meeting continued after Andrews's hurried departure as Gray tried to dissuade the veterans from precipitating a crisis by going ahead with a demonstration that would violate three proclamations. He would stop the demonstration peacefully if possible, he declared, but would resort to "other measures" if they insisted on forcing his hand. While the mayor and the veterans continued to argue, crowds were already gathering in Main Street, across from the city hall, in anticipation of the parade's 2:30 starting time. At fifteen minutes to two Acting Police Chief Newton telephoned the mayor to inform him of the crowds. Gray hurriedly left the hotel and rushed through back streets to city hall where Newton told him he thought the situation was already out of hand and that his force of special police could not restore order. Gray suggested that the RNWMP be called in, Newton concurred and the mayor drove to Mounted Police headquarters to ask Commissioner Perry to send his men out to patrol the streets. Perry complied and dispatched fifty-four men on horses and thirty-six in trucks.

By 2:30 the gathering crowds were filling the east side of Main Street between William and Rupert. A streetcar moving slowly north along Main was surrounded by several hundred people who tried unsuccessfully to stop it. When it forced its way through, they turned their attention to a southbound car, pulled its trolley off the wires and began to smash its windows. The crowd, now almost completely out of control, rocked the car back and forth, trying to tip it on its side, but when the task proved too great they broke the rest of the windows, slashed the seats and set the interior ablaze. While the attack on the streetcar was in progress, the Mounted Police arrived on the scene.

They swung north along Main from Portage Avenue, half in khaki coats and half in the traditional scarlet, batons in hand. Twice they charged north through the crowd and both times they met with flying stones and bottles. After the second charge one Mountie's horse tripped over a piece of streetcar fender lying in the street, threw its rider to the ground and began to

401

drag him wildly, his foot caught in the stirrup. Within moments several men separated themselves from the mob, grabbed the officer and began to beat him. When the rest of the force caught sight of their comrade they wheeled north once again, this time with revolvers cocked in their hands. Mayor Gray, watching anxiously from a parapet in front of city hall, decided to take further action and formally read the Riot Act. The time was now 2:35 and the crowd was given thirty minutes to get off the streets or be arrested. As Gray turned to go inside the building, he heard gunfire in the street below.[42]

The officer commanding the Mounted Police detachment, Inspector Mead, had concluded after the second charge that his men could not handle the large and excited crowd without extraordinary measures and ordered them to fire a volley into the throng. The command was given only moments after the Riot Act had been read and shooting continued intermittently for several minutes afterwards. One man was killed instantly and many others were wounded. It was claimed afterwards by Mayor Gray, the Manitoba *Free Press* and the Mounties that the order to fire was only given after the Mounties themselves had been shot at by unknown assailants in the crowd. They had certainly come under vigorous attack from bricks, stones and bottles, but the only shots fired that day came from police revolvers. Newspaper casualty lists published in following days listed all serious wounds suffered in the riot, including those of the RNWMP officers, not one of whom had been hit by a bullet.[43] Mayor Gray told reporters that he had not heard shots until shortly after he read the Riot Act and "presumed" they came from the crowd but, in fact, this was almost the exact moment when Mead was ordering his men to shoot. Mead himself, in early reports of the day's events, explained that he had ordered his men to use their sidearms only after he realized how hard pressed they were; he made no mention at all of being fired upon.

Panic swept the crowd as the bullets spattered and ricocheted against the streets and walls and people fell where they stood. Hundreds trying to escape police bullets swept down back alleys and ran up the streets where they met cordons of special police, armed with clubs and revolvers, thrown across Main Street and other streets and alleys in the vicinity of city hall. Now vicious fights broke out and many were arrested as Mounties and specials started to clear the downtown area. Meanwhile, Gray had driven to Fort Osborne Barracks when he heard the gunfire and asked General Ketchen to turn out the militia. The general complied, dispatched an emergency force and within minutes a mixed group of cavalry and the motor machine-gun section began to move into the downtown area in the auxiliary transport so obligingly provided by the Citizens' Committee.

By this time most of the crowd was trying in every way possible to escape the scene. Over eighty who were not successful were caught in the dragnet and arrested. The special police and the militia, aided by the Mounties, threw up cordons to block access to Portage and Main from Garry in the south to the CPR station in the north and remained on duty until midnight.

Soon all was quiet; the day known to history as Bloody Saturday was over.[44]

The events of June 21 climaxed the Winnipeg strike. The dénouement came four days later when the Strike Committee called off the walkout effective Thursday morning, June 26. The strikers had failed to achieve any of their objectives, and after six weeks of effort, the futility of the strike had become painfully clear. All that the strikers were able to gain was an agreement on the part of the provincial government to appoint a royal commission to conduct an impartial investigation into the causes of the dispute.[45]

In embarking on the course taken in the spring of 1919, the workers of Winnipeg were travelling a path few North American wage earners had trod before. There had been other attempted general strikes, the most complete in Seattle, Washington, in February 1919 involving sixty thousand workers, but they were either of short duration (Seattle's strike lasted four days) or incomplete. There were thus almost no campaign histories that could have been consulted and no previous successes or failures to guide the Winnipeg strikers. Therein lies the source of their failure to examine fully the consequences of what they were planning and to prepare themselves and their city for the days and weeks to come. This, more than anything else, assured the defeat of the strike and the resultant grave weakening of the city's labour movement.

403

Workers in Winnipeg and western Canada had spoken increasingly of general strikes since mid-1917, but rarely gave any consideration as to what a general strike would involve. They talked and wrote about general strikes either as political weapons to oppose conscription or as the ultimate manifestation of industrial conflict, this being especially true following the 1918 Winnipeg civic workers' victory. There was, however, never any thought given as to which essential services should be maintained, if any, and how this might be done. Workers were quite blind to the fact that they were going to be forced to assume some responsibility for the maintenance of society in the event they were to launch an open-ended general strike. This held true whether or not they were planning to create a revolutionary situation, since they could never separate themselves and their families from the rest of society.

Trapped into a situation in which they appeared to be assuming government authority, the Winnipeg strikers were not equipped or prepared to cope with the political and military implications of this new situation. By launching a general strike the workers had embarked on a radical course, but they were not radical enough to escape the consequences of their action. Once the unions had decided to shut down the entire city and keep it shut until they won, they ran directly into the power of three levels of government. And when the federal government decided to involve itself in countering a revolution that never existed, the workers were lost: their only choice was between unacceptable compromise, complete defeat or direct, perhaps armed, resistance.

The Winnipeg General Strike was not a revolution and was never planned to be one. It did, however, raise basic questions concerning the nature and composition of "constituted authority" as well as what qualifies as a *bona fide* challenge to that authority. There can be no doubt that the strikers intended to enhance their own position at the expense of the normal political and economic power of capital. In using as blunt an instrument as a general strike, however, they also ran the risk of challenging the *de facto* power of at least one level of government. General strikes are intended to bring the normal functions and activities of society to a standstill and they therefore transfer to the workers part of the option of what will continue to operate and what will not — this is inevitable if anarchy is to be avoided. To this degree the existing order *is* undermined, whether by accident or design and whether on a purely local level or a more national one.

The rapid increase of labour's power in Winnipeg was a shock to the cosy arrangements and alliances that had existed between capital and government for at least four decades. This threat to the status quo was compounded by the belief in some quarters that the workers were embarked on a campaign to supplant the municipal and even the provincial and national governments. The charge was not true, but it did reflect the unions' rapid rise to new positions of power. The leaders of the strike urged their followers to hold to a non-violent course so they could avoid open confrontation with the government and its police and military forces. They did not realize that this confrontation actually began at eleven A.M. the morning of May 15. Many years of mostly unsuccessful industrial struggles and the victorious sympathetic strike of 1918 had convinced them that a general strike would enable them to bring their full power to bear in an industrial dispute. This was a basic flaw in their thinking, however, because a general strike was not and could not be just another larger strike. By its very nature it is a political weapon and must, to a certain degree, challenge areas of authority of legally constituted governments. The strikers were, therefore, caught in a dilemma of their own making and the result was a crushing defeat.

In a very real sense the Winnipeg General Strike marked the end of an era in Winnipeg and western Canada. The Winnipeg strikers had manned the battle lines for their western brothers and their loss seriously undermined the strength of all western labour. The defeat of the strike assured the weakening of those unions and labour leaders who had championed its use and who had called it. The strike was, therefore, a key event in the climactic happenings of a postwar era of turmoil. Much of the vitality of a labour movement grown powerful and energetic during four years of war was sapped in the grinding and hopeless struggle of the six-week confrontation at Winnipeg.

Notes

1. See, for example, Testimony of T. R. Deacon, Evidence Presented to the Royal Commission on Industrial Relations, Winnipeg, 10 & 12 May 1919, Department of Labour Library, Ottawa.
2. D. C. Masters, *The Winnipeg General Strike* (Toronto: University of Toronto Press, 1950), pp. 8–10.
3. *Ibid.*, p. 7.
4. *Ibid.*

5. D. J. Bercuson, "Labour in Winnipeg: The Great War and the General Strike" (Ph.D. dissertation, University of Toronto, 1971), pp. 17–37.
6. See Canada Department of Labour, *Eighth Annual Report on Wholesale Prices in Canada, 1917*, and monthly tables in *Labour Gazette* for 1918 and 1919.
7. Bercuson, "Labour in Winnipeg," pp. 101–102, 105.
8. Martin Robin, "Registration, Conscription and Independent Labour Politics, 1916–1917," *Canadian Historical Review* 47 (June 1966): 101–118.
9. Bercuson, "Labour in Winnipeg," pp. 189–190.
10. *Ibid.*, pp. 175–178.
11. *Ibid.*, pp. 200–217.
12. T. J. Murray to Rigg, 28 May 1919, Rigg/Rees Papers, Public Archives of Manitoba; Manitoba *Free Press*, 25 May 1918.
13. *Western Labor News*, 4 October 1918.
14. *Ibid.*, 13 December 1918.
15. See P. Phillips, "The National Policy and the Development of the Western Canadian Labour Movement," in *Prairie Perspectives 2*, ed. A. Rasporich and H. Klassen (Toronto: Holt, Rinehart and Winston, 1973), pp. 41–61.
16. Bercuson, "Labour in Winnipeg," p. 134.
17. *Ibid.*, pp. 227–228.
18. Trades and Labour Congress of Canada, *Proceedings of the 34th Annual Convention* (Ottawa, 1918), pp. 32–33, 128–131.
19. Masters, *The Winnipeg General Strike*, p. 38.
20. *Western Labor News*, 16 June 1919.
21. *Ibid.*, 2 May 1919.
22. Bercuson, "Labour in Winnipeg," p. 289.
23. *Ibid.*, p. 291.
24. *Western Labor News*, 9 May 1919.
25. *Ibid.*, 16 May 1919.
26. *Ibid.*, 4 June 1919; Winnipeg *Citizen*, 20 May 1919.
27. *Western Labor News*, 17 May 1919.
28. Bercuson, "Labour in Winnipeg," pp. 312–314.
29. *Ibid.*, pp. 330–331.
30. Canada House of Commons, *Debates* (2 June 1919), pp. 3035–3043.
31. *Western Labor News*, 17 May 1919.
32. *Ibid.*, 22 May 1919.
33. Winnipeg *Citizen*, 10 June 1919.
34. Manitoba *Free Press*, 11 June 1919.
35. Ketchen to Ottawa, 17 June 1919, Department of National Defence Papers, File 5678, Public Archives of Canada (PAC).
36. *Western Labor News*, 12 June 1919.
37. Manitoba *Free Press*, 16 June 1919.
38. Robertson to Borden, 17 June 1919, Borden Papers, PAC.
39. Masters, *The Winnipeg General Strike*, pp. 103–104.
40. *Western Labor News*, 20 June 1919.
41. Manitoba *Free Press*, 23 June 1919.
42. *Ibid.*
43. *Ibid.*
44. *Ibid.*; *Western Labor News*, 23 June 1919.
45. *Enlightener (Western Labor News)*, 25 June 1919.

The Progressives*
WALTER YOUNG

The Progressives entered the campaign of 1921 with considerable enthusiasm. True to their philosophical origins, they did not campaign as a national party, although their leader, T.A. Crerar, did tour most of Canada. Instead, they campaigned almost exclusively in individual constituencies. Each electoral district was an autonomous unit in the party and as a result there was neither a national campaign nor an overall campaign strategy.

A national campaign would have been rather awkward, for there was a split within the movement. It was not serious in the beginning, but as the Progressives edged further into politics it grew and deepened. The division was between the Alberta wing and the Manitoba wing, or, more specifically, between Crerar and Henry Wise Wood. Crerar saw the election as an opportunity to bring the Liberal party to its senses, and to force a tariff reduction and free trade in agricultural products. He was not fundamentally opposed to the party system. He had been in the Borden cabinet and was no stranger to cabinet solidarity and party discipline. Wood, understandably, said of the 1921 election:

406

The issue is between the old party system and the system we have built up.[1]

Progressives of his persuasion characterised the old system as the tool by which the big interests had corrupted the electorate and had run the country to serve their own selfish ends.

A further bone of contention was the question of free trade versus government control in the marketing of grain. During the war the federal government had assumed control of the marketing of wheat. A board was established that fixed the price of wheat and controlled the marketing of the crops in 1917 and 1918. In 1919 the Canadian Wheat Board was set up to handle the selling of that year's crop, but the legislation was not renewed for 1920. The Manitoba wing of the Progressives was more interested in free trade and not much concerned about the demise of the wheat board. The Saskatchewan farmers, on the other hand, were well pleased with the effects of the wheat board and wanted to see the federal government stay in the business of marketing wheat. They believed this policy would result in stable prices and secure markets.

Of the two leaders of the "old line parties," as the farmers called them, Mackenzie King of the Liberals was the most shrewd. Prime Minister Arthur Meighen of the Conservatives displayed the short-sighted arrogance that became his trademark in politics and contributed materially to his lack of success. King saw the Progressives as impatient Liberals and attempted to

*From *Democracy and Discontent: Progressivism, Socialism and Social Credit in the Canadian West*, by Walter D. Young. Reprinted by permission of McGraw-Hill Ryerson Ltd.

placate the western farmers by telling them things about his tariff policy that he did not dare say in eastern Canada. Meighen either ignored the farmers' demands or referred to them as "Socialistic, Bolshevistic and Soviet nonsense." He described the governments they had formed in Ontario and Alberta as "freaks."

Meighen and King were campaigning to form a government—they were seeking power. The Progressive did not want power, they merely wanted representation. This fitted well their constituency by constituency campaign. The voters were not asked to elect a Progressive government, they were simply asked to elect a Progressive to represent them in Ottawa—an important distinction.

The Progressives at Ottawa

The election of sixty-five Progressives might appear to be a great start for a party but the results were actually a disappointment. Only one Progressive was elected east of the Ottawa river; the majority were from the prairies, with twenty-four from Ontario and five from British Columbia. They constituted a western block dedicated to the interests of the wheat farmer.

Although his party was the largest group in the House of Commons, Mackenzie King did not have a majority. Soon after the election he set about to bring the Progressives into some sort of alliance. The Progressives viewed his advances with mixed feelings. The Alberta wing, strongly committed to the idea of constituency autonomy and opposed to party politics, condemned any arrangement with the Liberals. The Manitoba wing wanted only to reform the Liberal party and would have entered into some agreement without much difficulty. But King did not have complete unanimity in his own party. The conservative wing represented by Sir Lomer Gouin and his Quebec colleagues, despised Progressivism and opposed any alliance.

King first offered cabinet representation to the Progressives in return for some kind of coalition arrangement. The offer was ultimately denied by King and, in any case, it was turned down by the Progressives. As a result of the reticence of the Albertans, the most the Progressives would agree to was conditional support of the Liberals. They recognized that there was likely to be more for them to support in the program of a Liberal administration than in that of the Conservatives.

In the discussions that took place before the opening of the new parliament, the division in the ranks of the radicals was evident. Crerar, as an experienced parliamentarian, was concerned about establishing the machinery of parliamentary discipline to ensure that the Progressives voted as a single unit, as a party, in fact. This involved the institution of a caucus, party whip and reasonable adherence to the direction of the parliamentary leaders. The Alberta Progressives opposed this approach, for they saw themselves as spokesmen for their constituents not as subordinate members of a political party. Despite his efforts and conditional agreement from his followers, Crerar

407

never achieved the kind of solidarity necessary to enable the Progressives to operate effectively in a parliamentary setting.

Although they were the second largest group in parliament, the Progressives did not choose to form the official opposition. This right they yielded to Meighen's Conservatives. The Progressives did not see themselves as an alternative government. They were a kind of pressure group, sitting in parliament to chastise the unfeeling and to assist those who wanted to help the farmers. By refusing responsibility and, by implication, demonstrating their lack of interest in forming a government, they made it possible for other politicians and the rest of the country to refuse to take them seriously. They rejected the opportunity to achieve the cohesion they so desperately needed to reach their goals.

The Progressives could not become the official opposition because of their principles. The Manitoba Progressives did not want to oppose the Liberals — they only wanted to reform them. The Alberta Progressives did not want to engage in the competitive processes of party government — they wanted to eradicate party government. For opposite reasons, therefore, the two wings of the Progressive group combined to pass up a chance to become a political party.

The Progressives were determined to demonstrate that they were an independent body, free to support the government or to oppose it in the light of their principles and the needs of their constituents. As Professor Morton has remarked:

It was a brave experiment, inspired by political naiveté, and marked by a curious over-emphasis on the importance of legislation and an ill-advised indifference to the importance of administration.[2]

It was a difficult position for the group to maintain, particularly as they lacked the unity such a role demanded. They were, in Morton's phrase, a "restive and unreliable band." Mackenzie King could count on Progressive support, however, for as much as the westerners disliked the Liberals, they liked the Conservatives even less.

Only the Albertan Progressives could regard the two old parties as indifferently steeped in iniquity.[3]

The rules of the House of Commons at that time were designed to facilitate the operation of a two-party parliament, composed of government and opposition. The Progressives did not fit the pattern. Because of the rules of the Commons, they found themselves unable to move a sub-amendment to the Conservative amendment to the government's budget. Thus they were deprived of a prime opportunity to criticise government fiscal policy, their chief concern at the time. Unable to get their own proposals before the House, they were forced to vote with the Conservatives. Their most significant achievement in the 1922 session was in gaining the government's agreement to reinstate the 1918 Crowsnest Pass rates on the shipment of grain and flour — to the advantage of the farmer.

Tension and Disintegration

By the end of 1922 cracks in the Progressive ranks were widening. Two Progressives slipped away to become Liberals. Crerar tried toward the end of the parliamentary session to bring his group closer to the Liberals by proposing some kind of working agreement between the two. The proposal was turned down and Crerar resigned as leader, to be replaced by Robert Forke. Forke was no less liberal than Crerar. His initial actions were toward establishing a national Progressive *party*. This move was opposed by the Alberta members and failed to succeed. Forke's failure in this regard — really the failure of the Progressives — marked the beginning of the end. There was nothing for them to do.

The two views on the movement's purpose turned the Progressives into a body of dissidents, in danger of disintegration. The Alberta view of the Member of Parliament as a delegate was simply inconsistent with the structure of parliament. The views of the Manitoba moderates were inconsistent with the radical strain in Progressive thought. Progressivism began to disintegrate through the centrifugal forces generated by the inconsistency and contradiction in its doctrine and composition.

In 1923 the Conservative party allowed the Progressives to make the major amendment to the budget motion. Forke made a frontal assault on Liberal tariff policy, calling for a reduction in the tariff on the necessities of life, more favourable terms of trade with Britain, reciprocity in trade with the United States and increased taxation on unearned incomes and luxury items. The ringing presentation of the bare bones of their policy united the Progressive as never before. The combination of the Progressive and Conservative assault on the Liberal budget reduced King's combined majority to 8. This was the Progressive's finest hour. Their course was downhill thereafter. In particular, they were beaten to a standstill in their attempt to amend the Bank Act in 1923 — although some of the reforms they advocated were later enacted.

The major break in Progressive ranks occurred in 1924. During the debate on the budget of that session, J.S. Woodsworth, Labour MP from Winnipeg North, moved an amendment that was substantially the same as that moved by Forke the previous year. The Progressives were in a difficult position. If they supported Woodsworth's amendment, the Liberal government could conceivably be defeated. If they opposed it, they would be repudiating their own principles. One of the main criticisms the Progressives made of the old parties was that they seldom stood by their principles.

Forke led most of his followers in opposition to Woodsworth's amendment on the grounds that there was more likelihood of a Liberal government enacting Progressive reforms than would ever be the case with the Conservatives. To defeat the government would, then, be folly. Fourteen Progressives disagreed and supported the Woodsworth amendment. As E.J. Garland of the breakaway group of Progressives declared on the floor of the House, his constituents would be:

. . . encouraged to know that even though our efforts are largely nullified by the attitudes of opposing interests, they have at least representatives who are pleading their cause without fear of party or press, and who will not be silent while injustice still stands.[4]

Six of the fourteen renegades left the Progressive party shortly after, constituting what became known as the "Ginger Group." In an open letter to Robert Forke they said:

As we see it there are two species of political organization — one the "Political Party' that aspires to power, and in so doing, inevitably perpetuates that competitive spirit in matters of legislation and government generally which has brought the world wellnigh to ruin; the other is the democratically organized group which aims to co-operate with other groups to secure justice rather than to compete with them for power. It is as representatives of this latter type that we take our stand . . .[5]

The Ginger Group was later joined by three more Progressives.

By 1925 the Progressive party was shattered beyond repair. Seventeen broke with the caucus and voted with the Liberals on the 1925 budget. When the election was called that year there was little to hold the group together. They had no funds and no national organization. Only 24 Progressive MP's were left when the votes had been counted. The Conservatives under Meighen had the most seats this time, but not a clear majority.

In the constitutional crises which followed, the Progressives played the part of makeweight and were responsible first for the defeat of King's administration and finally for the defeat of Arthur Meighen's. In the 1926 election Liberals and Progressives reached an agreement not to oppose one another in several ridings; in others "Liberal-Progressives" appeared. When the 1926 session of parliament opened there were only nine "pure" Progressives left.

The Lesson of Progressive Experience

To some extent the Progressives had achieved their goals. The eastern politicians and magnates had been jolted into an awareness of the needs of the farmers, even if these demands were not entirely met. The general spirit of reform, which had fostered the farmers' movements and had led to the creation of the Progressive party, had achieved some results in increasing the amount of social welfare legislation at the provincial level. But prosperity helped to take some of the steam from the movement, and the manifest failure of the party in parliament aided the process of diminution. Third parties, it seemed, had no place in the context of parliamentary government, and if they could not effect changes in the rules — as the Progressives had tried and failed to do — then they remained both vulnerable and impotent. This factor and the concessions Mackenzie King made to the west in the election of 1926, effectively brought an end to the career of the Progressive party. The Liberal-Progressives in the House of Commons insisted on keeping their dual identity but they attended the Liberal caucus and were seated in the House with the Liberals. Slowly but surely they were absorbed and digested by the Liberals.

The left-overs — those who sat as UFA members or Independent Progressives — were themselved absorbed in a different way by a different group. When the Progressives flared into prominence in the 1921 election, two Labour MP's were also elected: J.S. Woodsworth for Winnipeg North Centre and William Irvine for East Calgary. By 1923 Woodsworth had established his right to speak after Robert Forke as the leader of a party. Earlier Irvine had referred in debate to the presence of a "Labour Group" in the Commons; "Mr. Woodsworth is the leader," he said, "and I am the group."[6]

The Labour group had met occasionally with the more radical of the Progressives. After the Ginger Group had separated itself from the decaying carcass of the Progressive party, meetings of this group with the Labour group were more frequent and collaboration was the rule rather than the exception. By 1930 co-operation had proceeded to the stage that more formal arrangements could be considered. A document was drawn up which stated that the groups were "engaged in the common fight against a strongly entrenched system of special privilege," and affirmed the decision to work in unison to develop "a co-operative system of administration."[7] Each group was to retain its identity, and there was no intention to form another political party. A steering committee was elected, a secretary appointed, and a chairman was elected to act on behalf of all groups in the event that there was insufficient time for a conference. In effect, therefore, the document did lay the groundwork for a political party. Two years later the "co-operating groups" were to agree to begin building a new political party.

Much had happened between 1926 and 1932 to convince J.S Woodsworth and his colleagues in the House of Commons that there was enough support in the country to spell success for another organized attempt to break the two party monopoly. The onset of the depression and a series of crop failures once again brought the farmer up against the precarious nature of his occupation. There had been increased activity on the part of the various labour and socialist parties in the cities in the west. The failure of the Progressive party had certainly dampened the political ambitions of the farmers' organizations, but they had not disappeared.

What the Progressive experience had shown was the impossibility of effective parliamentary action by a loosely linked body of independents. The Progressives had assumed that government was essentially the process of law-making and that as long as you had a seat or two in the House of Commons you have a voice in making the laws. They had not understood the mechanism of parliament, nor had they realized that the centre of power was the executive, not the legislature.

The cabinet governs the country through the civil service, and cabinets are only interested in parties other than their own if those parties constitute a threat in the House of Commons. Had the Progressives been a single, united party, and had they been willing to play the parliamentary game with the Conservatives, they could have forced Mackenzie King to do more for the farmers — by threatening to defeat his government. But they had not been united and could never have been because the Alberta group at least,

411

and certainly several from the other provinces, had championed the view that the Member of Parliament ought not to be subordinate to the party. They had held that his first duty was to his constituents and his principles. It would have been odd, indeed, if having been elected because they opposed "partyism" the Progressives had turned around and adopted it.

If everyone playing a game follows one set of rules, those who join under their own different rules soon discover they have no hope of achieving any of their goals. It did not matter how valid the cause of the Progressives was, nor how accurate their criticism of the "old line" parties; they achieved little because they had not played the party game.

The Progressives had erred in thinking that it was parliament and the party system that were at fault and causing their trouble. To some extent the influence of American reform ideas and American experience had led to this misapprehension, for in the American Congress the individual member does have more influence than his counterpart in the Canadian House of Commons. Leadership in the Canadian House lies with the cabinet. Members, in effect, merely approve cabinet proposals or oppose them. The cabinet retains its right to lead the Commons and govern the country by virtue of the support it has in the House of Commons. Generally, this support is guaranteed because the prime minister and his cabinet colleagues are the leaders of the majority party in the Commons and that party, through strict party discipline, votes as a bloc. The addition of sixty-five undisciplined Progressives had alerted the Liberal and Conservative parties to the discontent of the farmers, but it did not force the government to make the concessions the Progressives had assumed their victory would bring.

412

*   *   *

When the CCF was established it appeared the lesson of the Progressive experience had been learned. Unlike the Progressives, the CCF was a vigorous champion of the parliamentary system and its members became particularly adept in using the institution to achieve the goals of the socialist movement. Social Credit, on the other hand, never demonstrated any great fondness for the institution, and on more than one occasion its members indicated that they considered it a nuisance. J.S. Woodsworth, M.J. Coldwell and Stanley Knowles of the CCF were all, at various times, described as great parliamentarians. William Aberhart of the Social Credit party rarely spoke in the Alberta legislature and W.A.C. Bennett of the B.C. Social Credit party considered that there was altogether too much talk in the chamber.

From the Progressive experience in the twenties and the agrarian opposition to "partyism", these two strands, the CCF and Social Credit, branch off, each running in different directions from the same source. In neither case was the position of the Member of Parliament — or of the provincial legislator — reconsidered in the light of Progressive ideas. For the CCF, the MP remained a representative and a party member; for the Social Credit party, he was an adjunct to the cabinet and the civil service, with a much more reduced role in the legislative process than even the normal parliamentary system envisaged. The Progressive ideal of members as delegates from their constituencies or from their economic groups languished and died, killed by the necessity of party unity that the cabinet system of parliamentary government demanded.

Notes

1. Cited in W.L. Morton, *The Progressive Party in Canada* (Toronto: University of Toronto Press, 1950), pp. 116/17, from *The Grain Growers's Guide*, Winnipeg, October 5, 1921, p. 27.
2. Morton, *op. cit.* pp. 152/53.
3. Morton, *op. cit.* p. 153.
4. Cited in Morton, *op. cit.* p. 193, from House of Commons *Debates*, 1924, p. 2214.
5. Cited in Morton, *op. cit.* p. 195
6. Cited in K.W. McNaught, *A Prophet in Politics: A Biography of J.S. Woodsworth* (Toronto: University of Toronto Press, 1959), p. 167.
7. P.A.C., Manuscript in Henry Spencer Papers (n.d.).

The Origins of the Maritime Rights Movement*
E. R. FORBES

Canadian historians have devoted considerable attention to post-war agitation on the Prairies; they have virtually ignored similar agitation in the Maritimes, the regional protest movement which became known by the slogan "Maritime Rights." The few comments it has received, in biographical literature or in sweeping analyses of long periods of history, have been largely concerned with its political manifestations.[1] Such a preoccupation is not surprising. Both Liberals and Conservatives were vociferous in their efforts to portray themselves as the champions of the movement. Shortly before the Antigonish-Guysborough by-election of 1927 a Protestant clergyman set out to review the issues of the campaign from the pulpit. Both candidates, he noted, were clamouring for attention as the defenders of "Maritime Rights." This aspect of their campaign, he said, reminded him of the behaviour of his own young children one evening when he and his wife were getting ready to go visiting. The little girl set up an awful howl from the moment the babysitter arrived. She bawled and bawled. Finally, just as her parents were going out the door, her brother turned, slapped her sharply, and declared, "Shut up, I wanna cry."

There was much more to "Maritime Rights" than the conspicuous wail of the politicians. One cannot begin to tell here the story of the movement — the intensive organizational campaign with its delegations to Ottawa, economic conferences, and country-wide speaking tours; the erratic swings

*Reprinted with permission from *Acadiensis: Journal of the History of the Atlantic Region*, Vol. V. No. 1 (Autumn 1975), pp. 54–66.

in the popular vote from one party to another as Maritimers searched desperately for solutions to their problems; and the inevitable royal commissions sent in to defuse the agitation[2] — but one can at least attempt a more basic introduction through the analysis of the motives of the different social groups which participated in it. Their behaviour suggests that the issues involved went much deeper than mere political manoeuvering or even, as professor G. A. Rawlyk has suggested, the attempt by the local "Establishment" to undercut other forms of social protest.[3] All classes in the region, although often in conflict on other issues, were united in their support of Maritime Rights. Each was aware that its own particular aspirations were incapable of realization until the region's declining influence was checked or reversed.

The social categories employed here will be those used by the people themselves. Maritimers spoke frequently in this period of their "classes." They were not referring to any clear Marxian structure nor did they imply the status-based stratification of the modern sociologist. Essentially they were talking about broad occupational interest groups. Such divisions were partly theoretical: the members of each group or "class" were assumed to have interests in common of which not all might be conscious. But they also had an empirical basis through such exclusively occupational organizations as the Maritime Division of the Canadian Manufacturers Association, retail merchants associations, the United Farmers, federations of labour and, by the end of the decade, the Maritime Fishermen's Union. These were the kinds of groupings to which New Brunswick Premier P. J. Veniot referred early in 1923 when he reported to Mackenzie King that, after looking "carefully into the [Maritime Rights] movement," he had found it was "purely non-political and embraces [the] efforts of all classes to obtain what is sincerely considered fair play for [the] Maritime Provinces."[4]

The development of Maritime regionalism, of which the Maritime Rights movement formed the climax, took place largely in the first two decades of the century. Previously, popular loyalties had been focused upon larger imperial or national entities or upon smaller political, cultural or geographical units. The shift was dictated by a growing realization of the need for co-operation. Co-operation was essential if the three Atlantic Provinces were to counteract the eclipse of their influence which resulted from the rise of the West and the growing metropolitan dominance of Central Canada. Another factor contributing to the growth of regionalism was the progressive ideology of the period, which increased the pressure upon the small governments for expensive reforms while at the same time suggesting the possibility of limitless achievement through a strategy of unity, organization and agitation. Consequently, regional awareness increased sharply in the three provinces. Their leaders joined forces to fight losses in representation, which followed every census after 1891; to increase their subsidies, which had fallen far behind those of the Prairies; and to defend the Intercolonial Railway, whose pro-Maritime policies came under attack from both the Prairies and Central Canada.[5]

The manufacturers' stake in the regionalization of the Maritimes was most obvious, particularly for the defense of the Intercolonial Railway. By the end of the 19th Century that railway had become an important agent of industrialization in the region. Its management had accepted the principle that half a loaf was better than none and had reduced rates to develop traffic. It created a basic freight rate structure which was between 20 and 50 percent lower than that in force in Ontario and offered in addition special rate concessions based upon "what the traffic would bear."[6] Built into the structure was a system of "arbitraries" or especially low rates between the Maritimes and Montreal on goods destined for points further west. These rates enabled the secondary manufacturers in the Maritimes to penetrate markets in Western and Central Canada to obtain the sales volume necessary for competitive production.[7] With such encouragement, capital investment in manufacturing in the Maritimes quadrupled between 1900 and 1920.[8] The old dream of some Nova Scotian entrepreneurs that their province would play the role of a great industrial metropolis to a Canadian hinterland was far from realization. But the Maritimers' optimism for their manufacturing potential persisted. The Halifax *Morning Chronicle* in 1906 explicitly touted Nova Scotia's pioneer programme in technical education as encouraging the industrialization which would reverse the region's declining status in Confederation. The Saint John *Standard* in 1916 enthused about a hydro-electric project to harness the Bay of Fundy tides, which, by providing cheaper energy for manufacturing, would raise the Maritimes "to a position of commercial supremacy as compared with any other part of the Dominion."[9]

Such aspirations received a severe check with the integration of the Inter-colonial into a national system. The happy partnership between the Inter-colonial management and the local producers had come under attack both from competing Central Canadian manufacturers and Prairie farmers preoccupied with their demand for the equalization of freight rates.[10] The Borden Government apparently decided to get rid of the anomaly of a Maritime-oriented railway once and for all. In November, 1918, it shifted the Intercolonial's headquarters to Toronto, transferred its senior officials to other lines and replaced them with appointees from the Canadian Northern. The following year, the Intercolonial was placed under the *de facto* jurisdiction of the Board of Railway Commissioners which raised the rates to the Ontario level.[11] The process was completed in time to provide an inflated base for the 40 per cent general rate increase of 1920. In Ontario and Quebec freight rates increased 111% between 1916 and September 1920; in the Maritimes basic rates rose between 140 and 216% and the simultaneous cancellation of special rates, such as the special commodity rate on sugar, led to still greater increases.[12]

The rate changes not only threatened the local entrepreneurs' dreams of industrial grandeur, but left them seriously exposed to the pressure for metropolitan consolidation. For many, the campaign for Maritime Rights became a struggle for survival. In 1919 a group of manufacturers mounted

415

a delegation to Ottawa, demanded the restoration of the Intercolonial to independent management and revived the Maritime Board of Trade as a channel for their agitation.[13] They continued to play a prominent role in the leadership of the movement through such representatives as W. S. Fisher of Saint John, a former Canadian Manufacturers' Association president, who served as a spokesman for another delegation to Ottawa in 1921, and D. R. Turnbull, managing-director of the Acadia Sugar Corporation, who, in 1925, became Nova Scotia's representative on the newly-formed Maritime Rights Transportation Committee.[14]

Maritime merchants were also seriously affected by the integration of the Intercolonial into a national system. The wholesalers were injured by the shift in supply purchasing for the railway from the Maritimes to Toronto.[15] They were weakened further, in relation to their metropolitan competitors, by the sharp increase in "town distributing rates" — especially low rates which had enabled them to import quantities of goods from Central Canada, break them up and send them out to individual towns and villages at little more than the cost of direct shipment. Similarly higher rates on the Intercolonial accelerated the shift away from Maritime ports as distributing points for products entering from abroad. H. R. Silver, a commission merchant, reported a decline in molasses shipments out of Halifax from 130 carloads in 1916 to 17 in 1921.[16] Retailers were also adversely affected. They had to pay more for their goods and had difficulty in passing the full charge on to their customers. The Halifax *Maritime Merchant* commented tersely in 1920 upon the general effect of the increase: "Added to the handicap already suffered by firms seeking western business, the new rate will be hard on the merchants and add materially to the cost the local consumer must pay."[17]

The issue which generated the greatest heat from the merchant and commercial interests of Halifax and Saint John was the development of their ports as entrepôts for Canada's winter trade. The two cities were engaged in a Darwinian struggle with the American seaports and with each other. The key to victory was volume and variety of traffic. The more traffic, the lower the port charges and ocean rates; the lower the rates, the greater the traffic. The Maritime ports were most conscious of their rivalry with Portland, Maine, which had traditionally enjoyed the advantage of a very active canvass for trade from the Grand Trunk Railway.[18] The Maritime ports' aspirations for Canadian trade, aroused initially by Confederation, had blossomed under the "national policy" of the Laurier Government. Laurier had promised that the National Transcontinental Railway would channel exports, particularly grain, through national ports. In 1903, he appointed a Royal Commission to investigate other means of routing trade through "all-Canadian channels," and in 1911, he pledged that his government would restrict the Imperial preference to goods entering through Canadian ports.[19]

Such expectations were rudely shaken by the federal take-over of the Grand Trunk. With it, the Canadian Government inherited a strong vested interest in the commercial success of Portland. At Halifax, prominent Liberals urged the return of a Conservative cabinet minister in the by-election of 1920 to give the Maritimes at least a voice in defending their port's interest.[20] Early in 1922 the Halifax and Saint John boards of trade appointed a joint committee, consisting largely of merchants and manufacturers, to co-ordinate their agitation on such issues as the restoration of the Intercolonial and the routing of trade through Maritime Ports.[21] The merchant's position in the Maritime Rights movement continued to be a prominent one through the organized activities of boards of trade and the role of individuals such as W. A. Black, of the leading merchant-shipping firm of Pickford and Black. At seventy-six years of age, against "his physicians' advice, his wife's fears and his family's opposition," Black came out of retirement to fight the Halifax by-election of 1923 on a platform of Maritime Rights.[22]

Another business group, the lumbermen, also joined the agitation. For them, the impact of the increased freight charges was compounded in 1921 by increased American duty on timber products under the Fordney tariff. Angus MacLean of The Bathurst Company, later president of the New Brunswick Lumberman's Association, appealed to Mackenzie King for relief on both issues.[23] When none was forthcoming he and other so-called "Lumber lords" of New Brunswick such as Archie and Donald Fraser, owners of the second largest lumber company in the Maritimes, threw their very considerable support behind the Conservative "Maritime Rights" candidates in the federal election of 1925.[24] In that year, MacLean became the titular leader of the protest movement as president of the Maritime Board of Trade.

Although labour in the Maritimes was at the peak of its "class" consciousness in 1919, it joined with the business groups in the agitation. Between 1916 and 1920, reported union membership in the Maritimes had quadrupled to about 40 000.[25] Spurred by the anticipation of a "new era" to follow the War[26] and beset by the grim reality of galloping inflation,[27] the workers attempted new techniques in organization and challenged their employers in a series of strikes in 1919 and 1920. At the same time they were conscious that their aspirations for a greater share of the fruits of their labour could not be achieved if their industries were destroyed from other causes. Early in 1919 the *Eastern Federationist*, published by the Trades and Labour Council of Pictou County, argued that the freight rate increases violated the "rights of the Maritime Provinces' people under the terms of Confederation."[28] After the Amherst "General Strike" in May and June of 1919, the *Federationist* was particularly incensed by reports that the Canada Car Company was planning to transfer its Amherst operation to Montreal. The thrust of the editor's bitterness was directed at both the capitalists involved and the trend towards metropolitan consolidation which posed a continual threat to Maritime industry and jobs.[29] Similarly the Halifax *Citizen*, the organ of the local Trades and Labour Council, severely criticized the removal of the railway headquarters from

417

Moncton and commended the activities of the Maritime Board of Trade president, Hance J. Logan, in seeking Maritime union as a counterweight to the declining political influence of the region. Bemoaning the unfair treatment accorded the Maritimes by the rest of the country, the *Citizen* concluded that there was "very little hope of any justice for us under present conditions."[30] The journal periodically returned to this theme and remained a consistent supporter of Maritime Rights.

The Railway Brotherhoods, which, after the United Mineworkers, constituted the largest bloc of organized labour in the region, were directly involved in the Maritime Rights campaign. During the first decade of the century the brotherhoods had won the acceptance of the principle of seniority in promotions and lay-offs on the Intercolonial.[31] In theory at least, the humblest employee could aspire to the highest office on the road. Under the new regime after 1918, that principle went by the board. According to one estimate, 400 employees were transferred out of the Moncton headquarters and any replacements came from other government roads. In addition, the repair shops declined and staff was reduced all along the line. To some workers it seemed the principle of seniority had been replaced by the principle that no Maritimer need apply.[32]

Labour did not need to be coaxed into the Maritime Rights movement by the Halifax *Herald* or other politically-oriented journals in the 1920's; large segments were already there, drawn by a consideration of their own immediate interest. The railway centres provided the most consistent voting support for Maritime Rights candidates throughout the 1920's. F. B. McCurdy attributed his victory in the important Colchester by-election of 1920 to the railway workers' belief that in the cabinet he would "be strong enough to afford some relief in the railway grievance." He blamed his defeat in the general election of 1921 on his inability to do so.[33] Labour also threw its support behind W. A. Black in the Halifax by-election of 1923.[34] Neil Herman, Labour-organizer, Social Gospel clergyman and sometime editor of the Halifax *Citizen* was a founder and executive member of the Halifax Maritime Club.[35] He later accompanied its president, H. S. Congdon, in a tour of Central Canada to drum up newspaper support for the movement. When the so-called "Great" Maritime Rights delegation went to Ottawa in February 1925, J. E. Tighe, president of the Saint John local of the International Longshoreman's Association, was one of four speakers who addressed the Members of Parliament on Maritime problems.[36]

The farmers were only slightly behind labour in their support for Maritime Rights. They too had expected to play a greater role in the new society which was supposed to follow the war; instead they were confronted by the realities of rural depopulation and community disintegration.[37] They challenged the business groups with new or intensified, political, occupational and economic organization. But their problems were in part those of the region. The new freight rates hit them, both as producers and consumers. Some were also angered by federal policies which seemed not only to encourage new immigrants to by-pass their region but also to promote westward migration at their expense. As much as they might resent the growth of industrial towns and their own relative loss in status, the farmers were conscious of their dependence on these towns for their markets. Even those who sold their apples or potatoes in Great Britain or the West Indies usually earned a significant proportion of their income in local markets — an important hedge against the sometimes widely fluctuating international prices.[38]

For a brief period the farmers' regional concern was obscured by their participation in what they believed was a national "class" movement. But their organizations, such as the Canadian Council of Agriculture, were dominated by the Prairies. Manitobans, T. A. Crerar and George Chipman, also sought to direct the movement in the Maritimes through the *United Farmers' Guide*. The *Guide*, theoretically the organ of the New Brunswick and Nova Scotia United Farmers Associations, was in fact a subsidiary of the *Grain Growers' Guide*.[39] The two regionalisms were soon in conflict. Western organizers tried in vain to get unequivocal statements against the tariff from the United Farmers of Nova Scotia and were cool to suggestions that "necessary" protection for local industries should be retained.[40] At the same time they offered no support for the Maritime positions on such issues as the Intercolonial, freight rates and subsidies. Most Maritime farmers realized they could not achieve their regional goals through a movement which was, in federal politics at least, "an agrarian and sectional bloc from the continental West, the representation of the monolithic wheat economy.[41] In 1921 support for the western-affiliated United Farmers Associations rapidly dwindled. By mid-summer "a majority" in the Maritime Co-operative Companies was reported anxious to dispose of the *United Farmers Guide* in which they had initially invested but were unable to control.[42]

The agricultural interests of Prince Edward Island had been involved in the Maritime Rights movement from the outset. At the Maritime Board of Trade meeting in 1919 they were happy to associate with the broader issues of the movement their own special problems. These were two: the need for a second car ferry and the completion of the widening of their narrow gauge railways to permit a more rapid, reliable and cheaper delivery of their products to mainland markets.[43] In 1921 the Mainland farmers met in conference with representatives of manufacturing, merchant and shipping groups to launch a delegation to Ottawa to demand the return of the Intercolonial to independent management.[44] Thereafter, farm leaders assumed an increasingly important role in the Maritime Rights agitation. In 1923, for example, A. E. McMahon, president of the United Fruit Companies and a former vice-president of the United Farmers of Nova Scotia, became president of the Maritime Board of Trade, and, a year later, of the Maritime Development Association. One of the primary purposes of the latter organization was the rehabilitation of the rural areas through immigration and colonization.[45]

419

The fishermen's contribution to the Maritime Rights movement was largely restricted to the intensification of the discontent which underlay it. Their aspirations had been relatively moderate. The victims of a declining salt fish trade with the West Indies, they hoped to restore their industry through the expansion of their sales of fresh fish in Central Canada and New England. The former had been encouraged by a federal subsidy of one third of the express rate to Montreal on less than carload lots, the latter by a *modus vivendi* with the United States which had permitted them to land and sell their catches directly at American ports.[46] In 1919, the federal subsidies on fresh fish were terminated just as the trade was hit by the higher freight rates.[47] Needless to say, the fish merchants passed on their losses to the largely unorganized fishermen. Meanwhile, the door to the New England market was slammed shut by the American cancellation of the *modus vivendi* and the introduction of the Fordney tariff.

In the election of 1921, some fishermen seem to have accepted the Liberal promises of reciprocity to restore the American markets.[48] When this failed to materialize, their desperate plight led many (for example, the Yarmouth halibut fleet) to pack up and move to the United States.[49] Those who remained formed one group in Maritime society which seemed genuinely prepared to contemplate secession in their frantic search for markets. It was surely no coincidence that both Howard Corning, who proposed the famous secession resolution of 1923, and the lawyer Robert Blauveldt, self-proclaimed secessionist and Maritime Rights publicist[50] were both residents of Yarmouth county.

The role of professional classes in the Maritime Rights movement was prominent, but their motivation ambiguous. It is often difficult to discern whether lawyers, doctors, clergymen, academics and journalists were speaking for themselves or for the other groups in society by whom they were directly or indirectly employed. Certainly they played an important function in articulating and rationalizing the aspirations of the other groups. This role was explicit in some cases. The Nova Scotia government retained H. F. Munro of Dalhousie University to aid in the preparation of its submission to the Duncan Commission. The boards of trade hired freight rate experts, professional organizers and lawyers to prepare, publicize and help present their cases before the federal government and its various commissions. Significant also was the relationship between Maritime Rights journalists and the interests who paid their salaries, or patronized their newspapers through advertising and subscriptions. The lumberman-industrialist, Angus MacLean, for example, was reportedly "the principal owner" of the Saint John *Telegraph Journal*.[51] That paper in 1925 promoted the cross-country speaking-tours of president J. D. McKenna and editor A. B. Belding as part of its campaign for Maritime Rights. Similarly C. W. Lunn, who was credited with the initial popularization of the defence of the Intercolonial as guaranteed under the "compact of confederation," aspired to a labour readership and was even hired for a brief period to write for the *Eastern Federationist*.[52] More tenuous but still significant was the relationship between clergymen and the congregations which they represented. It is clear, for example, that the priests who protested the Duncan Commission's failure to help the fishermen were acting as agents for the fishermen in their parishes. Their intervention resulted in the Royal Commission investigation of the fisheries in 1928.[53]

In articulating the progressive reform ideology, which provided an important element in the developing Maritime regionalism, the professionals' motivation was also ambiguous. As various American scholars have pointed out, "progressivism" with its optimism, social criticism and focus on government as an agent of reform might be inspired by many and mixed motives.[54] To farmers, labour and their representatives, "progressivism" could be the desire to improve the lot of the weak and exploited, namely themselves. On the part of the business-oriented it might be concern for efficiency, the replacement of old-fashioned party structures, and the development of a more dynamic role by government which might more effectively serve the interests of the entrepreneur. To the professionals, besides any humanitarian concern, "progressivism" might mean an improved status or an expansion of their role in society in social work, health services or the government bureaucracy.

In the Maritimes, the clergy and academics were most prominent in articulating the various strains of an amorphous progressive ideology. The clergy, imbued with the social gospel, promoted a variety of reforms ranging from prohibition to widows' pensions and occasionally engaged in wholesale attacks on the capitalist system.[55] Academics used a more secular terminology but they too championed a wide range of reforms for the welfare of the community. Dr. F. H. Sexton hailed Nova Scotia's programme of technical education — he happened to be its superintendent — as a valuable means of "social service" in improving the lot of the miners and industrial workers.[56] That it was also a service for local industry went without saying. Dr. Melville Cummings, of the Truro Agricultural College and Rev. Hugh MacPherson of Saint Francis Xavier University displayed a similar zeal for agricultural education and farmers' co-operatives as the means of rural regeneration. President George B. Cutten of Acadia University, having failed to persuade governments to undertake the hydro-electric development of the Bay of Fundy, organized the Cape Split Development Company in an attempt to interest private capital in the scheme.[57]

All these progressive proposals placed strong pressure upon provincial governments to inaugurate or expand programmes for which revenue was not readily available. This fact led progressive elements into an ephemeral campaign for Maritime union, which was expected to provide a more efficient use of available resources[58]; and into a more substantive campaign for Maritime unity, one object of which was to wrest from the Federal Government a "fair" share of Dominion revenues.

Increased federal subsidies were sought, for example, by professionals concerned about the declining quality of instruction in the schools as higher salaries drew experienced teachers westward. But, since fiscal need had never been accepted as a justification for higher subsidies, Maritime governments developed the claim that they were entitled to monetary compensation for grants of land from the public domain — grants such as had been given to Ontario, Manitoba and Quebec in the boundary settlements of 1912. They also demanded subsidies in lieu of the increasingly lucrative "school lands" funds held in trust by the federal government for the Prairie Provinces. The Maritime Educational Convention at Moncton in 1918 and a Catholic educational conference at Antigonish a year later both discussed the subsidy claims as a matter vital to educational reform.[59] In the latter year the Conservative Halifax *Herald* enthusiastically endorsed a Liberal resolution which outlined the Maritime claims in the Nova Scotian Legislature. The "serious material injustice" inflicted upon the Maritimes through "the unfair distribution which has been made of federal assets by successive governments" had, according to the *Herald*, starved local government services or supplied them" in such a niggardly manner that progress is almost impossible." The *Herald* advocated the launching of "a concerted movement and (sic) properly directed activity. *We suggest that a maritime popular league should be forthwith organized, with provincial and county and town and village branches in all parts of the Maritime provinces, until the whole country has been enlightened, aroused and arrayed in a support of the resolution unanimously adopted by the Nova Scotia legislature."* Although as their problems increased, Maritimers sought more fundamental solutions, the subsidy claims remained one of the basic components of the campaign for Maritime rights.

422

The Maritime Rights agitation which had emerged by 1919 was a regional protest movement which saw all classes united in their demands upon the rest of the country. This did not mean that different classes did not have distinct aspirations of their own; on the contrary, they were probably more conscious of them in 1919 than in any other period before or since. Each held a dream of progressive development in which its own collective interests were directly involved: for the manufacturers, their growth as the major industrial suppliers of the country; for the urban merchants, the final attainment of their communities' status as the entrepots of Canada's trade; for labour and farmers, the emergence of a new more democratic society in which they would break the economic and political dominance of the business classes; for the fishermen, the chance to rehabilitate their industry through the new fresh fish trade; and for the professionals, the elevation of Maritime society through education. But none of these aspirations was capable of realization with the continued decline of the economic and political status of the Maritimes in the Dominion. Just as electricity might channel the usually conflicting molecular energies of an iron bar to produce a magnetic force, so the federal government's adverse policies served to re-align the various "classes" in the Maritimes to produce a powerful social force — regionalism. This force, dressed up in a variety of complex rationalizations, became the Maritime Rights movement of the 1920's.

Notes

1. See J. M. Beck, *The Government of Nova Scotia* (Toronto, 1957), pp. 338–40; W. R. Graham, *Arthur Meighen Vol. II; And Fortune Fled* (Toronto, 1963), ch. 11; H.B.Neatby, *William Lyon Mackenzie King: 1924–1932; The Lonely Heights* (Toronto, 1963), pp. 67 and 220–24; K. A. MacKirdy, "Regionalism: Canada and Australia" (Ph.D. thesis, University of Toronto, 1959), pp. 245–50; and G. A. Rawlyk, "The Maritimes and the Canadian Community" in M. Wade, ed., *Regionalism in the Canadian Community, 1867–1967* (Toronto, 1969) pp. 113–5. The only previous study which focused directly on Maritime Rights was Michael Hatfield, "J. B. Baxter and the Maritime Rights Movement" (B.A. honours essay, Mount Allison University, 1969).

2. E. R. Forbes, "The Maritime Rights Movement, 1919–1927: A Study in Canadian Regionalism," (Ph.D. thesis, Queens University, 1975).

3. G. A. Rawlyk "The Farmer-Labour Movement and the Failure of Socialism in Nova Scotia," Laurier LaPierre *et al* eds., *Essays on the Left* (Toronto, 1971), pp. 37–8.

4. P. J. Veniot to W. L. M. King, 27 February 1923, W. L. M. King Papers, Public Archives of Canada (hereafter PAC).

5. See Canada, *Sessional Papers* (1910), No. 100; Halifax *Wesleyan*, 12 May 1909; Saint John *Standard*, 30 October 1913; W. Eggleston and C. T. Kraft, *Dominion Provincial Subsidies and Grants* (Ottawa, 1939) pp. 188–9; and the "Presentation to His Royal Highness in Council of the claims of the Provinces of New Brunswick, Nova Scotia and Prince Edward Island, for Compensation in Respect of the Public Lands of Canada, transferred to Certain Provinces of Canada or held in trust for their Benefit, January 29, 1913," R. L. Borden Papers, p. 5249, PAC.

6. R. A. C. Henry and Associates, *Railway Freight Rates in Canada* (Ottawa, 1939), pp. 266 and 268 and Transcripts of the hearings of the Royal Commission on Maritime Claims, pp. 462–5, Atlantic Provinces Transportation Commission (hereafter APTC).

7. See S. A. Saunders *The Economic History of the Maritime Provinces* (Ottawa, 1939), p. 27.

8. *Canada Year Book* (1922–3), pp. 220, 415–6.

9. Halifax *Morning Chronicle,* 17 August 1906 and Saint John *Standard,* 25 March 1916.

10. Judgement of the Board of Railway Commissioners, 15 March 1919, R. L. Borden Papers, pp. 131069–9, PAC; Canada, Debates (1917), pp. 787, 4339–77.

11. Transcript of hearings of the Board of Railway Commissioners, 1920, p. 11703, PAC.

12. Calculated from percentages in B.R.C. transcripts 1926, p. 6602, and from "standard mileage rates" in R. A. C. Henry, *op cit.*

13. Sackville, *The Busy East of Canada,* September, 1919.

14. "Report of Meeting with the Prime Minister and the members of the Government, Delegation from the Maritime Province," 1 June 1921, R. B. Bennett Papers, p. 10142, P.A.C. and F. C. Cornell to H. D. Cartwright, 12 October 1925, Maritime Provinces Freight Rate Commission Papers, APTC.

15. E. M. Macdonald to Mackenzie King, 8 December 1922, W. L. M. King Papers, PAC.

16. F. C. Cornell "Memorandum re the Transportation Problems and Freight Rate Structure of the Province of Nova Scotia," 1926, p. 10 and Transcripts, B.R.C., 1926, pp. 6765–7, PAC.

17. *Maritime Merchant,* 16 September 1920, p. 104.

18. Transcripts, Royal Commission on Maritime Claims, p. 2173, APTC.

19. "Report of the Royal Commission on Transportation . . . 1903," Canada, *Sessional Papers* (1906), No. 19a; Canada, *Debates* (1922), pp. 708–10.

20. Halifax *Herald,* 18 September 1920.

21. Minutes of the Council of the Saint John Board of Trade, 13 July 1922, New Brunswick Museum.

22. Hector McInnes to Arthur Meighen, November 1923, Arthur Meighen Papers, p. 051956, PAC.

23. A. MacLean to W. L. M. King, 25 April 1922 and 8 October 1924, W. L. M. King Papers, PAC.

24. J. C. Webster to Arthur Meighen, 26 September 1925, and R. O'Leary to Meighen, 3 September 1925, Arthur Meighen Papers, PAC.

25. *The Fifth Annual Report on Labour Organization in Canada 1916* (Ottawa, 1917) pp. 206–7 and the *Tenth Annual Report on Labour Organization in Canada 1920* (Ottawa, 1921), p. 279.

26. For examples of their optimistic rhetoric see the Sydney *Canadian Labour Leader,* 8 February 1918; the new Glasgow *Eastern Federationist,* 19, 26 April 1919; and the Moncton *Union Worker,* February, 1920.

27. *The Labour Gazette,* January 1921, p. 117.

28. *Eastern Federationist,* 8 March 1919.

29. *Ibid.,* 7 June 1919.

30. The Halifax *Citizen,* 21 May and 10 September 1920.

31. "Being an address by Mr. Geo. W. Yates, Assistant Deputy Minister of Railways, Before the History and Political Science Club of Western Ontario, Feb. 16, 1923", Arthur Meighen Papers, pp. 157485–9, PAC.

32. *The Busy East,* June and July 1923.

33. F. B. McCurdy to Robert Borden, 21 December 1921, Robert Meighen Papers, PAC.

34. H. L. Stewart to M. W. L. King, 9 December 1923, W. L. M. King Papers, PAC.
35. "Minutes of the Maritime Club of Halifax," 11 February 1924, H. S. Congdon Papers (courtesy of Mr. H. H. Congdon, Huntsville, Ontario).
36. Saint John *Telegraph Journal*, 27 February 1925.
37. See A. A. Mackenzie, "The Rise and Fall of the Farmer-Labour Party in Nova Scotia" (M.A. thesis, Dalhousie University, 1969), and L. A. Wood, *A History of Farmer Movements in Canada* (Toronto, 1924).
38. *Proceedings of the Select Special Committee of the House of Commons to inquire into Agricultural Conditions* (Ottawa, 1924), p. 475.
39. Three of the five members of the directorate were Manitobans. C. F. Chipman to "The Editor" *Maritime Farmer*, 13 March 1920, T. A. Crerar Papers, The Douglas Library, Queens University.
40. J. M. Pratt to T. A. Crerar, 9 November 1920, and G. G. Archibald to T. A. Crerar, 4 October 1920, *ibid*.
41. W. L. Morton, *The Progressive Party in Canada* (Toronto, 1950), p. 129.
42. S. H. Hagerman to G. F. Chipman, 18 June 1921, T. A. Crerar Papers, Douglas Library, Queens University.
43. *The Busy East*, September 1919. See also M. K. Cullen. "The Transportation Issue, 1873–1973" in F. W. P. Bolger, ed., *Canada's Smallest Province: a History of Prince Edward Island* (Charlottetown, 1973), pp. 255–7.
44. *Ibid.*, May 1921.
45. Charlottetown *Evening Patriot*, 23 January 1925.
46. *Report of the Royal Commission Investigating the Fisheries of the Maritime Provinces and the Magdalen Islands* (Ottawa, 1928), pp. 32, 61–5.
47. "Fifty-third Annual Report of the Fisheries Branch . . . 1919," *Sessional Papers* (1919), No. 44, p. 11.
48. G. B. Kenny reported to Hector MacInnes after a trip along the Eastern Shore that the Liberal candidates had "actually got many people to believe that real free trade with the U.S., is in sight." 21 November 1921, Hector MacInnes Papers, (courtesy of Donald MacInnes, Halifax, N.S.).
49. Transcripts of the hearings of the Royal Commission Investigating the Fisheries . . . 1928, p. 3476, APTC.
50. R. Blauveldt to H. S. Congdon, 30 September 1924, H. S. Congdon Papers.
51. J. H. McGaffigan to Arthur Meighen, 28 February 1924, Arthur Meighen Papers, PAC.
52. See Halifax *Morning Chronicle*, 16 November 1921; C. W. Lunn to H. S. Congdon, 13 April 1929, H. S. Congdon Papers.
53. Transcripts, Royal Commission to investigate the Fisheries . . . 1927, p. 6.
54. See for example R. H. Wiebe, *The Search For Order*, 1877–1920 (New York, 1967); Gabriel Kolko, *The Triumph of Conservatism* (New York, 1963) and D. W. Noble, *The Progressive Mind 1890–1917* (Chicago, 1970).
55. See E. R. Forbes "Prohibition and the Social Gospel in Nova Scotia," *Acadiensis* Vol. 1, No. 1 (Autumn 1971), pp. 15–19 and his review of Richard Allen, *The Social Passion* in *Acadiensis* Vol. II No. 1 (Autumn, 1972), p. 98.
56. Halifax, *Daily Echo*, 24 May 1913.
57. *Industrial Canada*, August 1918.
58. See J. M. Beck, *The History of Maritime Union: A Study in Frustration*, pp. 31–44.
59. O. T. Daniels, *The Claims of the Maritime Provinces for Federal Subsidies in Lieu of Western Lands* (Halifax, 1918) and *Proceedings of the Second Annual Educational Conference, Antigonish*, (1919).

Topic Eleven

Depression Era

In the 1930s, Canadians faced the worst depression in their history. It hit Canada very severely largely on account of the nation's reliance on foreign trade in what had become a nationalistic and protectionist era. Hardest hit were primary commodities. Wheat prices, for example, fell from $2.00 a bushel in the late 1920s to 34¢ a bushel in 1932. The resulting economic decline affected secondary and service industries. Between 1929 and 1933 Canada's gross national expenditure declined by 29%. Unemployment reached an all-time high of 20% across the country and as high as 35% in some regions. Thousands endured the humiliation of going on relief — a last, desperate solution to their critical situation.

At first Canadians expected the Depression to be a temporary phenomenon that would end as quickly as it began. But it did not. The Conservatives had come to power in 1930, and it remained for R.B. Bennett, the prime minister, to find a solution. At first, he tried to create "work and wages" for the unemployed through higher tariffs, unemployment relief and public works. Yet the jobless rate kept increasing. Frustrated and fearful of social upheaval, Bennett became less sympathetic to the unemployed, seeing them as an unnecessary drain on the state. James Struthers explains the transition in Bennett's attitude to the Depression and to federal government assistance to the unemployed, in "Two Depressions: Canadian Governments and the Unemployed in the Thirties and Eighties."

In the 1935 federal election, the Liberals defeated the Conservatives. William Lyon Mackenzie King, in office, proved slow to take action to deal with the Depression. He did so only when forced by public opinion and by powerful members of his cabinet. When he did act, he did so more out of a desire for "national unity" than out of a conviction for the radical policies that his government adopted. In "William Lyon Mackenzie King: The Conciliator in Politics," H.B. Neatby shows the gradual shift in the Liberal Party's economic position to the point where by 1940, the Liberals had introduced Keynesian economic policies to deal with the Depression.

To many Canadians, the two traditional parties, the Liberals and the Conservatives, appeared incapable of dealing with the unprecedented situation. They wanted new and daring action — one out of every five Canadians would vote for a new third party in the federal election of 1935. Led by the charismatic leader, William Aberhart, Social Credit offered a "solution" to the Depression, and swept the province of Alberta both federally and provincially in 1935. Harold Schultz explains the success of Social Credit in his "Portrait of a Premier: William Aberhart."

Students interested in the Great Depression in Canada should begin with *The Dirty Thirties: Canadians in the Great Depression*, edited by M. Horn (Toronto: Copp Clark, 1972), a collection of primary and secondary sources on the social and political repercussions of the Depression, and H.B. Neatby's *The Politics of Chaos: Canada in The Thirties* which contains biographical sketches of the political leaders. Neatby has also written the second, and third volumes of the official biography of Mackenzie King which covers the Depression years: *The Lonely Heights: 1924–1932* (Toronto: University of Toronto Press, 1963) and *The Prism of Unity* (Toronto: University of Toronto Press, 1976). James Struthers' work on unemployment relief in the Thirties is presented in greater detail in, *No Fault of Their Own: Unemployment and the Canadian Welfare State 1914–1941* (Toronto: University of Toronto Press, 1983). Also useful is Dennis Guest, *The Emergence of Social Security in Canada* (Vancouver: University of British Columbia Press, 1980).

There are a number of excellent studies of third parties during the Depression era. For the CCF see Walter Young's *The Anatomy of a Party: The National CCF* (Toronto: University of Toronto Press, 1969), and Kenneth McNaught's *A Prophet in Politics* (Toronto: University of Toronto Press, 1959), the only scholarly study of the party's first leader. Social Credit has been the subject of a series published in the 1950s by the University of Toronto Press. Students should examine in particular John Irving's *The Social Credit Movement in Alberta* (1959), and C.B. Macpherson's *Democracy in Alberta: Social Credit and the Party System* (1953). Also of interest is John Barr's popularly-written *The Dynasty: The Rise and Fall of Social Credit in Alberta* (Toronto: McClelland and Stewart, 1974).

Two Depressions: Canadian Governments and the Unemployed in the Thirties and the Eighties*

JAMES STRUTHERS

Like the 1930s, the 1980s increasingly appear destined to become the second decade in this century during which Canada's unemployment rate remains at double digit levels. Among the many parallels between the 30s and the 80s, none is more disturbing or paradoxical than the government response to the plight of the jobless. Despite rising unemployment throughout the late 1970s and early 1980s, unemployment insurance benefits and welfare assistance in Canada have become increasingly more difficult to get. In 1977, unemployment insurance was dramatically reformed to stiffen eligibility requirements and to reduce benefit levels. A further major tightening of the system is currently under consideration by the new Mulroney government. At the same time a growing number of provincial governments have severely reduced social assistance payments to single employables on welfare.[1]

Why are governments at all levels reducing support to the jobless precisely when their need has reached critical proportions? Politicians and economists have justified such cutbacks on the grounds that those out of work, in the words of one former prime minister, have become "too fussy about what jobs they'll take." As an Economic Council of Canada study put it, the very existence of unemployment insurance has "increase[d] the incentive to be unemployed or remain unemployed".[2]

But are unemployment insurance and welfare to blame for our enduringly high levels of joblessness? Are the unemployed themselves the authors of their plight? One way of finding an answer and gaining a perspective on the seriousness of "insurance-induced" unemployment[3] is to examine how another prime minister dealt with unemployment during our last great economic crisis — the Depression of the 1930s. That was the decade which produced our original unemployment insurance programme. It was also the decade in which many of the current contradictions surrounding unemployment policy in a market society first became apparent.

We usually think the Depression produced a straightforward, clearcut unemployment problem. Surely if ever there was a time Canadians could agree that the unemployed were out of work through no fault of their own it was in 1933 when the jobless rate reached the record level of almost 30%.[4] Yet, as will be shown later, such was not the case. To understand why first

427

*From the *Journal of Canadian Studies*, 14 (1) (Spring 1979): 70–80. Revised 1985. Reprinted by permission.

requires an understanding of what the Depression meant in social as well as economic terms.

Between 1926 and 1929 the Canadian economy and the Canadian labour force expanded at a phenomenal rate. During these three years 537,000 people entered the work force for the first time, expanding it by twenty-five percent.[5] Most of this growth occurred within cities, which absorbed seventy-seven percent of Canada's population increase during the 1920s. While agricultural income between 1926 and 1929 remained about the same, manufacturing, mining and construction income grew by 30%, 35% and 45% respectively.[6] In short, the creation of high-paying jobs, particularly in the durable goods industries, attracted hundreds of thousands of new workers into Canada's cities during the second half of the 1920s.

Most came from the countryside or abroad. Another large proportion were women.[7] For all of them, the entry into urban, wage-paying occupations was a form of social mobility, especially since the five years before 1926 were characterized by high unemployment.[8] Farm labourers got factory jobs for the first time; women moved out of the household into wage-paying occupations, and hundreds of thousands of immigrants rejected the lure of the "last, best West" for the more lucrative attractions of city living.

By 1931 their hopes had been shattered. Between 1929 and that year, the volume of employment contracted by exactly twenty-five percent and by 1933 it had shrunk by thirty-two percent, while national income as a whole was forty percent below 1929 levels.[9] In large part, the first to be thrown out of work by this collapse were those with the most tenuous attachment to the labour market, that is, those who got their jobs after 1926. Their numbers swelled rapidly. By January 1933, 718,000 were without work[10] and all governments, as well as the unemployed themselves, were faced with an agonizing moral dilemma. Did those who had entered the labour force for the first time in the late twenties have the right to work?

Almost 300,000 said no. They simply disappeared from the work force by 1933, either leaving the country, going back to housework or returning as unpaid labourers to their family farms.[11] But another 300,000 disagreed. That was the approximate number of individuals and heads of families who were collecting direct relief in the nation's cities by May 1933, pending a return of work.[12] "Under past conditions," the Dominion Bureau of Statistics pointed out a year later, "this surplus population would have emigrated on the depression; under a system of relief they remained."[13] And the question they raised for the employers who had lured them there in the first place, as well as for the governments who were responsible for their care, was simply this: how long should the state underwrite their hopes for social mobility by providing either work or relief in the cities until prosperity returned?

The first answer was provided by Mackenzie King. Faced with fighting an election during the first year of the crisis, he quickly discovered that one of the principal issues of the campaign was whether the federal government should provide unemployment relief for the jobless. King said no. Reasoning that "the men who are working are not going to worry particularly over some of those who are not,"[14] he refused either to call a conference on unemployment or to provide a federal contribution to municipal relief efforts as Ottawa had done during the last depression of 1920–22.

His opponent adopted the opposite position. R.B. Bennett promised that if elected he would "end unemployment" by providing jobs" for all who can and will work." "Someone is responsible for unemployment," Bennett argued, "not individuals, but governments." If given power, he would "abolish the dole" and provide "work and wages" for the unemployed.[15] An electorate uneasy over the growing numbers of idle men naturally preferred this more positive approach and rewarded Bennett with office in 1930. However, as King's defeated labour minister pointed out, they also gave him "a mandate to look after employment and unemployment, and no matter what the written word of the Constitution may be, the Canadian people have now placed this matter in the lap of the Federal Government."[16]

At first, Bennett did not shy away from this burden. Stiff hikes in the tariff, he was convinced, would soon give work in protected industries to all who needed it. In the meantime, to tide the jobless over the upcoming winter until these changes had had a chance to take effect, Bennett also provided $20,000,000 for unemployment relief — ten times more than Ottawa spent on this problem during the entire decade of the twenties. True to his pledge of giving work, not doles to the unemployed, Bennett also set aside $16,000,000 of this grant for support to municipal public works in order to provide jobs. Only $4,000,000 was to go for direct relief.

Though the amount was unprecedented, the method of distribution was not. The care of the unemployed was still "primarily a provincial and municipal responsibility," the 1930 relief act pointed out, Bennett's government was not assuming any "new constitutional obligations."[17] It was simply helping the provinces and cities tide the unemployed over the winter. These governments would administer the grant, contribute their own equal share, and decide how the money should be spent. Ottawa's help was financial only.

The help was also temporary, for the act expired at the end of March 1931 and was not renewed. Yet the number of jobless, contrary to expectations, did not decline over the summer months. By July 1931, usually one of the busiest times of the year, 18% of the work force was still unemployed.[18] Most worrisome among this group were thousands of seasonal labourers or "bunkhouse men," who usually resided in the cities over the slack winter months and departed for work on the nation's farms, railways and lumber camps in the spring. In 1931 they did not move out for there was nowhere for them to go. Yet since they were not municipal residents, the cities denied they had a claim for relief. As one social worker put it, "any humane treatment of these men . . . [would] make it impossible to eliminate the number."[19]

As a result, thousands began "riding the rods" looking for work or at least a meal and shelter for the night. Their "constantly increasing" num-

129

bers soon appeared to represent a "menace to . . . peace and . . . safety" in the eyes of Bennett's labour minister, Gideon Robertson, especially since few seemed "very anxious to obtain work" and "communist agitators and advocates [were] utilizing this method of travel to spread their propaganda." Consequently, in July he recommended that the first priority of any new relief legislation should be the "removal of thousands of transients from urban centres." They should be placed in relief camps constructed along the route of the proposed Trans-Canada highway and "put to work promptly under supervision equivalent to semi-military control." If they refused to go they would "forfeit their right to State Assistance."[20] For these men, at least, there could be no right to urban relief.

The new relief act introduced in late July incorporated Robertson's suggestions. To get the men out of the cities, Bennett provided financial support to provincial highway programmes and to ensure they would go, he pointed out that "where there is work there will be pay and . . . if an individual is capable of work and will not work, there will be no benefits."[21] More ominously, the 1931 relief act also gave the federal government sweeping powers under the "peace, order and good government" clause of the constitution to fine or imprison anyone disobeying orders or regulations issued under its terms.[22] It was the first sign that coercion might be necessary to provide work for all who were capable of doing it.

Nor was Bennett even sure, by 1931, that he could live up to that pledge. Instead, he would only promise that "no-one will be asked to accept direct relief for whom suitable work can be procured."[23] What constituted "suitable" work was unstated.

Once Britain went off the gold standard on September 21, even this limited commitment was abandoned. Since the value of the Canadian dollar was pegged to British sterling, the initial effect of this decision was to depreciate it in terms of American currency, thus raising the cost of paying back debts owed to U.S. creditors. Terrified that the nation's credit was now in peril, Bennett determined upon a policy of "most rigid economy" for his administration.[24] Before the British move, he had talked in terms of a $50,000,000 relief programme for the winter of 1931–32. Instead, he spent only $28,000,000. It was not enough to provide most of the unemployed with more than two week's work or a meagre $68 in earnings over that year.[25]

When the 1931 act expired in the spring, Bennett abandoned public works altogether. The new relief act, introduced in April, for the first time provided funds for unemployment relief only. Stung by business criticism that his relief programme was endangering the nation's credit and "holding back normal . . . development,"[26] and perplexed by the failure of his tariff hikes to create jobs, Bennett gave up his attempt to provide work for the unemployed. It was the ultimate irony. Having won office by promising to "abolish the dole," he was now forced to rely on it as the sole remaining unemployment policy of his administration.

However, more than financial reasons lay behind this decision. Once it became clear that the unemployment problem was more permanent than most had thought, attitudes towards it and towards the unemployed began to change. Bennett, for example, could accept the fact that most of the unemployed had lost their jobs through no fault of their own. What he could not understand was why so many had to depend upon the government to survive. "The people are not bearing their share of the load," he complained in October 1931. "Half a century ago people would work their way out of their difficulties rather than look to a government to take care of them. The fibre of some of our people has grown softer and they are not willing to turn in and save themselves."[27]

One reason, perhaps, was the existence of relief work itself. The wages were low, but not humiliating, and useful labour was performed in return. By working on such projects, men could still feel they had "earned" their living. As one M.P. noted, "many men who would never ask for direct relief will, without any feelings of humiliation, take a quota of relief work."[28] By abandoning such work projects, the government could reduce its responsibilities to only the genuinely needy. Direct relief, as one relief administrator pointed out years later,

was a disgrace. Men would say that never in the history of their family—and they'd usually mention something about the British Empire Loyalists or coming West with the first C.P.R. trains—never had they had to go on relief . . . I've seen tears in men's eyes, as though they were signing away their manhood, their right to be a husband and sit at the head of the table and carve the roast. It was a very emotional time, that first time when a man came in and went up to the counter.[29]

It was meant to be, for direct relief in most Canadian cities — true to the poor law tradition of "less eligibility" — was related not to need, but to the lowest wages for unskilled labour in the surrounding area. The stigma and humiliation of a degrading level of existence were the traditional tactics used for making it less appealing than the most brutal and unremunerative form of manual work. Now these tactics would be applied to all the unemployed in an effort to ensure that any kind of work in any part of the country would remain preferable to the "dole."

To underline this point, Bennett made two important modifications to his 1932 relief act. The first was to provide five dollars a month for unemployed men willing to work on farms in the four western provinces over the upcoming winter. The second was to establish a relief settlement programme. It provided $600 ($200 in grants and $400 in loans) to any unemployed urban family on relief with previous agricultural experience that was willing to resettle on one of the nation's 33,000 abandoned farms. It was strictly "a relief measure and not . . . a colonization scheme," Bennett's new labour minister, W.A. Gordon, pointed out, whose object was to "get . . . people back on the land . . . where they can . . . keep themselves . . . The question of selling . . . their surplus produce will have to come later on." Moreover, with a bushel of wheat going for the lowest price in recorded history, even Gordon was "at a loss to know whether to-day a man should be on a farm or in a city . . . no matter where [he] may be . . . he is in a very bad way."[30] Nevertheless, the programme carried a clear implication. Even the most miserable form of rural subsistence should be preferable to urban relief.

More tangible evidence of this hardening attitude towards the unemployed came that autumn. Over the summer, Bennett had appointed Charlotte Whitton, head of the Canadian Council on Child and Family Welfare, to investigate the soaring numbers dependent upon the dole in western Canada. Her October report was apocalyptic. The West, Whitton wrote, was not merely impoverished, it was becoming "pauperized." The widespread provision of direct relief had been taken up, not by the "emergency" unemployed but by the "permanently" jobless — that is, the hundreds of thousands of casual, unskilled farm labourers who were normally without work during winter months. As a result, it had succeeded only in "raising . . . the standard of employment and living of the great volume of the underemployed," and the whole problem was drifting towards "the inauguration of a system of permanent poor relief in the Dominion of Canada."[31]

432

Whitton went to great lengths to document how this was taking place. Farmers and their sons, for example, had been employed on relief projects in great numbers "when there was no actual question of the need of food, fuel, clothing or shelter for themselves and . . . when ordinarily the winter was a period of idleness." In southern Alberta, the large-scale provision of direct relief had "arrested . . . any natural disintegration" of dying mining communities and "served to 'suspend' them on direct relief." The same argument applied to "dead communities" in the northern and rural fringes of all provinces which were composed of "small packets of people, generally those with the least initiative and thrift" who had been "swept back or left behind as settlements moved elsewhere."

Unemployed women fell into the same category. Theirs was "not solely nor essentially an unemployment problem." Rather, it was a "social problem" arising from desertion, death, or illegitimacy and, as such, did "not form a justifiable charge on the [relief] legislation." Direct relief had also raised the standard of living of unemployed single men and immigrant families. Too many of the former who could have stayed on farms during the winter were "going to the cities where 'they could get two good meals and a bed a day on relief' and 'have a real rest for the winter.' " As for immigrants, the support they received from the dole was in many cases higher than what they could get while working. Whitton argued it was "neither just nor efficient to provide supplies on a scale neither attained nor desired by these people from their own resources or efforts." If the present system of subsidizing the existence of the marginally employed continued, she warned, "it becomes only a matter of time until the uninterrupted increase in all forms of social dependency becomes so great a burden on public funds that the whole substructure of public finance is undermined."[32] As a solution, she recommended the total reorganization of the relief system, under strict federal "leadership" (and employing the expertise of the social work profession) so that the casually unemployed could be taken off the dole before they became "permanently dependent at a scale of living which they never had and never will be able to provide for themselves."[33]

Whitton's report — the only one Bennett ever commissioned on unemployment relief — could not have been more tailored to confirm his own fears that widespread abuse of the dole was the real reason behind its rapidly increasing costs. However, the result was not what she intended. Rather than demanding that its administration be turned over to the social work profession through more rigid conditional grant legislation, Bennett instead resolved to get his government out of relief altogether. If the provinces and municipalities were wasting federal money, the solution was not to press for stricter standards through legislation, but simply to give them less money to waste. In short, by emphasizing the abuse rather than the inadequacy of the direct relief, Whitton destroyed any chance that it might be reformed.

Only one of her recommendations was adopted. In October 1932, Ottawa began the takeover of direct administration of relief to single homeless men "so that discipline may be enforced."[34] The department of national defence launched a pilot relief camp scheme employing 2,000 men clearing air-fields along the proposed route of the Trans-Canada Airway. The cost of their care could not exceed $1.00 a day, Bennett told General Andrew McNaughton, the principal author of the scheme; therefore, the men themselves received the princely "allowance" of twenty cents for their daily labours.[35] From Ottawa's point of view, the experiment was a great success and a year later the camps were caring for 20,000 single men working across the country on a wide variety of projects demanding unskilled, menial work.

The relief camp scheme has usually been viewed as a strictly cynical attempt to get the most dangerous class of unemployed out of the cities and under military supervision so that unrest could be avoided. Certainly, this was one principal object of the plan. Without the camps, McNaughton argued, it was "only a question of time until we had to resort to arms to restore and maintain order."[36]

Just as important, however, was the camps' function as a "workhouse test." Before they were established, single homeless men, especially in the West, had been receiving relief through government-funded hostels and subsistence relief camps operated by the provinces. As a result, by 1932, federal officials fretted that a "dole mentality was creeping into the minds of the single unemployed" and that many had "acquired the mental attitude that such assistance from the State was their inherent right."[37] The "moral purpose" of the DND camps, according to McNaughton, was to cure this "state of mind diseased by the demoralizing effect of compulsory idleness' by subjecting the men to the influence of "steady work, wholesome food and congenial surroundings."[38] In short, it was an attempt to preserve the work ethic among Canada's bunkhouse men until jobs returned. As Bennett's labour minister pointed out, if their "usefulness" was to be maintained, it was "essential" to demand that "work . . . performed by those in receipt of relief from the State."[39]

Precisely because they were a "workhouse test" rather than a means of providing work, the wages had to be kept at the extremely low rate of twenty cents a day in order to "encourage" the men, in McNaughton's words, to "return to normal industry as soon as opportunity offers."[40] From the men's point of view, however, this was ridiculous. Only the fact that they had been cut off from relief in the cities in the first place had forced them into the camps and once there they were forced to "work . . . to get what they obtained from the B.C. Government for nothing" — that is, subsistence.[41] As one man put it in 1933, "you come in broke, work all winter and still you are broke. It looks like they want to keep us bums all our lives."[42] It was just this contradiction that produced the "On-to-Ottawa" trek two years later.

Although flawed in conception, the camps represented Bennett's only extension of federal responsibility for the unemployed before his "New Deal" reforms of 1935. The remainder of his unemployment policy proceeded in exactly the opposite direction — towards reducing Ottawa's link with the jobless. Again, one reason was the soaring cost of relief. By April 1933, over, 1,500,000 people were dependent upon the dole for survival and it was costing Bennett's government over $31,000,000 a year in direct grants for their care. In addition, Ottawa had been forced to loan another $38,000,000 to the four bankrupt western provinces to keep them solvent. By abandoning public works for direct relief Bennett had hoped to move towards a balanced budget. Instead, by 1933 between a quarter and a third of the work force was unemployed and the federal deficit had ballooned to almost $160,000,000.[43]

Federal officials were not convinced that need alone explained these soaring expenditures. "Sufficient emphasis was not being placed upon the responsibility of the individual to maintain himself," Bennett's labour minister told the provincial premiers at a 1933 conference. "Wherever a province relieves the municipality of a share of the cost [of direct relief] the barriers are to that extent let down" and the same argument applied to Ottawa's share of the dole. If it were expanded, as the provinces demanded, relief administration would be "without restraint." Instead, W.A. Gordon put forward a different solution. "The land offers the best prospect for maintenance and independence of those who cannot find employment in the cities." To ensure the western provincial governments would pass this message on to their unemployed, Ottawa demanded that their deficits be kept below $1,000,000 a year as a condition for further federal loans.[44] In this way, perhaps, they might encourage the jobless more directly to take advantage of the relief settlement and farm placement schemes, and thus "assist . . . in the restoration of the balance between [the] urban and rural population which is so necessary."[45]

If Whitton's 1932 reports were correct, it would be relief itself that was attracting casual labourers from the country into the cities, and thus adding to Ottawa's already staggering deficit. This trend had to be reversed. The provinces would have to be forced to push the unemployed back to the land where they could become "self-sustaining," even if that land was plagued by grasshoppers and drought. As Gordon warned the House in March 1933, only with the "gradual turn towards other vocations than those which have afforded a certain sense of security to our people in the past" could relief be phased out.[46]

C.C.F. critics put it differently. Gordon's real intention, in their view, was to create a Canadian "peasantry" that would "form a labour reserve to be called upon at a time when working conditions in the cities improve."[47] One thing at least was clear. By 1933, "Back to the Land" was the Bennett government's only long-range solution to the unemployment crisis. It was to be achieved by forcing the unemployed out of the cities.

There were two ways of implementing this strategy, one administrative, the other financial. As it had done with single men, Ottawa could simply take over the administration of direct relief itself for all the unemployed and in this way ensure that their support was kept low enough to make subsistence farming attractive. This was never seriously considered. Apart from its constitutional ambiguities, it would necessitate creating a vast federal relief structure — something Bennett was loath to do when he still believed the Depression was an emergency and that Ottawa's responsibility for the unemployed was only temporary.

435

More importantly, direct federal administration of the dole posed an enormous threat to the "less eligibility" principle upon which poor relief was based. As a Department of Labour memo on the subject pointed out, Canada was a "country of such widely varied conditions" that unemployment relief could not be administered "with any standardized methods across the Dominion." Instead, it had to be "met on the basis of need existing in each district" and for this reason municipal administration of the dole was best suited for "adopt[ing] different and varying means to cope with the situation."[48] Ottawa could not provide one standard of support for Gloucester, New Brunswick and another for Toronto. The municipalities could, and that was why they had to be held responsible for relief, even if they were financially unable to bear the burden. Local variations in relief scales were not an unfortunate by-product of this policy, they were the reason for it. To abandon this approach might court disaster.

Hence Bennett opted for a financial solution. If Ottawa cut off all support for relief, the provinces and municipalities would be so financially hard-pressed that they would have no alternative but to impose rigorous relief standards upon the unemployed and weed out all those who, as Whitton claimed, were using the dole to improve their standard of living. In short, "less eligibility" could be enforced by shifting the burden of depression entirely onto the shoulders of the provinces, the municipalities and ultimately, the unemployed themselves. As the deputy minister of labour put it at the height of the crisis in May 1933, "there was the utmost need of impressing upon the municipalities that relief must be curtailed and the fact brought home to the individual that responsibility for caring for himself and his dependents devolved *solely upon himself*."[49]

Paradoxically, unemployment insurance appeared as one of the best ways of implementing this strategy. With so many out of work, it would be politically impossible for Ottawa to disavow all responsibility for the unemployed, especially after Bennett's extravagant promises in 1930. But, with the relief camp scheme, a modest programme of public works and a system of unemployment insurance, Bennett's principal advisor, Rod Finlayson, pointed out in 1933, "the administration of direct relief could then be entirely decentralized and its responsibility relegated to the provinces." In this way, Bennett's administration could "escape the charge that it has accepted a policy of dole."[50]

Deputy finance minister W.C. Clark agreed. "If you segregated . . . unemployment relief from the insurance scheme," he advised Bennett on the eve of the 1933 dominion-provincial conference,

you will make it much easier for your provinces to give you the new constitutional powers for which you are asking. Today, they are naturally hesitant about accepting a share in the cost of unemployment relief when the size of that burden is entirely uncertain. If you merely say to them that you will take care of the unemployment insurance programme, but that they must not expect such an insurance programme to do everything . . . they will, I think, be prepared to accept the major responsibility which they now have for unemployment relief.[51]

In short, accepting national responsibility for unemployment insurance would provide the perfect cover for abandoning all responsibility for direct relief.

Moreover, such a scheme need not be expensive. Benefits would be related to previous contributions, not need, and "insurance principles" would provide an effective ceiling to ensure they would not get out of hand. More importantly, Ottawa would only have to finance a minor share of the burden. Its major cost would be paid for by employers and the workers themselves.

It was powerful logic and by early 1934 it had won Bennett over. At another dominion-provincial conference in January, Gordon told the premiers that all federal support for relief would be phased out in the spring. In its place, Ottawa would launch a programme of "useful" public works and relief would be "restored" to the municipalities. At the same time, Bennett gave Finlayson the green light to prepare a draft unemployment insurance scheme.[52]

Over the winter, with the help of two actuaries and a British government official, Finlayson drafted the legislation, based largely upon the scheme in force in Great Britain. It was a highly conservative piece of work designed to preserve the "less eligibility" principle. Since the "heaviest incidence of unemployment," labour department officials noted, was among "manual and unskilled workers," they were largely left out of the plan by exempting most seasonal workers from contributions. Moreover, a uniform "flat-rate" of benefit was established at the miserable level of six dollars a week. "Unemployment insurance in itself increases . . . unemployment," Canada's chief actuary argued, and "this shows how dangerous and undesirable anything like generous unemployment benefits would be."[53]

The six dollar weekly payment did not pose such a threat. Even supplemented by dependents' benefits that would bring it up to $11.40 a week for a family of five, it was still well below the minimum budget of $17.30

which the Montreal Council of Social Agencies recommended was necessary to maintain health and decency for that same household in 1933.[54] However, just to make sure the work "incentive" was maintained, a further clause was added that benefits could in no case exceed 80% of wages, no matter how low. Although unemployment insurance would have a ceiling, there would be no floor. Finally, the stipulation that forty weeks' contributions over two years would be needed before benefits could be paid guaranteed that the scheme would only care for the most regularly employed, that is, those who needed it least. It also ensured no benefits would be paid for at least a year. The total cost of the plan, the actuaries estimated, might well come to $50,000,000 a year but Ottawa's share would only be one fifth of this amount.[55]

The bill was ready for Parliament by June and Finlayson urged immediate action. The longer Bennett delayed bringing down the legislation, "the more difficult it will become as a political undertaking." Modern social thinking now held that unemployment insurance was "only a first line of defence and that a well-organized national form of relief must be established as a last line." At the moment, however, relief was "repulsive" to the country. Thus, if Bennett brought down his public works bill

437

followed by insurance legislation, you have selected the most opportune time to get this job behind you as far as the political values are concerned. *This spring it could be done . . . without raising the relief question.* A year from now I am not quite sure that it could.[56]

Instead, Bennett ignored Finlayson's advice. His $40,000,000 Public Works Construction Act was introduced into Parliament in June. But there was no insurance bill. Nevertheless, at the same time Bennett announced that Ottawa would terminate its contributions to direct relief by June 15. The people had become "more or less relief-conscious," he argued two months later, "and were determined to get out of the Government, whether it be municipal, provincial or federal, all they could."[57] The time had come when it was necessary to draw the line.

The announcement provoked a storm of criticism. Provincial premiers claimed Bennett was trying to do something "that cannot be done." Mayors argued their already "meagre" relief scales could not be lowered. The R.C.M.P. requested an extra reserve in the West to deal with the anticipated unrest. Even within his own party, backbench M.P.s argued that Bennett's decision was a "neglect of duty" that would "spell disaster."[58] As a result, Bennett modified his stand. Instead of abandoning all support for relief, he only changed the policy of making a one-third percentage contribution. From August 15 onwards, fixed monthly grants-in-aid to the provinces based on need would replace percentage payments. And Ottawa alone would determine the need.

The premiers understandably were outraged by this arbitrary cut in federal support when over 1,100,000 were still on the dole, but Bennett remained unmoved. Relief had become a "racket," he told them at a hastily convened conference at the end of July. Adopting Whitton's views, he argued that at least twenty percent of the expenditure was going to "partially employed" workers whose wages were as high as before the Depression. Ottawa would not continue to "pay a subsidy" for these low-wage labourers who were now enjoying a "hitherto unknown" standard of living.

Nor would it permit the provinces to "scrap the constitution" by packing relief rolls with indigent unemployables who were normally a municipal responsibility. Up to now, Bennett pointed out, local governments had "not taken any steps to prevent abuses."[59] Limited to a fixed federal grant, they might. As the *Edmonton Journal* concluded, "the fixed budget plan . . . will have a tendency to make cities think twice before they increase relief scales for, hereafter, the whole burden of such increases is likely to fall on their own taxpayers."[60]

After totally alienating the premiers by these high-handed tactics, Bennett then asked them, one month later, whether they were "prepared to surrender their *exclusive jurisdiction* over . . . unemployment insurance."[61] His political timing could not have been worse. While the financially beleaguered western provinces could hardly refuse, Ontario and Quebec were in no mood to make any concessions after Bennett's ruthless cut in support for relief.

Realizing that agreement was impossible, the Tory leader soon abandoned his enthusiasm for another conference and by November it had been called off. Instead, he decided simply to seize the authority he needed for his insurance legislation and worry about the constitutional implications after the election. Thus, the Employment and Social Insurance Act, which had originally been designed as part of an unemployment package for the spring of 1934, instead went down in history as part of Bennett's "New Deal."

As a result, unemployment insurance has been mistakenly interpreted as an attempt to *expand* Ottawa's responsibilities in response to the crisis of the Depression.[62] As is evident from the previous analysis, this was not the case. Instead, it was part of a political strategy designed to *reduce* the existing and quite expensive federal obligation for direct relief. The reason was as much social as financial. Simply put, Bennett and his advisors were convinced, after 1932, that the dole itself was creating unemployment. As Gordon put it to the premiers in 1934, too many people had developed the attitude that "the state owed them a living." The more Ottawa paid for relief, the more

438

those unemployed would increase in numbers. To keep these numbers down, the essential thing, responsibility should rest first on the individual and secondly on the municipalities; even if at times this might result . . . in individual hardship.[63]

In other words, the only way of reducing unemployment was to reduce the level of support provided to the unemployed. By cutting back its own spending on the dole, Ottawa could ensure the effect would be passed on down the line. And unemployment insurance legislation could provide the perfect political cover for this retreat.

Behind this thinking lay the poor law principle of "less eligibility." As

Frances Fox Piven and Richard Cloward have pointed out, relief arrangements in any society "are ancillary to economic arrangements. Their chief function is to regulate labour. . . . To demean and punish those who do not work is to exalt by contrast even the meanest labor at the meanest wages."[64] Since depressions produce "meaner" wages, this function becomes more important as more people are thrown out of work. The result is a paradox. The claims of human decency and need are placed in conflict with those of a self-regulating labour market.

Rod Finlayson saw the point clearly. After the last round of federal cuts in relief in August 1934, one of his closest friends from Winnipeg pointed out that a transient family of four on relief in that city received only 5¢ per person per meal. "How is it humanly possible," he asked Bennett's advisor, "to raise a family under such conditions and what can we possibly expect from the rising generation when we are trying to bring up the children at the rate of 15¢ per day apiece?" Finlayson answered:

The basic problem is this. On the one hand, you have social economists, dieticians and others prescribing what people have to receive in order to live decently, and on the other hand, you have those who estimate what industry can pay, or in short, when you have a large proportion of your population unemployed, how much can those who have jobs pay toward the livelihood of those who have not?[65]

439

The answer, it seemed, was no more than would make relief more attractive than the worst-paid form of unskilled work. And to get people to take up subsistence agriculture on abandoned farms or to work for five dollars a month in rural Canada, this had to be low indeed.

Although living standards for the unskilled and unemployment benefits have increased substantially since the Bennett era, this basic moral problem remains. It is embodied in the growing attack on Canada's social programmes for those in need. Once again an economic crisis has boosted the unemployment rate to double digit levels and cut into the pay packets of the working poor. Once again governments have responded by *reducing* their level of support to the jobless on the grounds of reinforcing the work ethic.

At stake in this debate is not simply a difference of opinion over *whether* jobs are available or whether the unemployed are willing to work. Equally important is the question of what *kind* of jobs at what rate of pay. In short, in the 1980s, as in the 1930s, unemployment policy is above all a struggle over downward mobility, a conflict between the expectations of workers and the reality of what the labour market has to offer. In the 1930s this meant an attempt to force the urban unemployed "Back to the Land" or into relief camps or domestic service. In the 1980s it has meant pushing women back into the home or part-time work and college graduates into minimum wage jobs.

In both eras the basic tactic remains the same. The unemployed, government and business spokesmen claim, hold "unrealistic" expectations and feel "the state owes them a living". As a consequence, they must be punished by having their living standards reduced so that they will develop a proper "incentive" to work. In the 1980s, as in the 1930s or for that matter the 1830s, "less eligibility" remains a vital component of government unemployment policy. Then, as now, penalizing the jobless remains one of our principal means of motivating people to work.

Notes

1. For an excellent analysis of the 1977 changes to Canada's unemployment insurance system see Leslie A. Pal, "Revision and Retreat: Canadian Unemployment Insurance, 1971-1981", paper presented to the First Conference on Provincial Social Welfare Policy, Calgary, 5-7 May 1982. Recently the governments of British Columbia, Saskatchewan, and Quebec have signficantly reduced welfare assistance to single employables.
2. Prime Minister Trudeau's comments appeared in the *Toronto Star*, 17 August 1978: C. Green and J.M. Cousineau, *Unemployment in Canada: The Impact of Unemployment Insurance* (Ottawa: 1976), p. 115.
3. See Herbert G. Grubel, Dennis Maki and Shelley Sax, "Real and Insurance-Induced Unemployment in Canada", *Canadian Journal of Political Science*, VIII, no. 2, May 1975.
4. *Census of Canada*, 1931, vol. XIII, Monograph on Unemployment, p. 274. S.A. Cudmore of the D.B.S. put the rate at 33% in his January, 1934 "Report on Unemployment", Bennett Papers (PAC), vol. 782.
5. Bennett Papers, vol, 782, S.A. Cudmore, "Report on Unemployment," Jan. 4, 1934.
6. A.E. Safarian, *The Canadian Economy in the Great Depression* (Toronto: 1970), pp. 34-7.
7. The number of women in the labour force increased by 36% in the 1920s. Mary Vipond, "The Image of Women in Mass Circulation Magazines in the 1920s" in S. Trofimenkoff and A. Prentice eds., *The Neglected Majority* (Toronto: 1977), p. 117.
8. In the winters of 1921 and 1922 unemployment rose to over 12% of the work force. As late as 1925 it was still rising to over 10% in the winter. *Census of Canada*, 1931, vol. XIII, Monograph on Unemployment, pp. 275-6. For Ottawa's response to this problem see my "Prelude to Depression: The Federal Government and Unemployment, 1918-1929," *Canadian Historical Review*, September, 1977.
9. Bennett Papers, vol. 782, S.A. Cudmore, "Report on Unemployment," Jan. 4, 1934; Leonard Marsh, *Canadians In and Out of Work* (1940), p. 260.
10. *Census of Canada*, 1931, vol. XIII, Monograph on Unemployment, p. 274.
11. Marsh, *op. cit.*, p. 281.
12. *Report of the Dominion Director of Unemployment Relief*, March 31, 1941, p. 36.
13. Bennett Papers, vol. 782, S.A. Cudmore, "Report on Unemployment," Jan. 4, 1934.
14. King Diary (PAC), June 14, 1930.
15. Canada, House of Commons, *Debates*, Sept. 9, 1930, pp. 21-7.
16. King Papers (PAC), J-4 series, vol. 141, Peter Heenan to King, July, 1930.
17. *Statutes of Canada*, 21 George V, p. 1: "An Act for the granting of aid for the Relief of Unemployment," Sept. 22, 1930; Canada, House of Commons, *Debates*, Sept. 12, 1930, p. 174.
18. *Census of Canada*, 1931, vol. XIII, Monograph on Unemployment, p. 274.
19. Canadian Council on Social Development Papers (PAC), vol. 14, file 68, Ethel Parker to Charlotte Whitton, March 6, 1931.
20. Bennett Papers, vol. 778, Gideon Robertson to Bennett, June 19, 1931.
21. Canada, House of Commons, *Debates*, July 29, 1931, p. 4278 (my emphasis).
22. *Statutes of Canada*, 21-22 George V, Chapter 58, p. 429.
23. Canada, House of Commons *Debates*, July 29, 1931, p. 4277.
24. Bennett Papers, vol. 798, Bennett to R.B. Hanson, Oct. 22, 1931.
25. *Ibid.*, vol. 778, R.J. Manion to Bennett, July 1, 1931; *Report of the Dominion Director of Unemployment Relief*, March 30, 1935, p. 32; Harry Cassidy, *Unemployment and Relief in Ontario, 1929-1932* (Toronto: 1932), p. 145.
26. *Financial Post*, November 14, 1931.
27. Bennett Papers, vol. 794, Bennett to J.G. Bennett, Oct. 21, 1931.
28. *Ibid.*, vol. 793, undated, unsigned letter (*circa* March 1932) from a Saskatchewan M.P. to Bennett, p. 489188.
29. Barry Broadfoot, *Ten Lost Years* (Toronto: 1973), p. 70.
30. Bennett Papers, vol. 783, memo to W.A. Gordon on "Unemployment Relief — Land Settlement," March 29, 1932; W.A. Gordon to Bennett, April 6, 1932.
31. *Ibid.*, vols. 779-780, memo from Whitton to Bennett on "Unemployment and Relief in Western Canada, Summer 1932," pp. 478800-1, 478928-30, 478847.
32. *Ibid.*, pp. 478093-4, 478096-9, 478105, 478823, 478858-9.
33. *Ibid.*, pp. 478848-55, 478812.

34. *Ibid.*, vol. 793, Bennett to G.A. Sylte, October 5, 1932.
35. James Eayrs, *In Defence of Canada*, vol. 1, pp. 125–6.
36. McNaughton Papers (PAC), vol. 37, memo of meeting between W.A. Gordon and McNaughton, Oct. 3, 1933.
37. *Ibid.*, vol. 37, W.A. Gordon to F.J. McManus, Sept. 26, 1933.
38. Bennett Papers, vol. 783, memo by McNaughton on "The Department of National Defence Unemployment Relief Scheme with some observations concerning the United States Civilian Conservation Corps," October 1933.
39. McNaughton Papers, vol. 37, W.A. Gordon to F.J. McManus, Sept. 26, 1933.
40. Dept. of National Defence Records (PAC), vol. 2965, Memo of meeting between Harry Hereford, Andrew McNaughton and William Finlayson, July 6, 1933.
41. McNaughton papers, vol. 44, file 319, H.H. Matthews (D.O.C.B.C.) to McNaughton, June 16, 1933.
42. Dept. of National Defence Records, vol. 3181, quote from *Winnipeg Free Press*, Oct. 28, 1933.
43. *Report of the Dominion Director of Unemployment Relief*, March 31, 1936, pp. 36, 33; *Ibid.*, March 31, 1933, p. 25; *Census of Canada*, 1931, vol. XIII, Monograph on Unemployment, p. 274.
44. Bennett Papers, vol. 561, "Minutes of the Dominion-Provincial Conference, Jan. 17–19, 1933", pp. 346894–955; vol. 566, Bennett to the four western premiers, March 9, 1933.
45. *Ibid.*, vol. 561, "Memoranda Regarding Questions on the Agenda," Jan. 17, 1933.
46. Canada House of Commons, *Debates*, Feb. 24, 1933, p. 2464.
47. *Ibid.*, March 2, 1933, p. 2657.
48. Bennett Papers, vol. 781, "Memorandum *re* Heaps Motion," Nov. 16, 1932.
49. *Ibid.*, vol. 794, W.M. Dickson to A.E. Millar, May 29, 1933 (my emphasis).
50. *Ibid.*, vol. 813, memo from Finlayson to Bennett, n.d. (*circa* Dec. 1932–Jan. 1933).
51. *Ibid.*, vol. 810, W.C. Clark to Bennett, Jan 18, 1933.
52. *Ibid.*, vol. 181, "Minutes of Dominion-Provincial Conference, Jan. 17, 1934"; vol. 813, R.H. Coats to Rod Finlayson, Feb. 2, 1934.
53. Dept. of Insurance Records (PAC), vol. 1, A.D. Watson to R.K. Finlayson, April 11, 1934; memo on "Rates of Benefit," n.d. but *circa* April 1934.
54. *Ibid.*, memo on "Rates of Benefit."
55. *Ibid.*, vol. 1, Watson to H. Wolfenden, Jan. 12, 1935; G.D. Finlayson to A.D. Watson, "Memo on Coverage Exclusions and Exemptions, Eligibility Conditions, etc," April 6, 1934.
56. Bennett Papers, vol. 812, R.K. Finlayson to Bennett, May 25, 1934 (my emphasis).
57. *Ibid.*, vol. 790, Bennett to W.J. McCully, August 6, 1934.
58. *Ibid.*, vol. 792, L.A. Taschereau to Gordon, June 1, 1934; to Gordon, June 1, 1934; vol. 795, J.E. Brownlee to Bennett, May 9, 1934; vol. 797, T.D. Pattullo to Bennett, June 1, 1934; vol. 790, E. Wilton to Bennett, July 13, 1934; vol. 795, D.O.C., R.C.M.P., Edmonton June 3, 1934; vol. 792, Jimmy Stitt to Bennett, June 5, 1934.
59. *Ibid.*, vol. 182, "Minutes of the July 31, 1934 Dominion-Provincial Conference"; Bennett to Jimmy Stitt, July 30, 1934.
60. *Ibid.*, vol. 798, editorial from the *Edmonton Journal*, Aug. 16, 1934.
61. *Ibid.*, vol. 182, draft letter by Bennett to all provincial premiers, Aug. 31, 1934 (my emphasis).
62. See, for example, Richard Wilbur, "R.B. Bennett as a Reformer," Canadian Historical Association, *Annual Report*, 1969.
63. Bennett Papers, vol. 181, "Minutes of the Dominion-Provincial Conference, Jan. 17, 1934."
64. Frances Fox Piven and Richard Cloward, *Regulating the Poor: The Functions of Public Welfare* (New York 1971), p. 3.
65. Bennett Papers, vol. 792, E. Browne-Wilkinson to R.K. Finlayson, Aug. 17, 1934; Finlayson to E. Browne-Wilkinson, Aug. 21, 1934.

441

William Lyon Mackenzie King: The Conciliator in Politics*

H. BLAIR NEATBY

Mackenzie King is one of the best known and least liked of all our prime ministers. Even today he is a controversial figure; a man who had none of the obvious qualities of a leader and yet a man who survived for an incredibly long time in a very hazardous occupation — he was leader of the Liberal party for almost thirty years and prime minister for over twenty. And not only that, he left an indelible stamp on the country. Whether for good or ill, today's Canda is partly King's making.

Our concern is with the Mackenzie King of the 1930s. Even in those years his contemporaries were puzzled by the man. R.J. Manion, a Conservative opponent, commented that King was unpopular in the House of Commons and among most Canadians. How could such a man win elections? Manion could only suggest that he was an "opportunist, *par excellence*" and also very lucky.[1]

Prominent Liberals were just as ambivalent. J.W. Dafoe of the *Free Press*, for example, was a very partisan critic of R.B. Bennett but he also had reservations about King. Dafoe never sided with the Liberals who wanted to get rid of King — and there were many such Liberals in the early 1930s — but on the other hand he was never prepared to go farther than to say that King, for all his weaknesses, was the best man available. Most party leaders rouse more enthusiasm.

What is the explanation for this ambivalence? The simple answer is that Mackenzie King himself *was* an ambivalent figure. His career is strewn with apparent contradictions and inconsistencies. He seemed to be flabby and indecisive; never yes, never no, always maybe or partly, always the smoke screen of qualifications which concealed any decision, or hid the fact that no decision had been made. And yet this apparently indecisive man picked forceful and powerful colleagues; Gardiner, Dunning, Ralston, C.D. Howe — these men were not nonentities. What is more, King controlled and dominated these men. Ralston he dismissed abruptly, without warning. And C.D. Howe once said that the key to King's career was that King was a leader — a telling remark coming from C.D. Howe! The ambivalence shows up in King's policies too. He posed as a social reformer: the first Minister of Labour, the industrial consultant, the workingman's friend. And yet his record of social legislation is a meagre one, and is as easily explained by political opportunism as by political conviction.

King's political longevity becomes more credible if we begin with his

442

concept of political leadership. King did not believe in imposing his will or his policies on his party; he was not an authoritarian leader like Bennett. King believed that his party, and his cabinet, had to be consulted and had to be convinced before a policy could be adopted. He believed in participatory democracy, at least within the party. This didn't mean that he suppressed his own opinions — quite often it meant that he converted others to the policy he preferred. On other occasions, however, it could mean agreement on a policy or a compromise for which he had little enthusiasm. Political leadership for him was like being a conciliator in labour disputes; the successful conciliator is one who comes to understand the point of view of both sides, and who can thus suggest a compromise or a settlement which both sides can accept. The conciliator is not a passive bystander. He tries to create a satisfactory agreement, a consensus. He contributes his own ideas as well as his techniques for arriving at agreement. Although the final outcome cannot be dictated it is often the result of persuasion.

Mackenzie King's reaction to the depression illustrates his activities as a conciliator. Initially King, like many of his contemporaries, saw the depression as a temporary recession. It could not be ignored but at the same time it did not seem to demand drastic or radical measures. King, in the Liberal tradition, believed at first that the economy would recover with little help from governments. The important thing, from his point of view, was not to obstruct the process but to allow economic laws to operate. Canadian Liberals saw the protective tariff as the worst form of obstruction. By creating artificial barriers to trade, the tariff distorted national economies, and at the same time taxed the poor for the benefit of the rich. It was natural therefore for King in the early 1930s to blame the depression on the tariff which Bennett had just raised to unprecedented levels. Even as late as 1932 King was still focusing on the tariff as the real villain. In the session of that year the Liberal amendment to the budget declared that lower tariffs were "essential to a revival of trade, and improvement of business, and the return of prosperity."

By 1932, however, the traditional emphasis on the tariff no longer satisfied all Liberals. Western Liberals, for example, once so obsessed with the tariff issue, no longer cared. Lower tariffs might reduce the cost of farm machinery but what did this matter when wheat prices were too low to cover the costs of production, much less meet mortgage payments and provide a living? Most westerners by this time had decided that the depression posed new and urgent problems and could only be resolved by new and radical measures. Many of them had come to the radical and almost revolutionary conclusion that the answer lay, not in lower tariffs, but in inflation. Inflation would raise the prices of farm products. It would also raise the prices of the goods which farmers purchased but there would still be a net gain. Most farmers had mortgages on their land and machinery, mortgages based on the inflated prices of the 1920s but which now had to be repaid when dollars were scarce. Inflation, by lowering the value of money, would redress the balance, and make it possible to pay debts in devalued currency. Even in

1932 King had been under strong pressure from western Liberals to go beyond the tariff and opt for some form of inflation. Eastern Liberals were not sympathetic to the idea. They did not represent a debtor community; deliberate inflation was to them shockingly dangerous and even immoral. How could business survive if money had no stable value? There could be no Liberal consensus on inflation under these conditions and so King pacified the westerners by leaving inflation an open question. In the 1932 session at least, the party stayed united on its tariff resolution.

King, however, was sensitive to shifting political currents. Personally he would have been happy to continue to concentrate on the tariff issue; inflation seemed to him morally wrong and unlikely to foster economic recovery. But as party leader he could not ignore the feelings of his western followers. The party must be kept united. If Liberals could not agree to concentrate on the tariff, some new basis of agreement was needed. Inflation did not look like a promising avenue. In addition to King's personal misgivings, it was clear that eastern Liberals would not support that policy.

It was here that King illustrated his capacity for leadership—for his type of leadership. In the fall of 1932 he met with some prominent Liberals, a select group which included Vincent Massey and J.W. Dafoe as well as active politicians like Lapointe and Ralston. They argued about tariff policy, railway policy and, inevitably, about monetary policy. All of these men were Liberals with concern for the underprivileged but also with a healthy respect for free enterprise and existing social institutions. They were not likely to opt for simple panaceas such as printing money. All of them could remember the postwar inflation in Germany a dozen years earlier, when people had gone to the bakery with a wheel-barrow of paper marks for a loaf of bread. But on the other hand, what of the argument that the value of money had already changed during the depression? The depression could be seen as a period of deflation; to say that the prices had declined was only another way of saying that the value of money had increased. Would it be possible to manipulate the money supply to increase prices without having a runaway inflation? How could the money supply be safely adjusted? What about a central bank?

Mackenzie King was intrigued by the possibility. He had once been trained as an economist but he knew little about the complexities of velocity of circulation and rediscount rates, so he consulted Professor Curtis, an economist at Queen's University. From him King learned that a central bank would be necessary if a policy of controlled inflation was ever adopted, but that a central bank did not necessarily mean inflation. Here was the compromise King was looking for. He knew his party could not be united on a policy of inflation but both western and eastern Liberals might be persuaded to agree on the establishment of a central bank. The compromise might be summed up as "inflation if necessary but not necessarily inflation."

It was not enough for King to decide on a policy. Bennett was the kind of leader who announced his decisions in radio broadcasts but for King political leadership involved consultation and discussion. When Parliament reas-

444

sembled in January of 1933 King therefore announced to caucus that a Liberal platform needed to be hammered out and proposed a number of caucus committees to discuss the various planks. All of the committees — tariffs, railways, social welfare — encountered some difficulty in reaching agreement, but the committee on monetary policy was almost a free-for-all, as he knew it would be. King, however, used all his considerable talent as a conciliator. He attended all the meetings, began by suggesting the central bank as a possible basis of agreement, listened carefully to the contradictory views, drafted what he hoped would be an acceptable policy statement after three weeks, allowed the debate to continue for another two weeks, revised his draft slightly to meet the criticisms and finally got all members of the committee to agree that the draft was at least acceptable — as far as it went. The final consensus was that the Liberal party advocated a central bank. It went farther, however, and also stated that the supply of currency and credit should be determined by the needs of the community.

This was still vague. Liberals might still disagree on what the needs of the community were; but the platform was nonetheless a radical advance in party policy. The Liberal party had affirmed that government should control monetary policy, that it should manipulate currency and credit. Money was no longer sacrosanct; governments on this basis would be as responsible for the supply of money as they were for the level of tariffs or taxes. From King's point of view, what was even more important was that all members of the party had agreed. This policy represented a consensus on which the party was united. It was no mean achievement to have negotiated such a radical shift in policy without alienating any of his followers.

The Liberal platform of 1933 remained the official platform of the party through the election campaign of 1935. It had been difficult enough to arrive at a consensus and King had no urge to open up the Pandora's box and start all over again. In any case, he did not think it was necessary. He was sure that the Liberals would win the next election. It seemed the part of wisdom to be as flexible as possible; to adopt general principles without being committed to specific measures. The party favoured freer trade, closer co operation with provincial governments, more efficient administration — but few details were spelled out.

It required a good deal of self-confidence to avoid specific promises. Other parties were less reserved. R.B. Bennett had his New Deal. The C.C.F. had its Regina Manifesto of 1933. H.H. Stevens' Reconstruction party was promising a wide range of measures which would restore prosperity. Social Credit had its inflationary panacea. Many Liberals feared that they would suffer defeat if they did not participate in this auction. King, however, was convinced that the Canadian voters had had enough of reckless and unfulfilled promises. He was sure that they would have more respect for a party which offered a stable and responsible administration. In the welter and confusion of three new parties and a Conservative party which had changed its spots, the Liberal party would offer cautious reform. The Liberal slogan in 1935 was "King or chaos." As a slogan it reflected accurately enough the

445

political situation. The Liberal party was the only party with significant support across the country. If it did not win, there would be no majority government. The slogan also reflected King's view that the Liberal party would win without offering anything more specific. The voters confirmed his analysis: they returned 171 Liberals in a House of 245, the largest majority in Canadian history up to that time.

Any slogan, however, is an oversimplification. Chaos was still possible, even with King in office. The multiplicity of parties in 1935 was a reflection of fundamental divisions within the country. One out of every five voters had voted for new parties, radical parties, parties which had not even existed in 1930. And even within the older parties, Conservative and Liberal, there were differences and divisions which had not been resolved. These political divisions were based on deeply rooted divisions within Canada itself. The grievances of western Canada, for example, explain why both the C.C.F. and Social Credit parties drew their strength from that region. The Liberal party itself was a coalition of regional and cultural blocs, and there was no guarantee that it would hold together in the face of the continuing economic crisis.

Mackenzie King, when he returned to office in 1935, had no new or novel policies. In many ways he was still the King of an earlier era. In 1921 he had come into office during an economic recession. His government had economized, it had balanced its budget and even reduced the national debt, it had lowered tariffs and taxes. Within a few years prosperity had returned, and King believed that there was a cause and effect relationship. He was convinced that these policies had brought prosperity once and that similar policies in the 1930s would produce similar results. He did not close the door on new ideas, but he hoped that the tested remedies of the past would still be effective.

He began with the traditional Liberal policy of freer trade. Within three weeks of taking office he had signed a trade agreement with the United States. Negotiations had begun when Bennett was still Prime Minister but Bennett had not been enthusiastic. King had no reservations, although the implications were far-reaching. It was the first formal trade agreement with the United States since the Reciprocity Agreement of 1854 and it marked the turning away from the ever-increasing tariff barriers between the two countries which had reached their peak with the Hawley-Smoot tariff and the Bennett tariff, both in 1930. A further trade agreement was signed three years later, this time involving Great Britain as well as the United States. The trend was clearly towards increased trade with the United States. It is a trend which has continued ever since until today the relationship is almost symbiotic.

Freer trade, especially with the United States, was expected to benefit Canadian producers of natural products by increasing their markets. It was traditional Liberal policy and the effects would be gradual at best. The same traditional and cautious approach could be seen in the first budget of the new government. No new expenditures were proposed but corporation taxes

446

and the sales tax were increased. The aim was to balance the budget, to have the federal government live within its means.

Even monetary policy scarcely reflected the long-drawn-out discussion over inflation. R.B. Bennett had established a central bank in 1934. The Bank of Canada which he set up was a banker's bank, independent of the federal government and primarily concerned with financial stability. The Liberal government amended the constitution of the Bank of Canada to establish federal control and eventually federal ownership. It was thus in a position to determine the supply of currency and credit on the basis of the needs of the community. Under Graham Towers, however, the Bank of Canada had already established a policy of easy money. Chartered banks had plenty of easy money to lend at low rates of interest. The policy of easy money was continued but neither Towers nor the government under King was prepared to print more money.

Special measures were introduced for the drought areas on the prairies, where crop disaster continued to be almost the normal way of life. Some marginal crop land was turned back to grazing land and an insurance scheme was introduced to provide some income for farmers in a year of crop failure. The Wheat Board, established under Bennett, was continued under the Liberal government. What improvement there was, however — and there was some — had little to do with federal policies. Crop failures and acreage reductions in Canada and elsewhere in the world gradually eliminated the world wheat surplus and wheat prices increased, although they were still below a dollar a bushel. The price trend was at least encouraging, and if rains would come and if grasshoppers and rust and frost would stay away, the farmers could hope to get off relief.

At this stage there was nothing radical, nothing really novel, nothing that was not consistent with traditional and orthodox Liberalism. The orthodoxy of the new government is most clearly shown in its efforts to economize, to balance the federal budget. The greatest drain on the budget was still the heavy relief expenditures: unemployment relief and farm relief. Soon after taking office King appointed a National Employment Commission, which was asked to do two things. It was to reorganize the administration of all relief expenditures, in the hope that a more centralized and more efficient administration would eliminate duplication and reduce costs. It was also asked to recommend measures which might be taken to create employment opportunities and so remove men from the relief rolls.

The National Employment Commission was not able to introduce many economies. Most of the relief was administered by provincial and municipal governments and, even though the federal government was providing much of the money, there was little the federal government could do to change the system. It was a different story when it came to recommending positive measures to foster employment. The Commission argued that employment was not a local but a national problem. A factory might close down in Hamilton but the cause was elsewhere — in the declining purchasing power in the Maritimes or the prairies perhaps, where men could no longer afford to

447

buy the products of the factory. Two major conclusions were drawn from this analysis. Because the Canadian economy was national and not local or provincial in scope, unemployment must be seen as a national problem. The Commission therefore recommended that the federal government should take over the full cost of unemployment relief. The Commission went much farther, however; it argued that some positive action could be taken to reduce unemployment. Instead of economizing and trying to balance the budget, it recommended increased federal expenditures and reduced taxation in times of depression. The motor of the economy was seen as investment. When private enteprise was not prepared to invest money—when there was a depression — governments should deliberately incur deficits in order to counterbalance the deficiency. John Maynard Keynes had arrived in Canada.

Mackenzie King's initial response to these suggestions was more than negative: it was hostile. He paid little attention to the positive proposals; he was shocked even at the suggestion that the federal government should pay the full cost of unemployment relief. The federal government was having trouble meeting its financial obligations as it was; it seemed absurd to aggravate its problems by taking over more responsibilities. King was reacting like a traditional federalist, insisting that both levels of government, federal and provincial, should look after their own affairs. It was at this time, in the fall of 1937, that King decided to set up yet another royal commission — the Rowell-Sirois Commission on Dominion-Provincial Relations. If the federal system was going to be changed it would not be changed unilaterally, by having the federal government volunteer to take on new burdens.

But the positive proposals of the Employment Commission were not forgotten. The 1938 session might be the last session before the next election. King suggested to the Minister of Finance, Charles Dunning, that he plan a pre-election budget. For King this meant a balanced budget, for he was sure that responsible Canadians wanted a government which lived within its means. Charles Dunning agreed; he too believed that government deficits were undesirable, if not immoral. Dunning's first draft of his budget proposed a small surplus.

King and Dunning, however, were surprised to find that some cabinet ministers no longer believed in balanced budgets. Norman Rogers, Minister of Labour, had been converted by the Employment Commission. He argued that Dunning should budget for a deficit and talked of an additional $40 million for public works to inject money into the economy. Dunning threatened to resign if this policy was adopted; Rogers threatened to resign if it wasn't. Other cabinet ministers took sides. It was the kind of situation in which King the conciliator took over. He was not convinced by the arguments but he was, as always, convinced that the party must be kept united. Eventually he proposed $25 million of additional expenditure as a compromise and set up a cabinet committee to decide how the money would be spent.

The budget of 1938 was a turning point in fiscal policy in Canada. For the first time a government had consciously decided to spend money to counteract a low in the business cycle. In addition to the expenditures in the budget the government also offered loans to municipalities for local improvements and passed a National Housing Act to encourage the building of homes. Consistent with this Keynesian approach, the government also reduced some taxes and offered some tax exemptions for private investors. The idea of a static and balanced budget was gone. In its place was a fiscal policy of stimulating economic recovery by government deficits and by direct economic incentives.

The new fiscal policy did not work any miracles. Recovery would not come until the war, when deficit finanacing and government investments in the economy became a patriotic duty. But the budget of 1938 marks the beginning of a new concept of the role of government in Canada. Until then the federal government had concentrated on providing public services such as railways and canals, police forces and national defence, post offices, and more recently old age pensions and unemployment relief. The taxes it had collected were designed to pay for these services. It had now undertaken a new and significantly different responsibility: that of balancing the total *449* economic investment, private and public, in order to balance the national economy. The implications would be far-reaching. The government budgets of our day are dominated by this new role. Looking back to the 1930s we can now see that it was the most radical and most constructive innovation of that depression decade.

And yet it is still difficult to visualize Mackenzie King as a radical. He was not an innovator; he was not a man with original ideas. Indeed, he still continued to believe that eventually governments should balance their budgets and let free enterprise flourish. Certainly he did not appreciate the significance of the Keynesian revolution. King's strength was in his commitment to a policy of party unity, and in his capacity to accept and adopt new ideas when the alternative was a division within the party. This concept of policial leadership had brought King a long way since 1930. On monetary issues he had begun with the certainty that inflation was sin but had come to accept the idea of a central bank which might manipulate currency and credit on the basis of social need. On fiscal policy he had begun with the traditional ideas of a limited role for government with balanced budgets and had come to accept the idea of government responsibility for controlling the level of economic activity.

Under King the Liberal party did respond, gradually and tentatively, to the pressures of a revolutionary decade, and under his leadership it responded without disintegrating into warring fractions. To be leader of a still united party four years later was in itself no small achievement. The risk of party schisms had been real. More significant, the party still seemed to have popular support. Mackenzie King's policies had not been dramatic but his concept of political leadership had averted possible chaos.

Note

1. R.J. Manion, *Life is an Adventure* (Toronto, 1937), p. 290.

Portrait of a Premier: William Aberhart*
HAROLD J. SCHULTZ

Thomas Carlyle may have oversimplified the matter when he wrote that "History is the essence of innumerable biographies," but perhaps he was not far wrong. Certainly the early history of Social Credit in Alberta was in a very real way the story of William Aberhart, for it was his leadership and organization that provided the basic ingredients for the Social Credit victory at the polls in 1935. In achieving the premiership Aberhart's radio ministry, fundamentalist faith, methods of organization, and political manoeuvres made him one of the most controversial figures of his day, a man "more loved, and more hated, than any political figure in the history of Western Canada since the rebel Louis Riel."[1] No political label neatly explains this maverick figure any more than the term "Social Credit" really explains his party programme. But essential to any understanding of Aberhart as a politician is an awareness that Aberhart never relinquished his primary interests in teaching and preaching, and no portrait of the premier is complete without all three dimensions. The biblical oratory merely shaded into political evangelism as the school-teacher-premier continued to treat the province as one big classroom.[2] Like Gladstone he put a religious imprint on politics as surely as his personal life expressed a religious conviction — a conviction that was established long before he paid any attention to politics. It begins with his boyhood.

William Aberhart was born on December 30, 1878, on a prosperous farmstead near the town of Seaforth, Ontario. Here his German-born father and English mother raised eight children, including number four, William, Jr. Following in his father's footsteps held little appeal for William; he preferred browsing in books to farming and upon graduation wavered between teaching and preaching.[3] Finding no reason why he should not teach, he entered the Ontario Normal College at Hamilton and began his teaching career at Wingham, Ontario. Two years later he moved to Central High School in Brantford and his reputation, and salary, as an educator began to grow. Within three years he was married and principal of Central, but in spite of the promotion Aberhart was by no means convinced that teaching should be his final choice of career. While in Brantford he joined Dr. William Nicol's Bible class at Zion Presbyterian Church[4] and began a serious study of the Bible. The outcome was a "commitment to Christ" and serious consideration of the Presbyterian ministry.[5] Aberhart, however, was not one to take unnecessary risks either early in life or later in politics, and when the local presbytery could not guarantee him a stipend for the two years' training he would need at Knox College he hedged on a final decision.[6] While continu-

*From *Canadian Historical Review*, XLV (September 1964): 185–211. Reprinted by permission of the author and the University of Toronto Press.

ing his school duties he salved his conscience by taking a correspondence course from C.I. Schofield, an American Bible scholar best known for the Schofield Reference Bible. These studies intrigued Aberhart and whetted his interest in prophecy so that later, in Calgary, he was most attracted to the prophetic books of the Bible in his own Bible teaching.[7]

Aberhart enjoyed the correspondence course and realized that more education would be helpful in either teaching or preaching, but again, he could not afford the luxury of regular college attendance. Once again the alternative was correspondence courses. These had proved successful in Bible study, why not in academic study? Accordingly Aberhart enrolled with Queen's University in 1907 and marked "minister" as the intended profession on his application form. Outside of his favourite subject, mathematics, the extramural effort during the next four years was not outstanding; in fact, hardly passable. After failing Greek twice and Honour Political Science once, he salvaged a "C" in each course and so completed the needed credits for a B.A. degree in 1911.[8] By this time Aberhart was no longer in Brantford. Responding to the glowing reports of the educational opportunities in Alberta, the principal of Brantford Central offered his service and was accepted as principal of Alexander Public School in East Calgary. Assured of a two-hundred-dollar raise[9] he left Ontario and joined the more than one million who streamed into the Canadian prairies between 1896 and 1913. Five years after his arrival he became principal of Balmoral Heights and in 1927 the first principal of the new Crescent Heights High School.

451

It was at Crescent Heights that he built up a reputation as both an "excellent teacher and an able administrator" who believed in constant supervision and control of school activities.[10] Authoritarian in manner and a strict disciplinarian he was better able to talk to people than with them and the habit of "talking down" to children was carried over to his relations with his teachers at Crescent Heights[11] and later with his political colleagues. But his interest in students was intense and sincere and many students who would have failed without the extra time and encouragement he gave were helped in private tutoring.[12] In teaching arithmetic he would frequently invoke universals from the formulae he was working and apply them to the "mathematics of life." Often he would conclude by extolling four maxims for successful living: be enthusiastic, be ambitious, develop a distinctive personality, and have a hobby and "ride it hard."[13] All four maxims were practised by Aberhart and he had little trouble identifying his hobby. "I have been organizing all my life," remarked Premier Aberhart later. "There's nothing I'd rather do than organize. It's a hobby with me."[14] His love of organization helped make Crescent Heights Parent-Teachers Association the largest and most active branch in Alberta.[15] The portly principal, a formidable figure with his six-foot, one-inch frame, and two hundred and fifty pounds, relished picnics and games, particularly if he happened to be organizing them. One year his students wanted a movie projector but the school budget did not provide for any such frill. Aberhart thereupon incorporated a student "company" and the students bought in at ten cents a share. They put on movies, charged admission, and at the end of the year the company declared a dividend of twenty-five cents a share,[16] a dividend that came much more simply than the promised twenty-five-dollar dividend of 1935.

But education was only one of Aberhart's twin interests. The youthful urge to preach remained, and for a man who claimed he only needed (and frequently only had) four hours of sleep a night, teaching arithmetic and administering the province's largest high school were not taxing enough. What could he do in the evenings and on Sundays? One of the first things he did on Sundays was to organize a Young Men's Bible Class at Grace Presbyterian Church. "This Bible class which led to the construction of the prophetic Bible Institute and to the radio addresses which expounded Social Credit were direct highways leading to the Legislative buildings."[17] In the years that followed the Aberhart family transferred their membership to Trinity Methodist Church and eventually to Westbourne Baptist Church where Aberhart had intermittently filled the pulpit. At Westbourne Aberhart studied Baptist doctrines and became convinced of the validity of "water baptism" (immersion) and local church autonomy. Accordingly Aberhart and his wife were immersed and joined the church, which was a necessary step before Aberhart could accept ordination as a Baptist deacon.[18] By 1920 Aberhart had dubbed himself a Fundamental Baptist[19] and along with other fundamentalists of the 'twenties and 'thirties began to criticize the old-line churches for their modernism and apostasy. In particular he charged the major denominations with questioning the verbal inspiration of the Bible. Aberhart declared that it was not up to man to question the syntax or historicity of the Scriptures. Every word and comma of the Bible were to be accepted literally as the verbally inspired Word of God.[20] It followed, therefore, if every syllable in the Bible was inspired then the prophecies must also be inspired, and since not all the prophecies were yet fulfilled, some were yet to occur. These could be adduced if one could only decode the prophetic secrets found in the Scriptures. In religion, as in mathematics, Aberhart refused to admit mysteries or a choice of answers. In his Schofield Correspondence course Aberhart had picked up an interpretation that divided all human time into seven unequal periods or "dispensations." This arbitrary division of history brooked no uneasy compromise with modern geology or anthropology. The time-span of Creation was clear and simple. It "took place in six days of 24 hours each" and Adam was created the afternoon of the sixth day.[21]

Entrusted with these prophetic insights Aberhart joined with other likeminded men from various denominations to meet weekly for a study of the Bible and its prophecies. The group decided to organize and call themselves the Calgary Prophetic Bible Conference. As attendance jumped under Aberhart's leadership the conference moved to consecutively larger auditoriums so that by 1925 even the spacious Palace Theatre was filled each Sunday afternoon and Aberhart, on the urgings of his colleagues, began to experiment with radio. The lay preacher soon acquired a large following as scattered homes across the province tuned in to a new radio personality. As

452

W.E. Mann points out Aberhart helped fill an important religious vacuum in the scattered rural communities of Alberta that the major denominations had either neglected or lost by their increasing liturgical formalism and modernist sermons. The theological liberalism of the clergy may have appealed to the urban middle classes and the "better-class farmers and villagers," but by the same token it frightened many church supporters who felt that the doctrines of the Bible were being diluted. The new emphasis on social problems instead of personal conversion, of more concern for the here and now than for the hereafter, of criticism of biblical infallibility and rigid social norms rather than a proclamation of the verbal inspiration of the Bible and separation from the world, all raised deep-rooted questions in the minds of "the more puritan and evangelistically minded church supporters."[22]

In this situation Aberhart's position and personality struck a responsive note across the prairies. Here was a respected educator and layman who was independent of the old-line churches. Here was a preacher who was not an agent of any vested interest or established group, but one who preached the old faith with assurance and who could restore the confidence of those suspicious of the new style of interpretation. His personality also projected itself well. His obvious talent as a teacher and platform speaker, combined with a remarkable self-confidence, made him a highly successful radio preacher. Soon a radio audience of fifty thousand was tuning in every Sunday and within ten years an estimated three hundred thousand in and near Alberta were regular listeners, a number which gave his broadcast "a higher Hooper rating in Alberta than Jack Benny, whose program followed."[23] From this promising beginning Aberhart extended his religious work into new channels. A radio Sunday school was organized at the request of listeners. At first Aberhart used American Baptist materials from Philadelphia, but soon he was making up his own series of lessons and questions which he sent out to children free of charge. Volunteers collected the returned examination papers at prayer meeting Wednesday nights and marked them weekly. In 1926 four hundred and seventy-five enrolled and each year the number increased until the peak enrolment was reached in 1938–9 with 9,141.[24]

453

Aberhart turned over the Sunday School superintendency to a colleague, Charles Pearce, and now gave his attention to the more pressing task of building a Bible institute. The Bible Conference lacked regular facilities for its growing programme and at the same time a new Bible school would serve to combat "the skepticism and infidelity in our universities and in the so-called Theological Seminaries."[25] A building committee was set up and an intensive campaign launched. Here, as in his school administration, Aberhart mustered his organizing ability to sell his programme and each day the mail brought big and little donations from radio listeners. On Sunday, October 2, 1927, the new Calgary Prophetic Bible Institute opened with Aberhart preaching three times. That fall the Institute opened for resident students and thirty-six appeared. One was a lean, nineteen-year-old Saskatchewan farm boy named Ernest Manning.[26]

Aberhart's primary interest now became the Bible school and his personality dominated its programme as he served in the triple role of president of the Calgary Prophetic Bible Institute Church, Dean of the Bible Institute, and "apostle" of the Church.[27] When the Dean was away, Manning, after graduating, would fill in, but when Aberhart returned, Manning withdrew to the wings or behind the scenes. The doctrinal basis of the school, written by Aberhart, was strongly fundamentalist from the "Verbal Inspiration of the Scriptures" to "the awful and everlasting misery of the unbelieving wicked, in a literal lake of fire, prepared for a real, personal devil and his angels." At no time either before or after entering political life did Aberhart waver from or apologize for his theological position. His *Syllabus* very candidly explained that the Bible Institute would use every medium available to combat and resist "Modernism, Higher Criticism, Skepticism and Sectarianism in all its forms."[28]

In extending his religious programme Aberhart left little to providence. Convinced of the value of organization, he provided detailed instructions for his trainees. His followers could almost take a page out of his textbook in evangelism and apply it to the organization of a political campaign. Many did. Although his writings at this time were prepared for religious purposes, the principles and practices were equally applicable for the extension of Social Credit. In part two of *Personal Evangelism*, Aberhart provided fourteen pointers ranging from attention devices to tract distribution on the conduct of open air meetings. His section on "Cottage and Parlour Meetings" was shortly to double as the instructions on Social Credit study groups. Aberhart's directives were explicit and practical. "A small group of people might be widely scattered through a hall, but are packed together in a home, and so are drawn together." Organize carefully, taking into account "the location, the size, the suitability and accessibility" of a home. "Advertise the meetings. . . . Above all, do a great deal of Personal Invitation." Arrange for some music and "plan the program most carefully." Seat the people informally and have the meeting started before they realize it. "Yet be sure to control the meeting throughout." Organizers were urged to encourage every member present to take part in the service in some way (he then lists four ways: prayer, singing, Scripture reading, group discussion). Finally, "Take some simple subject for the message or discussion, at least for a beginning."[29]

In writing the textbooks for his students Aberhart, the Bible teacher, was essentially Aberhart, the schoolmaster. He wrote and spoke as one having authority. The course books were didactic and elementary, yet vigorous and readable as he substantiated his argument by graphic historical examples. After repeating the major points in each chapter he would review the entire chapter at the end of the unit just as he did in school. The correspondence booklets would close with a request urging the student to answer the "above questions carefully" and mail the same to "WILLIAM ABERHART, B.A." Each student's paper would receive "his personal supervision and correction of the same, if One Dollar is enclosed to cover postage, etc. This also advances the privilege of asking any three other Bible questions that you may desire."[30]

454

There was never any question of an alternate position to that provided in the studybooks. Every question had a right and wrong interpretation and the line of demarcation was clear.[31] Frequently fiat rather than fact was the basis of the argument, but this never seemed to disturb his students. For example, in his rejection of the Revised Version of the Bible, Aberhart pointed out its "impure" origins: "(5) This is MOST IMPORTANT. (A) The Revised Version was NOT TAKEN FROM THE AUTHORIZED VERSION, nor from the same sources as the AUTHORIZED VERSION. It was a NEW VERSION, from newly discovered MSS." Therefore, his syllogism concluded, the new version was evil.[32] In contrast the translators of the King James version were composed of "the best Hebrew and Greek scholars of the day" who had "a profound reverence for the Word of God" and used the manuscripts of Erasmus and Tyndale for their translations — manuscripts "preserved by the True Church" rather than by the corrupted Catholic church. This fact combined with the "godly desires of both Erasmus and Tyndale" are proof that "they were surely moved of the Spirit of God in these matters." The result was a version of "supreme scholarship . . . unequalled before or since." Aberhart clinched his explanation by concluding, "With these facts before us, our search for the truth is over. We have completed a careful investigation, and sought to honestly weigh the evidence. Our only possible conclusion is that our beloved Authorized Version is the perfect and infallible Word of God."[33]

This cast of mind was shortly to operate in politics and it was only natural for Aberhart with his authoritarian manner and fundamentalist faith to wrap his political programme in his piety and press on roughshod over the protests of his opponents. Their barbs were brushed off as the criticisms of the ungodly as he would fall back on biblical precedents to justify his course of action, saying Christ was criticized in like manner in his day. It was this didactic dogmatism and appeal to religious sanctions that drove Aberhart's critics frantic for they could not reply in kind. Although Aberhart's authority was part of his strength, it also proved a source of weakness for this very trait made relations with his colleagues exceedingly difficult. Over the years at the Bible Institute "a whole regiment" joined Aberhart, differed with him, and left. He would not brook insubordination; you worked with him or he worked without you.[34] The same situation prevailed during his premiership as several of his cabinet colleagues found it impossible to work with him and submit to this relationship. His political thinking, observed his ex-attorney general in 1937, was predicated on the theory of "the divine right of Aberhart."[35]

The new Bible school was in operation only three years when the depression first began to cast its shadows over the prairies. Up until that time Aberhart had taken no part in politics save for a nominal support of the conservative party and a personal friendship with Prime Minister Bennett. He had left politics to the politicians and preached his biblical prophecies unperturbed by political or economic affairs. But perhaps one of the most dangerous effects of the depression was that it started people asking questions. Aberhart began to examine the depression, disturbed by the inequality of it and the necessity of sending his high-school graduates into a jobless world. As he boarded the train for Edmonton in the summer of 1932 Aberhart still had no answer, but in Edmonton another teacher, Charles Scarborough, introduced him to the writings of Maurice Colbourne and his outline of a new economic theory called Social Credit. With concise algebraic equations and slogans Colbourne dramatized the irony of the continual struggle against scarcity in a machine age that had made scarcity obsolete and saw in Major Douglas's Social Credit theorems *a priori* laws that waited only for man's acceptance.[36] To Aberhart, the mathematician, the outline of Douglas' analysis and solution appeared to be a simple equation and certainly *a priori* presuppositions were not new to his fundamentalist teachings. For years he had noted the incongruity of governments paying people to destroy goods and of goods piled high on the store shelves both while people were begging for food, but had no money to buy it. Social Credit not only identified the banker as "the nigger in the woodpile" who was exploiting this paradox of "poverty in the midst of plenty," but also explained how to bring production and consumption into balance.[37]

456

Intrigued by Major Douglas' views Aberhart returned to Calgary and read everything he could find on Social Credit. Within weeks he began to introduce bits of Social Credit into his Sunday afternoon broadcasts and soon discovered that "he had tapped a great reservoir of public interest"[38] although this was hardly biblical exposition, or so some of his associates thought, and they urged him to confine himself to the Bible and set aside the economic doctrines. But when letters "poured in" telling him of a far wider ministry with many new listeners who now heard both his economic and religious message he elected to continue, for after all was not Social Credit merely the extension of religious truths, perhaps "an economic movement from God himself" he told a Strand Theatre audience in Edmonton.[39] However Aberhart made no effort to accommodate Major Douglas' view of human nature as essentially good with his own ten-year proclamation of the depravity of man and original sin. Although Social Credit could help solve economic problems, he would add, "there still remains a spiritual problem."[40] The similarity of Social Credit to Aberhart's version of fundamentalism was in its universals and *a priori* presuppositions that Douglas had unearthed. Aberhart could offer the same finality and assurances of truth as he could in his prophetic expositions. There was no room for error or any reason for question since "Social Credit is based upon the foundation of eternal principles. These can never be destroyed; they will be true for all men in all places at all times."[41] If challenged, a Social Crediter could always fall back on the argument that Social Credit, like the Trinity, was not understandable to non-converts[42] or a Social Crediter could testify, as Aberhart did in a legislative hearing, that "certain types of minds . . . do not lend themselves to progress."[43]

As the depression deepened Aberhart's message held more and more appeal. Soon the Institute's auditorium was packed as the teacher with the use of huge charts diagnosed the ills of the monetary system and sharpened the old U.F.A. indictment of the financial barons. The outcome was a new step in organization. Aberhart, the organization man in both high school and Bible school, continued his "hobby" in his new role of Social Credit spokesman. Soon Calgary and its environs was saturated with study classes and dedicated workers, such as Mrs. Edith Rogers, Joseph Unwin, and Earl Ansley, began to spread the Social Credit gospel to virtually every hamlet in the province, beginning in the south and moving northward. Shortly the mimeographed lessons that Aberhart wrote for his study classes were replaced by printed booklets and he began to answer invitations to lecture on Social Credit outside of Calgary. On Sundays his religious message shared the spotlight with Social Credit doctrines and in this way his firmly established religious organization conveniently doubled as a basis for the growth of the Social Credit movement.

Three elements contributed substantially to Aberhart's success in promoting his Social Credit doctrines. The first was Aberhart's respected career as a school-teacher and radio preacher. When he began to preach economics over CFCN in 1932 he was not handicapped by a reputation either as a socialist or as a known agitator. He was not even an American, but a pillar of local respectability. His lack of affiliation with any major religious denomination or political group was in his favour for both his religious and Social Credit movements shared the advantage of being "lay rather than professional movements, nonconformist in temper, hostile to the respectable well-to-do and to the eastern interests."[44] His strongest support at first came from the rural districts and small towns and among the "foreign elements . . . [who had] not been readily assimilated into the social life of the province."[45] This back-country religious rebellion soon became intertwined with a political separatist movement led by the same man, although its base of support was to grow strikingly.

457

Aberhart's second advantage was that neither political nor economic nonconformity was likely to be a liability in Alberta. If anything it was the badge of prairie independence to be worn with pride. Disenchantment with the monied and politically powerful east reached back at least to the 1911 election and even to territorial days, and both the Progressives and the U.F.A. had capitalized on this attitude to take Alberta outside of the main stream of traditional politics. In 1935 when a reporter asked what made a Social Credit government possible, he received the reply, "The late William Jennings Bryan."[46] But by 1932 the U.F.A. was in trouble. Tamed by time and success in office it was no longer the vehicle of prairie radicalism that it had been in 1921. It had weathered the election of 1930, but was immediately caught in the worst days of the depression and in an effort to keep financially solvent embarked on a very orthodox and unspectacular policy of government retrenchment. In 1931 the government suffered a serious political loss in the retirement of Henry Wise Wood from the presidency of the U.F.A. for with Wood went the almost religious zeal that had characterized the farmers' movement from its inception. In his place stepped Aberhart to put an even greater religious imprint on the new Social Credit movement and since no political tag was attached to Aberhart's lectures at first, many U.F.A. locals invited Aberhart to speak for social credit theories were not new to them. Many of their own leaders (George Bevington, William Irvine, Henry Spenser) had picked up the cry of monetary reform in the 'twenties and supplemented U.F.A. study materials with social credit literature. In fact, Aberhart's organization followed U.F.A. lines. The study groups compared to U.F.A. locals and shortly zones were organized similar to the U.F.A. districts.

However, neither of these assets would have coalesced effectively without the leadership of Aberhart to dramatize and organize this opportunity. The Social Credit movement centred on Aberhart and it was he who gave a sense of unity to the scattered groups.[47] As yet, Aberhart made no effort to form a political party. Rather his strategy in the winter of 1933–4 was to create a political pressure group that would force the Farmers' government to implement Social Credit economics and the hundreds of study groups, the petitions, and the Social Credit newspaper were all aimed at this objective. But by December, 1934, no party had unequivocally adopted Social Credit and an election was due within months. By this time the Social Credit leadership, like the Populists, and the U.F.A. in 1921, began "to realize that their non-partisan and bipartisan efforts were mainly wasted." Their organization, in evading the only practical means to implement their goals, was "like a gun that will do everything but shoot."[48]

Aberhart could now say he had no choice but to let the will of the people be heard by their own political voice. But first, once more, like Gideon, he tested the political fleece to gauge his strength; Aberhart was seldom one to forfeit the known for the unknown unless the venture was insured. Over the radio he asked for a straw vote in order to test the appeal of Social Credit. The response was so overwhelming (up to 93 per cent in many districts) that Aberhart no longer looked back, but only ahead to the task of electing Social Credit candidates to the legislature that summer. Aberhart had become the victim of his own proposals for a political party was the goal his proposals ultimately demanded. But perhaps he had become a willing victim even before the final rejection of his plan at the U.F.A. convention in January. His December writings and utterances would suggest this.[49] In two years Aberhart had become so involved in the movement and had been led on by the response of the crowds to a point where it would have been very unlike Aberhart to bow out and turn over his efforts to another. He was not a follower, and his followers considered only Aberhart their leader.

As Aberhart committed his following to political action in 1935 he already had the advantage of a closely knit and highly centralized organization. The study groups became political units, the Sunday services blended Biblical and political prophecy, and the lists of correspondents throughout the province who supported his Bible broadcasts served as points of contact for Social Credit organizers in hiring halls and getting out the advertising in each hamlet. Speakers, press releases, and more organizers kept emanating from the Prophetic Bible Institute to every polling district in Alberta. By election week his organizing capacity had resulted in handpicked candidates for each constituency, sixteen hundred Social Credit groups, and two skilfully conducted canvasses of the entire province. No political movement in Alberta ever provided so intensive an organization.[50]

The main feature of the Social Credit campaign, however, remained Aberhart himself. Already well known by radio he now stumped the hustings with his usual vigour and authority and the crowds that turned out to hear him broke all previous records.[51] Few groups were overlooked in the Social Credit's saturation campaign. They seemed to take "a leaf out of the book of Big Time Sullivan, the New York Tammany ruler" for they outorganized every other group. Even in such small places as Wainwright and Camrose four to five thousand people would turn out for the monster picnics and outings that were arranged. There would be bands, games, and amusements after which Aberhart would step to the platform to the tune of a martial hymn. Women baked cakes and men solicited contributions from the town merchants. "There were whist and euchre drives. And anybody who wanted to be anybody was on a committee."[52] To newspapermen covering the campaign, Aberhart was an "almost matchless manager of crowd psychology" who could adapt to his audience with deft ability. As a showman he exuded self-confidence and grasped "the subtle nuances of platform tactics" so that he induced his listeners to feel that they and he were in a "comradely communion" against the sinister forces of hell — forces usually identified as "they."[53] A forceful figure, he spoke powerfully and with his teacher's air of didactic dogmatism. Starting quietly with "forefinger in his vest pockets," he picked up volume and vehemence as he progressed. "We face a giant today. By ingenuity we can deprive him of his power. The sling of credit-loans-without-interest and the non-negotiable certified stones will destroy his grip and deliver us from his power."[54]

Aberhart enjoyed most playing the role of a provincial David, albeit a rather oversize one, fighting the eastern giant of finance as he would attack the "Fifty Big Shots of Canada" who allegedly were crucifying the will of the people.[55] The charge was at least as old as Bryan, but the appeal did not diminish, and always coupled with the charge was the respected religious identity of Aberhart. William Irvine, a U.F.A. leader, observed that Social Credit was "Douglas on the one hand and the Holy Ghost on the other" and Social Crediters appeared pleased with the definition.[56] In Edmonton at a Conservative rally, W.G. Ernst, M.P., frankly admitted that Social Credit without the Scriptures would not be hard to beat,[57] but how could opponents separate the two for Aberhart simply extended his religious mantle to envelop his economic preachings. Economic critics (and there were many, but most of them only angered Albertans by implying that voters were a bit addled if they listened to Aberhart) soon found themselves "in the position of an atheist" trying to ridicule faith itself.[58] Meetings opened with hymns. "O, God Our Help in Ages Past" was chosen the official theme song of the Social Credit League and a collection plate was usually passed around to defray expenses. And yet William Aberhart would have been out of character if he had acted otherwise. For ten years he was known outside of Calgary as nothing more than a radio preacher. A newspaper reporter admitted, "As to Mr. Aberhart's talks being flavored with religion — is it not inevitable considering his background? It would be surprising if it were otherwise."[59] Aberhart never demanded that his opponents take up his brand of campaigning, but, in turn, he had no intention of copying their style, even if it was not "cricket" in their minds not to play according to their rules of politics. When August arrived the voters, as in 1921, supported the party which promised to take "direct action" to overcome their problems and Social Credit swept the province with fifty-six out of the sixty-three seats in the legislature. The school-teacher's "educational" programme had won, not only a radio audience, but a premiership.

When Aberhart assumed office that fall he was fifty-six years of age and the main features of his personality and principles were already indelibly etched. His eight years as premier do not change this portrait appreciably for he continued to operate in the context he knew best — that of a teacher and preacher. His Bible Institute and radio ministry continued as he found that even in politics he preferred preaching to performing, and certainly he understood the principles of organization (his hobby) better than he understood Social Credit. These features show up almost immediately in his premiership for once in power Aberhart never introduced Social Credit as Douglas envisioned it, or as the pupil, using Douglas's terminology, promised it. The promised dividend of twenty-five dollars a month was to remain only a promise, for Aberhart remarked the week after the election that "75 per cent of those who voted for me don't expect any dividend, but hope for a just and honest government."[60]

Aberhart immediately embarked on a programme based on this assumption; besides, he knew how to go about implementing efficiency and organization in government, whereas he did not know quite how to implement Social Credit. In the campaign he had used Major Douglas' dictum of voting for results, not methods, but now he lacked the methods to achieve the promised results. This brings up the question of Aberhart's understanding of Social Credit. From a strictly economic point of view it is unlikely that "Aberhart ever understood the deeper implication of Douglas' monetary theories . . . [for] the fiscal policy of Aberhart was in practice financially orthodox and even conservative."[61] And yet Aberhart probably fulfilled his own concept of Social Credit, which was more humanitarian than economic in terms of his definition. In 1935 he claimed that the whole purpose of Social Credit was "to feed, clothe, and shelter the people."[62] In 1938 he defined Social Credit as "merely Christianity applied to every-day economics,"[63] and in an interview with the *New York Times'* correspondent (September 1, 1935) he saw Social Credit as a ray of hope for the "desperate young people" of the province. He also saw it as a possible alternative to socialism for Douglas (and Aberhart) would retain the capitalistic system. Capitalism was sick, but not beyond recovery. A "shot" of Social Credit would reduce the banker to size and restore the economy to health. In this way no existing privileges or institutes were threatened except those of the bankers, and they were seldom popular in Alberta anyway. Social Credit would not take away from the rich to pay the poor. Rather it would simply pay rich and poor a basic dividend.[64]

Aberhart seemed to think that good intentions would bring good results and in the manner of Micawber hoped that something would turn up if he offered good, Christian leadership. Operating on this premise Aberhart responded to the problems of the province in his first eighteen months in office with administrative reorganization and farm-labour legislation (the two voting blocs to which he owed his premiership). With his characteristic zest and thoroughness the new premier merged departments and eliminated waste in a determined effort to promote efficiency and a balanced budget. Such a policy proved beneficial, but hardly popular among ardent Social Crediters. In 1937 enough back-benchers revolted in the legislature to frighten the premier and his cabinet. These back-benchers, disillusioned by Aberhart's failure to implement a Social Credit scheme within the promised time, had the votes to topple the government at one time but hesitated to use them, hoping that Aberhart would bow out gracefully as Greenfield of the U.F.A. had done in 1925 in favour of Brownlee. This Aberhart had refused to do, and the insurgents had not known quite how to go about forcing the issue.[65] In the jockeying for position that followed the premier was able to use a hastily written Alberta Social Credit Act to wean away sufficient votes to stay in power. By June of 1937 the Social Crediters finally had two English technicians in Alberta to introduce Social Credit. They also continued to have Aberhart as their premier.[66]

Aberhart switched tactics after the insurgency and replaced his emphasis on "good government" with promotion of Social Credit policies under the aegis of Douglas' emissaries. By underwriting their measures Aberhart hoped to prove to his party that he was not only premier, but a Social Credit premier. For the next nine months a frontal attack on finance was the directive, even though Douglas himself admitted that such an attack had as much chance of survival as the "well-known celluloid cat in Hades."[67] Douglas was correct for Aberhart's "positional warfare" with finance resulted in the disallowance of thirteen Alberta statutes by the federal government and courts. It is doubtful if the cabinet really expected this legislation to evade federal or legal disallowance, for not even their own law officers would defend its legality, although one cabinet minister, Lucien Maynard, a barrister, used Aberhart's frame of logic to argue that the intent of the government was to "do good," therefore divine law, and therefore *intra vires*.[68] When the unfavourable decision of the Supreme Court was handed down, Aberhart said that the government would abide by its verdict and avoid all talk of sedition and secession. "The B.N.A. act [now became] the scapegoat,"[69] blamed for preventing the implementation of the premier's dividend. The feud with Ottawa had served its purpose. It had revealed to Social Crediters the power of finance in high places, united the Social Credit party, and provided Aberhart with a new role as the champion of provincial rights.

Aberhart announced in 1938 that the frontal attack on finance was over

461

and that Social Credit would adjust to the inevitable and take a new track for "a vessel has sometimes to sail against the very wind that is its only means of propulsion. To do this, the vessel pursues, you know, a zigzag course from side to side. It is called 'tacking in the wind.' "[70] The new tack was a return to the policy of 1936 with its emphasis on "good government," debt adjustment, and party organization. Speaking at his Bible Institute in 1939 Aberhart confided that if he, like Lincoln, could earn for himself "the title 'Honest Abe' " he would be "greatly satisfied" with his public career.[71]

Several of Aberhart's manoeuvres and statutes (particularly the bill to control the press) during this period brought charges of Hitlerism and fascism. In fact, the opposition parties were making this charge as early as 1935. Admittedly Major Douglas was strongly anti-semitic and one wing of the party in Alberta carried about and discussed the spurious *Protocols of Zion*; but Aberhart himself was never anti-semitic or a serious supporter of the regimentation that was characteristic of the corporate state. From the beginning Aberhart argued that Social Credit must come by voluntary co-operation, but Social Credit, as outlined by Major Douglas, was practically impossible without coercion. Certainly some of Aberhart's proposals, such as the use of scrip as legal tender, demanded state enforcement no matter what label was proffered the public for the entire province was not going to co-operate without a murmur as Aberhart was accustomed to expect from his religious following. The province was not a church and to get his programme in operation in Alberta was going to demand an element of coercion.

Dr. W.W. Cross, one of Aberhart's cabinet ministers and one of the few Social Crediters who really seemed to understand Social Credit, admitted as much[72] and Dr. R.M. Johnstone, western organizer for the Canadian Union of Fascists, was in essential agreement. He wrote:

Douglas in fact is in the predicament of having invented a machine he can't make work. There are a lot of good gadgets in it but the main drive shaft, and the power equipment requires a mechanism called THE CORPORATE STATE, which is altogether missing in Alberta. . . . Douglas . . . has blinders on insofar as he claims that his system essentially Socialistic in tone, IS A CAPITALISTIC PROPOSAL, AND MUST BE OPERATED UPON DISTINCTLY CAPITALIST PRINCIPLES. . . . Douglas went around the world ding-donging FASCISM AND FASCISTS. His only real friends in the background have been Fascists, since only through Fascist economics can it be operated.[73]

Another fascist complained that Social Credit was an imperfectly expressed form of fascism since Aberhart and some of his supporters were "still to an undue degree believers in the myth Democracy, and Abie is 'too full of the milk of human kindness to catch the nearest way.' "[74] Fascist organizer Johnstone tried to explain it by observing that only because of "certain religious quirks" had Aberhart not yet got around to realizing a full fascist ideology.[75] It is doubtful if he would have realized such an ideology even without his religious faith; on the other hand his fundamentalist cast may help explain some of his authoritarian statutes for he was used to speaking as one having authority and in most cases his political actions were no more autocratic than many of his religious rulings. Although he insisted on non-conformity to worldly standards at his Bible Institute there was, paradoxically, a rigid conformity in dress, belief, and behaviour demanded of those attending the Bible school and a conspicuous lack of charity to other non-conformists. Some phases of this viewpoint carried over into politics.[76]

The friction generated by Aberhart's style of leadership and efforts to implement Social Credit began to abate a bit as prosperity returned to Alberta, not as a result of dividends, but through such natural processes as rains, freedom from frost, and a revival of world trade. When war broke out the next year it was only proper and patriotic for the Social Credit Board to become more educational than economic for the government had promised not to introduce any controversial legislation so that undivided attention could be given to the war effort. Actually, the war undermined the original appeal of Social Credit for now Albertans had an abundance of purchasing power and a shortage of consumer goods. At the same time the war and the war-time powers acquired by the federal government reduced the role and prestige of the provincial premiers and forced Aberhart off the front pages for longer periods than he had been accustomed to expect.

463

In 1940 the opposition parties also tried to push Aberhart out of provincial politics as all the parties, except the C.C.F., pooled their organizations, candidates, and money in a determined effort to unseat Social Credit in its bid for re-election.[77] But the only thing they could agree on was their common dislike of Aberhart.[78] Social Crediters quickly capitalized on this by campaigning, "Vote FOR Something, Not Against Something." Perhaps more significant were the observations made by Elmore Philpott, a columnist for a Liberal paper. Reporting from the hustings, he noted that the farmers honestly believed that the choice was either Aberhart or the sheriff. The premier's debt legislation was no political mistake. The reporter's observations concluded: "Actually, as a politician Premier Aberhart is head and shoulders above most of his competitors throughout Canada. He is the only Canadian politician to realize and exploit the possibilities of radio. He is closer to the people than is any other public man in Canada by reason of his systematic use of the air lanes. Also he is a superb organizer. Already he has rural Alberta organized from end to end. His opponents have not."[79]

When the votes were all in Social Credit was returned to power with thirty-six out of fifty-seven seats and Aberhart began his second term.[80] The equation of Social Credit and Christianity continued through this term as Aberhart mixed the two with casual candour in his radio broadcasts. When requested by newspapermen to leave piety out of politics, Aberhart asked why "we shouldn't have a premier with a Bible in one hand. I suppose we should have a premier with a bottle of whiskey in his pocket. That would suit them better. Parents should think it over."[81] And yet in spite of his strict religious code that forbade smoking, drinking, and "wordly amusements" in his Bible Institute, he never tried to impose his standards on his colleagues. His tolerance of other faiths was attested in his selection of cabinet members who were Mormon, Anglican, Presbyterian, United Church, and Roman

Catholic. Only Manning followed Aberhart in his religious views, but the entire cabinet acknowledged the acumen of "the Chief" as a politician and organizer.

Any kind of organization appealed to the premier and in his first term (serving as Minister of Education as well) he had completely reorganized the rural school system over the opposition of ten thousand rural school trustees — a task that the U.F.A. government had continuously promised, but had never had the political courage to carry through. The Alberta Teachers' Association made no secret of its delight in seeing the demise of the U.F.A. administration with which it had been continuously at odds because of the delay of fundamental reforms in both organization and curriculum.[82] Over the noisy dissent of the trustees, Aberhart and Solon Low (another school-teacher) pushed through the bill to reduce the number of rural school districts from over three thousand to forty-five divisions. In addition Aberhart kept his campaign promise to revise the curriculum. Here he did not remain in "character" as the traditionalist his religious position might lead one to expect.[83] Aberhart, the disciplinarian and reader of Greek and Hebrew, observed that education was still aimed at university entrance in the province rather than preparation for "life," yet few students actually went on to university. He assigned the task of reforming the curriculum to Dr. H.C. Newland, Supervisor of Schools, and within a year a programme of progressive education called "the new enterprise or activity system" was introduced into elementary schools. The teacher was to be an evangelist of democracy and teach children not only to make a living, but "how to live."[84]

464

In his second term the premier selected another controversial area, municipal reform, and by 1943 the 143 rural municipalities were reorganized and consolidated over the bitter complaints of the traditionalists who disliked disturbing old patterns of government.[85] Here again, a dichotomy in Aberhart's thinking emerged. The premier bitterly opposed the growing powers of Ottawa and, even more, the prospect of an Atlantic community or "Union Now" which he claimed was a diabolical scheme leading towards world dictatorship, and yet he had no objections to an increased centralization in Alberta. Educational and municipal reorganization, the Marketing Act, and the government's entrance into the insurance business had all increased the powers of Edmonton and interfered more and more in private business and local government. Aberhart explained it by saying his "whole nature" reacted against "lackadaisical" methods of operation and that his political philosophy opposed the "general laissez faire attitude that seems to prevail."[86] When his projects were criticized by the opposition or blocked by Ottawa, he would frequently draw on the similar trials endured by one of his political heroes, President Roosevelt — "a much greater reformer than I [who] in his magnificent effort for progressive reform has come face to face with the same problem with his legislation."[87]

Probably no public figure supported the war effort more readily or more regularly than Aberhart. He was the first premier to urge conscription of manpower and the Alberta government was the first to give civil servants leave of absence to join the armed forces with their position of seniority guaranteed.[88] True to his prophetic orientation, however, Aberhart seldom preached on the war effort or its outcome without coupling it with his insights stemming from biblical prophecy. Fortunately for Canada the promises of God assured the victory to "our side" since this was a conflict between "paganism and Christianity."[89] The guarantee of ultimate victory was not based on armed strength, but on the conviction that the British Commonwealth and the United States were "truly God's battle axe" and Isaiah 54:17 promised their protection. This convenant was "clearly addressed to London and Washington" since the Commonwealth and the United States were "the servants of the Lord" in the war against Germany and Japan. Aberhart explained that without "any shadow of doubt" the members of the Anglo-Saxon race were favoured of God and were the descendants of the Old Testament Israelites: "The Angles who were so named because, as one of the Lost Tribes, they worshipped the golden calf; the Saxons who were so named because they were the sons of Isaac of Isaac-sons; and the Scoaths or Scots who lived in tents and who, even to this day, pride themselves on their woolen tartan cloaks of many colors."[90] As for Germany, Aberhart indicated that Germany's recurrent cycles of aggression and defeat were forecast in the Bible and would continue as long as Germany was allowed to remain a "united, powerful nation." Therefore he urged the Allies to divide Germany into small units after the war to prevent future aggression.[91] At the beginning of the war he gave a series of ten radio lectures on "The British Coat-of-Arms." In describing the inscription on the coat of arms ("Dieu et Mon Droit") the pedagogue explained that French was used because it was a more universal language. Besides, "the British who are proud of their Coat-of-Arms will naturally ask the meaning of the title and will be more deeply impressed" by the use of the French language.[92] The premier's interpretation of English history, as his interpretation of Bible prophecy, was uniquely his own.

Aberhart's intense interest in organization continued through the war years. In addition to reorganizing the government and the municipal units he turned his attention to party organization again. The premier had hoped that Social Credit provincial governments would provide the groundswell for a national movement. But when these failed to materialize in British Columbia and Saskatchewan, and when federal disallowance and court rulings outlawed any provincial Social Credit scheme, Aberhart began to see no alternative except a federal organization. The strategy was to be the same as that which had proved successful in Alberta. The plan was to build up an organization across the country and bring pressure on the established parties to implement social credit. If no response was forthcoming the organization would then take political action. The plan took shape at a three-day conference in Winnipeg, October 27–29, 1941, where seventy-five delegates, dominated by the Alberta bloc, met to launch their "educational" drive across Canada. The conference claimed that its purposes were to reform the monetary system and to "oppose and expose" attempts to weaken democracy by increased centralization.[93]

Aberhart, himself, never mentioned any federal aspirations even though

465

he was active in the national organization and began a series of weekly broadcasts of fifteen radio stations across Canada. His understudy and colleague, Ernest Manning, explained that Aberhart would never run for federal office unless he was drafted and pointed out that the purpose of the radio broadcasts was to educate the people. The people would then demand progressive leadership and draft Aberhart as in 1935. However, "one thing is certain," Manning concluded, "he will not thrust himself upon the people. But if they demand his leadership, he will see his duty."[94] Aberhart had never been one to commit himself until he could guarantee the outcome and meanwhile he would continue to organize and in his suite in Edmonton to study French. But death came before the premier could complete his organization of a national party. Taken ill while vacationing at his daughter's in Vancouver the end came suddenly for the prairie preacher and politician. His cabinet colleagues were summoned, but none reached him before he died early in the morning of May 23, 1943. He was sixty-four years old.

466

It is difficult to sum up or neatly categorize such a man's career for he defies any niche in which one could attempt to place him. In his final sermon preached at the Bible Institute before his death he indicated that he cared little what man said about his earthly career so long as God would commend him as a faithful servant.[95] At his teacher's funeral Aberhart's religious and political successor, Ernest Manning, agreed that Aberhart's finest service was his religious ministry to "thousands of homes across the Canadian West,"[96] but the very fact that Aberhart's religious ministry was primarily a radio ministry makes it impossible to assess the spiritual contribution that Aberhart made in Alberta. Observable events, unfortunately, are earth bound and therefore the premier's religious impact can be judged only in so far as it was recorded in human acts and actions.

His political career only seems to compound the confusion in assessing the man for Aberhart has been tagged with so many labels, ranging from "Fascist" to "Poujadist" to "William Jennings Bryan," that, at times, he seems to take on the habits of a chameleon and few definite statements stand up. And yet some constants emerge from his career. Perhaps most indelible was his fundamentalist cast of mind. His deep belief in the authority of the Bible (and in the authority of those who interpreted it correctly) and his equal interest in biblical prophecies, fulfilled and unfulfilled, marked his career and utterances at every turn. He frequently interpreted these biblical statements to fit the times (e.g., the guarantee of Allied victory in World War II), and in office, as before, he was always able to equate his programme with divine sanctions and seldom operated without this conviction. This meant that he was always in the right and "they" became the forces of darkness that had to be endured as best they could.

Before entering politics he had faced very little criticism. Whether teaching children in school in his authoritarian manner, or interpreting the Scriptures from the safety of his pulpit or a radio microphone, he was seldom confronted with controversy. His biblical study courses always gave *the* answer to each question and no alternative was even broached. From this insulated environment he entered politics late in life and never really accepted or appre ciated the give and take of political dialogue. He seldom spoke in the legis- lature, making only two addresses in his eight years, nor did he directly debate issues outside of the legislature, preferring to take to his pulpit and there move quickly into the clichés and rigid furrows of thought that he had used for so long. This is what drove his political opponents to distrac- tion. They could never confront him directly or argue a case with him accord- ing to their ground rules of debate. His habit of treating political warfare as a glorified "TV western" between the "good guys" and the "bad guys" went back to his years of teaching and preaching when he reduced either mathematical or biblical problems to their simplest denominator of right or wrong and then dramatized the telling of them. In politics he did the same with Social Credit, presenting it in such a grossly oversimplified form that Douglasites were left aghast and voters were lulled into accepting it for the proposal seemed so simple it *must* work.

But this fundamentalist cast did not operate in two other ways that would logically be identified with it, and in efforts to make Aberhart consistent writers have frequently misinterpreted these areas of action. First, he was by no means as conservative in education as he was in religion. As Minister of Education he put through the first far-reaching reforms in decades and ended up with a curriculum that was contrary to what one would expect from the authoritarian preacher and teacher. Secondly, his fundamentalist theology minimized the here and now in favour of the hereafter. The Chris- tian was to be "separate" from the world[97] for Satan was the Prince of this world and the Christian could never really be comfortable as a citizen in it, and yet Aberhart picked up Social Credit, in part, because of the injustices of the depression and the need to ameliorate the inequities of this life. As premier he put through labour legislation, increased old-age pensions, saved debtors from eviction, and set up rural health units and cancer clinics; it is, perhaps, significant that the brick and stone memorials to Aberhart today are a new hospital wing in Edmonton and a school in Calgary — the two areas he served best. All of these things were very much connected with a better life here and now; in fact they were some of the features of the social gospel that he condemned so roundly in his preaching. Actually Aberhart's political role, in performance if not in Social Credit ideology, comes closest to being that of a reformer just as he claimed to be a religious reformer in purifying Christianity from the evils of modernism. He was often compared to William Jennings Bryan and he liked to compare himself to President Roosevelt in the latter's effort to implement reform legislation. This was why B.T. Richardson noted that Aberhart, and all the rest of the Social Crediters except Low, Cross, and Ansley, never really understood the full implications of Social Credit but were Social Crediters because of their interest in either religious or monetary reform.[98]

Donald Smiley, in his interpretation of the Social Credit party, calls Social Crediters "Canada's Poujadists" and going back to the Aberhart regime, argues that "Social Credit is essentially anti-institutional and as such has

167

both radical and nihilistic elements.''[99] It is certainly true that Social Credit under Aberhart was always anti-banker and usually anti-eastern, but this was hardly radical and certainly not nihilistic; in fact it was in the tradition of the U.F.A. and the prairies to take this position. On the other hand it could be argued that Social Credit was successful in 1935 under Aberhart precisely because it incorporated many of the prevalent norms of the province. It copied the familiar U.F.A. organization in party structure, urged monetary reform as did many of the U.F.A. leaders earlier, and relied on two respectable institutions, capitalism and Christianity, as the staples in Aberhart's platform and preaching. If anything Aberhart toned down his earlier attacks on the older religious institutions after picking up Social Credit. Frequently the largest churches in the province held his conventions and numerous leaders of the United Church and Mormon communities publicly endorsed Social Credit, even running as candidates, while in Roman Catholic St. Paul he ran just as strongly as in Protestant areas. Only in winning loyal support from ethnic and religious groups formerly excluded from community or political leadership and in the *a priori* religious and economic preachings that Aberhart invoked did he depart from traditional norms.

468

In other respects Aberhart's approach to government seems to have been pragmatic rather than doctrinaire or nihilistic. The most revealing evidence of this approach was his organization of the government and his willingness to adapt his Social Credit platform to the exigencies of the times. At worst it can be termed opportunism; at best it might be called political acumen. He relied heavily on the precedents of the U.F.A. to build his organization, championed a programme of monetary and debt legislation in depression days, and stressed good government in power (note that the party was quite content to stand on its five-year record in the 1940 election). The premier's championing of debt reduction, provincial rights, labour legislation, and efficiency in government actually had very little to do with Social Credit economics. A Social Credit author explained that ''Social Credit is a mechanism; like a car offered a tired wayfarer. It doesn't matter where the man wants to go, or whether he is white, black or yellow, it will take him as far and as fast as he chooses to go, in any direction.''[100] Aberhart's direction was by a different route than that outlined by Major Douglas and it brought different results. Yet Aberhart, of course, retained his public devotion to Social Credit doctrines, even after Social Credit had become just another political party. The Social Credit theories became, just as Stephen Leacock predicted, ''a sort of sacred ideal . . . too holy for current use. Thus in the South Sea Islands the natives had a god so exalted they must not even pronounce his real name. He is just called Oom. Social Credit is going to be the Oom of the Canadian West.''[101]

In the beginning Aberhart wanted to believe that Social Credit was not just another political party and, like other reformers, believed that his programme was a panacea for the province. He pointed to Social Credit as a set of eternal principles, as unarguable as the Ten Commandments, which, if applied, would reform political and economic life. In this sense Social Credit was more a faith or a set of *a priori* principles than an economic doctrine but increasingly Aberhart found it difficult to relate this faith to the facts of political life. Once in power he found that his preachings outran his performance and the depression and "politics" still haunted the province and rivalries, revolts, and personal feuds existed even in his own party in spite of his hopes to the contrary. Aberhart found that he had no ultimate solution to the problem of economics and government and although his administration alleviated many provincial problems (eviction for debt, educational decay, poor working conditions in industry), it also brought new problems peculiar to itself (a loss of provincial credit, federal antagonism, and a rejection of "third parties" in national elections). Several of his colleagues experienced the same problem and became disillusioned,[102] but Aberhart's mind seemed to be made up of compartments and he appeared undisturbed by the contradictions between his professions as a preacher and his political manoeuvres as premier. And yet Aberhart never acquired a sudden piety as a cloak for politics for he had preached the same biblical message for decades before entering politics. He simply failed to relate the two at times.

469

As it turned out the majority of voters seemed no more disturbed than Aberhart by the contradictions between his profession and practice. One reason is that in 1935, of the two possible new options, Social Credit or C.C.F., Social Credit probably seemed the less radical to the ordinary voter for it promised to bring results without changing the basic economic habits of the province in the process. Perhaps that is why one Catholic writer gave Catholic sanction to Social Credit instead of C.C.F. policies, saying: "We may be magnificently social without being socialistic: Such is the case for the Crediters."[103] In the same year that Aberhart discovered Social Credit the U.F.A. Convention gave its "entire support" to the C.C.F. platform for a planned economy, but only the U.F.A. leadership really supported the programme; the rank and file shied away from such radical schemes.[104] Aberhart with his established religious and educational reputation and with his promise of "direct action" as the U.F.A. had promised fourteen years earlier seemed the better risk. Aberhart was known in the province too well and too long as a teacher and preacher to disturb Albertans simply because he wanted to be a politician. The person and the prospects of vigorous performance outranked the platform and party label.

William Aberhart had aimed high in each field he entered — teaching, preaching, and politics, but fundamentally, in all his relationships, he remained a teacher. He had spent most of his life in the classroom and it was an easy matter for Aberhart, the school-teacher and Bible preacher, to treat the province as if it were one big classroom and attempt to educate it as he saw fit. In his final years as premier Aberhart left a dictum that characterized his own public career. "Prudence," he said, "will get us what nothing else can. Remember prudence means a combination of two important qualities, piety and practical sagacity."[105] Never one to take an unnecessary risk, whether it was in moving to a new school without a guarantee or entering politics without two careful Gallup polls, he relied heavily, and wisely, on organization to achieve success in each of his three fields. Certainly as a political organizer he was above average. One wonders how he ever failed his Political Science course at Queen's.

Notes

1. Maxwell Vos, "Opium from Alberta," *New Statesman and Nation*, XLIV (Dec. 20, 1952), 747.
2. Aberhart's successor, Premier E.L. Manning claims that Aberhart was first and foremost a teacher. Interview with Premier Manning, Edmonton, Oct. 16, 1958.
3. Interview with Mrs. Wm. Aberhart, widow of Premier Aberhart, Calgary, July 18, 1958.
4. Now Zion United Church, *Zion Church 1852-1952*, a centennial booklet (Brantford, 1952), pp. 6-7.
5. Interview with Manning, Oct. 16, 1958.
6. *Edmonton Bulletin*, May 24, 1943.
7. Interview with Orvis Kennedy, Treasurer and National Organizer, Social Credit Association of Canada, former President, Alberta Social Credit League, S.C. Member of Parliament, 1938-40, Edmonton, Oct. 8, 1958. This same correspondence course with the same title, "Busy People's Bible Course," and 52 lessons was later offered at Aberhart's Bible Institute in Calgary, see the *Syllabus of the Calgary Prophetic Bible Institute* (Calgary, 1943-4), p. 3.
8. Jean Royce, Registrar at Queen's, to writer, Sept. 4, 1958, including Wm. Aberhart's academic record at Queen's.
9. Calgary School Board Records, L.A. Daniels, Asst. Superintendent, to writer, Dec. 9, 1958.
10. Interview with John J. Bowlen, M.L.A., 1930-44, Liberal House Leader, 1936-8, Lieutenant Governor of Alberta, 1950-9, Edmonton, Sept. 23, 1958. The only area in which all sixty-one persons interviewed by the writer were in agreement was on the matter of Aberhart's excellence as a high school teacher.
11. Interview with John Laurie, English teacher, Crescent Heights High School, 1927-54, Calgary, July 17, 1958.
12. Interview with Lem Fowler, agent for Burrough's and Company, Ltd., legal publishers, Calgary, July 20, 1958.
13. *Edmonton Bulletin*, May 28, 1943.
14. *Edmonton Journal*, Aug. 10, 1939.
15. Mabel Giles, *A Tribute to William Aberhart* (Calgary, 1944), p. 5.
16. Tone Cashman, *Ernest C. Manning* (Edmonton, 1958), p. 13.
17. *Edmonton Bulletin*, May 24, 1943.
18. Interview with E.G. Hansell, pastor, Westbourne Baptist Church, 1922-6, federal M.P. and Social Credit organizer, 1935-58, Director of Public Relations, Alberta Bible College, 1958- , Calgary, Oct. 22, 1958; and interview with Manning, Oct. 16, 1958.
19. Cashman, *Manning*, p. 9. "Fundamental" Baptist was a term coined by the Baptist ministers and churches who refused to go along with the Baptist conventions of Western Canada and Ontario and Quebec and pulled their churches out of the convention, charging a watering down of the traditional doctrines. See Wm. E. Mann, *Sect, Cult and Church in Alberta* (Toronto, 1955), pp. 43-58.
20. *Syllabus of the Calgary Prophetic Bible Institute*, p. 5. By the Bible Aberhart meant the King James Version. Only it was the true "preservation and revelation," see Aberhart, "The Latest of Modern Movements," *God's Great Prophecies* (Calgary, 192-).
21. Aberhart, *Systematic Theology: The Seven Dispensations,* "A" *Course* (Calgary, 1926), pp. 7-8.
22. Mann, *Sect, Cult and Church in Alberta*, pp. 51-4.
23. Cited in Barbara Moon, "Aberhart: The Man and the Shadow," *Maclean's*, LXVI (March 15, 1953), 52.
24. *Albertan Supplement* (Calgary), Feb. 22, 1936; interview with Charles Pearce, Treasurer of the Prophetic Bible Institute, 1929- ; Superintendent, Radio Sunday School, 1926- , Chairman, Provincial Marketing Board, 1955- , Edmonton, Oct. 8, 1958.
25. *Syllabus of the Calgary Prophetic Bible Institute*, p. 7.
26. From 1928 to 1930 Manning lived in the Aberhart home while the youth was finishing his Bible training. Since Aberhart lacked sons, Manning came closest to "filling the bill." Cashman, *Manning*, p. 11.
27. *Calgary Herald*, June 3, 1939. As premier he also held several cabinet posts at the same time.
28. *Syllabus of the Calgary Prophetic Bible Institute*, p. 9.
29. Aberhart, *Personal Evangelism* "B" *Course* (Calgary, 192-), pp. 24-7.
30. Aberhart, *God's Great Prophecies*, p. 14.
31. See Aberhart, *Ecclesiastes or the Findings of the Modernist Up-to-Date* (Calgary, 192-); *Apologetics* "B" *Course* (Calgary, 192-).

32. Aberhart, *Apologetics "B"*, p. 13.

33. *Ibid.*, pp. 18, 21–3.

34. Interview with Charles Pearce, Oct. 8, 1958, who stayed with him. Substantiated by Lem Fowler, Calgary, Sept. 17, 1958, who left.

35. John Hugill, *Edmonton Bulletin*, Sept. 23, 1937.

36. Colbourne, *Unemployment or War* (New York, 1928), pp. 252, 286, 306–7. Social Credit economics are presented in all of Major C.H. Douglas' works, e.g., *Credit Power and Democracy* (London, 1921). Knowledgeable examinations of Social Credit are provided by William and Kathryn Cordell, "Alberta and Social Credit," *North American Review*, CCLXI (March, 1936); E.S. Holter, *The ABC of Social Credit* (Toronto, 1944); Charles Sanderson, *Social Credit* (Toronto, 1936), and Richard Ford, "The Douglas Social Credit Scheme," *English Review*, LX (June, 1935).

37. John Lewis, *Douglas Fallacies* (London, 1935), p. 11.

38. H.D. Carrigan, "Aberhart — Man of the Century," *Busy Bee*, I (May–June, 1956), 28. Social Credit periodical.

39. *Today and Tomorrow*, Oct. 22, 1936.

40. As told to the writer by Cyril Hutchinson, Secretary of Prophetic Bible Institute under Aberhart, President of Berean Bible College, 1948– , Calgary, July 16, 1958; also in interview with Charles Pearce, Oct. 8, 1958. Note also Georges-Henri Levesque, *Social Credit and Catholicism* (Ottawa, 1936). This is a significant distinction that John Irving fails to make, "The Evolution of the Social Credit Movement," C.J.E.P.S., XIV (Dec., 1948), 324.

41. *Canadian Social Crediter* "Foreword" in all issues. When accused of pharisaism, the *Social Crediter* blandly replied, "Now where do we Crediters get this holier than thou attitude? We don't only *think* we are right, we *know* we are right. Primarily because our technique is based on a science and in that there are no half measures. You are either right or wrong." April 8, 1953, p. 2.

42. C.H. Douglas, *Social Credit*, Dec. 6, 1935, as cited in Wm. Hiskett and J A Franklin, *Searchlight on Social Credit* (London, 1939), pp. 6–7.

43. Aberhart testimony, *The Douglas System of Social Credit: Evidence Taken by the Agricultural Committee of the Alberta Legislature* (Edmonton, 1934), p. 13.

44. Mann, *Sect, Cult and Church*, p. 156. Alberta has the largest percentage of sects and cults of any Canadian province.

45. K.J. Binns, *Social Credit in Alberta* (Hobart, Tasmania, 1947), 8.

46. H. Napier Moore, "What of Social Credit?" *Maclean's*, XLIX (Jan. 15, 1936), p. 15.

47. For a detailed study of Aberhart's pre-election appeal from the point of view of a social psychologist, see John Irving's, *The Social Credit Movement in Alberta* (Toronto, 1959). In light of the key role that Aberhart plays in the realization of a Social Credit party in Western Canada it is rather surprising that the ten-volume Social Credit Series has dealt only with indirect or piecemeal segments of the story (e.g., *The Winnipeg General Strike, The Liberal Party in Alberta*) and has skirted the central figure except as he incidentally fits in. Only Irving deals in detail with Aberhart, and his book ends at the moment Aberhart and Social Credit come to power.

48. John D. Hicks, *The Populist Revolt* (Minneapolis, 1931), p. 206.

49. Note the *Alberta Social Credit Chronicle*, Dec. 7, 1934, and the *Edmonton Journal*, Dec. 27, 1934.

50. *Vancouver Province*, Aug. 23, 1935; *Lethbridge Herald*, Aug. 26, 1935.

51. See the *Alberta Social Credit Chronicle*, May 24, 1935, *Calgary Herald*, May 18, 1935.

52. Moore, "What of Social Credit?" 22.

53. Ken McConnell, reporter, *Vancouver Province*, May 25, 1943.

54. Cited in Moon, "Aberhart: The Man and the Shadow," 22.

55. Aberhart, *Social Credit Manual* (Calgary, 1935), p. 13.

56. *Edmonton Journal*, May 1, 1935.

57. *Calgary Herald*, April 29, 1935. Agreed the *S.C. Chronicle*, Oct. 5, 1934, "Social Credit without religion would be like an automobile without gasoline — it could not run."

58. *New York Times*, Sept. 1, 1935.

59. Homer Ramage dispatch, *Edmonton Journal*, April 8, 1935.

60. *New York Times*, Sept. 1, 1935.

61. *Encyclopedia Canadiana* (Ottawa, 1957), I, 35.

62. Aberhart, *Social Credit Manual*, p. 14.

63. *Today and Tomorrow*, Nov. 10, 1938.

64. Aberhart, *Social Credit Manual*, p. 14.

65. C.H. Stout, *Hanna Herald*, April 8, 1937.

66. See H.J. Schultz, "The Social Credit Back-benchers' Revolt, 1937," *C.H.R.*, XLI (March, 1960), 1–18, for a detailed study of this insurgency.

67. *Edmonton Journal*, July 22, 1938.

68. *Albertan*, Sept. 30, 1937. For an examination of this federal-provincial conflict, read J.R. Mallory, *Social Credit and the Federal Power in Canada* (Toronto, 1954).

69. A.L. Blue, Social Credit M.L.A., 1935–40, to writer, Sept. 21, 1958.

471

70. *Albertan*, March 14, 1938.

71. *The Times*, March 14, 1940.

72. *Hanna Herald*, May 27, 1937. B.T. Richardson, legislative reporter, after observing the S.C. members for three years claimed that only Cross, Solon Low, and Earl Ansley really understood Social Credit. The rest were just religious or monetary reformers, *Edmonton Journal*, Feb. 23, 1939.

73. Johnstone, Vidora, Saskatchewan, to J.J. Zubick, editor of the *Rebel*, Nov. 18, 1937, private correspondence in files of J.J. Zubick.

74. C. Brandel, editor of the *Thunderbolt* (official organ of the Canadian Union of Fascists) to J.J. Zubick, Nov. 26, 1937, private correspondence in files of J.J. Zubick.

75. Johnstone to Zubick, Oct. 2, 1937, private correspondence in files of Zubick.

76. Fundamentalists were particularly hostile to conscientious objectors during the war and certainly Aberhart showed little charity to the Hutterites. The regulations and practices at the numerous Bible schools in Alberta — e.g., Prairie Bible Institute at Three Hills, Canada's largest — demanded a conformity far in excess of what Aberhart was trying to get from the province.

77. *Edmonton Journal*, March 19, 1940.

78. *The Times*, March 14, 1940.

79. *Victoria Times*, Jan. 13, 1940.

80. H.J. Schultz, "A Second Term: 1940," *Alberta Historical Review*, X (winter, 1962).

81. *Edmonton Journal*, Jan. 7, 1939.

82. The A.T.A., XVI (Sept., 1935); Dec., 1935, 1.

83. And does lead John Irving to call him "an arch-conservative in education," *Social Credit Movement in Alberta*, p. 345.

84. Aberhart's address, *Albertan*, Nov. 9, 1936.

85. *Edmonton Bulletin*, Feb. 24, 1943; *Fort Record*, March 17, 1943.

86. Aberhart, *Post War Reconstruction*, series of weekly broadcasts, 1942-3 (3 books; Edmonton, 1944), Bk. I, 69-70. Broadcast of Dec. 14, 1942.

87. Speech in Alberta legislature, *Edmonton Journal*, Feb. 12, 1942.

88. *Edmonton Bulletin*, May 24, 1943.

89. Aberhart, *Post War Reconstruction*, Bk. I, p. 2. Broadcast of Nov. 9, 1942. Aberhart was by no means unique in taking this position. Such noted theologians as Emil Brunner were saying the same thing.

90. *Ibid.*, Bk. I, 16-17. Broadcast of Nov. 2, 1942.

91. *Edmonton Journal*, July 20, 1942.

92. Prophetic Bible Conference address, *Edmonton Bulletin*, Sept. 25, 1939.

93. *Today and Tomorrow*, Oct. 31, 1941.

94. *Edmonton Journal*, Feb. 2, 1943.

95. Mabel Giles, *Tribute to Wm. Aberhart* (Calgary, 1944), p. 16.

96. *Edmonton Bulletin*, May 31, 1943.

97. A position taken from Romans 12:2, II Corinthians 6:14-7:1, and I John 2:15-17.

98. *Edmonton Journal*, Feb. 23, 1939.

99. D.V. Smiley, "Canada's Poujadists: A New Look at Social Credit," *Canadian Forum*, XLII (Sept., 1962), 121.

100. W.A. Tutte, *Douglas Social Credit for Canada* (Vancouver, 1934), p. 257.

101. Stephen Leacock, *My Discovery of the West* (Boston, 1937), p. 134.

102. N.B. James, *The Autobiography of a Nobody* (Toronto, 1947), pp. 222-3.

103. Levesque, *Social Credit and Catholicism*, p. 21.

104. *Minutes of the 24th Annual Convention, United Farmers of Alberta* (Edmonton, 1932), p. 225. Robert Reid, former U.F.A. premier, estimated that only 15 per cent of the rank and file favoured the C.C.F. platform and that those in positions in leadership brought about the convention's stand, interview, Edmonton, Sept. 9, 1958.

105. Cited in Moon, "Aberhart: The Man and the Shadow," 59.

Topic Twelve
World War II

On September 1939 Canada declared war on Germany. It was the first time 473 in its history that Canada as an independent country — not a colony — had entered a war. The Canadian government waited one week after Britain before obtaining parliamentary approval to declare war. Yet no sooner had Canada weakened its military and economic ties with Britain when it strengthened them with the United States. Canada, it has been said, went from colony to nation, to satellite.

Canada, the only country in the Americas at war, had entered unprepared. Initially since Britain and France alone seemed capable of defeating Germany the danger of German invasion seemed remote. But the Germans' lightning sweep, the *blitzkrieg*, led to the defeat of the Low Countries, and the fall of France. The Germans prepared to invade England in the late spring and summer of 1940. As the Canadian government realized Canada's vulnerable position, it looked to the United States for protection and direction. The Ogdensburg Agreement of August 1940, which provided for the mutual defence of North America, symbolized the end of the British and the real beginning of American influence. At first, Canadian leaders optimistically believed that the mutual relationship could work to Canada's advantage. Jack Granatstein and Robert Cuff discuss the changing relations of Canada and the United States during the war in "Getting on with the Americans: Canadian Perceptions of the United States, 1939–1945."

On the home front, the War brought many changes too. The increased demand for manpower to serve in the armed forces, and to work in war production resulted in a demand for women in the workplace and in military-related activities. Women responded, contributing greatly to the war effort. Did the War, though, assist women's "emancipation"? is the question posed by Ruth Pierson in "Canadian Women and the Second World War."

The War affected all the population, but particularly those Canadians from countries at war with Canada, such as the Japanese Canadians living on the West Coast. Their very presence raised a cry of alarm among a white population already prone to racial intolerance. The Canadian government responded to the popular outcry, evicting Japanese-Canadians to inland British Columbia, or to points further east (disregarding the fact that the majority were born or had become Canadian citizens.) Peter Ward recounts the expulsion in "British Columbia and the Japanese Evacuation."

A good primary source of World War II is J.W. Pickersgill's *The Mackenzie King Record* (Toronto: University of Toronto Press, 1960–70), a four volume collection of excerpts from the Mackenzie King diaries. C.P. Stacey, the Canadian military historian, discusses the war years in *Arms, Men and Governments: The War Policies of Canada 1930–1945* (Ottawa: Information Canada, 1970). For an understanding of the conscription crisis in World War II, see J.L. Granatstein's *Canada's War: The Politics of the Mackenzie King Government, 1939–1945* (Toronto: Oxford University Press, 1975), and his *Conscription in the Second World War: 1939–1945* (Toronto: Ryerson, 1969), and Granatstein and Hitsman, *Broken Promises: A History of Conscription in Canada* (Toronto: Oxford University Press, 1977; new edition, 1984). R.D. Cuff and J.L. Granatstein's *Ties That Bind: Canadian-American Relations in Wartime From the Great War to the Cold War* (Toronto: Samuel Stevens Hakkert and Co., 1977), has essays relevant to the World War II period.

Ruth Pierson has researched women's roles during the war; in addition to the reading, see "The Double Bind of the Double Standard: Venereal Disease Control and the CWAC in World War II," *Canadian Historical Review*, 62 (March 1981): 31–58; "Jill Canuck: CWAC of all Trades, but no Piston-Packing Momma," Canadian Historical Association *Papers*, 1978, pp. 106–133; and "Women's Emancipation and the Recruitment of Women into the Canadian Labour Force in World War II," Canadian Historical Association *Papers*, 1976, pp. 141–174.

Peter Ward's *White Canada Forever: Popular Attitudes and Public Policies Towards Orientals in British Columbia* is a comprehensive study of the British Columbia response to Oriental immigration. For an alternative view, see Patricia Roy's "British Columbia's Fear of Asians, 1900–1950," *Histoire sociale/Social History*, 13 (May, 1980): 161–172. Ann Gomer Sunahara, *The Politics of Racism: The Uprooting of Japanese Canadians During the Second World War* (Toronto: Lorimer, 1981), is a carefully documented study of this same issue. It should be read in conjunction with Ward's study. A popular summary is: Thomas Berger's "The Banished Canadians: Mackenzie King and the Japanese Canadians", in his *Fragile Freedoms: Human Rights and Dissent in Canada* (Toronto: Clarke, Irwin and Company Limited, 1981), pp. 93–126.

Getting on with the Americans: Canadian Perceptions of the United States, 1939-1945*

J.L. GRANATSTEIN
R.D. CUFF

The Hyde Park Agreement illustrated as well as any international agreement could the joining of economic considerations with emotional considerations. The economic problems could readily be solved if there was a will to do so. But the emotional links between Canada and its vastly more powerful neighbour posed special problems that would persist, particularly as the war proceeded and forced the two countries into greater interdependency. Despite this, the Second World War is regularly trumpeted as the period in which Canada came of age. The nation contributed very substantially to the Allied victory in men, material, and foodstuffs, and as a result of this effort Canada emerged from the war as perhaps the leader of a group of middle powers. There was a very great distance between a middle and a great power, to be sure, but there can be no doubt that fortunate geographical circumstance and economic power had combined to give Canada a status far beyond anything she had enjoyed before.

475

But in a sense this was artificial. During the war, as Professor C.P. Stacey has effectively demonstrated in his magisterial study of Canadian war policies, Canada was essentially unsuccessful in getting much of a share in Allied decision-making.[1] Power was concentrated in the hands of the "Big Three" and there was no disposition to share it, no matter how valuable the contribution of Canada and other lesser states might be.

This was no less true of the United States than of the Soviet Union or Great Britain, and this came as something of a shock to Canadian statesmen. Relations with the Americans had been increasingly warm after 1935, and Prime Minister Mackenzie King for a time was fully convinced that his destiny was to serve as the linch-pin that would link Great Britain and her estranged former colony. With their heavy capital investment in Canada and a growing trade surplus to protect, American leaders reciprocated Mackenzie King's friendship, and a special relationship seemed firmly established. The outbreak of war made this a valuable asset to Canada and to Britain, and King was exceedingly successful in the way he exploited his position in the period before Pearl Harbour.

Perhaps he was too successful, for the war linked the two North American states into economic lockstep, while the military exigencies led to a large American presence in Canada. This state of affairs might have been mar-

*From _Ties that Bind: Canadian-American Relations in Wartime: From the Great War to the Cold War_ (2nd ed.), by R.D. Cuff and J.L. Granatstein (Toronto: Samuel Stevens Hakkert and Co., 1977), pp. 93-112, 191-194.

ginally acceptable to Canada if there had been an accretion of influence in Washington to offset it, but if such an intangible as influence can be measured, after mid-1941 there was probably an absolute decline. The effects were serious to Canada, and they preoccupied planners more and more as the war progressed and planning for the peace began.

The requirements of defence had begun to force closer cooperation on Canada and the United States even before 1939. A first meeting between military staff officers of both countries, arranged in secret and with the direct authorization of President Franklin Roosevelt and Prime Minister King, took place in January, 1938 and a second meeting followed eleven months later.[2] More important, since offered in a public statement, was Roosevelt's pledge in a speech at Queen's University in Kingston, Ontario in August, 1938: "The Dominion of Canada is part of the sisterhood of the British Empire. I give to you assurance that the people of the United States will not stand idly by if domination of Canadian soil is threatened by any other Empire."[3] "What I said at Queen's University," Roosevelt wrote in a private letter to Lord Tweedsmuir, the Governor General of Canada, "was so obvious that I cannot quite understand why some American President did not say it half a century ago."[4]

476

The importance of the American pledge became evident after September, 1939. The war was supposed to be one of "limited liability" for Canada, one that could be won without huge expenditures of men or money. The British and French shared similar views, too, and the Allied leaders and press talked optimistically of the blockade that would force Germany to its knees. The dreams of easy victory, however, dissolved into the reality of May and June, 1940. Suddenly Britain found herself in danger of invasion and bereft of her French ally. For Canada, the character of the war altered overnight, and the Dominion all at once became England's ranking ally. The prospect of a British defeat was real, and in the circumstances Canadians cautiously began to look to their own safety.

The United States was Canada's only salvation. This was clear. Fortunately, there had been no major gaffes to alienate the Roosevelt administration or the American public. War measures that would affect the United States, its citizens or its corporations had been canvassed fully in Washington before implementation.[5] And with a few exceptions Canadians managed to restrain themselves while the isolationists and interventionists hammered away at one another in the United States.[6]

The deliberate and cautious low profile maintained by Canada in the first months of the war was probably appreciated in Washington. As a result Canada was in a good position to deal with the United States in this time of troubles. The first task was to play the role of middleman between London and Washington. King had hoped for this earlier, but now in the very different circumstances of spring, 1940 he found this chore very difficult and taxing indeed.

The future of the Royal Navy in the event of a British defeat was obviously of great importance to Roosevelt. With the fleet in its hands, Germany could be a direct threat to America. Without it, or with the fleet in the

American service, there would be no practical risks at all. The problem was that some Empire statesmen, most notably Menzies of Australia, saw the fleet as a bargaining counter that could induce the United States to give aid to the foundering Allies. An appeal cast in those terms clearly offended Roosevelt, who told a Canadian emissary that the message seemed to say "If you don't help us at once we will let the Germans have the Fleet and you can go to Hell."[7] But what would happen to the Royal Navy "in the event of certain possible eventualities which could not possibly be mentioned aloud"?[8]

Roosevelt wanted Mackenzie King to convey to Prime Minister Winston Churchill the American hope that the Royal Navy would be preserved if the worst came to pass. In the event of a surrender, the President told H.L. Keenleyside, the External Affairs officer who served as King's emissary, the fleet should be dispersed to the Empire and the royal family despatched to Ottawa, perhaps, or to some other safe location. By that time, American opinion would be ready to help the Allies. But if Hitler took the Royal Navy, the result would be disaster. Japan would gain a virtually free hand in the Pacific and the empire would be divided between Germany and Italy. Then came the difficult part for Mackenzie King. Keenleyside told the Prime Minister that the President wanted him to persuade the other Dominions to make a joint appeal to Churchill not to surrender the fleet.

King was appalled since such a request could only imply a lack of faith in Churchill's determination. As he recorded in his diary, "for a moment it seemed to me that the United States was seeking to save itself at the expense of Britain. That it was an appeal to the selfishness of the Dominions at the expense of the British Isles. . . . I instinctively revolted against such a thought. My reaction was that I would rather die than do aught to save ourselves or any part of this continent at the expense of Britain." The worst was yet to come. After he sent Keenleyside back to see Roosevelt to clarify the point, King learned that he was expected to present the President's view as if it were his own. The result was that King spent a very difficult May 30th trying to draft a message so as to "meet the President's wishes . . . of having the message appear to be from myself rather than from him, while at the same time taking care to see that it was wholly his point of view that I was putting over and not my own."[9] The middleman's role was not an easy one, and Churchill's understandable irritation showed through his answering despatches. "Although the President is our best friend," he telegraphed to King, "no practical help has yet been forthcoming from the United States,"[10] a hard but true statement.

For Mackenzie King this period was an agonizing one. His world was crumbling, and he was near despair. Grant Dexter, the reporter for the *Winnipeg Free Press*, with the best contacts in Ottawa, saw J.L. Ralston, King's Minister of Finance, on June 7th and was told of the Prime Minister's condition:

Ralston had found King in his office at 2 a.m. working on this proposition [one of the liaison roles he was filling between Churchill and Roosevelt]. King had said that he was played out, finished and couldn't carry the load, or words to this effect. Ralston told me he said: "Chief

177

you've got to go through. The despatch you are working on may mean victory, the saving of civilization." King agreed.[11]

Of equal importance, particularly from the Canadian point of view, was the formal defence tie that was made with the United States in the summer of 1940. The idea was not a new one, but before the fall of France few would have believed it either necessary or expedient. Mr. Justice Felix Frankfurter, a close confidant of the President, told the Canadian Minister in Washington in early July that a common defence scheme was necessary.[13] Similarly a group of influential Canadians, mainly academics, younger politicians and lawyers associated through the Canadian Institute of International Affairs, had drawn up a "Program of Immediate Canadian Action" at a meeting in July. Their concerns were fixed on the potential economic difficulties Canada faced with much of Europe now closed to her trade, but even more they argued the need for "conversations with the United States aiming at a continental defence scheme. . . . Public opinion in Canada," they claimed, "is ready for a frank recognition by the government of the need for action." Time was of the essence and Canada had to take the initiative. "If Canada allows this opportunity to go by default and the United States is consequently [later] obliged to require us to cooperate, we might as a result be unable to maintain our independent identity."[14]

Economic issues also concerned official Ottawa. The Bank of Canada had set up a committee in June to explore what steps would be necessary if, as it was euphemistically stated, communications with the United Kingdom were cut. The results, the subsequent study argued, would be catastrophic, and there would be heavy unemployment as industries lost their overseas markets. Canada would have to appeal to the United States for assistance, Graham Towers of the Bank wrote to King, and almost the only card that Canada held was that "The United States will have to plan its defence on continental terms at least, and Canada will be an integral and necessary part of their plan."[15]

Certainly the Americans knew this, for their exports to Europe and Britain were in much the same position as Canada's. The result was a sharp turn toward hemispheric thinking in Washington. Bruce Hutchison, the reporter for the Sifton newspapers, visited Washington early in June and had an astonishing conversation with A.A. Berle, the theorist of the large-scale corporation who had served in Roosevelt's brains trust. By 1940, Berle was an Assistant Secretary of State and, as Hutchison put it a bit too fulsomely, "the President's very closest adviser and brain man." Berle's studies, the reporter noted in a memorandum that found its way to Mackenzie King, "now relate to the new American Empire. I can describe it as nothing else. He has been working, he said, on the re-organization of the economy of all North and South America, the new hemispheric concept." Where, Hutchison asked, did Canada fit in all this?

Well, [Berle said] it's a problem, but not as great as you might think. Don't forget that we are going in for huge armaments. This will provide a large employment for Canadians. Then

478

there are such factors as the end of Scandinavian paper exports. You will get this business in the U.S. Wheat is the headache. But there, too, we will have to make concessions. You people still talk Manchester Liberalism. All right, we'll apply it to wheat. We'll say to the wheat producers, we can take so much wheat at a fixed price guaranteed by the government. You can produce more than that if you please, but you'll take whatever price the market will pay. In the end, your wheat men will get less and many of them will move into other industries. That has to come with us and with you, too. It was coming anyway. My feeling, in fact, is that the war has made it possible to settle many such problems, including the future of trade between the U.S. and Canada, which we could not settle in peace time. In these times Congress will be willing to do many things it would never do before.

"His whole assumption," Hutchison concluded, "was that Canada's economy would be merged with that of the U.S., but he did not foresee political union."[16] Berle's scheme seemed predicated on a British defeat, of course.

Canadians could not publicly concede a British defeat as a possibility, although the Bank of Canada study indicated that planning for such an eventuality was in hand. H.L. Keenleyside wanted something more. "It is no longer any secret," Keenleyside wrote, "that the Government of the United States has been giving detailed and serious consideration to the possibility of reorganizing the whole economic life of the Western Hemisphere." Canadians had not studied this question at all, he argued, nor had they given much thought to the "military necessity for a revision of our external policies":

479

It would seem to be improbable that the United States, in the chaotic and dynamic world that is likely to emerge from the present war, will be prepared to continue indefinitely to protect Canada without demanding a measure of active cooperation in return. It is a reasonable assumption that the United States will expect, and if necessary demand, Canadian assistance in the defence of this continent and this Hemisphere. Concrete steps such as the construction of the Alaskan Highway, the defensive development of the Pacific Coast and the Maritime Provinces, the co-ordination of Canadian and United States war material . . . these are lines along which Washington is likely to require Canadian cooperation. If the United States is forced to defend the Americas against encroachments from across either Ocean, Canada will be expected to participate; thus the negotiation of a specific offensive-defensive alliance is likely to become inevitable.[17]

Indeed it would, and when Roosevelt telephoned Mackenzie King and invited him to Ogdensburg, New York in mid-August, King was only too pleased to go. The result of this meeting was the Ogdensburg Agreement, a simple statement that announced the creation of a Permanent Joint Board of Defence charged with beginning "immediate studies relating to sea, land and air problems . . . It will consider in the broad sense the defence of the north half of the Western Hemisphere."[18]

The Agreement was a logical extension of Roosevelt's pledge of 1938. What was striking about it, however, was that the board was declared to be permanent. Seen in retrospect, the Agreement marked the shift from Canada as a British dominion to Canada as an American protectorate. Some people realized this at the time,[19] but in the general relief that Canada's safety was assured in the face of Axis power only the very foolish felt obliged to say so in public.[20] There was one very important, very cool response from abroad, however. Churchill wired King that

I am deeply interested in the arrangements you are making for Canada and America's mutual defence. Here again there may be two opinions on some of the points mentioned. Supposing Mr. Hitler cannot invade us and his Air Force begins to blench under the strain, all these transactions will be judged in a mood different to that prevailing while the issue still hangs in the balance.[21]

Churchill's pique at Canada's scurrying to protect itself was understandable. But the British Prime Minister was wrong to assume that Canadian public opinion would permit the defences of Canada to be stripped so that aid could be sent to England without some guarantee of Canada's security. No Canadian government, charged above all with the defence of Canada, would have acted otherwise. The Ogdensburg Agreement, in addition, tied the United States closer to the belligerents, a positive gain for the Allied cause. In the long-run, however, Churchill was prophetic.

The post-Ogdensburg linkages between the two North American states developed apace. The PJBD began its meetings almost immediately and soon the Board was drafting plans and making recommendations to the two governments.[22] One of its suggestions, apparently advanced by the Canadian secretary to the PJBD, was that a Joint Committee should be appointed to report on the possibilities of increased economic coordination between Canada and the United States. This idea was extensively discussed within the Canadian government and with some Washington officials, including Berle, and it formed the subject of a formal Canadian note to the United States, delivered on March 17, 1941. "It is the belief of the Canadian Government," the aide-memoire stated, "that the promotion of economy and efficiency during the present period of crisis, the solution of the problems which will be posed during the period of transition from war to peace, and adequate and effective provision for the continuing requirements of hemisphere defence, all demand that early and detailed study be given to this question." The upshot was the establishment of the Joint Economic Committee in June, 1941. Its task was to study and report on the "possibilities of 1) effecting a more economic, more efficient and more coordinated utilization of the combined resources of the two countries in the production of defence requirements . . . and 2) reducing the probable post-war economic dislocations consequent upon the changes which the economy in each country is presently undergoing."[23] The Committee, like the Hyde Park agreement, was a Canadian initiative toward closer integration of the North American economy.

The Canadian aim in these critical months of 1940 and 1941 had been to bind the Dominion to the United States. In part this was a plain and simple desire for the protection that could be afforded by the American government. Part, too, was a clear desire to involve the United States more closely with a belligerent, to tie America and the Commonwealth closer together. To help Canada was to help Britain, and this was certainly the case with the Hyde Park Declaration, which ensured that Canada would not fall victim to an exchange shortage that could interrupt the flow of supplies to England.

In strictly Canadian terms, however, there were both assets and liabilities on the new balance sheet. The gains were in terms of security and the jobs, economic stability, and access to vital components that the new relationship with the United States brought. There was also a new influence in Washington. But Canada was also being linked inextricably into an American-dominated nexus, and its production and resources were increasingly coming to be thought of as joint assets. *The Canadian Forum* noted in June, 1941 that the Americans "are more and more tending to look upon the military and economic integration which is taking place between Canada and the United States as the starting-point. . . . They are hinting more and more openly that Canadian-American plans, military and economic, are not merely for the duration of the war."[25]

Even as the *Forum* wrote, however, the shift in American planning was in process. Talks with the British military had begun early in 1941, and joint planning was already far advanced. From the point of view of the War and Navy Departments in Washington it was much easier to negotiate with Britain alone rather than individually with Britain and her passel of Dominions. As a result when the Canadians tried in mid-1941 to secure U.S. permission to establish a military mission in Washington they were rebuffed. Repeated efforts were dealt with in a similar way, and it was not until July, 1942, that a full-fledged Canadian Joint Staff was created in Washington.[26] The hemispheric vision was gone after a year's existence. In its place was a global dream. Pearl Harbour forcibly fixed the new vision firmly in place.

481

For Canada the results would be pronounced. From being a vital link in the defence of the hemisphere in 1940–41, Canada had become a mere appendage of limited importance. The Canadian government had made agreements of far-reaching importance based on the continuance of an American hemispheric scheme, and now that scheme was dead. Roosevelt and King would still meet and talk in a friendly way, but no longer would the President feel obliged to deliver messages to London through the medium of Mackenzie King. He and Churchill met for the first time in August, 1941 off Newfoundland, a meeting at which the Canadian Prime Minister was prominent only by his absence. The realities had intervened.

The new Canadian position vis-à-vis the United States greatly concerned the Department of External Affairs, and Norman Robertson, the Under Secretary, prepared a long memorandum on the subject for the Prime Minister a few weeks after Pearl Harbour. Canadians, Robertson wrote, "have tended to take it for granted" that the United States "will always regard Canadian interest as a close second to their own and appreciably ahead of those of any third country." Now this was no longer so.

It is probably an inevitable consequence of the increasing involvement of the United States in the war and of its acceptance of leadership of the democratic cause that the President should tend more and more to deal directly with the Great Powers and find less time to spend on the specifically Canadian aspects of American international relations. Canada naturally loomed much larger in the American scheme of things when the President and both political parties in the United States were thinking primarily in terms of continental and hemispheric defence. Now that the world war is joined on both oceans, the United States is, not unnaturally, inclined to take Canadian concurrence and support entirely for granted.

The result was a shift in the tenor of Canadian-American relations, a shift that Robertson believed to be "rather abrupt and not too tactfully handled." Part of the problem was caused by the scattering of responsibility for foreign affairs among a plethora of new agencies and offices in Washington and partly by growing pressure there for a unification of Allied representation in the United States. Canadian matters were no longer always checked with the Department of State, as they had been before the war; and indeed the Department was rapidly declining in influence with the President at this time. Of course, contact between opposite members in various agencies in Ottawa and Washington was close and a useful aid to a speedy resolution of technical problems. But, Robertson argued, this gain was "offset by the loss . . . of the preferred position Canada had gradually consolidated through long years of close and friendly collaboration with the President and the Department of State."

Equally important was the shift in the American perception of power. Before the war, Robertson claimed, the U.S. believed it could save the world by "its example, by minding its own business, pursuing a fair and friendly policy toward its neighbours . . ." This era was now over and "we can see the United States turning everywhere to more direct and forceful methods of exerting its influence." This had been shown, for example, in the way the Americans had taken over the negotiations with Vichy France and in the way they had monopolized dealings with Japan before Pearl Harbour. The effect of this "new appreciation of the enormous strategic importance and strength of the United States" was a "new sense of . . . 'manifest destiny' and a corresponding disposition to take decisions and accept responsibilities. This change of attitude is very encouraging from the standpoint of the world in general but," Robertson warned, "it does imply quite an important modification of the special relationship in which Canada has hitherto stood with regard to the United States."

There were a host of examples that showed that the special relationship was gone. Robertson cited the "gradual assumption by the United States of hegemony in Newfoundland" as one and the negotiation of the Atlantic Charter by Roosevelt and Churchill alone as another. Equally important in his view was Canada's omission from the Anglo-American discussions of post-war commercial relationships then in progress although "the field of these negotiations is one in which, up until this year, Canada has taken a much greater initiative than any other part of the British Commonwealth."

Robertson was probably painting an idealized picture of the pre-1941 period, but that there was a shift in Canadian-American relations was clear. What was to be done? Probably the most able civil servant of his generation, Robertson could only suggest that Canada upgrade its Legation in Washington to embassy status and appoint as ambassador an individual who would also sit in the Cabinet War Committee in Ottawa.[27] The first part of this recommendation was to be carried out in 1943 without noticeable effect. Quite likely nothing that Canada could have done would have achieved much. The United States was now well and truly launched on a search for world power as pronounced as the reluctance to accept binding commitments had been during the interwar years.

Curiously, just at the time that some Canadians were beginning to worry about their declining relationship with Washington, the British were beginning to think that Canada's links with the United States were too close, that Ogdensburg and Hyde Park marked the seduction of Canada out of the empire and into the arms of America. Malcom MacDonald, the British High Commissioner in Ottawa who was very close to Mackenzie King, noted that "There may be some danger that Mr. Mackenzie King will be inclined to associate Canada too closely as a North American country with the United States as distinct from the United Kingdom." King's friendship with the President worried MacDonald, but the High Commissioner concluded that King's loyalty to the Commonwealth was "paramount in his mind as it is in the minds of his fellow countrymen."[28] Other British ministers were by no means as certain. "Bobbetty" Cranborne, the Secretary of State for Dominion Affairs, worried often about Canada's too-close relationship with the United States, and in a 1942 minute to a file he observed that "I do not like feeling that [Canada's] closest contacts are with Washington in matters of national defence."[29]

483

What of Mackenzie King? His career has been based in part of his desire to create closer ties with the United States and to cut away the bonds that entangled Canada in the affairs of empire.[30] But as MacDonald properly assessed him, he was a sentimental imperialist, a devotee of the British connection, and an almost fawning courtier before British royalty. To King, however, Roosevelt was almost a monarch, and the correspondence from Prime Minister to President was sometimes almost embarrassing in its devotion. After a visit to Washington in May, 1942, for example, King wrote that "I could not, if I would begin to tell you how much I enjoyed its every hour and, particularly, the intimate personal talks with yourself."[31]

This kind of hyperbole aside, King was very capable of assessing Canada's American problem realistically. He liked Roosevelt and admired him deeply,[32] and he knew that he could win important concessions for his country simply because his access to the president allowed Canada often to bypass the bureaucracy. In 1940, for example, he noted that "there is real purpose behind my seeing the President . . . I can do more in one week spent to that end than might be accomplished in months of remaining at Ottawa."[33] Still, Roosevelt was not the United States. The Alaska Highway, begun in 1942, was one issue that impressed upon King the need to protect Canada's sovereignty against the Americans. The road, he told Malcolm MacDonald in March, 1942 "was less intended for protection against the Japanese than as one of the fingers of the hand which America is placing more or less over the whole of the Western Hemisphere."[34] He told the same thing to another visitor: "it was not without some concern that . . . I viewed the Alaska Highway and some other things growing out of the war, . . . [and it] was clear to my mind that America has had as her policy, a western hemisphere control which would mean hemispheric immunity . . . from future wars but increasing political control by U.S."[35] In Cabinet, King "held strongly to the view with one or two others that we ought to get the Americans out of the further development there [Norman Wells, N.W.T.], and keep complete control in our hands.''[36] Again and again, King told his callers the same thing. With some it was what they wanted to hear, to be sure. He told the anglophilic Vincent Massey that "Canadians were looked upon by Americans as a lot of Eskimos,''[37] for example, but the refrain is so consistent that King certainly believed what he said.[38] Whether he did enough to counter American penetration is another question entirely.

King was not alone in feeling uneasy about American policy, as a whole series of assessments penned in the Department of External Affairs in 1943 and 1944 make clear. H.L. Keenleyside, for example, had detected a coordinated American effort to obtain post-war advantages in Canada as a result of United States wartime expenditures in the Northwest. The American people, he argued, "have begun to think in terms of postwar advantage . . . a popular feeling in the United States that the Administration will be failing in its duty if it does not provide now for the acquisition of post-war profit from wartime expenditure in foreign countries.''[39] Lester Pearson, the second-ranking officer in Washington, was similarly worried, and he regretted "that we should be so often forced into a position where we have to complain to the State Department about slights or injuries or omissions." There was another danger, Pearson added. "On instructions from Ottawa, we take a firm stand in Washington in opposition to certain United States demands. But as soon as pressure is exerted by the U.S. Government either here or in Ottawa, we give in . . . This kind of diplomacy, the strong glove over the velvet hand, has nothing to commend it.''[40] The same kind of feeling was expressed by Escott Reid, a young and able nationalist who before the war had been one of the leading neutralists in Canada. Reid had served in Washington early in the war and now he was back in Ottawa. Some Canadians, he observed in a memo sent to Norman Robertson, were expressing the fear that Canada was becoming an adjunct of the United States "without the formalities of annexation" simply because the Americans were becoming more insistent about demanding and getting their own way. To many Americans, their participation in the war "is a favour which the United States is conferring on humanity and which carries with it the right to run things their own way." This was particularly true of recent dealings with Canada, Reid said. Before the war, a patronizing "Good Neighbour" attitude had not been shown to Canada but now it was, and one reason for this change was just plain aggressiveness. One example Reid cited dealt with an argument over wheat sales. The American Embassy in Ottawa had told the Deputy Minister of Trade and Commerce "that if we did not sell the wheat at the low price demanded by the United States they would be forced to announce publicly that because of Canada's decision the United States would have to cut down on wheat shipments to the United Kingdom and the U.S.S.R." The message was clear: Canada would have to be prepared for "energetic, aggressive and at times inconsiderate policies on the part of the Administration in Washington and as close neighbours we may see more of this than most other people.''[41]

All these fears notwithstanding, however, the realities of geographical propinquity, of economic dependence, and of the potential problems of continental defence gave Canada little room for manoeuvre. The Cabinet War Committee finally decided in July, 1945 to maintain defence ties with the United States into the post-war world. The ministers' deliberations for more than a year had centred around successive drafts of a paper on "Post War Defence Arrangements with the United States," the major thrust of which was that the United States "may be expected to take an active interest in Canadian defence preparations in the future." The reason was clear: "Canada lies astride the overland route between the United States and the USSR." Any deterioration in Soviet-American relations would be embarrassing to Canada, the paper said, but in the event of any such embarrassment it was clear that Canada stood with the United States. As the paper also noted, "This closer tie-up with the United States need not conflict with the Canadian tradition of basing military policy and training upon British practice. However," the drafters of the report said, surely realizing the import of their words, "if Canada and the United States are to be efficient in the defence of North America, common experience between the national forces will be desirable."[42]

485

The government's decision was made, and so evidently was that of the informed public. This became very clear in 1945 when the Canadian Institute of International Affairs, its membership comprising virtually the entire Canadian foreign policy community, met at Kingston on May 26-27, 1945. The Canadian desk officer at the State Department in Washington, J. Graham Parsons, attended and addressed the meeting. His remarks and the reaction they received were reported to London by a British observer:

There was a high degree of acceptance of the proposition that Canada's future political alignment would be with the United States, and only secondarily with the British Commonwealth . . . The view . . . was tactfully encouraged by Mr. Parsons . . . He said that Canada's views and wishes exerted an influence on the United States administration out of all proportion to Canadian power, and added that on commercial policy Canada already enjoyed a consideration accorded to Great Powers alone. The enormous gratification of the company at this remark could not be concealed, and it apparently occurred to no one that it might be a bit exaggerated and of questionable validity in relation to the future.

Mr. Parsons went on to describe as a source of some embarrassment to the United States the elasticity of the present system under which Canada's interests are presented sometimes through Canadian diplomatic channels and sometimes through London . . . He said that the effect was that the State Department did not always know where Canada stood on particular issues.[43]

The shift was almost complete. Most Canadians now recognized that they lived in a North American nation and, although it would take a decade to become completely apparent, the Commonwealth tie was now in decay.

Two Canadian officials who spent much of the war in Washington summed it all up in an academic article written in 1945 that described the kind of cooperation that had existed in Washington:

There has been the open exchange of confidence between the Americans and Canadians, the warm welcome, the freedom from formality, the plain speaking, and the all-pervading frienship. Neither is it easy to enumerate the conditions which made the high degree of co-operation possible. Co-operation was, of course, a sensible course to follow. It stood on its own merits. However, commonsense is not always able to prevail over sovereignty, and self-interest, and special national interests. That the course was followed, or at least adopted so readily and successfully is due in part to the friendly disposition that existed, attributable no doubt to our common background of language and culture, and to the close trade and industrial relationship: in part it is due to the fact that our approach to problems is similar.[44]

Canadians and Americans were almost the same.

Over the course of the next few years, the pressing demands of international politics would force Canadians and Americans still closer together. Canadian policy-makers generally wanted this and pressed for it, seeing certain advantages for Canada in it. Their caution remained, however, and eventually they would begin to seek with increasing desperation for new makeweights to the United States. The United Nations, the North Atlantic Treaty Organization, even finally the Commonwealth — all would be tried and found wanting. The links that had been forged during the war were too strong. Those were "the ties that bind."

486

Notes

1. C.P. Stacey, *Arms, Men and Governments*, Ottawa, 1970, esp. chapter 4.
2. Public Archives of Canada, W.L.M. King Papers, "Memorandum to the Minister on Conversations held in Washington . . . 26 January, 1938," ff. C112708ff.; F.D. Roosevelt Library, Hyde Park, Roosevelt Papers, PSF State Dept., S. Welles to FDR, 20 December, 1937; *Ibid.*, PSF Welles, Welles to FDR, 10 January, 1938 and January, 1938; Directorate of History, National Defence Headquarters, 000.4 (D14), Memo, Gen. Anderson to Minister of National Defence, 23 November, 1938.
3. (United States Information Service), *Canadian-American Relations 1867–1967*, Ottawa, 1967, III, p. 34.
4. Roosevelt Papers, PPF 3396, FDR to Tweedsmuir, 31 August, 1938.
5. E.G., King Papers, Loring Christie to King, 23 February, 1940, ff. 241080ff.
6. See Stephen Leacock, *All Right Mr. Roosevelt*, Toronto, 1939. Even more foolish was a speech by Gordon Conant, Ontario Attorney-General. See *Toronto Star*, 4 April, 1940; King Papers, Christie to Secretary of State for External Affairs, 4, 11 April, 1940, ff. 241188, 241233–4. For a British response to Conant, see Public Record Office, London, Foreign Office Records, FO 800/398, Campbell to Lothian, 8 April, 1940, and FO 371/25224, Cavendish-Bentinck to Garner, 11 April, 1940.
7. King Papers, Black Binders, vol. 19, I, Memo, by Keenleyside, 29 May, 1940.
8. *Ibid.*, III, Memo by Keenleyside, 23 May, 1940.
9. J.W. Pickersgill, *The Mackenzie King Record*, Vol. I: *1939–1944*, Toronto, 1960, 117ff. The message is on pp. 120-1.
10. King Papers, Black Binders, vol. 19, III, Secretary of State for Dominion Affairs to Secretary of State for External Affairs, 5 June, 1940.
11. Queen's University, Grant Dexter Papers, Memorandum, 7 June, 1940. The memo goes on: "Which indicated Ralston's position fairly well. Willie may be doing all he says but, in any event, he sure has J.L. Buffaloed."
12. Library of Congress, Washington, Cordell Hull Papers, folder 194, Memo of Conversation with Canadian Chargé, 17 June, 1940; U.S. National Archives, Washington, State Department Records, 740.0011 Eur War 1939/4700, Memo by A.A. Berle, 12 July, 1940.
13. King Papers, Black Binders, vol. 20, file 77, Typed Diary Note, 13 July, 1940.
14. Copy in University of British Columbia, Alan Plaunt Papers, Box 9, file 1. Among the group were Brooke Claxton, M.P., John Baldwin of the CIIA, Frank Scott of McGill law faculty, Sen. Norman Lambert and others. See *Ibid.*, Box 8, file 20, Plaunt to Baldwin, 13 August, 1940. We are indebted to William R. Young for allowing us to use his notes from this collection.
15. King Papers, Towers to King, 15 August, 1940, ff. 25269ff.
16. *Ibid.*, Black Binders, vol. 19, Memorandum, 12 June, 1940.
17. P.A.C., Department of External Affairs Records, vol. 781, file 394, "An Outline Synopsis for a Reconsideration of Canadian External Policy with particular reference to the United States," 17 June, 1940.

18. *Canadian-American Relations 1867–1967*, II, p. 3.
19. See J.L. Granatstein, "The Conservative Party and the Ogdensburg Agreement," *International Journal*, 22, 1966–7, and James Eayrs, "The Road From Ogdensburg," *Canadian Forum*, 50, 1971, pp. 364 ff.
20. For press response, see King Papers, Notes and Memoranda, vol. 139 and *Ibid.*, Christie to Secretary of State for External Affairs, 10 September, 1940, ff. 241378ff.
21. *Ibid.*, Black Binders, vol. 20, file 77, Message of 22 August, 1940.
22. On the PJBD, see C.P. Stacey, "The Canadian-American Permanent Joint Board of Defence," *International Journal*, 9, 1954.
23. See documents on file 1497–40, part I, at the Department of External Affairs, Ottawa. See also, External Affairs Records, vol. 780, file 383 and vol. 826, file 725; State Department Records, 842.20 Defense/71, Memo by A.A. Berle, 17 March 1941.
24. On Hyde Park, see J.L. Granatstein and R.D. Cuff, "The Hyde Park Declaration of April 1941," *Canadian Historical Review*, 55, 1974.
25. "Pax Americana," *Canadian Forum*, 21, 1941, pp. 69ff. See also the notes on an interview with Berle in External Affairs Records, file 1497-40, 4 February, 1941.
26. The negotiations for the military mission are well handled in Stacey, pp. 354–7. Cf.S.W. Dziuban, *Military Relations Between the United States and Canada 1939–1945*, Washington, 1959, pp. 71ff. See also British documents on this question. Documents on Public Records Office, Dominions Office Records, DO 35/1010 pt. III/WG 476/4/6 and on DO 114/114, pp. 127ff.
27. External Affairs Records, vol. 810, file 614, Memo for the Prime Minister, 22 December, 1941. Cf. memos by Keenleyside in *Ibid.*, 27 December, 1941, and 14 April, 1942. For a U.S. appraisal of the new sensitivity in Ottawa, see State Department Records, 711.42/237, "Memo of Conversation with Norman Robertson . . . 19 February 1942." Prof. F.R. Scott characterized the new relationship with Washington as imposing a "dual colonialism" on Canada, adding the U.S. brand to the existing U.K. one. F.R. Scott, "Canadian Nationalism and the War," *Canadian Forum*, 21, 1942, p. 361.
28. P.R.O., Prime Minister's Office Records, Premier 4/44/10, extract from letter, August, 1941.
29. Dominions Office Records, DO 35/1010 A III/WG 476/141, minute, n.d. [early, 1942.]
30. See e.g., King's remarks to the Liberal caucus on 5 June, 1940, in Pickersgill, I, 87.
31. Roosevelt Papers, PSF Canada 1–42, King to FDR, 4 May, 1942.
32. *Ibid.*, PSF-1, Diplomatic correspondence-Canada, Archibald MacLeish to FDR, 15 February, 1941.
33. King Papers, Diary, 20 April, 1940, f. 392.
34. *Ibid.*, 21 March, 1942, f. 251.
35. *Ibid.*, 18 March, 1942, f. 243.
36. Pickersgill, I, pp. 644–5.
37. Vincent Massey, *What's Past is Prologue*, Toronto, 1963, p. 397.
38. But see State Department Records, 711.42/255, Memo, Hickerson to Hull, 20 May, 1943, which indicates real complacency about Canada-U.S. relations.
39. King Papers, "Evidence Relating to United States Efforts . . .", 11 December, 1943 ff. C241909ff.
40. *Ibid.*, "Certain Developments in Canada-United States Relations," 18 March, 1943, ff. C241878ff.
41. External Affairs Records, vol. 110, file 702, Memo for Undersecretary, 29 February, 1944.
42. External Affairs Records, file 7-AD(s), part II, and James Eayrs, *In Defence of Canada*, Vol. III: *Peacemaking and Deterrence*, Toronto, 1972, pp. 320–31, 375–80.
43. Foreign Office Records, FO 371/50365, "Notes on Annual Conference . . ." att. to Holmes to Stephenson, 15 June 1945. For a U.S. view of the same meeting, see State Department Records, 842.00/6–145, Atherton to Secretary of State, 1 June, 1945, and atts.
44. S.D. Pierce and A.F.W. Plumptre, " Canada's Relations with War-Time Agencies in Washington," *Canadian Journal Economics and Political Science*, 11, 1945, pp. 410–11.

487

Canadian Women and the Second World War*

RUTH ROACH PIERSON

When war broke out in September 1939, Canada was still in the grip of the Great Depression. Out of a population of 11 million, approximately 900,000 workers were unemployed and about 20 per cent of these were women. The Depression had not, of course, brought adversity to everyone. It was a time when goods and services could be bought cheaply. Many housewives were able to afford a new electric washing machine or vacuum cleaner, or to hire domestic help for the first time in their married lives. Many women, however, whose husbands or fathers lost everything in the crash, suddenly found themselves poor. It would be hard to say who was hit worst, the farm wives in the drought- and grasshopper-ridden prairies, the wives and daughters of men out of work and on relief, women raising families on their own, widows, or self-supporting older women who could not find jobs. Married women were simply not hired in the public service and in many private industries. In almost all the areas where women usually worked, in teaching, office work, telephone operating, sales clerking, textile and canning factory work, and nursing, there was wide-spread unemployment.

The one exception was domestic service. Poverty-striken wives hired themselves out as cleaning women in other women's houses and daughters of jobless fathers took positions as maids in the homes of the better off. During the Depression, employers — not employees — decided wages and working conditions. Various Royal Commissions found that women employed in the textile industry and garment trades, for example, were often exploited shamefully, through low pay, long hours, and a brutal pace of work.

For all those who had known the despair of unemployment or the nervous exhaustion of being badly exploited, the coming of World War II meant the opening up of new opportunities. Between September 1939 and mid-1941, military recruitment and war industry put an end to the unemployment of the Depression. By June 1941, the number of women workers was already higher by 100,000 than in 1931, an increase in keeping with the general upswing in employment. Soon after this date, an unusual demand for female labour outside the home began to make itself felt.

It is often assumed that war accelerates social change. This may be true of the wars that have taken place in this century and particularly of World War II, which saw the introduction of social welfare policies as well as of increased employment for women in Canada. What of the social position and role of women in Canada? Did World War II greatly or permanently alter

*From *Canadian Historical Association Booklet No. 37*. Copyright 1983 by Canadian Historical Association. Reprinted by permission.

the place of women in the labour market, corridors of power, and homes of the country?

Women contributed greatly to the Canadian war effort, in the armed forces, in factories, and in voluntary organizations. The three services of the Armed Forces were opened to women, other than nursing sisters, for the first time in Canadian history. In the course of the war, an unprecedented proportion of women left the domestic sphere to enter public employment and service. Women's voluntary labours were also mobilized on a vaster scale than ever before. Finally, a few women rose to positions of considerable responsibility and influence.

All this occurred under the shadow of a war which brought tragedy to those women whose brothers, fathers, sons, husbands and prospective husbands were injured or killed, or who lost European relatives to the Nazi policies of mass murder. For some of these women, the question of whether or not the economic and political status of women had improved during the war would assume particular significance as they sought to maintain families *489* and put their lives back together at the war's end. For all Canadian women, the efforts and sacrifices of the war had been linked to a wider role and larger responsibility in the nation's affairs. The question after the war was to what extent that wider role and larger responsibility would be maintained.

Women in the Armed Forces

The Armed Forces were the first to feel the pinch of a manpower shortage after the beginning of the war. As early as June 1940, National Defence Headquarters (NDHQ) began looking into the possibility of putting women into uniform and using them in support positions, to release men for active service elsewhere. Several months later, in February 1941, Britain requested that the Women's Auxiliary Air Force of Great Britain be allowed to recruit personnel in Canada for service with the Royal Air Force (RAF), or that the Royal Canadian Air Force (RCAF) form its own women's service. Canada responded to this request by preparing to raise a Canadian Women's Air Service.

These official plans coincided with the keen desire of thousands of Canadian women to serve their country in uniform. British Columbian women were the first to demonstrate this eagerness. A volunteer women's service corps had been formed in that province back in October 1938, on the model of the Women's Auxiliary Territorial Service of the British Army. With the actual outbreak of war, a host of unofficial women's paramilitary groups sprang up across Canada. About 6,700 women were enrolled in such organizations by 1941.

Women who joined these organizations were given training in military drill and etiquette, in physical education, and in jobs such as military clerical work, transport driving and motor vehicle maintenance, first aid, map reading, wireless and visual telegraphy, and cooking in large quantities. The organizations were self-supporting; the women had to buy their own outfits.

Some could affort only armbands. Others were uniformed very smartly in, for instance, a blue-gray tunic and skirt with maple leaf badges in gold, black beret, grey hose, and black brogues. The leaders organized themselves into hierarchies and assumed military titles such as colonel, major, and captain.

These women's organizations bombarded the Departments of National Defence and National War Services with requests for official recognition. Some clamoured to be sent overseas, but the government refused to allow this. The officials also knew that if they recognized some of the volunteer corps, they had to recognize all of them. Since not every single one could be trusted to be up to standard, they decided not to recognize any. At the same time, they could not afford to ignore the amount of womanpower in the volunteer corps. In the end, when the Departments of National Defence and National War Services were organizing the *official* women's services, they found their recruits among these women.

490   The first Armed Service to open its doors to women (other than nursing sisters) was the Air Force. The Canadian Women's Auxiliary Air Force (CWAAF) was brought into being in July 1941 and was an integral part of the Air Force from the start. The following spring it was renamed the Royal Canadian Air Force (Women's Division), commonly referred to as the WDs. The second service to move was the Army. The Canadian Women's Army Corps (CWAC) was formed in August 1941, but its full integration into the Canadian Army (Active) had to wait until the next spring. The last service to admit women was the Navy; the Women's Royal Canadian Naval Service (WRCNS) was formed in July 1942.

There were no uniforms ready for the first Army and Air Force recruits. Women from the volunteer corps were permitted to wear their old uniforms for the time being, but others had to make do with civilian clothes. One former member of the CWAC remembers how male soldiers made fun of the new female recruits drilling on the parade ground in their motley garb.

The Air Force, Army, and Navy used female labour in the ground crews, behind desks, and on shore, in order to release men for combat duty. The mottoes of the women's services tell the story: *We Serve That Men May Fly; We Serve That Men May Fight; We Are the Women Behind the Men Behind the Guns*. National Defence had been using female labour even before the creation of the women's services. Women had been working as civil servants in the offices of National Defence Headquarters, military districts, and naval and air bases. But now that female employees were in uniform and under service discipline, their labour was even more at the disposal of the Forces.

The occupations open to women in the Forces were initally limited and all non-combatant. The number of occupations, however, increased as the war went on. The Women's Division of the RCAF, which began with eleven basic trades, for example, had fifty by February 1943. And, in the Army, a few CWAC personnel were eventually assigned to operational duties with coastal defence units as kinetheodolite operators (testing the accuracy of height- and range-finders and anti-aircraft guns) and broadcasters and plottertelephonists in gun operations rooms. Recruitment propaganda, however, still assured the young Canadian woman that she would not be called upon to serve on the firing line: "You do not pull any triggers or throw any hand grenades." By March 1945, women in the CWAC were represented in fifty-five different trades, in addition to the general duty assignments carrying no trades pay, such as driver without technical training, laundress, medical orderly, batwoman, canteen helper, waitress, and officer orderly. Even among tradeswomen, however, the majority were assigned to office or kitchen duty. Of the almost six thousand CWAC tradeswomen stationed in North America in March 1945, fully 70 per cent were employed either as clerk (62.4 per cent) or cook (8 per cent). The secretary in uniform was the typical CWAC and this pattern of female employment was largely the same in the Navy and Air Force.

Nor was this employment pattern out of line with the desires, expectations, or work experience of the women. Of those applying to the CWAC up to mid-1942, over three-quarters were employed at the time of making application: 24 per cent of these were domestic servants, 24 percent office workers, 15 per cent store clerks, 10 per cent factory workers, and 4 per cent professional women and teachers. Approximately 70 per cent had had some high-school education, while only 6 per cent had attended university. Thirty-six per cent of those seeking admission wanted office work of some kind, 19 per cent wanted duties in the mess or canteen, 15 per cent wanted to be drivers, and 10 per cent store clerks.

The women accepted into the services did not receive the same pay as the men. At the time the women's services were begun, basic pay for all ranks was set at two-thirds that of the men. Furthermore, no dependents' allowances were provided to servicewomen. These inequalities in pay and benefits were cause for complaint on the part of women in the services. There was also a public outcry, led by the National Council of Women.

The Department of National Defence was sensitive to the criticism; for one thing, it was hindering recruitment. In July 1943, the minister announced adjustments in pay and allowances for women in the services. Among other improvements, basic pay was raised to 80 per cent of that paid to men in the same rank; and allowances would now be paid for the dependent parents, brothers, and sisters (but not husbands) of servicewomen. Although the Armed Services were ahead of private industry in narrowing the gap between men's and women's pay and benefits, the changes did not remove all inequalities. Many servicewomen still expressed dissatisfaction because their pay was not equal to that of the men they relieved.

By mid-1942, recruiting officers had come up against more difficult obstacles than unequal pay. Rumours were circulating about the morality of servicewomen and, consequently, discouraging enlistment. There were cases of venereal disease and pregnancy among unmarried servicewomen, and the incidence of the latter was apparently at higher rates than among the civilian population. Nonetheless, only a tiny percentage of servicewomen was actually involved, yet the rumourmongers sought to tar the entire women's services with the same brush. The Wartime Information Board (WIB) made a study of this "whispering campaign" and concluded that the rumours sprang from a prejudice against the Women's Services. Sexual respectability, the WIB recognized, was women's vulnerable point, "the traditional focus of attack by those who resent any extension of prerogatives." Wearing a uniform, marching, standing at attention, and saluting were traditionally masculine. Since a women who did these things was seen as unconventional and "unwomanly," it was easy to assume that she had broken with moral convention as well. There were in fact bitter denunciations of the women's forces in letters from servicemen overseas. Officers in charge of recruitment and public relations decided not to try to refute the rumours, but to play up the positive aspects of women's life in the services and to advertise parental approval of daughters' joining up.

492

Canadian women braved the opposition, which continued right to the end of the war. Almost 50,000 enlisted in the Women's Services in all: 20,497 in the CWAC; 16,221 in the Women's Division of the RCAF; and 6,665 in the WRCNS. An additional 4,439 served in the Nursing Services of the three Forces. Altogether they represented about 2 per cent of the female population of Canada between the ages of sixteen and forty-five. Some were stationed outside Canada: a total of 568 Canadian Wrens and approximately 740 members of the RCAF (WD) served in Newfoundland; smaller numbers of all three women's services held positions in the United States. The opportunity to serve overseas was reserved for those with the greatest seniority and best service records. In all, over 1,300 Canadian airwomen, some 2,000 members of the CWAC, and 530 Canadian Wrens served in the United Kingdom. Starting in May 1944, select groups of CWAC's were despatched to combat areas on the European continent, to serve in the rear of the Canadian Forces taking part in the invasion of Italy, and then France and Germany.

Civilian Employment for Women

By mid-1941, the reserve pool of male civilian workers had been largely exhausted. A government-appointed Labour Supply Investigation Committee noted the large reserves of female labour in the country and concluded that the complete mobilization of these reserves would be necessary for the success of the war effort. It calculated this female labour reserve at 561,000. The figure excluded all rural homemakers, on the grounds that they would be performing indispensible work on the farms, and 85 per cent of urban homemakers; to withdraw any more from the home would result in serious disruptions of family life, in the opinion of the committee. Thus, it was planned to use 15 per cent of urban homemakers in the workforce, or double the number already employed in August 1940. This was not out of line with actual trends. The percentage of the adult female population that was both married and employed had increased by 89 per cent over the ten previous years. Difficulties were anticipated, however. Although Quebec had the highest percentage of adult women in gainful employment (18.8 per cent in 1931), the committee recognized that there was in French Canada a long-standing tradition against women working outside the home. In the Prairie provinces and the Maritimes, a large proportion of the young employable women would have to be drawn from rural areas. To increase the number of women in employment from 876,000 in August 1940 to the projected 1,437,000 would require, therefore, an aggressive recruitment and placement programme, according to the committee. Its advice was heeded. The National Selective Service (NSS) was established by the government in March 1942.

Prime Minister Mackenzie King, in an address to Parliament, singled out the recruitment of women for employment as the most important single feature of the programme. A special Women's Division of NSS was created two months later, and in September 1942 a registration of women aged twenty to twenty-four was held. The objective of this inventory of Canada's womanpower was to determine how many single female workers were available to meet the increasing shortage of labour in essential war industries. Registration was compulsory for women in this age group, whether married or unmarried, but Selective Service officers were to restrict employment permits to single women or to married women without children, as much as possible.

Thus began the first phase of active recruitment of female labour. The registration itself stimulated young women to apply for jobs. In addition, NSS launched a nationwide publicity campaign using newspapers and radio to popularize war industrial work for young women. The September registration had revealed that in British Columbia, the Prairies, and the Maritimes there were more than twenty thousand young single women without home responsibilities and willing to work full-time. The government decided therefore to transfer women workers from rural areas to the centres of war industry in Ontario and Quebec; an estimated fifteen thousand women were transferred in this way.

The recruiting campaigns paid off. At the peak of female employment, in the autumn of 1944, more than 1,000,000 women were working full-time in Canada's paid labour force, a figure which does not include part-time workers, or the 800,000 women on farms who were doing their share, with or without wages, to meet farm production schedules. The largest number of women found jobs in the service sector, approximately 439,000 as of the autumn of 1943; 373,000 were in manufacturing, 180,000 in trade and finance, 31,000 in transportation and communication, and 4,000 in construction. The peak of female employment in war industry was reached in October 1943, when approximately 261,000 women were employed directly or indirectly in war production.

Women worked in war plants that made guns, ammunition, and tanks, in shipbuilding, and in aircraft production. In 1943, for example, shipbuilding employed over 4,000 women, still mostly as office workers, but also in some semi-skilled jobs as welders, riveters, electricians, drillers, painters, boilermakers, polishers, cleaners, rope slicers, tractor drivers, and occasionally

493

even as crane drivers. The Pictou shipyard in Nova Scotia, the first in North America to do so, employed 300 women in its wartime labour force of 1,300. Other shipyards in Nova Scotia and British Columbia soon followed suit. But it was in the rapidly expanding aircraft industry that women came to play an especially important part. In September 1939, only 119 women were working in aircraft plants. By February 1944, their number had risen to 25,013, almost a third of the work force. Canada's wartime production of Catalinas, Harvard training planes, Mosquito fighters and bombers, and the Norseman all depended heavily on women's labour.

Articles in technical journals and popular press alike attempted to justify women moving into new work roles by focusing on the suitability of their supposed character or skills. They maintained that women thrived on routine, "continued repetition of which would drive men to distraction." Women were regarded as faster than men at sorting small objects and at any task requiring digital dexterity. Women were in fact employed at electric welding, detail fitting, inspection, fabric work, the operation of lighter machines, and in stock rooms. They were also employed in offices and a few did drafting and layout work. Elsie Gregory MacGill, Chief Engineer at the Fort William plant, was one of Canada's best aircraft designers.

The war industry paid good wages. This accounts for the fact that from 1939 to 1944 women's industrial earnings increased more rapidly than men's. However, the average hourly earnings of women in industry were still only two-thirds those of men in 1944 (47.9 cents as compared with 71.2 cents), despite the lip service paid to the principle of equal pay for equal work. Still, women could earn more in war industry than in other jobs. For instance, the average hourly wage for women in the aircraft industry was 83 cents, compared to 48.7 cents in the women's clothing industry, or with the even lower 37 cents in the hosiery and knitted goods industry. About fifty thousand women left domestic service from 1941 to 1944 and the textile industry also complained to government about its loss of women workers. The government responded by designating production in some textile mills essential to the war effort. National Selective Service held drives in 1943 to recruit women for the textile industry in those centres where the labour shortage had become critical. This helped, but the Department of Labour was well aware that long hours, low rates of pay, and poor working conditions were responsible for the textile industry's difficulties.

In anticipation of labour shortages, several provinces changed their legislation affecting women's employment. In Quebec, for instance, an order-in-council was passed allowing war industries to employ women for night work and to allow them to exceed the maximum hours for women workers (ten a day or fifty-five a week). Some provinces considered employing women in mining operations. The Mines Regulation Act of Ontario prohibited the employment of any "girl or woman . . . in or about any mine, except in a technical clerical or domestic capacity." To get around this, the Cabinet issued a series of orders-in-council starting in August 1942 which permitted specific Ontario mining companies, such as INCO of Sudbury and Port

Colborne, to employ women in some fifty occupations above ground. This permission was given, subject to the observance of regulations safeguarding the health and welfare of the female labourers, such as a maximum eight hour day and forty-eight hour week, provision of separate washrooms, rest rooms, and changing houses for women, "suitable" supervision, and the use of no fewer than two women on any shift in an isolated location. In Manitoba, as well, arrangements were made through the federal government to permit women to work in surface mining operations. But in British Columbia and Alberta, the Coal Controllers' Office of the federal Department of Munitions and Supply ran up against the negative attitude of mine owners and strenuous opposition from the all-male United Mine Workers' Association when it sought to ease the shortage of male help in the mines there in May 1943. In the end, there was no relaxation of the statutes prohibiting women's employment as miners in those two provinces.

By mid-1943 there were labour shortages in many areas of the service sector, which depended on female labour. Women had been leaving not only for higher paying employment in war industries; by the summer of '43 more than twenty-five thousand women had joined the armed services. Hospitals, restaurants, hotels, laundries, and dry cleaners were clamouring for help, but the former surplus of female labour had evaporated. It became necessary to appeal to housewives and to groups that would not ordinarily take jobs. While the first recruitment had sought young unmarried women and then childless married women for full-time work, in mid-1943 NSS began to seek women with children for part-time employment.

495

The opening campaign for part-time women workers, mounted in Toronto in July, served as a model for similar campaigns in other Canadian cities throughout the autumn. NSS first made sure that employers in hospitals, restaurants, hotels, laundries, and dry cleaning establishments would agree to employ women part-time. NSS then directed its appeal to housewives or others who would do a part-time job for six days a week, several hours per day, or several full days each week. The drives sought part-time workers for essential services, but also in some cities for jobs in the textile industry. The Ottawa campaign aimed to get former female employees of the Civil Service, now married, to return to work to overcome the shortage of workers in the war departments of government.

Through 1943, NSS continued its recruitment campaigns for full-time women workers as well. When in late July a sudden need developed in Toronto for about 3,500 women to fill full-time high-priority jobs in war production, NSS hit upon the novel scheme of appealing to housewives to sign on for only three months' service. October and November saw drives to recruit female workers for the textile factories of Peterborough, Hamilton, Welland, St. Catharines, and Dunnville. An extensive campaign was planned for Montreal. But despite decades of high participation by Quebec women in the province's textile, electrical, and tobacco industries, there was considerable francophone opposition to the entrance of women into war industry. Various organizations, both religious and secular, passed resolutions deploring the employment of married women, particularly those with children, in war plants. The press warned that work in the production of shells and explosives was hazardous to the health of women, especially to their child-bearing capacity. But economic motives triumphed; the higher wages in war industries were as attractive to women in Quebec as in Ontario. About nine thousand women were employed in the Dominion Arsenals in Quebec City and Valcartier alone. Nonetheless, in November 1943, NSS officials and Montreal employers, fearful of renewed attacks on war industries, opted for small recruitment drives specifically for hotel, laundry, hospital, and textile workers rather than a large-scale campaign covering war industries as well.

The last major appeals to women workers occurred in 1944. In the first three months of that year, war industry declined slightly, and the number of women in the labour force actually fell by ten to fifteen thousand. Although the end of the war was in sight, NSS put out publicity asking that women remain on their jobs, until victory was secured. Then in June 1944 came a new emergency: the invasion of France. Ammunition plants in Ontario and Quebec had once again to operate at peak production for a brief period. The need for an estimated ten thousand new women workers gave rise to a last, large-scale recruitment campaign. The slogan was "Women! Back them Up — To Bring Them Back."

There has also been recruitment of women into agriculture. In all provinces, farmers' wives and daughters took over the running of farms in the absence of male relatives, but they needed help. A Dominion-Provincial Farm Labour Agreement was negotiated to help farm owners who were hard pressed to attract and hold workers against the lure of higher industrial wages. Ontario entered into this agreement in 1941 and British Columbia in 1943. In the latter, school girls and boys and female teachers were mobilized during holidays for agricultural work. The Ontario Farm Service Force divided female farm-labour volunteers into three brigades: the Farmerette Brigade for female students (sixteen and older) and teachers to work in fruit, vegetable, and truck farming during their holidays; the Women's Land Brigade for other non-farm women who could pitch in on a day-to-day basis or volunteer for year-round service; and the Farm Girls' Brigade for farm women under twenty-six who could lend a hand when and where necessary. National Selective Service helped to publicize the appeals for Farm Labour Service.

Young, unmarried women had been the first of the female population sought by the National Selective Service in its recruitment drives. Next were married but childless women. But from the very start, mothers in need of employment, including those with young children, took advantage of the increased job opportunities created by the war. It was discovered in September 1942 that many mothers working in Montreal's war plants had told their employers that they were single, because they had been afraid that they would not get jobs otherwise. It was evident that the special needs of working women, especially those with dependent children, would have to

496

be met. There were reports of "car babies" (infants locked in parked cars while the mother or both parents were at work). There was also concern over "latch-key" children as critics began to blame working mothers for juvenile delinquency.

The country was, however, increasingly dependent on the paid labour of women with young children. The Dominion government therefore took steps to make child care available to working mothers for the duration of the war. Late in July 1942, it agreed to co-operate on an equal-cost-sharing basis with any province interested in establishing day-care facilities for children of mothers in war industries ranging from care of school-age children and pre-school children to foster care for children under two. Only Ontario and Quebec, the two most industrialized provinces, actually took advantage of the Dominion-Provincial Wartime Day Nurseries Agreement, however. The programme was also slow in getting off the ground and limited in extent. Day nurseries did not start opening for example until 1943, and, at first, no more than 25 per cent of any nursery was to be open to children of mothers in jobs outside war industries. There was strong objection to this quota, however, on the grounds that it was unfairly discriminatory. In many cases, the woman doing the "non-essential" job was freeing a man or another woman for work in war industry. The agreement was finally amended in 1944 to include children of all working mothers, although children of mothers working in war industry still had priority at all times to any facility established under the agreement.

By September 1945 there were 28 day nurseries in Ontario accommodating about 900 children, and 44 school units accommodating about 2,500 children. At the same time in Quebec, there were only 5 wartime day nurseries, all in Montreal, and with an average enrolment of only between 115 and 120 children. After the war, government subsidies and interest came to an abrupt end. The Quebec government terminated the agreement in October 1945, despite appeals from social agencies, teachers, and working mothers. The programme lasted a bit longer in Ontario, while governments haggled over whether day nurseries were a federal, provincial, or municipal concern, but finally the Dominion government took the initiative and terminated the agreement. All the school-age centres were closed in Ontario as of the end of June 1946, though some of them reopened shortly afterwards; about half the pre-school nurseries survived the withdrawal of federal funds.

Volunteer Work

By far the largest contribution made by Canadian women to the war effort was through their unpaid labour in the home and their volunteer work. Women's domestic work was as crucial to most families in wartime as in peace, although the war did see a rise in communal kitchens and commercial laundries. The main purpose of these was to ease the burden on women working in "essential" industries, but who at the same time had to do equally essential domestic chores. Canadian society was almost totally mobilized to

497

fight the war and women were called upon as preparers of food, clothes makers, consumers, and managers of family budgets. Homemakers helped the war effort by coping with shortages, accepting rationing, and preventing waste; they also helped by saving and collecting materials that could be recycled for use in war production.

To increase Canada's food production, women cultivated "victory gardens" and canned the fruits and vegetables. Some learned for the first time how to remake old clothes, save scraps and oils for the ammunition industry, or pennies to buy war stamps. Women were told to "Dig In and Dig Out the Scrap" and save metals, rags, paper, bones, rubber, and glass. Someone had to collect the salvage. Someone also had to take in the contributions to Victory Loans and pass out information on how to practice domestic economies necessary for the war effort. Almost all of this was done voluntarily by women. Indeed, at the local level, women volunteers working in or outside the home or both, sustained a vast network of wartime services and activities.

498

The government stepped in, in the fall of 1941, to take charge of coordinating their efforts; a Women's Voluntary Services (WVS) Division was set up within the Department of National War Services. But the main burden of the programme was carried by local WVS Centres, which were set up eventually in forty-four cities. These centres kept a roster of the local societies and clubs performing war services, they recruited volunteers and placed them according to interest and ability, and they passed on information from the war departments of the federal government.

Most of the centres were staffed by volunteers, although a few of the bigger ones had paid secretaries or directors. Although they were mainly referral and coordinating agencies, the centres participated directly in many tasks, such as distributing rationing cards, recruiting and training volunteer staff for Wartime Day Nurseries, or helping with the National Clothing collection, which gathered 12 million pounds of used clothing for distribution in devastated countries.

Women who wanted to contribute voluntarily to the war effort, however, had not waited for action from the federal government. Immediately after the declaration of war, many volunteer organizations had sprung into being. In Winnipeg, for instance, early in the war, a group of women funded a Central Volunteer Bureau which registered volunteers and directed them according to their skills and interests to the appropriate club or agency. This bureau turned itself into the Women's Voluntary Services Centre of Winnipeg in October 1941, after National War Services set up its WVS Division.

In Ontario, the coordinating organization for women's volunteer war work resisted the federal government's takeover. It had been founded by a group of Toronto women, only one month before the creation of the WVS Division. Since they intended, once they got Ontario organized, to spread into other provinces and develop a national organization, they had called themselves the Canadian Women's Voluntary Services (Ontario Division). When the Canadian government decided to intervene, it notified them not only that their work would be superseded but that they would have to relinquish their name. The result was a furor. Members pelted the Department of National War Services with letters, protesting that unsalaried, charitable work was women's domain, questioning the government's right to intervene, and demanding to know why anyone should be getting paid to coordinate volunteer work anyway. In the end, the Ontario local lost the battle and was absorbed into the federal system.

Most of Canada's volunteer war work, then, was performed by millions of Canadian women, organized into hundreds of local societies and clubs and orchestrated by the local Women's Voluntary Services Centres under the direction of Ottawa's WVS. The latter worked to publicize voluntary work. From Ottawa's WVS Centre, for example, came the idea of "Miss Canada Girls." These young women promoted the sale of war savings stamps and other patriotic events in support of the war.

Local women's organizations were given the task of making "warsages," *boutonnières* with war savings stamps attached, and WVS Centres threw their weight behind the 1944 drive of the Postmaster General to get more letters written to members of the Armed Forces. On a regular basis, volunteers distributed salvage cards, staffed blood donor booths, informed apartment dwellers about window box victory gardens, and arranged hospitality and entertainment for servicewomen and servicemen on leave and far from home. Within the individual clubs, women sewed, knitted, and quilted, packed parcels, and put together "ditty bags" containing small necessities for the servicemen and women overseas. They also made jam, collected clothing bundles, and raised milk money for Britain.

499

In the countryside, it was the Women's Institute all across Canada that carried the burden of voluntary war work. Between 1943 and 1945, the Women's Institutes of Canada raised over half a million in cash and made almost the same number of garments for the Red Cross and others. After the war, Women's Institutes and WVS Centres alike organized committees to welcome returning veterans and to help foreign "war brides" of Canadian servicemen feel at home in their new country.

Another way in which women contributed to the war effort was by helping to monitor inflation. After the Wartime Prices and Trade Board established price and production controls in 1941–42, women's clubs across Canada appointed committees to keep an eye on prices and the availability of goods essential to housekeeping and family care. Women took pad and pencil to food, clothing, and hardware stores and made notes of prices that were out of line or products that were scarce. Once again women had taken the initiative, only to have the federal government step in to coordinate their activities when the Consumer Branch of the Wartime Prices and Trade Board came into being. Canada was divided into fourteen administrative areas, each with a Women's Regional Advisory Committee, sub-committees in urban centres, and corresponding members in smaller communities. In addition, every individual women's organization was to appoint a liaison officer to keep in touch with the local sub-committee. Through this network, a third of Canada's three million adult women was mobilized to keep a close watch on prices and production restrictions across the country and report to Ottawa.

The Leaders

A number of women rose to positions of public prominence and responsibilities in association with the war effort. Within the Armed Forces, the highest position a woman could have was head of one of the women's corps and in 1944 these positions were held by Wing Officer Willa Walker, Senior Officer, RCAF, Women's Division; Colonel Margaret Eaton, Director, CWAC; and Commander Adelaide Sinclair, Director, WRCNS. In government, women rose to high positions directing women's branches of federal war departments. For instance, Fraudena (Mrs Rex) Eaton was in charge of the Women's Division of National Selective Service in the Department of Labour; Nell (Mrs W.E.) West was made Director of Women's Voluntary Services in the Department of National War Services.

500

The leaders came mainly from the elite of Canadian society; they were either professional or businesswomen themselves, or married to successful business or professional men. They also had a record of public service. For example, Fraudena and Rex Eaton, born in Nova Scotia and graduates of Acadia University, moved as young adults to British Columbia, where Rex entered the lumber business, and Fraudena, community service. By the time of her appointment to National Selective Service, Fraudena Eaton's record included help with the foundings of the Elizabeth Fry Society, active membership in the Local, Provincial, and National Council of Women, seven years' service as the only woman member of the British Columbia Board of Industrial Relations, and organization of the Community Self-Help Association of Vancouver during the Depression. For a woman to hold high office effectively, being well connected sometimes helped more than anything else. Margaret Eaton, for instance, came from the Timothy Eaton family. When first approached to become an officer of the CWAC, she refused on grounds that her only qualifications were that she "knew the best night clubs in London and hunted with the best packs." But after being promoted to the position of Director, CWAC, it was precisely her high social standing that put her in such a "strong position *vis-à-vis* the boys": it was difficult for the male officers, no matter how high their title, to pull rank on her. The top ones, she recalled, never addressed her as "Colonel," but rather always as "Miss Eaton."

With few exceptions most women who held wartime governmental positions were appointed because the work was seen as within women's domain. For example, in keeping with the role of women as consumers, the position of head of the consumer division was given to a woman in both the Department of Agriculture and on the Wartime Prices and Trade Board. Miss Laura Pepper was made Chief of the Consumer Section, Department of Agriculture; Miss Byrne Hope Sanders, *Chatelaine* editor, was made director of the Consumer Branch, Wartime Prices and Trade Board.

In addition to creating leadership positions in government and armed forces, war increased the opportunities of women in the media. Women writers, broadcasters, and photographers were given special assignments to help with the mobilization of women. The journalist, Lotta Dempsey, wrote the lead article for each of the three special issues on "Woman at War" which *Mayfair* published in May, June, and July 1943. In 1939 Mrs Mattie Rotenberg, a homemaker with a Ph.D. in mathematics and physics from the University of Toronto and an interest in elementary education, began making public affairs broadcasts over CBC radio, on an afternoon programme for women. Her messages became progressively more concerned with women's rights as the war went on. The war also gave a boost to the career of Kate Aitken, a radio broadcaster, lecturer, and author. Her contributions to Canada's war effort included serving as Conservation Director for the Wartime Prices and Trade Board, touring Canada with her "Remake Revue" which showed women how to create new clothes from old, and using her broadcasts and cookbooks to instruct housewives how to cook good meals despite rationing.

501

But even at the young and flexible National Film Board of Canada, first created in 1939, of the nearly one hundred people employed in film production at the height of the war, only three or four women rose to prominence as directors and producers. The largest proportion of women were employed as secretaries, stenographers, and librarians, and as negative cutters, working for long hours with poor equipment amidst noxious fumes in a poorly lit, poorly ventilated room. The situation became even worse for women at the NFB after the war.

The Emancipation of Women

The attainment of such prominence by a few women, their replacement of men in some traditionally male occupations, and women's public involvement in the war effort on such a large scale led some people to believe that the war had emancipated women. The ceremonial launching of a ship that women workers had helped to build "from the first bolts and staves to the final slap of paint and piece of polished brass," moved Lotta Dempsey to suggest that the event symbolized the launching of women as well: ". . . the great and final stage of the movement of women into industry . . . on a complete equality with men." National Selective Service in 1943 spoke of the war as having "finally brought out the complete emancipation of women."

It was true that there appeared to be an equalizing of the roles of men and women in society. What was glossed over by those supporting this trend was that equalization usually involved a "masculining" of women's roles, rather than a "feminizing" of men's. Pants became acceptable attire for women. Women moved into male-monopolized fields, but the reverse did not happen. Women became truck drivers; men did not become day nursery attendants.

The extent to which women were becoming like men worried some Canadians. The fear that servicewomen would cease to be feminine and chastely monogamous, for example, was shown to be the main reason for opposition to women's joining the forces. Public applause for women's trailblazing in non-traditional fields often went hand in hand with assurances that things would return to "normal," once the war was over. Female applicants for war industrial work were assured that the job they were being asked to do would not diminish their femininity, while it would definitely speed up the return of Canadian men from overseas. A promotional photo series on "the typical Bren girl" showed her in her boarding house "dolling up" before an employees' party and jitterbugging after she got there. Similarly, public relations for the armed forces assured female recruits that they would not be required to do anything "unwomanly," and that being in the services would not stand in the way of their having dates.

For *Mayfair*'s 1943 celebration of Canadian women's contribution to the war effort, Westinghouse of Canada developed a series of large two-page ads on the theme "These Are Tomorrow's Yesterday." One pictured a nine- or ten-year-old boy writing to his mother in 1955 to tell her that he and his friends stumbled onto an "old book" on "Women at War" that had got them to talking about things back in 1943. The ad conveyed not only a tribute to Canadian women's role in Canada's struggle, but also the expectation that in ten or twelve years' time the women would all be back where they belonged, taking care of the home and rearing Canada's future generation, with the aid of Westinghouse appliances. In Quebec, *La Presse* exhorted women to remain feminine and attractive beneath their "external appearance of energy and will." For the men who were fighting, *La Presse* reminded the women of Quebec, your "beauty is a reward, a stimulant."

Postwar planners also saw most women returning to the home at the end of the war. One example is the sub-committee appointed by the federal government's Advisory Committee on Reconstruction to consider the postwar problems of women. While its final report agreed with the principle of women's right to work, whether married or not, it estimated that 45 per cent to 55 per cent of the six hundred thousand women who had entered the paid labour force since 1939 would be responding to "the normal urge towards marriage, and home, and family life," and would therefore be leaving their paid jobs at war's end. Another example is the L.C. Marsh Report on Social Security for Canada which emphasized that women's commitment was primarily to homemaking and childbearing and argued that most female industrial workers after the war would "retire voluntarily from the labour market through marriage;" that social security benefits for wives should be dependent on "recognition of the husband as the chief wage-earner;" and that a system of children's allowances should be paid to mothers as a way of promoting motherhood and mother's individual rights.

The Women's Sub-Committee strongly supported this stance. Its own report, however, had recognized the plight of unmarried women workers with adult dependents. But as far as married women workers with young children were concerned, the primary role envisaged for them was in the

502

home. The sub-committee recommended only part-time nursery schools; and it gave priority to finding sufficient well-paid employment for men since, when the husbands were employed, women could withdraw from wage work to devote themselves to home and family. The sub-committee thus implicitly accepted the reduction of women to the status of secondary earner. Moreover, while it insisted on the principle of equal pay for equal work, in considering what to do about the estimated 180,000 working women who would lose their jobs at the end of the war and for whom marriage would not come to the rescue, the sub-committee accepted the channelling of women into areas where they would be least in competition with men. Its list of possible professional careers for young middle-class women, for instance, included only the traditionally female occupations: school teacher, nurse, physiotherapist, dietician, librarian, personnel advisor, social worker. As for university positions, there would be only "a limited field" for women instructors, lecturers, and professors, but rather more opportunities "in professional schools such as household science, library, music, etc., and in extension departments for adult education." To soak up jobless working-class women, the sub-committee recommended domestic service, proposing training schemes for upgrading the status of maids and a change of terminology from "domestic servant" to the less stigmatizing one of "household worker."

In 1944 the only woman on the Economic Advisory Board of the Province of Quebec, Renée G. Vautelet, produced a similar report on the post-war problems of Quebec women, generally endorsing the recommendations of the federal sub-committee. In the Quebec report, women's role in the survival of the francophone culture and Quebec's rural economy took top priority. On the other hand, the report noted that almost half of all Quebec women between twenty and forty were not married and that many women needed therefore to seek employment outside the home. Nonetheless, it proposed that policies be developed to reduce industry's reasons for employing women in preference to men and that serious consideration be given to the possibility of recognizing legally the economic value of a woman's work within marriage, by giving the wife a legal right to a percentage of her husband's earnings.

Mme Vautelet, like so many others, saw domestic service as "one of our best post-war hopes" for absorbing surplus women workers into paid employment. Even during war, such Quebec groups as the *Jeunesse ouvrière catholique* had campaigned to persuade young rural women to stay on the farm and the daughters of urban working-class families to become maids. At the end of the war, the demand for household help grew sharply in many parts of Canada at the same time that there was fear of unemployment among discharged servicewomen and female war workers. As a result, the National Employment Service introduced the "Home Aide" project, an attempt to recruit domestic workers for light housework to be done in regular shifts and on a live-out basis, as its main job creation programme for women in the postwar period. Similarly, the Canadian Vocational Training Programme of the Department of Labour pushed Home Assistants' Courses for house-hold workers as the preferred rehabilitation training for demobilizing servicewomen and female war workers. But these training programmes alone could not bring about any real improvement in the working conditions of household help. For that, the whole category of domestics, from charwomen to parlourmaids, would have had to be brought under the federal Unem-ployment Insurance Act, as well as provincial legislation on minimum wage, maximum hours, and workmen's compensation. As it was, the "Home Aide" project left the issues of pay, work load, and hours to the good-will of the employer. Canadian-born women continued to show distaste for domestic service and the Canadian government resorted to its old method of using immigration to provide a supply of cleaning women for the middle- and upper-class homes of the nation. Two years after the war, the Department of Labour and the Immigration Branch were combing the "displaced per-sons' " camps of Europe for women between the ages of eighteen and forty, suitable for and willing to accept and remain in domestic employment.

504

The expendability of women's labour in the public sphere was illustrated most dramatically after World War II in the armed forces. During 1946, all three women's services were disbanded. Not until the Korean War in the 1950s were women enlisted again in the regular Forces. The Second World War experience was a clear case of last hired, first fired, not just of individ-ual women, but of an entire group of women. It proved that women could serve as a reserve army of labour for the armed forces, as well as for the civilian labour market.

But Canada's ex-servicewomen were not to be simply turned out into the cold. The country's generous rehabilitation programme for ex-service personnel was called in March 1945 "the most comprehensive of any yet advanced by any country." And Dr Olive Ruth Russell, appointed in January 1945 to the Department of Veterans' Affairs as an Executive Assistant spe-cializing in the rehabilitation of servicewomen, doubted that any other country had gone as far as Canada in "abolishing sex discrimination and the granting of equal status to women" in its legislation pertaining to ex-service personnel.

She was to a large extent justified in making that claim. Ex-servicewomen were equally eligible with ex-servicemen for the $100 clothing allowance, the rehabilitation grant of 30 days' pay and allowances, and the war service gratuity (of $7.50 for every 30 days of service overseas). For help with buying a home, repairing a house, buying furniture, or starting up a business, fe-male as well as male veterans could apply for "Re-establishment Credit." There was to be no discrimination on the basis of sex, with respect to the benefits and opportunities for university education, or vocational, techni-cal, or other non-university training. The Pension Act was amended to apply also to female members of the armed forces, and women were techni-cally fully eligible for the benefits of the Veteran's Land Act, the Reinstate-ment in Civil Employment Act, and the Civil Service Act which provided for preference for veterans. Dr. Russell acknowledged one minor exception to all this equality of status and opportunity: the out-of-work benefits provided by the Post-Discharge Re-Establishment Order were not available to a married ex-servicewoman whose husband was capable of supporting her.

There were, however, other sex-typed inequalities. As pensions were based on service pay, and as servicewomen's pay was only four-fifths that of servicemen's, the pension rates payable to former members of the CWAC, RCAF-WD, or the WRCNS, were four-fifths of the standard men's pensions. Furthermore, the preference that ex-service personnel were to be given in the civil service applied only to those who had seen active service overseas or on the high seas. Women were thus at a disadvantage, since only about seven thousand had been posted to overseas duty and none had seen service on seaborne vessels. As well, the Canadian Vocational Training programme, set up by the Department of Labour for former war industrial workes as well as ex-scrvice personnel, focused on training women in household service, practical nursing, or Home Making and Family Living.

Within these limitations, however, ex-servicewomen would appear to have made good use of their rehabilitation benefits. Of the almost 50,000 former members of the women's services, more than 25 per cent took advantage of the training and education benefits, a higher proportion than that of male veterans. Over 12,000 embarked on vocational, high-school, or university courses. In both academic and job training, however, the women tended to end up in traditionally female fields. Of the 2,600 enrolled in university, "encouragingly large groups" were to be found "in Public Health, Social Service and Education." Fully 85 per cent of the women taking vocational training chose the following five occupations, out of 91 for which courses were available: commercial (which included training for work as secretaries, stenotypists, clerks, and office machine operators); dressmaking; hairdressing or "beautician" work; nursing; and pre-matriculation. Half chose to be trained for a "commercial job", and more trained as beauty operators than the market could easily absorb. In 1946, 16,000 were already listed as married. That may account for the fact that, as of 31 March 1950, less than 3 per cent of female veterans (compared with 15 per cent of male veterans) had applied for out-of-work allowances. Almost 90 per cent of the $6.25 million in reestablishing credits claimed by women veterans was spent on home furnishings and equipment; this was evidence to the Deputy Minister of Veterans' Affairs that ex-servicewomen are "fulfilling their function as home makers."

Under the Veteran's Land Act, it was possible to get generous long-term financial assistance in buying a farm or rural land. But ex-service personnel had to qualify, and it was assumed that not many women would. To buy a farm, one had to have experience in farming or be willing to prove one's suitability by working with a farmer until the act's administrators were convinced. Very few women were able to benefit.

With the end of the War, there were fewer employment opportunities for women. For various reasons, they found themselves once more in positions subservient to men or pressed into the homemaker role. The amount of subsidized daycare shrank and the "marriage bar" was slid back into place

505

in the Civil Service, among other occupations. At the same time, the few women who had learned skills in non-traditional trades were eased out of work, to make room for the men returning from overseas.

Given these facts and the ideological pressures exerted from press and pulpit, it is difficult to know exactly how many of the women who had taken jobs during the war freely chose to quit at war's end. Dr Russell questioned two CWAC officers on the subject in 1944, both married women. One said, "I want to go home as fast as I can and make a home for my husband and have a family;" the other thought women should look after their own children, but she was sure she would eventually get restless at home and want an outside job as well. A 1944 Labour Department survey showed that 28 per cent of the women, as compared with 2 per cent of the men, intended to quit work after the war, but that meant that 72 per cent of the women wanted to stay in the work force.

An ex-servicewoman from Winnipeg, writing for the *Canadian Home Journal* in April 1945, said that sending women back home was "like putting a chick back in the shell — it cannot be done without destroying spirit, heart or mind." She exploded in anger at the idea that women during the war had been turned into competent, skilled workers only to be cast aside at war's end. On the other hand, the winner of the *National Home Monthly*'s contest in 1945 for the best letter on the subject, "If there's a job in industry for you after the war, do you want it?", expressed a definite preference for domesticity. "One thing I would like to make clear," she wrote, "I do not feel I am sacrificing myself for housekeeping. The thing I wanted most was a husband and home of my own." The postwar restrictions on women working outside the home took effect. Women's participation in the paid work force began to slide in 1945 and plummeted in 1946 to a quarter of the work force. The rate continued to decline until the mid-fifties. Only in 1966 did it climb back up to the 1945 level.

One trend that the postwar did not erase was the one concerning the marital status of employed women. In 1931 only one in ten working women was married and, at the beginning of the war, not many more. During the war, however, the proportion of working women who were married rose to one in three (35 per cent) by 1944. By 1951 it had dropped only to 30 per cent. But one needs to remember that there was also a rising marriage rate for women, and that they were marrying younger, after the war. A larger proportion of working women were married but, even so, only about one in ten married women worked outside the home, for women's proportion of the labour force as a whole had sunk to prewar levels.

Conclusions

Did the war "emancipate" women or raise their status? If "emancipation" means a genuinely equal sharing of power and responsibilities between men and women in both the public and the private spheres, the answer is no. Women's increased job opportunities during the war were not a recognition of their right to work, but rather because women were a convenient source of labour both for private industry and public service. Women were still used mainly for tasks already designated as female, and hence not in competition with men. Where women entered the military or took on traditionally male jobs in the civilian world, such as heavy machine operating or mining, there were many limits set to what they could do. The male monopoly on bearing arms went unchallenged.

At the same time, many people feared that the differences between men and women were breaking down, and that women were becoming masculine. Both private industry and government, in particular the Department of National Defence, tried hard to allay those fears and reassure the public that the woman in bandana and overalls, or in a khaki or blue uniform, was still feminine and chaste. Indeed, the largest number of women working in support of the war were those doing unpaid volunteer work — a traditionally female domain. Women volunteers found considerable scope for their great organizational and administrative abilities. Within the public sphere, however, no matter how high a woman's position, there was always a man, or a hierarchy of men, above her. Although women's labour was indispensable, the running of the war remained in the hands of a male elite.

507

To a large extent, the mobilization of women for the war effort was a clear case of state management of "human resources." There was propaganda for recruitment, there were tax incentives for working wives, and there was child care provided by government to mothers in war industries. But despite the fact that female labour in the public sphere was useful and cheap, the dominant message was that women's chief function was to bear and rear the next generation, as well as to create a home for a male worker. Only for the sake of the war was the state willing to accommodate the domestic responsibilities of women with jobs outside the home. After the war, government and industry halted those programmes or cut them back severely. Barriers to married women's employment dropped back into place.

With the evaporation of the labour shortage, preference for jobs was given to ex-servicemen. This situation, as well as the postwar baby boom and the end of state-supported child care, all encouraged married women to devote themselves to childbearing and housekeeping. A huge surge of advertising pushed the consumption of domestic commodities and romanticized the domestic woman. The family allowance system was designed to reduce a mother's need to work outside the home. These circumstances also persuaded young, single women to seek a husband, rather than to train for a career or a life of full-time, skilled wage work. The postwar dream of domesticity came true for many women — but not for all. The war had robbed many of their husbands and fiances. As well, almost fifty thousand Canadian servicemen had married overseas. Many of these unmarried and widowed women, as well as poor married women, now had to search for jobs in an economic climate unfavourable to women.

The massive mobilization of women during the war years thus failed to secure them a genuinely equal place in the postwar public world. The single older woman, the deserted wife or mother, or the woman whose husband earned too little or had no job remained in precarious positions. Unemployment insurance, introduced in Canada in 1940, would be able to use veterans' educational benefits to launch themselves on promising careers. But in the main, working women continued to be segregated into subordinate, poorly-paid job ghettos. The wartime situation had left intact, if it had not strengthened, the norm of the male as head of household and primary provider, for society's feeling of indebtedness to the returning soldier forced women out of non-traditional jobs and reinforced the economic primacy of males. The sexual division of labour reemerged stronger than ever.

Feminists who were active in Canada during the war had been hopeful about wartime developments. They could point to the fact that Quebec women were finally granted the provincial vote in 1940. But in most other areas of public life, the postwar world disappointed these feminist hopes. While some women had gained a new confidence and a new self-image through wartime service, many of them saw their expectations dashed. Traditional attitudes about women's role held sway once more and the contribution that women had made to the war effort was allowed to fade quietly from public memory.

508

British Columbia and the Japanese Evacuation*
W. PETER WARD

On 27 February 1942 the Canadian government announced plans to remove all persons of Japanese ancestry from the coastal region of British Columbia. During the seven months which followed more than 22,000 Japanese, aliens and Canadian citizens alike, were forced to abandon their homes and move eastward under government supervision. The majority were sent to settlements in the interior of the province, while others went to more distant points beyond the Rockies. Yet when war with Japan was first declared, on 7 December 1941, the federal government saw no need for such drastic action. Left to their own devices Prime Minister King and his cabinet would not have compelled most of the Japanese to leave the coast. After war's outbreak, however, the Liberal government could not resist the swelling tide of anti-Japanese feeling on the Pacific. Ultimately, King and his government concluded that only evacuation would quiet the popular outcry and avert public disorder.

But if the expulsion was a direct result of wartime stress, it was also the consequence of strained race relations in British Columbia. Since the late

*From *Canadian Historical Review*, 57 (3) (September 1976): 289–309. Reprinted by permission of the author and University of Toronto Press.

1850s west-coast society had been divided by a deep racial cleavage and, over the years, only limited integration had occurred in patterns of work, residential accommodation, and social contact. The white community had vented its persistent anti-Asian sentiments through petty discrimination, verbal abuse, and even mob violence. Driven by economic threats (both real and apparent) as well as cultural conflicts and psychological tensions, politicians, editors, farm and business organizations, patriotic clubs, and nativistic societies had all assailed the Asian immigrant at one time or another. Periodically, federal, provincial, and municipal governments had also approved legislation and enforced covenants which discriminated against Orientals. These official measures served to legitimate popular prejudice. In sum, long before Canada went to war with Japan, British Columbians had passively tolerated and actively promoted hostility toward their Asian minorities.[1]

Many whites who peered across this racial cleft viewed Orientals through a haze of prejudice, for their images of Asians were drawn from a few widely accepted negative stereotypes.[2] In the case of the Japanese these stereotyped attitudes, which hardened perceptibly during the interwar years, emphasized four characteristics: their unassimilability, their economic competitiveness, their high birth rate, and their lingering loyalty to Japan. None of these stereotypes was particularly accurate, although some did contain at least a kernel of truth. But it was their substance, not their accuracy, that mattered most to British Columbians.

During the early and middle 1930s anti-Japanese feeling was not particularly intense in British Columbia. But in the closing months of 1937 a new source of strain bore down upon the west coast's racial cleavage. Japan attacked China once again and, in Canada, reports of this aggression provoked the first strong outburst of anti-Japanese feeling in a decade. Much of it was directed at Japan herself. Across the nation indignant Canadians boycotted Japan's products and protested her war atrocities.[3] At the same time British Columbians aimed new barbs at the local Japanese. Animus was most intense in coastal centres — especially Vancouver, Victoria, and their surrounding districts — where provincial xenophobia traditionally had been strong. In part, at least, Canada's Japanese merely became the scapegoats of Japan's militarism. But some whites saw them as a separate cause for concern. Japan's military adventures had roused anxiety on the coast by stirring up the region's traditional fears of isolation and vulnerability, and this new, tense atmosphere breathed fresh life into the community's dormant animus. Moreover, it confirmed the threatening impression left by the popular Japanese image. Older Japanese stereotypes, like those which emphasized low standards-of-living and unfair competition, were burnished anew by abrasive racial tension. They shone even more brightly in the manacing light of Japanese militarism, for Japan was presumed to have designs upon British Columbia. It was rumoured that hundreds of illegal Japanese immigrants were present on the coast, that Japanese spies and military officers lived surreptitiously in the community, and that a Japanese

509

fifth column potential was growing in the province. Thus in 1937, when old antipathies fused with new anxieties, another wave of anti-Asian sentiment surged over the province.

Archdeacon F.G. Scott, a former popular Anglican wartime padre, precipitated the new outbreak in mid-November 1937, one week after the Japanese had taken Shanghai. In a widely-reported interview with the *Toronto Daily Star* he suggested that Japanese officers were living, disguised, in Japanese fishing villages along the west coast.[4] A few coastal residents ridiculed Scott's claims. Others, however, vouched for their truth, and his supporters won the day, for a public outcry followed his remarks. Captain MacGregor Macintosh, a Conservative member of the legislature of British Columbia, first endorsed Scott's report and then, early in 1938, raised charges of widespread illegal Japanese immigration.[5] Led by A.W. Neill, an Independent and perennial foe of the Oriental immigrant, provincial members of Parliament from all major parties demanded a halt to Japanese immigration.[6] Simultaneously, in Vancouver, Alderman Halford Wilson urged City Council to limit the number of licences for Japanese merchants and to impose zoning restrictions upon them.[7] Meanwhile, Vancouver's major daily newspapers launched their own anti-Japanese campaigns.[8] In Ottawa the prime minister received a flurry of protest notes while the outspoken Alderman Wilson's mail brought him letters of support.[9]

Judged in the light of past anti-Oriental incidents, this was not a major outburst. Its central figures, Wilson and Macintosh, made no attempt to organize a protest movement. They merely spent their energies in making public demands for more restrictive legislation. Nor was popular hostility as intense as it had been during the mid-1880s or the summer of 1907, when anti-Asian riots had occured in Vancouver. Because the level of social strain was relatively low and dynamic organizational leadership was absent, this precluded the development of a major racial crisis. Nevertheless, signs still pointed to increasing public tension, and the weight of this concern was soon felt in Ottawa.

But Prime Minister Mackenzie King was loath to grasp the nettle. King probably wished to placate British Columbia's xenophobes, or at least quiet them, if he could. At the same time, however, he was subject to countervailing pressures. He was anxious not to embarrass British interests in Asia by taking any initiative which might provoke Japanese ire. Japan's renewed militarism had heightened his own inherent sense of caution. But pressure from the west coast grew so intense that, ultimately, he could not ignore it. Urged first by Premier T.D. Pattullo of British Columbia and then by Ian Mackenzie, the only west-coast representative in the cabinet, King early in March 1938 promised a public enquiry into rumours of illegal Japanese immigration.[10]

But the mere promise of an investigation did not still the insistent demands for an end to Japanese immigration. Macintosh even called for the repatriation of all Japanese residents in Canada, regardless of their citizenship.[11] Then on 24 March the Board of Review charged with the investigation held its first public hearing in Vancouver. Over the next seven weeks it conducted a series of further meetings in major centres throughout the province and, once the hearings commenced, popular unease appeared to dissipate. The hearings themselves put an end to scattered public protest by offering a forum to the vociferous. Furthermore, the meetings forced critics to prove their allegations or remain silent, and many chose the latter refuge. In fact, public concern subsided to such an extent that, when the board's findings were published early in 1939, the report scarcely attracted notice.[12]

But while hostility ebbed appreciably it was not completely dispelled, and over the next two years the west-coast Japanese remained the targets of rumour, suspicion, and criticism. Then, in the spring of 1940, a wave of animosity began to well up once again. The anxious wartime atmosphere shaped by Canada's recent belligerency once more heightened traditional prejudices and aggravated racial tensions in west-coast society. At the same time, and for the same reason, Japan's Asian military campaign again began to rouse concern. The growth of general unease once more strengthened feelings of vulnerability and insecurity in the community. Prompted by mounting anxiety, the cry again went up that illegal Japanese immigrants were infiltrating the country; renewed demands were made for an end to all Japanese immigration as well as for stronger Pacific coast defences.

511

It was Alderman Halford Wilson who headed this new campaign of protest. Throughout the summer of 1940 he warned of Japanese subversion and called for closer restrictions on all Japanese residents.[13] Wilson still made no attempt to organize a popular movement but he did remain the most insistent of the Japanese community's critics. Himself aside, it is difficult to know for whom Wilson actually spoke. Few British Columbians in 1940 were willing to follow his lead in public. Yet undoubtedly there were many who endorsed the general thrust of his remarks, if not their specific aim. Certainly his crusade was a measure of the times, for anti-Japanese nativism was once more on the rise.[14] And in Ottawa as well as Victoria this resurgence soon became a source of some concern.[15] The worry was that Wilson's comments might put the torch to public opinion and touch off racial disorder.

While provincial and federal authorities grew increasingly alarmed at the prospect of racial turmoil, senior military officers in British Columbia were also concerned by the presence of Japanese on the coast. Intelligence officers had kept watch on the Japanese community since 1937 and, from the outset, they had accepted the prevailing assumption that Japanese residents, regardless of their citizenship, would endanger national security in time of war. As early as June 1938 the Department of National Defence had explored the prospect of widespread Japanese wartime internment.[16] In 1940, during the summer's crest of popular anti-Japanese feeling, the Pacific Command's Joint Service Committee approved contingency plans to meet both an external Japanese attack and an internal Japanese insurrection. The committee also endorsed an intelligence report which warned of possible sabotage from the west-coast Japanese fishing fleet. Japanese residents, it reported, 'could very easily make themselves a potent force and threaten the vital industries of British Columbia.' If war broke out, the committee believed, every Japanese resident in British Columbia should be considered a potential enemy.[17]

In contrast the RCMP tended to minimize the Japanese threat. Since 1938 officers in 'E' Division, stationed in Vancouver, had also kept the Japanese under surveillance. In 1940 they assigned three constables to observe the community and also employed Japanese informants. Through continual investigation the force concluded that Japanese residents posed no real threat to Canada. On the contrary, it observed what it believed to be convincing evidence of Japanese loyalty to Canada. Signs of this were especially clear in the community's strong support for Victory bond drives and Red Cross work, the Nisei desire to volunteer for military service, and the widespread wish amongst Japanese not to arouse white antagonism. 'This office,' the officer commanding at Vancouver reported late in October 1940, 'does not consider that the Japanese of British Columbia constitute a menace to the State.'[18]

Was there substance to this apparent threat of Japanese subversion? The Board of Review in 1938 had found no proof of wholesale illegal immigration. Nor had the RCMP discovered any indication of serious danger and, surely, this was the organization best able to judge.[19] It had scrutinized the Japanese community more carefully than had any other agency. Neither military intelligence nor popular rumour was founded on such close observation, and the claims of each should be judged accordingly. All available signs pointed in one direction only: no significant evidence of Japanese treachery could be seen at this time. Nor would any be discovered at a later date. The threat of Japanese subversion was in essence a fiction based on xenophobic traditions and perceptions clouded by fears and anxieties. Yet despite its insubstantial basis, the threat was real enough to many British Columbians and it was the goad which stirred popular animus to life once more.

This resurgence of anti-Japanese sentiment again placed the King government in an uncomfortable position. Whatever it felt about the demands of west-coast nativists, more than ever, in the summer of 1940, it wished to avoid irritating Japan as this might jeopardize British interests in the Pacific, if not induce war itself. As well, by this time Canada was preoccupied by European conflict and presumably the federal government wished to avoid distractions. Therefore it hesitated as long as seemed possible before taking action. But by September 1940, when rumours first were heard that Oriental Canadians would be included in the first call for military service, the question could no longer be ignored. Just as Japan announced her alliance with the Axis powers, these reports provoked a sharp cry of protest. Bowing before the rising winds of criticism, the Cabinet War Committee omitted Asian Canadians from the first draft and then formed a special committee to investigate the question of Orientals and British Columbia's security.[20]

The committee soon confirmed that anti-Japanese feeling was running high in the province and that this, rather than Japanese subversion, was the greatest potential source of danger to the community. Its major recommendations were therefore aimed at reducing public tension. In order to scotch persistent rumours of illegal Japanese immigration, it urged a new registration of all Japanese residents, both citizens and aliens alike. It also proposed the creation of a standing committee to advise the government on problems relating to Orientals in British Columbia.[21] King and his cabinet, because of the delicate state of Anglo-Japanese relations, were anxious to avoid even the threat of civil disorder in British Columbia. Thus they implemented these suggestions in the hope that they would promote public calm. Intent on disarming British Columbia's xenophobes, the government included MacGregor Macintosh on the Standing Committee. And in order to reassure the Japanese it nominated Professor H.F. Angus, a long-time champion of civil rights for Japanese Canadians.[22]

If the King government hoped its new initiative would calm popular fears, it must soon have been disabused of its optimism. During the first half of 1941 the public temper remained aroused. A few signs indicated, in fact, that some British Columbians were growing even more suspicious of the Japanese. Agitation thus continued, even though still no credible leadership had emerged to give protest a focus. Halford Wilson kept up his one-man campaign, repeatedly urging that, in the interest of national security, all Japanese fishing boats should be sequestered.[23] Furthermore, ongoing tension remained a source of concern to federal officials who still feared a racial incident. Wilson was singled out as the chief cause for alarm and unsuccessful efforts were made to persuade him to keep silent.[24] Meanwhile, in military circles, fear of public disturbance was matched by continued suspicion of the Japanese themselves. As an intelligence report noted in July 1941, widespread Japanese sabotage was unlikely in the event of war but it remained a possibility unless proper security precautions were taken and the Japanese themselves were protected from white provocation.[25]

In the final months before Pearl Harbor was bombed, racial tensions began to abate. But even then conditions favoured a new anti-Japanese outburst. Influenced by the community's xenophobia, its traditional racial cleavage, and its anxieties born of war and isolation, British Columbians continued to suspect their Japanese neighbours. The west-coast Japanese could not be trusted. Their allegiance was in doubt. Given the opportunity, it was assumed, some among them would betray the province to the enemy. The federal government, while alarmed by British Columbia's Japanese problem, was ill prepared to meet the issue head on. It feared that Japan might use a racial disturbance as a *casus belli*, but aside from forming the Standing Committee, it had done very little to prevent an outbreak.

Canada declared war on Japan on 7 December 1941, within hours of Pearl Harbor. The King government immediately recognized the likelihood of violent anti-Japanese demonstrations in British Columbia. At the same time it had to deal with a new enemy alien problem, for war's outbreak altered the status of many Canadian residents of Japanese origin.[26] Faced with the prospect of racial incidents as well as an alien menace, the dominion government quickly took pre-emptive action. Thirty-eight Japanese nationals were interned on the grounds that they might endanger the community and the west-coast Japanese fishing fleet was immobilized. On the advice of the RCMP, all Japanese-language newspapers and schools voluntarily closed their doors. Meanwhile, Prime Minister King, senior police and military officers, and Vancouver's major newspapers all reassured the public and called for calm. As King declared in a radio address to the nation on 8 December: 'the competent authorities are satisfied that the security situation is well in hand. They are confident of the correct and loyal behaviour of Canadian residents of Japanese origin.'[27]

But many west-coast whites were not so easily mollified. Neither prompt federal action nor loyal protestations from leading Japanese did much to assuage their fears. War's outbreak had once more opened the floodgates of fear and hostility. Roused by war on the Pacific, the west coast resumed its attack on the province's Japanese. Again, enmity was strongest in and around Vancouver and Victoria, long the province's two focal points of anti-Asian sentiment. In the week following Pearl Harbor some Japanese in Vancouver were victimized by scattered acts of vandalism. Several firms began discharging their Japanese employees. Fear of Japanese subversion again spread in the province.[28] In private, British Columbians began protesting to their members of Parliament. The weight of public concern also bore down on provincial newspapers. Columnist Bruce Hutchison informed the Prime Minister's office that, at the *Vancouver Sun*, 'we are under extraordinary pressure from our readers to advocate a pogrom of Japs. We told the people to be calm. Their reply was a bombardment of letters that the Japs all be interned.'[29]

To encourage calm, police, government, and military officials issued further assurances that the Japanese problem was well in hand.[30] But their statements seemed to have little effect. Popular protest continued to grow and, in response, alarm in government and military circles increased too. On 20 December F.J. Hume, chairman of the Standing Committee, told King: 'in British Columbia particularly, the successes of the Japanese to date in the Pacific have to a great extent inflamed public opinion against the local Japanese. People here are in a very excited condition and it would require a very small local incident to bring about most unfortunate conditions between the whites and Japanese.'[31] Major General R.O. Alexander, commander in chief of the Pacific Command, was also concerned: 'The situation with regard to the Japanese resident in British Columbia is assuming a serious aspect. Public feeling is becoming very insistent, especially in Vancouver, that local Japanese should be either interned or removed from the coast. Letters are being written continually to the press and I am being bombarded by individuals, both calm and hysterical, demanding that something should be done.'[32] Alexander feared that public demonstrations, to be held in the near future according to rumour, might lead to racial violence.

After a brief lull over Christmas the public outcry grew more strident than ever. Increasing numbers of west-coast whites, regardless of all reassurance, were certain that the local Japanese community endangered west-coast security. By early January 1942 patriotic societies, service clubs, town and city councils, and air-raid precaution units, most of them on Vancouver Island or in the Vancouver area, had begun to voice protest.[33] Repeatedly they urged that all Japanese, regardless of citizenship, be interned, as quickly as possible. Other spokesmen suggested somewhat less drastic action, but whatever the precise demands of the public they all assumed the need for some form of Japanese evacuation. And with each passing day opinion seemed to grow more volatile. Even moderates like J.G. Turgeon, the Liberal MP from the Cariboo, were alarmed at the seeming danger. On 6 January he warned the prime minister:

the condition of this province is dangerous, so far as the Japanese are concerned. If the Government do not take drastic action, the situation will get out-of-hand. The Government will suffer, and so will the Japanese, personally and through destruction of property.
I am therefore forced to recommend that very strong measures to [sic] taken, and quickly. Either delay, or lack of thorough action, may cause violence.[34]

Beneath this new hostile outburst, which war with Japan had precipitated, lay two primary social strains.[35] The first was British Columbia's traditional racial cleavage, one marked in recent years by strong anti-Japanese prejudice. This permanent gulf between whites and Asians had created enduring social tensions which perpetually tended towards outbreaks of racial animosity. The structure of west-coast race relations was conducive to such an end. The second strain was the growing sense of anxiety which accompanied war's outbreak, a condition created by the atmosphere of ambiguity which surrounded the Pacific war. In the weeks following Pearl Harbor the level of generalized public anxiety created by war increased appreciably. In itself the opening of a new theatre of war was a new source of unease because it raised new uncertainties in an already war-troubled world. More specifically, the ambiguity which enveloped Japan's military activities in the weeks after 7 December also conditioned the growth of anxiety. The startling number of her targets, the suddenness of her assaults, the speed of her military expansion, and the seeming ease of her victories surprised and frightened many west-coast whites. The enemy seemed everywhere in the Pacific. No one knew where he might next attack and some feared it would be British Columbia. In such conditions civil defence preparations themselves became a source of unease for they reflected the assumption that a Japanese attack was indeed imminent. During the first week of war air raid precaution units were called for duty, defence regulations were posted, and nightly blackouts were enforced. Far from offering reassurance these activities further unsettled an already apprehensive public.

In the years since the expulsion it has occasionally been suggested that two economic motives caused the anti-Japanese outburst: one the desire of some British Columbians to acquire Japanese property at bargain prices, the other a wish to rid the province, once and for all, of Japanese economic competition. These conclusions, however, are informed by little more than hindsight. There is no body of evidence to indicate that either factor significantly shaped public opinion or government policy. In the Fraser and Okanagan valleys some residents did request stringent restrictions on Japanese landholding, a proposal which reflected inter-racial tensions of economic origin. But the great majority of those who protested had no obvious economic interest to defend against Japanese encroachment and, evidently, no strong desire to profit at the expense of evacuees.[36]

It was because of wartime social strains that a sense of crisis mounted in British Columbia. And as these tensions grew they sharpened the coast's hostility toward the Japanese minority. Japanese militarism and the province's legacy of racial tension combined to cast the old image of the Yellow Peril in a new and lurid light. As many British Columbians peered through the fog of their anxieties they saw little but the menacing outline of Japanese subversion. Furthermore, while the growing sense of crisis narrowed whites' perceptions, these perceptions, in turn, intensified public unease. Thus, social tensions and racial imagery were mutually reinforcing. Had British Columbians seen their Japanese neighbours clearly, they would have observed an isolated, defenceless minority, gravely alarmed by its plight and anxious to demonstrate its loyalty to Canada. But fear and prejudice prevented them from taking a closer look. Consequently, the Japanese appeared nothing but a threat and therefore the call went up for their expulsion.

In addition, aroused public opinion pressed down upon a group of politicians particularly susceptible to prejudice against Asians. On a personal level most political leaders in British Columbia probably shared the stereotyped attitudes of their constituents. Furthermore, ever since Confederation anti-Orientalism had pervaded the provincial political culture. Over the years conservatives, liberals, and socialists alike had freely employed the rhetoric of racialism. The Conservative and Liberal parties had regularly nailed anti-Oriental planks to their election platforms, both federal and provincial, and after 1933 the CCF, despite its professed concern for civil liberties, had been divided on the question. Seldom, if ever, had the anti-Asian cry been a decisive issue in electoral contests: the broad consensus amongst west-coast politicians had prevented that. Yet, by World War II racial prejudice had long been common currency in political discourse. Some politicians merely dealt in the small change of petty racialism; others, like Wilson and Macintosh, traded in larger denominations — nativism and xenophobia. Ian Mackenzie, upon whom the weight of west-coast opinion fell in 1942, stood between the two extremes. He was undoubtedly confirmed in his anti-Asian sentiments, yet not outspoken so. Certainly, on the eve of war in the Pacific, most British Columbian politicians shared some of Mackenzie's convictions. Consequently, when anti-Japanese feeling welled up after Pearl Harbor, they also shared the public's growing concern and responded sympathetically to popular pressure.

In Ottawa Mackenzie King was also a target of rising protest. His experience with west-coast hostility toward Asians had been longer and more intimate than that of any other federal politician. In 1907 and 1908 he had held three royal commissions to investigate Oriental immigration and racial disturbances in Vancouver. Throughout the 1920s and 1930s, as prime minister, the issue confronted him repeatedly. As was usual with King, his comments on the Oriental problem were always extremely circumspect. Prior to his premiership he concluded that the roots of west-coast tensions were economic, not racial, and he saw their satisfactory resolution in negotiation with Asian nations to seek mutually acceptable immigration levels.[37] In office his government used both diplomacy and legislation to enforce restrictions on immigration from China and Japan. During the later 1930s, however, when anti-Japanese feeling increased on the west coast, King felt constrained from any further restrictive action by international tensions. His view of the issue after the outbreak of war with Japan remains unclear. He did not share the anxieties of west-coast residents yet he ultimately accepted the possibility of a Japanese invasion of British Columbia.[38] Probably his primary concern was for the instability of west-coast opinion and the threat to public order which it posed. If subsequent government policy was any measure of King's thought, he was willing to accept any expedient solution to reduce public tension.

517

Under heavy popular pressure the federal government ordered yet another review of the Japanese problem in British Columbia. On 8 and 9 January 1942 a committee of federal and provincial government, police, and military officials met in Ottawa to discuss means of allaying west-coast alarm. The central question explored was whether or not the Japanese should be removed from coastal areas; but the meeting could not agree on an answer. Several representatives who had just arrived from British Columbia, together with Ian Mackenzie, the meeting's chairman, argued that all able-bodied male Japanese nationals should immediately be removed. The majority of the delegates, however, few of whom had recently been in British Columbia, opposed such drastic action. Consequently the meeting submitted a moderate report which suggested both an extension of existing minor restrictions on the liberties of all Japanese and the creation of a quasi-military work corps for Canadian Japanese who wished to support the war effort.[39]

But the conference's report was only one opinion. From British Columbia there came ever more insistent demands for an evacuation programme and within the cabinet Ian Mackenzie, King's closest political friend from the province, pressed for such a solution.[40] Consequently, when the government announced its revised plans on 14 January, the new policy bore the unmistakable imprint of west-coast opinion. The King government accepted most of the Ottawa conference's proposals but in addition it proposed to remove all enemy aliens, regardless of age, sex, or nationality, from protected areas soon to be defined in British Columbia. The programme was aimed primarily at Japanese nationals although it embraced Germans and Italians as well. The statement also promised that a Japanese Civilian Corps would soon be formed for work on projects deemed in the national interest.[41] The covert hope was that Japanese-Canadian men would volunteer for it in large numbers, thus permitting the government to remove them from the protected areas without an unpleasant resort to compulsion.[42]

It was felt that, by yielding to some of the west coast's demands, the partial evacuation policy would calm British Columbian fears. Concerned for the safety of Canadian prisoners in Japan's hands, anxious to avoid needless expense and disruption in time of war, and touched with a lingering sense of justice and humanity, the King government refused to make further concessions. But the plan was also rather equivocal in that it neither defined the protected areas nor promised when evacuation would begin. In effect it still gave the federal government considerable freedom of action. For a few, brief moments the gesture seemed satisfactory. Premier John Hart of British Columbia, whose government had already demanded similiar measures, applauded the decision and the *Vancouver Sun* praised the King government's common sense. The storm of protest abated temporarily.[43]

518

Within ten days, however, agitation began to increase once again. The public outcry mounted throughout February until, during the last week of the month, it reached unprecedented volume. Pressed by the fear of enemy subversion, thousands of west-coast whites petitioned Ottawa for the immediate evacuation of all Japanese. Individuals, farm organizations, municipal councils, civil defence units, constituency associations, service clubs, patriotic societies, trades unions, citizens committees, chambers of commerce — even the Vancouver and District Lawn Bowling Association — all demanded the total evacuation of Japanese from coastal areas.[44] One group of prominent Vancouver residents telegraphed Ian Mackenzie that, 'owing to wide spread public alarm over enemy aliens on the Pacific coast and especially respecting those astride vital defence points and with a view to stabilizing public opinion and in the interest of public safety,' they urged the immediate evacuation of all Japanese.[45] Never before had west-coast race relations been so seriously strained.

By and large British Columbians appear to have reached their conclusions about the Japanese menace with little prompting. More or less simultaneously thousands recognized an obvious threat and identified the equally obvious solution. In the generation of this consensus neither popular leaders nor popular journalism played a predominant role. Halford Wilson and MacGregor Macintosh, once the two chief critics of the west-coast Japanese, were submerged beneath the rising tide of hostility. In fact the protest movement had no pre-eminent leaders whatsoever. Nor did provincial papers become leaders of opinion, even though some took up the popular cry. During the crisis west-coast journalism helped sustain the prevailing mood, but most papers merely reflected the popular mind. Agitation was the product of a widespread outburst of hostility, one which was rooted in longstanding antipathies as well as immediate wartime pressures.

The very structure of the protest movement supports this contention for it clearly revealed how extensive was the anti-Japanese consensus. Although public anxiety had flared up immediately after Pearl Harbor, no effective anti-Japanese movement had begun to emerge until late January. In its earliest stage protest was random; it had no central leadership and no institutional focus. But when the movement began to take form, protest was mobilized by a broad range of the traditional social, economic, administrative, and political organizations already entrenched in British Columbia. The Provincial Council of Women, the Vancouver Real Estate Exchange, the Canadian Legion in Gibson's Landing, the Kinsmen's Club of Victoria, the North Burnaby Liberal Association, the B.C. Poultry Industries Committee, the Corporation of the District of Saanich, the National Union of Machinists, Fitters, and Helpers (Victoria Local Number 2), and scores of other similar groups all pressed their demands for evacuation. These organizations not only represented major interest groups in the province but their influence cut across most social, economic, and political bounds in west-coast society. They represented the interests and opinions, the fears and hostilities of tens of thousands of British Columbians. If there were some who did not share prevailing attitudes, they remained largely silent when confronted by the tyranny of the consensus.

One further sign of mounting social pressure was the growing incidence of rumours of Japanese subversion. Some told of Japanese who owned high-powered vehicles and short-wave equipment, who lived near sites of great strategic value, who swelled with insolent pride at Japan's successive victories. Others hinted at active Japanese disloyalty — and, in the hothouse atmosphere of gowing public tension, stories grew to outlandish proportions. Military intelligence officers were informed in mid-January that Japanese in Vancouver had fixed infra-red and ultra-violet beacons on their roofs, devices which, when viewed through special binoculars, would guide enemy flights over the city.[46] Rumour, itself is usually the product of serious social strain.[47] These persistent rumours were one more indication of the growing racial crisis on Canada's west coast. The outbreak of war with Japan had spread a grave sense of looming threat amongst west-coast whites. Yet for all its immediacy this threat remained somewhat vague and nebulous. The enemy was identified, his whereabouts were not. Rumours helped resolve this ambiguity. They suggested that some of the enemy were very close at hand. While this in itself was cause for concern, it also helped to clarify the confusions of war with a distant, elusive power. Because rumours singled out the nearest available enemy they helped reduce the ambiguity which had spawned them in the first place. And, once in circulation, they, too, stirred the ever-widening eddies of hostility and alarm.

It seemed clear, as well, that one immediate reason for the renewed upsurge of protest in February was that many British Columbians, anxious for total evacuation, had misinterpreted the government's policy announcement of 14 January. The *Vancouver Sun* had taken it to mean that 'all Japanese and other enemy aliens' were to be removed from protected areas, an assumption shared by several provincial members of Parliament. 'My understanding' wrote Ian MacKenzie, 'was that all able-bodied, adult enemy aliens would have to be removed from protected areas. My further understanding was also that all able-bodied *Canadian nationals* would have to be moved, but that *first* they should be given an opportunity to volunteer in the Civilian Corps.'[48] This confusion aside, the federal government also failed to implement its programme immediately. Neither the evacuation plans nor the designated protected areas were announced until 23 January, and the delay itself provoked some concern. Furthermore, when finally announced, the plans indicated that evacuation was not to be completed before 1 April, a date which seemed far too remote to those who believed the Japanese threat was imminent. Once the plans were made public there was a further delay while the relocation machinery was set up. The task of arranging to move, house, and care for several thousand Japanese proved a time-consuming one and it was complicated further by the strong opposition of residents in the British Columbian interior, especially the Okanagan Valley, to proposals that the Japanese all be settled inland.[49] Several times the immediate departure of Japanese from Vancouver was announced and then postponed. Consequently, few, if any, Japanese left their homes before mid-February. In the eyes of concerned west-coast whites the government's partial evacuation policy increasingly seemed a mixture of confusion, delay, and prevarication. It appeared that Ottawa did not understand, let alone sympathize with, British Columbia's predicament.

Japan's startling military success continued to play on west-coast fears as well. By mid-January Japanese troops had overrun much of Malaya, the Philippines, Burma, and British North Borneo. They had occupied Thailand, captured Hong Kong (taking more than 1600 Canadian troops prisoner), sunk Britain's most modern battleship, and crippled her Pacific fleet. Late in January they had laid siege to the island of Singapore. News of this swift succession of decisive victories dominated the front pages of the provincial press. Furthermore, these accounts repeatedly emphasized that Japanese subversion and fifth-column activity had played a central role in Japan's programme of conquest. Already convinced of their own vulnerability, British Columbians grew more alarmed when worse news succeeded bad. As the military crisis deepened across the Pacific, so public tension grew on Canada's west coast.

Parliament reconvened on 22 January as the racial crisis mounted. Members of Parliament from British Columbia, no doubt as concerned as their protesting constituents, themselves began to press for total evacuation. Howard Green, the Conservative member from Vancouver South, opened the attack in the Commons on 29 January.[50] The threat of Japanese treachery confronted the Pacific coast, he said, and therefore all Japanese should be removed from the province. Other British Columbian members made similar claims before the House over the next three weeks. In private they were even more insistent. On 28 January British Columbians in the Liberal caucus demanded that Japanese Canadians who failed to volunteer for the Civilian Corps be evacuated as quickly as possible. In succeeding weeks, as popular protest reached its greatest heights, King faced successive demands for relocation from provincial politicians — Conservative, Liberal, and Independent alike.[51]

Meanwhile, government officials in British Columbia sustained their pressure as well. At the height of the popular outcry the attorney-general of British Columbia told Ian Mackenzie:

> Events have transpired recently which add to the danger we have already been subjected to by the presence of Japanese on this Coast.
>
> I cannot urge too strongly the seriousness of this situation and the danger the people of British Columbia feel upon this matter.
>
> Nothing short of immediate removal of the Japanese will meet the dangers which we feel in this Province.[52]

At the same time the minister of labour campaigned for total evacuation. The lieutenant-governor informed Mackenzie King that he had 'rarely felt so keenly about any impending danger as I do about the Japanese on this coast being allowed to live in our midst.' He suggested that, at very least, Japanese males be quickly interned. Since mid-January senior officers of the Pacific Command had grown more concerned as well. By the time public protest reached its peak, they, too, subscribed to demands for total evacuation.[53]

521

It was Ian Mackenzie who ultimately bore the brunt of this storm of protest. First he received warnings and notes of alarm, then petitions urging evacuation, and finally demands that he resign. But Mackenzie shared the concerns of his west-coast constituents. In the first weeks after the outbreak of war he grew convinced that all able-bodied Japanese men should be removed from strategic areas. In consequence, he considered the partial evacuation policy inadequate. He also believed that the 1 April deadline was too remote. Furthermore, as pressure upon him grew, Mackenzie's alarm at the instability of public opinion increased in like proportion. On 22 February, when news reached him of a series of mass protest meetings planned for 1 March, his anxiety heightened further.[54] Two days later he informed cabinet colleagues of the heated state of west-coast opinion and of a call for his own resignation. As he told the minister of justice:

> The feeling in British Columbia in regard to the Japanese is so aflame that I consider we should take the necessary powers (if we have not got them now) to remove Canadian Nationals, as well as Japanese Nationals, from the protected areas.
>
> I have no report on how the Vancouver Corps has succeeded, but I greatly fear *disorder* from reports actually received, unless all able-bodied males of Japanese origin are immediately evacuated.[55]

Publicly Mackenzie appeared unperturbed, urging calm on his west-coast correspondents, but privately he was extremely exercised.[56]

Within the cabinet others shared something of Mackenzie's alarm, particularly his concern for possible public disturbances. The prime minister agreed that there was 'every possibility of riots' on the west coast, and feared that in such an event there would be 'repercussions in the Far East against our own prisoners.' The situation was awkward, he recognized, because 'public prejudice is so strong in B.C. that it is going to be difficult to control.'[57] Thus, under heavy external pressure and alarmed by the evident danger of racial violence, the federal government finally took decisive action. On 24

February, only hours after Mackenzie had written his warning to cabinet colleagues, the government approved an enabling measure which permitted total evacuation. Three days later the announcement was made that all persons of Japanese ancestry would have to leave the protected zones.[58] In the hope of reducing social tensions the King government had finally capitulated to public pressure.

The province did not all at once breathe a sigh of collective relief. Tension remained high for several days thereafter. From Ottawa Ian Mackenzie believed that public disorder was still possible. Hostility surged onward in the Okanagan Valley, where many local residents feared that the new federal policy would bring a large Japanese influx. Slowly, however, the strain of racial crisis began to ease. The two mass meetings held on 1 March were quiet and orderly. Mackenzie received a note of praise from supporters in Vancouver. The flood of protests to Ottawa began to recede.[59]

522

When the cabinet approved the order which permitted evacuation, the editors of the *Sun* looked forward to the day the move would be complete. They hoped that the coast was 'Saying Goodbye, Not Au Revoir' to the Japanese.[60] But while some had undoubtedly seen the crisis as a chance to solve the province's Japanese problem for all time, this scarcely explains the previous weeks' outburst of hostility. War with Japan had sharpened the animus, narrowed the vision, and roused the fears of a community already deeply divided along racial lines. In the minds of west-coast whites intimations of vulnerability and isolation had long nursed a sense of insecurity, and after Pearl Harbor many British Columbians had felt themselves exposed as never before to attack from Japan. In addition they had grown convinced that the resident Japanese were a threat to the community's security. These beliefs had virtually no foundation in fact. In essence they were facets of the traditional Japanese image held by white British Columbians, stereotypes further distorted in the heat of war. Its fears fed by these perceptions, the west coast loosed a torrent of hostility. Sensitive to the public temper, and alarmed by the prospect of racial disturbance, the federal government attempted preventative action. But neither minor restrictions on civil liberties nor the promise of partial relocation could satisfy the west-coast public for long. It demanded total Japanese evacuation. In the end its wishes were met.[61]

Notes

1. The major works on Orientals in Canada are Tien-fang Cheng, *Oriental Immigration in Canada* (Shanghai 1931); Charles H. Young and Helen R.Y. Reid, *The Japanese Canadians* (Toronto 1938); Charles James Woodsworth, *Canada and the Orient: A Study in International Relations* (Toronto 1941); Forrest E. LaViolette, *The Canadian Japanese and World War II: A Sociological and Psychological Account* (Toronto 1948); William Peter Ward, 'White Canada Forever: British Columbia's Response to Orientals, 1858–1914' (PHD thesis, Queen's University, 1972).
2. On the nature and significance of Oriental stereotypes see Ward, 'White Canada Forever,' 37–67 and 132–48, and LaViolette, *The Canadian Japanese*, 3–28.
3. A.R.M. Lower, *Canada and the Far East — 1940*, Institute of Pacific Research Inquiry Series (New York 1940), 23–8.

4. *Vancouver Sun*, 17 Nov. 1937.
5. *Vancouver Sun*, 24 Nov. 1937; *The Colonist* (Victoria), 19 Jan. 1938.
6. Canada, House of Commons, *Debates*, 17 Feb. 1938, 550–75.
7. *The Province* (Vancouver), 22 Feb. 1938.
8. *The Province*, 2, 17, 18, and 24 Feb. 1938; *Vancouver Sun*, 10, 12, 14, and 28 Feb. 1938.
9. Two representative letters to King are: R.S. Hanna to King, 14 Feb. 1938, William Lyon Mackenzie King Papers, MG 26, J2, vol. 147, file 1-209, Public Archives of Canada [PAC]; Forgotten Native of Japanada to King, nd, ibid. Letters to Wilson in 1938 can be found in the Halford Wilson Papers, vol. 1, file 1, Public Archives of British Columbia [PABC].
10. T.D. Pattullo to King, 26 Jan. 1938, King Papers, MG 26, J1, vol. 256, 218388–9; Ian Mackenzie to King, 26 Feb. 1938, ibid., vol. 253, 216060; King to Mackenzie, 1 March 1938, ibid., 216062–3A. At this time Mackenzie was the minister of national defence. After the outbreak of war he was transferred to Pensions and National Health.
11. *Vancouver Sun*, 23 March 1938.
12. The Board of Review concluded that rumours of illegal Japanese immigration had been greatly exaggerated. It estimated that about 120 Japanese were living illegally in the province. Board of Review [Immigration], *Final Report*, 29 Sept. 1938, 38.
13. H.L. K[eeyside], Memorandum, 11 June 1940, Department of External Affairs Records, RG, G-1, vol. 2007, file 212, part I, PAC; *The Province*, 7 and 15 Aug. 1940.
14. See also Wilson Papers, vol. I, file 4; *Vancouver Sun*, 29 June and 10 Aug. 1940; *The Province*, 21 and 24 Aug. 1940.
15. K[eenleyside], Memorandum, 11 June 1940, External Affairs Records, vol. 2007, file 212, part I, PAC; Gray Turgeon to King, 7 Aug. 1940, King Papers, MG 26, J1, vol. 297, 252824–5; King to Lapointe, 8 Aug. 1940, ibid., 252828.
16. Extract from Report on Japanese Activities on the West Coast of Canada, 10 March 1937, External Affairs Records, vol. 1803, file 729, PAC; Major General E.C. Ashton, chief of the General Staff, Memorandum, Acquisition by Japanese Interests of Timberland and Mineral Concessions on the Pacific Coast, 13 Nov. 1937, Ian Mackenzie Papers, MG 27, III-B-5, vol. 30, file x-23, PAC; L.R. LaFlèche, deputy minister, Department of National Defence, to F.C. Blair, director of immigration, 2 June 1938, Department of National Defence, to F.C. Blair, director of immigration, 2 June 1938, Department of National Defence Records, file HQ 6-0-7, Department of National Defence Archives.
17. Brigadier C.V. Stockwell, district officer commanding Military District 11, to the secretary, Department of National Defence, 4 Sept. 1940, Defence Records, file HQS, VS 38-1-1, vol. 5.
18. Superintendent C. E. Hill, 'E' Division, RCMP, to the Commissioner, 25 Aug. 1938, Government of Canada, Immigration Branch Records, RG 76, vol. 86, file 9309, vol. 16, PAC; R.R. Tait, assistant commissioner, RCMP, to Keenleyside, 28 Oct. 1940, External Affairs Records, vol. 2007, file 212, part I, PAC. The entire contents of this file substantiate the observations made in this paragraph.
19. The RCMP did, however, identify a small number of Japanese who might endanger the state in time of war and these individuals were arrested and detained immediately after war on Japan was declared.
20. Pattullo to King, 23 Sept. 1940, King Papers, MG 26, J1, vol. 293, 248363; King to Pattullo, 27 Sept. 1940, T.D. Pattullo Papers, Vol. 70, file 4, 21, PABC; Wilson to the Finance Committee, City of Vancouver, 24 Sept. 1940, Wilson Papers, vol. 1, file 4; A.D.P. Heeney, Memorandum for the Prime Minister, 27 Sept. 1940, King Papers, MG 26, J4, vol. 361, file 3849.
21. Report and Recommendations of the Special Committee on Orientals in British Columbia, Dec. 1940, typescript, ibid. The committee also recommended that, because testimony before it almost unanimously favoured a complete end to Japanese immigration, the government should forbid it when the international situation permitted. This recommendation was not published because King feared it might strain existing relations with Japan and inflame anti-Oriental opinion in British Columbia. Government of Canada, Privy Council, Minutes and Documents of the Cabinet War Committee, RG 2, 7C, vol. IV, Minutes, 2 Jan. 1941, 8–9, PAC; Keenleyside to Sansom, [3 Jan. 1941], External Affairs Records, vol. 1868, file 263, part IV, PAC; Additional Statement by the Members of the Special Committee on Orientals in British Columbia for consideration by the Prime Minister and members of the Cabinet War Committee, nd, King Papers, MG 26, J1, vol. 307, 259432-3.
22. Keenleyside to King, 2 Dec. 1940, King Papers, MG 26, J1, vol. 289, 244808–10.
23. *The Province*, 9 Jan. and 11 Feb. 1941; *Victoria Times*, 26 Feb. 1941; *Vancouver Sun*, 8 April and 26 July 1941. One sign of growing suspicion was the increasing sensitivity of west-coast whites to Japanese using cameras. For example see *Nanaimo Free Press*, 8 Feb. 1941.
24. Keeleyside to S.T. Wood, commissioner, RCMP, 20 Feb. 1941, External Affairs Records, vol. 2007, file 212, part II, PAC; F.J. Mead, assistant commissioner, RCMP, to the commissioner, 28 Feb. 1941, ibid.; H.F. Angus to Mayor F.J. Hume, chairman, Standing Committee on Orientals, 25 July 1941, ibid.
25. Flying Officer W.A. Nield, Report on the State of Intelligence on the Pacific Coast with Particular Reference to the Problem of the Japanese Minority, 27 July 1941, Defence Records, file HQ S67-3, vol. 1.

523

26. All Japanese nationals immediately became enemy aliens and, in addition, restrictions imposed upon them were also imposed upon all Japanese Canadians naturalized after 1922.
27. LaViolette, *The Canadian Japanese*, 44; Declaration of the Existence of a State of War Between Canada and Japan, 8 Dec. 1941, King Papers, MG 26, J5, D58190-4; *Vancouver Sun*, 8 Dec. 1941; *Nanaimo Free Press*, 8 Dec. 1941; *The Province*, 8 Dec. 1941.
28. After Pearl Harbor the major daily newspapers in Vancouver and Victoria published steady streams of letters on the Japanese problem, most of which voiced suspicion of the west coast Japanese and demanded federal action to remove the threat which they posed. For reports of vandalism see *The Province*, 8, 9, and 11 Dec. 1941. For rumours of Japanese subversion see Weekly Internal Security Intelligence Report, 13 Dec. 1941, Western Air Command, Defence Records, file HQ S67-3, vol. 1. With the exception of fishermen, those Japanese who lost their jobs were soon reabsorbed by the labour market. C.H. Hill, assistant commissioner, RCMP, Intelligence Report, 16 Dec. 1941 and 13 Jan. 1942, External Affairs Records, file 3464-G-40, Department of External Affairs, Archives Branch [EAA].
29. Hutchison to Pickersgill, [16 Dec. 1941], King Papers, MG 26, J4, vol. 347, 239219-20.
30. *The Province*, 19 Dec. 1941; Hill to the commissioner, RCMP, 20 Dec. 1941, External Affairs Records, file 3464-H-40C, EAA.
31. Hume to King, 20 Dec. 1941, External Affairs Records, vol. 1868, file 263, part IV, PAC.
32. Alexander to chief of the General Staff, 30 Dec. 1941, Defence Records, file HQ 6-0-7. Alexander's concern was shared by those officers commanding Canada's Pacific coast naval and air forces. Commodore W.J.R. Beech to the general officer commanding-in-chief, Pacific Command, 27 Dec. 1941, ibid.; L.S. Stevenson to the secretary, Department of National Defence for Air, 2 Jan. 1941, Defence Records, file HQ S67-3, vol. 1. In Ottawa the chief of the General Staff did not subscribe to these fears. Lt.-Gen. K. Stuart to Keenleyside, 26 Dec. 1941, External Affairs Papers, file 3464-H-40C, EAA.
33. Petitions to the federal government can be found in King Papers, MG 26, J2, vol. 294, file p-309, vol. 14; Mackenzie Papers, vol. 24, file 70-25, vol. 1; ibid., vol. 25, file 70-25, vols. 2 and 3; ibid., vol. 25, file 70-25E; External Affairs Records, file 773-B 1-40, parts I and II, EAA.
34. Turgeon to King, 6 Jan, 1942, External Affairs Records, file 773-b-1-40, part I.
35. For a useful theoretical discussion of the hostile outburst as a social phenomenon see Neil J. Smelser, *Theory of Collective Behavior* (New York 1962), especially Chap. VIII.
36. *Langley Advance*, 15 and 22 Jan. 1942; see also note 49.
37. W.L. Mackenzie King, *Industry and Humanity: A Study in the Principles Underlying Industrial Reconstruction* (Toronto 1918), 75-6.
38. King Diary, 20, 23, and 24 Feb. 1942, King Papers, MG 26,J13.
39. Conference on the Japanese Problem in British Columbia, Minutes, 8 and 9 Jan. 1942, External Affairs Records, vol. 1868, file 263, part IV, PAC; Mackenzie to King, 10 Jan. 1942, Mackenzie Papers, vol. 32, file x-81; Keenleyside to Mackenzie, 10 Jan. 1942, *ibid*. The minority recommendation for partial evacuation was appended to the report.
40. Pacific Command to National Defence Headquarters, 12 Jan. 1942, telegram, Defence Papers, file HQ 6-0-7; Mackenzie to King, 10 Jan. 1942, Mackenzie Papers, vol. 32, file x-81.
41. Statement of the prime minister, 14 Jan. 1942, Mackenzie Papers, vol. 24, file 70–25, vol. 1.
42. Mackenzie to Bryce M. Stewart, deputy minister of labour, 23 Jan. 1942, Mackenzie Papers, vol. 32, file x-81, vol. 2; Keenleyside to Mackenzie, 26 Jan. 1942, *ibid*.; Keenleyside, The Japanese Problem in British Columbia, Memorandum to Mr. Robertson, 27 Jan. 1942, *ibid*..
43. *Vancouver Sun*, 14 Jan. 1942; the lull was obvious to military intelligence officers in British Columbia. Major C.H. Bray, Intelligence, Pacific Command, to the director, Military Operations and Intelligence, National Defence Headquarters, 29 Jan. 1942, Department of Labour Papers, RG 27, Lacelle Files, vol. 174, file 614.02:11-1, vol. 1, PAC.
44. See above note 33.
45. M.C. Robinson and others to Mackenzie, 23 Feb. 1942, Mackenzie Papers, vol. 25, file 70–25, vol. 2.
46. Weekly Internal Security Intelligence Report, 17 Jan. 1942, Western Air Command, Defence Records, file HQ S67-3, vol. 1. For another example of rumour see Gwen Cash, *A Million Miles from Ottawa* (Toronto 1942), 25-6.
47. On the nature and significance of rumour see Gordon W. Allport and Leo Postman, *The Psychology of Rumor* (New York 1965), especially Chap. II.
48. *Vancouver Sun*, 14 Jan. 1942; Mackenzie to Stewart, 23 Jan. 1942, Mackenzie Papers, vol. 32, file x-81, vol. 2. The emphasis was Mackenzie's.
49. Although some fruit and vegetable growers in the Okanagan Valley requested Japanese workers for the duration of the war in order to ease the wartime labour shortage, the proposal roused a strong outburst of bitter opposition in the valley. Protest was channeled through municipal councils, newspapers, boards of trade, and dissenting farm organizations. In addition, proposals that the Japanese be moved east of the Rockies met opposition from several provincial governments. *Penticton Herald*, 15, 22, and 29 Jan. 1942; *Kelowna Courier*, 22 Jan. and 12 Feb. 1942; Keenleyside, Memorandum for Mr. Robertson, 4 Feb. 1942, External Affairs Records, file 3464-G-40, [EAA].

50. House of Commons, *Debates*, 29 Jan. 1942, 156–8.
51. Mackenzie to Robertson, 28 Jan. 1942, Mackenzie Papers, vol. 32, file x-81, vol. 2; R.W. Mayhew to King, 12 Feb. 1942, King Papers, MG 26,J1, vol. 330; G. McGeer to King, 13 Feb. 1942, Gerald Grattan McGeer Papers, box 2, file 9, PABC; Olaf Hanson and others to King, 21 Feb. 1942, King Papers, MG 26,j1, vol. 336.
52. R.L. Maitland to Mackenzie, 17 Feb. 1942, Mackenzie Papers, vol. 32, file x-81, vol. 2.
53. *Vancouver Sun*, 16 Feb. 1942; Pearson to A. MacNamara, associate deputy minister of Labour, 17 Feb. 1942, Labour Records, RG 27, Lacelle Files, vol. 174, file 614.02: 11–1, vol. 1; W.C. Woodward, lieutenant-governor, to King, 11 Feb. 1942, King Papers, MG 26, j1, vol. 336; Alexander to the secretary, Chiefs of Staff Committee, Department of National Defence, 13 Feb. 1942, Defence Records, Chiefs of Staff Committee, Miscellaneous Memoranda, vol. 3, Feb. 1942; Joint Services Committee, Pacific Coast, Minutes, 19 and 20 Feb. 1942, *ibid.*
54. Mackenzie to L. St. Laurent, 14 Feb. 1942, Mackenzie Papers, vol. 24, file 70–25, vol. 1; Mackenzie to King, 22 Feb. 1942, King Papers, MG 26,j1, vol. 328.
55. Mackenzie to St. Laurent, 24 Feb. 1942, Mackenzie Papers, vol. 25, file 70–25, vol. 2. At the same time Mackenzie sent similar letters to colleagues King, Power, Ralston, Macdonald, and Mitchell.
56. Mackenzie to J.R. Bowler, dominion secretary, Canadian Legion, 26 Feb. 1942, *ibid.*
57. King Diary, 19 Feb. 1942.
58. Order-in-Council PC 1486, 24 Feb. 1942; House of Commons, *Debates*, 27 Feb. 1942, 917–20.
59. Cash, *A Million Miles from Ottawa*, 33; *The Province*, 2 March 1942; *The Colonist*, 3 March 1942; Ann Thompson, Vancouver Liberal Council to C.N. Senior [private secretary to Mackenzie], 27 Feb. 1942, Mackenzie Papers, vol. 25, file 70–25, vol. 2.
60. *Vancouver Sun*, 26 Feb. 1942.
61. While racial tensions swelled in British Columbia after Pearl Harbor, a similar crisis occurred on the American Pacific Coast. There, as in Canada, residents in coastal areas who were of Japanese origin were forced to move inland to camps constructed for their reception. The American decision for evacuation, however, was based solely on military considerations and was taken by military officers who had been given a free hand by President Roosevelt. There was no collaboration between the Canadian and American governments in the decision-making process and, while the events of the two evacuations ran in close parallel, neither country's policy appears to have influenced the other. For accounts of the American evacuation see Morton Grodzins, *Americans Betrayed: Politics and the Japanese Evacuation* (Chicago 1949); Stetson Conn, 'The Decision to Evacuate the Japanese from the Pacific Coast (1942),' *Command Decisions*, ed. Kent Roberts Greenfield, Prepared by the office of the Chief of Military History, Department of the Army (New York 1959); Roger Daniels, *Concentration Camps USA: Japanese Americans and World War II* (New York 1972).

525

Topic Thirteen
Foreign Policy: Interwar and Cold War Eras

Canada's relations with Britain and with the United States have dominated our foreign policy. Our aim has been to seek a balance between these two major powers, thus enabling Canada to play the role of middleman, and preventing absorption by either power. Up until World War II, this meant finding an American counterbalance to Britain as a means to achieve independence from British control. Since World War II, our effort has been to find forces outside North America, notably the United Nations, the Commonwealth of Nations, and the North Atlantic Treaty Organization (NATO), to offset the powerful American presence.

This obsession of aligning ourselves with the British and the Americans has both positively and negatively influenced Canadian foreign policy. During the 1930s, our preoccupation with gaining independence from Britain caused us to overlook the serious international situation which led to World War II. Independence became a rationale for refusing to support the League of Nations, the only international organization capable of controlling European aggression. In " 'A Low Dishonest Decade': Aspects of Canadian External Policy, 1931–1939," James Eayrs reviews Canada's foreign policy in the 1930s.

Since the Second World War Canada has taken an active role in international affairs, through the United Nations, the Commonwealth of Nations, and NATO. These organizations, according to Edgar McInnis, enabled Canada to continue its traditional role of mediator, now between the superpowers, the United States and the Soviet Union, rather than between Britain and the United States. He discusses this role in "A Middle Power in the Cold War."

To some commentators, "middle power status" and "functionalism" (a policy of trying to affect world change by piecemeal and pragmatic means) serve as only polite euphemisms for our subservience to American foreign policy. To these observers Canada's foreign policy since World War II has been towards an integrated North American defence system, and an uncritical acceptance of the American view of the world to the point where Canada no longer has an independent foreign policy. Kenneth McNaught argues this viewpoint in "From Colony to Satellite."

James Eayrs in *In Defence of Canada*. Vol. II: *Appeasement and Rearmament* (Toronto: University of Toronto Press, 1965), provides an exhaustive analysis of Canadian foreign policy in the late 1930s. Two alternatives to Eayrs' critical views of Canada's position of isolationism are H. Blair Neatby's "Mackenzie King and National Unity," in H.L. Dyck and H.P. Krosby, *Empire and Nations: Essays in Honour of Frederic H. Soward* (Toronto: University of Toronto Press, 1969), pp. 54–70; and J.L. Granatstein and R. Bothwell, " 'A Self-Evident National Duty': Canadian Foreign Policy, 1935–1939," *Journal of Imperial and Commonwealth History*, 3 (1975): 212–233. A good documentary collection on the 1930s is R. Bothwell and G.N. Hillmer, *'The In-Between Time': Canadian External Policy in the 1930's* (Toronto: Copp Clark, 1975). For an overview of the interwar years see C.P. Stacey, *Canada and the Age of Conflict*: vol. 2, *1921–1948: The Mackenzie King Era* (Toronto: University of Toronto Press, 1981). I. Abella and H. Troper, *None Is Too Many: Canada and the Jews of Europe, 1933–1948* (Toronto: Lester and Orpen Dennys, 1982) deals with Canada's failure to allow European Jews into Canada.

527

On the cold war era, see James Eayrs's *In Defence of Canada* Vol. III: *Peacemaking and Deterence* (Toronto: University of Toronto Press, 1972), and Vol. IV: *Growing Up Allied* (1980). The critical question of Canadian-American relations in the postwar years is dealt with in John W. Holmes, *Life With Uncle: The Canadian-American Relationship* (Toronto: University of Toronto Press, 1981), and his *The Better Part of Valour* (Toronto: McClelland and Stewart, 1975). See as well: Allan E. Gotlieb, "Power and Vulnerability; Canadian and American Perspectives on International Affairs," in E. Feldman and N. Neville, eds., *The Future of North America: Canada, The United States and Quebec Nationalism* (Montreal: Institute for Research on Public Policy, 1979) pp. 109–131; and Stephen Clarkson, ed., *An Independent Foreign Policy for Canada?* (Toronto: McClelland and Stewart, 1968), and his *Canada and the Reagan Challenge: Crisis and Adjustment, 1981–1985*. Two special issues of *International Journal* should be examined, that of the summer 1967 offered retrospective looks at Canadian foreign policy, and the summer 1976 issued concerned "The U.S. and Us." Students should also consult the relevant sections of R. Bothwell, I. Drummond and J. English's *Canada Since 1945: Power, Politics, and Provincialism* (Toronto: University of Toronto Press, 1981).

"A Low Dishonest Decade": Aspects of Canadian External Policy, 1931–1939*

JAMES EAYRS

There has not yet taken place in Canada that debate on the wisdom of appeasement in which British statesmen and scholars have been engaged since the appearance of Professor Feiling's *Life of Neville Chamberlain*. If this seems a remarkable fact, it is not hard to explain. Had the Canadian government of that day urged a more sturdy resistance to the Nazi tyranny, it is doubtful that events would have taken a significantly different course. German policy was unresponsive to the action or inaction of the Dominions; and it seems unlikely that Chamberlain would have been deflected from the path of the appeaser any more by the Prime Minister of Canada than he was by the Prime Minister of New Zealand, which is to say not at all. Canada's external policy during the years 1931–1939, so far from requiring extended apology, appears to most of its historians to possess the self-evident vindication of having brought a united and determined nation to Britain's side on September 10, 1939. The evidence which might sustain a contrary interpretation is still scanty. Documents from the files of the Department of External Affairs have yet to be published; the private papers of the Prime Ministers of the period are withheld from the scholar's domain;[1] both R.B. Bennett and Mackenzie King retained a jealous hold upon the External Affairs portfolio and conducted foreign policy possessively, even stealthily, so that few of their colleagues and subordinates have been able to throw strong light upon shadowy though crucial episodes; and a tradition unlike that prevailing at Westminster (where politics and literature—or politics and journalism—honorably combine) assists in their concealment. These are some (but by no means all) of the circumstances accounting for the remarkable early appearance of an Authorized Version of events not yet three decades removed.

The time is now approaching when a revisionist interpretation will be possible; one or two significant steps in this direction have already been taken.[2] The present paper has a more modest purpose. It attempts to discuss some aspects of Canadian external policy during the 1930's to which insufficient attention has perhaps been paid, and to bring to more familiar themes evidence previously overlooked. Although the title[3] may suggest an excess of moral indignation, its point of view is rather that of Lord Vansittart, who, writing of Dominion policies during the period in which he labored with such prescience and to such little avail, remarked, perhaps too generously: "One could not blame them, one could not admire them, one could not admire anybody."[4]

*From *The Growth of Canadian Policies in External Affairs*, ed. by H.L. Keenleyside. Copyright © 1960 by Duke University Press. Reprinted by permission.

I. The New World and the Old

In 1919 Canadians turned away from Europe, leaving behind their dead. However misguided it might appear to those of a later generation drawn as their fathers had been into "the vortex of militarism," isolationism in Canada was a natural response to the four-year ordeal on the Western front. The Great War remade the map, but left unchanged the scale and the projection. How could a conflict in which major gains were measured by hundreds of yards, and a million lives exchanged for a few desolated acres of mud, affect in any way the traditional concepts of geography? It brought half a million Canadians to Europe but Europe no closer to Canada. The world was still wide. To the Oceans and the Fleet might now be added as purveyor of security the great and friendly guardian to the South. Canada was a "fire-proof house, far from inflammable materials";[5] and its fortunate inhabitants peered indistinctly at the distant continent from which invasion seemed so improbable. "At present danger of attack upon Canada is minor in degree and second-hand in origin," Mackenzie King had insisted as late as 1938;[6] and although his military advisers were less certain of Canada's immunity,[7] their misgivings were not allowed to disturb unduly the complacency of the public or the size of the defense estimates.

Isolationism was the product of geography; it was shaped by distrust, a distrust born of the Great War and confirmed at the council tables of Paris. "It was European policy, European statesmanship, European ambition, that drenched this world with blood," N.W. Rowell told the First Assembly of the League of Nations. "Fifty thousand Canadians under the soil of France and Flanders is what Canada has paid for European statesmanship trying to settle European problems. I place responsibility on a few; I would not distribute it over many; but nevertheless it is European."[8] These bluntly accusing words, an official of the Canadian delegation wrote privately at the time, "hurt and stung many people," and in his view "marred the performance."[9] But they conveyed, however tactlessly, the sense of Canadian feeling; and the Prime Minister wrote to their author to express his "appreciation of the stand you took in stating to the Conference, as frankly as you did, the price the world has paid for the European diplomacy of the last hundred years."[10] Nor, as it seemed, had the trauma of the trenches changed Europe for the better. Ancient enmities and grievances arose once more, or were replaced or supplemented by new disorders; the scope for intrigue and for disaster was if anything enhanced. "Everywhere there are signs of trouble," wrote one of Canada's representatives at the Paris Peace Conference in 1919. "Egypt is now disturbed with the fever for self govt. — the vicious results of Wilson's doctrine of ill or nondefined self determination. Asia Minor and Turkey are disorganized — Roumanians threatened on three sides by Bolshevists and Hungarians — Russia poisoned and poisoning — Hungary communist and Germany in near chaos. 'Tis surely a sad mess out of which to evolve a new Europe."[11]

Distrust and disapproval of Europe's statecraft and statesmen passed easily into an assertion of North American moral superiority. In Canada as in the United States there was nourished the conviction that the New World in its national life and international behavior exhibited standards above and beyond those of the Old. Like Mr. Herbert Hoover, Canadians

returned in 1919 from several years abroad . . . steeped with two ideas: first, that through three hundred years [North] America had developed something new in a way of life of a people, which transcended all others of history; and second, that out of the boiling social and economic cauldron of Europe, with its hates and fears, rose miasmic infections which might greatly harm or even destroy . . . the hope of the world.[12]

Rare was the Canadian who, addressing himself at Geneva or at home to the theme of his country's place in world affairs, did not elaborate this contrast. ". . . we think in terms of peace," remarked Senator Dandurand in 1924, "while Europe, an armed camp, thinks in terms of war."[13] "After listening to and participating in the proceedings of the League," Mackenzie King declared in 1928, "I have come back to Canada with a more profound conviction than ever that there is no land on the face of the globe in which the lot of men, women and children is cast in a pleasanter place than in this Dominion."[14] In 1936 he referred to Canada's "tremendous, absorbing and paramount tasks of achieving economic development and national unity, which with us take the place of the preoccupation with the fear of attack and the dreams of glory which beset older and more crowded countries";[15] a few weeks later, at Geneva, he contrasted his country's friendly relations with the United States and Europe's "violent . . . propaganda and recriminations hurled incessantly across the frontiers, the endeavours [in Europe] to draw all countries into one or other extremist camp, the feverish race for rearmament, the hurrying to and fro of diplomats, the ceaseless weaving and unravelling of understandings and alliances, and the consequent fear and uncertainty of the peoples";[16] and in March 1939, soon after Hitler's seizure of Czechoslovakia, he referred despairingly to the "continent that cannot run itself," in implied contrast to that North American continent which could.[17]

Such comparisons were frequently joined to moral exhortation. The rostrum of the Palais des Nations became for successive Canadian spokesmen a pulpit from which Europe was urged to forswear her foolish ways, to abandon intrigue, violence, hostility, to adopt those institutions which (they claimed) had brought a century of peace to North America. Canada and the United States, Mackenzie King informed the Ninth Assembly of the League of Nations, had ceased "to rely upon force, we have looked to reason as the method of solving our differences, and reason has supplied us from time to time with conference, conciliation or arbitration in a form . . . sufficient to settle our various differences as they have arisen."[18] Let there be a European Rush-Bagot Treaty, a European International Joint Commission — tranquility would follow for a hundred years. As a prescription for Old World ills, these New World remedies were altogether inadequate, arising as they did from a wholly different situation.

The toad beneath the harrow knows
Exactly where each tooth-point goes;
The butterfly upon the road
Preaches contentment to that toad.

Moreover, they were compounded of a series of fictions unrelated to things as they were. "Not a single soldier, not a single cannon," the Canadian delegate had told the Fifth Assembly of the League, faced the famous frontier. This was simple falsehood. The International Joint Commission had been able to function without major difficulty only because each government had refrained from submitting disputes other than those over waterways. As for the Rush-Bagot Agreement, "the truth is," Mackenzie King had written privately in 1922, "our American friends have been steadily evading [it], until it has become more or less of a mockery to speak of its terms in the manner in which we do."[19]

However ill-justified, Canada's moralizing at Europe led logically not to isolation but engagement. Ought not the practitioners of the New World's higher morality try by more active participation in the affairs of the Old to lead it into the paths of righteousness? That is not what happened. More potent than the zeal of the missionary was the desire to escape contamination. The less the New World came in contact with the Old, the better; the more, the greater the chance of succumbing to those "miasmic infections" which threatened to invade and to destroy the healthy bodies politic of North America. "Bolshevism," wrote the editor of the *Canadian Annual Review* in 1918, "had a basis wherever Russians and Jews and other foreigners gathered together" in Canada's cities; if foreigners brought Bolshevism, Canadians should keep clear of foreigners. "We are told there are enormous numbers of people on the continent of Europe who want to come [here]," remarked a former Minister of Immigration in 1922. "I want to say I regard it of the dimensions of a national menace that there is any danger whatever of the bars being let down."[20] Questioned in 1920 on Canada's readiness to accept a mandate for Armenia, the Leader of the Opposition wrote that the proposal "would provoke general protest from one end of the Dominion to the other," for "a sort of reaction has set in . . . with respect to interference by the Governments of this Continent with European Affairs."[21] As the twenty years' crisis developed and deepened, isolationism became if anything more firmly rooted in the Canadian people and their governors. Early in 1922 the Canadian government refused to contribute funds in the form of an interest-free loan for the relief of famine in Russia, and turned down a Soviet request for credit to buy Canadian seed wheat. In 1924 it ignored an appeal to contribute to the relief of famine in Albania. In 1925 it refused the invitation to sign the Geneva Protocol, and it was largely at Canada's insistence that an article was inserted in the text of the Locarno Agreements specifically exempting the Dominions from their provisions. ". . . I do not see," Ernest Lapointe observed some years later, "that Canada should assume obligations in connection with the boundaries between France and Germany . . . [or] guarantee any boundaries in central Europe or else-

531

where. . . ."[22] And an influential member of the Canadian government wrote before sailing for the Imperial Conference in the spring of 1937:

The conference will be interesting, and probably in some ways revealing; but the more I see of the whole thing, the more I am certain that our destiny is on the North American continent and that if Europe is going to insist on destroying itself, it is no part of our mission to destroy ourselves in attempting to prevent it. . . .[23]

2. The League and the Nation

If other countries entered the League of Nations in something of the spirit expressed by Smuts' phrase — "the tents have been struck and the great caravan of humanity is once more on the march" — Canada may be said to have been mainly concerned lest she be called upon to do more than her share of the work in breaking camp or be compelled to march without the consent of her Parliament. It is usual to attribute the reserve with which Canadians watched the Geneva experiment to the coercive characteristics of the Covenant, and to suppose that so long as the League confined itself to conciliatory methods it could count upon Canadian approval. This view has the weighty support of Professor Mansergh, who writes that "from the first the League was welcomed as a means of furthering international co-operation, as a forum for debate and discussion," and that it was only "as a means for enforcing, as distinct from maintaining, peace" that it aroused the suspicion and censure of successive Canadian governments.[24] Certainly it is difficult to overestimate the agitated concern lest through Articles X and XVI of the Covenant the newly independent Dominion be placed at "the beck and call of a Council not responsible to the nation for its actions," or, even worse, become involved "in conflicts in some far-away section of Europe, or in some distant portion of South America."[25] Fears such as these lead to that policy; "remarkable," as Professor Mansergh observes, "for its consistency," by which Canada tried at first to have Article X removed entirely from the Covenant; that proving unsuccessful, introduced an interpretative resolution which, though it failed by one vote to receive the unanimous support required for adoption, had the desired effect of weakening the obligations of League membership; and finally, when the League was confronted with the two decisive tests of its procedures for collective security, did what could be done to weaken the effectiveness of sanctions.

But this interpretation may be misleading. It implies a degree of attachment to the League as a non-coercive agency for peaceful conciliation which, whatever might be said in public, no Canadian Minister really felt. For Canadian suspicion of Geneva derived basically from Canadian distrust of Europe; and it was as a European institution that the League appeared from Canada. "The League was born ostensibly as a world League," commented a former official of the Department of External Affairs in 1926, "but really is a European League with the non-Europeans tacked on. The most distinctive and powerful New World people went out of it." A Canadian had no more legitimate concern "with the administration of Danzig or of the Saar Valley" than had "a Nova Scotian . . . [with] the municipal government of Vancouver."[26] "Let us . . . conciliate Quebec and Ontario," remarked a member of Parliament in 1923, "before we start conciliating Roumania and Ukrainia."[27] "The League of Nations is a preposterous and expensive farce," wrote Sir Clifford Sifton, "and amounts to nothing more than a part of a machine designed to involve us in European and Imperialistic complications. Canada ought to call a halt on this business."[28] The views of those in office were much the same. Sir Joseph Pope, the Under Secretary of State for External Affairs until 1925, dismissed the Covenant as "not worth the paper it is written on," and wrote in his diary: "Our reps are making a great stir at the League of Nations, advertizing Canada and incidentally themselves. I think it all absurd, and am convinced that Canada's true policy right now is to develop her resources and to leave European questions such as the Bessarabian frontier &c to our Imperial statesmen and the trained experts of Downing Street."[29] His successor, O.D. Skelton, while holding "the trained experts of Downing Street" in somewhat lesser regard, was no more sympathetic to the Geneva experiment. Mackenzie King, as his official biographer remarks, "was the type of uplifter who might have been expected to give the League his full and enthusiastic support," but his attitude towards the League in its formative years "was one of studied neglect."[30] In the 1930's this was to develop into an attitude of profound hostility, especially after the "Riddell incident" of November 1935. W.A. Riddell, the Canadian Permanent Delegate at Geneva, left in some perplexity as a consequence of the General Election a few days earlier, proposed on his own initiative the imposition of certain sanctions against Italy, and in the brief period until his action was repudiated by the Canadian government, set Canada's policy upon a course it had never before taken. In his published recollection of this celebrated episode, Dr. Riddell attributes his repudiation partly to the fact that the Prime Minister and the Under Secretary of State for External Affairs were at the time out of the country, leaving the Department of External Affairs in charge of "two French Canadians," Ernest Lapointe and Laurent Beaudry. On reporting to Mackenzie King in Ottawa, Dr. Riddell writes, he found him, "as always, most gracious," while Lapointe seemed "cold, critical and overbearing."[31] But beneath a mask of practiced cordiality King was no less angered than Lapointe, probably more so, by Riddell's initiative. A Canadian newspaperman has recorded an interview with the Prime Minister soon after the event:

533

Had a few words with Mr. King re the Italo-Ethiopian settlement and he spoke with surprising frankness. I never knew before Mr. King's general attitude towards the League and foreign affairs. King complained angrily about Dr. Riddell's gasoline [sic], steel and coal proposal. "I am certainly going to give him a good spanking", was the way he put it. . . . He said that excessive idealism in politics should be avoided. Canada's policy, he believed, should be dictated by considerations of geographical location and population. After all we are but 10 millions on the north end of a continent and we should not strive to over-play our part . . . He is very dubious about foreign commitments, and, also, about getting into the League too deeply. He said that the only real difference of opinion he had ever had with Lapointe was with regard to Canada's acceptance of the presidency of the League Assembly [in 1925]. He had opposed it on the ground that it would stimulate League thought in Canada, tend to lead us more deeply into League affairs and, possibly, foreign commitments.[32]

"We should not strive to over-play our part." This theme was henceforth to be heard in nearly all of the Prime Minister's infrequent public statements on the European crisis until the outbreak of war, a refrain in praise of diffidence. "After all, . . . there is such a thing as a sense of proportion in international affairs," he said in the House of Commons in February 1936. "Do hon. members think that it is Canada's role at Geneva to attempt to regulate a European war. . . ?" If he had not disavowed Riddell's proposal, "the whole of Europe might have been aflame today."[33] A few days later he added: "Our country is being drawn into international situations to a degree that I myself think is alarming."[34] Within a fortnight Hitler was to invade the Rhineland.

3. The Law and the Jungle

If distrust of European politics contributed to isolationist sentiment in Canada in the years between the wars, it also helped to thwart understanding of what was happening to Europe during the deepening crisis of the later 1930's. With a very few exceptions, notably J.W. Dafoe,[35] Canadians did not recognize Fascist Italy and Nazi Germany for what they were. Totalitarianism was thought to be merely an aggravation of that *malaise* from which Europe traditionally suffered; there was little if any suspicion that it might be a distinctively twentieth-century phenomenon arising from the tensions and insecurities of twentieth-century man. The fascist apparition was no new menace for which the old responses would no longer suffice, but a rebirth of the intrigues, the rivalries, the nationalisms of prewar European diplomacy. Thus it required no special explanation; created no new problems; needed no exceptional precautions.

A significant section of the Canadian public was indeed disposed to view fascism in its Mediterranean setting not merely without alarm but with undisguised approval. The lofty sentiments of Fascist doctrine elaborated by Mussolini's publicists, with their apotheosis of order, discipline, family, nation, their pseudo-syndicalist remedies for industrial unrest, gained powerful support among the elite of French Canada. "The work of Mussolini and of the Fascist Party finds among a certain number of my compatriots admirers," remarked Mr. Paul Gouin in 1938. "They have the same attitude towards the corporative movement of Salazar. . . . We may ask ourselves if it would not be to the advantage of our Province and of Canada to borrow what is best in these different formulae, while naturally avoiding their excesses."[36] Few French-speaking Canadians saw anything for adverse comment in the description of General Franco's forces offered by the newly appointed Papal Delegate to Canada and Newfoundland as that "army of heroes, justly called Christ's militia,"[37] any more than they resented the valedictory pronounced by Maxime Raymond in the House of Commons on the occasion of the departure of the Mackenzie-Papineau Brigade: "This, I admit, does not give me any sorrow; it will rid us of these undesirable people, provided they do not return home here."[38] If there was no emulation in French Canada of General O'Duffy's Blueshirts, who went from Eire to fight in Spain for Franco, it was due not to want of sympathy for the Nationalist cause but to the even stronger hold of isolationism.

National Socialism was something else again. No religious or ideological link could bind Quebec to a regime which had so soon and so obviously singled out the Catholic Church for brutal destruction. But diagnosis of the Nazi movement was hindered in Canada by the magnitude of domestic crisis and by the isolationist tradition. Events in Germany were consistently misconstrued as a nationalist revival of the conventional type, distinguished, perhaps, by the odd fanaticism of its leaders, by the strut and swagger of its rank and file, but for all that a movement which might be comprehended in traditional terms, appeased and contained by traditional methods. When Hitler entered the Rhineland there was aroused among English-speaking Canadians little of the emotion produced by Mussolini's attack on Ethiopia. On the contrary, there was a widely held conviction that in reoccupying the demilitarized zone Hitler was only avenging the wrongs of Versailles, taking possession of what rightfully belonged to Germany. Why shouldn't a man walk into his own backyard? With the significant exception of Dafoe's *Free Press*, nearly all Canadian newspapers urged, on March 9, 1936, a sympathetic understanding of Hitler's position. "Canadians who do not allow themselves to be swayed by a personal dislike for Hitler and his unpleasant colleagues," wrote the editor of the Vancouver *Sun*, "will feel a measure of sympathy for this new attitude of the German people. . . . Canada is only a spectator. There are not enough moral principles at stake to induce her to become otherwise. . . . Whatever morality lies in the scales seems to be, this time, on Germany's side of the balance." "After eighteen years," the Edmonton *Bulletin* observed, "Europe can afford to restore Germany to full standing in the concert of nations." "Nothing can ever be gained," argued the editor of the Montreal *Gazette*, "by persistently treating Germany as though she were national enemy No. 1 in perpetuity. It would likewise be dangerous and futile to regard Adolf Hitler in no other light than as one whose designs are wilfully antagonistic to forces that hate war."

It is possible that had Canada been represented in Germany by a diplomat of insight and influence, a less reassuring image of National Socialism would have reached its government and people. As it was, the Canadian government, having no diplomatic mission at Berlin, necessarily relied on whatever Whitehall might select for its instruction from the despatches of Sir Nevile Henderson — despatches which conveyed a sadly erroneous interpretation of Nazi policy.[39] This unhelpful source was supplemented by the assessment of the Canadian High Commissioner at London, so closely associated with the group which moved with such great and disastrous effect between Cliveden, Printing House Square, and Downing Street that nothing he learned from its members seems likely to have provided a useful corrective to the misleading despatches passed on by the Dominions Office. "Walked about the grounds in the forenoon with Vincent Massey, talking politics," wrote Thomas Jones in his diary on June 7, 1936. "I begged

535

him to stress the urgency of dealing with Germany and not to wait upon France.''[40]

But the most misleading impression was derived more directly. In 1937 Mackenzie King decided to go from the Imperial Conference to Germany. There he met and talked with Hitler and other leading personalities of the Third Reich. It was not a wholly useful confrontation. It is true that King did not allow so unique an opportunity to pass without stressing in Berlin what he felt unable to disclose in London, namely, that in the event of ''a war of aggression, nothing in the world would keep the Canadian people from being at the side of Britain.''[41] Heeded or not heeded, this message was at least delivered, and more valuable service could hardly have been rendered. But its value was diminished by the way in which the Canadian Prime Minister fell victim to the Führer's remarkable capacity for mesmerizing his visitors. ''There is no doubt that Hitler had a power of fascinating men,'' Mr. Churchill wrote in his memoirs; and added the sage advice: ''Unless the terms are equal, it is better to keep away.''[42] As between the Prime Minister of Canada and the perpetrator of the Nazi *Schrecklichkeit* the terms were far from equal. The extent of Hitler's advantage may be measured by the opinions with which King returned to Canada. According to Mr. Bruce Hutchison, to whom he related them soon afterward, King found Hitler

536

a simple sort of peasant, not very intelligent and no serious danger to anyone . . . obsessed with the recovery of neighboring territory inhabited by Germans, a natural feeling. When he had brought these territories into the Reich . . . he would be satisfied . . . he would not risk a large war. His ambitions were centered entirely in Germany and the narrow irredentist regions beside it. For this reason [there would be] . . . no early trouble in Europe. . . .[43]

And to the Canadian people Mackenzie King declared, three weeks after his talks with the German leaders:

Despite every appearance to the contrary, I believe the nations of Europe have a better understanding of each other's problems to-day than they have had for some years past. Moreover, despite all appearances, they are prepared, I believe, in an effort to work out a solution, to co-operate to a greater degree than has been the case for a long while. . . . Of this I am certain . . . that neither the governments nor the peoples of any of the countries I have visited desire war, or view the possibility of war between each other, as other than likely to end in self-destruction, and the destruction of Europe civilization itself.[44]

That the destruction of European civilization was precisely the object of the man he had so recently talked with in the Reichskanzlei was a thought unlikely to have crossed the mind of the Canadian Prime Minister; for, as was remarked of him in a different connection, ''Mr. King never quite got it into his head during his economic studies at Toronto and Harvard that our civilization is dominated by carnivorous animals.''[45]

4. Empire and Reich

In 1923 the Prime Minister of Canada had protested vigorously and decisively against the Imperial Conference ''assuming the rights of a cabinet in the determination of foreign policy. . . , expressing approval of the present [British] Government's foreign policy. . . , trying to shape the affairs of Europe."[46] By 1937 Mackenzie King's suspicions of "Downing Street domination" had been sufficiently allayed to allow him to do what he had never done before—to endorse at an Imperial Conference a united Commonwealth policy on international affairs. As it happened, the policy for which the Dominions offered their collective approval and support was the ill-fated policy of appeasement. ". . . the settlement of differences that may arise between nations," asserted the section of the *Proceedings* of the Conference dealing with foreign affairs, ". . . should be sought by methods of co-operation, joint enquiry and conciliation . . . differences of political creed should be no obstacle to friendly relations between Governments and countries . . . nothing would be more damaging to the hopes of international appeasement than the division, real or apparent, of the world into opposing groups."[47] These sentiments, which, as Professor Mansergh rightly remarks, are "hardly consistent with the dignity of a great Commonwealth confronted with the shame less aggression of European tyrants unmatched for their cruelty and faithlessness since the Dark Ages,"[48] continued to be uttered by Mackenzie King during the interval between the end of the Conference and the beginning of war. For the first time since becoming Prime Minister in 1921 he found himself able to pay public tribute to "the unremitting care and anxiety which those responsible for the foreign policy of Britain have devoted to their task"; he spoke of "their strong and determined effort to establish peace."[49] This was followed by a series of press statements in praise of British policy. When the news of the proposed mission to Berchtesgaden reached him, Mackenzie King announced that he had "conveyed to Mr. Neville Chamberlain the deep satisfaction with which my colleagues and I have learned that his proposal for a personal conference with Herr Hitler . . . has been agreed to" and described "this far-seeing and truly noble action on the part of Mr. Chamberlain" as "emphatically the right step." A further statement issued after the British Cabinet's decision to support the principle of self-determination for Sudeten Germans referred to the "courage and vision" displayed by the Government of the United Kingdom in seeking "to avert recourse to force by finding a peaceful and agreed solution of the present clash of interests in Central Europe." Following Chamberlain's radio address of September 27, 1938 ("How horrible, fantastic, incredible it is that we should be digging trenches and fitting gas-masks because of a quarrel in a far away country"), Mackenzie King proclaimed the Canadian government's "complete accord with the statement Mr. Chamberlain has made to the world today." Word of the impending visit to Munich called forth the most ecstatic endorsement of all:

The heart of Canada is rejoicing tonight at the success which has crowned your unremitting efforts for peace. . . . My colleagues in the Government join with me in unbounded admiration at the service you have rendered mankind. . . . On the very brink of chaos, with passions flaming, and armies marching, the voice of Reason has found a way out of the conflict.

It may be safely assumed that these utterances were carefully noted and transmitted to Berlin by the German Consul General at Ottawa, Herr Windels; and to the extent that the disordered diplomatic apparatus at the Wilhelmstrasse was capable of bringing them to the attention of the Führer they can only have reinforced his belief that the British Empire was too weak and too craven to oppose his plans for the subjugation of Eastern Europe as a prelude to the destruction of the West. Appeasement, the only foreign policy on which the Commonwealth has ever been in substantial agreement, thus came close to accomplishing its ruin. Offered in the hope of peace, it led it straight to war.

Yet while Mackenzie King had by 1937 become able to support Britain's appeasement of Germany, his earlier fear of centralized control persisted in the realm of defense. All attempts on the part of the United Kingdom to co-operate militarily and industrially with Canada in advance of the outbreak of war were rebuffed. "From 1936 onwards," the official history of the Royal Air Force recalls reproachfully, "Canada, which enjoyed an ideal strategic position and a convenient proximity to the vast industrial resources of the United States, was repeatedly approached [with the request to make facilities available for training of pilots and aircrew]; but the Canadians, largely for domestic reasons, felt unable to accept our proposals. . . ."[50] At the Imperial Conference of 1937 "the principal Supply Officers' Committee tried to pilot through . . . an agreement with Canada about wartime supplies of bauxite and aluminium," but failed largely because of Canadian opposition.[51] In the summer of 1938 the Board of Trade entered into negotiations with the Canadian government to make provision in advance of war for adequate supplies of certain strategic materials; but Ottawa being unwilling to assume such commitments, by September 1939 "virtually no preparations had been made for the war-time purchase of raw materials in North America."[52] Munitions fared little better; with the exception of a contract for Bren machine guns, nothing was done by the Canadian government to assist United Kingdom defense officials in their effort to stimulate the manufacture of arms in the overseas Dominions.[53]

It is thus a major irony of Commonwealth history that Canadian influence on British policy was at this stage brought to bear in the worst of all possible ways. In external policy, as Professor Mansergh observes, "what was most of all required was not a greater consensus of Commonwealth opinion but the more vigorous expression of independent and conflicting opinion";[54] in defense policy what was most of all required was a united effort to create a deterrent of imperial power. The Canadian response was to voice with unaccustomed fervor approval of British statecraft while resisting Britain's efforts to improve the Empire's defenses. While "No evidence so far published suggests that doubts about the unity of the Commonwealth were a major factor in encouraging German aggression,"[55] a firmer signification of the Commonwealth's will to resist might have given Hitler pause; in any event the opportunity was both too good and too rare to be squandered. Certain it is that a fuller measure of defense preparation would have made his defeat less costly and precarious. The margin of superiority with which

538

Britain faced the Axis in the summer of 1940 remained excruciatingly narrow. Had the R.A.F. failed, for want of aircraft or of pilots, to deflect and defeat the Luftwaffe, would not those responsible for Canadian policy during the prewar years have to share the blame?

5. Statecraft and Unity

On January 20, 1937, the Canadian Prime Minister spoke in confidence to a meeting of his parliamentary supporters. He urged them to reject the views of Mr. Arthur Meighen, the Conservative Leader in the Senate, "that the amount in the [defense] estimates was not enough, that we were concerned with the defence of the Empire as a whole; that the first line of our defence was the Empire's boundaries." Equally he urged them to reject the alternative offered by J.S. Woodsworth, the leader of the socialist group in the House of Commons, who, he said, "would do nothing at all" for defense. "The safe policy is the middle course between these two views. . . . Let us explain that policy to our people and let us above all strive at all times to keep Canada *united*."[56] This insistence upon the overriding importance of national unity appears again and again in Mackenzie King's statements on external policy during the years immediately preceding World War II. It served to explain his reluctance to participate in projects or pronouncements likely to deter potential aggressors. To do so, as he remarked in the House of Commons on May 24, 1938, "would bring out deep and in some cases fundamental differences of opinion, [and] would lead to further strain upon the unity of a country already strained by economic depression and other consequences of the last war and its aftermath."[57] Of the wisdom of this policy its architect betrayed neither doubt nor misgiving, and believed it fully vindicated by events. On September 8, 1939, he spoke as follows in the House of Commons:

539

I have made it, therefore, the supreme endeavour of my leadership of my party, and my leadership of the government of this country, to let no hasty or premature threat or pronouncement create mistrust and divisions between the different elements that compose the population of our vast dominion, so that when the moment of decision came all should so see the issue itself that our national effort might be marked by unity of purpose, of heart and of endeavour.[58]

It is a matter for debate whether this "supreme endeavour" was not altogether too restricted. Politics is the art of the possible. But how much was possible during the years before the war? More, perhaps, than the Prime Minister of Canada allowed the nation, or himself, to believe. Never was Mackenzie King more satisfied than when enunciating the dictum that his country was difficult to govern. It was, and is, difficult to govern, in the sense that government is at all times and in all places an exacting and complicated craft. Compared to the ordeals which nearly every twentieth-century nation has undergone — destruction and occupation in war, civil conflict, malevolent and scouring tyrannies — Canadians might consider their situation extraordinarily favorable. Nor were those wearying comparisons between the continent of the undefended frontier and "the continent which cannot run itself" too easily reconciled with plaintive references to exceptional domestic difficulties invoked to justify inaction. So much harping upon the need for unity and the obstacles in its path exaggerated the degree of internal discord, just as repetition of the difficulties encountered in governing the country obscured the fact that it was a good deal less difficult to govern that most. Was it not misleading "to emphasize the precariousness of Canada's export markets, but not the value of her exports; to speak of regional and cultural tensions within but not of the growing sense of unity; of the conflicting pulls of geography and history to which indeed every 'settled' country is subject, but not of the immense strength of Canada's position in the heart of the English-speaking world"?[59] When the history of these years is set out in detail, many of the portents of disunity in the Dominion will be seen to have been greatly overdrawn. For example, it is commonly believed that had the United Kingdom gone to war over Czechoslovakia in September 1938, the C.C.F. (Socialist) party in Canada would have demanded a policy of neutrality. But Professor McNaught has discovered that "correspondence in the Saskatchewan C.C.F. files . . . leaves no doubt that the C.C.F. leaders who defeated the Woodsworth-Farmer neutrality motion in the emergency National Council meeting in [September] 1939 had concluded at least as early as September, 1938, that 'it is already decided that if Britain declares war, Canada must accept the situation.' "[60]

A direct result of reducing Canadian policy to the lowest common denominator of public agreement was the condition of the nation's defenses, "utterly inadequate," as the official historian of the Canadian Army observes, "by comparison with the scale of the coming emergency."[61] Another harmful consequence was the effect upon United Kingdom policy. Just as the Canadian government seized with alacrity upon stress and strain in the Dominion's domestic affairs as an excuse for passivity in all external policies save that of appeasement, so the British government fastened upon the difficulties of members of the overseas Commonwealth to justify its own cautious conduct. Disunity in the Dominions plays a major part in the arguments of apologists for Britain's prewar policy. "The fact remains that the Commonwealth Governments were unwilling to go to war on the issue of Czechoslovakia," a former British Foreign Secretary has written of that period. "Dominion opinion was at the time overwhelmingly against a world war. This opposition was continually in our minds. Time after time we were reminded of it, either by the High Commissioners in London, or by Malcolm MacDonald, the Secretary of State for the Dominions. As early as March 18, 1938 we had been told that South Africa and Canada would not join us in a war to prevent certain Germans from rejoining their Fatherland."[62] While "The actual policy Mr. Chamberlain followed in September 1938 owed little or nothing to dominion inspiration,"[63] there can be no doubt that dispiriting responses from the Dominions were used by him to discourage those within the British Cabinet who urged a less cowardly posture in the face of German threats.[64] In Canada's case their effect was the more damaging for their misrepresentation of the real intention of its government. For had war broken out at the time of Munich, the Prime Minister "was prepared to call Parliament within two weeks and submit to it a policy of Canadian participation. . . . The Cabinet was unanimous."[65]

Over half a century ago the French historian André Siegfried had noted the timidity of Canada's political leaders. "They seem . . . ," he wrote, "to stand in fear of great movements of public opinion, and to seek to lull them rather than to encourage them and bring them to political fruition."[66] It will be observed that Canadian political leadership at the time of M. Siegfried's examination was provided by Sir Wilfrid Laurier; and that it was upon Sir Wilfrid Laurier's leadership that Mackenzie King had faithfully modeled his own. "You do Sir Wilfrid Laurier an injustice in regarding him as an opportunist," King had written a friend during the controversy over naval policy in 1909. "He is other than that. . . . We have had no man in Canada who had done as much to reconcile differences of race and creed and to make of the people one nation. If he hesitates to go to the length that some desire, it is because he does not wish disruption and believes that a united progressive Canada is a more valuable asset to the Empire, and will be so through time, than a Canada divided in opinion, or professing an obligation it is not in a position to meet."[67] But hesitation for the sake of unity was not the inevitable response of all Canadian leaders to the tensions of their plural society; there were those to whom its tensions the more insistently demanded bold and imaginative statecraft. "In our Dominion where sections abound," Mr. Arthur Meighen once declared, "a Dominion of races, of classes and of creeds, of many languages and many origins, there are times when no Prime Minister can be true to his trust to the nation he has sworn to serve, save at the temporary sacrifice of the party he is appointed to lead."[68] Faithfully practicing this doctrine, Mr. Meighen was compelled to retire from public life. Mackenzie King's very different concept of political leadership, no less faithfully practiced and resulting in political longevity only once surpassed in the history of the Commonwealth, must face a very different kind of criticism. It "would have been improved," his official biographer has conceded,

541

had he been more venturesome and more willing to offer forthright advice to the nation. King's tactics enabled him to secure and retain office — the indispensable first step. But King, too frequently, stopped right there; and because he was reluctant to press on and try to realize some independent conception of the national interest, his policies slipped into the mire of pure expediency. King was always reluctant to venture into the unknown. He avoided taking risks, and he would postpone action, if by so doing he could ensure a greater degree of safety. He dreaded unnecessary discussion which might lead to disagreement and even threaten the existing party solidarity on which the whole security of his position rested. He was not prepared to use his own power extensively in an effort to modify the character and scope of those common elements on which he sought to base his policy. He was too willing at times to yield his own judgment when confronted with opposing opinion. He was slow to admit that he had a duty as leader to exert a moderate pressure in the direction in which he believed the country should move.[69]

This verdict is the more severe coming as it does from "one who is in general sympathy with Mr. King and his work and career."[70] There is no part of Mackenzie King's long responsibility for Canadian affairs to which it may with more justice be applied than to his conduct of external policy during that "low dishonest decade" when the world lay "defenceless under the night" and so few free men in power dared to "show an affirming flame."

Notes

1. The Bennett Papers have been deposited by Lord Beaverbrook, their owner, at the Library of the University of New Brunswick. The King Papers are in the Public Archives of Canada and became the property of the Crown in 1975. The present writer, having assisted in the preparation of the official biography of W.L. Mackenzie King, has had access to this immense collection; he has permission from Mr. King's Literary Executors to quote from the King correspondence to the end of 1923, the period covered by the published first volume of the official biography.
2. See K.W. McNaught, "Canadian Foreign Policy and the Whig Interpretation: 1936-1939," Canadian Historical Association, *Report of the Annual Meeting* 1957, pp. 43-54.
3. It is taken from the poem by W.H. Auden, "September 1, 1939": "As the clever hopes expire/Of a low dishonest decade."
4. *The Mist Procession: The Autobiography of Lord Vansittart* (London, 1958), p. 529.
5. League of Nations, Official Journal, Special Supplement No. 23, *Records of the Fifth Assembly* (1924), p. 222. It is interesting that this most celebrated of Canadian utterances on foreign affairs goes unremarked in the unpublished autobiography of Senator Raoul Dandurand, its author.
6. Canada, *House of Commons Debates*, 1938, III, 3179.
7. See Colonel C.P. Stacey, *Six Years of War: The Army in Canada, Britain and the Pacific* (Ottawa, 1955), p. 10.
8. League of Nations, *Records of the First Assembly* (1920), p. 379.
9. Loring C. Christie to Sir Robert Borden, Dec. 12, 1920, Borden Papers (Public Archives of Canada).
10. Arthur Meighen to N.W. Rowell, Jan. 10, 1921, Rowell Papers (P.A.C.).
11. Diary of Sir George Foster, entry for April 7, 1919 (P.A.C.).
12. *The Memoirs of Herbert Hoover: The Cabinet and the Presidency, 1920-1933* (New York, 1951), p.v.
13. League of Nations, Official Journal, Special Supplement No. 23, *Records of the Fifth Assembly* (1924), p. 221.
14. "Address Delivered by the Right Hon. W.L. Mackenzie King on November 9th, 1928, at a Banquet of the League of Nations Society in Canada" (Ottawa, 1928), p. 22.
15. Canada, *H. of C. Debates*, 1936, IV, 3862.
16. League of Nations, *Verbatim Record of the Seventeenth Ordinary Session of the Assembly*, Sept. 29, 1936, p. 1.
17. Canada, *H. of C. Debates*, 1939, III, p. 2419.
18. League of Nations, Official Journal, Special Supplement No. 64, *Records of the Ninth Assembly* (1928), p. 60.
19. Mackenzie King to Wallace Nesbitt, Oct. 2, 1922, King Papers.
20. Sir Clifford Sifton, "Immigration," in *Addresses Delivered before the Canadian Club of Toronto, 1921-2* (Toronto, 1923), pp. 185-186.
21. Mackenzie King to Aneuran Williams, Feb. 18, 1920, King Papers. A portion of this letter is quoted in R. MacGregor Dawson, *William Lyon Mackenzie King: A Political Biography*, Vol. I, *1874-1923* (Toronto, 1958), p. 404.
22. Canada, *H. of C. Debates*, 1928, II, 1960.
23. T.A. Crerar to J.W. Dafoe, April 17, 1937, Dafoe Papers (P.A.C.).
24. Nicholas Mansergh, *Survey of British Commonwealth Affairs: Problems of External Policy, 1931-1939* (London, 1952), p. 112.
25. Canada, *H. of C. Debates*, 1919 (Special Session), pp. 102, 103.
26. Loring C. Christie, "Notes on the League of Nations Meeting of March, 1926," April 14, 1926, Borden Papers.
27. Canada, *H. of C. Debates*, 1923, IV, 4001.
28. Sir Clifford Sifton to J.W. Dafoe, Nov. 19, 1920, Dafoe Papers.
29. Entry for Dec. 11, 1920, Pope Papers (P.A.C.).
30. Dawson, *op. cit.*, p. 403.
31. W.A. Riddell, *World Security by Conference* (Toronto, 1947), p. 140.
32. Grant Dexter to J.W. Dafoe, Dec. 17, 1935, Dafoe Papers.
33. Canada, *H. of C. Debates*, 1936, I, 97, 98.
34. Quoted in F.H. Soward, *et al.*, *Canada in World Affairs: The Pre-War Years* (Toronto, 1941), p. 23.

35. Of whose newspaper it was well remarked that "what the *Free Press* thinks today, Western Canada will think tomorrow and the intelligent part of Eastern Canada will think a few years hence." Frank H. Underhill, "J.W. Dafoe," *Canadian Forum*, XIII (Oct. 1932), 22.

36. Quoted in Henri Saint-Denis, "Fascism in Quebec: A False Alarm," *Revue de l'université d'Ottawa*, Jan. 1939, p. 4. See also "S," "Embryo Fascism in Quebec," *Foreign Affairs*, XVI (April 1938), 454-466.

37. *Le Devoir* (Montreal), July 14, 1938.

38. Canada, *H. of C. Debates*, 1937, I, 910.

39. During the Munich crisis in the fall of 1938, Henderson wrote of "Hitler's own love for peace, dislike of dead Germans and hesitation of risking his regime on a gambler's throw." Quoted in Felix Gilbert, "Two British Ambassadors: Perth and Henderson," in Gordon A. Craig and Felix Gilbert, *The Diplomats, 1919-1939* (Princeton, 1953), p. 543.

40. Thomas Jones, *A Diary with Letters, 1931-1950* (London, 1954), p. 218. See also Thomas Jones to Lady Grigg, March 8, 1936, *ibid.*, pp. 179-181; *The History of 'The Times': The 150th Anniversary and Beyond, 1912-1948*, Part II, 1921-1948 (London, 1952), p. 938; John Evelyn Wrench, *Geoffrey Dawson and Our Times* (London, 1955), p. 369.

41. Canada, *H. of C. Debates*, 1944, VI, 6275.

42. Winston S. Churchill, *The Second World War*, I: *The Gathering Storm* (London, 1949), p. 250.

43. Bruce Hutchison, *The Incredible Canadian* (Toronto, 1953), p. 226.

44. Speech given over the National Network of the Canadian Broadcasting Corporation, July 19, 1937.

45. Frank H. Underhill, "The Close of an Era: Twenty-five Years of Mr. Mackenzie King," *Canadian Forum*, XXIV (Sept., 1944), 125.

46. Quoted in Dawson, *op. cit.*, p. 474.

47. Imperial Conference, 1937, *Summary of Proceedings*, pp. 14, 16.

48. Mansergh, *op. cit.*, p. 89.

49. Canada, *H. of C. Debates*, 1938, III, 3182.

50. Denis Richards, *Royal Air Force 1939-1945*, I: *The Fight at Odds* (London, 1953), pp. 72-73.

51. *History of the Second World War*, United Kingdom Civil Series, M.M. Postan, *British War Production* (London, 1952), p. 89.

52. *History of the Second World War*, United Kingdom Civil Series, J. Hurstfield, *The Control of Raw Materials* (London, 1955), p. 254.

53. See *History of the Second World War*, United Kingdom Civil Series, H. Duncan Hall, *North American Supply* (London, 1954).

54. Nicholas Mansergh, *Survey of British Commonwealth Affairs: Problems of Wartime Co-operation and Post-War Change, 1939-1952* (London, 1958), p. 17

55. Mansergh, *Survey...: Problems of External Policy*, p. 446.

56. Quoted in Stacey, *op. cit.*, p. 14.

57. Canada, *H. of C. Debates*, 1938, III, 3184.

58. Canada, *H. of C. Debates*, 1939 (Special War Session), I, 25.

59. Mansergh, *Survey...: Problems of External Policy*, p. 111.

60. McNaught, *op. cit.*, p. 54 n. 40.

61. Stacey, *op. cit.*, p. 35.

62. Viscount Templewood, *Nine Troubled Years* (London, 1954), p. 323.

63. Mansergh, *Survey...: Problems of External Policy*, p. 439.

64. See *Old Men Forget: The Autobiography of Duff Cooper* (London, 1954), pp. 239-240.

65. "Back Stage in Ottawa," *Maclean's Magazine*, II (Nov. 1, 1938).

66. André Siegfried, *The Race Question in Canada* (London, 1907), p. 142.

67. Mackenzie King to Lord Stanhope, July 23, 1909. Quoted in Dawson, *op. cit.*, p. 215.

68. Arthur Meighen, *Unrevised and Unrepented: Debating Speeches and Others* (Toronto, 1949), p. 319.

69. Dawson, *op. cit.*, pp. 417-418.

70. *Ibid.*, p. viii.

543

A Middle Power in the Cold War*
EDGAR McINNIS

Like most other lands, Canada finds her policies conditioned by her structure and her history. Her national interests grow out of her economic framework and her internal social and political balance; their expression is affected
by sentiments and traditions whose roots reach back into earlier centuries.
The structure may change as the nation develops. The traditions may be
modified as new conditions call for new responses. But, short of total catastrophe, the social and economic bases of a nation are never completely wiped
out by technological changes or even by political revolutions, and the past
imposes its continuity on the successive adaptations that are expressed in
changing policies.

544   A nation's policies are also conditioned by environment. No country is so
completely self-contained that it can avoid the need to project its national
interests beyond its own borders in the effort to realize its national purposes. Yet there are limits to its ability to impose its own aspirations on the
rest of the world. Other nations have different sets of interests that they are
not ready to abandon, and one of the tasks of foreign policy is to take the
maximum advantage of favorable opportunities in the world situation, and
to reduce to the minimum the effects of adverse factors on the country's
own national development. In this field, too, there is the constant need to
adapt to changing conditions. The economic situation of a particular country may be drastically altered by the development of new trade routes that
bypass old entrepôts or the appearance of new products that tend to super-
sede old staples. Its political and strategic position can be changed by the
decline of old empires and the rise of new super-states, or the development
of new weapons that pose new security problems. Yet here also there is seldom a complete expunging of the old lines of external policy or a comprehensive severance of traditional friendships and connections.

The story of Canada's postwar foreign policy is one of adaptation to these
two sets of factors, domestic and external. It is possibly the latter that has
called for the more drastic adjustments. Domestic evolution has been striking in many ways, but changes in the fundamental pattern have perhaps
been less revolutionary than the upheavals in the general world balance. Yet
the repercussions of world events have had their effects on Canada's internal conditions and outlook, adding their weight to the effect of changes in
the domestic sphere; and these in their turn have reacted on the conduct of
foreign policy and the attitude toward world issues.

There are two essential facts about Canada's structure that retain their

*From *The Growth of Canadian Policies in External Affairs*, ed. by H.L. Keenleyside. Copyright © 1960
by Duke University Press. Reprinted by permission.

historic validity even in the present day. Socially and politically, she is conditioned by the continued existence of a dual culture and a dual language. Economically, she still relies to a very large extent on the production of natural staples for sale in the world markets. In both respects there have, of course, been very real changes from even a generation ago. The significance of cultural divisions has altered and in some respects undoubtedly diminished. The range of natural products has broadened; some have risen in importance while others have declined; new elements of maturity have been added to the economy in such sectors as processing and transportation. These are factors that modify the form in which Canada's national interests can best be expressed or implemented; they do not essentially alter the ultimate roots from which those interests spring.

In this area the most pertinent change of all arose from the change of status that had been achieved during the interwar years. Emergence into nationhood had been a gradual process, and even after the formal barriers to independent action had been removed, the habits and attitudes of the colonial era were slow to disappear. These inhibiting influences were largely swept away by World War II. Canada emerged as a nation in her own right, with a sense of her separate identity and her equal place in the ranks of the other sovereign members of the world community. She had become aware of the privileges and opportunities of nationhood; she had come by experience to realize also its responsibilities. If there were restraining considerations, they no longer arose from legal limitations as such (even though these may have had their lingering psychological legacies) but from a sense of the limited influence that a nation of Canada's capacities could exert on world politics. Within that framework there was a new sense of national self-confidence that found expression in active and constructive efforts in the field of foreign policy.

Along with this, and expressing the new attitudes that developed with a growing sense of national identity, there emerged new figures to shape the form and substance of Canadian external policy. Mackenzie King had been concerned with the protracted struggle to free Canada from external controls. For a quarter of a century he had fought the battle for full independence in the sphere of external relations. He had become habituated to look with distaste on the restraining effects of any outside commitments, not merely toward the empire which orbited around Westminster, but almost equally toward the world collective system with its center in Geneva. Freedom of national decision was his cardinal objective in external affairs, and having gained this from London, he had no inclination to accept any diminution of such freedom in the name of collective action.

His successors typified the evolution of the Canadian outlook as it adapted itself to changing world conditions. Louis St. Laurent became the first man to hold as a separate office the Secretaryship of State for External Affairs. An internationalist in the classic liberal tradition, he entered upon his ministry at a time when the aggressive policy of the Soviet Union revealed unmistakably the rising totalitarian threat to democratic freedoms throughout

545

the world. His response was based on a conviction that free nations must stand together to preserve their liberties, and that Canada, whose national security was bound up with that of the other Western democracies, must make her contribution and subordinate her right of unhampered decision to the needs of the common cause.

This was the approach that was developed to fruition by Lester Pearson. He was by no means the sole contributor to the evolution of Canada's postwar policy. Political decisions were intimately bound up with other vital aspects such as finance and trade, production and defense. The ministers in charge of these departments under St. Laurent as Prime Minister were vigorous personalities who were usually ready to fight for their own views in opposition to their colleagues when occasion arose. Yet, while there might be sharp differences on specific questions, there was a broad consensus on overall objectives, and this was embodied and implemented through the policies of Lester Pearson as the architect of Canada's postwar external relations, which reached their mature form under his direction.

546

For Canada, as for the other Western democracies, the dominating fact was the cold war with its inherent threat to world peace and stability. The territorial conquests of communism, backed as they were by the massive military strength of the Soviet Union, would if unchecked bring the destruction of the kind of world in which Canada as a free democracy could hope to survive and prosper. Physical force was needed to contain Soviet aggression, and this meant the creation of a military balance of power with the attendant risk of armed conflict resulting in a third world war. Canada's position, if she were involved in such a war, would be much more vulnerable than in previous conflicts. Her virtual immunity from direct attack had been wiped out by the advent of the nuclear-rocket age. Her ultimate security was bound up with that of the Free World, yet participation in the defense of strategic areas beyond her own borders would expose her to new hazards and exact a new and formidable price.

In the interwar years there had developed a certain current of neutralist opinion in Canada though it never rose to major significance. In the postwar period only a shadowy remnant survived. Even the divergence between the two main racial groups, previously so acute in the field of external affairs, virtually disappeared. There was no longer ground for the suspicion that Canada was being dragged into a conflict on behalf of British imperial ambitions, or for the illusion, which in the thirties had induced a wilful blindness toward the brutal menace of Nazism, that militarism could be induced to yield to reason and totalitarianism enlisted in the defense of Christian civilization. The enemy was clearly identified and clearly recognized as an enemy, and French-speaking Catholic Canadians were certainly not behind their English-speaking Protestant compatriots in their resolve to resist the threat to the foundations of the society to which they were so deeply attached.

The result was a national consensus on basic objectives that gave concrete substance to Canada's new sense of national self-confidence as Canadians became habituated to the realities of national independence. Internally, the foundations were laid for the development of a positive foreign policy; external conditions called for positive decisions in a way that was almost inescapable. Canada found herself impelled by the demands of the postwar situation into an active and sustained role in world affairs. The nature of the existing balance was clear. The need to maintain it on a favorable level was urgent. The obligation to make a contribution to this end commensurate with the national resources was one which practically all Canadians accepted as necessary and inevitable.

Given this agreement as to ends, the means of attaining them became consequently restricted to a relatively narrow range of choice. Canada could hardly hope by her own unaided efforts to mould the scheme of things to her heart's desire. In her direct contacts with other countries she could press her own interests on her own initiative; in the wider sphere of world politics, she could make little impression by trying to go it alone. To attain her objectives, she must be ready to act with other like-minded states who shared her basic aims. Foremost among such states were her traditional associates, Britain and the United States. In that respect the historical continuity of her external policies was carried on unbroken into the postwar era. At the same time, the new conditions called for new adaptations. The relative weight given to these two major partners tended to change; the wider scope of the new problems called for wider associations; and the consequences of Canada's maturing independence were reflected in modifications of her attitude toward the leadership that she had earlier looked for from the United Kingdom and the ascendancy in world affairs more recently acquired by the United States.

This last element in particular was illustrated by the emergent concept of Canada as a Middle Power. She was no longer content to act simply as an auxiliary to one or other of the larger nations in the realm of external affairs. Her policies were her own, based on a reasoned concept of her own national interests; and while they coincided in the main with those of the other democracies, especially the English-speaking ones, she held herself free to assert her own point of view when policies diverged. Yet dissent was bound to be limited by practical considerations, and not least by the realization that a refusal to act with others might leave her impotent to take any effective action at all.

As between impotence and acquiescence, the desirable thing seemed to be the attainment of a recognized right of influence over decisions affecting Canada's interests and obligations. While she could not pretend to the stature of a Great Power, she was reluctant to be lumped together with all the smaller ones. She had greater resources than most of them; she was expected in a crisis to make a much greater contribution to the common cause. The war had called forth an effort second only to those of the Great Powers, and the demands of peace might be equally exacting. What she aspired to was a degree of influence comparable to the scale of her participation. It looked for a time as though the battle for status that Canada had successfully waged within the Commonwealth would be carried into the wider sphere of the community of nations.

In actual fact, of course, this aim was never pressed to a formal issue. The tentative effort to get the Middle Powers recognized as a special category within the United Nations failed at San Francisco, and any hope of attaining it as a general feature of the international structure was soon tacitly abandoned. Not only was there certain to be controversy over what states should be admitted to the ranks. There was the more operative consideration that the line was almost impossible to draw on a basis of either distinct interests or separate functions. There were relatively few cases in which the interests that were pursued by the middle-sized nations were distinct in character from those of their associates, small as well as great. There were a few cases — for example, the commissions that supervised the settlement in Indo-China, or the agreements on the composition of the United Nations Emergency Force — where distrust of the larger states and lack of resources on the part of the smaller ones imposed a special role on the Middle Powers; but such instances were relatively few and did not lead to any clear-cut division that would give the middle states a separate and clearly recognized position.

548

Yet the fact remained that Canada faced a real dilemma when it came to reconciling the range of her external involvements with her available means for implementing them. Isolated voices have occasionally been raised to urge that Canada should stand aloof from specific commitments in favor of a policy of non-alignment. In theory at least this would leave her free to formulate her own independent policies on particular issues as they arose, to decide the type of action that she could most effectively take in any given situation, and to use her potential weight in the power balance as a leverage on the side of moderation and compromise. This tends to ignore the extent to which Canada is in practice committed by the very nature of her interests to the common cause of the Free World as a whole, and to overrate her ability to exercise pressure based on an assumed freedom of choice that does not in fact exist, at least so far as fundamental issues are concerned. The alternative is to accept the facts of life, to recognize that Canada must join in a common effort on behalf of common aims, and to be reconciled to the secondary position that she will in consequence find allocated to her in the councils of the world community.

If the choice of the second of these alternatives has been almost instinctive on the part of the Canadian people as a whole, it also finds solid support from sound practical considerations. Soviet communism is a threat to the existence of the democratic society with which Canada's own vital interests are inescapably bound up. The threat cannot be met by individual nations acting independently, or even by the Great Powers among the democracies acting in concert. The full collaboration of all interested nations is needed if an effective balance is to be created and maintained; and Canada, unable in this situation to assure her national interests by her own unaided resources, has inevitably been impelled to look to a collective system within which those resources can be utilized with cumulative effect.

One result is that the United Nations bulks larger as an operative factor in Canadian foreign policy than did the League of Nations in the years between the wars. There was a genuine attraction to the principles behind the League, to the concept of a world organization as a remedy for international anarchy, but this was accompanied by a reluctance to entrust to a collection of foreigners the right to exercise any portion of Canada's newly won sovereignty. In the end there was an equal reluctance on the part of the Canadian government itself to take action in the name of international law and order that might embroil it with other states, however deplorable their conduct might be in defiance of the letter and spirit of the covenant. Aversion to the use of sanctions, pious reliance on moral force, and an increasingly stubborn clinging to the policy of non-commitment were the main features of Canada's attitude toward the collective system on the eve of World War II.

The inadequacy of such an approach was made all too plain by the outcome. If peace was to be sought through a world organization — and this was an aspiration to which the appalling experience of the war gave fresh urgency — a necessary minimum of power must be devolved on such organization by the member states. It was evident that the main strength must come in the first instance from the Great Powers. This was recognized by Canadian political leaders, but they were not satisfied with the prospect of a system that would leave the right of decision as well as the obligation of action solely in the hands of the larger states. If power and responsibility were to go together, as Mackenzie King asserted, then a secondary state such as Canada was entitled to a voice in decisions commensurate with the demands that she would be expected to meet. The converse of this was the recognition that Canada must be ready to make a contribution commensurate with her resources if her claim to an adequate voice in decisions was to be justified. There was little dissent from the logic of this proposition. "The Canadian people," said Mr. St. Laurent, "wish Canada to be a part of the international organization and to do whatever may be required in order to be a full partner in it. I believe that whatever may be required is a price that Canada is prepared to pay to make the organization effective, if it can be made effective."

This is not to say that Canada was yet prepared to subordinate her right of independent decision wholly to the authority of an international body. Indeed, it would be hard to find any sovereign nation that was willing to submit its destinies to the dictates of a world superstate. What can fairly be claimed is that Canada does not lag behind other member states in her readiness to strengthen the direct authority of the United Nations in matters concerned with the prevention of aggression and the peaceful settlement of disputes, and that she has repeatedly shown her willingness to join in cooperating with the organization and with her fellow-members in actions that are calculated to contribute to world peace and stability.

This attitude has been consistently maintained through all the vicissitudes that have beset the United Nations since its foundation. There has been a measure of disappointment over the failure of the organization to fulfil all the hopes that were initially placed in it, a certain disillusionment

549

about its capacity to achieve the aims for which it was designed; there has been little tendency to abandon it as wholly ineffective or to discard it as an instrument for the advancement of world order. On the contrary, there has been a continued emphasis on the United Nations as a major area of Canada's interests and activity. If its limitations have been made evident by experience, they have been accepted realistically; and far from leading to lukewarmness or indifference, they have if anything increased Canada's concern to strengthen the positive and constructive elements that the United Nations organization still contains. The weakness of the League was made an excuse for a policy of wary aloofness and the avoidance of commitments. It is symptomatic of Canada's advance in national maturity and self-confidence that the deficiencies of the United Nations have had almost the opposite effect, and that Canada, instead of trying to evade her responsibilities under the Charter, has been prepared to fulfil and even to extend them in a number of significant respects.

550   To no small degree, indeed, it is participation in the work of the United Nations that on the one hand enables Canada to develop the advantages that attach to her position as a Middle Power and, on the other hand, illustrates the limitations inherent in such a position. The United Nations, and particularly the Assembly, represents diplomacy by conference organized on a continuing basis. Up to a point this gives an opportunity to a secondary power to make a larger impact than is usual through the kind of bilateral contacts that are customary in conventional diplomacy, to win the trust and respect of other states, and thus to increase its influence over major decisions in which it is concerned. This is particularly evident in cases where neither the Great Powers nor the smaller states are appropriate instruments for dealing with some important international issue. In such cases, and especially where the issue is vested with a colonial aspect, Canada ranks with India and the Scandinavian countries as the states that are normally called on to make a leading and a constructive contribution. When economic matters are in question, the combination of states is somewhat different, but here too Canada is in the forefront because of her advanced technology and standard of living and her ability to provide capital assistance on a scale second only to that of the large Powers. Yet the need to accept these obligations is accompanied by only a limited capacity to lay down the conditions under which they shall be implemented. Canada's aid may be important and desirable in a given situation; it is rarely so indispensable that other states can be pressured into following Canada's lead against their better judgment or to their apparent individual disadvantage. In the Suez crisis, for example, Canada was able to play a leading part in the establishment of UNEF. Her best efforts were not enough to secure the creation of a permanent stand-by force as a regular instrument for dealing with future crises, or even to get a determined and concerted attempt at a final settlement of the Middle East problem that had bedeviled world politics for the past decade.

The positive side of Canadian foreign policy, and the accompanying willingness to accept increased external obligations, are even more strikingly apparent when we turn to the North Atlantic Treaty Organization. Here is a concrete illustration of the contrast between Canada's prewar and postwar attitudes toward external commitments. The decline of the League resulted in an apprehensive aloofness from all such engagements, whether under the Covenant or through promises of support to other Powers, including the United Kingdom. The frustrations of the United Nations in the sphere of security led, not to a discouraged resignation, but to a determined search for an effective alternative that would fill the resulting gap, and to an equally resolute acceptance of the burdens that must be borne as a consequence of Canada's participation as a full member of NATO.

In a sense, NATO was an extension of Canada's traditional connections and her long-standing interest in a favorable world balance. Twice within a generation Canada had been drawn into major conflicts born of authoritarian and militaristic threats to the democratic way of life. The security of Western Europe was clearly essential as a bulwark for the kind of world in which Canada could hope to survive and prosper. The United Kingdom *551* was a bastion that must be maintained if Western Europe was to be preserved. The strength and resources of the United States must be enlisted if democratic resistance was to command the necessary power, as well as the confidence and resolution without which the will to resist might all too readily be dissipated. When Mr. St. Laurent, in 1948, called for the creation by the nations of the Free World of "an overwhelming preponderance of force over any adversary or combination of adversaries," he made it clear that this was to be "under the leadership of Great Britain, the United States and France," and in fact the support of at least the first two of these Powers was essential in Canadian eyes for any effective system of collective security.

At the same time, Canada's participation in NATO was something more than simply a new expression of an old-standing orientation. Right up to 1939, Britain was the touchstone for Canada's attitude toward the European balance. If Britain stayed aloof from a European conflict, it was quite inconceivable that Canada should plunge into the hostilities. If Britain were drawn into a major war, it was virtually impossible for Canada to stay out. The latter situation still obtained, for the survival of the United Kingdom remained vital to Canada's national interests. But Western Europe was also vital, and Canada's entry into NATO was an explicit recognition of this salient fact. Her participation in European affairs was no longer remote and indirect, dependent on her connection with Britain; it was direct and immediate as a full partner in a common enterprise on behalf of Western security.

Two factors of special significance were inherent in this development. The first was the emergence of the United States from a long-standing tradition of isolation to the assumption of an active world leadership. Quite apart from the fact that this provided the Atlantic alliance with the solid core around which the other members could rally, it also released Canada from her prewar dilemma of reconciling her policy with divergent attitudes on the part of the United Kingdom and the United States. The two countries were now close partners in world politics, and with this fact as an established base, Canada was enabled to look beyond her most immediate connections and to frame her policies with broader considerations in view.

The second aspect was the change that has already been mentioned in the area of domestic opinion, particularly in French Canada. If on the one hand the continuance of co-operation with Britain through NATO gratified those groups in English-speaking Canada who still cherished the idea of the imperial connection, on the other hand Canada's independent membership in a wider grouping removed the stigma of subservience to Westminster that had previously been a chief ground for French-Canadian opposition to external commitments. Canada's entry into NATO was clearly and unquestionably a strictly Canadian decision based on a conception of Canada's own national interests to which all groups within the country subscribed.

In effect, what resulted was a new departure, of major significance as a stage in the evolution of Canadian foreign policy, yet growing out of considerations that were traditional as well as basic. The North Atlantic region had always been for Canada an area of primary concern. This was implicit in her constant efforts to harmonize her policies with those of both Britain and the United States. Now that a solid basis for harmony had been achieved, the wider interest could become explicit in its expression. It was an adaptation of historic factors to the demands of a new situation; and with the establishment of NATO, Canada's longest-standing external connections were supplemented and rounded out in the regional grouping that was henceforth a major pivot of Canada's approach to world affairs.

The postwar years saw a comparable adjustment in Canada's attitude toward another grouping that also represented a major and traditional interest. The Commonwealth of Nations was now undergoing a striking transformation. The emergence of the old Commonwealth during the interwar period — a development to which Canada had made a leading contribution — had set in motion forces that were having ever-broadening effects. The new Commonwealth that evolved after the war was different in composition, different in outlook, and involved considerable adjustments in the attitude toward the structure of the Commonwealth as an institution.

The relationship that was established by the Balfour Report and the Statute of Westminster left Canada's aspirations very largely satisfied. Her persistent aim had been to achieve for Canada the unqualified right to manage her own affairs, external as well as internal. This involved a rejection of any centralized machinery that might conceivably result in the subordination of separate and independent decisions to the consensus of other Commonwealth members, or even more distasteful, to the overriding weight of the Mother Country. It was a struggle for sovereign status as the basis for a continuing connection, and this absorbed Canada's efforts to the virtual exclusion of other aspects. There was relatively little attention devoted to the question of the composition of the Commonwealth. There was, of course, the anticipation that India would in due course take her place on an equal footing with other members. There was also a tendency to assume that the existing members would continue to stick together, and a genuine regret when Ireland decided to sever her Commonwealth connection. In addition, there was an almost automatic tendency to look at the Commonwealth through the perspective of Britain as the center and the motive force. There was a sentiment of fraternity with the other fellow-Dominions, a desire to retain the sense of united purpose and outlook that the Commonwealth seemed to provide; there was relatively little direct contact for specific common purposes with Australia or New Zealand or South Africa, and relatively little feeling of close and continuous co-operation except in matters in which co-operation with Britain on the part of each individual Dominion was the central motivating factor.

There is reason to believe that Canada would have been prepared to see this situation continue indefinitely. It was a pattern that met her concept of a settled and satisfactory relationship, and she had little or no incentive to press for further changes. The changes that came about in the postwar period were the result of pressures from other quarters, from newer or even from still aspiring members as they emerged from colonial status. But if Canada played no part in initiating the new advance, she did nothing to hamper it. Her attitude was one of benevolence toward other embryo nations who were moving along the path that Canada had pioneered, of approval for Britain's far-sighted policy in conceding a broadening measure of freedom to her former dependencies in response to the rising demands of nationalism, and even of complacence toward the formal changes in the structural and symbolic aspects of the Commonwealth that accompanied the new advance.

There can be little doubt that the dynamic and dramatic new phase that began with the admission of the new Asian states to full membership resulted in a fresh upsurge of interest in the Commonwealth on the part of a considerable section of the Canadian public. There remained, of course, an underlying attachment to the British connection, and to the Commonwealth as an emanation of Britain's imperial greatness. At this level, however, there was a tendency to take the existing relationship for granted and to bring it under discussion chiefly when it looked as though events were threatening to weaken that connection in its economic or political aspects. But there was a second and newer level from which the extension of the principle of free association to the countries of Asia and Africa was viewed much more in the light of its bearing on the world struggle to uphold the ideals of freedom and democracy than from the narrower point of view of its significance for Britain's power position. From this aspect, the Commonwealth appeared as a unique instrument for maintaining the links between Asia and the West, a bridge between the Western democracies and the uncommitted nations that were of such potential importance for the world balance, a means for creating a sense of common interest and establishing an awareness of common ideals. Canadians who were hardly concerned over whether Canada had any influence in Australia and who had long ago given up any idea that Canada could exert any influence over the Nationalist government in South Africa were urgently desirous that every effort be made to establish close and friendly

553

contacts with India and to show generosity and helpfulness toward the newer Commonwealth members. In these cases, Britain was no longer looked on as the normal intermediary. There were positive attempts to form direct links that would establish Canada as a friend in her own right and as a Western nation to whom the newer states could freely extend their trust and friendship in return. And if these objectives were incompatible with the concept of unity based on common allegiance, as laid down in the Balfour Report, then Canada was prepared to see the older conventions adapted to the new conditions, to accept the disappearance of the Common Crown as the necessary price for holding the newer members in continued association, and to help in working out the formula that enabled those members to replace the monarchy by a republican regime and still remain within the Commonwealth.

Thus, while the North Atlantic stood out as the prime area of Canada's interests and activities, her Commonwealth connection resulted in a wider geographical involvement and a selective extension of her external associations. Even further, her membership in the United Nations opened worldwide horizons and symbolized her inescapable concern with world affairs in their broadest sense. Her national interests were bound up with world peace and stability. She might have no direct stake in internal developments in Egypt or Indonesia, but when repercussions from those developments threatened to disturb the international economy or the existing political balance, Canada could hardly remain indifferent.

At the same time, there was a natural desire to refrain from getting involved in areas of purely general and indirect concern. There were limits to Canada's material resources, and perhaps even more, as a middle-sized state, to her resources in personnel. The burden of her existing commitments was far from negligible in relation to her size and capacities. It seemed in principle desirable to concentrate her efforts on those areas where her interests were most immediate and where her contribution would be most effective. It was with reluctance and at times with considerable perturbation that Canada found herself compelled by circumstances to extend her direct activities to spheres with which she was unfamiliar and from which she had previously been able to stand aloof.

Here was an illustration of the obligations consequent on participation in collective activities under the conditions created by the postwar balance of power. Great Powers as well as smaller ones found their main strength pinned down at the points of maximum danger and had limited resources to spare for secondary areas. It could no longer be taken for granted that they would in all circumstances assume a unilateral obligation to maintain stability in specific regions, even in ones in which they had special interests. This was accentuated when situations arose in which, for political reasons, it was desirable to exclude the Great Powers from participation in special arrangements. Taken together, these factors meant that other nations must be prepared to assume obligations in cases that the larger states would previously have dealt with on their own initiative. Canada had lost the kind of immunity from regional involvements that she had enjoyed in the early years of nationhood. Korea and Indo-China and Sinai were successive episodes that underlined the implications of Canada's position as an upholder of collective security and a foremost member in the ranks of the secondary states.

At the same time, such developments did not mean that the secondary states, once charged with these special responsibilities, were also vested with the power to decide or dispose of the issues that were involved. The Great Powers might not be all-powerful, but they had by no means abdicated. They still carried the decisive weight in world politics; they still provided the strength without whose backing their smaller associates would be largely ineffective. Canada might find herself drawn into new commitments, not only because her contribution was needed to supplement that of her larger associates, but as the result of a crisis created by their mistakes or misjudgments — factors over which she had little if any control. She had not only an important stake in the collective system as such — she had more than ever before a stake in the soundness of the individual policies pursued by her larger associates.

555

This meant, first and foremost, the policies of the United States. As a neighbor, the United States was of ever-increasing importance to Canada; as the leader of the Free World, its policies were now of almost daily concern to the mass of Canadian citizens.

Up to a point, the direct relations of the two countries followed much the same pattern as had developed during the past century or so. Friendship with the United States had throughout that period been a cardinal principle of Canadian policy. It had not always been easy to get the corresponding expressions of American good will translated into concrete measures, or to persuade Americans to treat Canada as an independent nation in her own right. The Good Neighbor policy of Franklin D. Roosevelt, however, ushered in a new phase in which Canada was accepted as an equal as well as a friend when it came to formal diplomatic dealings; and if on specific issues there were still grounds for complaints about lack of consideration for Canadian interests, these sprang rather from disparity in size than from any deliberate disregard of Canada's sovereign status.

What has occasionally been a matter for concern is the degree to which the actual exercise of sovereignty might be circumscribed by the growing influence of American interests over certain key aspects of Canada's national structure. This is both a consequence of the closer integration of the two countries during recent years and an illustration of the dominant place that the United States now occupies in the realm of external factors affecting Canadian policies and interests. The basic elements in the pattern may not have changed, but there have been striking changes in scale and shifts in emphasis; and in two spheres particularly — in economic relations and defense — there have been new developments that have significantly modified the shape of Canadian-American relations during the past decade.

Among the most consistent aspects of Canadian policy has been the constant effort to secure wider access to the American market. With the spectacular postwar upsurge of exports to the United States, it might seem paradoxical that the Canadian reaction was not so much satisfaction at this achievement as apprehension and irritation over American trade policies. There had been successive reductions in the American tariff since 1933, yet the persistence of protectionist pressures made for continual uncertainties about the future which were given substance by occasional concessions to American producers, either through increased duties or through quotas and embargoes. Moreover, while the American tariff structure in general favored the entry of Canadian primary products, it still raised barriers against manufactured goods, and Canadians who aimed at developing a national economy that would be more advanced as well as more diversified felt that the lines of evolution were being distorted by this imposition of stiff rates against their finished products. And although the fact that the United States took 60 per cent of Canada's exports might in one aspect be a cause for gratification, in another it increased Canadian uneasiness at this high degree of dependence on a more powerful neighbor over whose policies Canada had at best a very limited influence.

556

Added to the strains that arose in the direct relations of the two countries were the occasional points of friction resulting from their more general policies in the matter of world trade. In principle Canada and the United States were advocates of a lowering of trade barriers and a system of multilateral exchange. In practice it seemed at times that the United States was urging a strict adherence to these objectives by other countries while insisting on special exceptions for itself. The use of escape clauses not only had direct effects on Canadian exports such as minerals and dairy products; it also limited the contribution that the United States, as a creditor nation, needed to make to the world trade balance if a multilateral system was to be made freely operative. It meant that Canada's trade deficit with the United States, which in 1958 amounted to $1300 million, could not be fully offset by sales to other countries, since those countries in their turn found it hard to earn the dollars they needed by selling in a protected American market. And when the United States embarked on a policy of disposing of commodity surpluses by sales abroad on special terms, Canada felt that, besides being restricted in her ability to sell to the United States, she was being undercut by unfair practices in the alternative markets for her exports, especially the export of wheat. Taking it all in all, trade questions gave rise to the sharpest controversies between the two countries and provoked the stiffest protests from Canada against American policies.

Another major aspect of economic relations was the large-scale American investment in Canada during the postwar years. It was again paradoxical that this too gave rise to mixed feelings, though rather from apprehension over its political implications than from any serious resentment against American policies as such. There were occasional grounds for protest over such matters as the application of American laws to Canadian subsidiaries, but the real concern was over the extent to which key segments of the Canadian economy had fallen under outside control and the possibility that this might add a further element of distortion affecting the lines of Canadian economic development. This led every now and then to dark mutterings about the danger that economic infiltration might end up undermining Canadian sovereignty. It never resulted in concrete steps to restrict American investment, whose vital importance for the expansion of the Canadian economy was spectacularly evident, or even to use measures beyond persuasion and publicity to secure for Canadians a share in the direction of foreign-owned enterprises within their borders.

Similarly, in matters of defense, there were expressions of concern over the alleged attrition of Canada's independence accompanied in practice by a realistic acceptance of the demands of the actual situation. Of all the elements in postwar Canadian-American relations, this was the most novel as compared to the situation in the past. It was different not only in degree but in kind from the type of co-operation that even World War II had imposed. The nuclear-rocket age that staked the survival of the Free World on the striking power of the United States meant also that this power must be shielded from the long-range intercontinental blows to which it was now vulnerable. Canada's geographical position made her an essential element in the shield. The defense of North America was a continental problem that demanded integrated planning and operation. It was not enough for Canada to think in terms of protecting her own soil — she must collaborate to the maximum in the protection of the United States as the heartland of Western security. And if she could not fulfil this essential role on her own soil with her own resources, she must admit American supplementary activities within her own borders and the consequent American authority over such activities. As costs increased with advancing technology, so did the need to let the United States undertake the steps that Canada could not carry out by herself, and to provide the necessary facilities within Canada for the resulting American operations. The construction of the DEW Line, the creation of an integrated air defense through NORAD, the abandonment of the Arrow in favor of the BOMARC, were successive stages in the diminution of Canada's control of defense activities on and over her own soil; the acquisition of nuclear weapons or warheads will carry this a stage further. The problem of retaining effective sovereignty while agreeing to the concessions involved in this developing co-operation has not yet become acute, but it is evident that it lies implicit in this completely new relationship.

In another aspect, the progressive integration for purposes of defense illustrates the new level in relations that has developed during the past two decades. It is no longer merely a question of keeping Canada's separate policies in reasonable harmony with those of the United States and of minimizing any divergences that may arise in their respective courses of action in world affairs. The two countries are linked in common enterprises that call for joint rather than simply parallel action, and Canada has found herself obliged to consider positive efforts to act in concert with the United States to a far greater extent than ever in the past.

Involved in this development was a certain shift of emphasis from the

557

United Kingdom to the United States as the main pole of Canada's external policy. This did not necessarily imply any diminution of Canada's attachment to Britain or any lessening of interest in Britain's position as a strong and stable factor in the world balance. It was simply an inevitable fact that the much greater power and resources of the United States had now been thrown actively into world affairs. Decisions that in the days of American isolation had to be taken without American participation now needed the consent and support of the United States if they were to be made effective. Support from Great Britain was still desirable and in some cases equally essential; but the power center of the Free World was now the United States, and neither Canada nor the other secondary nations could realistically ignore that salient fact.

Indeed, even the direct relations of Canada with her great neighbor, vital as they were to her national development, were at times overshadowed by concern over the policies pursued by the United States in the broader field of world affairs. This concern was not confined to questions with which Canada herself was associated, such as the efforts at disarmament or the development of NATO as an effective instrument of security. There were issues in which Canada was not directly involved and on which she differed sharply from the position of the United States, yet whose consequences she would inescapably share if they should take the form of a major conflict. The clearest example was the China policy of the United States, to which Canada specifically refused to pledge support, yet with full awareness that if American policy should lead to full-scale war, Canada could hardly stand aloof. The assumption by the United States of a leading role in world affairs gave Canada a powerful added incentive for maintaining the closest possible contact, and for using every available opportunity to influence American policy along lines that she could approve and support.

Perhaps those opportunities were not always used to the full. Perhaps, indeed, they were actually fewer than circumstances might at first lead one to expect. It could hardly be denied that if the United States was of paramount importance in Canadian eyes, Canada on her part was more than ever of real importance to the United States as a neighbor and customer and ally. Yet there were distinct limits to the use that could be made of this situation as a basis for pressure on Washington. There were few ways in which Canada could use her potential nuisance value without the risk that the harm might in the end be chiefly to herself. Threats by Canada of economic retaliation, of a refusal of defense facilities, of curtailing or withholding co-operation through NATO or the United Nations, were less likely to bring a change in American policies than to weaken the unity for common purposes that was one of the chief Canadian interests in the field of external affairs.

Here was a further illustration of how desirable it was for a Middle Power such as Canada to seek collective action wherever feasible as the most effective means for implementing her own policies in foreign affairs. The leverage that she could by herself exert on the policies of her larger associates was limited at best. She had to rely chiefly on reason and persuasion — qualities that were most likely to be effective when exercised in concert with others. By the same token, opportunities for the exercise of an effective initiative were more likely to present themselves under these conditions than they would to a smaller power acting in isolation. It may be that even in this wider sphere Canada was more diffident than she need have been about trying to give a lead. Partly this was a survival of the old habit of waiting for a lead from her larger associates; partly, too, it sprang from the realization that effective action could be taken only within the limits that those associates would accept, with a resulting tendency to wait until those limits were defined before trying to frame the kind of policy that would be practical and realistic. It is not impossible that a continued growth in maturity and national self-confidence may gradually overcome some of these inhibitions and stimulate a more forward policy on the part of Canada in the years ahead.

And here again it is the situation created by the cold war that provides the most likely incentive for such a development. The first problem was to find a way of preserving the free nations against the imminent threat, not only to their individual national existence, but to the survival of the kind of world within which they could continue to exist as the kind of nations they wanted to be. In this matter, Canada took a real initiative which made its contribution to the creation of NATO and the emergence of a collective system of Western defense. There is a continuing task of maintaining and strengthening that system, but along with that goes the need to search for means of relaxing the tensions that imperil world peace and stability, and ultimately of ending the cold war itself if that can be done by any means compatible with the preservation of the essential interests of the Free World. These are objectives that have been consistently inherent in Canada's foreign policy throughout the postwar years. She has lent support to all practical efforts toward these ends, whether through negotiations on disarmament or by efforts to strengthen the peace-preserving functions of the United Nations. As is her habit, she has tended to let the Great Powers play the foremost part in trying to work out a basis for agreement. Indeed, in matters in which she was not directly involved in the first instance, such as the question of a German settlement, she has been content mainly to put the expression of her interest on formal record, and has refrained from pressing for an active share in the immediate negotiations or from complicating matters by demanding a recognized status for herself. Nonetheless, she has made clear her desire for continued efforts at a rapprochement with the Soviet bloc and for a serious exploration of every advance, however unpromising, that comes from that quarter. In this she has been against the attitude of rigidity and rejection that some of her associates have at times exhibited, and has been prepared to recognize that mutual concessions may be the necessary price for a genuine appeasement in the true sense of that much-abused word. It is very possible that the Berlin crisis marked the opening of a new phase in which consolidation and adjustment will be the dominant themes in international relations, and in which the imagination as well as the tenacity of

559

national leaders will have to be exercised to the utmost. There is no likelihood that this will bring any change in the basic aims that Canada has traditionally pursued, or in the identity of her fundamental objectives with those of her traditional associates, or in the closeness of co-operation with her historic partners in world affairs. The real task will once again be to work out the most favorable adaptation to changing conditions; and Canada, whose postwar policies have by no means been devoid of flexibility, may yet find new and still wider scope for a constructive application of that quality in the phase that lies before us.

From Colony to Satellite*
KENNETH McNAUGHT

560

Survival by Balance

The most consistent theme running through the sometimes tenuous tale of Canada's relations with the outside world has been a concern for survival. It was the dominant theme in the Old Province of Quebec and was strongly reinforced in all of British North America by the Loyalist migrations. The War of 1812, the nuisances of border raids in the 1830's and 1860's, the complicated pressures of American expansionism in the 1880's and 1900's produced strong reiterations of the survival theme. These were marked by successive decisions against political union with the United States. Canadians generally, both French- and English-speaking, agreed that the surest safeguard of independent Canadian survival was maintenance of the British connection. While we accepted this necessity (with varying enthusiasm), we did so with considerable care. If ultimate military protection against the only imminent threats, those posed by American expansionism, required "loyalty" to Britain, super-heated Britishism in such manifestations as the Imperial Federation League was rejected even by that most notable of British-born subjects, Sir John A. Macdonald.

Nineteenth-century Canadian foreign policy was thus based on a consciously-formulated concept of balance. The principal counterweight to dependence on Britain was encouragement of trade with the United States. Of almost equal significance was the steady Canadian refusal to give military support to British policies elsewhere in the world. And when unpleasant side-effects resulted from dependence upon British diplomacy Canadians exhibited some very positive counteracting nationalism.

The imperial basis of Canada's world view came into question with the mounting insistence that overseas dominions contribute substantially to the maintenance of Britain's world position. As long as the demands were not too great we accepted a cautious growth of commitment, although Canadian control of the forces involved became increasingly a criterion.

Unity through Isolation

After 1918 Canadians began to redefine their external relations. Borden and Meighen failed notably to salvage a Britain-centred world view. Under British leaders like Curzon and Amery equal partnership in formulating common imperial policies meant about the same as "consultation with allies" does now to men like McNamara and Rusk. And in these circumstances Mackenzie King reacted more decisively than he ever did in domestic affairs.

King's concept of national interest, which was his sole touchstone in any consideration of external objectives, was summed up in the one word "unity." Knowing well that French Canada was, to a man, opposed to the Borden-Smuts Commonwealth, King dismantled it between 1922 and 1939. In so doing he had, undoubtedly, the support of a majority of Canadians — French Canada plus a wide range of native-born English-speaking Canadians. Ostensibly King was returning to that concept of balance which had been distorted in the twenty years preceding 1918. Yet, in practice, King and Lapointe emasculated the revived strategy of balancing of external influences by failing to use our independence to any real purpose. Their total disinterest in the League of Nations symbolized their policy of ignoring international issues lest, as Lapointe put it, "we divide the country right away."

While the government defended its virtual silence on foreign policy by saying it left us free to decide our own course, in fact we were not free. In the guise of independence, we went to war in 1939, just as we had 25 years before, in defence of policies in whose formation we had refused to participate. The government went through the motions of a separate declaration, seconded with sombre lack of enthusiasm by J. A. Blanchette:

561

"It cannot be reasonably contended, after due reflection, that it would not be wise to co-operate to a reasonable extent with France and England in the present conflict, taking into account, however, our resources and our capacity, and without sacrificing our vital interests. . . ."

The tragedy of the 1930's was that those "vital interests" were not defined. In 1939 the unresolved question was, like the depression, simply swept under the rug. And, as with the depression, the drift of affairs, rather than any mastery of purpose, "resolved" the foreign policy problem.

Our American Century

In 1940 we passed from the British century of our history to the American century. We became dependent upon the United States for our security. We have, therefore, no choice but to follow American leadership.

Do we, as Frank Underhill maintains above, have no choice but to follow American leadership? A Yes to this question could come only from an unrepentant Calvinist.

In the 1940's as well as in the 1950's our external objectives were defined almost by default because governmental actions were hardly debated and only superficially explained. The Canadian-American defence agreements of 1947 set the pattern. As the undeclared "policy" of drifting into the American orbit continued unabated it produced the retroactively debated and documented North American Air Defence Command (Norad). The government veiled the real assumptions of defence integration in a manner startlingly similar to its ceremonial renunciation of prior commitments in the 1930's. Mr. King described the northern radar plans as civilian in character and announced that the armed forces of the United States and Canada would merely make contributions to the system. Even Mr. Diefenbaker had the courage of his illusions to declare that Norad did not place the RCAF in North America under American control because a Canadian officer was named deputy commander. Because the opening of the cold war made the political course of commitment to the United States the easiest path to follow, no efforts to maintain a balance were seriously considered. As a result we ended up more subservient to American than we ever were to British direction since our commitments are, for the first time in our history, supported in advance by military pacts and establishments — as well as by unimpeded economic integration.

Two potential countervailing forces were the Commonwealth of Nations and the United Nations. With respect to the Commonwealth, we simply carried on the artificial game of independence — by vastly exaggerating the importance of formalizing our freedom from British influence. At the very time when Britain ceased to be even an imaginary restraint upon our independence we made a great to-do about terminating the "colonial relationship." No one would argue that these things should not have been done; they should have been done more completely and cleanly than they were. But they should never have been billed as the completion of our independence at the very time when our actual policy was to enter a web of unprecedented dependence upon the United States. And closely related to all this was Ottawa's reluctance to take any serious initiative or to seek a real leadership role in the emergent multi-racial Commonwealth, one of the most usable North-South bridges in a perilously divided world.

In the United Nations, Canada seemed to wish to use her independence to advance the international rule of law. But there too our role was closely circumscribed by the same political timidity which had hobbled us in the inter-war years. We allowed ourselves to be dominated by fear of domestic division and by a curiously outdated assessment of the nature of national power in the post-1945 world. King and St. Laurent used the shibboleths of "middle power status" and "functionalism" to cover what was in fact a nervous retreat from independent initiative. Initiative and influence they proclaimed, must always be strictly proportional to military power, even if "middle powers" such as Canada should have slightly greater influence than small powers.

Despite Canada's participation in all agencies and peace-keeping operations she was reluctant to give leads in basic policy matters. Middle power functionalism remained a synonym for big power and, increasingly, for American decisions. Mackenzie King, as Bruce Hutchison remarked, wrote off the UN as "a failure" within a week of its founding. In 1947 Mr. St. Laurent added his interpretation of functionalism: "There is little point in a country of our stature recommending international action, if those who must carry the burden of whatever action is taken are not in sympathy." The doctrine was plausible as long as "stature" was seen exclusively in terms of military power and, indeed, in terms of nuclear power. Functionalism thus led inexorably away from serious UN commitment and towards subservience to the larger powers. It was a highly convenient rationalization for our political decision to accept a re-clothed world-order of regional military alliances. Once it was accepted we found ourselves under the alleged necessity of playing ball with the power which lay at the centre of all the freshly constructed western regional alliances. Thus, although we are not members of Seato and although both our material and ideological interests are at variance with American policy in Southeast Asia, our spokesman felt compelled to justify the American invasion of Vietnam, to subvert our position on the ICC and to furnish hospitals to Saigon because to do otherwise would make our general position of commitment to the United States too uneasy.

563

Satellite Status Confessed

The most recent version of King-St. Laurent functionalism goes under the name of "quiet diplomacy." The doctrine that only quiet, behind-the-scenes, confidential methods should be applied by Canada-size powers was succinctly stated by Prime Minister Pearson in March, 1967. In a public letter replying to an appeal by 360 University of Toronto professors to dissociate Canada from the American war in Vietnam, he wrote:

Confidential and quiet arguments by a responsible government are usually more effective than public ones. . . . Too many public declarations and disclosures run the risk of complicating matters for those concerned   The more complex and dangerous the problem, the greater is the need for calm and deliberate diplomacy.

But Mr. Pearson in the same letter went behind the reasons of diplomatic method to other, more profound reasons for his unwillingness to rock the North American boat. He, like Professor Underhill, pointed to the World War II origins of our entanglement in continental defense. He reviewed the extent to which defence production has been integrated, the technological and mass production advantages we receive and then declared that because of these developments we could not, in fact, refuse to contribute to the American war effort in Vietnam:

For a broad range of reasons, therefore, it is clear that the imposition of an embargo on the export of military equipment to the USA, and concomitant termination of the Production Sharing Agreements, would have far-reaching consequences which no Canadian government could contemplate with equanimity. It would be interpreted as a notice of withdrawal on our part from continental defence and even from the collective defence arrangements of the Atlantic Alliance.

No more concise or authoritative statement has been made on the subject. After his letter no one can maintain that acceptance of continental integration in defence production and planning leaves us free in general foreign policy — leaves us free to accept one part of the American alliance structure while rejecting other parts of it. Nor can anyone seriously doubt that it is this integration that has produced, as James Eayrs has put it, the smooth Canadians who haunt the corridors of Washington with their confidential, ineffective briefs.

The process by which we accepted the bipolarization of the world was both curious and facile. During the second half of 1947 and through 1948 Canada did appear to define an external objective. It was the objective described by Senator Vandenburg, George Kennan and Harry S. Truman — the objective of crippling communist power by encirclement of Russia. For the Canadian government this essentially American objective was overwhelmingly attractive and Canada leapt with agility to its support. The concept of a deeply divided world within which the West was imminently threatened by aggressive communist imperialism and which required a unified military response was attractive because it settled the Canadian foreign policy question automatically. Moreover, it settled that question along lines which could and did eliminate any serious internal political division.

But, most people say, it is all very well after the crisis is past to discourse upon the other side of the case; in fact the real danger was so great that we only saved Europe and ourselves from having to cower under the Kremlin's knout by building the Nato shield. While one may agree that a genuine dilemma existed in 1949, one should be quite equally aware that a crucial commitment was made to an increasingly military assessment of the situation — and that this emphasis remained while any justification for it grew steadily less credible as the Communist military threat declined. While the original case for Nato may or may not be convincing, the case for maintaining the alliance as the centre of our foreign policy is entirely without substance.

From the Canadian point of view, the case for disbanding Nato (or for simply withdrawing from it) seems virtually unanswerable — except from the abashedly continentalist premises put forward by the Prime Minister and which imply acquiescence in Washington's ideological anti-communism. The case for leaving Nato depends upon one's interpretation of its present and likely future role as well as upon an assessment of its impact upon Canadian foreign policy.

The impact of Canada's membership in Nato has determined our other external policies. The basic premises of the alliance's dominant member have governed our position on all major questions — recognition of China, disengagement in Europe, nuclear disarmament, the creation of a genuine

UN police force. While it can be argued that we have been able to play honest broker on occasion (e.g. Suez) the initiatives of this sort that we have taken have always been either in conformity with US policy or they have been such as to cause the US minimum discomfort. Whenever basic questions affecting the US position arise, our commitment to "nuclear security" and production agreements has been decisive. The effects of total loyalty are sometimes veiled, as in the case of Cuba — where we do not formally toe the line but where we are excruciatingly careful not to mount any trade campaign or to facilitate Russian-Cuban air communications. Loyalty is unveiled in hotter situations such as Vietnam where the government defends openly the legal and moral position of the United States and concedes that our position on the ICC is not that of an independent but that of a representative of "the West." One does not envy Mr. Chester Ronning, who no doubt found it difficult explaining in Hanoi why we send aid only to Saigon — an aid policy which enabled General Westmoreland and the State Department to list Canada as one of the "supporting" allies in Vietnam. Indeed this automatic loyalty in situations deemed crucial by Washington is taken absolutely for granted.

565

But it is not just by choice that we forego within the alliance system the rights and opportunities of independent initiative in major matters. Despite the rhetoric of equal partnership and consultation, Nato remains a military alliance dependent upon United States decisions and it is now abundantly clear that real influence will not be shared by the power that controls the essential nuclear component of the system. As long as Canada accepts the alliance basis of security she will accept the shackles of nuclear loyalty and the stigma of total commitment. Thus we violate our liberal traditions by refusing entry to deserters from the US army under a "Nato commitment." As Melvin Conant put it somewhat harshly a few years ago: "Fifteen years of effort to meet the security requirements of the air age have concluded with the prospect that the Canadian role from now on will be marginal and certainly not consequential."

Even apart from the question of hobbling ourselves by accepting the nuclear measuring rod, there is the question of the general effect of Nato upon the most dangerous of the world's outstanding problems. Clearly, Nato stands as the principal obstacle in the path to a German settlement. (To argue as von Rickhoff does, that Nato has achieved "the incorporation of West Germany within the Atlantic community of nations" makes light of the fact that we do not even recognize the existence of East Germany!) Nato stands also as the symbol, in an image-minded age, of western commitment to a cold-war interpretation of international affairs. On these grounds alone Canada should withdraw her Nato contributions and should give notice that she will exercise her right under Article 13 of the Treaty to withdraw from the alliance in 1969. Just as our acceptance of Nato was an implicit definition of external objectives, so our withdrawal from it should be the occasion for redefinition of such objectives.

A Return to "Balance"?

If we cannot return to the simple formulae of earlier times, we can define from the frustrations of our alliance experience a more fruitful set of policies.

What we lost in the Nato period should be our chief guide in the future. We abandoned any serious concern for our national independence and based policy upon considerations that are wholly archaic — especially in the light of American predominance, nuclear weaponry and the rise of Afro-Asia from imperialist control; and we have almost wholly ignored the glaring inequality of welfare and opportunities amongst the world's peoples. In "defence" matters we have ignored the obvious reality that the only serious threat to our own territory stems from our proximity to the centres of US nuclear power — and the presence of Bomarcs which have been described by Mr. McNamara as bait for Russian missiles. The "nuclear umbrella" is for us a nuclear lightning rod. New definitions of foreign policy should aim at rectifying such crippling inadequacies of assessment and they should take into account changes within Canada as well as changes abroad.

Since Canada's security, prosperity and any hope she may have of exercising a beneficent influence abroad all depend upon the maintainance of peace and are hindered by continuance of cold war divisions it should follow that her principal external objectives should be to achieve: 1) enhancement of the United Nations at the expense of regional alliances; 2) absolute priority for nuclear disarmament; and 3) top spending priority for foreign aid.

These three objectives are obviously interrelated and rest upon certain assumptions about the post-1945 world which are implicit in the foregoing discussion, but which deserve explanation.

The most important assumption is that after the nuclear revolution in the nature of military power Canada can no longer seek to measure her influence in terms of the dominant military weaponry. She cannot hope to build a nuclear weapons system and therefore cannot be completely Gaullist; she is therefore, if she continues as a committed party to the arms race, completely dependent upon American decisions. Moreover, the evidence of the past twenty-two years leads irresistibly to the conclusion that no one can help to moderate the arms-race tensions simply by pious participation and disarmament conferences while wearing prominently the US arm-band. Yet, while nuclear disarmament is already a subject to produce yawns it is, nevertheless, one which must lie at the heart of our international objectives. Few people now doubt that the *gravest* danger facing the world is unlimited nuclear war and that limited nuclear war is, at the very least, unlikely. While we remain committed to Nato we are also committed to the use of nuclear weapons on our behalf, and in some cases by our own forces — that is, committed to risking the destruction of civilization. Although we have learned to live with the bomb, we do not have to love it. If our foreign and defence policies are to be founded on morality and realism they must exclude membership in alliances which depend upon nuclear power. Even in terms of

566

seeking to persuade others to deny themselves the bomb (i.e. the limited goal of non-proliferation) our present position is hypocritical.

A militarily non-aligned Canada could do more than a committed Canada to mobilize a growing pressure within the United Nations for acceptance of the most advanced disarmament offers that have been made by both the United States and Russia during the ebb and flow of past disarmament talks. While the history of the arms race is not such as to encourage ill-considered optimism neither is the present instability of terror something to induce lethargy and a failure of nerve. Surely the most striking facts ignored by advocates of cautious debate, quiet diplomacy and iron-clad guarantees is that twenty-two years of such methods have succeeded only in producing the most dangerous arms-race in history — whose most recent peak is the edgy debate about anti-missile systems and the development of Chinese nuclear capacity. It is clear that in this field words are no substitute for actions. Our most significant action would be immediate renunciation of nuclear weapons and withdrawal from nuclear alliances. The cries of hypocrisy that would be raised in some quarters would have much less base than those which can now be *legitimately* raised.

567

Much of what I have been suggesting by way of redefining our international objectives has already been canvassed by our government. But in each case the extent of the tentative moves has been minimized by the facts and psychology of commitment to the American military alliance. We do not, for example, really wish to keep any military force in Germany and it is evident that in terms of power our presence there is ridiculous. Thus we have elected a kind of equipment-erosion method of withdrawing from the scene — a method that impresses no one, but which is required in order not to offend American political-strategists openly. We have expanded our aid to the West Indies and Afro-Asian states but on a scale that should make us blush. Many people hope that Norad will be phased out in the face of new airscreen devices developed in the US, but we retain in Canada the useless and dangerous Bomarc missiles. We are rearranging our own military forces so that their essential role will be that of mobile emergency forces for peace-keeping operations. But we have made no real progress toward the establishment of a fullfledged UN police force. The concept of do-it-yourself stand-by forces clearly falls far short of the police project proposed by Tryggvi Lie as early as 1949. Since it is not possible, save in the case of individual or collective mania, to use nuclear power, the roles of economics, diplomacy and minor specialist military force have all been remarkably enhanced. Our role in peace-keeping must be complemented by a serious commitment to the concept of international equality. In our own country we have decided that, on grounds both of justice and utility, we must establish basic minimum standards of welfare and that we must work for the realization of equality of opportunity. The same grounds should be the basis of our approach to international affairs. Utilitarian reasons also require the effort to establish international equality of opportunity — for the seeds of conflict and of extremist nationalism find favourable ground in the desperate inequalities that divide the affluent from the underprivileged world. Without entering the debate about the most efficacious methods of raising welfare and opportunity levels in Latin America and Afro-Asia it is more than apparent that we now devote to the problem only a tiny proportion of the manpower and resources that we consider appropriate in other fields. Here again, as in the area of nuclearism, our intentions and policies will be convincing and have influence to the extent that they are whole-hearted and unambiguous.

Clear-cut, non-alliance objectives would thus be in the Canadian national interest in two senses: they would be our only possible contribution to the kind of world in which alone it is possible for a country such as ours to exist, and they would in themselves strengthen our national experiment by extending to our foreign policy the principles of tolerance, compromise and equality which we endeavour to establish at home. While to some the detailed implications of the policy basis I have suggested will appear to be merely anti-American, in fact this bogey is now an irrelevant, timorous excuse for inaction. Imperial Washington's loyalty requirements are tougher than were those of Imperial London. But the conditions of the present require, just because this is so, a vigorous response and return to a concept of survival and balance in our external relations.

568

Topic Fourteen

Post-World War II Economic and Social Developments

Since the Second World War, Canada has experienced many economic and social changes. An expanding population — through natural increase (Canada had the highest birthrate of any industrial country in the world in the immediate postwar era) and immigration — has created a much larger market than existed before the war, thus creating new opportunities for industrialists. Our abundance of natural resources, and a continuing world-wide demand for them, have also helped to give Canadians one of the highest standards of living in the world. But the capital for this expansion came (and continues to come) largely from the United States in the form of direct investment in Canadian industries and control of Canada's natural resources. By the mid-fifties the situation was critical, with an estimated foreign investment of $17.4 billion. The Liberal government in 1955 established a Royal Commission on Canada's Economic Prospects as a preliminary step to study the question. In the 1960s and 1970s, the debate intensified. One side of that debate is presented in "Regression to Dependence" and "Metropolis and Hinterlands" — both excerpts from Kari Levitt's *Silent Surrender*.

"The Second World War marked the end of the old order of Canadian society," according to S.D. Clark in "Movements of Protest in Postwar Canadian Society." The sociologist examines the impact on Canadian society in the 1960s that resulted from Canada's population boom, the shift from rural to urban society, and a growth in the number of students attending post-secondary institutions of education. Although Clark's paper looks at developments from the perspective of the 1960s, many of his observations are still relevant today.

R. Bothwell, I. Drummond and J. English in *Canada Since 1945: Power, Politics, and Provincialism* (Toronto: University of Toronto Press, 1981), provide a good overview of political, economic and social developments since World War II. An earlier treatment is provided by Donald Creighton in his *Canada: 1939–1957: The Forked Road* (Toronto: McClelland and Stewart, 1976).

On the question of economic nationalism and foreign investment, students should consult G.J. Aitken's *American Capital and Canadian Resources* (Cambridge: Harvard University Press, 1961) for development through the 1950s. For the views in the 1960s and 1970s, see the publications of the University League for Social Reform: *Nationalism in Canada*, ed. by P. Russell (Toronto: McGraw Hill, 1966); *Close the 49th Parallel etc.: The Americanization of Canada*, ed. by I. Lumsden (Toronto: University of Toronto Press, 1970); *The Prospect of Change: Proposals for Canada's Future*, ed. by A. Rotstein (Toronto: McGraw-Hill, 1965). A more recent economic study is Glenn Williams, *Not For Export: Towards a Political Economy of Canada's Arrested Industrialization* (Toronto: McClelland and Stewart, 1983).

For a review of Canada's social development in the post-World War II era (besides the relevant chapters in *Canada Since 1945* — cited above), students should consult the *Canadian Year Book* which contains factual material for each year. On cultural, educational and literary life in the post-World War II period, see Julian Park, ed., *The Culture of Contemporary Canada* (Toronto: Ryerson, 1957), and Carl Klinck, ed., *Literary History of Canada: Canadian Literature in English*, 3 vols. (Toronto: University of Toronto Press, 1976). George Woodcock's *Canada and the Canadians* (Toronto: Macmillan, 1970) looks at Canadian development from a social and cultural perspective.

570

Regression to Dependence*
KARI LEVITT

Some sixty years ago Sir Wilfrid Laurier declared that the twentieth century belongs to Canada. By the middle of the century it had become clear that Canada belongs to the United States. Indeed Canada provides a dramatic illustration of the stultification of an indigenous entrepreneurial class and the regression to a condition of underdevelopment in spite of continuous income growth.

Until recently the change in Canada's status has largely gone unnoticed. Most Americans are barely aware of the existence of Canada; if they were, it would not be necessary for our political leaders to remind them so often and so politely that Canada is not the fifty-first state of the Union, nor the thirteenth district of the Federal Reserve System. Canadians tend to be more impressed by their relative wealth than by their neo-colonial satellitic relationship to the United States. As for the rest of the world, it is not really interested.

The instrument by which the Canadian economy has been recolonized

* Chapter 4 from *Silent Surrender: The Multinational Corporation in Canada*, by Kari Levitt. Copyright 1970 by Macmillan of Canada. Reprinted by permission of Gage Publishing Limited.

since the days of Sir John A. Macdonald and Sir Wilfrid Laurier is that of direct investment — more specifically U.S. direct investment. The distinction between the import of foreign capital by the sale of bonds or debentures or non-controlling equity stock, and the intake of direct investment in the form of subsidiaries and branch plants controlled by externally-based parent corporations is crucial. In the former case control remains with the borrower; in the latter it rests unequivocally with the lender. Liabilities incurred by debt borrowing can be liquidated by the repayment of the loan. Direct investment creates a liability which is, in most cases, permanent. The following description of the difference between direct and portfolio investment is taken from a study prepared by an organization representing American corporations with interests in scores of foreign countries.[1]

Direct investment refers to an investment made to create some kind of permanent organization abroad — plants, refineries, sales offices, warehouses — to make, process and market goods for local consumption and, in some instances, for sale in third areas. Such operations typically combine U.S. personnel, technology, knowhow, machinery and equipment, to expand the productive capacity of the countries in which the investment is made and to open important markets for the products of the investing country. Venture capital engaged in the location, extraction and refining of mineral resources; in developing agricultural resources; in establishing manufacturing, trade and banking enterprises; and in building and operating public utilities that serve foreign areas — all these represent direct investments.

It is important to distinguish between direct investments and the other forms of private investments abroad — banking and portfolio. A bank loan or credit to a foreigner is strictly a financial transaction between the lender and the borrower with a fixed maturity; . . . the bank may require the borrower to deposit some collateral. A portfolio investment may take two forms — purchase of foreign bonds and debentures or purchase of foreign stocks by a U.S. resident. Purchases of bonds and debentures are, like bank credits, at fixed terms with no equity interest; purchases of stocks involve equity interest, but generally not controlling interest. Only when 25 per cent or more control is attained is the investment considered a direct investment. This assumes some measure of managerial influence.

571

This exposition stresses the acquisition of markets for the investing country as a prime motive for direct foreign investment. The literature of underdevelopment, including that written on Canada, has emphasized the expectation that the host country will acquire markets when it takes in direct investment. The contradiction is more apparent than real; in general the host country acquires a market for its raw materials and becomes a market for the manufactured goods of the investing country. Direct American investment in Europe has concentrated on producing and selling manufactures in these markets; in the underdeveloped countries of Latin America and the Middle East it has concentrated on extracting raw materials. In Canada we are in the unique situation of playing host to large American investments both in the resource and in the manufacturing sectors. As a result Canada has acquired markets for its industrial raw materials and has become a market for manufactured goods produced by American corporations located both here and in the United States.

Prior to the First World War Canada was the prototype of a borrowing country, old style. It contained the highest concentration of British portfolio

TABLE I – **Foreign direct investment in Canada, 1945 and 1965**

	U.S. direct investment (*millions of dollars*)		All other foreign direct investment (*millions of dollars*)	
	1945	*1965*	*1945*	*1965*
Wood and paper products	316	1 164	32	195
Iron and ore products	272	1 769	5	244
Non-ferrous metals	203	1 021	8	91
Vegetable and animal products	184	798	63	181
Chemical and allied products	118	947	26	224
Non-metallic minerals	39	160	4	102
Textiles	28	97	28	44
Miscellaneous manufactures	31	142	2	6
TOTAL MANUFACTURING (*Excluding petroleum refining*)	*1 191*	*6 098*	*168*	*1 087*
Petroleum and natural gas	141	3 600	—	930
Mining and smelting	215	1 875	22	143
Utilities (excl. pipelines)	358	286	17	20
Merchandising	147	695	55	362
Financial	198	1 041	141	644
Other enterprise	54	345	6	82
TOTAL	*2 304*	*13 940*	*409*	*3 268*

Source: Dominion Bureau of Statistics: *Canadian Balance of International Payments, Third Quarter 1968*, p. 25, December 1968.

572

investments to be found in any major area of the world; 14 per cent of all British foreign capital was invested in Canada, compared with 20 per cent in the United States and 20 per cent in all of Latin America.

Within fifty years Canada had become the prototype of a borrowing country, new style. By 1964, 80 per cent of long-term foreign investment in Canada was American, $12.9 billion in the form of U.S. direct investments in branch plants and subsidiaries. Canada, a relatively small country, accounted for 31 per cent of all U.S. direct investment abroad, more than the total U.S. investment in Europe, more than in all of Latin America.

As a result of the penetration of the Canadian economy by direct investment some 60 per cent of Canada's manufacturing industry, 75 per cent of her petroleum and natural gas industry and 60 per cent of her mining and smelting industry are now in the control of foreign corporations. This contrasts with the situation only twenty-five years ago when 38 per cent of manufacturing and 42 per cent of mining and smelting were under foreign control (see Tables I and II).[2]

The switch from portfolio to direct investment and the associated displacement of Canadian by American entrepreneurship has taken place against a relatively diminishing need for foreign capital. It has been estimated that the book value of all foreign assets in Canada in 1926

TABLE II – **Non-resident control as a percentage of selected Canadian industries 1926 — 1963**

Percentage of total controlled by all non-residents	1926	1939	1948	1963
Manufacturing	35	38	43	60
Petroleum and natural gas	—	—	—	74
Mining and smelting	38	42	40	59
Railways	3	3	3	2
Other utilities	20	26	24	4
TOTAL	17	21	25	34
Percentage of total controlled by US residents				
Manufacturing	30	32	39	46
Petroleum and natural gas	—	—	—	62
Mining and smelting	32	38	37	52
Railways	3	3	3	2
Other utilities	20	26	24	4
TOTAL	15	19	22	27

Source. Dominion Bureau of Statistics, *Canadian Balance of International Payments, 1963, 1964 and 1965,* August 1967, p. 127.

573

amounted to 117 per cent of Canada's annual output (G.N.P.). By 1948 the corresponding figure has declined to 50 per cent. Since then it has risen to 61 per cent.[3] A similar picture emerges from the trend in the cost of servicing foreign borrowing. These diminished from 3 per cent of G.N.P. in the late twenties, rose to 6 per cent in the depressed thirties and fell to a mere 2 per cent over the period 1957 to 1964. Interest and dividend payments abroad as a percentage of export earnings declined from 16 per cent in the twenties and 25 per cent in the thirties to 9 per cent in the recent period.

The use of the value of foreign assets in Canada as a measure of the contribution of foreign capital to Canadian productive capacity invites two words of caution. First, this measure of "capital inflow", includes the appreciation in the book value of direct investment due to the ploughing back of retained earnings. This reflects the fact that a significant portion of foreign assets in Canada have been financed from Canadian savings. Second, the measure is a gross figure; in order to obtain an estimate of Canada's net indebtedness it is necessary to subtract the value of Canadian assets abroad. For both these reasons the value of foreign assets in Canada exceed significantly the sums of the net inflow of capital as shown in Canada's balance of payments.

Prior to the First World War Canada, like the United States, was unquestionably short of capital. She borrowed heavily, lent almost nothing abroad. At the time of the wheat boom in the early years of the twentieth century net capital imports reached a peak of $42 per person during the five years 1909–1913.

In the 27-year period spanning the Depression and the Second World War (1930 to 1947) there was no increase in the value of foreign assets in Canada. Indeed during the Second World War and the immediate postwar period Canada had attained a level of economic strength and maturity of fiscal and monetary institutions which enabled her to export capital on a large scale, and to contribute to the financing of the British war effort and post-war reconstruction. In the ten years 1940 to 1950 Canada's surplus on current account totalled $6.5 billion. Between 1946 and 1950 the *net export* of capital averaged $8 per head.[4]

The acceleration in the loss of control over the manufacturing and mining industries commenced with the decade of the 1950s. Since 1950 there has been a deficit on current account on the balance of payments in every year except one, and during the boom of the 1950s net capital imports averaged $12 per head. After the recession of 1957–58 capital continued to flow into Canada despite rising rates of unemployment and a slowing down of the growth of output. During the ten-year period 1957 to 1967 Canada's net indebtedness more than doubled from $11.8 billion to $24 billion.

574

Those who believe that all the fuss about foreign ownership and control is misguided nationalism, have taken comfort in the diminishing dependence of Canada on external sources of finance. The figures, however, lend themselves to a different interpretation; it is simply not true that Canada is short of capital. The expensive infra-structure required by her peculiar geography has long been put in place and paid for. Levels of per capita income are second only to the United States and the rate of personal savings is higher. The brutal fact is that the acquisition of control by U.S. companies over the commodity-producing sectors of the Canadian economy has largely been financed from corporate savings deriving from the sale of Canadian resources, extracted and processed by Canadian labour, or from the sale of branch-plant manufacturing businesses to Canadian consumers at tariff-protected prices. Thus, over the period 1957 to 1964 U.S. direct investment in manufacturing, mining and petroleum secured 73 per cent of their funds from retained earnings and depreciation reserves, a further 12 per cent from Canadian banks and other intermediaries and only 15 per cent in the form of new funds from the United States. Furthermore, throughout the period payout of dividends, interest, royalties and management fees exceeded the inflow of new capital.

Pattern of Investment from Confederation to Centennial

The chart on the next page illustrates the stages by which the British-financed east-west national economy has yielded to the new mercantilism of direct foreign investment of American corporations. (See also Tables III and IV.)

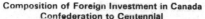

**Composition of Foreign Investment in Canada
Confederation to Centennial**

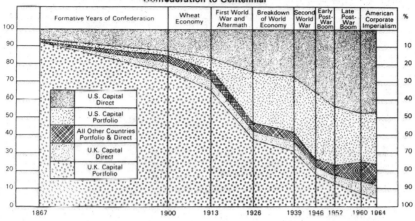

575

In 1867, there was little foreign capital in Canada. Of $200 million, $185 million was in the form of U.K. bonds; the remaining $15 million was American direct investment.

In the formative years (1867–1900) of the Canadian nation-state, there was an inflow of $815 million of U.K. bond capital and $160 million of U.S. direct investment.

In the period of the wheat boom (1900–1913), there was a total increase in indebtedness of $2545 million, in the form of portfolio investments, predominantly British, and $530 million in the form of direct investment, mainly American. By 1913 foreign capital in Canada was $3850 million of which $3080 million was portfolio debt, almost all of it British. Significantly, of the remaining $770 million of direct investment, $520 million was American. As in Australia, India, Latin America and the United States, British portfolio capital was used primarily to finance the construction of a

TABLE III – **Foreign Capital Invested in Canada, Selected Year Ends**
(book value of assets in millions of Canadian dollars)

	1867	1900	1913	1926	1939	1946	1952	1960	1964	1965
U.K. direct		65	200	336	366	335	544	1 535	1 944	2 013
portfolio	185	1 000	2 618	2 301	2 110	1 333	1 340	1 824	1 519	1 485
Total	*185*	*1 065*	*2 818*	*2 637*	*2 476*	*1 668*	*1 884*	*3 359*	*3 463*	*3 498*
U.S. direct	15	175	520	1 403	1 881	2 428	4 532	10 549	12 901	13 940
portfolio		30	315	1 793	2 270	2 729	3 466	6 169	8 542	9 365
Total	*15*	*205*	*835*	*3 196*	*4 151*	*5 157*	*7 998*	*16 718*	*21 443*	*23 305*
Other direct			50	43	49	63	144	788	1 044	1 255
portfolio		35	147	127	237	290	358	1 349	1 404	1 449
Total		*35*	*197*	*170*	*286*	*353*	*502*	*2 137*	*2 448*	*2 704*
All direct	15	240	770	1 782	2 296	2 826	5 220	12 872	15 889	17 208
All portfolio	185	1 065	3 080	4 221	4 617	4 352	5 164	9 342	11 465	12 299
GRAND TOTAL	200	1 305	3 850	6 003	6 913	7 178	10 384	22 214	27 354	29 507
Direct as percentage of total foreign investment	*7.5*	*18.5*	*20.0*	*30.0*	*33.5*	*39.0*	*50.0*	*58.0*	*58.0*	*58.3*
U.S. as percentage of total foreign investment	*7.5*	*15.5*	*21.5*	*53.0*	*60.0*	*72.0*	*77.0*	*75.0*	*78.5*	*79.0*

Source: Dominion Bureau of Statistics, *The Canadian Balance of International Payments, 1963, 1964 and 1965* and *International Investment Position*, p. 126, and *Quarterly Estimates of the Canadian Balance of International Payments, Third Quarter 1968*, p. 17.

TABLE IV – **Changes in Canadian Long-Term Indebtedness, Select Periods**
(in millions of Canadian dollars)

	U.K.	U.S. (Direct)	U.S. (Portfolio)	Other	Total
Formative years					
1867–1900 (33 years)	+880	+160	+30	+35	+1 105
Wheat economy					
1900–1913 (13 years)	+1 753	+345	+285	+162	+2 545
First World War					
1913–1926 (13 years)	−181	+883	+1 478	−27	+2 153
Breakdown of world economy					
1926–1939 (13 years)	−161	+478	+477	+116	+910
Second World War					
1939–1946 (7 years)	−808	+547	+459	+67	+265
Early postwar boom					
1946–1952 (6 years)	+216	+2 104	+737	+149	+3 208
Late postwar boom					
1952–1960 (8 years)	+1 475	+6 017	+2 703	+1 635	+11 830
The Sixties					
1960–1965 (5 years)	+139	+3 391	+3 196	+567	+7 293
TOTAL INFLOW (1867–1964)	+3 498	+13 940	+9 365	+2 704	+29 507
INFLOW 1952–1965 (13 years)	+1 614	+9 408	+5 899	+2 202	+19 123

Source: Derived from Table III

transcontinental system of communication geared to the growing markets for foodstuffs and agricultural raw material required by metropolitan industrialization in Europe. The borrowers were Canadian entrepreneurs, both public and private. Canada was indeed short of capital — but not of entrepreneurship. Control over commodity-producing sectors remained in Canadian hands. The number of well-known Canadian businesses established before the First World War bears testimony.

During the First World War and its aftermath, there was large-scale liquidation of British investments and a corresponding increase in American portfolio investment. As a result of British financial weakness and some acceleration of U.S. direct investment, American ownership of total foreign assets in Canada has topped the halfway mark at 53 per cent by 1926. Direct investment as a percentage of all foreign investment stood at 30 percent.

In the breakdown of world economy (1926–1939), the rate of foreign capital inflow slowed down in Canada, as everywhere else in the world. During these thirteen years the value of foreign assets increased by only $910 million, compared with the increase of $2153 million in the previous thirteen years or indeed the increase of $2545 million during the years of the wheat boom. British assets declined, while the book value of American direct investment continued to increase by $478 million, in spite of the Depression.

During the Second World War when Canada became a heavy net exporter of capital, foreign indebtedness increased by only $265 million, but American direct investment increased by $547 million, reflecting heavy liquidation of $808 million of British assets. By 1946 the American share of Canada's foreign liabilities had climbed to 72 per cent and direct investment liabilities accounted for close to 40 per cent of all Canada's external indebtedness.

The early stage of the postwar boom (1946–1952) was dominated by the

Korean War and the stock-piling of raw materials by the United States. Canada's foreign indebtedness rose by $3208 million in six years. Of these investments, two-thirds were in the form of U.S. direct investment, mainly in resource industries. By 1952, direct had exceeded portfolio investment, and the American share of Canada's foreign debt had reached 77 per cent.

The later stage of the postwar boom (1952–1960) witnessed the largest inflow of capital in Canada's history. Over half of the total increase in foreign liabilities of $11 830 million came in the form of U.S. direct investment ($6017 million), much of it in manufacturing. Portfolio borrowing also increased because the boom caused a severe shortage of capital in the public as well as the private sectors. Tight monetary conditions drove regional and local governments as well as corporations to New York to borrow funds. By 1960, 58 per cent of Canada's long-term indebtedness was in the form of direct investments. Forty-eight per cent of all foreign capital in Canada was directly controlled by American corporations.

577

In the sixties, there are indications of a change in the pattern of investment. Although half of the increased indebtedness of $7293 million in the five years 1960–1965 was U.S. direct investment, the share of Canada's debt represented by such investments had levelled off at 58 per cent. In part this is to be explained by the relative shift of U.S. direct investment toward Europe in the 1960s, and in part by the unusually heavy portfolio borrowings on the American capital market by provincial governments and corporations.

These briefly are the trends. Total reliance by Canada on foreign capital has declined. Yet the degree of dependence and the degree of control by metropolitan enterprise have increased. The key to this apparent paradox lies in the misleading practice of treating direct investments as capital inflows, presumed to be similar to portfolio borrowings. In fact, the element of capital transfer is only incidental to the process of direct investment, which involves a transfer of market organization, technology, and marketing channels. There is no explicit borrower, as in the case of portfolio capital. Direct investment comes for reasons of its own. Loans floated in foreign countries can, in due course, be redeemed, leaving no trace of foreign ownership. Direct investments have no necessary termination. Lenders of portfolio capital are attracted by a market rate of return. Direct investment capital comes for reasons which are quite different. Aitken has perceptively described the impact of direct investment on the Canadian economy:

Direct investments typically involve the extension into Canada of organizations based in other countries; these organizations establish themselves in Canada for purposes of their own and bring with them their own business practices, their own methods of production, their own skilled personnel, and very often their own market outlets. If all Canadian borrowings from other countries were to cease tomorrow, these direct investment organizations would continue to exist and function. Many of them, indeed, would continue to expand, financing their growth from retained earnings. And the corporate linkages which integrate them — and the sectors of the Canadian economy that they control — with organizations in other countries will survive.[5]

Notes

1. *The United States Balance of Payments*, An Appraisal of U.S. Economic Strategy, International Economic Policy Association (Washington, D.C., 1966), pp. 24, 25.
2. These figures exclude the estimated book value of foreign branch plants of Canadian enterprises which themselves are controlled abroad. The inclusion of these branch plants of branch plants would raise the value of direct investments in Canada from $17.2 billion in 1965 to $22.9 billion.
3. A. E. Safarian, *Foreign Ownership of Canadian Industry* (Toronto, 1966), p. 10.
4. Calculated by P. Hartland, and quoted in Aitken, *American Capital and Canadian Resources* (Cambridge: Harvard University Press, 1961), p. 60.
5. Aitken, pp. 66–67.

Movements of Protest in Postwar Canadian Society*

578 ## S.D. CLARK

Though the decade of the 1960's has just now come to an end, it may not be too soon to attempt to seek some understanding of those forces of social unrest and protest which, in our society as elsewhere, have attracted so much attention in the years since the decade's beginning. The decade began with the ushering in of that state of political and social ferment in French Canada which has found its clearest expression in the movement directed towards the separation of the province of Quebec from the federal union. If the clamourings of dissent have been less shrill in other parts of the country, they have nevertheless been sufficiently loud and persistent to make themselves clearly heard. The rise of a hippy cult among the young people of our larger cities, the development on our university campuses of a militant student movement, the increasing readiness of dissident farmer and labour groups to resort to violent forms of protest, the new militancy of such professional groups as teachers and nurses, the stirring movement of native Indian protest in fringe areas of the north, offer themselves only as some of the more striking examples of a type of social protest against established authority which appears today to have become so widespread in our society.

It is easy to dismiss these movements of unrest and protest in Canada as simply emanations of movements growing up across the border in the United States. Certainly, there has been a strong connection between what has been happening in Canadian society and what has been happening in American, and Canadians may have some cause for annoyance about the work among the more restless elements of our population by agitators from outside the country, particularly when violence results. But the existence of a connection with outside movements offers no explanation for the development of movements of unrest and protest here; if it did, there would be nothing that

*From *Transactions of the Royal Society of Canada*, Series 4, Vol. 8, 1970, pp. 223–237. Reprinted by permission of the author and The Royal Society of Canada.

has happened in Canadian history that could not be explained in this manner. If the troublous occurrences of the 1960's are to be understood, it is to an examination of developments within our own society that we must turn. Many of these developments had their beginnings with the Second World War.

It is not necessary here to detail the many far-reaching changes that have taken place in Canadian society since the Second World War came to an end. The sheer growth of Canada's population from twelve million to twenty million people, the large-scale shift of population out of rural into urban areas, the crowding into our larger cities of great masses of immigrants from Europe, the mass movement of population from the cities to the suburbs, the change in the age composition of the Canadian population, the increased importance of such forms of industrial and business enterprise as house-building, construction, and household finance offering new opportunities for economic advancement, the opening up of new areas of economic enterprise and the establishment of new centres of urban development in northern regions, the upgrading of the labour force with technological developments and the increase in the numbers of women working, and the growth in the number and proportion of young people attending post-secondary institutions of education have been developments which offer some indication of the dimension of the changes taking place in Canadian society. What has occurred represents more than changes in the scale of Canadian society — a larger population, bigger cities, more young people going to university. Changes in scale have brought with them changes in the quality of Canadian social life. It is perhaps no exaggeration to say that the Second World War marked the end of the old order of Canadian society. What we have been witnessing in the years since is a wave or avalanche of social changes which, for the country as a whole, not inappropriately may be called "a quiet revolution."

579

In terms of the concern of this paper, the most significant development growing out of the changes taking place in Canadian society since the Second World War has been the sudden emergence of new large bodies of the population, what might here be called publics, actively involving themselves in the political and social affairs of the nation at large. Canadian society before the war could be described as one composed of a very narrow and almost self-perpetuating urban middle class and a very large rural and working class within which there were offered few opportunities for economic and social advancement. John Porter's Vertical Mosaic offers perhaps as good a portrayal as any of the chief characteristics of Canadian society as it once was. If read as a supplement to the work of H.A. Innis, it serves to show how the nature of economic development of the country led to the creation of a social system in which a large proportion of the population stood outside and divorced from the main areas of economic and social activity. The exploitation of the nation's wealth-producing resources became lodged largely in the hands of great, powerful corporate enterprises located in the major centres.

There did develop, of course, at various times in Canada's history, areas of economic activity in which individual enterprise played an important part and out of which there grew strong forces of social change. The breakdown of the monopoly control of the fur trade in the years immediately after 1660 and again after 1760, the early establishment of the lumbering industry in New Brunswick and Upper Canada, and of the mining industry in British Columbia, the Yukon, and northern Ontario and Quebec, and the opening up of the wheat-farming areas of Western Ontario after 1850 and of Western Canada after 1900 offer examples of developments where for a time economic activity broke through the bounds of corporate control. But the forces favouring large-scale forms of economic organization and centralized control soon asserted themselves, even in areas of development such as these. It was basically a bureaucratically structured type of society which Canada produced. Within such a society there were offered few opportunities for advancement to the higher levels of the organizational structure, in business, politics, education, religion, and community affairs. The stability of this society over the years could be maintained by large-scale emigration to the United States. As immigrants or migrants from rural areas filled up the lower levels of the social hierarchy, the pressure upon the higher levels was relieved by the movement of people across the border. The consequence was that large sections of the Canadian population could remain permanently isolated from the secondary structure of the society, dependent largely upon primary group forms of social organization and fellowship developing from within themselves.

For purposes of the present discussion, prior to the Second World War six such segments or blocs of the Canadian population may be identified: the population of French Canada; the large rural immigrant population of the western prairies; the population of those extensive marginal farming and fishing areas which extended from Newfoundland, Cape Breton, and eastern New Brunswick through northern Quebec and Ontario to central Manitoba and into Saskatchewan and Alberta; the new growing masses of unskilled workers gathering within and on the outskirts of our industrial centres; the native Indian and Métis population; and, finally, suffering legal as well as economic and social disabilities, the women and the young people of the nation. Though there was considerable overlapping in the composition of these six population groups, taken together they constituted nevertheless a sizable proportion of the total Canadian population. If some other smaller identifiable groups were added, such as the racial minorities, the proportion would be even larger.

All of these segments of the population had at least two things in common. The one was that they lacked the capacity within themselves to participate in any really meaningful way in the economic, political, and social affairs of the country. They had the character of political blocs rather than of publics. That is to say, they acted in terms of a collective judgment, dictated by custom or a traditional authority, rather than in terms of individual judgments. Thus one could speak of a French-Canadian bloc, a farm bloc, or an ethnic bloc in the years before the Second World War. The actions of such segments of the population were highly predictable for the reason that, for the most part, such actions did not arise out of group debate and the decisions of autonomous individuals. Behaviour was an expression of the ethos of the group.

The second thing these segments of the population had in common was closely related to the first. They constituted distinctive cultural islands within the larger Canadian society. In their values and social attitudes, and, indeed, as well, in their manner of speech, dress, and behaviour, there was no mistaking these people. In truth, before the Second World War, the Canadian society had very much the character of a social mosaic. The assimilative forces of the urban middle class culture extended only very little beyond the bounds of the tight little urban complexes that housed the middle class society. Even as late as the Second World War there was much that remained about the Canadian urban community that had the character of the military fort or company town. The population that spread out from the urban core, into those working class residential areas immediately adjacent and beyond into rural areas, shared only in a very small way in the dominant urban middle class culture and way of life.

581

It is the contention of this paper that the social unrest of the years since the Second World War has grown out of the social situation created by the developments of the postwar period, where the barriers to mobility characteristic of the prewar society have to a very great extent broken down. What resulted has been the unleashing of new, powerful assimilative forces in society and a very great mixing up of the Canadian population. Many of those segments of the population which formerly had been largely isolated from the mainstream of Canadian life have been drawn into urban middle class society and become involved in the problems and the affairs of the world at large. What once were cultural blocs of the population have now taken on much of the character of political publics.

In seeking, however, to relate the growth of social unrest to this breaking down of barriers to mobility within postwar Canadian society, we immediately confront what appears to be a social contradiction. Instead of an increased involvement in the affairs of the society at large, what seems to be sought by people, wherever social protest develops, is a dropping out, a separation from the society at large. Thus the French seek to separate from the English, the West from the East, the suburbs from the city, the native Indians from the Whites, and, in a manner like that elsewhere in the Western World, young people from old and women from men. The rhetoric of social protest plays upon the differences between people. The separatist movement in French Canada seeks justification in the belief that a wide cultural gulf separates the French from the English; the demands of youth become caught up in the concept of the generation gap; suburban residents plead the lack of understanding of city governments divorced from their problems and needs; Western Canada urges the distinctive character of its wheat economy (now giving way to other forms of economic enterprise) as the reason for threatening to withdraw from the federal union; the new red power ideologists argue the inherent distinctiveness (and superiority) of the native Indian's way of life in mounting a campaign to preserve it; even women, in the ideology of new left feminists, claim a physiological and cultural make-up so different from that of men that their true nature can be realized only by the separation of their world from the world of men.

It could scarcely be denied that there are important differences that separate people. There is no mistaking young people from old, or women from men, and the physiologist's or ethnologist's measuring instruments are hardly necessary to distinguish between French and English, suburban residents and city dwellers, native Indians and Whites. Yet, if the situation now is compared with that of fifty, or even twenty-five years ago, what is apparent is that the differences between people, rather than increasing, have markedly diminished.

582

Youth offers a striking example. We have heard much in recent years about the generation gap. So persuasive has been the belief that there has developed a gap between the younger and older generations that the assumptions upon which it is based have been little questioned. We live in a world, the argument goes, changing so rapidly that people who grew up twenty-five or more years ago can have no understanding of the needs and problems of young people growing up today. Theirs is a world entirely different. There develops easily out of this notion of the generation gap the whole range of demands made by youth spokesmen. Whether what is being questioned is the teaching programs of our universities, the laws administered by our courts, or simply the bewildering efforts of parents to provide for the wants of their children, resort can readily be had to the doctrine that only the young people themselves are qualified to prescribe for their needs. What may be relevant for the world of the adult has no relevance for the world into which young people have moved, or so we are led to believe.

It is true that youth today finds itself in a world undergoing rapid change. The effect of this change, however, has not been to widen the gap between youth and adults, but to narrow it. What has happened is the sudden catapulting of young people into the adult world.

It will be argued that young people years ago grew up faster than they do today; they were, many of them, farmers, fishermen, lumbermen, before they were twenty. Now the young person may be twenty-five or more before he is ready to earn his livelihood. Such an argument, however, overlooks two important facts. First is the fact that the young person growing up to become a farmer, fisherman, or lumberman fifty years or so ago moved scarcely at all out of the narrow and circumscribed world of his childhood. Participation in the wider world of business, politics, and community affairs was largely denied him, whether as a young person or as an adult. The second fact that tends to get overlooked is that growing up has no necessary relationship to earning a livelihood. Young people can be part of an adult world and yet be far from ready to earn their own livelihood. Such would certainly appear to be true of our young people today.

The effect of the developments of the past quarter century within our society has been to break down the barriers separating youth from adults. In truth, fifty years ago one could speak of a generation gap, a youth culture. Young people were then not expected to share in the interests and experiences of adults. They had no ready means by which they could acquire the sort of knowledge adults possessed. If, on occasion, they tried to behave like grown-ups, their manner of dress, behaviour, and speech, and their limited understanding of the world about, made evident the great gulf that separated them from adult society, and particularly from the society of adult males. Children shared much of the shyness of their mothers with respect to the affairs of men.

In the changes that have been taking place within our present-day society there have been brought together a generational revolution and a social class revolution. The generational revolution has had its beginnings in the changed situation in the home. Here, with the growing importance of the mass media and the penetration of the influence of outside educational bodies, the young person has become exposed to almost the whole range of knowledge and experience of the grown-up. The late show on television may still protect the young from things they ought not to know, but scarcely more than in a symbolic way. It would not be easy today to define the boundaries of an adult universe of discourse from which the young are excluded.

Children grow up fast in the modern home. It is not in the home, however, but in the high school and university that the really important social revolution has occurred in the years since the Second World War. The phenomenal increase in the proportion of young people going on to high school and university has been a development in itself of considerable social significance. Even more significant, however, has been the role of the high school and university in breaking down the ethnic and social class barriers separating people. Our secondary and post-secondary institutions of education have come to constitute the chief melting-pot in our postwar Canadian society. Within the society as a whole there has been a rising up of people in the economic and social hierarchy, partly by the shift of people to a higher occupational stratum, partly by a social upgrading of occupations. To a considerable extent, however, the barriers to the mixing of people of different social background, and especially where social class differences have been reinforced by ethnic differences, have remained intact. Residential segregation has acted to check forces of assimilation even when economic circumstances have changed. Within the high school and university, however, barriers to the mixing up of people have come near to completely breaking down. Here the whole population has been pitched, suddenly and completely, into an urban middle class society, and in numbers very great.

It has been the coming together of these two forces of change, the sudden breaking down of the barriers separating young people from adults, and the equally sudden breaking down of the barriers separating people of different social class and ethnic background, that has made our high schools and universities such important centres of dissent. An increasing number of young people, through high school and university attendance, are now finding themselves very much involved in the affairs of the world at large. They have acquired a type of citizenship which imposes upon them the obligations of the adult.

Yet they have carried into this adult middle class society the disadvantages of their age and, for many of them, their social background. Young people find themselves in the adult world, even though this adult world assumes they are still too young to accept the responsibilities of adulthood. The position of dependency forced upon the young person in high school or university as a consequence of his being unable to earn his own livelihood acts strongly to limit the adult privileges accorded him, but the disadvantages suffered by young people arise out of a social situation that extends far beyond the dependency relationship of the high school or university student. It reaches out to the state, with its denial of citizenship to persons under twenty-one, and back into the family, and the retention there of forms of parental authority which are a product of a former age. Where such disadvantages associated with age become joined to disadvantages associated with ethnic or social class origin, the malaise experienced can become acute.

It has been among the most mature of these young people, among those most fully assimilated to the values and ways of life of the adult world, that the expression of this malaise has gathered the greatest force. Thus there has developed the apparent social contradiction that the more like adults young people become the more stress they place upon their differences. Like all disadvantaged minorities, young people can only press their claim for a greater share of society's privileges by giving emphasis to those qualities that distinguish them from others. Distinctive manners of speech, dress, and conduct become important means of setting young people apart, as a group. In the ideology of youth protest there is much that is remindful of religious sectarianism and its damning of the world beyond it as one of sin and evil, the world of anti-Christ. What the young seek are privileges now enjoyed by their elders, but they can only advance their claim to these privileges by discrediting those who now hold them. Such is the strategy of all protest. It would do the university student, for instance, little good to seek a greater share in university administration by urging the extent of his experience while admitting to the still greater experience of those whose authority he challenges. The student challenge is made a threat because it grows out of the conviction that the experience of the generation who are now students has a greater value than that of the generation who have passed beyond student years. The conviction serves to strengthen the force of the challenge but even more to weaken the resistance of the challenged. The older generation has let itself be persuaded that its experience, indeed, is not relevant to the problems the younger generation faces.

The hippy cult exemplifies in extreme form the way in which the effort of young people to make a place for themselves in the adult world has led to their apparent rejection of this world. It has been very largely middle class young people who have become caught up in the hippy movement. These

584

have been the young people who are the most sophisticated, urbane, the most exposed, particularly in the family situation, to the adult social world. At the same time, they have been the young people who perhaps more than any others have been made to suffer the disadvantages of youth. The parents of these young people have attained their middle class social position by a variety of means: some by inheriting family businesses, some by qualifying themselves professionally, some by successfully building up new businesses, some by financial speculation. Whatever the means by which they attained their middle class social position, however, they have been of the view that, given the conditions of economic advancement in the postwar world, the only way to ensure that their children maintain the social position they have achieved is by education. Any other form of preparation for participation in the adult world would be so fraught with risks that it could not be contemplated. The time was when the young man of nineteen could go to sea, or try his hand at various jobs, and settle down in his mid-twenties to become a successful businessman (or, indeed, a professional). Increasingly, however, the opportunities open to people have become dictated by the needs of a bureaucratic structure, and nowhere more so than for those seeking a middle class social position. Thus it has been in our society that the range of choice of a vocation has been the most restricted for the body of young people who are the most socially and intellectually mature. The son of the farmer or workingman could choose education as one of various means of equipping himself for life in an adult world, but the son of the middle class parent has been given no choice.

Within the hippy cult, thus, protest becomes directed very much not only at the adult world but at the world of the middle class as well. Dropping out means repudiating the route to middle class social status: accepting the discipline of education, and acquiring the manners, the form of speech, the values of the middle class adult. Around the act of dropping out is built a whole set of beliefs and acts directed to the end of unmistakably setting the hippy apart from his middle class fellowmen. Because he is, indeed, so middle class in his way of upbringing, and so adult in his range of knowledge and social demeanour, the effort to appear different forces him to resort to highly extreme manners of dress, speech, and behaviour. The farm boy, struggling to rid himself of the awkward ways of dressing, speaking, and behaving carried with him from his rural society, may be left wondering about the efforts of the city boy intent on making himself more socially awkward than he was as a farm boy when he took his first step into the urban middle class social world. What he is not likely to appreciate, however, is how the middle class young person can feel trapped in the very social system that assures him of his middle class social status. It is no accident that the feeling of being trapped has developed most strongly among young people in those minority ethnic groups which have experienced a swift rise to middle class status. Here the highly hazardous means employed by the older generation to secure social advancement has made education vital as a way of maintaining within the newer generation the status achieved.

585

It has been only a very small number of young people who have been attracted into the hippy movement, but the indictment of urban middle class society which finds such clear expression within the hippy philosophy has won widespread endorsement. Symbols of middle class affluence have been made objects of derision and condemnation. Much of this denunciation of the middle class way of life has been caught up in the language of social reform. It is made to appear to develop out of a concern for the welfare of the poor, the down-trodden, the less socially fortunate. In the protestations of young people generally there is built up an image of middle class society as one that is wholly given up to the pursuit of materialist ends.

It would, of course, be unfair to suggest that young people have had no genuine interest in the cause of social reform. The ideology of youth protest has made a strong appeal because it could draw upon that large store of human sympathy and idealism which all young people possess. The indictment of middle class society has led to the pointing up of very real faults in this society. One might note the current attention being given to the problem of pollution, the public concern about which owes much to the fervour of young people in attacking what they have come to view as a major social evil. What is important to recognize, however, in seeking an understanding of youth protest, is that the indictment of middle class society does not arise out of a concern about particular faults of this society but rather that the concern about particular faults arises out of the indictment of the society.

Youth protest, whether of the sort manifested on university and high school campuses or within the hippy cult, represents only one of the many forms of social protest which have made themselves felt in Canadian postwar society. The protest of youth has importance not only because it exemplifies so clearly the nature of protest movements in general but because it has cut across a great many of the other areas of protest in Canadian society — French Canada, the native Indian population, the new ethnic minorities, the disadvantaged professional groups, the service occupations.

In turning attention to these other areas of social unrest, what becomes evident is that here, as in the case of young people, it has been the sudden breaking down of the barriers isolating great bodies of the population from the affairs of the society at large that accounts for the unrest even though, where protest has developed, it has taken the form of seeking withdrawal from the larger society. It is easy to be taken in by the rhetoric of protest, whether it comes from youth and their talk about the generation gap, or from various other socially disadvantaged groups and their talk about cultural pluralism. A term such as assimilation has become, even in the language of the social scientist, a word of opprobrium. We speak now of a "mosaic" when all the forces in our society are directed to reducing the cultural differences that separate people. Thus, fifty years ago, the European immigrant, located largely in the rural areas of Western Canada or in the mining towns of northern Ontario or Quebec, was very much divorced from Canadian urban middle class society. So as well was the population of French Canada, apart from a small minority, and, whether of immigrant,

586

French, or Anglo-Saxon origin, the large unskilled labouring masses gathered in the growing industrial cities. What the developments of the postwar period have done is to propel great numbers of these and other elements of the population into urban middle class society.

It has been this sudden move upwards into the middle class of large bodies of people that has given such social significance to the new residential developments of the city since 1950. The suburbs, and the new high-rise apartment house complexes, have been, next in importance only to the universities, the great gathering places of the new middle classes. As would be expected, it has been people of Anglo-Saxon origin who have led the way into these new residential areas of the city. People of Anglo-Saxon origin, of rural or working class background, were the first recruits to urban middle class society as the forces of economic growth made themselves felt in the years after the war. Over the years since 1950, however, the composition of the new urban residential population has undergone a significant change. In the province of Quebec, a growing proportion of this population has become French Canadian; in other parts of Canada, and as well in the province of Quebec, it has come to be made up increasingly of people of diverse ethnic and racial background. The two metropolitan communities of Montreal and Toronto have felt most fully the effects of the change in the composition of the population, but, wherever in Canada urban growth has occurred, there has been a move upwards in economic and social status of large bodies of the population.

587

What has been produced by urban growth has been a number of new publics. Suddenly, in a manner almost as if overnight, many thousands of people, locating in the new, growing residential areas of the city, have found themselves involved in the affairs of society at large — the urban community, the province and nation, the world beyond. These have been, for the most part, people who previously had not been called upon to concern themselves with matters beyond their immediate primary group, their family, neighbourhood, circle of friends, or fellow-workers. A very large number of them had been young people only just entering the labour force and acquiring politically the right to vote. Many of them had moved out of occupations, or rural or urban residential areas, where they had developed no strong sense of responsibility for the affairs of the community at large. Still others had been largely isolated, socially and politically, within ethnic enclaves. Urban growth has operated as a powerful force of social mobility, but it has operated also, and in a very important way, as a social levelling force. People settling in the new residential areas of the city — in the suburbs and in the high-rise apartment house complexes — have moved up in the social hierarchy, but, in moving up, they have lost many of those social characteristics that gave them distinctiveness as social groups. Everyone in these new residential areas of the city has become an urban middle class person; everyone, that is to say, except those people locating in areas that developed as exclusively working class areas, or areas set apart for the urban poor or the urban rich.

In assessing the nature and extent of unrest in Canadian society since the Second World War, it could hardly be suggested that the great masses of people crowding into the new growing suburban areas or into the high-rise apartment house complexes have been a strong force of dissent. These are people who could be described with good reason as conservative. But so, it should be noted, and for reasons not greatly different, could the population of young people be so described, even that of the universities. People settling in the new residential areas of the city, like young people, have been persons on the make, and this striving to get ahead has given to them a character of conservatism. Nevertheless, not unlike young people, the new urban residential population has been one suffering certain disadvantages, and this has been particularly true of those elements of the population which, because of their ethnic or social background, have found themselves, while being pulled into the urban middle class society, not made fully a part of it. The suburban community of St Leonards outside the City of Montreal offers a far from isolated example of such a population. Wherever in Canada urban growth has occurred there has been a catching up in the forces of mobility-generated elements of the Canadian population which, now suddenly approaching middle class social status, have been made to feel their disadvantaged position.

588

Among such elements of the population, feelings of unease, social alienation, or disaffection have found expression in various ways and forms. Under conditions producing feelings of intense hostility there may be a blind striking out in all directions. In situations where alienation is only barely felt, however, the protestation may assume the form simply of talking vaguely about "they" or "them" as the persons responsible for what appears to be ailing. Whatever the particular form, the expression of feelings of disaffection in all cases becomes directed at the world outside, the world in which people are becoming caught up. It is only, however, with the development of an ideology that this world takes clear shape and can be made an object of attack. Thus, for the French-Canadian separatist, the world outside that is made to appear a threat to what he holds dear is that of English-speaking Canada. For the left-wing political activist, it is American society. For the red power advocate, the society of the white man. Though the indictment takes on a particular reference, for particular elements of the population — English Canada, American society, the society of the white man — what in reality are being attacked are the values and ways of life of urban middle class society. It is this society that is made to represent the world outside from which it is necessary to withdraw if salvation is to be attained.

Thus the advocates of red power, though some of them may boast university degrees as distinguished as the Ph.D., would have their fellow Canadian Indians throw off the ways of the white man and return to the simple life of their native past; a form of garb, unmistakably Indian in cut and material, is made to serve as a symbol of the Indian's distinctive culture. In French Canada, language has become the chief rallying point in the growing demand for separation; without a language difference, nothing much remains to distinguish the middle class French Canadian from the middle class English Canadian. For the new left political movement, the appeal has depended upon creating the idea that Canadian values and the Canadian way of life are different from the American and can only be preserved by resisting the inroads of American values of ways of life.

This play upon their differences, and seeking to withdraw from the world outside, become important strategies of protest for any disadvantaged social group. Canadian Indians would certainly face disaster if they acted seriously upon the urgings of their red power leaders, but if Indians are to secure a redress of the social wrongs done them, the most effective means is by developing a militant sense of group identity. The same can be said of the French-Canadian separatist movement, or any movement of protest that has developed out of a situation where the population suffers certain disadvantages. Black power in the United States offers a striking example of how a disadvantaged social group is compelled to resort to the weapon of social withdrawal as a way of asserting its rights. The more the forces of social change lead to a breaking down of the barriers to participation in the wider society the more urgent becomes the need to develop symbolic forms which give emphasis to the distinctiveness of those elements of the population which are disadvantaged. Thus, in no paradoxical fashion, the identity of Canadian nationhood has grown in strength out of those very social forces that have been made to appear a threat to its existence.

589

Yet, if the concern is for the welfare of the individual rather than that of the group, account has to be taken of the price paid by the effort to secure the withdrawal of disadvantaged population elements from the world outside. The ideology of hippyism has given to the group of young people caught up in this movement a very strong sense of distinctiveness, and, in weighing the impact of the movement upon society, the very characteristics which have made it appear objectionable have been those which have made it an influential social force. But for many of the young people drawn into the hippy movement, particularly of lower, or working class social background, the price paid has been a very heavy one. A movement of social protest inevitably engenders within it powerful vested interests. Unfortunately, from the point of view of the mass of the following, it is those persons who have the least to lose from the act of withdrawal who come to exert the greatest influence in promoting the cause of withdrawal. They are the ones most fully assimilated into the urban middle class culture.

The student protest movement offers a good example. The spokesmen for this movement, for the most part, have been young middle class people brought up in homes stocked with books, and in families with an academic or professional tradition, who have had no cause to be greatly concerned about their future careers. Because they have been highly middle class in their manner of life and range of knowledge, they have been the ones who have felt most keenly the disadvantages of youth. In leading the attack upon the structure of the university they could thus demonstrate a high degree of competence in judging for themselves the worth of various academic offerings. In courses of study where the content and the evaluation of performance are left to the student's own determining, the experience gained by a person possessed of a sound intellectual discipline can be highly rewarding. The Oxford undergraduate, in the time when none but the élite of English society found their way to university, had little need of professors, prescribed programs of study, reading lists, and examinations.

In the recent restructuring of our Canadian universities, the lead has been taken by those students who because of their intellectual and social background have stood to suffer little personally from the breaking down of prescribed programs of study, formal methods of teaching, and objective evaluation procedures, but the restructuring has made a strong appeal to the general student body for the reason that this has been a student body with no strong intellectual tradition and which, as a consequence, has found attractive means of escaping the rigorous discipline of the learning process. In the years since the war, an increasing proportion of the Canadian university population has been drawn from the ranks of the working and new middle classes. Thus the very social conditions which have made decisive leadership on the part of the universities important, have resulted in the serious weakening of that leadership. Ironically enough, in attacking the university as an elitist institution, what our student radicals have produced is a university more elitist still. It is a university designed to serve the needs of a select body of middle class students, without regard for the needs of the large body of students who lack the means to take advantage of a type of educational experience which leaves very largely to the individual the determination of the character of his instruction.

What protest has essentially meant, whether voiced by student leaders, French-Canadian separatists, red power advocates, or, in its most extreme form, by the prophets of the hippy cult, has been an attack upon the means of qualifying for full participation in the urban middle class society. The protest had justification in injustices suffered. Redress required the development of a sense of group identity on the part of the socially disadvantaged, and such a development could come about only by a repudiation of the urban middle class society into which people were being drawn. To the extent, however, that the repudiation of the middle class society has been acted upon, the effect has been to cripple the individual's capacity to achieve full middle class status. A great number of those young people who have endorsed the hippy philosophy will never recover, or be able to achieve, the kind of middle class security, well-being, and health which they have been led to scorn. The still unresolved struggle between the separatist and labour movements in the province of Quebec grows out of the simple issue of the extent to which the individual should be left free to seize whatever opportunities for advancement are offered him, without regard to the consequences upon language and culture. The middle class leaders of the separatist movement may have much to gain by destroying the English-speaking establishment, and making of themselves a new establishment, but for the people as a whole the gains are problematic. Likewise, the effort of Canadian Indian leaders to preserve the isolation of their people within the larger society can be seen to serve their interests as Indian leaders and makes understandable their bitter opposition to the government white paper on Indian policy, but the consequences, if the effort succeeds, may be costly to the Indian people. On the larger Canadian national front, as well, ordinary people, industrial workers, farmers, and such, may have good reason to pause and consider the consequences upon their welfare of the current attack upon the penetration into the country of American economic and cultural influences made by middle class political and intellectual leaders whose standard of living would not seriously suffer from a policy of economic and social isolation and who can aspire to becoming a part of the new Canadian establishment. What Canadians want is to enjoy the same middle class way of life Americans enjoy, but the new left-wing ideology of Canadian nationalism would have Canadians be persuaded that this way of life is one that should be rejected.

But such, it must be said, is the way of revolutions, and the world has been better for at least some of them. The destroying of an old establishment leads to the creation of a new one, and for the people as a whole there may appear little improvement. The French-Canadian workers of Quebec Hydro now have to fight a management that is French Canadian. The time perhaps is not far distant when university students will discover that governing councils composed of students can be as authoritarian, as ill-considered in their judgments, as governing councils composed of faculty. But what is important, in any revolution, is its effect in destroying the privileged position within the social system undergoing revolution of particular classes or groups of persons. It would be hard to deny the important role protest has played in improving the position within the Canadian political structure of the French-Canadian people. It may come hard for a faculty member to admit it, but it is possible that, however dearly the present generation of students will pay for the damage done, in the long run our universities will be the better for the upheaval they have been experiencing.

591

Topic Fifteen
Regionalism

592   The existence of regions is basic to the study of Canadian history. However defined, these regions have had unique identities which have set them apart from each other, and at times in opposition to the aspirations of the central government — and to the existence of a national identity.

Canadian historians, geographers and literary critics have long debated the nature and characteristics of Canada's regions. Initially they were defined in geographical terms: the North, the Pacific, the Prairies, Central Canada, and the Atlantic. It was believed that the unique environmental features of each area dictated the characteristics of its people and defined its distinctive culture. This "environmental determinist" approach, however, failed to take into account how Canadian regions have changed through history.

A new and dynamic approach to regionalism has emerged which defines regions in terms of their relationship to each other, and especially to the nation as a whole. Regions are not static, but dynamic functional entities which change over time, due to their historical evolution, and their associations with other regions, and with the central government.

The following readings recognize the historical evolution of Canadian regions since World War II. They deal with the nature of four "regions" of Canada — the North, the West, Quebec, and Atlantic Canada — attempting to show their similarities to other Canadian regions, and at the same time, their uniqueness, due to their own historical development. In "The North in Canadian History: An Outline," Richard Diubaldo discusses the changing images of the North and how the region had gradually taken on greater importance. Gerald Friesen in "The Prairie West Since 1945: An Historical Survey" examines the ways in which the modern West of the post-World War II era has become more like the rest of the modern world, and yet at the same time, has retained, and indeed strengthened, its regional identity. In "French Canada and English Canada: Conflict and Coexistence," Richard Jones reviews the historical evolution of Quebec since the 1960s, in terms of this region's association with the rest of Canada. David Alexander in "Canadian Regionalism: A Central Problem," raises some general questions about the nature of Canadian regionalism from the vantage point of present-day Atlantic Canada.

On the general subject of Canadian regionalism see "Regionalism/Le Regionalisme," a special issue of the *Journal of Canadian Studies*, 15 (Summer 1980), and *Perspectives on Regions and Regionalism in Canada/Perspectives sur les regions et le regionalisme au Canada*, edited with an introduction by William Westfall (Ottawa: The Association for Canadian Studies, 1983), as well as Mason Wade, ed., *Regionalism in the Canadian Community 1867–1967* (Toronto: University of Toronto Press, 1969). The historical association of the West and Atlantic regions with Canada is examined in D. Bercuson and P.A. Buckner, eds., *Eastern and Western Perspectives* (Toronto: University of Toronto Press, 1981). A classic view of Canadian regionalism still remains Goldwin Smith's *Canada and the Canadian Question* (1891), reprinted in the *Social History of Canada* series (Toronto: University of Toronto Press, 1971).

On the question of defining the North see W.L. Morton's "The 'North' in Canadian Historiography," *Royal Society of Canada, Transactions*, Series 4, vol. 8 (1970): p. 31–40. The image of the North is the subject of Chapter 1 of Louis-Edmond Hamelin's *Canadian Nordicity: It's Your North, Too* (Montreal: Harvest House, 1979), while Carl Berger's "The True North Strong and Free," in *Nationalism in Canada*, edited by Peter Russell (Toronto: McGraw-Hill, 1966), pp. 3–26, deals with the symbolic importance of the North in Canadian history. The most comprehensive history of the early North is Morris Zaslow's *The Opening of the Canadian North: 1870–1914* (Toronto: McClelland and Stewart, 1971), which includes an excellent bibliography.

On the modern West see the relevant chapters in Gerald Friesen's *The Prairies: A History* (Toronto: University of Toronto Press, 1984), and the collection of essays in A.W. Rasporich, ed., *The Making of the Modern West: Western Canada Since 1945* (Calgary: University of Calgary Press, 1984), from which the Friesen reading is taken. An interesting account of the decline of regionalism in the modern West is R. Gibbin's *Prairie Politics and Society: Regionalism and Decline* (Toronto: Butterworths, 1980).

For overviews of Quebec since World War II consult: Kenneth McRoberts and Dale Posgate's *Quebec: Social Change and Political Crisis*, revised edition (Toronto: McClelland and Stewart, 1980); Henry and Sheilagh Milner's *The Decolonization of Quebec* (Toronto: McClelland and Stewart, 1973), and Henry Milner's *Politics in the New Quebec* (Toronto: McClelland and Stewart, 1978).

Denis Monière reviews the development of political thought in Quebec, in *Le developpement des ideologies au Québec: des origines à nos jours* (Montréal: Editions Quebec/Amerique, 1977), which has been translated as *Ideologies in Quebec: The Historical Development*, by Richard Howard (Toronto: University of Toronto Press, 1981).

Quebec's past, present, and future, is examined by sociologist Marcel

Rioux in *La Question du Québec* (Paris: Seghers, 1969), translated into English as *Quebec in Question* by James Boake (Toronto: James Lewis and Samuel, 1971). Historian Ramsay Cook's views on the Quebec question are presented in "The Paradox of Quebec," in *Entering the Eighties: Canada in Crisis*, edited by R.K. Carty and W.P. Ward, (Toronto: Oxford, 1980) pp. 46–59; and "Has the Quiet Revolution Finally Ended?" *Queen's Quarterly*, 90 (Summer, 1983): pp. 330–342.

Two recent studies of Quebec politics in the late 1970s and early 1980s are Graham Fraser's *P.Q.: René Levesque and the Parti Québécois in Power* (Toronto: Macmillan, 1984) and L. Ian MacDonald, *From Bourassa to Bourassa: A Pivotal Decade in Canadian History* (Montreal: Harvest House, 1984).

David Alexander's writings on Atlantic Canada are available in *Atlantic Canada and Confederation: Essays in Canadian Political Economy*, compiled by E. Sager, L. Fischer, and S.O. Pierson (Toronto: University of Toronto Press, 1983). On the history of the Atlantic region see the journal *Acadiensis* (1971–   ). A volume of essays on post-Confederation Atlantic Canada, drawn from back issues of *Acadiensis* is available: *Volume Two: The Atlantic Provinces After Confederation* (University of New Brunswick, Fredericton, Acadiensis Press, 1985).

594

The North in Canadian History: An Outline*
RICHARD J. DIUBALDO

The summer of 1980 witnessed the celebration of the 100th Anniversary of the transfer of the Arctic Islands from Great Britain to Canada. The occasion was marked with a number of events including a symposium sponsored by the Royal Society of Canada and held in Yellowknife, N.W.T., and symbolic trips and speeches made by the Governor-General of Canada. On the whole, however, the events went unnoticed in the south, which takes the northern reaches of Canada and its people, native and white alike, for granted. It is as though there exists an attitude similar to the one expressed by Lord Durham in the late 1830s regarding the history and culture of French Canadian society. In this case it is the north which appears to have no history, no deserved uniqueness. It remains a frozen, desolate and barren wilderness in the nation's consciousness.

Most often the terms "North" and "Arctic" have been used interchangeably, accepted as synonymous, but that is incorrect. Strictly speaking, the Arctic is the area north of 66°30′N. latitude (i.e. the Arctic Circle), the line above which the sun would not rise in the winter solstice, nor set in the summer solstice, but conditions above and below that latitude vary to such a degree that other definitions have been put forward in an attempt to give

*From *Fram*: The Journal of Polar Studies, (1984 Winter Issue): 187–196. Reprinted by permission.

some precision. Besides, Canada's north is more than just her Arctic. Efforts to demarcate the north, though, have added to the general confusion, and one can only highlight a few of these propositions to illustrate the problem of what and where the north is.

The line of permafrost, the presence of perenially frozen ground below the surface, can be used to delimit the region, yet not all would accept this concept simply because of the discontinuous nature of permafrost in more southerly latitudes. Temperature, too, has its limitations because there has never been universal agreement as to which isotherms should be employed: mean winter temperatures; the growing temperature, etc. The same can be said for the use of the treeline as a boundary as it, too, is open to dispute. To these essentially geological and climactic factors, we could add human and economic definitions: the extent and limit of commercial agriculture or the accessibility of the area to the "outside" world, and the nature and density of communication and transportation networks. In fact, over twenty criteria have been used to delineate the "North" and it becomes obvious, at least from a geographer's point of view, that a combination of select elements is necessary. It has fallen to one of Canada's foremost geographers, Louis Edmond Hamelin, to attempt the task. Using a sophisticated quantitative approach, Hamelin has put forth the idea of "nordicity" based on what he has called the "isonord" — a line which divided north from south. In Hamelin's scheme, this line would run roughly mid-way through British Columbia, east to Edmonton, thence down to about Winnipeg, and then made a gently sweeping arc from just north of Lake Superior to the Gulf of St. Lawrence and beyond northern Newfoundland to Iceland. By this, at least two-thirds of Canada would be considered as belonging to the north.[1]

595

To preserve one's sanity and make one's task easier here, the "north" in this essay will encompass political boundaries, specifically the Yukon and the Northwest Territories. These two districts were carved from territory acquired, shortly after Confederation in 1867. Two events occurred which turned the young Dominion's eyes to its western and northern frontiers. The first, the transfer of Rupert's Land to Canada had been long sought by Ontario politicians and businessmen anxious to expand their western horizons beyond the north shore of Lake Superior. Provision had been made in the British North America Act for the incorporation of this North-Western Territory, formerly controlled by the Hudson's Bay Company. The final transfer of this vast, poorly explored territory took place in 1870. Canada was now thrust westward and northward, possessing a huge area stretching from Lake Superior to the Rockies and from the 49th parallel to the virtually unknown shores of the Arctic Ocean.

The second event which turned Canada's gaze northward occurred in 1880 when Great Britain, by Order-in-Council, transferred the then-known Arctic Islands to Canada. Canada had never really given thought to acquiring this particular territory and had to be prodded by Imperial authorities. The British Government, for its part, was worried that if no official status were given to these islands, the United States especially would claim the area and limit possible Canadian expansion. Only a few Canadian politicians considered the territories to be of any potential value, and fewer still talked of this northward expansion as a natural part of Canada's own brand of manifest destiny.

The Yukon was created in 1898 when the Klondike gold rush required an administrative unit separate from the Northwest Territories. In 1905, Alberta and Saskatchewan were whittled from the remaining territory, and with the boundary adjustment to Manitoba in 1912 the Northwest Territories took its present shape. Today, in area this represents about 3,000,000 square km, or 40% of Canada's land mass, in which a total of 65,000 people live out of a population of over 23,000,000. Though sparsely populated, these territories bring to Canada and Canadians numerous treasures, both tangible and intangible.

Transcending the political boundaries, are those symbols, myths and aspirations which are northern in orientation and genuinely Canadian in content. One of the most enduring has been the concept of "The True North Strong and Free." That short phrase, found in the English version of Canada's national anthem, sums up a major theme in Canada's intellectual history and her search for identity. It is, or was, a deliberate choice of words by Robert Stanley Weir who penned them in 1908 — not randomly selected merely to rhyme with "We stand on guard for thee." Simply put, the notion conjures up images of what Canada is and will be, and can be found in a large body of Canadian literature, historical or otherwise. Canada and Canadians, in this view, are a product of the country's northern location, her deep winters and her heritage of northern, essentially European, races. There was a vital link between climate and character in which the former, through severe cold and arctic-like conditions, produced or reinforced hardiness, ruggedness and strength in her inhabitants. Added to this geographical determinism was a dash of racialism: the legacy of northern peoples who were perceived as the finest blossoming of the human race because of their moral superiority and power, as opposed to southern degeneration and weakness. More than that, it had been the Teutonic tribes of northern Europe which had produced the seeds of Liberty, and would, through the generations, create those flowers of Liberty, English Common Law and the Parliamentary system.[2]

To some, it seemed logical that nations occupying the northern latitudes, especially those bordering the Arctic Seas, would be the future empires of the world. To Vilhjalmur Stefansson, one of Canada's greatest arctic explorers, theorist and publicist, there was an inevitable conclusion to be drawn by what he termed "The Northward Course of an Empire." By 1922, he was convinced that the course of history had "proved" that higher civilizations and great empires succeeded one another in a northerly direction; that such phenomena were a function of latitude and mean temperature. For Canada to realize her full potential, Stefansson felt that her citizens and politicians must be made to look upon the north as valuable territory that could be exploited and developed to achieve supremacy. Otherwise, Cana-

596

da's destiny would be perverted. Antiquated and negative notions about the north had to be obliterated:

We have not come to the northward limit of commercial progress. There was many a pause but no stop to the westward course of empire until we came to the place where East is West. In that sense only is there a northward limit to progress. Corner lots in Rome were precious when a banks of the Thames had no value; the products of Canada were little beyond furs and fish when the British and French agreed in preferring Guadeloupe. But values have shifted north since then and times have changed, . . . There is no northern boundary beyond which productive enterprise cannot go till North meets North on the opposite shores of the Arctic Ocean as East has met West on the Pacific.[3]

The far north was not unfriendly or hostile, but habitable, liveable and fruitful; its flora and fauna, and still uncovered mineral resources would fuel and sustain a great civilization. As well, Canada's northern shoreline controlled a large portion of the Arctic basin. The greatness of ancient Rome had been founded on its ability to exploit and control the Mediterranean Sea. Canada, too, Stefansson said, had its Mediterranean, a polar one, which had remained frozen and inaccessible because of insufficient technology until the 20th century. But now, by the first quarter of this century, dirigibles, airplanes and submarines signalled the dawn of a new epoch for Canada and her Arctic. Once the Dominion understood its strategic position and the historical imperative — the "Coldward Course of Progress" — and developed the north, Canada would establish herself as a world power.[4]

Almost forty years later, one of Canada's most eminent historians, W.L. Morton, would see in Canada's northern frontier the "key" to Canadian history. To Morton, Canadian life is marked by a northern quality with its strong seasonal rhythms which "runs through every Canadian psyche."[5] Canada was unique, set apart from the United States, because it is a northern country possessing a northern way and a northern destiny:

. . . we should see our country as a distinctive and integrated nation. Not as a second class United States, not as a United States failed, but a different enterprise to be played on the frost bound and rocky northern half of the continent as a part of the manifold drama of human history. I would not for the moment be political, but I must say it is important that Canadians should have, if not a vision at least a notion, or conceit of themselves, as a northern people, that with Stefansson we should dare call the Arctic friendly, that we should believe that we are called, not to people the last best West, but in the dour fashion of our northern forebears, to make something of . . . a challenging, a tough but rewarding proposition, our north.[6]

When Morton made these observations in 1960, much had transpired since the time of the 1880 transfer to make the north ultimately a part of the Canadian experience. Mostly, there were a series of modest, unrelated endeavours, but they were in keeping with Canada's low-key approach to a region which would remain, for a long time to come, far down on the nation's list of developmental priorities.

Canadian acceptance of these new territories in 1880 had been too casual, for the government failed to assert vigorously her sovereignty over the Arctic Islands. Priorities were much further south: administration and peopling of its western lands and the building of the Canadian Pacific Railway.

The higher latitudes of Canada still had the unofficial status of a no-man's land—an area perhaps to be developed in the future. Very little was done on an official level to investigate the region, and only the Hudson's Bay Company continued to be a permanent fixture as it became more than just a fur trade company, transforming itself into the major transport and supply agency of the region. A handful of men from the Geological Survey and Dominion Lands Branch of the Department of the Interior reconnoitered the northern mainland and west and east of Hudson Bay to the Yukon during the 1880s and 1890s. The main areas explored were the Peace River country, Great Slave Lake, the waterways of the great Mackenzie River basin, and portions of Ungava. Their findings, which received little popular acclaim at the time, from Fort Chimo to Fort Yukon not only filled the blank spaces on the map of northern Canada, but helped to uncover untapped resources. The oil-laden Athabaska Tar Sands and the iron-bearing rocks of Central Ungava, for instance, were discovered by these unsung heroes.

598

As for the waters and islands of the Arctic, they commanded little or no attention. The only official investigation of northern waters was conducted in 1885 when Lieutenant A.R. Gordon, commanding the sealing ship *Neptune*, investigated the navigational possibilities and resources of Hudson Bay. Penetration of the Arctic Archipelago was left, in the main, to non-Canadians: Scottish whalers in Hudson Bay, and American whalers stationed at Herschel Island in the western Arctic from 1889 on.

Canadian authorities seemed little disposed to worry about foreign activities in the northern territories. In the long run the territory might have been lost to the Dominion by sheer negligence. Canada in fact did not formally acknowledge the 1880 transfer of territory until the 1890s. In 1895 and 1897, two Orders-in-Council were passed declaring that all northern territory between 141 West Longitude (the main Alaska-Canada Boundary) and a vague line running west of Greenland belonged to Canada. The Orders-in-Council also created three new northern districts for administrative purposes: Mackenzie, Yukon and Franklin. Arctic Islands which had been discovered to that date were placed within the District of Franklin.

The action was none too soon, for, at that very moment in Canada's history, the North made world headlines. Gold was discovered in 1896 in the Yukon in a stream called Rabbit Creek, renamed appropriately, Bonanza Creek. The entire world was briefly caught in the grips of gold fever. *Fortunes* would be made and lost in the rush to the goldfields. Men walked away with millions in gold dust and nuggets stuffed in satchels, blankets, and even jam jars. By 1899 Dawson, with a population of about 40,000 had become the largest city in Canada west of Winnipeg, and by 1903 modern society was transplanted into the North. Dawson became an opulent and garish settlement with all the amenities of western civilization: government institutions, hospitals, churches, schools, sidewalks, a water system, electricity, saloons, and theatres. By 1901 the centre of the Yukon could even boast telegraph and telephone connections with the outside world. Dawson was a boom town, but its destiny was tied to gold. Once the easy gold was gone, as it was by 1903, Dawson declined. The population in 1908 was about 8,000; in the

1920s and 1930s it stabilized at approximately 4,000 people. The mining of gold was taken over by more efficient, capital-intensive methods, such as hydraulic mining and dredging. The advent of such expensive enterprises meant the end of older methods of placer mining by individuals.

Overseeing all of this development were the North-West Mounted Police, who had moved into the area just before the discovery of gold. Until other government agencies and private institutions arrived on the scene, the police were jacks-of-all trades as well as the symbol of law and order. Klondike society, it should be mentioned, consisted largely of American citizens, men and women who might flout Canadian law and request that Washington, already involved in an imperialist adventure (in the Spanish-American War), make the Yukon part of the United States. Whether this threat was real or imagined, the territory was stamped Canadian mainly through the early efforts of the police. Between 1898 and 1903 the force had never totalled more than 300 men in a population of over 40,000. To their tribute, the Yukon never experienced the lawlessness and violence so prevalent in American territory where camps like Skagway were controlled by "Soapy Smith" and his henchmen. Only twelve murders in thirteen years were reported in the Yukon.

Nevertheless the American challenge remained. In 1903 the United States were victorious in their claims regarding the boundary of the Alaska Panhandle; the Dominion claimed it had been sold out by a mother-country anxious to establish friendlier ties with the Americans at the expense of Canada. Since the Alaska Boundary dispute the attendant American aggressiveness had posed a threat to northern boundaries, Canada commissioned an examination of her claim to the Arctic. The Dominion was to be rudely shocked by the findings.

A confidential 1904 report by W.F. King, the Dominion Astronomer, concluded that Canada's title to the Arctic Archipelago was incomplete and imperfect. Canada, King argued, has been tardy in acknowledging the 1880 transfer, leaving it to nationals of other states to penetrate the Arctic. The most direct threat to Canadian control of the entire Archipelago came from Norway which, as a result of Otto Sverdrup's discoveries between 1898 and 1902, could have claimed Axel Heiberg and the Rignes Islands (now known as the Sverdrup Islands) on the basis of prior discovery. Americans also had been active in the North since the middle of the nineteenth century. Most American expeditions to the northlands had been privately sponsored, but they frequently built cairns, deposited written records and raised their country's flag. Though there were few definite territorial claims, the Americans might argue that they had been far more active in the North than the Dominion. King further pointed out that American whalers regularly operating and wintering in the vicinity of Herschel Island and Hudson Bay might entertain attitudes which could threaten Canadian sovereignty. Unless Canada demonstrated that she could exercise effective occupation, King implied, she was in danger of losing complete and unquestioned control of some of the Arctic territories.

A relatively low-key and sometimes muddled programme was inaugurated by Ottawa to secure Canadian suzerainty and to find out more about these northern regions. Lawlessness at the winter headquarters of the American whaling fleet in the Beaufort Sea and the alleged debauchery of the sailors with the Inuit (Eskimo) led the North-West Mounted Police to establish, in 1903, posts at Herschel Island and on Hudson Bay. The Police presence, it was also hoped, would notify other states that Canada controlled these waters and territories. Ironically, though Canada claimed that her establishment of these posts in 1903 was designed to protect Inuit who were left exposed to white man's ways and vices, very little was readily done to protect the natives of the area who were left exposed to the onslaught of the white man. The most damaging contact, in the immediate sense, was the lucrative, but short-lived, whaling economy which began in earnest in 1889.

600

The whale was prized for its baleen, a plastic-like fibre found in its mouth, used by the animal to strain plankton from seawater. Until the fashion changed in women's undergarments and the introduction of plastics, baleen was used largely for stays in rigid corsets, umbrellas and so on. Its blubber was boiled down to provide oil for lubrication and lighting. Whalers wintered in the Arctic for several seasons at a time, pursuing the *Balaena mysticetus* into its last retreat and eventually bringing it to the brink of extinction. Ultimately whalers began to use the Inuit as part of their crews, and suppliers of local food supplies. The whalers ranged far and wide and in many cases their incidental victims were the Inuit themselves, who became dependent on white man's goods — foods, guns and liquors — to the point where they began to lose their ability to fend for themselves. Syphilis and measles killed at least one-fifth of the population of the Mackenzie delta area and their numbers continued to decline, though the figures are deceptive since the whalers boosted the population by importing Alaskan Eskimos. By 1900 most of the original Inuit of the delta area had been replaced in this fashion.

Care and education of the Inuit had been left mainly to missionaries who, although sincere, contributed to the breakdown of Inuit society and to the natives' inability to cope with the advance of white civilization. The primary task of the missionary was to Christianize the Inuit and if possible ease the impact of white civilization. Missionaries had to be more than men of God. They learned the language of the natives, compiled grammars of native tongues and with the aid of small government grants were responsible for their meagre education. Few succeeded in cushioning the shock of contact with a radically different culture.

In 1906 Canada resolutely claimed the Hudson Bay as belonging wholly to Canada and empowered government agents to collect fees from every vessel in these waters. Although foreign whaling captains chafed under what they considered an imposition, no serious difficulties were encountered. Their token adherence to Canadian regulations was seen as a demonstration of Canada's ability to control these waters and surrounding territory. Control over the Arctic Islands, on the other hand, was a more complicated matter.

Canada toyed with the idea of applying the so-called sector principle to the archipelago. In 1907 Senator Pascal Poirier suggested that the Arctic be divided like a pie, the North Pole as the centre. Norway, Sweden, Russia, and the United States would each be given its share. The Dominion's slice would lie between 141 West Longitude to roughly 60 West Longitude, there encompassing a triangle stretching from Canada's mainland Arctic coasts to the North Pole. The solution seemed a simple one, but the United States as a supreme maritime power would never accept boundaries which would restrict her movement on the high seas. The territorial waters of any state, by international agreement, were supposed to extend only three miles from the mainland. Poirier's northern boundaries extended hundreds of miles beyond Canada's mainland. Nevertheless, in 1909 Captain Joseph Bernier, who made several forays into the North aboard the *Arctic* between 1906 and 1911, formally claimed the Arctic "sector" for Canada.

Officially, Canada has never adopted the sector principle; unofficially, she has acted until very recently in accordance with this doctrine. Canadian maps, even today, show Canada's boundaries in the North as pie-shaped, extending from the Pole, but this has never been recognized by other countries, especially the United States.

The Canadian government continued to worry about the activity of the Americans in what she considered her rightful territory. Robert Peary, for example, claimed the North Pole for the United States in 1909, but the American Congress made no move to formalize the discovery. In addition American scientific societies had been sending expeditions to the North. These included activities of the American Museum of Natural History of New York and the National Geographic Society of Washington. Both were interested in scientific investigation, but also in the possibility of discovering the much talked about mysterious polar continent said to exist north and west of the Canadian mainland. These activities constituted an implicit threat to Canada's sovereignty should they succeed in making any new discoveries.

In 1913 these societies prepared a joint expedition to the Arctic under the command of a Canadian-born American, Vilhjalmur Stafansson. The Canadian government succeeded in persuading the American societies to relinquish their control, and the expedition became a wholly Canadian project. Stefansson became a British subject once again at the request of the government. The result was the Canadian Arctic Expedition of 1913–18, which included members of the Geological Survey and other scientists concerned with marine biology, oceanography, and the study of Inuit. Although handicapped by hasty planning and fraught with internal dissension, the expedition marked the high point of Canadian interest in the North to that date. The greatest blot on the expedition, however, occurred when the primary government ship, the *Karluk*, became caught in the ice north of Alaska, drifted in a north-westerly direction and was finally crushed by the relentless ice pressure. Before she sank, the crew and government scientists abandoned the ship, some setting off for the distant Siberian coast, never to be heard of again; others managed to reach Wrangel Island, a tiny island 100 miles due north of Siberia. There the *Karluk* survivors remained until the summer of 1914 where on July 1st, it was alleged, the island was claimed for Canada.

The expedition's scientific reports gave Canada and the World more knowledge of Canada's northern coast and islands than ever before. Stefansson, for his part, was able to explore 100,000 square miles of Arctic territory, travelling roughly 20,000 miles by sled and dogteam and discovering the last major bodies of land in the Arctic Archipelago. Stefansson discovered Brock and Borden Islands (1915) and Meighen and Lougheed Islands (1916). In his unprecedented and spectacular exploration, he managed to outline for the first time the continental shelf from Alaska to Prince Patrick Island and to reveal the submarine mountains and valleys beneath the Beaufort Sea. All this, he claimed with some exaggeration, was accomplished while living off the land, or, more correctly, the marine resources of the Arctic Ocean.

602   Stefansson returned from the Arctic convinced that the region was the land of the future and that the country which possessed and developed it would be the greatest power in the world. Canada and the British Empire could realize their destiny by controlling this strategic polar "Mediterranean." The Arctic Islands would serve as bases for airplanes, dirigibles, and submarines. In 1919 such ideas anticipated the polar air route and submarine voyages of half a century later, but when Stefansson tried to demonstrate their practicability, they served only to embroil Canada in a serious and complicated international incident over ownership of Wrangel Island, about 100 miles due north of Siberia and certainly outside the Canadian "sector."

Stefansson wanted Canada to lay claim to Wrangel Island as part of a general effort to secure Arctic islands. The government of Arthur Meighen turned down the idea. Undaunted, Stefansson, one of the last "red-hot imperialists," created a private company and occupied the island in 1921 in the hope that the Canadian government would officially recognize it as part of Canadian territory. Meighen's successor, Mackenzie King, complicated matters by stating before the House of Commons in 1922 that Wrangel Island was part of Canada. The U.S.S.R. protested that this was a violation of Soviet territory. The United States, hampered by the Washington Conference disarmament agreements (1922) which had reduced her strategic presence in the Pacific north-west, hinted that she might occupy certain islands north of Canada to re-capture her position in the Pacific. By claiming Wrangel Island, north of Siberia, Canada had moved out of her unofficial sector, in theory denying her claims to the Arctic Archipelago. The matter was finally resolved when the British Government eventually recognized the island as part of the U.S.S.R. The United States seemed content about the fate of Wrangel Island but a U.S. State Department official reiterated in 1926 that Canadian claims to the entire Arctic Archipelago were "not worth a damn." In that same year, the Soviet Union adopted a sectoral approach to its Arctic territory and although this could have conceivably strengthened the Canadian position, the Soviet sector has never been accorded international recognition.

Canada, happy with this turn of events, returned to a low-profile approach in the Arctic in the 1920s. The Dominion scrapped a secret expedition to the North to avoid publicity about the frailty of her claims. The misadventure of Wrangel Island had almost cost her the territorial integrity of the Arctic Archipelago, and so Canada avoided any northern confrontations at all costs. Rather, she relied on annual R.C.M.P. patrols, and the establishment of police posts on both flanks of the Archipelago, and other kinds of government activity to consolidate theoretically unclaimed territory. Along with the continuing efforts of the Geological Survey, small scale exploration by private industry and the advent of bush piloting, there were the beginnings of a communications network in the Mackenzie Valley and Yukon under the auspices of the Royal Canadian Corps of Signals, and the start of an aerial photo reconnaissance programme.

With the Depression of the 1930s, the fortunes of Canada took a nose- *603* dive. This was doubly so in the North. Problems of economic distribution in the south sapped the time, energy and attention of most Canadians. The north was again put on the shelf — if it had ever been off. World War II would change all this.

In the 1940s, greater responsibility for the north and its people were literally forced on Canada—at least onto the Canadian military, Canadian politicians and bureaucrats in departments such as External Affairs. The shocking exposé of neglect on the part of Canada toward its Inuit (Eskimo) population would force Ottawa to finally offer coherent programmes in the fields of health and education to a people for whom, up to this point, the government had denied any formal responsibility.[7] This had only begun to change after 1939 when the Supreme Court of Canada declared, in one of its stranger decisions, that Eskimos were Indians, hence under the provisions of the British North America Act. Before that, the Canadian Government had argued that they were merely Canadian citizens, pure and simple, with no special status. In late 1953, the Department of Northern Affairs and National Resources was established, now known as the Department of Indian Affairs and Northern Development. Its creation was a redress of generations of negligence, for as Prime Minister Louis St. Laurent observed, Canadians had "administered these vast territories of the North in almost continuing state of absence of mind."[8]

Of equal importance, had been American wartime activity and American postwar aspirations in Canada's north. Canadian control of her own territory could have been undermined if the United States had had its way in the mid-1940s. The United States had conducted a series of military and construction activities in north-western and northern Canada, known as the Northwest Defense Projects, involving at its peak in 1943 over 37,000 Americans. The Alaska Highway, the Canol Project (pipelines linking Norman Wells to Whitehorse and Alaska), the Northwest Staging Route to Alaska (a series of northern airfields parallelling the U.S. built highway), and the North-west Staging Routes to the European theatre of war, gave the Americans great insight into, and a taste for, the vast mineral potential and strategic value of Canada's northern hinterland.[9] Canadians had to take the lead in developing their backyard; otherwise the north could be lost by default should the United States do more than Canada. Besides, wrote External Affairs' Escott Reid in 1943, such a northern focus could prove therapeutic to Canadians:

After the emotional debauch of the war there is going to be a bad hangover in all the former belligerent countries. In order that people's lives will not feel too empty, some peacetime equivalents to the exciting national objectives of the war must be found. The opening of a new frontier in the Canadian North can, I think, become a national objective of some importance to the Canadian people. Even if, from the point of view securing the highest possible national income, the Canadian North is not worth a large expenditure of national energy and capital, a very large expenditure might nevertheless be justified in an effort to realize an inspiring and somewhat romantic national objective.[10]

604

By the 1950s, the north and things northern would become stylish.

The perceived menace of the Soviet Union by the United States after 1945 and a fear on the part of Canada that the United States might violate Canadian sovereignty if Ottawa refused to cooperate with her against the U.S.S.R. would help push Canada into the sabre-rattling posturing of the Cold War.[11] Continental defense, meaning defense against Soviet nuclear attack over the Pole, became the stuff of headlines and after-dinner talk. Canadians could not help but notice their country's participation in a series of joint military exercises, *radar* lines being built across her north, climaxing in the mid-1950s with the Distant Early Warning (DEW) line flung across Canada's Arctic Islands and reinforced with the creation in 1958 of NORAD, the North American Air Defence Command. The north was now more than just mysterious, and romantic. It had become fashionable and, by the dictates of the international situation, it was dangerous — it was news. Canadians were told that the north was also our salvation in such bleak and threatening times. Said statesman-historian, Hugh Keenleyside at the height of the Cold War,

The North has been referred to as the frontier. But the frontier is more than a geographical area; it is a way of life, a habit of mind. As such, it plays a most significant role in the national life. . . . As long as the frontier remains, there will be Canadians who will never succumb to the dogmas of the totalitarian or the power of domestic tyranny. The frontier is a bastion of freedom, and the North a permanent frontier.[12]

Yet by the late 1960s the north was being looked upon as more than just a battlefield; the Cold War was entering, it appeared, an era of detente. Newly-discovered oil deposits off the north shore of Alaska quickened the pace and expectations of energy-hungry nations in the south for this precious commodity. There was now more to the north than radar and interception, smiling natives, soapstone carvings and a sprinkling of mineral resources. The attempt of the U.S.S. *Manhattan*, a proto-type of future Arctic supertankers, to force its way through the ice-clogged Northwest Passage in 1969, once again raised anxieties in Canada. The ostensible purpose of the voyage was to demonstrate the practicability of such ships in the Arctic. The voyage was only a partial success. Despite her powerful engines, the *Manhattan* was frequently caught in the ice and had to be helped by Canadian icebreakers like the *John A. Macdonald*. Nevertheless, Ottawa regarded the *Manhattan* voyage as a foreign challenge to Canadian claims to exclusive jurisdiction in those waters. Canada did not employ the sector principle to assert her claims, but passed, in Parliament, the Arctic Waters Pollution Act in 1970, which sought to control the passage of ships through its high northern waters. Canada asserted that it was the only country which had not only a direct interest in protecting these waters from possible calamities and contamination, but the technological expertise as well. The United States, for its part, has not recognized this Canadian action as having any force in law. Given this, it appears that although much has happened in the last 100 years to bring the north closer to the south and vice versa, some things never change.

Notes

1. John E. Sater, *The Arctic Basin* (Washington: Arctic Institute of North America, 1969), pp. 1-4; Louis-Edmond Hamelin, *Nordicité canadienne* (Montréal: Editions Hurtubise HMH, 1975).
2. For an excellent treatment of this theme see, Carl Berger, "The True North Strong and Free," in P. Russell, ed., *Nationalism in Canada* (Toronto: McGraw-Hill, 1966), pp. 3-26.
3. Vilhjalmur Stefansson, *The Northward Course of Empire* (London: Harrap, 1922), p. 19
4. See, Richard J. Diubaldo, *Stefansson and the Canadian Arctic* (Montreal, McGill-Queen's University Press, 1978), chap. 7.
5. W.L. Morton, *The Canadian Identity* (Madison: University of Wisconsin, 1961), p. 93.
6. W.L. Morton, "The North in Canadian History," *North* 7 (Jan-Feb. 1960), 29. In Quebec such sentiments were mirrored in the construction of a parallel myth. Its shifting, advancing north would anticipate a greatness still to come. The north was a Promised Land, whose conquest was the special providential mission of its people, a people who would, in turn, be spiritually regenerated or revitalized in the process. See, Christian Morissonneau, *La Terre Promise: Le mythe du nord québécois* (Montreal: Editions Hurtubise HMH, 1978).
7. See Diamond Jenness, *Eskimo Administration: Canada* Technical Paper No. 14 of Arctic Institute of North America (Montreal: The Arctic Institute of North America), 1964.
8. Cited in R.A.S. Phillips, *Canada's North* (Toronto: Macmillan, 1968), p. 161.
9. See Richard J. Diubaldo "The Canol Project in Canadian-American Relations; The Canadian Historical Association, *Historical Papers* (1977), pp. 179-195.
10. Public Archives of Canada (PAC), Privy Council Records, Record Group 2/18, vol. 21, File A-25-3, Escott Reid to Norman Robertson, 30 July 1943.
11. For the vexing question of sovereignty and Canadian anxieties over unilateral actions by the United States see R.J. Diubaldo and S.J. Scheinberg, *A Study of Canadian-American Defence Policy (1945-1975) — Northern Issues and Strategic Resources* (Operational Research and Analysis Establishment, Department of National Defence (Ottawa, 1978), especially pp. 12-28.
12. Hugh Keenleyside, "Human Resources and Problems of the Canadian North," *Transactions of the Royal Society of Canada (1950)*.

The Prairie West Since 1945: An Historical Survey*

GERALD FRIESEN

It is a truism that prairie society changed rapidly in the four decades after 1940. Observers of the region might single out such local trends as the migration of farm residents to the cities, the entry of women into the workforce, and the participation of Indians in political debates as indicators of a social upheaval. But these particular changes also affected Argentina and Australia and midwestern America. Like the spread of transnational corporations and made-in-Hollywood "entertainment" — two other noteworthy developments of the era — these trends were not unique to the prairie West but, rather, affected many parts of the developed world. And yet, despite the apparent homogeneity of modern social history, the prairie community also witnessed a flowering of distinctive local cultural expressions and seemed to be the home of distinctive political and ethnic loyalties in these decades. What was the "state of the region"? Was it indeed just a neighborhood of a global metropolis? Or did elements of a distinctive society and culture continue to exist? This paper will sketch some of the political, economic, and social trends of the era in order to suggest the nature of the "delicate balance" which must be struck in the study of small communities in the modern world.

606

Prairie demographic trends demonstrate that significant social changes carried the region closer to international norms in the decades after 1945.[1] Of these trends, the most striking was the decline in rural population and the growth of cities. Though half of prairie residents lived on farms in 1941, only 10 percent did so in 1981. Because the village proportion of the total remained nearly constant, the proportion of prairie residents living in towns and cities over 1,000 population rose from 38 percent to 71 percent. By 1981, a demographic milestone had been passed: for the first time, over 50 percent of the prairie population lived in its five metropolitan centers. Within these generalizations is hidden an important change in the balance of urban power. Winnipeg, which was as large as the combined population of the other four prairie metropolises at the start of this period, was slightly smaller than Calgary and Edmonton by 1981. And the prairie population declined in relation to the national population because, despite a sharp rise in Alberta, neither Manitoba nor Saskatchewan kept pace with Canada's steady growth.

The nature of the prairie economy changed considerably in these four decades, as the urban-rural balance suggests. Agriculture's share of the wealth produced in the provinces (census value added) in 1941 was 50 percent of

*From *The Making of the Modern West: Western Canada Since 1945*, ed. by A.W. Rasporich. Copyright 1984 by University of Calgary Press. Reprinted by permission.

the regional total; in 1978 it was under 15 percent. In Alberta, indeed, agriculture contributed just 8 percent of census value added by 1978. The economic boom was based upon the mining sector, whose proportion of regional wealth (cva) grew from 8 percent in 1941 to 41 percent in 1978. With such changes in population concentration, in place of residence and in the nature of economic activity, the prairie provinces also experienced a significant redistribution of the labor force. The proportion engaged in agriculture declined from 48 percent in 1941 to 10 percent in 1981. The most important increase occurred in the tertiary sector, where the proportion of managerial, professional, clerical, sales, and service workers grew from 30 percent of the paid labor force in 1941 to 59 percent in 1981.

There were dramatic changes in the household, too, after World War II. Life expectancy rose sharply, from the low sixties to the low seventies for men, and from the mid-sixties to the high seventies for women. The number of divorces increased rapidly, from about 230 in each prairie province in 1941 to an average of over 4,000 per province per year in the early 1980s. Family size decreased. The proportion of women over fifteen years, including married women, in the paid labor force increased from 20 percent to 52 percent in these four decades. The level of education rose and, both in rural and in urban communities, the attainments of prairie children became comparable to those in the rest of Canada and North America.

To these numerical measures of change must be added the qualitative evidence which suggested the transcendence of urban and rural differences. Farm people moved to the cities by the tens of thousands in these decades, it is true, but the life of the city also invaded the countryside. The rapid adoption of the car, truck, combine and tractor, the spread of rural electrification and the consequent changes in the farm household, the complex demands of crop selection and cultivation, the growing importance of farm finance, as well as school consolidation and centralization of economic and social services brought rural work processes and material culture closer to their urban counterparts than at any time in the preceding century. The prairie provinces also led the continent into another international trend of the era, the welfare state. It was quite possible in the 1930s to live in fear of illness, to suffer serious food shortages, and to be clothed and housed at the barest minimum standard. These problems were mitigated in the postwar decades as the prairie West joined western Europe in attempting to guarantee that the state would intervene to provide health and income assistance.

The Canadian West became increasingly homogeneous and increasingly like the rest of the developed world between 1945 and the early 1980s. It was much more urban than rural; it was less dependent on agricultural income; the largest proportion of its labor force was in the so-called tertiary-sector occupations including the liberal professions and managerial and clerical jobs; it was still heavily engaged in natural resource production and tied to world markets, true, but it had a reasonably diversified base of resources and its per capita personal income hovered around the national average; it had been swept by new trends in family formation, as had the rest of the

607

developed world, and it had succumbed to the trappings of material culture that guided, amused, adorned or eased daily living in Lyons and Belgrade and Wichita and Leeds. Finally, it was part of the North Atlantic welfare state and, depending upon the perspective of the observer, might have seemed just another neighborhood within a single homogenized global metropolis.

This assumption of growing global uniformity which would swallow up a distinctive prairie society was prominent in Canadian scholarship. One influential work of this type was George Grant's *Lament for a Nation*. Grant argued that, in the years after 1945, Canada's ruling class, the people who controlled its great corporations, became a northern extension of the continental ruling class, just as the nation's economy became a branch plant and the nation's military became an errand boy. In the modern age, he wrote, it was possible for many citizens to live outside the dominant assumptions of their world: democracy could not save Canadians from absorption into a "homogenized continental culture." His argument was based upon the assumption that Canada was "a local culture" and upon the assertion that "modern civilization," especially "modern science," made all local cultures obsolete. His essay reached a stinging conclusion: because conservatism was impossible, and because Canadian existence had hitherto been predicted upon the conservatism of Canadian society and its leaders, then the existence of Canada — a local conservative culture — was impossible.[2]

Grant had considerable support for his generalizations in the 1960s. A distingished Canadian economist, Harry Johnson, argued that Canada was increasingly a part of the larger North American economy: "Both politically and economically, the general trend of world evolution is toward . . . political and economic organization on a continental . . . rather than national scale."[3] The best known Canadian student of communications in the 1960s, Marshall McLuhan, was making comparable statements about the effects of the electronic media, though one was never certain whether he saw the global village as a harmonious utopia or a centralized tyranny.[4] A paper presented by E. K. Brown upon the proper audience and context of Canadian imaginative writing, though published in 1943, remained an important force in literary criticism. Brown deplored the possibility of a descent into "regionalist art" in Canada, arguing that such art would "fail because it stresses the superficial and the peculiar at the expense, at least, if not the exclusion, of the fundamental and universal. The advent of regionalism may be welcomed with reservations as a stage through which it may be well to pass, as a discipline and a purgation. But if we are to pass through it, the coming of great books will be delayed beyond the lifetime of anyone now living."[5] Finally, John Porter's studies of Canadian society denied the existence of coherent class cleavages and suggested that Canadians were becoming more like each other: "the maintenance of national unity has over-ridden any other goals there might have been, and has prevented a polarizing, within the political system, of conservative and progressive forces." He also argued that "There is . . . little conflict between those who have power and those who do not. It is not a question of conflicts between the 'ins' and the 'outs', but rather of conflicts between those who are 'in'."[6] Prairie Canadians, in this perspective, were entering a new phase in national existence. They were moving beyond regionalist art and regional or even national economic policy; they were accepting greater homogeneity in culture and, apparently, were less distinguishable from other communities in the developed world.

The perspective which emphasized homogeneity and internationalism has shaped aspects of prairie scholarship. The economist, Paul Phillips, based a recent essay upon the assumption that regionalism had always been a central characteristic of the Canadian economy but that, in recent decades, the multinational corporation and continental capital integration, not the Canadian government, were the crucial forces in decision making.[7] The historian, J.E. Rea, in his discussion of "the most persistent social theme" in prairie history, "the struggle for cultural dominance," suggested that ethnic minorities were assimilated in post-1945 decades: "What has evolved is a Prairie culture which is more diverse, but not essentially different from that established at the end of the nineteenth century. The premises of the Ontario migrants, and the social institutions which they planted, have generally remained intact."[8] The political scientist, Roger Gibbins, perceived a "decline of political regionalism" in the prairie West and made it the central theme of his *Prairie Politics and Society*. Among the reasons for the decline, he argued, were the urbanization of the population, the erosion of ethnicity, the transformation of agriculture and, finally, "the loss of a distinctive prairie culture, or the lost opportunity to create a distinctive prairie culture" which he associated with pressures from urban multinational mass media.[9] What these prairie scholars had in common was the assumption that the forces of modern economic organization, modern transportation and communications technology, and even of modern politics were eliminating the possibility of local autonomy, region-wide political identity, and a distinctive local culture.

609

There is merit in this view. No one would wish to deny it. But it is only half a story for a student of regional society. We must also look at the other side under these same headings of economic structure, social organization and regional perspective. The argument for a decline of local control over the economy, for example, should be tempered by recognition of areas of considerable regional power. As long as prairie-based cooperatives owned three-quarters of the country elevators and were relatively responsive to their membership, there was a measure of local control in the wheat economy. As long as the Wheat Board acted as the central agency for the sale of Canadian grain, and was reasonably responsive to the needs and desires of its constituents, its important functions were subject to a measure of local control. And as long as decisions on freight rates remained within the political system, even there a measure of local control was possible. It is true that determinants of prices and yields were still beyond the farmers' grasp but security of return had become greater than ever before, due in good measure to the efforts of the local Pools and the local agricultural scientists and extension educators. These trends did not suggest homogenization or loss of local autonomy.

Within the rest of the prairie economy, the strength of the thesis regard-

ing international capital flows and transnational enterprises must be acknowledged. But, at the same time, given the inevitable context of an increasingly integrated global economy, the degree of local control over the nonag-
ricultural portions of the prairie economy merits a closer look. Three developments contradict the conventional wisdom. First, cooperative enterprises
and credit unions were extremely important in the prairie economy. In the
early 1980s, five of Canada's ten largest cooperatives were based in the prairie West and the prairie credit unions possessed assets of nearly $7 billion.[10]
Second, the number and importance of prairie-based industrial enterprises grew substantially in the four decades. Though in several cases these
corporations were themselves transnational enterprises, their owners, the
prairie super-rich, demanded recognition as local entrepreneurs who reflected
a regional bias in their approach to the economy. The power associated with
such families as Richardson, Poole, Mannix, Southern, Webster, Child, Sea-
man, Scurfield, Simpson, Banister, Cohen, Searle, McKinnon, Asper,
Simkin, Torchinski, Friesen, Lyons and Ward could not be discounted. And,
to the degree that this power was exercised with the future of the community of the region in mind, must be recognized as another kind of local
control.[11] The third theme in prairie economic self-determination concerned the role of the state. Prairie governments had always been prepared
to intervene in the economy on behalf of the local citizens. By the early
1980s, it was a rule of thumb that Canadian governments—that is, all levels
of government—spent, on direct purchases and transfers of income, roughly
40 percent of the total value of goods and services produced in Canada.[12]
Large state-owned institutions such as the three prairie telephone corporations, the two power corporations, the Alberta airline (Pacific Western), the
Alberta Energy Company and Treasury Branches, the Saskatchewan Crown
Investments Corporation and the Alberta Heritage Fund and even that
unusual hybrid, "NOVA-An Alberta Corporation," were subject to direction from the people's representatives. Though one might debate the true
nature of state capitalism and corporate socialism, one must still acknowledge that the degree of local control over the local economy was much greater
in 1980 than in 1940.

610

If the argument for increasing international homogeneity and multinational power could be contrasted with a trend to local control in the case of
the prairie economy, a similar duality could be posited in the case of social
organization and social structure. Ethnicity, native-white relations and social
class were the chief subjects at issue. The conventional wisdom in North
American sociology, a product of Robert Park's work many years ago, was
that ethnic minorities inevitably were assimilated during the passage of several generations. This perspective seemed reasonable because it corresponded
to daily observations on the replacement of folk architecture by suburban
tract home, the decline of traditional language use, the exogamy of young
people and the uniform secularism of daily life, to cite but a few obvious
illustrations. But the field work of prairie sociologists such as Alan Anderson and Leo Driedger in the early 1970s found evidence which did not entirely

confirm the Park thesis. Despite a significant province-wide decline in the use of traditional languages, Anderson discovered widespread use of ethnic languages and other important characteristics of group identity in the rural bloc settlements of north-central Saskatchewan.[13] Driedger catalogued continuing minority group loyalties and institutional completeness within Winnipeg's ethnic communities and then adopted the concept of "cultural pluralism" to depict the social organization of the prairie West. He had found relatively meltable and unmeltable individuals and groups, in other words, and the latter — the "unmeltables" — created institutions parallel to those of the mainstream and climbed parallel ladders to success.[14]

This distinction between cultural assimilation, defined as adaptation to mainstream values and material culture, and structural assimilation, defined as entry into the important institutions of mainstream society, itself raised problems but it did emphasize the continuing importance of ethnic identity in the prairie West. Similarly John Porter, Wallace Clement and Raymond Breton noted the "gatekeeping" activities and the overrepresentation in the national elite of Canada's "charter" ethnic groups.[15] If some groups were rewarded, others were denied. Surely ethnic consciousness was the product of such experiences. Howard Palmer recently associated the tides of nativism in twentieth-century Alberta with the rise and fall of prejudice throughout the English-speaking world, but he did not argue that nativism had disappeared. Indeed, the hostility expressed toward the so-called "visible minorities" from South and East Asia, the "indigeneous minorities" — Canada's native peoples — and the "unassimilable minorities," such as the Hutterites, ensured that ethnic identity and conflict remained a part of prairie society.[16]

Native identity, like ethnic identity, did not disappear during these forty years. There were 68,000 native people in the prairie West in 1941, most of whom lived in rural surroundings, and about 200,000 in 1981. By the latter date, natives constituted about 7 percent of the Manitoba and Saskatchewan populations and about 4 percent of the Alberta population. About one-quarter of the registered Indians lived off their reserves by 1976 and it was estimated that this proportion would reach one-third by the mid-1980s. In the five prairie cities in 1981 estimates of the native proportion of the population varied from about 2 percent in Calgary (about 7,000), to 4 percent in Edmonton (about 15,000), 15 percent in Regina (about 20,000), 6 percent in Saskatoon (about 7,000), and about 5 percent in Winnipeg (about 22,000).[17] Generalizations concerning the economic and social status of the urban and rural native population appeared frequently in the press and, almost without exception, emphasized that native birth rates were higher than white, that native unemployment rates were higher and native household incomes lower than whites, that transfer payments were a primary source of native income, and that violence was endemic in native communities. The catalogue of negatives was so well-known that it must have had some accuracy but it also rang chords which were familiar to students of prairie immigration history. The questions asked and the values implicit in the analysis sounded very much like the social surveys of central European immigrant communities in the prairie West before 1930. Like those surveys, contemporary reports reflected a concern for the members of the native community but they also imposed goals that were not necessarily those of the natives.

A different perspective upon the prairie native community was presented by the sociologist, Linda Gerber, whose research into reserve communities was based upon the concepts of institutional completeness and personal resource development. Her survey of over 500 reserve bands in Canada demonstrated that adaptive strategies which concentrated upon either the development of individual skills or upon community development policies had become a focus of local native politics. In the late 1960s and early 1970s, she wrote, the bands in the southern two-thirds of each prairie province differed from their counterparts in the rest of Canada: "The typical prairie band is larger and grows rapidly due to the unusually high fertility rates. It is remarkably cohesive, well-developed at the community level, and relatively likely to retain the use of native languages. The typical nonprairie band is the obverse in many respects, being more fully integrated into the mainstream through education, employment, and off-reserve residence." Her conclusion was that "the communal prairie bands and the individualistic bands of the other provinces employed different strategies of adaptation to modern conditions," and that "ethnic differentiation" and the development of an Indian "institutional framework" were becoming more evident in the prairie West.[18]

Native identity in the region was consolidated in the decades after 1945. Campaigns for native rights and celebrations of native culture produced a clearer and more insistent articulation of native perspectives than had occurred in the preceding half century. Despite the assimilationist drive of the federal government, indeed, the natives forced the larger society to acknowledge a new political status—or statuses—for them. And within the larger Canadian native community, the distinctive characteristics of the three prairie provincial associations and of the Métis and nonstatus Indian communities were evident.

Ethnic and native studies are familiar aspects of social history. Class analysis is not. It has not always enjoyed favor in national historical scholarship and it continues to pose serious problems even for its most committed practitioners. And yet a tentative version of class appeared in discussions of the prairie experience between 1880 and 1940 and, as a clear trend in modern political studies literature suggests, class-based analysis of the post-1945 era preoccupied a number of Canadian scholars. Tom Peterson's interpretation of Manitoba politics, for example, argued that the fundamental cleavage in the province between the early 20th century and the 1960s had been ethnicity, but that class loyalties transcended ethnic divisions in the late 1960s and 1970s. Nelson Wiseman and Wayne Taylor measured class and ethnic loyalties in Winnipeg elections in the 1940s and 1950s and found them to be significant. Other recent studies, such as Richards and Pratt's *Prairie*

612

Capitalism, suggested similar conclusions for rural society. The crude categories of the Marxian dialectic might not have been the proper abstract formulation of social divisions in the postwar prairie West but some type of categorization still seemed necessary. Prairie people were not, as the pioneer cliché had it, "all just folks together," nor did they lose their class identity in a modern homogeneous society.[19]

Studies of prairie literature took a different course. Dick Harrison, the literary critic, recently suggested that the history of prairie literature must first treat the "struggle for an indigenous prairie fiction;" its task was to reconcile "the incongruities between the culture and the land." W.L. Morton's literary confession emphasized similar themes.[20] Even Wallace Stegner contended with this kind of problem:

> Contradictory voices tell you who you are. You grow up speaking one dialect and reading and writing another . . . all the forces of culture and snobbery are against your *writing* by ear and making contact with your natural audience. Your natural audience, for one thing, doesn't read — it *isn't* an audience. You grow out of touch with your dialect because learning and literature lead you another way unless you consciously resist.[21]

This is the gap between nature and culture, America and Europe, West and East, country and city, body and mind which has been expressed many times from many perspectives. But in the decades after 1945 in the prairie West, one was struck not by an exceptionally-wide gap between literature and life, nor indeed by the absence of an audience, but by the very eagerness for locally-created, locally-inspired art, and by a distinctive but not exceptional quest to bridge the gap between "memory" and "history." Was this not the inspiration for the Golden and seventy-fifth provincial birthdays in Alberta and Saskatchewan, the centennials of Manitoba, Winnipeg, Saskatoon, Regina and Canada and the boom in local history publications, heritage movements and family reunions?[22] A regional voice and a regional audience — two very different things — had developed in the prairie West after World War II. As John Hirsch said of the Manitoba Theatre Centre, which was founded in 1957–58 but whose formative years were in the preceding decade, there came together in Winnipeg the physical and financial support, the artistic talent, and best of all, the audiences to support an institution devoted to drama. In the postwar decades, the prairie West was prepared to see its life translated into and its perceptions shared by literature.

The expression of this interest in one's past and one's environment often began at an artistic level inferior to that of the metropolises of the English-speaking world. Despite a continuing self-consciousness, however, there was, especially in literature, and here the growing influence of the university was evident, a growing maturity. The finest prairie writers had learned to speak of local concerns in an international idiom. And, for that reason, the language of their imagination created a vision that became a focus for the community. It also attracted international attention. Northrop Frye has suggested that the best literature seems to depend upon local identification. And he went on to defend its quality in Canada, to argue that the gap between colonialism and maturity had narrowed:

. . . there is no reason for cultural lag or for a difference between sophisticated writers in large centres and naive writers in smaller ones. A world like ours produces a single international style of which all existing literatures are regional developments. This international style is not a bag of rhetorical tricks but a way of seeing and thinking in a world controlled by uniform patterns of technology, and the regional development is in a way of escaping from that uniformity.[23]

Every type of cultural expression has its own technology and its own historical rhythms of patronage, circulation, production, content or language and form. Thus, what may have been true for prairie literature had no necessary relationship to developments in architecture, film, television, newspapers, painting or other kinds of cultural production. Two brief observations upon their development might be hazarded. First, one saw in each of these areas the contradictory pressures toward a distinctive indigenous expression, on the hand, and toward international uniformity, on the other. Second, communications technology was changing so rapidly in these decades that generalizations about international cultural homogeneity — as in the common fear of Hollywood and American network television — like generalizations about the disappearance of "genuine culture" entirely, were premature.

This discussion of economic decision making, social composition, cultural expression and literary achievement in the prairie West omits one theme that is central to society and to historians' analysis of its evolution. That is politics. As the decades of the twentieth century passed provinces became increasingly important units in Confederation. With the growth of provincial responsibilities, provincial wealth, and local bureaucracies, as Alan Cairns has suggested, provincial identities began to take shape.[24] One aspect — even creator of — these identities was the provincial party system. A distinctive local blend of personalities and popular preferences molded distinctive provincial governments and political institutions. In the years after 1945, the various communities in each province — native, ethnic, class, occupational, rural and urban — became more closely integrated into a single community. The political parties reinforced provincial distinctiveness by pursuing significantly different brands of political education. The result was the development of ideological divisions within each prairie province, and, thus, an indigenous two-party system. These were not simply brokerage parties, in other words, but rather were parties based upon ideological differences. The disappearance of the national governing party, the Liberals, from the prairie scene ensured that federal-provincial conflict would be bitter; disagreement between the two levels of government was probably inevitable but the Liberal failure made such disagreement a more serious event. Finally, despite the separatist backlash, which was the right-wing ideological expression in Alberta, the prairie West continued to be Canadian.[25] Its local politics possessed distinctive elements, but its distinctiveness did not imply disloyalty.

In these forty years, the prairie West was affected profoundly by international forces but it also retained elements of individuality. The sweeping generalizations concerning cultural homogeneity and the concentration of global decision making presented only one perspective on a complex story. As W.L. Morton commented, "there are sections as well as nations, nations as well as civilizations. The sub-society which is a section . . . possesses some degree of integrity and character. That character . . . may be defined, and the relations of the sub-society with other societies explored." In a later essay, he added: "Federally created, the West was self-defined . . . (It) knew in its bones that it was an independent creature which had determined its own life within known and accepted limits."[26] The West was a distinctive community from the mid-seventeenth to the mid-nineteenth century; the diplomatic and economic rhythms of native-European relations ensured that the dramatic changes of these two centuries would occur in relative peace and according to the dictates of local forces. The prairie West adapted to the industrial capitalism of the North Atlantic world in the last half of the nineteenth century, as did much of the globe, and became a separate Canadian region with interests, issues, and an outlook of its own despite vast areas of experience in common with Canadians from other parts of the country. In the first four decades of the twentieth century, it adjusted to the strains of rapid population change, the challenges of ethnic and political disagreements and the crises of the Great Depression and two World Wars while remaining within the Canadian economic structure and the parliamentary system. Its experience was no less distinctive in the four decades after 1945. As in the past, so in recent years, world issues were also prairie issues. But it would be one-sided to talk about international homogeneity and transnational decision making as if they were the only aspects of prairie experience that mattered. As ever, local will, local interests and local memory constituted the other side of the "delicate balance" that was prairie experience.[27]

615

Notes

1. The following paragraphs are based upon the appended tables.
2. George Grant, *Lament for a Nation: The Defeat of Canadian Nationalism* (Toronto: 1965)
3. Harry G. Johnson, *The Canadian Quandary: Economic Problems and The Policies* (Toronto: 1963, 1977), p. 103.
4. Marshall McLuhan, *Understanding Media: The Extensions of Man* (Toronto: 1964, 1966).
5. E.K. Brown, "Canadian Poetry," in *Contexts of Canadian Criticism*, edited by Eli Mandel (Chicago: 1971), pp. 29–47.
6. John Porter, *The Vertical Mosaic: An Analysis of Social Class and Power in Canada* (Toronto: 1965), pp. 27, 369.
7. Paul Phillips, "National Policy, Continental Economics, and National Disintegration," in *Canada and the Burden of Unity*, edited by David Jay Bercuson (Toronto: 1977), pp. 19–43. I would like to thank Doug Owram for an advance copy of his "The Economic Development of Western Canada: An Historical Overview," Discussion Paper 219, *Economic Council of Canada* (November 1982).
8. J.E. Rea, "The Roots of Prairie Society," in *Prairie Perspectives I*, edited by David Gagan (Toronto: 1970), p. 54.
9. Roger Gibbins, *Prairie Politics and Society: Regionalism in Decline* (Toronto: 1980). p. 93.
10. Canadian Co-operative Credit Society Limited, *Annual Report* (1982), p. 20; *The Financial Post 500* (June 1982), p. 100.
11. Based upon *The Financial Post 500* (June 1982).
12. Marsha Gordon, *Government in Business* (June 1982), p. 100.
13. Alan Anderson, "Linguistic Trends among Saskatchewan Ethnic Groups," in *Ethnic Canadians: Culture and Education*, edited by Martin L. Kovacs (Regina: 1978), pp. 63–86 and "Ethnic Identity in

Saskatchewan Bloc Settlements: A Sociological Appraisal," in *The Settlement of the West*, edited by Howard Palmer (Calgary: 1977).

14. Leo Driedger, "In search of cultural identity factors: a comparison of ethnic students," *Canadian Review of Sociology and Anthropology* 12 (1975), pp. 150–62.

15. Leo Driedger, "Multicultural Regionalism: Toward Understanding the Canadian West," in this volume. I would like to thank Professor Driedger for permitting me to see an early draft of this paper.

16. Howard Palmer, *Patterns of Prejudice: A History of Nativism in Alberta* (Toronto: 1982).

17. Stewart J. Clatworthy and Jonathan P. Gunn, : "Economic Circumstances of Native People in Selected Metropolitan Centres in Western Canada" (Institute of Urban Studies, University of Winnipeg, December 1981).

18. Linda Gerber, "The development of Canadian Indian communities: a two-dimensional typology reflecting strategies of adaptation to the modern world," *Canadian Review of Sociology and Anthropology* 16 (1979), pp. 404–24.

19. Nelson Wiseman and Wayne Taylor, "Class and Ethnic Voting in Winnipeg during the Cold War," *Canadian Review of Sociology and Anthropology* 16:1 (1979), pp. 60–76; Wiseman and Taylor, "Ethnic vs Class Voting: The Case of Winnipeg, 1945," *Canadian Journal of Political Science* 7 (1974), pp. 314-28; John Richards and Larry Pratt, *Prairie Capitalism: Power and Influence in the New West* (Toronto: 1979).

20. Dick Harrison, *Unnamed Country: The Struggle for a Canadian Prairie Fiction* (Edmonton: 1977), p. xii and W.L. Morton, "Seeing an Unliterary Landscape," Mosaic 3:3 (Spring 1970), pp. 1–10; also Eli Mandel, "Writing West: On the Road to Wood Mountain," in *Another Time*, edited by Mandel (Erin: 1977), pp. 68–78.

21. Wallace Stegner, *Wolf Willow: A History, A Story and a Memory of the Last Plains Frontier* (New York: 1955, 1966), pp. 25–6.

22. David E. Smith, "Celebrations and History on the Prairies," *Journal of Canadian Studies* 17:3 (Fall 1982), pp. 45–57.

23. Northrop Frye, "Across the River and Out of the Trees," in *Northrop Frye: Divisions on a Ground: Essays on Canadian Culture*, edited by James Polk (Toronto: 1982), p. 31.

24. Alan C. Cairns, "The Governments and Societies of Canadian Federalism," *Canadian Journal of Political Science* 10:4 (December 1977), pp. 695–725.

25. Larry Pratt and Garth Stevenson, eds., *Western Separatism: The Myths, Realities and Dangers* (Edmonton: 1981); David E. Smith, *The Regional Decline of a National Party: Liberals on the Prairies* (Toronto: 1981).

26. W.L. Morton, "The Bias of Prairie Politics," in *Context of Canada's Past: Selected Essays of W.L. Morton*, edited by A.B. McKillop (Toronto: 1980), p. 159 and Morton, "A Century of Plain and Parkland," in *A Region of the Mind*, edited by Richard Allen (Regina: 1973), p. 179.

27. Carl Berger, *The Writing of Canadian History: Aspects of English-Canadian Historical Writing: 1900–1970* (Toronto: 1976) contains a chapter on "William Morton: The Delicate Balance of Region and Nation," pp. 238–58.

English-Canadian Attitudes to French Canada, Yesterday and Today*

RICHARD JONES

I

Historically, much has been made of Anglo-French antipathy in Canada and it is undoubtedly true that many incidents of an ethnic, linguistic or religious nature have occurred. Racial and religious prejudice and different national objectives, as well as insecurity on both sides, have been at the root of these conflicts. It is easy to understand French-Canadian and Catholic fears at a time when educational "rights" were being trodden upon and "democratically" suppressed by Anglo-Protestant majorities in New Brunswick, Manitoba, Alberta, Saskatchewan, and Ontario. It is perhaps more difficult to believe that Anglophone fears were equally as genuine. Yet many English-speaking Protestants were convinced that Catholic "papist" influence was a real and growing threat to Canada. They felt that a strong French-speaking minority or even a majority was a distinct possibility in Ontario as French Canadians overflowed into the province from neighbouring counties in Québec, and that French-Canadian "domination" was preventing loyal British Canadians from properly accomplishing their imperial duties. 617

It was in 1917 during the conscription crisis that Anglo-French relations in Canada ebbed to their lowest point. Unionists were quite rabid in their determination to "make Quebec do her duty." In the course of the 1917 election campaign Sir William Hearst, the Ontario Premier, declared at Georgetown:

The issue today is: Shall Canada have a Union Government of all provinces and parties outside of Quebec, or shall a solid Quebec control the destiny of a divided Canada? Ontario must stand by the Union of the eight provinces, and must do so in a manner so emphatic and conclusive that Quebec domination will never again be attempted."

Pro-Unionist, pro-conscriptionist newspapers joined in the fray. "Men are not volunteering in English-speaking Canada for the express purpose of preserving to French Canadians the freedom to stay at home while others brave the dangers of war," editorialized the Toronto *Mail and Empire*. The same newspaper suspected the presence of "the 'hidden hand' of the Kaiser behind Québec's desire not to reinforce troops overseas" and urged: "English Canada must deny Quebec and Germany's desire." At the time of the disastrous Halifax explosion in December 1917 the *Winnipeg Telegram*

*Revised by the author from an article first published in *The Quarterly of Canadian Studies*, 4 (1976): 105–114. Reprinted by permission of the author.

bemoaned the fact that the catastrophe had befallen such a patriotic and decent city and suggested that "in Quebec it would have been of inestimable value as an object lesson to those who made so little of the danger . . . of this war to Canada."

Meanwhile, Henri Bourassa, embittered by the virtual abolition of French-language schools in Ontario, his faith shaken in a Confederation that continually denied the rights of French-speaking and Catholic Canadians, drew the conclusion that insofar as the survival of French Canada was concerned, the "Prussians of Ontario" were a far more dangerous and immediate threat than the Prussians of Germany. Clearly, French-English relations in Canada were at their nadir. It is true that the 1917 experience would be repeated during the Second World War, but this time the political sagacity of Prime Minister Mackenzie King did much to mollify opinion.

Partisan political interests also contributed to racial bitterness. Throughout the lean years of the twentieth century, many Conservatives blamed Québec and her Liberal loyalties for their misfortunes, and they not infrequently appealed for Anglo-Saxon unity in the face of what they esteemed to be Québec's domination over Canada. "It is time to make [French Canadians] understand once and for all that we are English in an English country," proclaimed the Toronto *News* in 1900, for example. Some Anglo-Canadians whose sentiments ran along the same lines listened and undoubtedly voted for Conservative candidates. The theme did not change even when an English-speaking Canadian took over the leadership of the Liberal party after Laurier's death in 1919. During the election campaign of 1921, the Toronto *Telegram* could still advise its readers that W.L.M. King's victory (over the conservative, Arthur Meighen) would signify that "Quebec, which refused to fight when Canada was in danger, would govern the country whose liberty had been brought by the other provinces at the price of their blood." After the election and King's victory, the weekly *Orange Sentinel* headlined: "French Canadians to govern Canada for five years!"

Liberal propagandists in Quebec were often not satisfied to proclaim simply that their party was the party of national unity; they did not fail to realize that they could turn Conservative denunciations of French Canada to their political advantage. Liberal newspapers in the province printed the defamatory remarks of Conservative dailies in Toronto in order to convince Québec voters — if this were really necessary! — that there was no home for them in the Tory party.

Intergroup tensions involving French- and English-speaking Canadians are virtually a constant in Canadian history since the early nineteenth century and latent animosities have been quick to flare up given the particular incidents or conditions. Those of an older generation who, today, yearn nostalgically for the good old days of "*bonne entente*" and national unity, thus appear to gloss over much of Canadian history.

618

II

This text seeks to explore English-Canadian reaction to the evolution of French Canada since 1960. In Québec, particularly in nationalist circles, it was easy to gather the impression that a large number of Anglo-Canadians continued to be dedicated advocates of the cultural assimilation of French Canada, and that they sincerely believed that Canada was, or should be, an English-speaking country. This is scarcely surprising. Throughout the 1970s, the Official Languages Act was the object of vigorous criticism in English Canada, so much so that Francophones became increasingly skeptical of the federal government's promises to work towards equality in its own back-yard. Indeed, when the bill was adopted by the House of Commons in 1969, seventeen Conservatives, led by former Prime Minister John Diefenbaker voted against it. During the debate one Tory member even maintained that "the cold hard fact is that Canadians of French origin should be learning English as fast as they can instead of the English learning French," because "English is the easier and more reasonable language to learn." Then in 1972 at the time of the federal election campaign, a backlash against bilingualism contributed to the decline of Liberal fortunes in a certain number of con-stituencies in English Canada. Moreover, a host of other incidents and events have been easily construed in Québec as evidence of the unextinguished desire of Anglophones to, at best, relegate French Canada to inferior status. A serious of disputes over French-language schools, particularly in Ontario, helped stoke the fire of ethnic conflict. In Manitoba, the Conservative party campaigned vigorously against proposed new services in the French lan-guage and several local referenda turned down the plan overwhelmingly. In New Brunswick, a government-commissioned report called for equal French and English provincial government services; public hearings on the ques-tion in late 1984 provoked violent outbursts from many Anglophones. More soberly, perhaps, business worried over the cost of bilingualism requirements.

The use of French in air-to-air and ground-to-ground communications in Québec also aroused considerable animosity. When the Canadian Airline Pilots Association, supported by the English-language controllers, struck Air Canada illegally in June 1976 over the federal government's policy of implanting bilingualism at certain airports in Québec, Prime Minister Pierre Trudeau termed the conflict "the gravest threat to national unity since the debate over military conscription during the Second World War." In addi-tion, Québec's language legislation, notably the Bourassa Liberal govern-ment's Bill 22 (adopted in 1974) and the Parti-Québécois government's Language Charter (voted in 1977), provoked enormous antipathy in English Canada and undoubtedly contributed to the departure of nearly twenty per cent of Québec's Anglophones from the province. If language legislation stemmed from French Canadians' sensitivity to real or perceived threats to their existence, then English Canada's reaction simply confirmed the valid-ity of those fears.

Still, the notion of linguistic equality has made considerable headway in

619

Canada since the early 1960s. But throughout the period, those Anglo-Canadians accepting the principle of equality of the two communities have generally viewed the problem as being a question of individual free choice. Just as in Québec, until the adoption of Bill 22 by the Bourassa government in 1974, all parents could choose the language of instruction for their children, so believers in linguistic equality began to admit that French Canadians in other provinces should have the same right. It should be noted that we are talking here of "rights," not "obligations." The fact that many French Canadians outside Québec opted for an English-language education for their children, even when French-language schools were available, while within Québec virtually all English-speaking citizens, as well as new Canadians of non-English, non-French origins, enrolled their children in English-language institutions, was irrelevant. What was important, in the opinion of more liberal-minded Anglo-Canadians, was that the rights of the French-speaking outside Québec could and should be recognized. English Canada should be as generous to her French-speaking minority as Québec was to her English-speaking minority.

620

To a growing number of Francophones, however, individual freedom of choice was not the solution to the French-speaking community's woes. Statistics demonstrate all too clearly that French Canada outside Québec was being decimated by assimilation, and demographers were predicting that French Canada, in addition to forming a diminishing proportion of Canada's total population, would be increasingly concentrated within the province of Québec. The 1971 census showed that fully 54.9% of so-called French Canadians in the English-speaking provinces were using English as the main language of communication at home, that 39.2% had English as their mother tongue — that is, the first language learned and still understood — and that 33.5% — fully a third of French Canadians outside Québec — were unilingual Anglophones! In the far western provinces, precisely three quarters of French Canadians spoke English at home.

The 1981 statistics, though not yet complete, show that French as the language of the home has continued to decline outside Québec. Such, then, is the sorry state of the French-Canadian diaspora. Within Québec, the French-speaking majority of nearly 80% was holding its own but doing very little assimilating. The vast majority of immigrants who arrived in the province in the years after the Second World War learned English as their second tongue and enrolled their children in the English-speaking school system. The "problem" was particularly evident in Montreal where most immigrants settled. So-called "freedom of choice" seemed to be working against French Canada. The attraction of the English language on a continent peopled by 250 million Anglophones was evident, and in the eyes of many French Canadians, the cards seemed to be stacked in advance against French Canada.

While Anglo-Québeckers and other English-speaking Canadians continued to praise freedom of choice and to demand that it be legislated into law in Québec, more and more French-speaking Québeckers came to see legislative action by the Québec government as a necessity to assure the long-term survival of French Canada. At first, the Québec government seemed to heed the partisans of free choice: indeed in 1969 Jean-Jacques Bertrand's Union Nationale government adopted Bill 63, which guaranteed free choice of language in the schools. This law, bitterly decried by nationalist groups, was finally abrogated by the Bourassa government and replaced in 1974 by Bill 22 which for the first time curtailed access to English-language schools in Québec. English Canada reacted bitterly to the new policy and newspapers editorialized that at a time when English Canada was ever more ready to recognize French-language rights, Québec should not go against the current and revoke rights that it has always recognized for English speakers. The Union Nationale party under its new leader Rodrigue Biron began to advocate a return to free choice and large numbers of English-speaking voters actually deserted Robert Bourassa's Liberals and voted for the Union Nationale in the 1976 election. Their gesture aided the Parti Québécois in winning power on November 15. As it had promised, the Parti Québécois government repealed Bill 22 and replaced it by Bill 101, the French language charter. Bill 101 perhaps clarified the numerous ambiguities of Bill 22 in relation to the language of instruction but it also went further in limiting access to English schools; in addition, it stiffened the clauses relating to the language of work and publicity. English Canada could certainly not respond with enthusiasm to the new law. But it can probably be said that by the end of the decade those most concerned by the law, Anglo-Québeckers and neo-Québeckers, became at least resigned to the inevitable. There would be no return to free choice in Québec in the foreseeable future. Polls, although somewhat ambiguous, show that most French Canadians think Québec needs a language law although, in some respects such as the language of advertising, they would favor a softening of Bill 101. The courts also contributed to weakening the law. Still, the workplace has become undeniably more French, large numbers of Anglophones have become bilingual and, by 1985, more than half of so-called "Allophone" children, neither English- nor French-speaking, were enrolled in French schools. The relative success of Bill 101 has surely had a positive effect on French Canada, perhaps diminishing the degree of insecurity and making possible a type of coexistence with English Canada.

621

III

Evolution in Anglophone opinion in regard to French Canada was thus slow — painfully slow — and to a degree at least, it came about as a result of the threat of separatism. Premier Daniel Johnson's slogan, "Equality or Independence," may have been seen by some Anglo-Canadians as a form of blackmail but it undoubtedly made gentle persuasion a little firmer.

Complicating this trend towards greater cultural equality was the constitutional question: what was to be the place of the province of Québec in the Canadian Confederation? When Québec Premier Maurice Duplessis died in September 1959 and the Union Nationale government, in power since

1944, was finally ousted by a largely reborn Liberal party under Jean Lesage in the June 1960 elections, English Canada rejoiced. After all, Duplessis had had a bad press outside Québec and his party's apparent demise brought forth few regrets. The period of reforms instituted over the next few years by the new Liberal government at almost all levels of Québec society was quickly baptized the "Quiet Revolution." But as long as this remarkable upheaval seemed limited to problems associated with the political, economic and social modernization of Québec, as long as Québeckers aspired simply to catch up with the rest of Canada and North America, change could only be approved by English Canadians. Nationalizing the hydro-electric system (as Ontario had done decades before), establishing a government holding corporation, completely restructuring the educational system, creating a Ministry of Cultural Affairs, reforming labour legislation, and cleaning up corrupt electoral practices scarcely affected the rest of Canada nor Québec's position within Confederation.

622   Still, throughout the 1960s, greater political and fiscal autonomy was a guideline for both Liberal and Union Nationale governments and a growing segment of Québec's population leaned towards special status for the province or even independence. Indeed at the first interprovincial conference in more than three decades, held in Québec City in December 1960, Québec's new Liberal Premier, Jean Lesage, handed out copies of the Tremblay Report on constitutional problems to the other premiers. This report, submitted four years earlier, was an exposé of classical federalism and a veritable Bible of autonomism.

In the course of his six years in office, Lesage was involved in numerous confrontations with the federal government over such issues as tax-sharing, provincial opting-out of shared-cost projects, the establishment of a Québec pension plan independent of the federal plan, and federal intervention into certain fields of action (such as loans to municipalities) judged by autonomists to be of provincial responsibility. These recurring incidents, however serious they may have been, were still a far cry from separatism, and it is well known that certain other provincial premiers, such as British Columbia's W.A.C. Bennett, maintained as strident a tone as Lesage.

Towards 1966 and 1967, with the return to power of the Union Nationale, Québec's political claims began to evolve considerably. Premier Daniel Johnson argued that changed Canadian conditions made a new constitution imperative; a completely revised constitution would modify the separation of powers in favour of the provinces, and notably Québec, and would offer solid guarantees — this time — that provincial autonomy would be respected.

The *Toronto Star*, discussing Québec's "demands," linked together very neatly the province's claims to greater autonomy and French Canada's desires for linguistic equality.

If Quebec insists on autonomy, English-speaking Canadians will be less and less inclined to concede to French Canadians a strong influence in the federal government; moreover, in the other nine provinces, they will be less sympathetic in regard to the cultural and linguistic rights of Francophones.

The *Star* was simply admitting what many English Canadians were thinking and continued to think. If Québec wanted cultural equality for French-speaking Canadians, it would have to be satisfied with political equality as one of the ten provinces, renouncing any claims to "special status." It could not both have its cake and eat it too!

Official English Canada seemed to become much more conciliatory on both the cultural and the constitutional questions for a brief moment at the end of 1967 and at the beginning of 1968. In November the provincial premiers gathered together in Toronto for the Confederation of Tomorrow Conference. Premier John Robarts appeared favourable to the implantation of most of the attributes of official bilingualism in Ontario and Premier Louis Robichaud promised to put both languages on an equal footing in New Brunswick. In a moving speech Premier G.I. Smith of Nova Scotia affirmed that he had a greater attachment for Canada than for a constitution. Even Premier Manning, who on the first day of the conference had taken an uncompromising stand against broader constitutional guarantees for the French language, seemed to join in the new spirit. "I want to see the legitimate interests of Quebec met," he declared. And on the subject of constitutional change he voiced the opinion that the B.N.A. Act had "nothing sacred about it" and that if the Canadian people so desire, it could be altered drastically. Had Daniel Johnson's more or less subtle hint — he promised to do his best to fight separatism by seeking rights for French Canadians outside Québec — helped to sway certain English-speaking premiers?

623

This theme of accommodation also dominated the first meeting of the federal-provincial Constitutional Conference, held in Ottawa in February 1968. In a speech described by Daniel Johnson as "unprecedented in the history of Confederation," Premier Robarts stated specifically what Ontario would do in order to fulfil its obligations towards its French-speaking citizens: there would be language courses for civil servants and bilingual public services, members of the Legislative Assembly would have the right to speak either English or French in the House, certain municipalities would function bilingually, and so forth. At the conclusion of the conference the provinces were committed to the acceptance of the recommendations of the Royal Commission on Bilingualism and Biculturalism as well as to a search for means to implement them. In addition, elaborate machinery was set up to consider every aspect of the B.N.A. Act.

IV

This chapter of constitutional revision ended with the failure of the Victoria conference in June 1971. At that meeting, the seventh in the series that had begun in 1968, the federal government put forth an amending formula to the British North America Act that would permit the patriation of the Canadian constitution. In addition the separation of powers between the two levels of government was discussed, with Premier Bourassa insisting on constitutional recognition of provincial legislative primacy in the sphere of social policy. When Ottawa failed to yield to demands formulated by Bourassa and his social affairs minister, Claude Castonguay, Québec vetoed the proposed charter. Actually, Québec public opinion was quite divided on the question — but for considerable nationalist agitation, Premier Bourassa might well have signed the Victoria charter. Commenting on Québec's decision, a somewhat bitter Pierre Trudeau said: "It's not likely that we're going to have other conferences on division of powers." One Liberal member of Parliament went even further, declaring: "We have to take a firm line toward the province of Québec. We can't keep giving in and vacillating." And the *Globe and Mail*, "Canada's National Newspaper," editorialized: "Mr. Bourassa has proved that Quebec Premiers do not come to the bargaining table to bargain but to demand, to tell the rest of Canada, 'I deliver the pattern of the future and you abide by it.' " And it urged that the rest of Canada cease yielding to Québec.

624 In examining the various political options presented in Québec, English Canada was constantly searching for anti-separatist professions of faith. When Paul Gérin-Lajoie submitted his report on the constitution to the Liberal party in 1967, one Toronto Newspaper asked if the ex-education minister were suggesting that his party reject separatism while at the same time accepting it in a slightly modified version and calling it by another name. Another Toronto daily agreed: "Perhaps René Lévesque was right in saying that the minimum demanded by Quebec greatly surpasses the maximum that the most well disposed of English Canadians are ready to concede." In any case it was quite natural that Anglophones welcomed the results of both the 1970 and 1973 provincial elections as proof that Québec was firmly opposed to separatism and in favour of remaining in Confederation. Robert Bourassa based his sales campaign for federalism on its "profitability" for Québeckers, in terms of dollars and cents. English Canadians, however, seemed to ignore these unpleasing realities.

The arrival of the Parti Québécois in power in November 1976 seemed to presage important changes on the Canadian constitutional stage. For the first time in Québec, a separatist party took office pledging to hold a referendum on the province's political future and openly favouring the cause of "sovereignty-association," that is, political sovereignty for Québec together with an economic association with the rest of Canada. Patriation of the Canadian constitution and even a revision of the current distribution of powers between the governments obviously seemed unimportant in the light of Québec's new policy. Over the next four years, English Canada announced firmly and nearly unanimously that sovereignty-association was unacceptable and would not be negotiated with Québec. When the Québec government published a white paper in the fall of 1979 on the "new entente" proposed between Canada and Québec, Joe Clark, then prime minister of Canada, judged the suggested treaty of association to be incompatible with the idea of federalism while Premier William Davis of Ontario, supported by the provincial legislature, affirmed that he would not negotiate such an accord with Québec. The four western premiers also reacted quite negatively, stating that sovereignty-association was in the interest neither of the West nor of the rest of Canada.

Prime Minister Pierre Trudeau intervened in a palpitating referendum campaign in the spring of 1980, declaring that a "yes" vote would lead to an impasse. On the other hand he promised that if Québec voted "no," he would immediately put into motion the wheels of constitutional reform. On May 20, nearly 60% of Québeckers, including about half of the French-speaking population, voted "no" to the question submitted by the Lévesque government. The Québec lion appeared to have been shorn of its teeth. Although the Parti Québécois was reelected in April 1981 to a second term, disappointing most English-Canadian observers who would have preferred Claude Ryan's Liberals, Lévesque's promise not to hold a new referendum was reassuring.

The federal government's efforts at constitutional reform after 1980 brought it into a collision course not only with Québec but with seven other provinces. However, in late 1981, all the English-speaking provinces reached an agreement with Ottawa on the substance of a new constitution. Québec alone was left out and, though many observers might regret the province's isolation, they scarcely saw in it a danger for the country.

By the mid 1980s, Québec seemed to have returned to the ranks and assumed a less dramatic place on the inside pages of English-Canadian newspapers. With the referendum defeat, the improved relations with the Mulroney government, the decision of the Parti Québécois to relegate its project for sovereignty to the indefinite future and the internal strife that provoked a veritable schism within the party, Québec no longer appeared a menace. Moreover, the province's economic problems gave it new worries. Nevertheless, French Canada, both within Québec and outside, has made considerable progress since 1960 and there is no reason to believe that English Canada, in spite of the difficulties of adaptation, wants to turn the hands of the clock back now.

625

Canadian Regionalism: A Central Problem*
D. ALEXANDER

In the nineteenth century, many countries were formed from disparate parts in order to capture the increasing returns to scale in manufacturing and raw material production offered by the industrial revolution. Over the last century world industrial output has exceeded by many times the entire production of mankind's history before 1850. To accomplish this wider markets

*From *Atlantic Canada and Confederation: Essays in Canadian Political Economy*, comp. by E. Sager, L. Fischer, and S. Pierson. Copyright 1983 by University of Toronto Press. Reprinted by permission of University of Toronto Press. Originally presented to the Conference on Canadian Regionalism, Memorial University of Newfoundland in 1975, revised and published as "Weakness at the Centre" in *Canadian Forum*, 61, 665 (1976).

were essential, as well as larger political units to organize the necessary overhead structures. The economic limit to scale advantages may be a global unity, imposed by international corporations or achieved through the extension of customs unions over an ever-widening surface. But for the foreseeable future customs unions and free trade areas will probably be constrained by diminishing returns to scale in administration and the disinclination of people in rich areas of the world to acquire political obligations to those in poor regions, especially if there are other ways to exploit them and their resources.

The minimum economic size of a viable political unit is unknown, for it varies with time and a host of special circumstances. It is clear, however, that the bias of advantage is towards increasingly large units, and once again the Economic Council of Canada is fussing about Canada being economically too small.[1] But while economists press us ever forward to the purity of a single world economic and political market, and businessmen follow yapping at their heels, in a number of the large political units formed in the past people demonstrate a distressing inclination to restore the old patchwork of kingdoms and grand duchies. Scotland is unhappy with the Act of Union; the Basque country dislikes Spain; Bretons cannot stand Frenchmen; and we could even see a sovereign state of Alberta or Newfoundland before there is one in Quebec.

In countries where discontented regions are politically impotent and the possibility of separation is poor, grievances have a habit of becoming ancient artifacts. They begin with the people of the region identifying some grievance, assigning it an exogenous origin, and demanding a solution from outsiders. Externally the grievance is regarded as insignificant, lacking a solution, or having its cause somewhere else—mainly in the region itself. The aggrieved then become embittered, turn in upon themselves, and manifest hostility towards the exogenous enemy in usually futile ways. The region's enemy regards this behaviour as distasteful, revealing both a shocking nativism and a peculiar inability to see the grievance within the context of national interest. As the new federal deputy minister of finance was reported to have said to the provincial government, if Newfoundland thinks it will have any share in the regulation of offshore gas and oil development, then it is suffering delusions of grandeur. It simply would not be good for Canada as a whole.

Albert Breton has dismissed nationalism, and by extension regionalism, as a dirty little plot of the middle class to secure income transfers from the working class.[2] With a little imagination the thesis could be applied to Quebec's *Action française* in the 1920s and perhaps to the Saint-Jean-Baptiste Society today. But it would be a trifle difficult to extend it to the Parti Québécois support in the east end of Montreal or to the manifestos of the Common Front, particularly that of the Confederation of National Trade Unions (CNTU).[3] Moreover, the nativism of the CNTU document is very muted, and what surfaces most strongly is the material grievance of a province that acquired the dregs of the National Policy industrialization, spiced with resent-

626

ment of anglophone domination, whether from Westmount, Ottawa, or New York. The voices of the Saint-Jean-Baptiste Society and fashionable Montreal might be those of cultural nativism, but they would be politically unimportant if they were not also grounded in the material grievances of the Quebec working class.

It has been easy in Canada to dismiss the regional protest of the Maritimes as an illogical and petty resentment of the inexorable march of industry into southern Ontario. The inability of Maritimers to arrest the slide can, at the same time, be explained in Roy George's fashion as the result of excessive social and cultural homogeneity — a polite way of indicating that natives have become xenophobic to the point of self-destruction.[4] It has been much more difficult to manufacture the same argument for the west, because that region is hardly homogeneous in its population, and its output has made massive contributions to Canada's trade. None the less the west's protest has been met with mumbles of regret, genuflexions to impossible conditions in international markets, and when conditions became absolutely appalling, shipments of used clothing from the Ladies' Auxiliary of the Belleville United Church. It is fortunate for Canada that there is one example of intense regional complaint that cannot be dismissed as nativism or as the result of poor external markets. In Alberta nativity is virtually conferred by residence (although it takes a few days longer if one is from Ontario or speaks French), and the protest is associated with immense, if temporary, strength in the domestic Canadian market. It is scant wonder that Albertans are furious when virtually everything they buy from central Canada is priced above world levels, whereas almost everything they sell is required to be traded below world prices. When Alberta or any other region queries this odd arrangement, the CBC immediately launches a documentary special to discover whether the residents are 'good Canadians.'

627

It is hardly an original argument, but it is none the less true, that much of the regional discontent in Canada is rooted in the economic structure of the country as it has developed out of the National Policy. Ontario and Quebec acquired the protected industrial sector, but as the Wonnacotts have shown, southern Ontario had the additional advantage of location at the apex of the U.S. industrial triangle and so participated in American intra-corporate transfers of resources and semimanufactures.[5] By that same National Policy the west was settled for food production, initially for the British market. When that turned sour in the 1930s some rather desperate scrambling was required to reorient the grain economy into a genuinely international market, and with their other primary exports the Prairies have been settled on a relatively firm economic base. British Columbia was and remains a world in its own, for while its economy is volatile the rich mineral, forest, and ocean resources have made the province prosperous and basically indifferent to the rest of the country.

The Cinderella has been Atlantic Canada. It is the only region which secured no economic benefits (in the economist's sense) from Confederation. The nature of its economic base — ocean resources and derived maritime activities—required the energies and services of a national state with a genuinely international orientation. This is precisely what Upper Canada is not and never has been. Scott Gordon has commented on the oddity of Lower and Upper Canada, founded as export regions, persistently demonstrating a passionate mercantilism even during the flowering of international liberalism in the mid-nineteenth century.[6] This mercantilism was manifested not only in industrial protection but (whenever trade was unavoidable) in a desperate search for some bilateral arrangement which could be dressed up as a 'special relationship.' The collapse of the Liverpool grain market and the slow realization in the 1920s and 1930s that Britain would not impose food taxes for the benefit of Canada and Australia forced the federal government through the Wheat Board to poke a timid toe into international trade. But, that development apart, the really tough world of international trade was avoided in the early decades of Confederation by border transactions in Ontario forest and farm products with the United States, British requirements for cheap food, and since 1945 by prostrating the country before the raw material requirements and intra-corporate transfers of the American industrial machine.

628

As an international trader Canada is a joke. In 1971 our commodity exports were valued at $17.3 billion. Some 30 per cent of this represented intra-corporate transfers by U.S. energy and automotive companies. Of the remaining $12 billion some 37 per cent also went to the United States, the bulk of which again amounted largely to transfers by U.S. corporate parents. This leaves $5.6 billion, or a third of commodity exports, entering overseas markets. About $1.5 billion represented food shipments and a further $1.5 billion sales of unprocessed raw materials. Out of a total foreign trade of $17.3 billion, no more than $2.7 billion or 16 per cent were overseas shipments of fabricated products. If forest products are removed from this—the bulk of it newsprint—only some $1.9 billion or 11 per cent of commodity exports and 2 per cent of gross national product remains. It would be too embarrassing to subtract overseas shipments of partially processed minerals, for we would then be left with virtually no overseas trade in mildly sophisticated fabricated products. With an overseas trade amounting to less than 6 per cent of GNP and in fabricated products to less than 3 per cent, it is safe to say that Canada is no international trader to turn hair grey in Hamburg or Tokyo. For eastern Canada, where land resources and location discouraged replication of the Ontario/Quebec pattern, and where ocean resources required a national government with a real international focus, Confederation amounted to a disaster. Among the frightened little fellows at C.D. Howe's Department of Trade and Commerce, Peoria was almost Samarkand.

The Maritimes had been reduced to sullen resentment long before Newfoundland was forced into the eastern mould. This country was an international trader, at least on the export side. Its foreign trade ratio at the end of World War II was a staggering 150 per cent of national income and its export trade was distributed among a score of countries in two hemispheres. Newfoundland's problem was that it was too small to carry the overhead charges of national status or to overcome by itself the inter-war and post-war problems of trade and payments bilateralism and currency inconvertibility. Union with a large international trader could ease these problems, but unfortunately economic geography limited the choice to North America. Henry Mayo predicted Newfoundland's fate brilliantly in his 1948 DPHIL thesis at Oxford.[7] He saw that the structure of the international economy, despite Bretton Woods, would no longer permit the existence at reasonable living standards of a tiny country with Newfoundland's location. Union with a larger power was inevitable and he saw no practical political choice other than Canada. Canada, however, would offer the country no economic benefits because the structure of the two economies were competitive and economic benefits were reserved for the centre. Nevertheless, Canada would offer an assured avenue for emigration, lower living costs, and minimum guarantees for those who remained in the province. But Mayo believed that Newfoundland had a poor future as a self-supporting entity, either as an independent country or as a Canadian province. To the anti-Confederates, who saw the opening of the U.S. market for frozen groundfish as a way of avoiding both the difficulties of overseas trade and the distastefulness of union with Canada, Mayo pointed out that the technical coefficient of frozen fish production for the United States would provide employment equivalent to that of a medium-sized pulp mill.

629

Mayo's predictions proved enduring. The province has acquired prosperity of sorts through the expansion of various income transfer programmes, a long construction boom, and the results of their derived expenditure. The province has turned to massive northern resource schemes as the locus of mineral and energy exploitation has shifted away from the frontiers established in the early decades of this century. But these have returned minimal benefits for residents because Newfoundland lacks the scale and technical depth to provide capital and management inputs, and Ottawa, with its customary obeisance to political power in certain provinces, has insisted that the economic rent from Labrador flow to Quebec. The efforts to generate development which will actually confer benefits to residents comes down to a decision by the Department of Regional Economic Expansion whether Moncton or Corner Brook would provide the best location for a hockey-stick plant.[8] In the course of the comedy the one demonstrably attractive pole for economic growth, the fishery, has been wound up and alienated to distant-water fishing nations.

Prior to Confederation the Newfoundland government was on the right track when it planned post-war reconstruction around the fishery. The one major error, which unhappily coincided with the Canadian disease, was to assume that the country could safely abandon its international trade in fish products for a bilateral exchange with the United States. This was a mistake for the simple reason that the American market was not sufficiently large, in terms of the access to it which Newfoundlanders could reasonably expect, either to employ the labour force or to utilize the open-access resource around its shores. When a country is located on a major world resource characterized by open access, it must establish production control over that resource and forge trade links with all consuming countries. If it does not do so it will lose control of the resource. As an independent country Newfoundland would probably have lost control of the resource because in the short run it lacked the capital resources to exploit it and the trade and military power to prevent foreign fishing. This process had begun in the 1920s when Spain and Portugal began investing in national fishing fleets and returned to the Grand Banks after a few centuries' absence. But the real onslaught came after 1945 when northern and eastern Europe followed the Iberians. Canada had the potential commercial strength to persuade these countries to trade rather than fish. But with its timid bilateral orientation towards the United States, and its chronic inability to recognize and meet the minimal requirements of its international export regions, it encouraged Newfoundland to adjust itself to income transfers and a miserable little trade with Boston and Chicago in frozen fillets and blocks. This was accomplished by denying the saltfish trade the short-run assistance necessary to keep it in the European and Brazilian markets during the post-war exchange crisis, and ignoring the possibilities for expanding output of all fisheries products for trade into western and eastern Europe. An international trade effort of these dimensions alone would have staunched the investment in distant-water fleets, employed the labour force, and justified capital expenditure in the primary fishery. Instead Ottawa insisted on an inadequate U.S. trade in conformity to the branch plant mentality of Ontario and Quebec. A similar solution for prairie wheat was avoided only because the United States — regrettably no doubt from Ottawa's point of view — was a net exporter of grains.

Newfoundland's landings of fishery products tumbled by the 1970s to about 14 per cent of all catches in Newfoundland waters. In 1968 some 15,000 fishermen employing $54 millions of capital equipment (in 1954 prices) landed 280,000 metric tons of cod, red-fish, flounder, halibut, and other groundfish. In 1905–24 on average 35,000 fishermen using in real terms about 10 per cent of the capital landed 170,000 tons of codfish alone, and in some years equalled in cod the present catch of all groundfish.[9] The depression in the fisheries has meant that Newfoundland suffers the worst features of the Atlantic Canadian malaise. It does not share the benefit of military expenditures in the Maritimes, the regional droplets from federal government offices in Moncton and Halifax, or the coastal ports and rail lines for break-bulk shipments to central Canada. Newfoundland is also uncompetitive with the Maritimes in attracting by subsidization the branch plants that neither Ontario nor Quebec is interested in having.

What is impressive about central Canada and its national government is not strength and power but weakness. The national government does not behave like one. The economic nationalism of Ontario provokes howls of laughter in the export regions, but once the tears are dried there is sober speculation about what the centre is dreaming up next. We can be sure that André Raynauld and the Economic Council were not moved to preach free trade in the interests of export regions, and a careful reading of *Looking*

Outward shows that it is nothing more than an acknowledgment that the inefficient industrial sector of Ontario/Quebec can survive only by seeking complete absorption into the United States. That is the legacy of Sir John A. Macdonald and all the earlier and later mercantilists of Upper Canada.

Perhaps the current revival of economic nationalism in Ontario is a long-awaited revulsion against the crude bilateralism which has emasculated that province and intensified the resentment of Quebec against the twin enemies of American and anglophone imperialism. Perhaps it offers a slight hope to the export areas of this country that Canada will begin to think about multilateralism and regional economic development. But I fear that Ottawa will still be reduced to palpitations of the heart when shown an irrevocable letter of credit drawn on the Bank of Brazil against a shipment of small Madeira.

Notes

1. Economic Council of Canada, *Looking Outward: A New Trade Strategy for Canada* (Ottawa 1975).
2. Albert Breton, 'The Economics of Nationalism,' *Journal of Political Economy* 72 (1964).
3. Daniel Drache, *Quebec — Only the Beginning: The Manifestoes of the Common Front* (Toronto 1972).
4. R.E. George, *A Leader and a Laggard: Manufacturing Industry in Nova Scotia, Quebec, and Ontario* (Toronto 1971).
5. Ronald J. and Paul Wonnacott, *Free Trade Between the United States and Canada* (Cambridge, Mass. 1967).
6. Scott Gordon, 'The Historical Perspective: Nineteenth Century Trade Theory and Policy: *Canada and the International* Economy, ed. H.E. English (Toronto 1961).
7. Henry Mayo, 'Newfoundland and Canada: The Case for Union Examined' (unpublished DPHIL thesis, Oxford University 1948).
8. See G.K. Goundrey, 'The Newfoundland Economy: A Modest Proposal: *Canadian Forum* LIII (March 1974).
9. Calculations from an unpublished manuscript by the author.

TO THE OWNER OF THIS BOOK:

We are interested in your reaction to **Readings in Canadian History, Post-Confederation, 2/e**. Through feedback from you, we can improve this book in future editions.

1. What was your reason for using this book?

   _____ university course   _____ continuing education course

   _____ college course   _____ personal interest

2. Approximately how much of the book did you use?

   _____ ¼ _____ ½ _____ ¾ _____ all

3. What is the best aspect of the book?

4. Have you any suggestions for improvement?

5. Is there anything that should be added?

Fold here

POSTAGE WILL BE PAID BY

ANTHONY LUENGO
Publisher
College Editorial Department
HOLT, RINEHART AND WINSTON
OF CANADA, LIMITED
55 HORNER AVENUE
TORONTO, ONTARIO
M8Z 4X6

Tape shut